Wills, Trusts, and Estate Administration for the Paralegal

Second Edition

West's Paralegal Series

Consulting Editor, William P. Statsky

Wills, Trusts, and Estate Administration for the Paralegal

Second Edition

Dennis R. Hower
University of Minnesota

West Publishing Company

St. Paul New York Los Angeles San Francisco

COPYRIGHT © 1979 By WEST PUBLISHING COMPANY

COPYRIGHT © 1985 By WEST PUBLISHING COMPANY
50 West Kellogg Boulevard
P. O. Box 64526
St. Paul, Minnesota 55164–0526

96 95 94 93 92 91 90 89   8 7 6 5 4

Library of Congress Cataloging in Publication Data

Hower, Dennis R.
  Wills, trusts, and estate administration for the paralegal.

  Includes index.
  1. Wills—United States. 2. Trusts and trustees—
United States. 3. Probate law and practice—United States.
I. Title.
KF755.H68 1985   346.7305'4   84–20996
ISBN 0–314–85314–6   347.30654

To
Rock

Summary of Contents

Contents

Appendices

Preface

A new vocational opportunity has emerged within the legal profession. It is called paralegalism. By definition, a paralegal is a person trained to perform legal skills who works under the supervision of an attorney or who is otherwise authorized by law to use those skills.

While this text is primarily for paralegals, it can also be used by trust officers working in banks and personal representatives selected and appointed to handle the affairs of a deceased person.

As an adviser and instructor in the paralegal program at the University of Minnesota, I have become aware that a serious deficiency in our program, and similar pioneer programs around the nation, is the lack of appropriate textbook materials for legal specialty courses. The detailed work required in a paralegal career necessitates resource books that explain the practical, everyday duties of the paralegal in the basic fields of law and that prepare the paralegal to undertake these skills. These books should also serve as a reference to other related materials and as a supplement to the lecture and discussions presented by the instructor in the specialty classes. The purpose of this writing is to meet this need in the area of wills, trusts, and estate administration.

The text identifies the responsibilities and duties that can be performed by the paralegal under the supervision of the attorney handling an estate. After reviewing the general principles of law and terminology that are basic to an understanding of the field of estate administration, a chronological treatment of the procedural steps required to complete the administration is presented including an update of the current federal and state tax consequences with the appropriate tax forms.

The administration of estates is a complex field utilizing interrelated principles of law that apply throughout the procedure discussed. Some of these principles and associate definitions have been intentionally repeated in several different sections or chapters to decrease the need for cross references to other pages or chapters in the text. However, frequent cross references are necessary and are used to establish cohesiveness within and among the chapters.

Terminology is a problem. Much confusion exists when describing or defining how the decedent's property is transferred and when naming the persons entitled to receive such property. The statutes of the various states, some authors of legal texts, and practitioners have contributed to the confusion by failing to select and use uniform terms. Such terms as devise, legacy, bequest, heirs, distributee, legatee, devisee, next-of-kin, successor, and the like are examples. Since several terms are used interchangeably, it is easy to understand the cause of the confusion. To avoid any such problem in this text, those terms recommended and defined by the Uniform Probate Code, hereinafter referred to as U.P.C., will be used. The terminology of the U.P.C. is cited both within the chapters of the text and in the glossary. The entire text of the U.P.C., without comments, has been included in Appendix C.

A few sample forms for the preparation of wills, the creation of trusts, and the administration of a decedent's estate are included in the body of the text, but most will be found in Appendix A. It should be emphasized that the forms and the statutes of the state in which a paralegal practices must always be checked, since the courts of that state will use forms different from those illustrated. This effort will be encouraged by frequent questions asking the student to compare his or her own state's provisions, court rules, and probate forms with those given in the text.

The author is indebted to the American Law Institute for granting permission to cite numerous sections of the Restatement (Second) on Trusts, and to the National Conference of Commissioners on Uniform State Laws and the American Bar Association for permission to include the Uniform Probate Code in this text.

DENNIS R. HOWER

Wills, Trusts, and Estate Administration for the Paralegal

Second Edition

Chapter 1

Introduction and the Sources of Law

The chapters of this book follow a consistent pattern: the Scope of the Chapter; the Competencies the student should acquire from the chapter; the body of the chapter, supplemented by terminology, appropriate statutes (using the Uniform Probate Code for comparison), student assignments (within the chapter or at the end of the chapter). *Sample forms referred to in the text are found in Appendix A.*

The reader will undoubtedly come across unfamiliar legal terms. In each case, he or she is urged to turn to the extensive Glossary at the end of the book for the definition of the term or a reference to a page where the definition may be found. Another study aid is student assignments requiring answers to questions and problems based on the statutes, probate code, and court rules of the state in which the paralegal intends to reside and work.

Scope of the Chapter

This chapter contains an introduction to the objectives of the text and the format of the succeeding chapters, followed by a topic fundamental to all legal texts: the forms or sources of the law in the United States.

Competencies

After completing this course, the paralegal should have acquired the following general competencies:

• Mastery of the technical vocabulary necessary to understand and use the legal language in the practice of the profession and to develop the habit of thinking in legal terms

• An understanding of the functions of wills and trusts

1

• An ability to undertake a preliminary draft of the basic instruments in these two fields of law

• An ability to recognize various problems and the legal implications of situations as they arise in the field of estate administration

• An ability to think critically and constructively in analyzing existing legal principles, cases, and problems in the field of estate administration

• A knowledge of the paralegal's own functions and those of the employer, and a recognition of the authorized limits of the paralegal's practice

Introduction and General Comments

The purpose of this text is to aid in training paralegals in the field of estate administration. The intent is to provide the student with the general theory and procedures, both legal and administrative, employed in the preparation and handling of wills, trusts, and estates. It is hoped that the paralegal student, after studying this text and completing an estate administration course, will understand the basic concepts in the field; be able to apply these concepts to the skills needed to perform the tasks of a probate paralegal; recognize the immense complexity of estate administration; and realize that only through continued study combined with practical experience can the professional competency required of a paralegal be obtained.

The text will explain the techniques and technicalities involved in handling both an estate where a will exists and an estate of a person who has died without a will. The goal is to equip paralegals with sufficient background in terminology and procedures so that they can knowledgeably complete and file the numerous and complicated forms involved in estate administration and attend to correspondence concerning the estate. Material is included to familiarize the student with the methods of obtaining pertinent information from a client in order to assist the supervising attorney with the preparation and execution of wills and trusts. The paralegal must perform this work in a precise and consistent matter. Because the attorney-supervisor, clients, and courts will rely on the competency of the paralegal, there can be no room for guesswork.

A number of laws (statutes) have been enacted by the legislatures of each state to regulate the transfer of a deceased person's belongings to his or her heirs. Very few states have identical laws. For illustrative purposes, sample pages concerning the law of wills from books containing the statutes of two states, Minnesota and Pennsylvania, are included in this chapter. The probate laws of your state are probably similar to the laws of the states and the practices cited in this text, but not precisely the same. The materials presented are general rules of law based on the customs and practices followed by attorneys in carrying out the specific statutory provisions of their own states.

Sources of Law

When faced with a legal problem, you have undoubtedly asked yourself, "What is the law on this matter?" "Where does the law come from?" "How are laws made?" "Where can I find the law?" The answers to these questions lie in pinpointing the origins (sources) of laws. The laws administered by our courts originate in: constitutions, federal and state; statutes, federal and state; and common law, or case law (law made by judges, case by case).

Constitutional Law

America's greatest contribution to the legal system to which we subscribe is the federal Constitution. The United States Constitution contains the basic list of the rights and powers possessed by the federal government and by the people. It is the supreme law of the land and is the controlling standard against which all other laws must be measured to determine their validity. While the U.S. Constitution provides a framework for federal and state statutes, it does not expressly refer to the fields of wills, trusts, and estate administration, which, as we shall see, are state law issues.

Since, in addition to the federal Constitution, each state has its own constitution, a dual constitutional system exists in this country. The Tenth Amendment of the federal Constitution states: "The powers not delegated to the United States by the Constitution, nor prohibited by it to the States, are reserved to the States respectively." The state constitution becomes the fundamental law of that particular state, but if it is in conflict with the federal Constitution, the latter is superior. Like the federal Constitution, individual state constitutions have little to say directly about wills and estate administrative law. The state constitutions, however, give to the state legislatures the authority to enact laws in broad areas, including wills, trusts, and estates.

Statutory Law

Statutory law is another source of law. There are state statutes and federal statutes. Federal statutes are written laws enacted by the federal legislature—Congress. State statutes are those laws enacted by the state legislatures. The federal statutes are subordinate to the federal Constitution, while a state statute must not conflict with either the federal Constitution or the constitution of the state in which the statute was enacted.

Exhibit 1.1 shows law books, called codes, that contain federal and state statutes. Within such compilations, statutes are systematically arranged according to subject to facilitate reference. The book on the left in the exhibit is the official primary source of U.S. (federal) statutes passed by Congress. It is called the United States Code (U.S.C.). The book in the middle is one volume of the United States Code Annotated (U.S.C.A.), which contains the statutes enacted by Congress and annotations of the laws passed, i.e., commentary on the law, cross references, historical data, and excerpts from cases that interpret the statutes. As in the case of the federal and state constitutions, the federal statutes, except for estate tax consequences, have little to say directly about the law of wills, trusts, and estates. It is left either to the states and their legislators to enact legislation directly affecting these fields of law, or to judges by their decisions to create case law that is legally enforceable in such fields. The book in the center of Exhibit 1.1 is an example of a state statutory code, volume 52 of the Minnesota Statutes Annotated (Minn.Stat.Ann.) which contains statutes enacted by the Minnesota legislature with annotations similar to those in the U.S.C.A. To illustrate the type of information contained in these source books, an example of a page from a volume of the Minnesota Statutes Annotated concerning the statutes in wills and estates is shown in Exhibit 1.2. A page from the law of wills from the Pennsylvania Statutes Annotated is shown in Exhibit 1.3.

Because the Constitution of the United States allows the states to enact their own statutes, state laws often lack uniformity. To help alleviate the confusion of having 50 states with different procedures for handling decedents' estates, the National Conference of Commissioners on Uniform State Laws and the American Bar Association undertook the task of preparing model uniform statutes and recommending their adoption by the states. Such uniform codes are not the law of a particular state until that state adopts them.

The Uniform Probate Code is one model. The Uniform Probate Code proposed by the American Bar Association is an attempt to standardize the various state probate procedures now in existence. Its purpose was to counter the widespread criticism of the present probate system in the

Exhibit 1.1   Some Books Containing Federal and State Statutes

Exhibit 1.2   Sample Page from Minnesota Statutes Annotated

ARTICLE II

INTESTATE SUCCESSION AND WILLS

PART 1

INTESTATE SUCCESSION

Laws 1974, c. 442 and Laws 1975, c. 347, enacted the provisions of Chapter 524 of the statutes. Chapter 524 replaced certain of the subject matter contained in Chapter 525 of the statutes. For table showing the disposition of Chapter 525 see the preliminary matter of this volume.

Minnesota in 1974 and 1975 enacted only section 2–110 [M.S.A. § 524.2–110] of the portion of Uniform Probate Code relating to Intestate Succession. Provisions relating to Intestate Succession are retained in Chapter 525 at section 525.13 et seq.

524.2–110.   Advancements

If a person dies intestate as to all his estate, property which he gave in his lifetime to an heir is treated as an advancement against the latter's share of the estate only if declared in a contemporaneous writing by the decedent or acknowledged in writing by the heir to be an advancement. For this purpose the property advanced is valued as of the time the heir came into possession or enjoyment of the property or as of the time of death of the decedent, whichever first occurs. If the recipient of the property fails to survive the decedent, the property is not taken into account in computing the intestate share to be received by the recipient's issue, unless the declaration or acknowledgment provides otherwise.

Laws 1975, c. 347, § 22, eff. Jan. 1, 1976.

* * * * *

PART 5

WILLS

Minnesota in 1974 and 1975 did not enact sections 2–503 and 2–511 of the Uniform Probate Code relating to holographic wills and testamentary additions to trusts respectively. For provisions relating to probate of wills made out of this state see M.S.A. § 524.2–506. For provisions relating to testamentary additions to trusts see M.S.A. § 525.223.

524.2–501.   Who may make a will

Any person 18 or more years of age who is of sound mind may make a will.

Laws 1975, c. 347, § 22, eff. Jan. 1, 1976.

Exhibit 1.3 Sample Page from Pennsylvania Statutes Annotated

CHAPTER 25

WILLS

§ 2501.   Who may make a will

(a) **Persons 18 or older.**—Any person of sound mind 18 years of age or older may by will dispose of all his real and personal estate subject to payment of debts and charges.

(b) Repealed.

1972, June 30, P.L. 508, No. 164, § 2, eff. July 1, 1972. As amended 1972, Dec. 6, P.L. ——, No. 331, § 2; 1974, Dec. 10, P.L. ——, No. 293, § 6, imd. effective.

§ 2502.   Form and execution of a will

Every will shall be in writing and shall be signed by the testator at the end thereof, subject to the following rules and exceptions:

(1) **Words following signature.** The presence of any writing after the signature to a will, whether written before or after its execution, shall not invalidate that which precedes the signature.

(2) **Signature by mark.** If the testator is unable to sign his name for any reason, a will to which he makes his mark and to which his name is subscribed in his presence before or after he makes his mark, shall be as valid as though he had signed his name thereto: Provided, That he makes his mark in the presence of two witnesses who sign their names to the will in his presence.

United States by providing an alternative system which, if adopted by a state, would be uniform, less expensive, less time-consuming, and more efficient than the present system of administering a decedent's estate. It includes both formal and informal proceedings. At this writing, Alaska, Arizona, Colorado, Florida, Hawaii, Idaho, Kentucky, Maine, Michigan, Minnesota, Montana, Nebraska, New Mexico, North Dakota, and Utah have adopted the Uniform Probate Code. Eleven other states have adopted some of the code's provisions. The current trend of state legislatures is to adopt the Uniform Probate Code. The Uniform Probate Code is found in Appendix C of this text. Exhibit 1.4 shows law books that contain the Uniform Probate Code (left) and the State of California Probate Code (right).

Familiarity with the probate code of the state in which the paralegal resides and works is essential. To illustrate some of the characteristics that are common to state probate codes and the Uniform Probate Code, Exhibits 1.5, 1.6, and 1.7 show titles with excerpts from the tables of contents of two state codes and the Uniform Probate Code. The common features of the codes illustrated in the exhibits include a codification (systemization) of the individual state's statutes covering the specific subject matter desired, e.g., a unit on wills, their execution and revocation; a unit on intestate succession or descent and distribution; a unit on administration of estates (probate); a unit on guardians; and other common topics. But note that they each use different ways of organizing their ideas, e.g., they all deal with the estate of a missing person, but only California has a section by that name. Your state will have its own categories. In addition, each chapter is subdivided into various specific topics with each given a code section number. For reference, the topics are listed in an index at the end of the code and the appropriate section number is given. The index is a useful means of finding the relevant code provision when performing legal research.

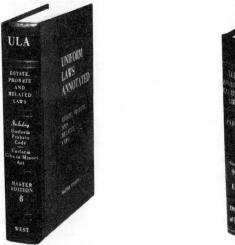

Exhibit 1.4   Two Law Books Containing Probate Codes

Exhibit 1.5   Excerpt from Table of Contents of Texas Probate Code

TEXAS PROBATE CODE

Acts 1955, 54th Leg., p. 88, ch. 55

Approved April 4, 1955, effective Jan. 1, 1956

As amended to September 1, 1977

An Act to establish and adopt a probate code for the State of Texas by revising and rearranging the statutes of this State which pertain to descent and distribution, wills, administration of decedents' estates, actions to declare heirship, guardianship, and other probate matters; and by making various changes in, omissions from, and additions to, such statutes; defining the meaning of certain words and terms used in the code; and fixing the effective date of the code; providing for the application of the code; validating certain proceedings had under existing and prior statutes; repealing statutes and all laws or parts of laws in conflict with the code; containing a severability clause; and declaring an emergency.

Be it enacted by the Legislature of the State of Texas:

Exhibit 1.6   Excerpt from Table of Contents of California Probate Code

THE
PROBATE CODE
OF THE
STATE OF CALIFORNIA

AN ACT to revise and consolidate the law relating to probate, including the custody, disposal by will, succession, administration and distribution of estates of decedents, estates of missing persons, the custody and administration of estates of persons, under guardianship, the custody of persons under guardianship, and the management, control and disposition of community real property and homestead property of insane or incompetent persons; and to repeal certain provisions of law therein revised and consolidated and therein specified; and to establish a Probate Code.

Stats.1931, c. 281, p. 587.

Approved May 11, 1931.   In effect August 14, 1931.

The people of the State of California do enact as follows:

Sections 1 to 399 are set out in this volume

Title of Act amended by Stats.1935, c. 712, p. 1922, § 1; Stats.1941, c. 1220, p. 3031, § 1.

Exhibit 1.7 Excerpt from Table of Contents of Uniform Probate Code

UNIFORM
PROBATE CODE

Official Text Approved by the National Conference of Commissioners on Uniform State Laws

AN ACT

Relating to affairs of decedents, missing persons, protected persons, minors, incapacitated persons and certain others and constituting the Uniform Probate Code; consolidating and revising aspects of the law relating to wills and intestacy and the administration and distribution of estates of decedents, missing persons, protected persons, minors, incapacitated persons and certain others; ordering the powers and procedures of the Court concerned with the affairs of decedents and certain others; providing for the validity and effect of certain non-testamentary transfers, contracts and deposits which relate to death and appear to have testamentary effect; providing certain procedures to facilitate enforcement of testamentary and other trusts; making uniform the law with respect to decedents and certain others; and repealing inconsistent legislation.

COMMENT

The long title of the Code should be adapted to the constitutional, statutory requirements and practices of the enacting state. The concept of the Code is that the "affairs of decedents, missing persons, disabled persons, minors, and certain others" is a single subject of the law notwithstanding its many facets.

Exhibit 1.7 *(continued)*

ARTICLE I

GENERAL PROVISIONS, DEFINITIONS AND PROBATE JURISDICTION OF COURT

PART 1

SHORT TITLE, CONSTRUCTION, GENERAL PROVISIONS

Section
1-101. [Short Title.]
1-102. [Purposes; Rule of Construction.]
1-103. [Supplementary General Principles of Law Applicable.]
1-104. [Severability.]
1-105. [Construction Against Implied Repeal.]
1-106. [Effect of Fraud and Evasion.]
1-107. [Evidence as to Death or Status.]
1-108. [Acts by Holder of General Power.]

PART 2

DEFINITIONS

1-201. [General Definitions.]

PART 3

SCOPE, JURISDICTION AND COURTS

1-301. [Territorial Application.]
1-302. [Subject Matter Jurisdiction.]
1-303. [Venue; Multiple Proceedings; Transfer.]
1-304. [Practice in Court.]
1-305. [Records and Certified Copies.]
1-306. [Jury Trial.]
1-307. [Registrar; Powers.]
1-308. [Appeals.]
1-309. [Qualifications of Judge.]
1-310. [Oath or Affirmation on Filed Documents.]

PART 4

NOTICE, PARTIES AND REPRESENTATION IN ESTATE LITIGATION AND OTHER MATTERS

1-401. [Notice; Method and Time of Giving.]
1-402. [Notice; Waiver.]
1-403. [Pleadings; When Parties Bound by Others; Notice.]

Common (Case) Law

Common law is based on the unwritten principles of law that had their origin in England. These principles were developed according to the customs and traditions of the "community" or on what was "equitable, fair, or just." Thus, a controversy taken to the courts involving simple issues was decided by the established customs of the community. But if a controversy concerned matters for which there was no applicable custom, the court (judge) decided according to his idea of fairness and justice. English common law principles spread to this country. Over the years in the United States, the written court decisions based on the common law principles came to be called *case law* because the decisions resulted from prior decisions in similar cases. Today the terms common law and case law have become synonymous, and legal writers tend to use the terms interchangeably. If a court is confronted with a case involving issues to which no constitutional provision or federal or state statute is wholly applicable, the court looks to previous decisions, i.e., common (case) law, for guidance. If no prior similar cases are available, the judge's decision necessarily creates new case law.

In summary, courts serve two major functions: they interpret and apply the constitutional and statutory law, and they create their own law by looking to prior cases when no constitutional law or statutory law exists to resolve the dispute before them. Such "judge-made" law is called case (common) law.

Points to remember about common law are that it must not conflict with constitutional or statutory law and that it can be altered by statute. Following is an example of a decision based upon common law.

WINDUST v. DEPARTMENT OF LABOR AND INDUSTRIES

Supreme Court of Washington, 1958.
52 Wash.2d 33, 323 P.2d 241.

MALLERY, Justice.

Aubra H. Windust died on March 29, 1954, at the age of sixty-one years, while working for the Glacier Sand and Gravel Company as an operator of a ready-mix concrete truck.

On April 28, 1954, his widow filed a claim for a pension with the department of labor and industries, which the supervisor rejected upon the ground that there was no injury within the contemplation of the workmen's compensation act. The board of industrial insurance appeals sustained the supervisor's order and claimant appealed to the superior court. From its judgment of dismissal, she appeals to this court.

As a driver of the ready-mix concrete truck, one of the workmen's customary duties was to walk out on the catwalk on the side of the truck, step up about two feet and look into the drum to see how much concrete was in it. He fell dead, on the day in question, just as he was stepping up to look into the drum. Appellant contends this act incident to his employment constituted an *injury* under the workmen's compensation act. It is not denied that the workman had been looking into the drum to ascertain the amount of remaining concrete, whenever his duties required it, for approximately ten years.

The workman's death was due to a myocardial infarction involving the interventricular septum caused by fatty deposits on the inside of the heart arteries, known as arteriosclerosis, which so narrowed them that not enough blood could pass through to supply the heart muscle.   Dr. Sloan's testimony followed the customary pattern that, if the workman had not engaged in his work but had been receiving proper medical treatment at the time he looked into the drum, he would not have died.

This satisfied the rule of McCormick Lumber Co. v. Department of Labor and Industries, 7 Wash.2d 40, 108 P.2d 807, 815, which is:

> "* * * An accident arises out of the employment when the required exertion producing the accident is too great for the man undertaking the work, *whatever the degree of exertion or the condition of the workman's health.*"

This formula justifies holding that the recurring duties of a job and acts incident thereto constitute *injuries,* whenever a workman's heart ailment has progressed to the point where a restriction of activities is essential to his survival.

The rule of the McCormick case has represented for many years the decisional weight of authority in this state.   If the doctrine of *stare decisis* is applicable to cases which interpret a statute, we are not now free to depart from that rule, notwithstanding its obvious conflict with the statute.

The statute in question is RCW 51.08.100 [cf. Rem.Rev.Stat. (Sup.), § 7675; Rem.Supp.1941, § 7679–1].   It provides:

> " 'Injury' means a sudden and tangible happening, of a traumatic nature, producing an immediate or prompt result, and occurring from without; an occupational disease; and such physical condition as results from either."

This situation, in which the statute is amended or repealed by a court-made rule, warrants an examination of the doctrine of *stare decisis* and the proper occasion for its application.   This is its definition in Webster's New International Dictionary (2d ed.):

> "Literally, to stand by decided matters; * * * as implying the doctrine or policy of following rules or principles laid down in previous judicial decisions unless they contravene the ordinary principles of justice.   This principle had an important part in the development of the English common law."

Indeed, the common law is comprised of that body of court decisions in the nonstatutory field to which the doctrine of *stare decisis* applies.   The rule of law of those cases was promulgated by the courts for the inescapable reason that pending litigation had to be disposed of, even though there was no legislative enactment that governed the issue therein.   Uniform and equal justice naturally required subsequent adherence to such decisions in the absence of pertinent legislation.   In the sense that the promulgation of a rule of law is legislation, the courts can and do properly legislate in nonstatutory fields.   Every case governed by *stare decisis,* rather than statute law, is a proper occasion for judicial legislation.   However, the courts may only so legislate in fields left vacant by the legislature.   A legislative enactment, intended to be comprehensive upon a subject, pre-empts that field, with the result that the court's constitutional function with regard to it is thereafter limited to an interpretation of what the legislature meant by the language used in the statute.

Whenever a judge makes a decision in a case involving previously undetermined issues, case law is created.   The judge, in effect, makes

law. The ruling may establish a precedent for another judge to follow in a subsequent case having similar facts. Since uniformity and consistency in deciding cases is desirable, the practice of following previous court holdings established the doctrine of *stare decisis,* a Latin term meaning "to stand by decisions." The law made by the highest court in a state is binding on other courts in the same state when similar cases arise, until that highest court itself changes its view of the law in a subsequent case. After precedents have been followed in a number of cases with similar facts, they become firmly established in our common or case law.

Following the principles of *stare decisis* is a valuable but not invincible aid in rendering decisions. The U.S. Supreme Court can overrule any state or lower federal court decision. State supreme courts can overrule the decisions of lower-level courts within the state court system. If the facts in a second case are distinguishable from the original, or if changing economic, social, or political conditions make the doctrine outmoded, the doctrine of *stare decisis* may not be followed. The court may decide a subsequent case differently, in which case it would be said that the decision "overruled" the prior case that had established the original precedent. The source of most of our laws pertaining to contracts, property, trusts, and agency relationships is common (case) law.

Here is an example of case law concerning wills.

IN RE ESTATE OF WILLIAMS

(1965 Fla.) 182 So.2d 10.

O'CONNELL, Justice.

The District Court of Appeal, Third District, has certified to us, as passing upon a question of great public interest, its decisions in In re Williams Estate, Fla.App.1965, 172 So.2d 464, and In re Estate of Zarkey, Fla.App.1965, 172 So.2d 465.

In each of these cases the county judge refused to admit to probate a will signed by the testator with a mark, similar to an X, on the ground that the making of a mark was not sufficient signing of the will under the provisions of F.S. Section 731.07, F.S.A. On appeal the district court affirmed the county judge in each case. The factual circumstances in both cases are so similar as to require no discussion.

The single issue for decision is whether, under the wording of Sec. 731.07, a testator may execute his will by making his mark, as distinguished from writing his alphabetical name. The county judges and the district court held that a will could not be validly executed in this manner. We cannot agree.

The pertinent portions of the controlling statute read:

"731.07 Execution of Wills—Every will, other than a noncupative will, must be in writing and must be executed as follows:

"(1) The testator must sign his will at the end thereof, or some other person in his presence and by his direction must subscribe the name of the testator thereto.

"(2) The testator, in the presence of at least two attesting witnesses present at the same time, must sign his will or cause his name to be signed as aforesaid or acknowledge his signature thereto."

We are here concerned only with the requirement that the "testator must sign his will at the end thereof * * *." The county judges and the district court were of the view that in order to "sign" the testator must write his alphabetical name. The respondents, of course, agree with this, while the petitioners argue that one may "sign" by making his mark.

In the construction of any statute it is always our duty to give effect to the legislative intent where such is ascertainable. However, we find nothing in the statute itself which gives support to either of the definitions urged to be given the word "sign."

This being so, we think we must then decide in that way which gives effect to the will of the testators involved unless some countervailing factor of public policy prevents.

We are surprised that the question here presented is one of first impression in this state. The only Florida case dealing with the question of signing by mark is Bruner v. Hart, 1910, 59 Fla. 171, 51 So. 593, in which this court held that a witness to a deed could subscribe as a witness by affixing his mark, rather than by writing his alphabetical name. In so holding this court stated that a person could witness by mark unless such method was forbidden by statute and noted that the applicable statute did not forbid a witness "subscribing his name by making his mark." A witness to a will is now required to actually sign his name to the will. F.S. Sec. 731.03(16), F.S.A.

It is interesting to note that in Bruner v. Hart, supra, the two grantors also signed the questioned deed by mark. Surprisingly the deed was not attacked on this ground. This would seem to indicate that the parties in that case conceded that a grantor could "sign" by mark, but questioned only whether a witness could "subscribe" by mark. It is not unreasonable to assume that a like and widely held concession that a testator could sign his will by mark may account for the fact that no case in point has previously been presented to the appellate courts of this state.

We have carefully read the three cases cited by this court in support of the holding in Bruner v. Hart that a witness could subscribe by mark. Two of the cited cases decided that a witness to a will could subscribe as an attesting witness by mark. Garrett v. Heflin, 1893, 98 Ala. 615, 13 So. 326; and Pridgen v. Pridgen's Heirs, 1852, 13 Ired. 259, 35 N.C. 259. In the Pridgen case that court discussed the early English cases and statutes dealing with the execution of wills, explained that the word "signum" (from which our word sign is derived) meant no more than a mark, and expressed the view that sign and subscribe meant essentially the same thing when used in a statute. This seems to be the prevailing view in this country.

There can be no doubt that the effect of this court's decision in Bruner v. Hart is that a person can meet the statutory mandate of subscribing his name by making his mark rather than writing his alphabetical name. If there is a difference in meaning in the words "sign" and "subscribe" it is that "subscribe" is more limited than "sign". This logically leads to the conclusion that if one can subscribe by making his mark he can certainly sign by the same means. We so hold.

The great majority of the courts which have dealt with cases like these involving similar statutes hold as we do here, that a mark made by the testator at the proper place on his will with the intent that it constitute his signature and evidence his assent to the will is sufficient to satisfy the statutory requirement that he "sign" his will. See Annotations in 31 A.L.R. 682, 42 A.L.R. 954, 114 A.L.R. 110, and 98 A.L.R.2d 841.

We have not ignored respondent's contention that public policy, which is to protect testators and their heirs from fraud, would be best served by refusing to accept as properly executed under the statute a will signed by the testator with only his mark. In support of this contention respondents argue that it is impossible for handwriting experts to determine the authenticity of a mark as might be done with a handwritten alphabetical name. They also argue that if a testator cannot write his name and is not permitted to sign by mark, he will be forced to have another person subscribe his name for him. This they say will be added protection because a person requested to sign the name of another will not be likely to do so without first determining the identity of the purported testator.

It is true that even a handwriting expert would have difficulty determining who made a mark in the absence of distinguishing characteristics by which certain comparisons can reasonably be made. If proof of the execution of a will rested entirely upon the identification of the mark or signature of the testator the respondents' argument would be difficult to overcome. But such is not the case. The greatest protection against fraud, and the greatest aid in proof that a testator did in any manner sign his will as his, is furnished by the statutory requirement that it be done in the presence of, or acknowledged in the presence of, at least two attesting witnesses.

Furthermore, the alternative method for the execution of a will, by which some other person may subscribe the testator's name, really seems to offer even less protection than the testator's mark.

This is so because the statute does not require the person signing for the testator to be identified in the document. True, a careful lawyer supervising the execution of a will would see that such person's identity was reflected in some manner at the end of the will. Nevertheless, the statute does not require it nor does it prescribe how it shall be made known that the testator's name was subscribed by another or how such person is to be identified in the document.

Therefore, we fail to see how fraud on testators would be prevented in any meaningful way by a holding that our statute requires that a person must either subscribe his alphabetical name or have another person to do so for him. Rather, we hold, as do most jurisdictions, that a testator may "sign" his will by making a mark. It is a matter of fact to be proved in proper proceedings whether the testator made the mark with the intention that it evidence his assent to the document.

If this cause accomplishes nothing more than to call attention to the inadequacies of Section 731.07(1) and (2) it will have served a useful purpose. We have no doubt that the appropriate committees of The Florida Bar and the Legislature will give attention to making the changes which are necessary to make clear whether a person should be able to sign his will by mark, and to prescribe the formalities to be followed and recorded as a part of the will when the testator signs by mark or another person subscribes the name of the testator at the testator's direction.

For the reasons given above the decisions of the district court are reversed and the cause remanded for further proceedings consistent herewith.

It is so ordered.

Assignment 1

1. Is there a separate index in your state code devoted solely to wills, estates, and trusts? If not, where is the index system your code uses?

2. Is there a general index at the end of the entire code? List five of the main headings in the area of wills, estates, and trusts.

3. Are there any forms in your code on wills, estates, and trusts? If so, pick any one of them and identify it.

4. In the law library nearest you, go to the card catalog. Make a list of every book that contains material on wills, estates, and trusts *for your state*. (Eventually you will want to examine all these books.)

Assignment 2

1. Has the Uniform Probate Code (U.P.C.) been adopted in your state code? If so, on what date was it adopted?

2. Examine your state's probate code and the U.P.C. at the end of this text. Give one example of a difference between the two codes in a statutory section on the same topic.

3. Using the Glossary, define the following terms: *Uniform Probate Code (U.P.C.), stare decisis, common law, codification, statutes, citation.*

Chapter 2

Estate Planning
and Introduction to
Estate Administration

Scope of the Chapter

This chapter begins with a discussion of the need of every person to have an estate plan. The legal instruments, i.e., trusts and wills, which are developed and used to implement the estate plan will be covered extensively in later chapters. Also included in this chapter is an illustrative survey of the tasks performed by a paralegal in the administration of the estate of a decedent. The dialogue presented is for introductory, overview purposes only. At this point the student is not expected to master the terms used to identify and explain the estate administration process. In later chapters, terminology and procedures will be repeated and discussed in more detail. The glossary in the back of the text should be used as a reference to define unfamiliar terms.

Competencies

After completing this chapter, the paralegal should be able to:

• Understand and explain the need for estate planning
• Identify the people who play a necessary role in the administration of a decedent's estate
• Begin to understand and become familiar with the general procedures of estate administration
• Begin to recognize and learn the terms associated with estate administration

The Need for Estate Planning

Estate planning is the determination and utilization of a method to accumulate, manage, and dispose of real and personal property by the owner of the property during the owner's life and after the owner's death. Estate planning is accomplished by the means of such devices as trusts and wills. The purpose of estate planning is to identify, preserve, and expand or increase the assets owned and to provide for distribution of these assets, with the least possible tax expense, to those persons and institutions the owner wishes to benefit during life as well as after death. If estate planning is properly performed, the intent and desires of the owner will be accomplished and the beneficiary-recipients will receive the maximum benefit and enjoyment of the property.

Unfortunately most people have neither an estate plan nor a will. They are so involved in their daily activities that they give little thought to the consequences of their deaths. Many do realize the importance of purchasing life insurance to protect their dependents, and as people grow older they are apt to give some thought to their mortality. But many people die prematurely, leaving dependents unprotected, and all too many people die without having made provisions through a valid will for those for whom they care. The consequences of these acts of procrastination can be tragic.

The chapters in this book will detail how the creation and use of trusts and wills can resolve and avoid the unfortunate consequences. For now, it is important that the paralegal understand the need for estate planning and be prepared to assist parties who have the responsibility for planning estates and estate administration. These parties will include the paralegal's supervising attorney and the personal representative of the decedent's estate. In addition to the attorney, numerous other individuals are qualified to give estate planning advice. They include trust officers from banks and trust companies, accountants, investment advisers, and some life insurance agents. Since this text is primarily concerned with the work of a paralegal, we will focus on the functions of the attorney, the representative of the decedent's estate, and the paralegal student. The role of these parties is the topic of the rest of this chapter and part of the next.

We begin with an overview of the administration of a deceased person's estate. The purpose is to acquaint the paralegal student who is unfamiliar with the legal terms and procedures of estate administration with a broad, general view of the estate administration process using a dialogue among the essential parties. In later chapters the legal terms and concepts, plus the step-by-step procedures for handling an estate, will be covered in greater detail. Repetition of essential information is the best way for a beginning student to understand this complex legal field and become qualified to perform the necessary paralegal functions.

Introduction to
Estate Administration: A Dialogue

The following discussion describes the probate procedures involved in a typical case. The participants include the decedent's named personal representative (the executor), the attorney for the estate, and the paralegal. The participants and facts of the case are as follows:

Participants

- Decedent—John Smith

- Executor—William Smith

- Attorney—Ms. Brown

- Paralegal—Ms. Jones

Facts

John Smith, the decedent, died August 15, 1983, owning property in two states, State A and State B. He was domiciled at 1024 Pleasure Lane, Heavenly City, in Cotton County, State A, owning his home there. In addition to the homestead held in joint tenancy with his wife, John owned the following property: a car, licensed in State A and owned in his name only; stocks and bonds owned jointly with his wife; a savings account jointly owned; a checking account in his name only; a life insurance policy with his wife named beneficiary; some valuable paintings given to him by his grandfather; and a summer cottage in his name only, located in State B. John had only a few debts at the time of his death, and no one owed him any money. He was survived by his wife, Mary, and only child, William, age 22.

An attorney, Ms. Brown, had previously been retained to help with the drawing of John Smith's will. Ms. Jones, the paralegal, had collected all the pertinent information from John Smith and had written a preliminary draft of the will, which had then been finalized in a meeting between John Smith, Ms. Brown, and Ms. Jones on January 10, 1981 (see Exhibit 2.1). The final draft of the executed will had been placed in a vault in Ms. Brown's office.

The provisions of John's will left his wife all property not already transferred to her by joint ownership, gift, or other means. William Smith, son of the decedent, had been named executor of the will. He had made all the necessary funeral arrangements for his father's burial, and knowing he had been named executor, went to the office of Ms. Brown to discuss the handling of the administration of his father's estate.

In the presence of the paralegal (Ms. Jones), the attorney (Ms. Brown), and the executor (William Smith), the following dialogue takes place.

Attorney: Come in and sit down, William. Here is your father's will. As you know, you have been asked to be his executor.

Executor: (Reads the will) Before his death, my father and I discussed the handling of his estate. I knew he had named me executor, and I agreed to serve. But we also decided, and my mother agreed, to ask you, Ms. Brown, to act as my attorney and advise me in carrying out the duties of the executor since I have no experience in these matters and feel I should learn and understand completely the responsibilities.

Attorney: I will be happy to serve as your attorney. It has been the practice of this law firm when advising clients named as executors to work with our paralegal in the field of estate administration. As you know, William, Ms. Jones helped both to collect the necessary data for and to prepare the preliminary draft of your father's will. Now, under my supervision, she will handle many of the details necessary to help settle your father's estate. She will participate in all our conferences on administration, and she will keep you informed of all meetings, hearings, correspondence, and the current status of the administration of your father's estate. She will be available to answer some of the questions you might have about your executor's duties. Others she will discuss with me, and we shall then communicate the information to you. Please feel free to ask either of us any questions or contact us at any time you have matters which you want to discuss.

Executor: Yes, I have met Ms. Jones. My father told me how pleased he was with the help she had given him in drafting his will. I am very happy that Ms. Jones will be working with us.

Paralegal: Thank you. Before we begin our discussion about estate administration, let me review for you the things that have been done to this point. As you know, our firm assisted your father in planning for the distribution of his estate after his death. Ms. Brown discussed with your father the purpose of and need for a will. I compiled checklists of all the property which your father owned or in which he had any interest. After discussing the estate plan with Ms. Brown, I then drew up a preliminary draft of the will. Ms. Brown, utilizing methods that took advantage of all possible tax considerations, drew up the final draft of your father's will in its present form. The will ensures that the estate will be distributed according to your father's wishes.

Attorney: Let's get started. What we try to accomplish, William, when we assist executors, is to explain the basic course of conduct that must be followed procedurally in administering an estate from beginning to end.

Executor: A few years ago my uncle died without a will. I recall my aunt talking about it. Are procedures in the administration of the estate the same when a person dies with or without a will?

Attorney: I intend to discuss with you procedures that occur whether a decedent dies *testate,* meaning with a will, as in your father's case, or *intestate,* which means without a will, as in your uncle's case. In either case, a *personal representative* must be appointed to administer the decedent's estate. In the situation such as your father's, where someone has died leaving a will, the personal representative named in the will is generally called an *executor,* if a man, or an *executrix,* if a woman. When a person has died without a will, the personal representative is referred to as an *administrator,* if a man, or an *administratrix,* if a woman. An executor is named in the will and then confirmed by the court to handle the estate. An administrator, however, must be appointed by the court when there is no will. You, William, will perform the duties of an executor.

Exhibit 2.1 John Smith's Will

LAST WILL AND TESTAMENT
OF
JOHN SMITH

I, John Smith, residing at 1024 Pleasure Lane, Heavenly City, Cotton County, State A, declare this instrument to be my Last Will and Testament, hereby revoking all former Wills and Codicils by me made.

Article I

I direct that all my just debts, funeral expenses and expenses of administration be paid out of my estate.

Article II

I give all of my property, now owned or hereafter acquired by me, to my wife, Mary Smith.

Article III

In the event my said wife, Mary Smith, shall predecease me, or if we should die in a common accident, then I give all of my said proprety, now owned or hereafter acquired by me, to my son, William Smith, now residing at 1024 Pleasure Lane.

Article IV

I hereby nominate and appoint my son, William Smith, Executor of this, my Last Will and Testament. In the event he should predecease me or should be unwilling or unable to serve in that capacity, then I hereby nominate and appoint my brother, Joseph Smith, Executor of this, my Last Will and Testament. I hereby give and grant unto my said Executor full power to sell and convey, lease or mortgage any and all real estate that I may own at the time of my death or which may be acquired by my estate, without license or leave of court.

Article V

No bond shall be required of the individual named above as Executor of this Will.

IN WITNESS WHEREOF, I have hereunto set my hand to this my last Will and Testament this 10th day of January, 1981.

_____

THIS INSTRUMENT, consisting of one (1) typewritten page, including this certificate, each bearing the signature of the above named Testator, was by him on the date thereof signed, published and declared by him to be his Last Will and Testament, in our presence, who, at his request and in his presence, and in the presence of each other, we believing him to be of sound mind and disposing memory, hereunto subscribed our names as attesting witnesses.

_____ residing at _____

_____ residing at _____

Executor: Well, how do we begin? What must I do?

Attorney: The basic duties that must be performed by any personal representative are these:

1. All your father's assets must be collected.

2. His debts, claims against the estate, and taxes due must be paid.

3. The remainder of his estate or property must be distributed according to his will within guidelines set by the *statutes* or laws of this state.

When a person dies, the county and state in which the decedent resides at death, the *domicile*, is the proper *venue*, or place, for the *"domiciliary" administration* of the decedent's estate. In this state, as in most states, the court that handles the decedent's estate is called the *probate court.* Each county has its own probate court. The right, power, and authority a probate court has to hear and decide these matters is referred to as the court's *jurisdiction.* Jurisdiction of the probate court over the administration of a decedent's estate continues until the proceeding is finished. Since your father also owned *real property,* your summer cottage in State B, a second or *"ancillary" administration* must be commenced in that state. The county in which the property is located is the proper venue for the ancillary proceeding. Ms. Jones will give you additional information and assistance in handling such matters.

Executor: So far I believe I understand the basic functions that must be performed and how the probate court fits into the picture. Since my father named me executor, do I give the money and property to the people mentioned in his will?

Attorney: Not right away. Although you have been named executor, you have no authority to act as representative until you petition to and are appointed by the probate court. This will be done once your father's will has been validated and accepted by the probate court. Now that we are ready to discuss procedural steps and the checklist of information necessary to accomplish them, I am turning you over to Ms. Jones to have her go through the steps with you. As we previously mentioned, if you have any questions about your responsibilities, please call. We shall see that any problems are resolved.

Executor: Thank you for the information, Ms. Brown. If I have any problems, I'll be sure to ask you. Good-bye, and thanks again.

Paralegal: As Ms. Brown mentioned, in order for you to become authorized as executor, you must petition the court to admit and accept your father's will. This is done by filling out one of the numerous forms required for estate administration. We have in our law office all the necessary forms that you must complete as part of this administration. In addition, we will set up what is called a "tickler" system, which lists chronologically all the important steps and dates in the stages of the administration of the estate.

Here is an example of a "tickler" form. (See Exhibit 2.2) Using both this system and a list of procedural steps will help reduce the possibility that some important detail or significant date might be forgotten, with resulting damage to the beneficiary's (*successor's*) interest and with potential liability to you, the executor.

Executor: In that case, let's set up this "tickler" system right away. If we each have a copy, then we can remind one another of the essential steps and important dates. Right?

Paralegal: Yes. This is exactly what we will do. But remember, you must first get your position as executor authorized as well as establish the necessary ancillary

Exhibit 2.2 Sample "Tickler" Form

ESTATE OF JOHN SMITH

"Tickler"

ESTATE OF _____ deceased, _____, 19___

Date of Death _____ Domicle _____

Probate Court _____ County, File No. _____

Name, Mailing Address and Telephone of Representative:

_____

Ancillary Administration Necessary _____

Date of Last Will _____

Probate Court File No. _____

Proceeding	Due or Dated	Filed or Paid
Petition for probate, administration, etc.		
Hearing on Petition for Probate		
Letters issued		
Inventory and appraisal		
Personal property tax	Feb.	
Real estate taxes: (First half	May 31	
Second half) if necessary	Oct. 31	
Last date for spouse's election		
Property set apart for surviving spouse and/ or minor children		
Maintenance ordered		
State and other inheritance tax waivers obtained		
Last date for filing claims		
Claims hearing		
Decedent's final income tax returns due		
Federal		
State		
Fiduciary's final income tax returns due		
Federal		
State		
Last date for filing claims with leave of court		
Optional alternative valuation date		
Federal estate tax return due		
State inheritance tax due		
Partial payment of inheritance tax (amount)		
Closing letter (federal estate tax)		
Date maintenance ends		
Final account		
Hearing on final account		
Discharge of representative		

administration in State B where the summer cottage is located. You recall that administration in your father's county of residence is called the "domiciliary" administration. Administration necessary in any other state is "ancillary." Although your father left a will naming you as executor of his estate, a person must also be appointed in State B to handle the ancillary administration. Even though there is a will, that person is called the *ancillary administrator,* not the ancillary executor.

Executor: Now I understand the term. But how is the ancillary administrator authorized, and what does he or she do?

Paralegal: You and your your mother are given the opportunity to select the person to act in this representative, *fiduciary* capacity. As a representative of the estate, the ancillary administrator must submit a petition for appointment to the probate court of the county in which the *real property,* the cottage, is located, using a form similar to the one you will use for authorization in our state. Once authorized by the local county probate court in State B, the ancillary administrator will:

1. Collect the local assets

2. Pay the local creditors and taxes, if any

3. Transfer the balance of the estate to you, the domiciliary representative

Some states allow the domiciliary representative to apply for appointment as ancillary administrator if there is no law to the contrary. We shall check this out because, if it is allowed, your acting as ancillary as well as domiciliary representative might be desirable. If there are creditors of your father in State B, you will be faced with the choice of paying their claims out of ancillary assets or the domiciliary estate funds. If you want to protect the summer cottage against being sold to satisfy such debts, you must discuss this with Ms. Brown.

Executor: By all means, I will consult with Ms. Brown. We would not want to sell the summer cottage unless necessary, since both my mother and I enjoy it so much.

Paralegal: Once you petition the court for probating of the will, and the court has proved and accepted it, you will be the authorized personal representative—the executor. The probate court signs an order admitting the will as valid and issuing to you *Letters Testamentary.* This particular legal form is the authorization given to executors to handle the administration of a decedent's estate. If your father had died intestate, without a will like your uncle, either your mother or you as *next-of-kin* would petition the probate court for general administration of your father's estate, requesting that the probate court appoint one or both of you as administrators. The form used to authorize an administrator is called *Letters of Administration.*

Executor: Then, Letters Testamentary authorize an executor named in a will to handle the decedent's estate, and Letters of Administration authorize a general administrator to do the work when the decedent dies leaving no will. Are the duties of the executor and administrator the same?

Paralegal: Basically, yes. Administrators do much the same thing as executors, but they must rely on the state laws to guide their actions, whereas executors follow the provisions of the will within statutory limitations, of course.

Executor: I've heard that in some cases an estate can be probated in a more simple manner—informally, I believe it is called. Is this possible?

Paralegal: That is a good question. Many states, including our own, have adopted the *Uniform Probate Code*'s recommendations for administration of decedents' estates. Two forms of probate procedures are included in the Code: *formal* or *solemn* and *informal* or *common.* Some states use only the formal procedures;

some follow the Uniform Probate Code and use both formal and informal procedures; others use a variation of these forms.

Basically, formal probate, also called supervised probate, indicates proceedings conducted before a *judge* with the requirement that *notice* be given to all *interested persons* so they might be present to contest the will or, in *intestacy* cases, to contest the appointment of a general administrator. Informal probate, on the other hand, is also known as unsupervised probate since it is necessary only to present a will or petition for administration to an appropriate court representative, who may be a judge but likely will be a *registrar* or *clerk*. After the will has been admitted or the administrator appointed, no notice to interested parties is necessary. The administration of the decedent's estate can thus be rapidly completed. Another advantage of informal probate is that it may reduce the expenses of administration, including the elimination of the need for an attorney to assist in the procedures. Every personal representative should consider administering an estate informally.

After hearing of the person's death, interested parties such as beneficiaries, successors, or creditors of the decedent who want to contest the validity of the will or the appointment of the administrator must request a formal hearing. An original informal proceeding then becomes a formal one, with all associated procedures. Because of the size of your father's estate and the real property involved, you will have to discuss with Ms. Brown the type of proceeding to be followed.

Executor: So what exactly would be the advantages of formal as opposed to informal probate for an estate like my father's?

Paralegal: Basically, the choice of formal or informal probate depends on a number of variables, like the nature of estate assets and the preferences of the representative. The probate court must supervise formal probate, while it does not have to supervise informal probate unless someone who has an interest in the estate requests it. The representative might feel that it would be better for the court rather than the registrar to oversee administration of the estate because of problems presented by certain assets. Since your father's estate hasn't been inventoried or valued yet, I can't give you facts or figures. However, Ms. Brown will advise you of the method that would better suit your case. One word of caution—informal probate sounds effortless, but I assure you it isn't. It leaves the representative to administer the estate with the help of the registrar. The court will step in only when requested, but knowing when to request the court's help isn't all that easy.

Executor: I can see that the procedures can be complicated. What information is needed to commence the formal probate?

Paralegal: First, we shall need a *petition to prove the will* (see Form 1).[1] It requests the following information:

- The name of the decedent
- His last residence
- His birthdate
- The place and date of his death
- The name and address of the executor
- The date and original copy of the will being probated
- The estimated value of the decedent's estate, including both real and personal property

---

1. All forms referred to in the text are found in Appendix A at the end of the book. The forms used in each state will vary, so the forms in Appendix A are shown for illustrative purposes only.

- The names and addresses of the decedent's known heirs and successors
- The request by the petitioner that notice that the will be admitted to probate be given to all the decedent's creditors, and that the petitioner (you) be appointed executor and Letters Testamentary issued

The petition, like so many of the forms we use, must be verified, that is, signed and sealed by a notary public.

Executor: What happens after the petition is completed?

Paralegal: We file the petition with the probate court, which establishes the court's jurisdiction over the estate, and the probate judge sets a date and time for the hearing on the petition. This order also limits the time for any of your father's creditors to file their claims and sets the date for hearing any disputed claim. Notice of the hearing is given to all interested parties either by direct mail to each heir, devisee, or successor, or by publication once a week for three weeks in a legal newspaper within the county for the benefit of creditors. Copies of this notice are also given to the state's tax department.

Executor: What happens at the hearing?

Paralegal: Before the actual hearing, we correspond with the witnesses to your father's will and make arrangements to have them meet you and Ms. Brown at the judge's chambers on the hearing day. Ms. Brown will have with her at that time the necessary forms for presentation to the court. You and I shall prepare these forms with Ms. Brown's supervision. The forms include:

- A *proof of publication* of notice of the hearing (Form 2)
- An *affidavit* stating when and where publication was made, obtained from the newspaper publishing the notice (Form 3)
- An *order admitting the will to probate* (Form 4), which states that this is the last will of the decedent, grants *Letters Testamentary* (Form 63), and specifies the amount of *bond* (Form 101), if required
- The representative's *oath of office,* which is usually on the same form as the bond but is sometimes on a separate form in other states (Form 59)
- The *certificate of probate* certifying that the will attached to it is the decedent's last will which the court allows, thus verifying its validity (Form 5)

We shall also prepare Letters Testamentary for the signature of the probate judge. These authorize you to act as the executor of your father's estate. Remember, had your father died intestate like your uncle, we would prepare Letters of Administration instead.

Executor: Yes, I understand that clearly now.

Paralegal: The final forms we prepare and present to the court are:

- The *order appointing the appraisers,* which names the persons who will appraise or value the estate (Form 6)
- The *notice to the surviving spouse,* your mother, of her *right to renounce* or waive what your father left to her in the will and take, instead, a percentage of his total probate estate, as she is allowed by statute (Form 7). Widows or widowers who receive little under their spouse's will find this *statutory election,* also known as the "forced share," advantageous, but since your father left your mother everything, she will obviously not pursue this right.

Executor: All right. We have the forms and the witnesses to my father's will at the courtroom. Are we ready for the hearing?

Paralegal: Yes. As petitioner, you will take the stand and be sworn in. Ms. Brown will elicit from you the information contained in the petition. Under oath, you will verify that it is correct and request appointment as executor of your father's estate. Then Ms. Brown will ask the witnesses who *attested* and *subscribed* to your father's will to take the stand and under oath testify that your father *acknowledged* the document as his last will and signed it in their presence and that they each signed as attesting witnesses. They will also testify that your father was of sound mind at the time he signed the will. Ms. Brown then asks the court to admit the will to probate and that you be authorized as executor.

Executor: What happens if my father's brother, Uncle Joe, objects to the will?

Paralegal: Good question. That's called a contest of the will. The probate court would then have to set up a separate hearing date for the will contest. Do you expect this to happen?

Executor: No, I was just wondering about the procedure.

Paralegal: In that case, I assume the probate judge will agree to the requests made by Ms. Brown. The execution of the will is thereby proved, and probate of the estate can begin.

Executor: What happens next at the hearing?

Paralegal: The probate judge asks you to take the required oath and sign the executor's bond if the judge deems it necessary. Since your father's will specifically requested that his representative be exempted from this, the judge will try to comply with the request, unless our statute requires the personal representative to be bonded in estates like your father's. A bond guarantees to the court and to those parties with an interest in the decedent's estate (creditors, successors, and the like) that you, the executor, will act in a fiduciary manner and perform your duties faithfully. The amount of the bond is determined by the court, and if it is needed, we will seek the lowest amount possible to lessen the bond premium expense.

After you have signed the bond and it is approved by the court, Ms. Brown asks the court to appoint two persons, previously agreed on, as appraisers for your father's estate. Not all states require appraisers, but ours does. Before the hearing, we will contact and receive the consent of these persons to act as appraisers. They are paid for their work out of the assets of the estate by you, the executor.

Finally, Ms. Brown requests the clerk to issue Letters Testamentary to you. These become your official authorization from the court to act as executor of your father's will and estate. You will use the Letters to obtain the assets of your father's estate that are currently in the possession of others such as banks and corporations. A few of the forms I have mentioned are provided by the court, but it will be necessary for us to prepare most of the forms we previously discussed.

Executor: The procedures are just as complex as I imagined. What next?

Paralegal: Well, remember we discussed ancillary administration?

Executor: Yes, in connection with the summer cottage.

Paralegal: That's right. We petition the county probate court in State B, where the cottage is located, asking that you be appointed ancillary administrator. I shall check to make sure you qualify. If I remember correctly, State B does not require the personal representative to be a resident of that state. I will check on this and on all similar matters under instructions from Ms. Brown before we act. It you are appointed, you will follow procedures similar to those we have discussed. You should notify creditors, if any, collect other assets, and pay taxes and debts. Doing these things will prevent creditors from attaching the cottage to satisfy debts, so you will be able to transfer it to your mother according to your father's wishes.

Executor: I am sure my father had no debts in State B where the cottage is located.

Paralegal: We must still go through these procedures, but the ancillary administration should create no problems.

Executor: Good.   Let's get back to our state procedures.

Paralegal: The next step is to prepare a complete inventory of your father's property with an estimate of the value of each asset.   I prepare an *inventory and appraisal form* (Form 65), which Ms. Brown reviews.   The two appointed appraisers will value the inventory according to one of the methods allowed by the Internal Revenue Service—assigning to each asset either the value it had at the time your father died or the value it had six months after his death.[2]   We will discuss the tax advantages of both methods and choose the one we think best once we have completed the inventory.   The inventory and appraisal serve as a basis for the federal and state tax returns that must be filed and provide information to all interested parties concerning the value of the estate.   You will also find them helpful when filing your *final account* (Form 72) after completing all required procedures.

Executor: I was wondering about the taxes.   What taxes must be paid and when are they due?

Paralegal: This area, resolving tax problems, is probably one of the most important functions Ms. Brown and I will help you perform in administering the estate.   Death tax laws, both state and federal, are very complex.   Ms. Brown determines whether any of the following tax returns must be filed and paid: *federal estate tax* (Form 119), *State A and B inheritance tax* (Form 71) *and/or estate tax* (Form 8), *federal and state individual income tax* (Forms 9 and 10), *federal and state fiduciary income tax* (Forms 11 and 12).

Now you see why the "tickler" system and the checklist we previously discussed are so valuable.   They help to avoid forgetting any important step or date in the administration of the estate.   They are especially useful and timely when dealing with potential tax problems.

I prepare all the necessary tax returns, and then we review them thoroughly with Ms. Brown.   She then files them, along with your check as executor for any tax payments due, with the appropriate federal or state tax department as well as the probate court.

Executor: I am glad we have the opportunity to review the tax consequences together because I know very little about this area, but I have been interested in it.

Paralegal: Well now, let's discuss the major items of property that compromise your father's estate.   As you know, your duties as executor are basically to collect the estate assets, to pay your father's creditors and necessary taxes, and to distribute the remaining assets according to the provisions of his will.

Some of your father's property was owned by him and your mother in *joint tenancy* and will automatically pass to her by "*operation of law.*"   This results from the *right of survivorship,* which means that the surviving joint tenant (your mother) gets the property without having to wait for a court order.   The home, the stocks and bonds, and the savings account automatically belong to your mother because she is a joint tenant owner.   These property items, along with the benefits from your father's life insurance policy, are called "*non-probate*" assets since they do not have to be disposed of by will nor do they *descend* to an heir as intestate property.   Other

---

2.   Internal Revenue Code (I.R.C.) § 2032.

items, which he owned, were in his name alone, such as the car, the paintings, and the summer cottage. These are *probate assets,* and, I might add, anything he may have owned as a tenant-in-common with someone else would be a probate asset also. Tenancy-in-common is a form of ownership between two or more persons. It differs from joint tenancy in that each co-owner can transfer his or her property interest not only while alive as in joint tenancy but also, unlike joint tenancy, after death, i.e., through a will.

As executor, you will collect and preserve only *probate assets* such as the car, paintings, and checking account. All probate and generally all nonprobate assets are included, however, in the decedent's estate for computing death taxes. There are additional procedural steps we must follow to clear the passage of the nonprobate property to your mother.

Executor: What do we need to do now?

Paralegal: At this time, you must open an account at your father's bank in your name as executor of his estate. Here is an example of what the check imprint on your father's account should look like (see Exhibit 2.3). You can then submit to the bank Letters Testamentary authorizing you to withdraw your father's checking account and have it transferred to the estate account. All the estate funds you collect must be deposited into this account, and receipts for such funds and any disbursements you make must be retained. You will need the canceled checks and other receipts or vouchers you receive during the administration of the estate when you present your *final account* to the probate court. It is essential that you keep complete and accurate records of all transactions affecting the estate, because the court will hold you personally responsible for any discrepancies or negligence.

Executor: What about some of the other property that I can't deposit—the probate assets I believe you called them—like the car, the paintings, and dad's life insurance?

Paralegal: Let's back up one moment and discuss again which are probate assets and which are nonprobate assets. Probate assets are those that can be passed by will or by intestate succession statutes. They include property owned solely in the decedent's name or, as previously mentioned, owned as a tenant-in-common. No other person takes them automatically when the owner dies. The car and the paintings that belonged to your father are probate assets because he alone owned them. The life insurance benefits are different. When the owner dies, the named

Exhibit 2.3 Sample Check Imprint for Deceased's Estate

No. _____

Heavenly City, State A _____, 198 __

PAY TO THE
ORDER OF _____ $_____

_____ DOLLARS

FIRST NATIONAL BANK
Heavenly City, State A

Estate of John Smith, deceased, by *William Smith*
Executor*

*Or other titles for the personal representative may be used.

beneficiary more-or-less automatically becomes the owner of the benefits—because life insurance benefits are derived from a contract between an insured person and an insurer (the insurance company) to pay a certain sum of money to a third person, the beneficiary, should the insured die. When your father died, your mother, whom he named beneficiary, became entitled to the insurance benefits directly, without having to wait for the probate court's approval.

Executor: Then the insurance benefits are nonprobate assets like the property my parents owned as joint tenants?

Paralegal: That's right. You must notify the insurance agent of your father's death and see that the agent receives the policy so that your mother can be given its proceeds. Remember, however, that we still must report this insurance as part of your father's *gross (total) estate* for tax purposes, unless he had relinquished the "*incidents of ownership* " on the policy. If your father contacted his insurance agent three years before his death and gave up certain contractual rights under the policy, such as the right to change the beneficiary and the right to borrow on or assign the policy, then the amount of the policy will not be part of his gross estate for tax purposes. We must check this out.

Executor: It's getting complicated.

Paralegal: Right now I'm sure it seems complicated. But let me assure you that if we work on this together in a systematic manner, everything will go smoothly.
Let's see. We were discussing the car and the paintings. The title to the car must be transferred to your mother. This cannot be accomplished until you receive Letters Testamentary. The following, however, will be necessary:

• The title *registration card* (Form 13) or certificate of title must be executed (filled in with any required information and signed by you as executor).

• A transfer fee of $5.00 must accompany the executed registration card or certificate and be mailed within 14 days of the date of transfer to the register to avoid penalties.

• A certified copy of Letters Testamentary—your authorization from the court to act as executor.

• A certified copy of the *Decree of Distribution* (Form 14) or *Order Setting Apart Personal Property* (Form 67). (We will discuss this in greater detail later.)

The paintings, like the car, are part of the inventory, and title will be transferred to your mother after creditors' claims and taxes due are paid. Determination of your father's debts and payment of those claims are other topics we must discuss.

Executor: Suppose my mother wanted to obtain and use some of the probate property now. Could she?

Paralegal: Yes. Some states, including ours, allow a surviving spouse and/or minor child to petition the probate court for a *maintenance allowance* and the receipt of certain *personal property* reserved for them by law. Your mother can petition for these things as the surviving spouse. Because your father was solvent and left his entire estate to your mother, however, I do not believe this will be necessary. If some unknown creditors of your father with considerable claims appear, we will then review the situation.

Executor: If the creditors do appear and there isn't enough property in my father's estate to pay all of them, would my mother still receive these things?

Paralegal: Yes. This is true in our state. Such claims of the spouse are given priority even over funeral expenses as well as various other debts within statutory limitations. Now concerning creditors' claims, do you remember what was said during our previous discussion about creditors and the hearing on the petition to approve the will?

Executor: Yes.   You mentioned time limits are set for filing creditors' claims against my father's estate.

Paralegal: Right.   When that time expires, we shall check to determine whether any filed claims should be contested.   If you reasonably believe a particular claim is not legitimate, you will file an *Objections to Claim* form (Form 15) with the probate court and serve a copy on the alleged creditor.   Contested claims are not heard on the same date as uncontested claims.   A separate hearing date is set, at which time the court will decide which contested claims are to be allowed.   Since it appears that your father had only a few debts and you have already acknowledged their validity, a hearing for contested claims may not be necessary.   If one is necessary, however, you must pay the claims the court allows.

Executor: How do I pay the claims?

Paralegal: By writing checks on the estate account.   Remember to ask for receipts from each creditor so that the receipts and the canceled checks can be filed with the court as evidence of payment.   Be cautioned that overpayment to a creditor, or payment of an invalid claim, makes you, the executor, personally liable.   This means that you must be very careful not to pay any doubtful claim until the hearing is over.

Executor: What if debts occur during our handling of the estate?

Paralegal: These expenses, including the fee our law firm will charge for its assistance in handling the estate, are priority debts according to statute and are paid just before you make the final distribution of the assets of the estate.   As executor, you also are entitled to reasonable compensation as the personal representative of the estate, which is another priority debt.

Executor: My father mentioned that to me, but I do not intend to charge a fee.

Paralegal: That, of course, is entirely up to you.   After claims are paid and receipts filed, the *final account* can be prepared.   Each state generally sets, for settlement of an estate, a time limit, which the court may extend for proper reasons.   This state allows the personal representative, you as executor, one year from the date of the appointment to settle the estate.   Again, a hearing is held for final settlement, and forms must be prepared.

Executor: What forms are required, and what is the procedure?

Paralegal: To close the estate after having distributed its assets—

• You must submit a *final account* containing a listing of all the assets you have collected, such as personal property and monies from sales, rents and other sources.

• You must list the liabilities you claim as credits against the estate, including payments for expenses of administration, creditors' claims allowed by the court, funeral expenses, taxes due, and other necessary and proper expenses.   Your account must show in detail these receipts and disbursements.

• You must prove that you have distributed the *remaining assets* of the estate, and this figure must correspond to the inventory actually remaining.

• You must sign and file a *petition for settlement and distribution* (Form 16).

The court will then issue an *order* (Form 73) setting a hearing on the final account so parties interested in the estate can have the opportunity to be present and make any objections to the accounting.

As with the hearing to prove the will, *notice* (Form 56) must be published once a week for three consecutive weeks in a local newspaper for the probate court. Copies of the notice must be sent to all heirs, devisees, or successors as well as to the state Department of Taxation within a specified statutory time period before the hearing. In our state, it is 14 days. *Proof* of this publication and mailing must be filed with the court (Forms 3 and 56).

Executor: Then is the hearing held?

Paralegal: Yes. At the hearing, if satisfied that the final account is correct and that all the taxes due have been paid, the probate judge will sign an order allowing the final account. Proof of payment of necessary taxes is provided by a certificate of release of tax lien. All the tax returns I have previously mentioned must be filed and any tax due must be paid before the court will determine the persons entitled to the remaining assets of the estate. The court will then issue the *Decree of Distribution* (Form 14) assigning these assets. The Decree of Distribution states that notice of the final account and settlement was given; that the decedent died testate; that the final account was approved and allowed; that all allowed claims were paid; that all other expenses, such as funeral and administration expenses have been paid; and that all heirs or successors are named and the share of the decedent's property to which each is entitled is listed.

Executor: Is that it? Am I then finished with my duties?

Paralegal: No. You must record a certified copy of the Decree of Distribution with the county recorder's office, specifically the register of deeds, for the real estate that your father willed to your mother. Other documents might also have to be recorded in State B, depending on its own laws.

Finally, you can distribute the estate in compliance with the Decree of Distribution. Each distributee or recipient must sign a receipt for the property passed to him or her, and you must file the receipts with the court. The last act is *petitioning* the court for your discharge as personal representative (Form 78). In this case, the court will sign an *order* discharging you, as executor (Form 79). A certified copy of this order should be sent to the surety company that holds your executor's bond. With that, you will have completed your responsibilities.

Executor: And there are quite a few! I very much appreciate your taking the time to explain the probate procedures to me. It gives me a much clearer picture of what happens in an administration and what duties I have to perform.

Paralegal: Well, I enjoy being able to assist you in these matters. I am sure we shall work well together. There are some matters we might need to cover more fully, such as what happens if you decide to sell any of your father's real property, but we can wait to discuss those with Ms. Brown when they arise. Now let's go set up our "tickler" system.

Assignment 3

1. Using the Glossary if necessary, define the following terms: real property, surety, executor (-trix), administrator (-trix), testate/intestate, creditor, maintenance allowance, assets, gross estate, intestate succession.

2. Look in your state's statutes and find the section covering estate administration. Cite the section.

3. How long does your state allow for the completion of an estate administration?   Cite the section in your state's statute.   How is an extension of time obtained?

4. What are the general steps taken by an executor (-trix) in estate administration as discussed in this chapter?   Do they differ with those in your state?

5. What are the primary duties of the representative of the estate?

Chapter 3

The Participants and the Proper Court

Scope of the Chapter

The chapter reviews the role of the participants in the administration of an estate and the basic functions of the participants and the proper court, often called the probate court. Important terms associated with the selection and function of the court, such as *probate, jurisdiction, domicile, venue,* and *ancillary administration,* are defined and explained in the second half of the chapter.

Competencies

After completing this chapter, the paralegal should be able to:

• Identify the participants essential to estate administration and explain their basic functions

• Identify the proper court that supervises the administration and distribution of a decedent's estate

• Explain what is meant by the term "jurisdiction"

• Identify the various elements of jurisdiction required by a specific court, such as the probate court

• Determine the proper place (county/state) to commence probate proceedings of a decedent's estate

• Recognize the necessity for establishing a second or ancillary administration of a decedent's estate when property of the decedent is located in another state.

The Participants

The following people are involved in the administration of a decedent's estate: the *personal representative* [1] *of the estate* —either named in the will (executor or executrix) or in intestate cases appointed by the probate court (administrator of administratrix) for formal proceedings, or by the probate court, registrar, or clerk in informal proceedings; the *attorney; paralegals;* and the *probate court judge or registrar* (could be the same person), or *clerk.*

We begin our discussion by defining some important terms more precisely.

Executor (-trix)
The executor or executrix is the man or woman designated in the will to carry out (execute) its provisions and handle the affairs of the decedent's estate.

General administrator (-trix)
The general administrator is the general representative selected and appointed by a probate court to administer the estate of a person who dies without leaving a will.

Administrator de bonis non
The administrator *de bonis non* —also called administrator D.B.N. (means administrator of goods not administered)—is the court-appointed representative who replaces a previous administrator who has failed to complete the administration of an intestate estate for any reason, including death of the original representative or other cause terminating authority prior to or during administration of the estate.

Administrator cum testamento annexo
The administrator *cum testamento annexo* —also called administrator C.T.A. (means administrator with the will annexed)—is the representative appointed by the court in cases where the maker of a will does not name an executor or executrix or the person so designated does not serve because of qualification or competency deficiencies.

Registrar
The registrar is the judge of the court or the person designated by the judge to perform the functions of the court in informal proceedings.

Clerk
The clerk (of the probate court) is the administrative assistant to the court (judge), who administers oaths and authenticates and certifies copies of instruments, documents, records of the court, and the like.

---

1. The Uniform Probate Code (U.P.C. § 1–201) uses the term "personal representative" to identify anyone who administers a decedent's estate. It discontinues the use of such terms as executor, general or special administrator, etc.

The Personal Representative

The term "personal representative" or *"fiduciary"* refers to the person entitled and authorized, either by selection of the deceased or by the probate court (judge) or registrar, to handle the administration of the estate. It includes *executors, general administrators,* (administrators *de bonis non* [D.B.N.] and administrators *cum testamento annexo* [C.T.A.]) and *special administrators* all of whom act in a "fiduciary" capacity. This means that the personal representative must use care, diligence, and prudence at all times while in the performance of various duties. Guardians, trustees and agents are also fiduciaries.

In Chapter 12 the special functions performed by some of these and other representatives are defined and discussed. In general, however, the role of the personal representative is:

1. To collect, take charge of, preserve, and manage the estate of the decedent.

2. To settle and pay out of estate funds all just claims and other liabilities, such as taxes against the estate.

3. To distribute the remaining assets of the estate to the successors (beneficiaries) according to the decedent's will, if any, or according to intestate succession statutes. The authority of the representative to administer the property left by the decedent is governed by the will and by state statutes.

The representative distributes only the probate property of the decedent's estate, i.e., the assets that are disposed of by will or that descend as intestate property. The representative does not have administrative power to distribute non-probate property—such as jointly owned property, the proceeds from an insurance policy payable to a named beneficiary other than the decedent's own estate, and the like. Statutes generally require that the representative report all the property (probate and non-probate) in the estate for tax purposes. These requirements and non-probate assets will be discussed in greater detail in Chapter 13, page 335.

Because the personal representative is responsible to the court, the representative must discharge these fiduciary duties with the highest degree of care and integrity, since formal probate proceedings are closely scrutinized by the probate court. Even in informal proceedings, if a personal representative breaches the fiduciary responsibilities, any heir, devisee, or creditor can petition the court for a formal proceeding (see page 381).

The list of representative's duties below is not intended to be all-inclusive. These functions vary from state to state. In addition, many duties performed in estate administration depend on the provisions of a will, if one exists, and the amount and nature of the assets the decedent owned. The personal representative will generally perform these tasks with the advice and assistance of a lawyer and the paralegal.

Pre-Probate Duties

1. Upon request, assist with funeral arrangements.

2. Find and review any existing will.

3. Hire attorney to help with the administration of the estate.

4. Convene a conference of family members and other interested persons to discuss provisions of the will or intestate laws, as well as election rights, maintenance, and the like.

5. Locate and notify witnesses of the testate's death.

6. Discontinue utilities if advantageous and notify the post office to forward mail.

7. Determine appropriate probate proceedings—formal or informal.

Probate Duties

In addition to the following, the filing of all required legal documents, petitions, and accounts, as discussed in detail in Chapters 13 and 14, will be presumed duties of the representative.

1. Arrange for probate of the will or for general administration if there is no will.

2. Give notices of decedent's death and representative's appointment to appropriate parties (successors, heirs, creditors and financial advisers of decedent).

3. Give notice of rights to surviving spouse and/or minor children.

4. Open estate bank account.

5. Obtain authorization as personal representative from the court.

6. Arrange for bond if necessary.

7. Protect, collect and preserve assets:
   a. Find and review all documents and papers, e.g., business records, tax returns, insurance policies, concerning decedent's financial affairs.
   b. Take possession of all personal property not set aside for spouse and/or minor children, including safe deposit contents, stocks and bonds, automobiles, household and personal effects, etc., and transfer all cash from such sources as savings and checking accounts, life insurance payable to estate, and the like into the estate account.
   c. Inspect all real estate and review all written documents, including leases, mortgages, contracts for deed, and deeds to the property.
   d. Protect both real and personal property with adequate insurance coverage.
   e. Collect information on all non-probate assets to be used later in preparing tax returns.
   f. Collect all debts owed decedent and place such funds in the estate account. Make sure decedent was not involved in any pending litigation. If the decedent or the estate is entitled to sue

others, e.g., debtors and the like, then the representative must perform these tasks.

g. File claims for any Social Security, veterans pension plans, etc., to which the decedent's estate is entitled.

h. Determine if any gifts were made by decedent during the last three years prior to death or gifts for which a gift tax return must be filed.

i. Determine if ancillary administration of out-of-state assets is necessary and make appropriate arrangements for such administration when required.

8. Distribute the family allowances, including support and maintenance to surviving spouse and/or minor children, as determined by statute.

9. Once determined and collected, appraise and inventory all assets valued at the date of decedent's death or the alternate evaluation date.

10. Examine all claims made against the estate; determine their reasonableness, validity, and priority; defend the estate against any improper claims.

11. Defend the estate against any litigation filed against the estate.

12. Pay all allowed claims against the estate according to their statutory priority.

13. Prepare and file all necessary tax returns—federal and state.

14. Terminate the ancillary administration, if one exists, including the payment of any debts or taxes due.

15. Obtain receipts or vouchers for all disbursements and prepare all necessary data for final account.

16. Distribute the remaining assets of the estate according to the will or the intestate statutes.

17. After final accounting, obtain discharge from the court.

18. Cancel the representative's bond, if one was necessary, with the surety (bonding) company.

The Attorney

In many cases the personal representative appointed by the decedent is a relative or friend. Such a person may lack the knowledge, experience, or expertise to handle an estate. Because of the complexity of administration, the representative may elect to request the assistance of an attorney. This assistance becomes the role of the attorney unless, as in some instances, an attorney is named executor or executrix.

It is not necessarily true that an attorney named in a will by the decedent to assist in probating the estate will be the one to do so. An attorney is retained only by the representative of the estate, who has the sole discretion in determining who will be hired.

Having been retained to help the representative settle an estate, it is the attorney's duty to inform the successors to the estate that the attorney works *for the representative* and not for them. In case of conflict, e.g., if named successors to the will want to sue the estate, they must hire their own attorney. They cannot retain the same attorney representing the estate, because that would create for the attorney a conflict of interest. The attorney, like the personal representative, has a fiduciary responsibility, a basic duty of loyalty to the client, and cannot become involved in a situation where a conflict may evolve or where a personal interest in the outcome of the proceedings exists.

Assignment 4

Sharon is the personal representative of her father's estate. Sharon hires Tamara Colby, an attorney, to help administer her father's estate. All of Sharon's brothers and sisters were named as devisees in their father's will except Charles. Charles intends to contest the will. Answer the following according to your own state's laws:

1. Could Charles hire Tamara to represent him in the will contest?

2. If Tamara and Sharon's father were partners in a business, could Tamara accept the position offered by Sharon?

3. Could the attorney who drafted the will act as the attorney for the estate?

4. Charles owns his own business. Tamara has on occasion been retained to handle various legal problems for the business. There are no legal actions of the business pending at this time. Could Tamara accept the position offered by Sharon?

The Paralegal

The paralegal must act under the direction and supervision of an attorney and cannot give legal advice without first discussing and clearing it with the attorney. Many tasks must be performed in the administration of decedents' estates, but not all of them require the individual performance of an attorney. It is the paralegal's role to complete and assist in completing as many of the tasks as possible.

The specific duties the paralegal performs when assisting the attorney and the personal representative in estate administration will be discussed in a later chapter. An overview of paralegal tasks in wills, trust, and estate administration follows.

Wills

Tasks of the paralegal concerning wills include (1) collecting all data necessary for making a client's will; (2) discussing with the attorney the contents of the will (the need for incorporating trusts, tax considerations, including methods of diminishing taxes, and clarification of devises, devisees, etc.); (3) preparing a preliminary draft of the will; (4) assisting in the execution of the final draft of the will.

Trusts

Tasks of the paralegal in relation to trusts include (1) obtaining from client data needed for the creation of a trust (trust purpose, parties, property to be transferred, powers of trustee, etc.); (2) drafting a preliminary trust; (3) reviewing the preliminary draft with client and attorney; (4) assisting in final execution of the trust.

Estate Administration

Pre-probate tasks of the paralegal in estate administration include (1) locating the will, if one exists; (2) setting up a family conference and giving notice to all members and devisees; (3) assisting in a review of the will or in intestacy procedures with family and devisees; (4) explaining the "tickler" system and probate procedures; and (5) setting up "tickler" with representative, preparing for the maintenance and monitoring of the procedures (dates for filing, correspondence, filing of documents, etc.). *Probate tasks* of the paralegal include (1) helping to collect assets; (2) handling correspondence with parties holding assets (insurance companies, banks, etc.), creditors, and devisees; (3) assisting in preparing preliminary drafts of legal documents associated with administration; (4) maintaining records of all collected assets (filing of documents, creditors' claims, etc.); (5) preparing preliminary drafts of necessary tax returns; (6) filing legal documents (from original petition to final account); and (7) filing tax returns after review with attorney.

These and other specific duties the paralegal must learn to perform will be the topics of succeeding chapters. The paralegal's handling of such tasks frees the attorney from the time-consuming but important details of estate administration, thus decreasing the cost of legal services.

Paralegals are responsible for seeing that these matters move smoothly and chronologically. Indirectly the paralegal makes possible greater attorney-client rapport by allowing the attorney more time to advise the client and can free the attorney from numerous tasks and client queries not involving the dispensing of legal advice.

The Probate Court

Another participant with an essential role in the administration of a decedent's estate is the judge. The words "court" and "judge" are frequently used synonymously in statutes and in legal writings. As a courtesy, the judge who presides over a court is referred to as "the court." Throughout the remaining chapters of this text, the words will be used interchangeably. Chapters 13 and 14, pages 335 and 379 discuss the rule of the court in greater detail.

In general it is the function of the probate court to ensure that the personal representative properly administers the estate so that (1) family allowances and maintenance are granted; (2) creditors who have valid claims are paid; (3) taxes owed are paid; (4) the remaining property goes to the rightful successors according to the testator's wishes as expressed by the provisions of the will if a will exists or, in the alternative, according to the controlling state intestate succession statutes; and (5) disputes that may arise in the course of the administration of the estate are settled.

Terminology relating to the probate court will be covered in the next section of this chapter. Other functions that may be performed by the probate court, but will not be discussed in this text, concern adoption, divorce, guardianships, and commitment proceedings.

Assignment 5

1. If May B. Brown was appointed executrix of her mother's estate, did her mother die intestate or testate?

2. Does either an executor (-trix) or administrator (-trix) have the duty to collect money from insurance policies naming a specific person as the beneficiary? Do they have this duty if the beneficiary predeceased the decedent?

3. To whom is a personal representative responsible?

4. Look up the sections in your state's statutes defining the appointment and duties of the various personal representatives mentioned in this chapter. Cite the sections.

Terminology Relating to Probate Proceedings

Probate

Probate refers to a proceeding in the appropriate court (called, in various states, the orphan's, surrogate's, probate, or prerogative court) to prove that a certain document is a will. The usual designation, *probate court,* will be used throughout this text. Originally an adjective, probate is today commonly used as a noun meaning "probate proceedings." Probate proceedings differ from other court proceedings in that they are directed solely to the proving of a will and to the administration of the decedent's estate, and sometimes to other matters related directly to them, such as settlement of a dispute between a plaintiff and a defendant. Plaintiff-defendant suits, known as *will contests,* i.e., a contest between two devisees who claim that the same piece of property was willed to each of them, may arise after the document is proved to be a will.

Jurisdiction

Jurisdiction is the authority by which a particular court is empowered by statute to decide a certain kind of case and to have its decision enforced. The court that has authority (jurisdiction) over the administration of decedents' estates is most often called the probate court.

In general, the jurisdiction of a probate court extends to the administration and distribution of a decedent's estate, including the primary function of proving that a certain legal document is a will. The statutes or constitutions of each state detail the powers and duties of the probate court. A typical statute on the subject is New Mexico's:

N.Mex. Comp.Laws § 16–4–10, 1953, Jurisdiction of the Probate Court

The probate courts have concurrent [i.e., the same] jurisdiction with the district courts [i.e., the general trial court] of:

(A) The probate of last wills and testaments, the granting, repealing, and revoking of letters testamentary and of administration, the appointment and removal of estate representatives, the settlement and allowance of accounts of estate representatives, and the determination of heirship; and
(B) The hearing and determination of all controversies respecting wills, the right of executorship and administration, the duties, accounts, and settlements of estate representatives and any order, judgment, or decree of the probate courts with reference to those matters of which the probate courts have exclusive original jurisdiction.

Note that in this statute the probate court operates at the level of the district court. In other words, in New Mexico there is a probate division of the state district courts instead of a separate probate court. In other states, the probate court may be a division of a system of courts (e.g., of the county courts, as in certain counties of Minnesota and Oregon) or a separate court (as in New York State, where it is called the surrogate's court).

Note also that the powers of the probate court are enumerated in the New Mexico statute. It may make decrees (decisions) respecting these matters only, and with limitations on matters related to these matters (e.g., it does not ordinarily determine title to property; however, if the solution bears directly on the court's performance of one of its enumerated powers, it will decide that question). The New Mexico statute is typical of state statutes giving certain powers to their probate courts. If the states did not give these powers by law, the probate courts would not be able to function at all because they are purely "creatures of statute," unlike other courts, which have some basis in common law.

A probate court's jurisdiction with respect to the kind of decision it may render is unique. No other court has the power to assess the validity of a decedent's will or to adjudicate matters concerning the estate. Although the probate court's jurisdiction is limited to powers given it by statutory law, it has "superior" jurisdiction in the matters on which it rules. That is, its decisions can be overruled only by the state supreme court.

A probate court has jurisdiction over decedents who were domiciles, i.e., legal residents, of its territory.[2] Domicile has been defined as "the place adopted by a person as his or her permanent place of habitation, and, to which, whenever absent, he or she has the intention of returning." A permanent legal address is determined by where one lives, banks, goes to church, buys license plates, and votes. If an uncertainty does arise, e.g., if a person abandons his or her domicile in one place and has not yet taken up another before dying, probate proceedings are usually conducted in the county where the assets of the decedent's estate are located.

Example: Whitney legally resides, i.e., is domiciled, in Kennebec County, Augusta, Maine. The Probate Court of Kennebec County in Maine would be the proper court to probate his will. Whitney moves his household goods from Augusta to Hartford, Connecticut, but dies before establishing legal residence there. If he still owned land in Augusta, the Probate Court of Kennebec County would probably remain the proper court to probate his will.

Personal representative

The personal representative is the person who acts as liaison between the decedent's estate and the court to which the decedent's will is submitted. If the personal representative has been named in the will to carry out such liaison duties, he is called an executor (a woman is an executrix); if the court appoints the personal representative because no valid will exists, he or she is an administrator (administratrix, in the case of a woman). Generally, the executor and administrator perform similar duties, face similar liabilities, and hold similar powers. In sum, the court that has jurisdiction over the estate of the decedent manages this estate through the personal representative.

Example: Howard appoints the Third State Bank to oversee the distribution of his estate to the persons named in his will. The Third State Bank is Howard's personal representative and executor.

Example: Howard dies without a will. The probate court appoints his sister, Nanette, to oversee the distribution of his estate to the persons whom state law declares to be the heirs of Howard. Nanette is Howard's personal representative and administratrix.

Venue

Venue is the particular place (either city or county) where a court having jurisdiction may hear and determine the case. "Venue" and "jurisdiction" are not interchangeable words, although they are closely related. "Jurisdiction" is abstract, denoting the power or authority of a

---

2. Domicile and residence on frequently used interchangeably, but they are distinguished in that domicile is the legal home, the fixed permanent place of habitation, while residence is a transient place of dwelling. Domicile, not residence, determines venue. For further discussion, see page 148.

court to act; "venue" is concrete, denoting the physical place of a trial. "Venue" approximates the definition of territorial jurisdiction and will be used throughout this text to signify the location of the proper probate court.

In determining which probate court is the proper one to handle the decedent's estate, the question of the court's jurisdiction is primary. After that has been resolved, the question of venue arises. Usually venue corresponds to the decedent's place of domicile (legal abode) or to the decedent's residence at death. In other words, the proper venue (place) for the probate administration of the estate of a deceased state resident is usually the county in which the decedent was domiciled at his or her death. The venue for out-of-state residents (domiciles) is generally the county in which the non-resident left property.

Example: Ralph Schollander wrote a will three years ago, identifying himself as a resident "of the . . . County of Multnomah, State of Oregon." Last year he moved to Malheur County (Oregon) to live with his sister. Should Ralph die in Malheur County, venue for the probate of his will would be a question for the probate court of Multnomah County to decide. It would have to consider, among other things, whether Ralph intended to give up legal residence in Multnomah County and establish it in Malheur County (i.e., to remain there indefinitely).

An example of statutory regulation of venue is Cal. Prob. Code § 301 (West 1956), *Jurisdiction and venue:*

> Wills must be proved and letters testamentary or of administration granted and administration of estates of decedent had, in the superior court:
>
> (1) Of the county of which the decedent was a resident at the time of his death, wherever he may have died;
> (2) Of the county in which the decedent died, leaving estate therein, he not being a resident of the state;
> (3) Of any county in which he leaves estate, the decedent not being a resident of the state at the time of his death and having died out of the state or without leaving estate in the county in which he died; in either of which cases when the estate is in more than one county, the superior court of the county in which a petition for letters testamentary or of administration is first filed has exclusive jurisdiction of the administration of the estate. (Compare U.P.C. § 1–303.)

Note that Letters Testamentary or Letters of Administration refer to the written authorization that the decedent's personal representative must obtain from the proper court, e.g., a probate court, before beginning the administration of the estate. Note also that to "prove" a will is to admit it to the probate process in order to establish it as the properly executed last will of a decedent.

In addition to its value in determining the venue of a probate proceeding, the fact of the decedent's domicile aids the court in establishing *in rem* jurisdiction over the estate's probate assets. Similarly, when two or more states are involved in the probate of a single will, the one that can claim the testate as its citizen will collect the greater share of the state inheritance taxes (see page 359). The fact of domicile controls not only the state's power to levy taxes, but also its right to collect taxes on decedent's property passed by will. Therefore, the tax liability of an estate may vary noticeably, depending on the inheritance tax demands, if any, of the state in which the estate assets are situated.

Ancillary administration

Ancillary administration is a secondary administration procedure to dispose of that portion of the decedent's estate left in a state other than the one of domicile. When a person dies leaving assets in two or more jurisdictions (states), separate administration procedures, one domiciliary and one or more ancillary, are necessary. Usually the testate or the court of the state of domicile appoints a personal representative to handle the administration in each state where the decedent's assets are located. Occasionally, the personal representative of the domiciliary state will also be allowed to administer the ancillary proceedings in foreign (out-of-state) jurisdictions, but this is rare.

Example: Lina resides in Virginia and owns a summer home in North Carolina. Several years ago she mortgaged the home to a bank in Raleigh. Should she die without having paid the mortgage, the bank, an "interested party" by virtue of being her creditor, would have no notice of this fact. An ancillary administration of her North Carolina property would be necessary.

Therefore, as previously noted, when the located of a portion of the real property owned by the deceased at death is in a state other than the domicile, such property is administered under the laws of the state where the real property is located. On ancillary administration, see also page 339.

Assignment 6

1. Using the California code section (page 47, above) as a guide, construct three hypothetical situations to illustrate venue.

2. Maura Hanlon, legally a resident of Amarillo, Texas, dies in Waterford, Ireland. She had not given up residence in her home state and had owned real property both in Amarillo and in Tulsa, Oklahoma. Where should Maura's will be probated? (Be sure to consult the Texas statute.) Find a statute of your own state resolving the question if Maura had resided in your state.

Chapter 4

The Concept of Property Relating to Wills, Trusts, and Estate Administration

Scope of the Chapter

Everyone owns some kind of property. Included in this chapter is the terminology related to property and estate administration, and related statutes. Also discussed are the ways or forms in which property can be owned; each form of ownership is identified, defined, and explained. Estates in real property (freeholds and leaseholds) are also covered.

Competencies

After completing this chapter, the paralegal should be able to:

• Identify, explain, and classify the various kinds of property

• Recognize and understand the terminology associated with property law

• Distinguish the various forms of ownership of real or personal property and explain the requirements for their creation

• Understand and explain why courts do not favor the creation of joint tenancies between parties other than spouses

• Identify the community property states and differentiate between community and separate property

• Explain the kinds, methods of creation, and characteristics of estates in real property

Terminology Relating to Property and Estate Administration

Estate

An estate (also called a gross estate) is the whole of the property, real and personal, owned by any person, or all the assets owned by a decedent at the time of death (see page 421).

Example: Janet Brown is single. She owns her own home, furnishings, household goods, and clothing. She has money in savings and checking accounts, stocks and bonds, and valuable jewelry. She also owns a lake cottage with a boat and motor. All these property items, real and personal, constitute Janet's *estate* or *gross estate*.

Tenancy

Tenancy is an interest in or ownership of property by any kind of legal right or title. In this chapter, the term is used in its broadest sense and is not limited to the more restricted meaning of one (called a tenant) who has temporary use and possession of real property, e.g., an apartment, owned by another (called the landlord). See examples on page 62.

Joint tenancy

Joint tenancy refers to the ownership of real or personal property by two or more persons (joint tenants) by gift, sale, or inheritance. Joint tenants have the same interest, acquired by the same conveyance, commencing at the same time, held by the same undivided possession, and each has the *right of survivorship,* by which a deceased joint tenant's interest in the property automatically goes to the surviving joint tenant or tenants.

Example: Harold Carlson sells his farm to William Leavitt and Mary Wilson as joint tenants with the right of survivorship. Harold transfers the title of the farm to William and Mary by delivering a deed to them. William and Mary are now co-tenants or co-owners and hold title to the farm as joint tenants. If William dies first, Mary would receive William's interest in the farm because of the right of survivorship.

Tenancy-in-common

Tenancy-in-common is the ownership of real or personal property by two or more persons under different titles but by unity of possession. See page 70. Each person has the right to hold or occupy the whole property in common with the other co-tenants, and each is entitled to share in the profits derived from the property. There is no right of survivorship in tenancy-in-common. Therefore, unlike a joint tenancy, when a tenant-in-common dies, the decedent's interest goes to an heir or as directed in a will.

Example: Jeff Morrow dies with a will. In the will, he gives one-half interest in his Picasso original to his only living relative, his nephew

Charles Morrow. The other half of the ownership rights in the painting Jeff gives to his two close friends, Mike Thompson and Dave Brown, equally. Charles, Mike, and Dave are co-owners of the Picasso painting as tenants-in-common. If Mike Thompson should die, his one-fourth interest in the painting would be transferred according to his will, if he has one, or to his heir (closest relative) according to state law. (For further discussion, see Chapter 5, page 99.)

Conveyance
Conveyance refers to any transfer by deed or will of legal or equitable title to real property from one party to another, e.g., from one person to another person, a corporation, or the government.

Transfer
A transfer is an act of the parties (e.g., individuals, corporations, or the government) by which the title to property is conveyed from one party to another.

Will
A will is a legally enforceable written declaration stating how the maker wishes property distributed after death (see Chapter 5, page 88).

Deed
A deed is a written, signed document that transfers title or ownership of real property such as land.

Title
A title is the right to or ownership of property.

Legal title
A legal title is a title that is complete, perfect, and enforceable in a court of law, granting the holder the right of ownership and possession.

Equitable title
An equitable title is a right of the party to whom it (the equitable title) belongs to have the legal title transferred to him or her, such as a person in possession of real property, like a home, who has equitable title while that person pays off the installment (on a mortgage) on the home to the legal title owner, e.g., the bank. Once the last payment is made, legal title will be transferred to the possessor by the delivery of a deed.

Interest
The terms "interest" and "title" are not synonymous. An interest is any right in the property, but may be less than title or ownership. For example, a renter has an *interest* in the apartment which the renter leases, but not the title.

Unity of possession
Unity of possession is one of the essential elements of concurrent forms of ownership, i.e., ownership involving two or more persons. It requires that concurrent owners must hold the same undivided possession of the

whole property, and each owner has the right to share proportionately in profits derived from it, e.g., cultivated crops or livestock.
Example:

Blackacre—a farm

Roy	Alice
Vera	

Alice, Roy, and Vera each have the right to possess the whole property concurrently with the other co-tenants. None has the right to exclude the others from possession of all or any part of the property, and each has the right to share in profits derived from the use of the farm.

Right of survivorship

The right of survivorship is an important characteristic of a joint tenancy which, on the death of one joint tenant, passes the decedent's interest in the property to the surviving joint tenants, with the last joint tenant entitled to the whole property.
Example:

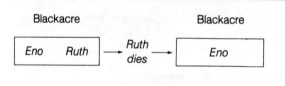

Eno and Ruth are joint tenants who concurrently own Blackacre. Ruth dies. Eno owns the undivided whole property in severalty (single ownership).

The land goes directly to Eno *without* passing through Ruth's estate. Even if Ruth had a will, the will would not affect property owned as joint tenants.

Undivided interest

An undivided interest is a right to an undivided portion of property that is owned by one of two or more tenants-in-common or joint tenants before the property is divided (partitioned). A farm, including the buildings (house, barn, etc.), the personal property (tractor, other machinery, and livestock), and the land itself, owned in joint tenancy or tenancy-in-common creates an *undivided interest* for each co-tenant. In a practical sense this means that each co-owner has a right or interest in the entire farm, but cannot claim a specific portion of the property, e.g., the house or the livestock, as the co-owner's own individual property. After partition, each person (co-owner) owns the apportioned part of the property in severalty, i.e., in single ownership. (See Partition, below.)

Example:

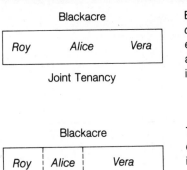

Each of the three joint tenants has a one-third *undivided interest* in the whole property. Each has the equal right to use and possess the whole property and to share equally the profits from the crops, buildings, and livestock.

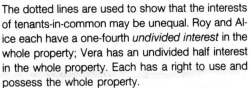

The dotted lines are used to show that the interests of tenants-in-common may be unequal. Roy and Alice each have a one-fourth *undivided interest* in the whole property; Vera has an undivided half interest in the whole property. Each has a right to use and possess the whole property.

Partition

Partition is the dividing of property held by joint tenants or tenants-in-common into distinct portions so that the individuals may hold the property *in severalty,* i.e., in single ownership.

Example: If a concurrently owned farm, Blackacre, is partitioned it is divided into separate parts:

Blackacre	After Partition	Blackacre	After Partition
Roy Alice Vera	Roy | Alice | Vera	Roy Alice Vera	Roy Alice Alice Alice Vera
Joint Tenancy Equal Parts (cannot be unequal)	Each owns the divided property as a single owner, i.e., *in severalty.*	Tenancy- in-Common Unequal Parts (could be equal)	Roy 1/5 Alice 3/5 Vera 1/5

Once the property has been partitioned, the former co-tenants each own a portion of the property in severalty. The joint tenancy property will be partitioned into equal parts; the tenancy-in-common property will be partitioned into equal or unequal parts.

Example:

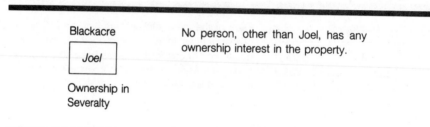

Blackacre

Joel

Ownership in
Severalty

No person, other than Joel, has any
ownership interest in the property.

Severalty

Property in severalty is property held by one person only, without any
other person having an interest or right in the property.

Severance

Severance is the act of severing, separating, or partitioning. With
respect to joint tenancy, severance is the destruction of any one of the
four essential unities accomplished by one of the joint tenants transferring inter vivos (while alive) the interest in real property to another by
deed (see pages 67 and 68).
Example: Maureen and Rick own a farm, Blackacre, in joint tenancy.
Rick sells his one-half undivided interest to Juanita. The joint tenancy
is severed. Maureen and Juanita each now own a one-half undivided
interest in Blackacre as tenants-in-common. When Rick sold his interest, the unities of time and title were destroyed (see page 68).

Disposition

Disposition is the parting with, transfer of, or conveyance of property.
Example: X owns Blackacre in severalty. There are no encumbrances,
e.g., mortgages, liens, and the like, on the property. X sells Blackacre
to A. A owns Blackacre in severalty, and X no longer has any interest
in the property. X has *disposed* of Blackacre.
Example: X owns Blackacre in severalty; however, it is encumbered by
a mortgage. X devises Blackacre through his will "to B and his heirs."
When he dies, X has *disposed* of Blackacre. B takes Blackacre in
severalty subject to the mortgage (i.e., B will have to pay off the
mortgage). X's heirs have no interest in the property.

Testamentary devise

Under the orthodox terminology, a testamentary devise is a transfer of
real property through a will. Compare Uniform Probate Code terminology, page 96.
Example: In George's will he states, "I give and devise my farm,
Blackacre, to my son, John." When George dies, John receives the
land through a testamentary devise.

Judgment

A judgment is the official decision of a court of justice establishing the rights and claims of parties in a lawsuit submitted to the court for determination.

Foreclosure

Foreclosure is the termination of all rights in property of the person (the mortgagor) who, in writing, pledges the property for the purpose of securing a debt.

Example: Amy buys a summer cottage for the price of $30,000. Amy pays a down payment of $10,000 and secures a mortgage from a lender (mortgagee) for the balance of $20,000 with monthly payments of $185. Amy fails to pay the monthly mortgage payments, i.e., Amy is "in default" on the payments. The mortgagee (lender) can foreclose on the mortgage. Generally, the property is sold under court order at a foreclosure sale. The mortgagee is entitled to be paid the balance owed on the mortgage out of the proceeds of the sale. The mortgagor (borrower) is entitled to the proceeds from the sale which exceed the mortgage balance less the expenses required to handle the foreclosure.

Freehold estate

A freehold estate is a right of title to land, an estate in land of uncertain duration. Two types of freehold estates are fee simple estates and life estates.

Fee simple

A fee simple estate is a freehold estate which is absolute and unqualified; the largest estate and the most extensive interest that can be enjoyed in real property. It is not limited in duration, or in the owner's method of disposition. The owner has the unconditional power to dispose of the property during life by deed, after death by will, or, upon death intestate, the property descends to heirs and legal representatives of the owner.

Life estate

A life estate is a freehold estate in which a person, called the life tenant, holds an interest in land during his or her own or someone else's lifetime.

Example: X devises Blackacre through a will "to Abby for life, then to Betty and her heirs." Abby has a life estate and has the right to the use and possession of Blackacre during her lifetime. When Abby dies, Betty gets the property in fee simple.

Lien

A lien is a claim or charge on property for payment of some debt. An estate in real property includes the right to possession and enjoyment of it, while a lien on real property is the right to have it sold or otherwise applied in satisfaction of a debt.

Example: X owns Tanglewood, a lake cottage. X hires A to put in new electrical wiring at a cost of $2,000. X neglects to pay A for the work.

A may then file a "mechanic's lien"[1] within a statutory time period (usually within 90 days of completion of the work) at the office of the County Recorder, e.g., the Register of Deeds.[2] If X does not pay A within a statutory time period (e.g., one year), A may obtain a court order for the property to be sold. The lien will be satisfied (i.e., paid) out of the proceeds of the sale. A mortgage is another example of a lien on real property.

Dower

Dower, at common law, is the wife's right to a life estate in one-third of the real property which her husband owned during the marriage. Most states (except community property states) have replaced common law dower with statutes that give one spouse (wife or husband) the right to an "elective" share of the other spouse's property. The spouse may renounce the will and "elect" to take the statutory share (see Forced Heirship, Inchoate Dower, and example below).

Example: Melvin died in Iowa, willing his real property to his wife, Isadora. Isadora has the option of taking the devise in the will or a portion of Melvin's real and personal property according to the Iowa Code Ann. § 633.237 (West 1964).

Curtesy

Curtesy, at common law, is the right of the husband to a life estate in *all* his wife's real property owned during marriage. A husband was entitled to curtesy only if the married couple had a child born alive.

Example: John and Mary Jones are married. Their only child, Jimmy, is now ten years old. If Mary owned real property before the marriage and died intestate, John would be entitled to the right of curtesy in those states that follow the common law rule.

Forced heirship

Forced heirship, also "forced share," is the absolute right of an heir (e.g., spouse) to receive a statutory share of a decedent's estate. A statute granting such a right of election to take "against the will" is called a "forced share" statute or an "election" statute. That part of a decedent's estate obtained through the statute in this manner is then called the "forced" or "elective share." The right of a spouse to a statutory share, whether or not the decedent includes the spouse in the will, or whether the decedent dies intestate, is the spouse's elective share (see Chapter 7, page 166). In addition, statutes in virtually all states require parents to provide for the support of their minor children.

Example: In his will, Joe leaves a small portion of his estate to his wife, Mary. Under the statute granting an "elective" share, Mary deter-

---

1. A mechanic's lien is a claim created by law that secures payment for labor performed or materials furnished in building or repairing an item of real property.

2. The office that records documents, e.g., a deed, that affect the title ownership of the real property.

mines that her "elective" share of her husband's estate would be greater than the amount she would receive from his will. Mary elects against the will.

Inchoate
Inchoate means incomplete, partial, unfinished, begun but not completed.

Inchoate dower
An inchoate dower, at common law, is the wife's interest in the real property owned by her husband during his life while the husband is still alive. It is a claim contingent on the wife's surviving her husband. The right of dower becomes vested (established, settled) in the wife when her husband dies. Forced share statutes have abolished or greatly modified dower as a means of providing for a surviving spouse (husband or wife).

Co-tenants
Co-tenants, also co-owners, are two or more persons who own interests in the same real property, e.g., joint tenants, tenants-in-common, and tenants by the entireties.

Tenancy by the entireties
Tenancy by the entireties refers to an estate available only to a husband and wife. It is essentially a "joint tenancy" modified by the common law theory that husband and wife are one person, but it is distinguished from the usual joint tenancy in that it cannot be terminated by one joint tenant's inter vivos conveyance of his or her interest. Neither one of the tenants by the entireties can convey (transfer) the property or sever the tenancy by the entireties without the consent of the other spouse. The predominant and distinguishing feature of both joint tenancy and tenancy by the entireties is the "right of survivorship" (see page 52). Most states have abolished tenancy by the entireties as against public policy because it imposes a restriction on alienability (transferability) of real property. States that still allow a conveyance to a husband and wife in tenancy by the entireties demand that strict language requirements be met in the words of the instrument of conveyance.

Example: A will states: "I hereby give and devise Blackacre to Jim and Trudy Nelson, husband and wife, in tenancy by the entireties." But if the will had been worded "I hereby give and devise Blackacre to Jim and Trudy Nelson, husband and wife, with the right of survivorship," the devise might have been interpreted to be a joint tenancy, and therefore severable.

Half-blood
Half-blood is a term denoting the degree of relationship that exists between those who have the same mother *or* the same father, but not both parents in common.

Example: Jean is the daughter of Jim and Agnes; Leonard is the son of Jim and Eleanor (Jim's second wife). Jean and Leonard are brother and sister by half-blood.

Grantor

A grantor is the person who makes a conveyance (transfer) of real property to another.

Grantee

A grantee is the person to whom the conveyance of real property is made.
Example: Abner conveys Blackacre, a farm, by deed to his friend, Charles. Abner is the grantor; Charles is the grantee.

Reversion

Reversion, or reversionary interest, refers to the interest in real property that a grantor retains when a conveyance of the property by deed or by will transfers an estate that is smaller than what the grantor owns. At some future time the real property reverts back to the grantor.
Example: John owns Blackacre, a farm, in fee simple. By deed, John conveys the farm to "Betty for life." Betty gets a life estate (which is smaller or less than a fee simple estate). John retains a reversionary interest in the farm. When Betty dies, the farm reverts (returns) to John.

Remainder

A remainder is a *future* estate in real property which will take effect on the termination of a prior estate created by the same instrument at the same time.
Example: John owns Blackacre, a farm in fee simple. John conveys the farm by one legal document (e.g., a deed) to "Betty for life, then to Robert and his heirs." This conveyance creates a life estate for Betty and a remainder, i.e., a future interest, in Robert which will not take effect until Betty dies. Robert takes his interest, which will be a fee simple estate, not from Betty, but from the original grantor, John. Because he receives a remainder of the real property which is conveyed by the same instrument which transferred the life estate to Betty, Robert is called the *remainderman*.

Classification of Property

Each person during a lifetime accumulates a variety of property items collectively called an *estate*. Such property can be classified as either *real* or *personal*.

Real property

Real property (realty or real estate) is land and generally whatever is built or growing on or affixed to land. It includes land, buildings, and fixtures. A fixture is real property that may have once been personal property but now is permanently attached to land or buildings. An example of a fixture on land is a tree. In a building, a fixture could be the carpeting nailed to a floor, a built-in dishwasher, and the like.

Personal property

Personal property, also referred to as "chattels personal" or movable property, is everything subject to ownership which is not real estate and includes such items as clothing, household furnishings, stocks, money, contract rights, life insurance and similar holdings. A *chattel* is an item of personal property.

Personal property can be subdivided into two categories: tangible or intangible.

Tangible personal property

Tangible personal property is property that has a physical existence, i.e., it can be touched. Examples would be a ring, a watch, a car, or an appliance.

Intangible personal property

Intangible personal property has no physical existence but is only a right to receive something of value. Examples would include cash, bank accounts (savings and checking), shares of stock of a corporation, corporate and government bonds, government benefits such as Social Security and veterans benefits, profit-sharing plans, pension plans, life insurance proceeds, patent rights, royalties, and claims against another person for property damage, personal injury, or death.

The paralegal's role in helping the personal representative collect, preserve, and distribute these personal property assets will be discussed in future chapters. Listing all the decedent's assets and classifying them properly is essential to administering an estate. Therefore it is important for the paralegal to be able to identify property as real or personal property.

Assignment 7

Place a mark (X) under the column that best classifies each of the items listed below.

Item	Real Property	Personal Property
Car		
Cash in checking account		
Right to renew lease		
Home		

Assignment 7 *(continued)*

Item	Real Property	Personal Property
Proceeds of life insurance policy		
Furniture		
Stocks and bonds		
Furnace		
Clothing		
Dishwasher (built-in)		
Dishwasher (portable)		
Mobile home		
Houseboat		
TV roof antenna		
Bookcase		

Statutes Governing Passage of Property

States have the power to enact statutes governing the passage of property from one generation to another or from the deceased to someone in his or her own generation. The states derive such power from their right, under the U.S. Constitution, to levy and collect taxes and from their duty to protect the citizenry.

Example: If Jane Doe dies owning property including her home (real property) and items of personal property such as her household furniture and small savings and checking accounts, what are the respective rights of Jane Doe and her creditors?

As an owner of an estate, a citizen such as Jane Doe has the right to have her property distributed as she wishes, so long as those desires do not conflict with the rights of others, e.g., a spouse, children, or creditors. Generally, a spouse cannot be disinherited, and minor children are entitled to support (see page 168).

Creditors of each citizen have the right to be compensated for their claims, and the state by statute establishes procedures whereby the creditor may make a claim against the decedent's estate whether or not the decedent has made a will (see page 360).

Generally, each state requires careful recording of all activity involving a decedent's estate so that it can accurately and fairly calculate the amount of tax which should be taken from the estate of the decedent. Here the state becomes a "creditor"; the estate owes the state an estate tax (see page 460).

The state protects the decedent's rights by enacting statutes to ensure that each person will be allowed to make a will. If someone dies without a will, the state's statutes also provide for distribution of the property to those whom the decedent would probably have chosen if the decedent had made a will. These are called *descent and distribution* or *intestate succession statutes.* Exhibit 4.1 is an example of an intestate succession statute (for further discussion see Chapter 5, page 99).

Exhibit 4.1 New York State's Intestate Succession Statute

N.Y.Est. Powers & Trusts Law § 4–1.1 (McKinney 1981),
Descent and Distribution of a Decedent's Estate

The property of a decedent not disposed of by will, after payment of administration and funeral expenses, debts and taxes, shall be distributed as follows:

(a)   If a decedent is survived by:

(1)   A spouse and children or their issue, money or personal property not exceeding in value two thousand dollars and one-third of the residue to the spouse, and the balance thereof to the children or to their issue per stirpes.

(2)   A spouse and only one child, or a spouse and only the issue of one deceased child, money or personal property not exceeding in value two thousand dollars and one-half of the residue to the spouse, and the balance thereof to the child or to his issue per stirpes.

(3)   A spouse and both parents, and no issue, twenty-five thousand dollars and one-half of the residue to the spouse, and the balance thereof to the parents. If there is no surviving spouse, the whole to the parents.

(4)   A spouse and one parent, and no issue, twenty-five thousand dollars and one-half of the residue to the spouse, and the balance thereof to the parent. If there is no surviving spouse, the whole to the parent.

(5)   A spouse, and no issue or parent, the whole to the spouse.

(6)   Issue, and no spouse, the whole to the issue per stirpes.

(7)   Brothers or sisters or their issue, and no spouse, issue or parent, the whole to the brothers or sisters or to their issue per stirpes.

(8)   Grandparents only, the whole to the grandparents. If there are no grandparents, the whole to the issue of the grandparents in the nearest degree of kinship to the decedent per capita. [See page 104.]

(9)   Great-grandparents only, the whole to the great-grandparents. If there are no great-grandparents, the whole to issue of great-grandparents in the nearest degree of kinship to the decedent per capita. Provided that in the case of a decedent who is survived by great-grandparents only, or the issue of great-grandparents only, such great-grandparents or the issue of such great-grand-parents shall not be entitled to inherit from the decedent unless the decedent was at the time of his death an infant or an adjudged incompetent. Provided, further, that this subparagraph nine shall be applicable only to the estates of persons dying on or after its effective date.

(b)   If the distributees of the decedent are in equal degree of kinship to him, their shares are equal.

(c)   There is no distribution per stirpes except in the case of the decedent's issue, brothers or sisters and the issue of brothers and sisters.

(d)   For all purposes of this section, decedent's relatives of the half blood shall be treated as if they were relatives of the whole blood.

(e)   Distributees of the decedent, conceived before his death but born alive thereafter, take as if they were born in his lifetime.

(f)   The right of an adopted child to take a distributive share and the right of succession to the estate of an adopted child continue as provided in the domestic relations law.

(g)   A distributive share passing to a surviving spouse under this section is in lieu of any right of dower to which such spouse may be entitled.

Assignment 8

Define the following words contained in the New York statute (Exhibit 4.1) by using the Glossary at the end of this book (all these terms will be defined and discussed in later chapters): *dower, right of succession, distributees, issue, distributive share, spouse, degree of kinship, per capita, per stirpes, residue, intangible personal property, half-blood, spouse's forced or elective share.*

Forms of Property Ownership

Various forms of property ownership exist, ranging from one person holding the entire interest in an item of real or personal property to situations where two or more persons share concurrent ownership rights as co-owners (co-tenants). The most common forms of property ownership are *tenancy in severalty* (individual ownership) and *concurrent ownership* (joint tenancy, tenancy-in-common, tenancy by the entireties, and community property).

Tenancy in Severalty

Tenancy in severalty (ownership in severalty, or individual ownership) means that one person is the sole owner of real property, such as land, or personal property, such as a car. As an individual, the owner in severalty, has absolute ownership of the real or personal property with exclusive rights, privileges, and interests in it. The owner may voluntarily dispose of the property while living, either by gift or sale, or may dispose of it at death through a will. If no such disposition has taken place at the time of death, the property remains in the owner's estate and passes to certain specified takers under intestate succession statutes.

Example: John buys Joe's car. The title is transferred to John. John is the sole owner of the car. He owns it in severalty.

Example: Mary is given a ring by her aunt. Once delivered, the ring belongs to Mary, solely. She owns it in severalty.

Example: Uncle Henry died. In his will, he left his lake cottage to his niece, Kathy. Kathy owns the real property in severalty.

Forms of Concurrent Ownership

Cases where more than one person shares ownership rights in property are forms of *concurrent ownership*. The most common forms of such multiple ownership are joint tenancy, tenancy-in-common, tenancy by the entireties, and community property.

Joint Tenancy

A joint tenant interest in property is acquired when two or more persons as co-owners have possession with the common law requirements known as the "four unities": unity of time, unity of title, unity of interest, and unity of possession. A simple conveyance (transfer) of property to two or more persons as joint tenants does *not* necessarily create a joint tenancy *unless* the four unities also exist. These "unities" are defined by common law as follows:

Unity of time For unity of time to exist, joint tenant owners must take their interests in the property at the same time. To satisfy this requirement, the joint tenants must receive their interest in the property together.

Example: A single conveyance of property from Mary to Amy and Betty as joint tenants dated July 15, 1984 would create a joint tenancy. If, however, Mary were to convey the property to Amy and Betty as joint tenants in a single transfer taking effect on different dates, Amy receiving an interest on July 15, 1984 and Betty receiving an interest a day later, then the conveyance would fail in its attempt to create the interest desired and a tenancy-in-common would exist between Amy and Betty. Some states require an express statement creating a joint tenancy and avoiding a tenancy-in-common.

Assignment 9

Howard conveys a farm, Blackacre, by deed to "Brown and Jones as joint tenants and not as tenants-in-common." Would such a conveyance create a joint tenancy in your state?

Unity of title For unity of title to exist, the tenants must receive their title (ownership rights) from a single source, e.g., the same will or deed.

Example: When Mary, in a single deed, transfers property to Amy and Betty as joint tenants, unity of title exists and a joint tenancy is created. On the other hand, when Mary transfers property to Amy and Betty by will *and* deed respectively, or by more than one deed, the use of multiple instruments of transfer fails to meet this (i.e., unity of title) requirement, resulting in the creation of a tenancy-in-common between Amy and Betty.

Most states do not allow the creation of a joint tenancy wherein the grantor names himself or herself and another or others as joint tenants. For example, if Brown conveys a farm, Blackacre, which he inherited and now solely owns, to "Conrad and himself (Brown) as joint tenants with the right of survivorship," a joint tenancy, generally, does not result because of the lack of unities of time and title. The parties do not receive their interest in the property simultaneously since Brown already owned the farm, nor do they receive their title from one document since Brown received his title through inheritance.

Assignment 10

Determine whether your state statute would allow a joint tenancy to be created in the manner presented in the last example.

Unity of interest For unity of interest to exist, each tenant must have an interest in the property identical with that of the other tenants, the interests being of the same quantity and duration, e.g., fee simple estate, life estate, and the like.

Example: If Mary were to convey property to Amy, Betty, and Carol as joint tenant owners each holding an equal life interest, a joint tenancy would be created. But, in the above conveyance, if Mary had given Amy and Carol each one-sixth shares of the ownership rights and Betty a two-thirds share, then the unity of interest requirement would not be met, and Amy, Betty, and Carol would own the property as tenants-in-common and not joint tenants, even though the conveyance specified that they were to be joint tenants.

Assignment 11

If Keller attempted to create a joint tenancy by transferring by deed his farm, Blackacre, to three friends, Hudson, Daniels, and Miller, he would fail if he transferred a life estate to Hudson and fee simple estates to Daniels and Miller. What form of ownership has Keller created according to your state statutes?

Unity of possession To have unity of possession, an individual joint tenant must own an undivided whole of the property held in joint tenancy. As part of the group that owns all the property, each joint tenant has an equal right to possess the entire property.

Example: A conveyance of a farm, Blackacre, from Mary to "Amy and Betty as joint tenants with the right of survivorship," with no restrictions on the amount of their respective possession rights would successfully create joint tenancy ownership. In contrast, if in the above conveyance Mary had attempted to limit the possession rights of either Amy or Betty ("to Amy and Betty as joint tenants, with only Betty having the right to possess Blackacre"), the transfer would fail to create a joint tenancy for want of the possession unity, and Amy and Betty would be tenants-in-common.

Summary Example: Williams conveys a farm to A, B, and C on June 1, 1984 (unity of time), by a single deed (unity of title). Each co-owner receives one-third undivided interest (unity of interest) of the whole property, and each has an equal right to possession of the whole (unity of possession). All four unities are present. Therefore, a valid joint tenancy has been created if Williams has complied with other state statutory requirements, e.g., used language indicating that he desired to create a joint tenancy, such as "to A, B, and C as joint tenants and not as tenants-in-common."

Assignment 12

1. If Robert Miller owned a farm in your state and died leaving by will the farm to "my three sons, Roger, John, and James as joint owners with equal shares," what form of ownership would the three sons have? Go to your state statutes and look up forms of ownership, specifically joint tenancy. Then answer according to the laws of your state.

2. If Robert Miller in the problem above had devised the farm "to my three sons, Roger, John, and James as joint tenants and not tenants-in-common," would a joint tenancy be created according to the laws of your state?

3. Joyce, 21, and Ellen, 20, are sisters. When Aunt Mary dies, she leaves her country home "to Joyce immediately and to Ellen on her twenty-first birthday, as joint tenants with the right of survivorship." What form of ownership has Aunt Mary created?

The legal document in Exhibit 4.2, a deed, is executed to illustrate the creation of a joint tenancy with the required four unities. Notice that the conveyance reads "to Roger L. Miller, John M. Miller, and James R. Miller as joint tenants and not as tenants-in-common." This language is necessary to create the joint tenancy. Since Roger, John, and James receive their co-ownership at the same time (August 1, 1984,—the date on the deed); by the same legal document (the deed); with the same undivided interest in the whole (equal interest); and with the right to possess the entire property (equal possession), all four unity requirements are satisfied.

Assignment 13

Assume you own the house in which you now live. Draft a deed conveying the house to your two best friends as joint tenants.

Assignment 14

Minn. Stat. Ann. § 500.19 (West 1947) is a typical state statute that discusses forms of ownership. Read the statute and comments.

Exhibit 4.2 Sample Deed Showing Creation of a Joint Tenancy

Individual (s) to Joint Tenants

Form No. 5-M—WARRANTY DEED

No delinquent taxes and transfer entered; Certificate of Real Estate Value ( ) filed ( ) not required
Certificate of Real Estate Value No._____
_____, 19_____

_____
County Auditor

by_____
Deputy

STATE DEED TAX DUE HEREON: $ __282.70___

Date: __August 1_____ , 19 _84_

(reserved for recording data)

FOR VALUABLE CONSIDERATION,_____
Henry J. Smith and Sara M. Smith,   husband and wife   , Grantor (s),
                                          (marital status)

hereby convey (s) and warrant (s) to _Roger L. Miller, John M. Miller, and James_
_R. Miller_____ , Grantees as joint
tenants, real property in __Brownstad_____ County, Minnesota, described as follows:

Lot 4, Block 12, Moser's Addition to Fairview Village.

(if more space is needed, continue on back)

together with all hereditaments and appurtenances belonging thereto, subject to the following exceptions:

_____
Sara M. Smith

Affix Deed Tax Stamp Here

_____

_____
Henry J. Smith

STATE OF MINNESOTA   } ss.
COUNTY OF __Brownstad_____   }

_____

The foregoing instrument was acknowledged before me this __1st__ day of __August_____ , 19 _84_ ,
by _Henry J. Smith and Sara M. Smith, husband and wife_____
_____ , Grantor (s).

NOTARIAL STAMP OR SEAL (OR OTHER TITLE OR RANK)

SIGNATURE OF PERSON TAKING ACKNOWLEDGMENT

Tax Statements for the real property described in this instrument should be sent to (Include name and address of Grantee):

My commission expires on:
August 4, 1985

THIS INSTRUMENT WAS DRAFTED BY (NAME AND ADDRESS):

I.M. Attorney
Plaza Bank Building
Minneapolis, MN 55455

Roger L. Miller
1704 Northland Road
St. Paul, MN 55243

Subd. 1 Estates, in respect to the number and connection of their owners, are divided into estates in severalty, in joint tenancy, and in common; the nature and properties of which, respectively, shall continue to be such as are now established by [common] law, except so far as the same may be modified by the provisions of this chapter.

Subd. 2 Construction of grants and devises. All grants and devises of lands, made to two or more persons, shall be construed to create estates in common, and not in joint tenancy, unless expressly declared to be in joint tenancy.

Notice in Subdivision 1 of the statute that the Minnesota legislature establishes by written law the forms of ownership it recognizes. For example, joint tenancy and tenancy-in-common are mentioned, but not tenancy by the entireties, which will be discussed later in this chapter. Also notice that *common law* or case law (see page 12), is allowed to determine the "nature and properties" of the forms of ownership Minnesota is herein acknowledging. Minnesota common law requires that the four unities—time, title, interest, and possession—be present in order to create a joint tenancy.

Check your own state statutes and determine which forms of ownership they recognize. Cite the statutes.

Besides the four unities, certain other characteristics distinguish joint tenancy from tenancy-in-common and other forms of co-ownership.

Joint tenants are entitled to the equal use, enjoyment, control, and possession of the land since they have an equal and undivided identical interest in the same property. Each joint tenant is considered to be the owner of the whole property and also of an undivided part. The undivided interest means that no joint tenant can say he or she owns a specific or individual part of the property. If a joint tenant did own a particular portion of the property, it would be owned as a single owner, *in severalty,* not as a co-owner, *joint tenant.*

When a joint tenant dies, the surviving joint tenants receive the interest of the deceased, i.e., the undivided part, with nothing passing to the heirs (successors) of the decedent. The passage of a deceased joint tenant's ownership rights directly to the other living co-tenants is the major distinguishing characteristic of joint tenancy and is called the *right of survivorship.* Each joint tenant has this right of survivorship, which defeats the effect of a will since a joint tenant cannot transfer jointly owned property by a testamentary devise.

If all the joint tenants die except one, without having *severed* (transferred by deed) any of their interests while alive, the remaining joint tenant owns the property *in severalty,* which means that the joint tenancy is destroyed and the lone survivor owns the property solely. Severance occurs when a joint tenant owner conveys an interest in the property during the joint tenant's lifetime, thereby destroying one of the four essential unities (time) and terminating the joint tenancy. Such an *"inter vivos"* conveyance, a transfer of interest while the joint owner is alive, is the *only* way a joint tenancy can be severed. When a joint tenancy is severed in this manner, the remaining joint tenants and the new tenant are tenants-in-common, with the new tenant having no right of survivorship. (See the examples below.)

Example: To illustrate joint tenancy ownership, suppose X dies, willing a farm to A and B as joint tenants. If during their lifetimes neither A nor B conveys his or her interest in the farm to another person and A dies, B becomes the sole owner (*in severalty*) of the farm through right of survivorship.

X	wills	A and B	A dies	B owns property
(decedent)	property	joint tenants		*in severalty*

Assume that X dies and wills the farm to A, B, and C as joint tenants. C later conveys, by deed, an undivided one-third interest in the farm to D. This conveyance, as a severance, terminates the joint tenancy between (A and B) and (C) and creates a tenancy-in-common form of ownership between (A and B) and (D). Since they have done nothing to change (sever) their form of ownership, a joint tenancy still remains between A and B. Therefore, if A were to die having made no conveyance of an interest, B would receive A's interest in the farm through right of survivorship. The result would then be that B and D would own the farm as tenants-in-common, B owning a two-thirds interest and D owning a one-third interest of the whole property. The unities of time, title, and interest having been destroyed, only the unity of possession remains.

Example:

X	wills	A, B, C	C	to D
dies	property	joint tenants	conveys his ⅓ interest	

Result: A and B own a ⅔ interest in the farm as joint tenants (each owns a ⅓ undivided interest). Tenancy-in-common exists as between (A and B) and (D).

Then:

A	B takes A's ⅓ interest	B and D are tenants-in-common
dies	as surviving joint tenant	⅔ interest for B
		⅓ interest for D

What happens on the death of B or D will be dealt with in the discussion of tenancy-in-common.

Assignment 15

Apply the previous illustration to the following cases and then answer the questions.

Case 1   Alice died, providing in her will that her farm, Blackacre, should be conveyed to her three nephews, Able, Baker, and Charlie, as joint tenants. Able was married and had eleven children; Baker was divorced and had two children; Charlie was a bachelor. Able's will left all his property to his wife, Agnes. Able dies. Who owns Blackacre? What form or forms of ownership exist between the owners?

Case 2   Suppose in Case 1 all the facts were identical except Able sold and deeded his interest in Blackacre to Dolan, and Charlie gave and deeded his interest to Elaine, his girlfriend. Who owns Blackacre? What form or forms of ownership exist between the owners? What happens to Baker's interest in the property when he dies? Does Able's wife, Agnes, have any interest in Blackacre?

At one time, common law preferred the creation of a joint tenancy over the creation of a tenancy-in-common when an instrument of conveyance was unclear concerning which of these two interests was intended by the grantor. Today the reverse is generally true, and by statute a tenancy-in-common is preferred over a joint tenancy in most states since the legislatures believe the decedent's property should pass to successors or devisees and not to surviving joint tenants. An example of one such statute is Minn. Stat. Ann. § 500.19(2) (West 1947), *Construction of grants and devises.*

Unless the parties have shown an express intent in a will or deed to create a joint tenancy, the law today presumes that a tenancy-in-common has been created. For this reason, it is important, if a joint tenancy is desired, to be very cautious in the wording of the instrument of conveyance. For example, a deed or will should read: "To Adam and James as joint tenants and not as tenants-in-common" (see Chapter 7, page 171, on drafting wills). Notice the wording required to create a joint tenancy in the states of New York and Illinois. N.Y.Est. Powers & Trusts Law § 6–2.2 (McKinney 1967) provides that a grant of an estate (interest in property) to two or more persons "creates in them a tenancy-in-common, unless expressly declared to be in joint tenancy." The Ill. Rev. Stat. ch. 76, § 1 (1966) states that the deed of conveyance must expressly provide that the property interest is granted "not in tenancy-in-common but in joint tenancy."

Assignment 16

Using your state's codes, find and cite appropriate statutes, if any, that determine the form of ownership that would be created by the following conveyances by deed: (1) "to A and B jointly," (2) "to A and B as joint owners," (3) "to A and B equally," (4) "to A or to B," (5) "to A and to B." If your statutes or case law do not address themselves to this problem find a statute from another state that does.

Tenancy-in-Common

Tenancy-in-common exists when two or more persons own separate undivided interests in property such as land. The interests may be equal or unequal. When there are two tenants-in-common, each may own one-half of the property, i.e., an equal interest, or one may own three-fourths of the property and the other one-fourth, i.e., an unequal interest. Neither owns a specific portion of the land, each having an undivided interest in the entire property.

Example: X may expressly create a tenancy-in-common in the following way:

June 1, 1983, X deeds	to A, ¼ interest in Blackacre	and	to B, ¾ interest in Blackacre

as tenants-in-common;

or

X deeds	to A, ½ interest in Blackacre	and	to B, ½ interest in Blackacre

as tenants-in-common

While joint tenants must have an *equal* undivided interest in the whole, equal *or* unequal interest characterizes a tenancy-in-common. Of the four unities of time, title, interest, and possession which must be present to create a joint tenancy, only the unity of possession is a requirement for tenancy-in-common. Tenants-in-common may own different interests in terms of quantity and duration, and they may receive their interests from different parties through different instruments of conveyance at different times.

As previously mentioned, a tenancy-in-common is also created when a person making a conveyance (grantor) fails to properly express in words the terminology required to establish a joint tenancy; also, once a joint tenancy is validly established, if one of the joint tenants makes an inter vivos conveyance by deed to another person, the joint tenancy is severed and a tenancy-in-common is created for the new owner.

Example: Most states today prefer the establishment of tenancy-in-common over a joint tenancy. Therefore, if William Kennedy dies providing in his will that Blackacre is to go "to my sons, Joseph and Robert jointly in equal shares," the realty will pass to the two sons as tenants-in-common in states with such a preference. Note that there was no explicit statement in the conveyance that a "joint tenancy" was to be created.

Example: In another case, suppose William Kennedy creates a valid joint tenancy by providing in his will that Blackacre should go "to my sons, Joseph and Robert, as joint tenants with the right of survivorship and not as tenants-in-common." Joseph and Robert are joint tenants. Robert, by deed, sells his interest in Blackacre to Charles Brown. The result is that the original joint tenancy is severed by Robert's inter vivos conveyance and a tenancy-in-common is created between Joseph and Charles.

Assignment 17

1. If Michael conveys one-third of his farm, Blackacre, to Fred on August 15, 1984, and the remaining two-thirds to Bob on September 20, 1984, what form of ownership will Fred and Bob have according to the statutes or case law in your state?

2. If Peter and Mary are joint tenants, and Peter gives his interest in the property to Paul by a valid conveyance, what form of ownership exists according to your state law?

The state of New York, by statute, handles the transfer of property to two or more persons in the following way:

N.Y. Estates Powers & Trusts Law § 6–2.2 (McKinney 1967),
When Estate Is in Common, in Joint Tenancy or by the Entirety:

(a) A disposition of property to two or more persons creates in them a tenancy in common, unless expressly declared to be a joint tenancy.
(b) A disposition of real property to a husband and wife creates in them a tenancy by the entirety [see below, page 000], unless expressly declared to be a joint tenancy or a tenancy in common.
(c) A disposition of real property to persons who are not legally married to one another but who are described in the disposition as husband and wife creates in them a joint tenancy, unless expressly declared to be a tenancy in common.
(d) A disposition of property to two or more persons as executors, trustees or guardians creates in them a joint tenancy.
(e) Property passing in intestacy to two or more persons is taken by them as tenants in common.

Example: Phyllis, a resident of New York, dies without leaving a will. Her husband, Martin, has died a year earlier. She leaves a house, which had been in her name only, and no debts. The law of descent and distribution of the state of New York entitles their children, Joan and Jack, to take the house in tenancy-in-common.

Assignment 18

1. If Susan Sowles, a resident of New York, died without a will, owning a lakeshore cottage in upstate New York, and her only heirs were her three children, what form of ownership of the cottage would result for the benefit of the three children?

2. If Mary Main, also a resident of New York, died leaving a will transferring her homestead to her two nephews, who were the executors of her estate, what form of ownership would exist between the nephews? Cite the section and subdivision in New York Estates, Powers, and Trusts Law where this information is found.

Each tenant-in-common may transfer an interest by gift, will, or sale, or may pledge it as security for a loan. When a tenant-in-common dies without having conveyed his or her share of the property, it goes to his or her devisees or successors. The *right of survivorship* that accompanies a joint tenant interest does not exist with a tenancy-in-common. For example, A, B, and C each own an undivided one-third interest in property as tenants-in-common. Upon A's death *intestate,* A's interest in the property will pass by descent to A's successors and not go to B and C.

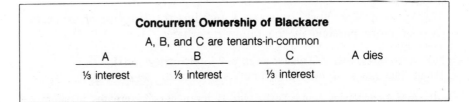

Result: A's successors receive A's ⅓ interest (by descent). (A's successors and B and C, are tenants-in-common.)

If A died testate (with a will) in the above case, A's will determines how and to whom A's interest in Blackacre will be distributed. Such a testamentary transfer is not possible in a joint tenancy. If one is attempted in a joint tenancy, the provision in the will is not followed, since the property held in joint tenancy is automatically transferred to the surviving joint tenant.

Assignment 19

Abner, Boswell, and Clarence are owners of Blackacre as joint tenants. Clarence sells his interest and delivers a deed to Boswell. Abner gives, by delivering a deed, his interest to Ruth. What form of ownership exists? Name the owners and the amount of their interests. Explain what would happen to Boswell's interest if he died testate or intestate.

When a tenant-in-common disposes of an interest by gift, sale, or will, the new owner is also a tenant-in-common with the remaining co-tenants-in-common. Tenancy-in-common is destroyed by merger, i.e., when entire ownership rights vest in (pass to) one person.
Example: A and B are tenants-in-common. A purchases B's interest. A now has the complete ownership of the property *in severalty.*
The deed in Exhibit 4.3 illustrates the creation of a tenancy-in-common.

Tenancy by the Entireties

Tenancy by the entireties is a specialized form of joint tenancy which may be held only by a husband and wife. In addition to the four unities of time, title, interest, and possession required for joint tenancy previously mentioned, tenancy by the entireties requires a fifth unity— the unity of person. A husband and wife are considered one person in a tenancy by the entireties.

Most statutes concerning tenancy by the entireties are worded like the New York statute (N.Y. Est. Powers & Trusts Law § 6–2.2 [McKinney 1967]):

> A disposition of real property to a husband and wife creates in them a tenancy by the entirety, unless expressly declared to be a joint tenancy or a tenancy in common.

Each tenant by the entireties has an absolute right of survivorship, i.e., on the death of one spouse complete ownership of the property passes *in severalty* to the surviving spouse. Neither party (spouse) can (i.e., has the power to) individually transfer the property by deed during the spouse's lifetime or by will after death.

Tenancy by the entireties cannot be terminated except with the consent of both parties. This characteristic distinguishes tenancy by the entireties from joint tenancy since joint tenants do not need permission from the other joint tenants in order to transfer (by deed) their interests. Unless the husband and wife join in (i.e., sign) the conveyance (transfer), it is invalid.

Property held in tenancy by the entireties is protected from a creditor of one spouse foreclosing on or enforcing a judgment (court decision) against it, and a judgment against one spouse is not a claim (lien) against the property (see N.Y. statute above, § 6–2.2, note 144). On the other hand, if a judgment exists against both spouses, it can become a lien against the property, and a creditor can foreclose.

A tenancy by the entireties is destroyed by a divorce or a conveyance by deed made with the consent and signatures of both husband and wife. Since a divorce (or dissolution as it is now called in some states)

Exhibit 4.3   Sample Deed Showing Creation of a Tenancy-in-Common

Individual (s) to Individual (s)

Form No. 1-M—WARRANTY DEED

No delinquent taxes and transfer entered; Certificate
of Real Estate Value (   ) filed (   ) not required
Certificate of Real Estate Value No._____
_____ , 19 _____

_____
County Auditor

by_____
Deputy

STATE DEED TAX DUE HEREON: $ __282.70__

Date: __September 12_____ , 19 _84_

(reserved for recording data)

FOR VALUABLE CONSIDERATION, _____
David L. Smith and Sally J. Smith, husband and wife _____ , Grantor (s),
                                                    (marital status)
hereby convey (s) and warrant (s) to _____ Warren P. Jones and Mary S. Jones, husband
and wife as tenants in common _____ , Grantee (s),
real property in __Lowry_____ County, Minnesota, described as follows:

Lot Two (2), Block Five (5), Samuel's Addition to Lake Park.

(if more space is needed, continue on back)
together with all hereditaments and appurtenances belonging thereto, subject to the following exceptions:

_____
Sally J. Smith

Affix Deed Tax Stamp Here   _____

_____
David L. Smith

STATE OF MINNESOTA   }
                                       } ss.
COUNTY OF __Lowry_____   }

The foregoing instrument was acknowledged before me this _12th_ day of _September_ , 19_84_ ,
by __David L. Smith and Sally J. Smith, husband and wife__
_____ , Grantor (s).

NOTARIAL STAMP OR SEAL (OR OTHER TITLE OR RANK)

_____
SIGNATURE OF PERSON TAKING ACKNOWLEDGMENT

Tax Statements for the real property described in this instrument should
be sent to (Include name and address of Grantee):

My commission expires on:
August 4, 1985

THIS INSTRUMENT WAS DRAFTED BY (NAME AND ADDRESS)

I.M. Attorney
Plaza Bank Building
Minneapolis, MN 55455

Warren P. Jones
1400 River Street Drive
Minneapolis, MN 55455

destroys the unity of person, the divorced couple become tenants-in-common of the property (see N.Y. Statute above, § 6–2.2, note 138).

Tenancy by the entireties is not recognized in many states. A conveyance seeking to create such an interest may result in the creation of a joint tenancy. In some states that do recognize tenancy by the entireties, however, a conveyance to a husband and wife as "joint tenants" is held to create a tenancy by the entireties.

The policy reasons for abolishing the common law tenancy by the entireties include the following. First, property owned in this form is not subject to creditors' claims of a deceased tenant (spouse); second, there is uncertainty as to what language creates this form of ownership; and finally, when marital problems and disagreements arise, the mutual consent required in order to transfer the property held in tenancy by the entireties may be difficult to obtain.

Assignment 20

1. John and May are married and live in Duluth, Minnesota. The deed conveying their property states: "to John A. Kowalski and May F. Kowalski, husband and wife, as joint tenants and not as tenants-in-common." (a) Is this a tenancy by the entireties? Cite the Minnesota statute. (b) Would this conveyance create a tenancy by the entireties in your own state?

2. What five unities are necessary for the establishment of a tenancy by the entireties? Explain each one.

3. Which unity that must exist in a tenancy by the entireties does not exist in joint tenancy?

Community Property

According to common law, in all states a widow was entitled, on the death of her husband, to a life estate in one-third of the real property which her husband owned at any time during their marriage. This life estate in favor of a wife is called *dower*. Modern statutes have greatly modified the dower right and have changed the rights a married woman has in her husband's estate. At common law, the dower right is limited to a particular person (widow) and to a specific estate (life estate).

Recognizing these limitations, California, Arizona, Idaho, Louisiana, Nevada, New Mexico, Texas, and Washington have adopted by statute another system—*community property*. It gives to the surviving spouse (husband or wife) the protection that the common law supplied inadequately through dower. The theory behind this form of property ownership is that a husband and wife should equally share the property acquired by their joint efforts during marriage. Each spouse is deemed to own half of all that is earned during a marriage regardless of whether one earned more money than the other or whether one spouse actually earned nothing.

Community property states recognize two kinds of property: separate property and community property. *Separate property* is that which the husband or wife owned at the time of marriage or which he or she acquired during marriage by inheritance, will, or gift. Separate property is entirely under the management and control of the spouse to whom it belongs no matter in which of these ways he or she acquired it, and it is completely free from all interest and claim on the part of the other spouse. All other property acquired during the marriage in any manner is *presumed* to be *community property.* The presumption may be rebutted by valid evidence that proves the property to be separate property.

Below is a list of factors to consider in determining the existence of separate or community property of the married couple:

• The language of the conveyance (deed or will)

• The intent of the grantor, if the conveyance is made by deed, or of the testator (-trix) if made by will

• Whether the property is given as a gift to one or both spouses

• Whether the property is inherited by one or both spouses

• Whether separate property of a spouse is sold or exchanged for other separate property, or the purpose of the sale is to use the proceeds for community purposes

• The purpose and use of property acquired or obtained by the married couple

Examples: (1) In a community property state, when a deed conveys property to a husband and wife, it is community property. (2) On the other hand, a deed which expressly states that the property is the separate property of either husband or wife creates a presumption that it is indeed the separate property of that person. (3) A married woman's father dies, conveying property in his will to her. Such property is separate property belonging to the married woman. (4) If a married woman's father dies intestate, i.e., without a will, and she is her father's only heir, she will receive his property as her own separate property. (5) An employer gives $1,000 to a married man living in California, and the man's wife claims the money is salary. Testimony, as evidence, is given by the employer establishing the fact that the $1,000 was a gift. Therefore, it becomes part of the husband's separate property.

Either spouse may, without the consent of the other, dispose of *separate property* by gift, sale, or will; mortgage it; or replace it with other property, with the newly acquired property also being *separate property.* A typical statute is Cal. Prob. Code § 20 (West 1956):

> Every person of sound mind, over the age of 18 years, may dispose of his or her separate property, real and personal, by will. . . .

Formerly, a husband had the sole control over community property and could convey or mortgage it without the wife's consent. Today, statutes have been enacted in the community property states requiring the signatures of both spouses with any transfer or mortgage of community property.

Since each spouse owns one-half of the community property, on the death of either (in the majority of the community property states), the surviving spouse is entitled to his or her one-half of the community property. The decedent's will, if one exists, or the community property state's statutes, determine the disposition of the remaining one-half. Under no circumstances can either spouse dispose of more than one-half of the community property by will. A typical community property state statute illustrating the disposition of such property is Cal. Prob. Code § 201 (West 1956):

> Upon the death of either husband or wife, one-half of the community property belongs to the surviving spouse; the other half is subject to the testamentary disposition of the decedent, and in the absence thereof goes to the surviving spouse, subject to the provisions of sections 202 and 203 of this code.

If the couple is divorced, the court generally divides the community property so that each party receives an equal share (see Cal. Civ. Code § 4800 [West 1983]). In most community property states, even without divorce, spouses may at any time enter an agreement dissolving the community relationship and divide the property. The equal share received by each spouse is then his or her separate property.

Assignment 21

1. John and Mary Doe live in a community property state. John dies. The property owned by John and Mary is: a house in joint tenancy, two cars in both names, a camper given husband by his father, savings and checking accounts in both names, a boat purchased by Mary before their marriage, furniture and household goods, a stereo and TV sets purchased during their marriage. Which of this property can John transfer or convey in his will?

2. Doug died, providing in his will, "I give and devise Blackacre to my best friends, Jim, Carl, and Alan, as joint tenants with the right of survivorship and not as tenants-in-common." What form of ownership is created for Doug's three friends? Is it a concurrent ownership?

3. In the question above, Alan is married and has two children; Jim is married and has six children; Carl is single. Alan's will leaves all his property to his wife. Carl, who wants to move out of state, finds a buyer for his interest in Blackacre and sells the property, transferring by deed the title to the buyer, Jeff. Six months later, on his way to work, Alan is killed in an automobile accident. (a) Who owns Blackacre? (b) What form of ownership exists? (c) What effect did Jeff's purchase have on the ownership before the accident? (d) Why would a court prefer the creation of a tenancy-in-common over a joint tenancy in the hypothetical case above?

Assignment 22

If possible, obtain your own family documents and determine the forms of ownership in which your family property is held, e.g., house, stocks, bonds, savings account.

Estates in Real Property

The law of real property divides the rights of ownership in real property into two categories: *freehold estates* and *leasehold estates*. The categories are distinguished by the extent and duration of the individual's interest. In other words, freeholds and leaseholds in real property are classified according to how long and how much an interest a person has in realty. The following illustrates the classification of estates that will be discussed:

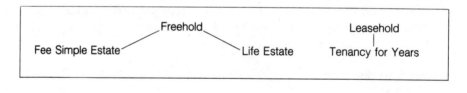

Freehold Estates

Fee Simple Estate

A fee simple estate, also known as an estate in fee, a fee simple absolute, or simply as a fee, is the largest estate possible. An individual holding a fee estate has the absolute and unlimited interest in the real property. The fee estate is not subject to any restrictions. The owner is entitled to all rights and privileges incidental to the land, and the ownership runs forever. The following are characteristics of a fee simple estate:

• *A fee simple estate is transferable during life.*
Example: Jane Doe owns a farm, Blackacre, in fee simple. While living, she can sell the farm or give it away simply by transferring the title to the real property as a fee simple estate to another person by delivering a deed. Jane Doe sells Blackacre by deed to Tom Brown:

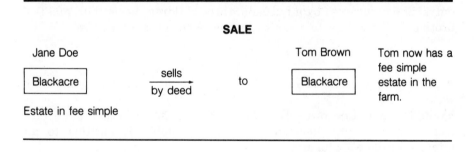

SALE

| Jane Doe | | | Tom Brown | Tom now has a fee simple estate in the farm. |

Jane Doe gives Blackacre to Tom Brown by delivering the deed to the farm to Tom:

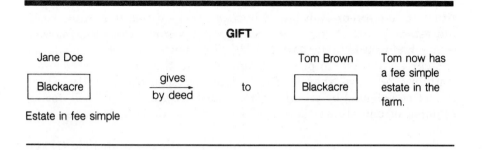

GIFT

- *A fee simple estate is transferable by will.*

Example: Jane Doe owns Blackacre in fee simple. In her will she gives the farm, Blackacre, to her niece, Sheila Johnson. When Jane dies, Sheila will own Blackacre as a fee simple estate:

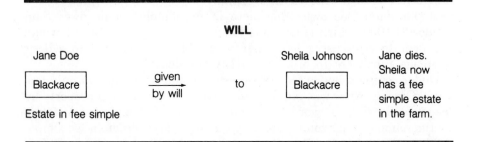

WILL

- *A fee simple estate descends to heirs if not transferred through a will.*

Example: Jane Doe owns Blackacre and dies intestate. The state in which the farm is located will generally determine the heirs of Jane who are entitled to the farm in fee simple.

Assignment 23

Assume Blackacre in the above example is located in your state. Jane Doe dies intestate owning Blackacre, the family home, in her name only. She is survived by a husband, three children, her father, and two brothers. According to your state law, who owns Blackacre?

• *A fee simple estate is subject to the rights of the owner's surviving spouse.*
Example: Jane Doe owns Blackacre. She dies. Whether Jane dies testate or intestate, her surviving spouse, John, is entitled to an interest in Jane's property.

Under common law the wife's interest in her husband's estate was called *dower,* and it entitled her to a life estate in one-third of the real property which the husband owned during the marriage. She could not be deprived of her dower right by her husband's will. Reversing the situation, under common law, a husband was entitled to *curtesy,* i.e., a life estate in *all* of his wife's real property but only if the married couple had a child (issue born living). Very few states retain the dower and curtesy rights. In place of them, most states grant *either* spouse a statutory "elective share" of the decedent spouse's property which cannot be defeated by an inter vivos transfer by deed or by will (for an example of one state's "forced share" or "election" statute, see page 167).

The policy reasons for replacing dower and curtesy include (1) the inadequate support provided a surviving spouse by the common law rules and (2) the complications that occur in transferring or clearing title to real property, i.e., the passing of a free and legal title to the land for the benefit of prospective purchasers or for future heirs or devisees.

• *A fee simple estate is subject to claims from creditors of the fee owner both before or after the owner's death.*
Example: Jane Doe owns Blackacre in fee simple. Jane owes Sam Bender $10,000, which is now due for payment. If Jane could not pay this debt to Sam using her other assets, Jane may have to sell or mortgage Blackacre in order to satisfy the debt.

Under common law, a fee simple estate could be created in only one way. The fee owner was required to convey the title to real property by deed or will using the words to "A *and his heirs.*" (The letter A stands for the name of a person.) The words *and his heirs* create a fee simple absolute estate for A and were the only words allowed by common law to create this estate. Today a fee simple estate can be created by any words that indicate an intent to convey absolute ownership, e.g., "to A in fee simple," "to A forever," or simply, "I give the land to A." In most states, however, the words "to A and his heirs" are commonly used even today to create a fee simple estate. The fee simple estate gives the holder of such an estate the maximum quantity of rights that exist in real property. Generally, whenever any real estate, e.g., a house, is purchased, the buyer becomes the fee owner.
Example: Steven Brown buys a business including the land and building in which the business operates. When the current fee owner, Janet Williams, transfers the deed to Steve, he becomes the sole owner of the property *in severalty* and holds the real property in a *fee simple estate.*

The transfer of the deed accomplishes the following: (a) Steven now holds legal title to the property; (b) Steven, as sole owner, owns the property *in severalty*—single ownership; (c) Steven receives a *fee simple estate* in the realty since this is the estate Janet held and transferred to Steven by deed. All the rights associated with a fee owner are now Steven's.

Example: Susan and David Martin contract to buy a home from Stan Williams. When Stan delivers the deed to the real property (house) thereby transferring legal title to the Martins, the deed reads "to Susan Martin and David Martin, husband and wife as joint tenants in fee simple." Susan and David own the property as joint tenants with a fee simple estate. They are the fee owners.

Keeping in mind the characteristics of joint tenancy ownership and fee simple estates, the following summary of the principles of law apply:

• A fee simple estate allows the fee owner, while alive, the right to sell or give the property to another. But since the property is held in joint tenancy by a husband and wife, both joint tenants must join in the conveyance (sale or gift) to pass the title to the new owner(s). Thus, both Susan and David (in the previous example) must sign a deed transferring their home to another as part of a sales contract or as a gift.

• Although another characteristic of a fee simple estate allows a fee owner to transfer the property through a will, since Susan and David are joint tenants neither can will his or her interest in the home to another because a joint tenancy has the right of survivorship, i.e., when a joint tenant dies, the decedent's interest automatically passes to the surviving joint tenant by operation of law. Thus the survivor of Susan or David, holding a fee simple estate as a single owner, could transfer the estate by will, but while both are alive, neither could pass the property by a testamentary disposition until after the death of the first joint tenant.

Assignment 24

Zachary, a Montana farmer, deeds 20 acres of his land to his daughter, Catherine, in fee simple when she becomes engaged to Frank. Catherine marries Frank, and they have two children. Upon Catherine's death, Frank claims that he, and not the children, is the owner of the land as a joint tenant with the right of survivorship. Is Frank's claim correct? Explain.

Life Estate

The second type of freehold estates is the life estate (see page 55). The person holding such an estate in real property is called the *life tenant*.

A life estate is one that lasts for the lifetime of an individual (generally the grantee). The following are characteristics of life estates:

• *A life estate may last for the lifetime of the original owner (the person who conveys the estate).*
Example: Sam conveys Blackacre to "Shirley for the life of Sam." Shirley has a life estate based on Sam's lifetime. Shirley is the life tenant.

• *A life estate may last for the lifetime of the person enjoying the estate (the person to whom the estate is conveyed).*
Example: Sam conveys Blackacre to "Shirley for life." Shirley receives a life estate based on her own lifetime.

• *A life estate may last for the lifetime of a third person.*
Example: Sam conveys Blackacre to "Shirley for the life of Julie." Shirley has a life estate based on Julie's lifetime.

• *A life estate cannot be transferred by will, unlike a fee simple estate.* Life tenants may, however, convey their interests in the land by sale or gift to a third person.
Example: Shirley, a life tenant, sells her lifetime interest in Blackacre to Laverne. When Shirley gives a deed to Laverne, Laverne becomes the new life tenant and holds the property till Shirley dies. Shirley can sell only her interest in Blackacre, i.e., a life interest called a life estate.

• *Upon the death of the life tenant, the life estate terminates and no interest remains to be passed to heirs or by will.* The property returns (reverts) to the person who created the life estate by conveying the property by deed or will. Such a person is called the *grantor*, and the person receiving the property is the *grantee*.
Example: Peter Alexander owns a farm, Blackacre, in fee simple. By a deed, Peter conveys (transfers) the property to "Edward Robinson for life." Peter is the grantor; Edward is the grantee and life tenant. Edward has the right to use and possess Blackacre or to convey his life estate to another for his own lifetime. When Edward dies, the life estate ends, and the property returns (reverts) back to the grantor, Peter. If Peter dies before Edward, then the property reverts to Peter's estate and Peter's will, if he has one, or state intestate succession statutes, if he has no will, determine which devisees or heirs of Peter will receive the property.

Assignment 25

Jane Smallwood owns a lake cottage. In a deed she conveys the cottage "to my father, Brent Smallwood, for life, then to my sister, Sue Smallwood for life." Jane outlives her father but dies before her sister,

Sue. Is Brent a life tenant? Who gets the property when he dies?
What interest does Sue have at the time of Jane's conveyance? Explain what will happen to the property, and why, after the death of
Sue.

The person holding a fee simple estate may want to pass or transfer
the entire estate to another. For example, Bill Maxwell holds Blackacre, a farm, in fee simple and wants to convey the property to his son,
James. As we have seen, such a conveyance could be accomplished by
deed (while Bill is alive) or by will after death by the words "to James
Maxwell *and his heirs,*" or simply "to James Maxwell in fee simple."

Suppose, however, that Bill wanted to create a life estate in Blackacre before transferring the property to his son. How is this done?
Answer: Bill conveys again by deed or by will, "to my sister Helen for
life, then to James forever." Such a conveyance creates a life estate for
Helen, followed by a future fee simple estate for James. Notice that in
this case the grantor, Bill, terminates his right to a reversion, i.e., the
right to have the property revert (return) to the original grantor (see
page 000). A reversion exists only when the grantor holding a fee
simple estate conveys an interest in property by deed or will that is less
than the entire fee simple estate. Only a grantor is entitled to a
reversion.

Example: Bill conveys Blackacre "to James for life." Result: James
receives a life estate with a reversion to Bill on James' death. If Bill
predeceases James, then Bill's heirs (by intestate succession) or devisees
(by will) received the property.

Example: Bill conveys Blackacre "to James for life, then to Mary for
life." Result: James receives a life estate that passes as a future life
estate to Mary. Mary on James' death becomes the life tenant and
holds the property until she dies. After Mary dies, or if Mary dies
before James dies, then the property reverts to Bill, if alive, or to Bill's
heirs or devisees.

Example: Bill conveys Blackacre to "James for life, then to Mary *and
her heirs.*" Result: James receives a life estate. When James dies the
property does not revert to the grantor, Bill, but instead passes as a
future fee simple to Mary. Since Bill had a fee simple estate and
conveyed the property by deed or will giving a fee simple estate to
Mary, his reversionary interest in Blackacre terminated. Mary, once
becoming the fee owner, is entitled to do with the property as she
pleases, i.e., sell it, give it to another, or convey it after death through
her will. The same result as in this case would have occurred if Bill
had conveyed Blackacre "to James for life, then to Mary," or "to Mary
forever," or "to Mary in fee simple." In such cases, in which a person,
e.g., Mary, is entitled to the remainder of an estate in real property
after another prior claim has expired, the person is called the *remainderman* (see page 58).

Assignment 26

According to your own state laws, what kind of an estate in real property would Mary Williams receive if her Uncle Charles deeded a farm to her in the following ways? (1) "to Mary"; (2) "to Mary and her heirs"; (3) "to Mary in fee"; (4) "to Mary forever"; (5) "to Mary for life"; (6) "to Mary for the life of Helen"; (7) "to Mary for as long as I live."

Leasehold Estates

Various types of leasehold estates exist. For the purposes of this text, only one example will be identified and explained.[3] For a more complete discussion, see textbooks on real property.[4] The leasehold discussed here is a tenancy for years.

Tenancy for Years

A tenancy for years creates an interest in real property that will last for the period designated, e.g., a tenancy for ten years. Such a tenancy is created and terminates according to its own terms. No notice to terminate is required.

Example: John Kellar owns a farm, Blackacre, in fee simple. John conveys the farm by deed to "Maude Owens for ten years." Maude holds Blackacre as a tenancy for ten years. She has the right to use, possess, or even to sell her *interest* (see page 000) in the property. At the end of the ten-year period, however, Maude's interest ends, and the property reverts to John because of the grantor's reversionary interest.

Assignment 27

On the basis of the above discussion, and after reviewing freehold estates, answer the questions below.

Amy conveys by deed her lake cottage to "Clare for life, then to Maxine for twenty years, then to Elizabeth and her heirs."

1. What kind of estate does Clare have?

2. Who receives the property when Clare dies?

3. If Maxine dies before Clare dies, who receives the property on Clare's death?

4. Does Amy have a reversionary interest in the property? Explain.

---

3. Other leaseholds include tenancy at will, tenancy at sufferance, and tenancy from month to month.

4. E.g. William E. Burby, *Real Property*, 3d ed. (St. Paul: West Publishing Co., 1965), p. 123.

5. What interest does Elizabeth hold?

6. There are two remaindermen involved in the conveyance. Who are they and explain why they are so classified?

7. Do the heirs of Elizabeth have any interest in the property by this conveyance?

Leaseholds, such as the tenancy for years, also include the standard landlord-tenant relationships. If Harold signs a lease, i.e., a contract to take possession of real property for a specified time period while agreeing to pay rent while in possession, such a contract creates the estate called the tenancy for years. It is not the function of this text to review in depth this area of contract and property law, but it is important to identify where the landlord-tenant relationship fits into the terminology and legal concepts previously discussed. Confusion between such terms as landlord-tenant and joint tenancy, tenancy-in-common, tenancy by the entireties, and tenancy for years must be avoided.

Chapter 5

The Laws of Succession, Death Testate or Intestate, and the Purpose of A Will

Scope of the Chapter

Before the specific procedures and forms necessary for the administration of a decedent's estate can be understood, basic vocabulary must be mastered. In this chapter, the terms associated with the persons and proceedings involved in the law of succession are addressed. The two sets of terminology, used both in practice and by legal writers—the orthodox (traditional) and the Uniform Probate Code's—are identified, defined, and discussed. The terminology and definitions recommended by the Uniform Probate Code (U.P.C.) are stressed and will be used throughout the remainder of the text.

First under discussion are terms related to *testacy*—death with a will. A sample will is included with an illustrative review of the terminology. Next under discussion are terms related to death without a will—*intestacy*. The use of intestate terminology is illustrated. The chapter concludes with the advantages and occasional drawbacks of wills, and the use of will substitutes.

Competencies

After completing this chapter, the paralegal should be able to:

• Recognize, understand, and use the basic terms associated with testacy and intestacy

• Understand the difference between orthodox and U.P.C. terminology, for gifts made by will, for persons named to receive such property, and for property conveyed according to intestate succession statutes

- Read a will and identify the parties and gifts using both orthodox and U.P.C. terminology
- Recognize and identify lineal and collateral relationships and know the difference between them as they relate to the right to inherit a decedent's property under intestate succession laws
- Interpret state intestate succession statutes and determine who is entitled to receive what property under such laws
- Know the difference between relationship to the decedent by consanguinity (by blood) and by affinity (by marriage) as it relates to the right to inherit a decedent's property under intestate succession laws
- Understand the difference between the right of heirs of an intestate to take their share of the estate per capita or per stirpes
- Understand the process of escheat (the right of the state to take the decedent's property)
- Understand why most people should have a will
- Determine when it is appropriate to use "will substitutes" to convey the decedent's property

Death with a Will—Testacy

When death occurs, it is necessary to determine whether the decedent has died testate or intestate. These terms refer to death with a valid will (testacy) or without a valid will (intestacy). The difference between testacy and intestacy is critical in situations where the client has left a will that is challenged as ineffective or invalid. If the challenge is successful and the will is declared invalid, the state intestacy statutes determine who receives the decedent's property, and these recipients may not be the same as those individuals mentioned in the will.

When a will exists, the paralegal must know all the techniques of determining whether the will is valid. If it is not valid, the paralegal must be able to analyze the intestate statutes in order to determine to whom the property will go (see requirements for executing a valid will, pages 129–136). Before learning how to collect information for the preliminary draft of a client's will and then how to write the preliminary draft, the student must understand certain basic terms.

Orthodox (Traditional) Terminology

Orthodox terminology
Orthodox terminology is the traditional definitions of words relating to wills and probate matters, used universally before the adoption into law of the Uniform Probate Code (U.P.C.)

Deed

A deed is a written instrument or document, signed, sealed, and delivered, by which one person conveys (transfers) title (ownership) to real property such as land. The essential difference between a deed and a will is that the former passes a *present interest* and the latter passes *no interest* until after the death of the maker (see Form 17).

Seal

A seal is an impression on a piece of wax or other substance affixed to a paper or legal document in order to legally authenticate it.

Decedent

The decedent is the deceased person, referred to as having died testate or intestate.

Testate

Testate, as an adjective, means having made a valid will; as a noun, it means one, either a man or a woman, who has made a valid will.

Execution of a will

Execution of a will refers to the complete process of drawing up a will, signed by the testate, and witnessed (attested) and signed (subscribed) by the witnesses.

Testator

A testator is a man who makes a will.

Testatrix

A testatrix is a woman who makes a will.

Will

A will is a person's legally enforceable declaration, usually in writing, stating how the maker wishes his or her property distributed after death. Prior to death, the maker may modify the will by the addition of a *codicil* or revoke the will either by destroying the original or by issuing a new will. A will has legal effect only upon the death of the testate (see page 206 for a sample executed will).

Codicil *republish of the will*

A codicil is a supplement or addition to a will which may modify or revoke provisions in the will but does not cancel (invalidate) the will. A codicil must be executed with the same formalities as a will.

Executor

The executor is a man named in the will to be the personal representative of the estate and to carry out the provisions of the will.
Example: John Jones executed a valid will designating within the instrument that his brother, Bob Jones, be executor of his (John's) estate. Upon John's death, Bob assumes his duties as executor.

Executrix

The executrix is a woman named in the will to be the personal representative of the estate and to carry out the provisions of the will.

Guardian

A guardian is the person or institution named by the maker of a will to care for the person and/or property of a minor, handicapped, or incompetent person.

Trust

A trust is a right of property, real or personal, held by one person (trustee) for the benefit of another (beneficiary). The trustee holds *legal title* to the property; the beneficiary holds *equitable title*.

Testament

A testament is a will.

Testamentary trust

A testamentary trust is a trust created in a will (see page 197). It becomes operative only after death.

Inter vivos trust

An *inter vivos* trust is a trust created by a maker (settlor) during the maker's lifetime. It becomes operative during the lifetime of the settlor.

Trustee

A trustee is the person or institution named by the maker of a will or a settlor to administer property for the benefit of another according to provisions in a testamentary trust or an *inter vivos* trust.

Beneficiary

The beneficiary, in the terminology of wills, is the person or institution to whom the maker of a will gives personal property through the will. **Example:** Sam gives his daughter his collection of books through his will. The books are personal property, and Sam's daughter is the beneficiary.

Beneficiary of a trust

The beneficiary of a trust, during the existence of the trust, is the person or institution to whom the trustee distributes the income earned from the trust property. When the trust terminates, the trustee conveys legal title to the property held in trust to the beneficiary or to some other person designated by the settlor (grantor) by a deed (*inter vivos* trust) or by a will (testamentary trust).
Example: X conveys by will a farm, Blackacre, "to A in trust for the benefit of B." In the will, X describes the trustee's (A's) duties in regard to managing the property and distributing the income therefrom to B. The will then directs A to convey legal title to the property to B when B attains the age of 21 years. B would be the beneficiary of the trust.

Legal title

Legal title, as it pertains to trust law, is the form of ownership of trust property held by the trustee giving the trustee the right to control the property. Legal title is the antithesis of equitable title.

Example: When property is entrusted to Ray (trustee) by will for the benefit of Bill, Ray holds legal title, while Bill holds equitable title. Bill also holds the right to have the legal title transferred to him at some future time (e.g., when he reaches the age of majority).

Equitable title

In trust law, equitable title is the form of ownership of trust property held by the beneficiary of the trust, giving the beneficiary the right to enjoy the trust property.

Example: Johnson conveys (transfers by deed or will) Blackacre (a farm) "to Howard in trust for the benefit of Sue." Johnson is the grantor (if a deed was used) or testator (if a will was used). Howard holds legal title, and Sue holds equitable title. The holder of legal title is called a "trustee," and the holder of equitable title is called a "beneficiary" (see page 214).

Operation of law   *automatically because the law exist.*

Operation of law refers to the manner in which rights pass to a person by the application of the established rules of law, without the act, knowledge, or cooperation of the person.

Example: Mike and Mary own their home as joint tenants. Mike dies. Because of the right of survivorship, Mike's interest in the home automatically passes to Mary by operation of law.

Disposition

Disposition is the parting with, transfer of, or conveyance of property by deed or will.

Example: Maxine by deed conveys (sells) property "to Michael Ford and his heirs." Maxine's conveyance is a disposition of the property.

Example: William by deed conveys property "to Samuel in *trust* for the benefit of George." Samuel holds legal title, George holds equitable title, and William has made a disposition of the property.

Example: Shirley by will conveys property "to Sally Short and her heirs." A disposition of the property will occur when Shirley dies.

Bequest

A bequest is a gift of personal property, other than money, through a will.

Example: Patrick conveys by will a *bequest* of all his household furnishings to his sister.

Legacy

A legacy is a gift of money through a will.

Example: Judy conveys by will a *legacy* of the money in her $10,000 savings account to her son.

Devise

A devise is a gift of real property through a will. In U.P.C. terminology, "devise" refers to gifts of both real and personal property (see Table 5.1, page 96).

Example: Herman conveys a farm, Blackacre, by will to his son and daughter in joint tenancy. Herman's gift is a devise.

Devisee

The devisee is the recipient of a devise.

Residue

The residue is any property of a testator or testatrix remaining in the estate after all gifts mentioned in the will have been delivered.

Example: Jane Brown in her will conveyed all her real and personal property to designated relatives, but forgot to provide in her will for disposition of $700 in her personal checking account and $400 worth of government bonds. This property, the $700 in cash and $400 in bonds are the residue of Jane's estate (i.e., what is left over or not disposed of by the will or by deed prior to Jane's death). In this case, the recipient of the residue of the estate is determined by the intestate succession laws of the state in which Jane lives. Another way of transferring the residue of a decedent's estate is to include a residuary clause in the will. In the above case, Jane could then leave any unmentioned or forgotten property of her estate to the named residual beneficiary (for a sample residuary clause, see page 190).

Attest

To attest is to witness the making of the final draft of a will (see sample clause, page 201).

Subscribe

To subscribe is to sign one's name as a witness to the final draft of a will.

Holograph

A holograph is a will drawn entirely in the maker's own handwriting. State laws establish the conditions for a valid holographic will.

Nuncupative will

A nuncupative will is an oral will spoken in the presence of a witness or witnesses which is valid only under exceptional circumstances, such as the impending death of the person "speaking" the will. Nuncupative wills are prohibited in some jurisdictions.

Probate

Probate is the procedure by which a document alleged to be a will is established judicially as a valid testamentary disposition; as a verb, it is the process by which a proper court declares the will to be a valid testamentary disposition.

Publish

To publish is to make something known to the public for a purpose, e.g., to publish a last will.

make it known

nasty things about someone but once you give it to a 3rd person, it now it is publish

Sound and disposing mind and memory

To say that one has a sound and disposing mind and memory is to say that he or she has testamentary capacity, i.e., is able to know and understand the meaning and consequences of a will (said of the testate).

Seisin (or seizin)

Seisin is actual possession, where the possessor intends to claim the land as a fee simple or life estate. Seisin is not the same as legal title. The difference between legal title and seisin is that the person who holds seisin over the land does not necessarily hold legal title to it.

Example: Amy takes possession of a farm, Blackacre, which she has recently purchased from Beth. Beth gives Amy a deed that conveys Blackacre. Amy has seisin, or is said to be seized with the land. In this instance, Amy also has legal title.

Example: Raul owns Whiteacre in fee simple, but he is not in possession of the property (he lives in another state). Sam, a trespasser, takes physical possession of Whiteacre (i.e., lives on it) and claims to own it. Sam has seisin, but Raul still owns the property and holds legal title. Raul has the right to institute legal action (i.e., action in ejectment) to remove Sam from possession of Whiteacre.

Seised (or seized)

Seised means in actual possession of land.

Bond

A bond is a certificate whereby a "surety company" agrees to pay money if the personal representative of a deceased fails to faithfully perform the duties of administering the decedent's estate (see Form 28).

Surety

Surety is a guarantee of an individual or company that, at the request of another, usually called the principal, it will undertake to pay money or to do any other act in event that the principal fails to perform as agreed, e.g., the surety of a personal representative's bond.

Hand and seal

Hand refers to a person's signature; seal, authenticated by a seal, refers to the affixing of a seal followed by the signatures of witnesses.

Declare

To declare is to solemnly assert a fact before witnesses, as where a testator declares a paper signed by him to be his last will and testament.

Illustrating the Use of Testate Terminology

To better understand the meaning and usage of the above terms, read the facts below and the accompanying will.

The Facts

Sheila Swanson, desiring that all the property she owns be distributed at death according to her wishes, draws up a will specifying the persons to whom the property in her estate shall be distributed and which items of real and personal property will go to each person. She leaves a fur coat along with all her other clothing to a sister, Myrtle Jones. Sheila also gives $20,000 to each of her children living at her death. To a close cousin, John Stewart, Sheila leaves her one acre of land in Northern County. The sum of $100,000 is left in trust for her surviving grandchildren, to be administered by Glen Howard of the Fullservice Bank. The rest of her estate is given to her husband, Frank, but if he does not survive her, then her surviving children receive the property in equal shares. In the event that Sheila and her husband die at the same time (as in a common accident) before her children have grown up, she appoints her sister, Myrtle, to take care of them. Viola Larson is named to oversee the management and distribution of the estate according to the dictates of the will, which is signed and witnessed by Charles Larson, Althea Gibbons, and Harold Smith.

LAST WILL AND TESTAMENT OF SHEILA SWANSON

I, Sheila Swanson, of the City of Winslow, in the County of Northern, and State of Maine, being of sound mind and memory, and not acting under duress, menace, fraud, or undue influence of any person whatsoever, do make, publish, and declare this instrument to be my Last Will and Testament. I do hereby cancel, revoke, and annul all former wills and testaments or codicils by me at any time made.

First: I direct that all my just debts, funeral and burial expenses be paid out of my estate as soon after my death as can conveniently be done;

Second: I give my fur coat and all other personal clothing to my sister, Myrtle Swanson;

Third: I give my one acre of land with the following legal description, "Lot 1, Block 4, Brauer Addition," located in Northern County to my cousin, John Stewart, and his heirs;

Fourth: I give from the assets of my estate $20,000 to each of my children living at my death;

Fifth: I give $100,000 to Mr. Glen Howard of the Fullservice Bank to hold in trust for the benefit of my grandchildren. See attached testamentary trust. (For example of such trusts see Chapter 8, page 197.)

Sixth: All the rest, residue, and remainder of my estate, real and personal of any kind, of which I die seized or possessed or to which I am entitled at the time of my death, I give to my husband, Frank, if he survives me, and if he does not survive me, or we die in a common accident, I give my residuary estate to my children that survive me in equal shares;

Seventh: In the event of a common accident in which both my husband and I die, I nominate and appoint my sister, Myrtle Jones, to be the personal guardian over any of my minor children living at the time of our deaths;

Eighth: Finally, I nominate and appoint Viola Larson to be the executrix of this my last will and testament and direct that she not be required to give any bond or security for the proper discharge of her duties.

IN TESTIMONY WHEREOF I hereunto set my hand and seal on this _____ day of _____, in the Year Nineteen Hundred and _____.

[*Signature*] _____

[*Address*] _____

The foregoing instrument, consisting of two pages, including this page, was, at the date hereof, signed, sealed, published, and declared by Sheila Swanson, the testatrix above named, at _____ in the State of _____ as and for her last will and testament, in our presence, who, in her presence, at her request, and in the presence of each other hereunto set our names as witnesses.

Names	Addresses
_____	_____
_____	_____
_____	_____

[*Signed by three witnesses*]

Review of Terminology

If Ms. Swanson dies now, her death will occur *testate* because she has left a will. For her will to have validity as a written legal document directing the distribution and disposition of an estate on death, it must be *executed* carefully to comply with the requirements established by statutes or common law controlling *testate succession*. The fact that Mr. Larson, Ms. Gibbons, and Mr. Smith were *attesting* and *subscribing witnesses* to the will is an example of such statutory control.

Because Sheila Swanson as testatrix can change her mind and dispose of her estate prior to death in any manner she chooses, subject to but a few restrictions,[1] she might execute a *codicil,* i.e., a written modification of the will which, while not canceling the will, could have added to, deleted from, or otherwise changed various provisions to keep it up-to-date with Sheila's wishes. She also retains the option to cancel or destroy the will and either to substitute a new one in its place or to decide never to make a new will, in which event she would die *intestate*.

---

1. It is Sheila Swanson's prerogative to change the terms of her will to reflect changes in her marital or family status (e.g., dissolution of her marriage or birth or death of a successor), in the inheritance tax laws (e.g., by modifying a provision, she may lessen the tax on a certain devise), or in the status of her property (e.g., she may have gained an asset which she would like to devise).

The *beneficiaries* under the will are Sheila's children and grandchildren living at her death, her sister Myrtle, cousin John, and husband Frank; these are the persons to whom she intends to leave her estate. Before any of the interests pass to these recipients, the will must be *probated,* declared by a court to be a valid testamentary disposition. This procedure for approving a will and overseeing its administration is discussed in detail in later chapters.

Comparison of Orthodox and U.P.C. Terminology

The clauses directing the passage of identified property have certain labels, as do their recipients. The *Uniform Probate Code (U.P.C.)* has replaced a few of the orthodox (traditional) definitions and uses of these words. Table 5.1 compares the orthodox testacy and intestacy terminology with the U.P.C. terminology (see Appendix C, U.P.C. § 1–201).

Assignment 28

1. Rita Caldwell, a widow, died testate, giving her house (through her will) to her daughter, Susan Nestor; her gun collection and her lake cottage to her daughter, Carmen Caldwell; $3,000 and her jewelry to her favorite niece, Jana Nelson; $12,000 and her china and silver pieces to her longtime housekeeper, Jaylene Bouchard; $12,000 to the March of Dimes; an acre of land to her church; a one-half undivided

Table 5.1 Orthodox and U.P.C. Terminology Compared

Testacy Terminology	Orthodox	U.P.C.
Gift of personal property through a will (other than money)	Bequest	Devise
Gift of real property through a will	Devise	Devise
Gift of money through a will	Legacy	Devise
Designated recipient of money through a will	Legatee	Devisee
Designated recipient of personal property through a will (other than money)	Beneficiary	Devisee
Designated recipient of real property through a will	Devisee	Devisee
Intestacy Terminology		
Person entitled by statute to real property of intestate	Heir or heir-at-law	Heir
Person entitled by statute to personal property of intestate	Distributee or next-of-kin	Heir
Testacy or Intestacy Terminology		
Person, other than creditors, entitled to the real or personal property of a decedent under the will or through intestate succession	No all-inclusive word	Successor
Person, other than a creditor or purchaser, who has actually received real or personal property from the decedent's personal representative	No all-inclusive word	Distributee

interest in real property (Blackacre) held in joint tenancy with her sister, Bonnie Gatson, to her brother, Alex Nelson; and all remaining household furnishings to her sister, Bonnie Gatson.

   a. What would each of the persons named in the will be called, using orthodox terminology? Why? Using U.P.C. terminology?

   b. What would each of these "gifts" be called, using orthodox terminology? Using U.P.C. terminology?

   c. Which of these conveyances (transfers) to a named recipient can *not* be made legally? Why not?

The deceased forgot to include in her will a "residuary clause," i.e., a clause specifying who should get all the rest and residue of her estate. She had $4,000 in a checking account.

   d. Who would get the $4,000, and what would the person be called in orthodox terminology? In U.P.C. terminology?

2. Lawrence Bellamy died without a will, leaving the following property: $80,000 in checking and savings accounts; stocks valued at $58,000; a homestead (Blackacre, valued at $100,000); an office building (valued at $300,000); household furnishings (valued at $25,000); an art collection (valued at $150,000); a one-half undivided interest in real property (Greenacre) held in tenancy-in-common with his brother, Robert Bellamy (the entire property being valued at $60,000); a new set of encyclopedias (valued at $580); a man's diamond ring (valued at $4,000); and a large number of old family pictures and bric-a-brac of little material value but possibly having value as family mementos to some or all members of the family. Lawrence left surviving him a wife, Susan; four children, Joe, Nancy, Tim, and Sara; his father, William; two first cousins, Allen Green and Hortense Green; an aunt, Terry Orwell; and a housekeeper, Alice Graham, who had faithfully performed duties for the family for several years.

   a. What would each of the persons who receive any of the deceased's property be call in orthodox terminology? In U.P.C. terminology?

   b. According to your state statutes, what would each of the "gifts" be called in orthodox terminology? In U.P.C. terminology?

Now that both orthodox and U.P.C. terminology have been covered, refer to page 941 and the Sheila Swanson case. The following discussion illustrates the use of both the orthodox and U.P.C. terminology. The first term listed is the orthodox term; the corresponding U.P.C. term is placed in parentheses.

Thus, the distribution of Sheila's one acre of land is a *devise,* the gift of real property by will, and its taker, cousin John, is a *devisee* (or *successor*). Sheila devised the land to him. The $20,000 to be received by Sheila's surviving children, a gift of money, is a *legacy (devise),* Sheila's children being the *legatees* (*devisees* or *successors*) of this gift of money. Myrtle, because she is receiving personal property under the will, is a beneficiary (*devisee* or *successor*) but the distribution of the fur coat and other clothing to her, since it is not money, is known as a *bequest* (*devise*). Sheila bequeathed (devised) the clothing to her. Although it is important to keep the latter distinction in mind, in modern practice the terms *bequest* and *legacy* are used interchangeably. Generally, if the orthodox terms such as "bequeath" or "bequest" are used in a will, they stand for a gift of any personal property, including money. In preparing wills today, however, most attorneys prefer to use the phrase "I hereby give" in place of the words "I hereby bequeath."

The $100,000 earmarked for the grandchildren constitutes a *testamentary trust* (i.e., a trust created by the will) with Mr. Howard of the bank as its administrator, the *trustee*. Since Viola Larson has been named to handle the estate, she is its *executrix*. Had Viola's husband, Charles, been given the responsibility instead, he would be the *executor* of the estate. Sheila's sister, Myrtle, has a role beyond that of a beneficiary (successor). As the person designated to care for the testatrix's minor children at her death, if Sheila's husband, Frank, is also deceased, Myrtle is a *guardian* for Sheila's children.

Assignment 29

Read the following will, then answer the questions at the end.

LAST WILL AND TESTAMENT OF JOHN JONES

I, John Jones, of the City of _____, in the County of _____ and State of _____, being of sound and disposing mind and memory, and not acting under duress, menace, fraud, or undue influence of any person whatsoever, do make, publish, and declare this instrument to be my Last Will and Testament. I do hereby cancel, revoke, and annul all former wills and testaments or codicils by me at any time made.

First: I direct that all my just debts, funeral and burial expenses be paid out of my estate as soon after my death as can conveniently be done.

Second: I give and bequeath to my son, James, my diamond ring, and all my other personal jewelry and effects.

Third: I give and bequeath to my said son, James, the sum of five thousand dollars.

Fourth: All the rest, residue and remainder of my estate, real and personal, of whatsoever character and wheresoever situated, of which I shall die seized or possessed or to which I shall be in any way entitled at the time of my death, I give, devise, and bequeath to my wife, Mary, if she shall survive me, and if my said wife shall not be living at the time of my death or we both should die in a common accident, I give, devise and bequeath my residuary estate to my son, James, absolutely.

Fifth: I nominate and appoint Bill Brown to be the executor of this my Last Will and Testament, and I direct that my said executor shall not be required to give any bond or security for the proper discharge of his duties.

IN TESTIMONY WHEREOF I hereunto set my hand and seal on this _____ day of _____, in the Year Nineteen Hundred and _____.

[*Signature*] _____

[*Address*] _____

The foregoing instrument, consisting of two pages, including this page, was, at the date hereof, signed, sealed, published, and declared by JOHN JONES, the testator above named, at _____ in the State of _____ as and for his Last Will and Testament, in our presence, who, in his presence, at his request, and in the presence of each other have hereunto set our names as witnesses.

Names	Addresses
_____	_____
_____	_____
_____	_____

[*Signed by three witnesses*]

1. Who is the testator?

2. Is there a testatrix?

3. Did John Jones die testate or intestate?

4. Is there a guardian or trustee named in the document?

5. Is the document a will or a codicil?

6. What is the diamond ring given to James called according to the U.P.C.?

7. Is there a devisee named in the will?

8. Who are the beneficiaries named in the will?

9. Who is the personal representative?

10. Does the document contain a testamentary trust?

11. Has the will been attested and subscribed?

12. Is this an example of a nuncupative will?

Death Without a Will—Intestacy

When a person dies without a will or with an invalid will, the state in which the decedent resides at death for personal property purposes and the states in which the decedent owned real property at death determine by statute how and to whom such property, both real and personal, passes. The following chart demonstrates how intestacy occurs:

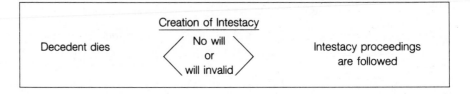

Terminology Relating to Intestacy

The following terms are associated with the persons and proceedings involved in the law of intestate succession.

Intestacy
Intestacy is death without a will.
Example: Ann owns property and dies, either leaving no will at all or leaving an invalid will. Her estate will descend under intestate succession laws.

Intestate
As an adverb, intestate means having not made a will; as a noun, it is a decedent who has not made a valid will.

Succession
Succession is the devolution (transfer or passage) of title to property under the law of descent and distribution. Succession occurs in testacy as well as intestacy.

Intestate succession laws
Intestate succession laws are statutory laws passed in each state determining the manner in which a decedent's property will be distributed when death occurs without a valid will.
Example: Abby dies with no will or an invalid will. Her estate descends to her heirs and next-of-kin if her state's intestate succession laws so provide.

Heir or heir-at-law
In orthodox terminology, the heir or heir-at-law is the person entitled by statute to the real property of an intestate decedent.
Example: If her mother dies intestate, Georgia would receive part of her mother's real estate. Georgia is her mother's heir (heir-at-law).

Distributee or next-of-kin
In orthodox terminology, the distributee or next-of-kin is the person to whom personal property of the intestate decedent is distributed.

Example: Mark Rutledge dies intestate. His personal property passes to his wife, Joanna, and child, William. In some states his parents also would receive his personal property. These persons are Mark's next-of-kin.

Kindred
Kindred refers to persons related to one another by blood.

Administrator
The administrator is a male personal representative appointed by the probate court to handle the estate of an intestate decedent.

Administratrix
The administratrix is a female personal representative appointed by the probate court to handle the estate of an intestate decedent.

Lineal
As a noun, a lineal is a person related to an intestate decedent in a direct line either upward in an ascending bloodline (e.g., parents, grandparents, or great-grandparents) or downward in a descending bloodline (e.g., children, grandchildren, or great-grandchildren). See Figures 5.1, 5.3, and 5.5.

Figure 5.1 Examples of Lineal Ascendants and Descendants

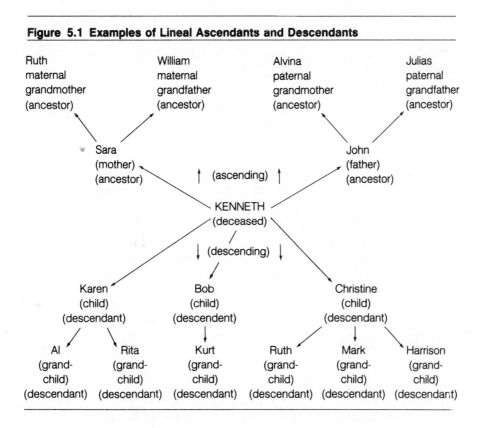

Ascendant or ancestor

An ascendant or ancestor is a claimant to an intestate's share related to the decedent in an ascending lineal blood line.
Example: The parent of a decedent.

Descendant

A descendant is a claimant to an intestate's share related to the decedent in a descending lineal blood line.
Example: A child of a decedent.

Collateral

As a noun, in testate terminology, a collateral is a person not in a direct line of lineal ascent or descent who traces a kinship relationship to an intestate decedent through a common ancestor (e.g., brothers, sisters, aunts, uncles, nieces, nephews, cousins, and other such relatives), forming a collateral line of relationship (see Figures 5.2, 5.3, and 5.5).

Affinity

Affinity refers to relationship by marriage.
Example: In Figure 5.3, Nathan's wife is related to Joe by affinity. Generally, she cannot inherit under intestate succession laws.   The

---

Figure 5.2 Examples of Collateral Relatives

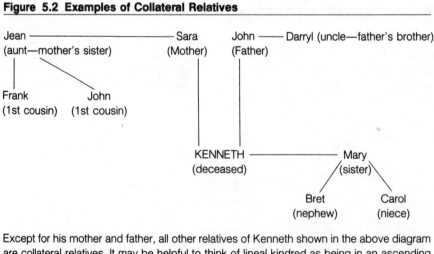

Except for his mother and father, all other relatives of Kenneth shown in the above diagram are collateral relatives. It may be helpful to think of lineal kindred as being in an ascending or descending vertical line, i.e.,

D

And to think of collateral kindred as being in a horizontal line (or to the sides of the decedent), i.e.,

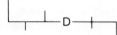

Figure 5.3 Examples of Lineal and Collateral Relationships

Joe (deceased) — Keith, David, Molly	Joe's three children are in his direct line—also called descending lineal bloodline.
Mother—Father (parents); Joe and Brenda (sister); Joe's children: Keith, David, Molly; Brenda's children: Fran (niece), Larry (nephew)	Here, the common ancestors of Joe (decedent) are Joe's mother and father, who are also Brenda's parents. Brenda is Joe's sister, a collateral relative (kin). Brenda's children are also Joe's collateral kindred (Joe's niece and nephew).
Mother—Father — Nathan—Wife (uncle); Joe, Brenda	Nathan, the brother of Joe's father (Joe's uncle) is Joe's collateral kin. Nathan is married; his wife is neither a direct lineal relative nor a collateral relative for purposes of intestate succession, i.e., she would not be related to Joe *by blood*.
Mother—Father — Nathan—Wife; Joe, Brenda, Sally (first cousin), Susan (first cousin)	Nathan, Joe's uncle, has two children, Susan and Sally, who are Joe's and Brenda's first cousins (see Figure 5.5) and are collateral kindred.
Grandmother—Grandfather — Sam—Shirley (grand-uncle); Mother—Father, Nathan—Wife; Joe, Brenda, Susan, Sally; Mary, Sue, Alice (first cousins once removed)	Sam is Joe's grand-uncle who has three children, Mary, Sue, and Alice. They are Joe's first cousins once removed (see Figure 5.5). Sam, Mary, Sue, and Alice are collateral kindred. Sam's wife, Shirley, is not a collateral relative. She is not related to Joe by blood.

decedent and the person related to him by affinity have no common ancestor. This rule, of course, does not apply to the spouse of the decedent even though husband and wife are related solely by marriage (by affinity).

Consanguinity
Consanguinity refers to relationship by blood through at least one common ancestor.
Example: A child, grandchild, grandparent, aunt, uncle, cousin, and the like related to the decedent through a common ancestor. Janice Rule is the granddaughter of Elliot Sanderson. She is related to her grandfather by consanguinity.

Per capita

The term per capita means "equally to each person." When all heirs entitled to a portion of an intestate decedent's estate are related to the deceased in the same degree of relationship (same-generation ascendants or descendants), each receives an identical portion, all sharing equally. **Example:** Three children, the only heirs of an intestate, take equal shares per capita (see example under Per Stirpes, below).

Per stirpes

Per stirpes rights refers to a situation when heirs entitled to a portion of an intestate decedent's estate are related to the deceased in different degrees of relationship (intergenerational ascendants or descendants) with some heirs having predeceased the intestate, the descendants of such persons receive their shares through the predeceased heirs. An example of a statute regulating per capita and per stirpes rights to an intestate's estate is Idaho Code § 15–2–103 (1979) on the share of heirs other than surviving spouse:

> The part of the intestate estate not passing to the surviving spouse under Idaho Code § 15–2–102 of this part, or the entire intestate estate if there is no surviving spouse, passes as follows:
>
> (a) To the issue of the decedent; if they all are of the same degree of kinship to the decedent they take equally [per capita], but if of unequal degree, then those of more remote degree take by representation [per stirpes].

Example: Mary, a widow, has three children—Jim, Nora, and Kathryn. Jim is married and has two children—Matt and Colleen. Nora is single. Kathryn also was married and had three children—Charles, Darlene, and Elaine. Kathryn died of cancer two years ago. Now Mary dies. (Refer to Figure 5.4.) If Mary dies intestate, leaving an estate valued at $225,000 after payment of debts, taxes, and all other expenses, and her only surviving relatives are two of her three adult children and her five grandchildren (three of whom are the children of her deceased daughter, Kathryn), her estate would be distributed as follows:

- $75,000 to Jim (son) per capita
- $75,000 to Nora (daughter) per capita
- $25,000 to Charles (grandchild) per stirpes

Figure 5.4 Mary's Descendants

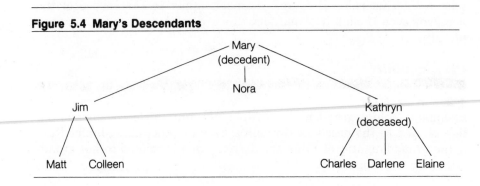

- $25,000 to Darlene (grandchild) per stirpes

- $25,000 to Elaine (grandchild) per stirpes

If Kathryn had still been alive at her mother's death she would have taken a per capita share of $75,000 (one-third of the total estate). Since Kathryn was deceased at her mother's death, Kathryn's children receive Kathryn's share through Kathryn, taking per stirpes. This means that Kathryn's share was divided equally among her children, each child taking a third of their mother's share. Each took only one-ninth of the total estate, whereas the two children of the decedent, Mary, each took one-third. The three children of Kathryn take per stirpes (by right of representation), i.e., they "represent" their mother. The other two grandchildren of the decedent receive nothing because their father, Jim, who was the son of the decedent, Mary, survived his mother.

Escheat

Escheat is the passing of property to the state when an intestate decedent leaves no surviving relatives entitled to inherit the intestate's estate.

Example: Bob dies intestate, leaving an estate valued at $100,000. There are no surviving relatives. The property "escheats" to the state; the state enjoys complete ownership and can use the property as it sees fit, sell or lease it just as an individual owner could do.

Some potential assets of the estate, such as life insurance policy proceeds, do not necessarily escheat if the decedent has no surviving heirs. A person who takes out a life insurance policy is allowed to name a primary beneficiary to receive the proceeds in case of the insured's death and a contingent beneficiary to receive the proceeds should the primary beneficiary die before or at the same time as the insured.

Example: Malcolm names his nephew and only blood relative, Donald, primary beneficiary of his insurance policy but does not name a contingent beneficiary. If both Malcolm and Donald should die in a common accident or within a few hours of one another, the proceeds of the policy would revert to Malcolm's estate. Since Malcolm has no other living relatives, his estate would escheat; the point is, however, that the proceeds do not automatically escheat. They go back to the insured's estate, which itself may or may not escheat, according to the intestate succession laws of the state.

Uniform Probate Code Terminology

As previously mentioned (page 96), orthodox and Uniform Probate Code definitions of terms are used interchangeably in common practice, not only in testate but also in intestate proceedings. This leads to much confusion. To avoid misunderstandings, we will hereafter use the following definitions as specified in the U.P.C. (see U.P.C. § 1–201, in Appendix C).

Devise

As a noun, devise means the testamentary disposition of real or personal property; as a verb, it means to dispose of real or personal property by will.

Devisee

A devisee is any person designated in a will to receive a devise. In the case of a devise to an existing trust or trustee, or to a trustee in a trust created by will, the trust or trustee is the devisee; the beneficiaries of the trust are not devisees because they do not receive the trust property directly from the decedent through the will. Rather, the trustee receives the property from the decedent through the will, then in turn distributes the income from the trust or conveys the trust property to the beneficiaries.

Distributee

As defined by the U.P.C., the distributee is any person, other than a creditor or purchaser, who *has received* property of a decedent from the personal representative.

Heirs

Heirs are those persons, including the surviving spouse, who are entitled under the statutes of *intestate succession* to the *real* or *personal* property of a decedent.

Successors

Successors is an all-inclusive term meaning those persons, other than creditors, who are entitled to real or personal property of a decedent *either* under the *will* or through *intestate succession.*

Because the law of intestate succession controls the distribution of an intestate decedent's estate, the testamentary terms "devisee," "legatee," and "beneficiary" do not apply since no testamentary gift has been made by the deceased. The state, by statute, determines the heir(s) or successor(s) (terms used by the U.P.C.) to whom the intestate's property will be given.

Under such intestate succession laws, sometimes called *statutes (laws) of descent and distribution,* a hierarchy of potential heirs of a decedent is outlined. As seen from the sample statutes, generally the *surviving spouse* is first in line to receive the estate of the deceased, with the intestate's lineal descendants—blood relatives in a direct line of descent below the decedent on the family tree (children, grandchildren, great-grandchildren, and so on) following (see previous discussion, page 104). When no lineal descendants are surviving, *lineal ascendants* are looked to as potential heirs. (Lineal ascendents are blood relatives in a line directly above the decedent on the family tree and include parents, grandparents, great-grandparents, and so on.) Next in order come *collateral heirs:* blood relatives not in a direct descent line, such as brothers, sisters, and their offspring, who come before aunts, uncles,

Figure 5.5 Family Tree Chart

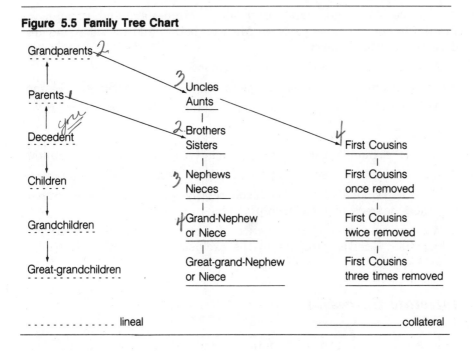

and cousins. Collateral heirs are referred to as above or below the decedent and to the sides. For example, a collateral heir above the decedent and to the side is an uncle. An example of a collateral heir below the decedent and to the side would be a first cousin once removed (see Figure 5.5).

In determining which collateral heirs receive the property, to the exclusion of others, it is often necessary to ascertain the *degree of relationship* between the decedent and the particular heirs in question. This is accomplished by counting up on the family tree chart from the *decedent* to the *closest ancestor common* to both the decedent and the possible *heir,* and then counting down to the heir. In so counting, the decedent is excluded and the possible heir is included. For example, in determining the degree of relationship of a *grand-nephew,* count up to the parents (1), and then down through brothers or sisters (2), and nephews and nieces (3), to grand-nephew (4); thus a grand-nephew is related in the 4th degree. Similarly, a first cousin is also related in the 4th degree (parents [1], grandparents [2], uncles and aunts [3], to first cousins), while a first cousin once removed is related in the 5th degree.

Assignment 30

Armond died in Great Falls, Montana. Either by choice or through oversight, Armond had neither married nor drawn a will. At his death, Armond had the following blood relatives surviving him:

- A brother, Niles, living in Sacramento, California
- A sister, Lorraine, living in London, England

- A niece, Francine, living in Fridley, Minnesota, and a nephew, Frank, living in Albany, New Mexico, both children of Armond's deceased brother, Harry
- A mother, Lila, who lived with Armond
- An aunt, Rose, Armond's mother's sister, living in Bangor, Maine
- A first cousin once removed, Judy, living in Lawrence, Kansas

Answer the following questions.

1. Who of Armond's surviving blood relatives are lineal descendants?

2. Who of Armond's surviving blood relatives are lineal ascendants?

3. Who of Armond's surviving blood relatives are collaterals? What are their degrees of relationship?

4. What is the order of inheritance of Armond's surviving relatives? Which heir receives property to the exclusion of others?

Intestate Succession Laws

Besides determining the distribution of an intestate's estate as a whole, intestate succession statutes (also known as laws of descent and distribution) frequently provide rules for the descent of an intestate's property. Pertinent Minnesota statutes, typical of those in many other states, are used here as a model to describe the operation of intestate succession.

The Minnesota statute concerning the descent of the "homestead" is as follows:

Minn. Stat. Ann. 525.145 (West 1975) *Descent of Homestead*

(1) Where there is a surviving spouse the homestead, including a mobile home which is the family residence, shall descend free from any testamentary or other disposition thereof to which such spouse has not consented in writing or by election to take under the will as provided by law, as follows:
(a) If there be no survivng child or issue of any deceased child, to the spouse;
(b) If there be children or issue of deceased children surviving, then to the spouse for the term of the spouse's natural life and the remainder in equal shares to such children and the issue of deceased children by right of representation.
(2) Where there is no surviving spouse and the homestead has not been disposed of by will it shall descend as other real estate.
(3) Where the homestead passes by descent or will to the spouse or children or issue of deceased children, it shall be exempt from all debts which were not valid charges thereon at the time of decedent's death; except that the homestead shall be subject to a claim filed pursuant to section 256B.15 for medical assistance benefits. If the homestead passes to a person other than a spouse or child or issue of a deceased child it shall be subject to the payment of the items mentioned in section 525.16. No lien or other charge against any homestead which is so exempted shall be enforced in the probate

court, but the claimant may enforce such lien or charge by an appropriate action in the district court.

The homestead is defined as the house and adjoining land occupied by the owner (decedent) as a home. The amount of land comprising the homestead may be limited in acreage by statute. Many states also impose a monetary limit.

Minn. Stat. Ann. 510.01 (West 1947) *Homestead Defined; Exempt; Exception*

The house owned and occupied by a debtor as his dwelling place, together with the land upon which it is situated to the amount hereinafter limited and defined, shall constitute the homestead of such debtor and his family, and be exempt from seizure or sale under legal process on account of any debts not lawfully charged thereon in writing, except such as are incurred for work or materials furnished in the construction, repair, or improvement of such homestead, or for services performed by laborers or servants.

Minn. Stat. Ann. 510.02 (West 1947) *Area, How Limited*

The homestead may include any quantity of land not exceeding 80 acres, and not included in the laid out or platted portion of any city. If it be within the laid out or platted portion of such place its area shall not exceed one half of an acre.

It is common practice for spouses (husband and wife) to have title to their home in joint tenancy form of ownership. When such is the case and one of the spouses has died, it does not matter that death occurs without a will regarding the transfer of the homestead. As previously mentioned, the decedent's interest in jointly owned property of any kind, real or personal, as a result of the right of survivorship, automatically passes to the surviving joint tenant. Thus, in the case of a homestead, when a husband dies, owning a home in joint tenancy with his wife, the house belongs to the wife automatically whether his death has taken place with a will or without. Because it is not affected by either intestate succession statutes or wills, jointly owned property is an example of *non-probate property* (see Chapter 13, page 357).

In some states, such as Minnesota, when it is not in joint tenancy ownership and the decedent leaves no will, the homestead descends to the surviving spouse in the following manner:

• If there is no surviving child or offspring (issue) of such child, e.g., a grandchild of the decedent, the homestead goes solely to the spouse.

• If a child or issue thereof (the child's child) survives, then the spouse gets only a life estate in the homestead. After the surviving spouse's death, the remainder goes in equal shares to the decedent's children or their issue by right of representation (see page 108).

• When the spouse does not survive the decedent, the homestead is transferred just as all other real property (see page 108).

• When the homestead is passed by intestate succession, or by will, to the surviving spouse, children, or their issue, it is exempt from all debts that are not valid encumbrances (claims) against it. An existing mortgage or tax lien are examples of valid encumbrances.

To illustrate the passage of a homestead upon the intestate death of its owner, consider the following assignment.

Assignment 31

Henry and Wilma are husband and wife. They have been married for the past 32 years, and Henry owns their house in his name only. Henry suddenly dies without having executed a will, leaving surviving his widow, Wilma; two children, Abby and Beth; and six grandchildren, Cindy and Daniel, Abby's children, Elaine and Fred, Beth's children, and George and Ida, children of Henry's already deceased child, Stanley. The house, in which Henry and Wilma lived, has a lien against it for partial non-payment of 1974 property taxes and a 30-year mortgage with 5 years remaining. According to your state laws, how, to whom, and in what shares will the house descend? Is the descent of the homestead free from claims against it?

The Minnesota Law (Minn. Stat. Ann. § 525.15 [West 1975]) *on the Family Allowance for Spouse and Children is:*

After the decedent dies, with or without a will, before any debts are paid or benefits under a will distributed, the personal property of the deceased's estate shall be disposed of as follows:

(a) The surviving spouse receives the decedent's clothing and $6,000 worth of household goods, furnishings, and appliances.
(b) The spouse may select also other personal property up to a maximum of $3,000.
(c) In addition, if all the personal estate of the decedent is included in (a) and (b) above, except for one car, then the spouse receives the car.
(d) When no spouse survives, the minor children of the decedent receive all allowances the spouse could have received.
(e) A reasonable maintenance allowance for the spouse and minor children is granted by the probate court during administration of the decedent's estate for a period of time prescribed by state statute, e.g., up to 18 months in some cases. An extension of the prescribed time is allowed under certain circumstances.

See also page 359 on family allowances.

Assignment 32

Benjamin and Christy, husband and wife, have been married ten years. They have three children, Andrew, Shannon, and Lincoln. Benjamin is killed in an airplane mishap. He has no will, and his wife and children

survive him. Christy has been advised that probate might be lengthy.
The extent of Benjamin's estate encompasses (a) a $100,000 house; (b)
household furnishings, clothing, and other like items valued at $20,000;
(c) additional items of personal property amounting to $15,000; (d) a
$10,000 family car. Christy estimates that upkeep for the family
during probate of her husband's estate will cost $400 per month. At
death, Benjamin's estate had $200,000 in assets and $5,000 in liabilities.

Answer the following according to the family allowance procedures
under Minnesota Law, mentioned above.

1. What, from which source, and how much can Christy seek as the
allowance to a surviving spouse?

2. Will Benjamin's children be entitled to receive the allowance, and if
so when?

3. Does the family allowance in this case include the car?

4. Will the family receive a sum of money to maintain it for the balance
of the time it takes to administer Benjamin's estate? If so, how long?
If not, why not?

5. Check to see if your state has a family allowance statute. If it does,
answer the questions above according to your own state laws.

On the descent of other property, Minn.Stat.Ann. § 525.16 (West
1975) states that subject to the family allowances which are granted in
cases of both testacy and intestacy, the first items paid out of the estate
are the expenses of probate administration, followed by funeral expenses, debts and taxes under federal law, then expenses of the last
illness, debts and taxes under state law, and finally all allowed creditors' claims. The balance of the estate, both real and personal property, descends and is distributed as follows:

1. Personal property: The surviving spouse receives one-third of personal property unhindered by any testamentary disposition to which
the survivor has not consented in writing or by election to take under a
will as provided by law.

2. Real property: The surviving spouse acquires an undivided one-third
interest in all real property which the decedent possessed or owned at
any time while married to the spouse, unless the spouse consented to its
disposition in writing or elected to take under a will.

3. If the spouse alone, or the spouse and only *one* child or offspring of a
deceased child survive, the share the spouse receives under the provisions of clauses (1) and (2) above increases to one-half instead of one-
third.

4. Subject to provisions (1), (2), and (3) above, the decedent's entire estate, real and personal, *except as otherwise disposed of by will* descends and is distributed as follows:

a. In equal shares to surviving children and to the offspring (issue) of deceased children by right of representation (see page 104).

b. If no child or issue of any deceased child is surviving and the intestate leaves a surviving spouse, then the latter takes everything.

c. If there is no surviving issue or spouse, then the decedent's father and mother equally, or the one surviving parent alone, receive the estate.

d. When neither children, offspring of children, spouse, nor father or mother survive, then the surviving brothers and sisters in equal shares and the offspring of any deceased brother or sister by right of representation acquire rights to the decedent's estate. If there are no surviving brothers or sisters, then the offspring of deceased brother and sister receive equal shares if they are all of equal degree. If not, then those in the nearest degree receive equal shares and those in a more remote degree receive by right of representation, e.g., a grandnephew is one degree more remote than a nephew.

e. If there is no surviving child, offspring thereof, spouse, father, mother, brother, sister, nor offspring of deceased brother or sister, then the next of kin in equal degree are given equal shares. But when two or more collateral kindred in equal degree claim an interest through different ancestors, those collaterals claiming through the nearest ancestor receive interests to the exclusion of those collaterals claiming through a more remote ancestor, e.g., a grandnephew and a first cousin are in equal degree (4th degree), but the grandnephew claims through the nearer ancestor (the parents), while the first cousin claims through the more remote ancestor (grandparents) (see Table 5.5).

f. When a minor dies leaving no spouse or offspring surviving, all the decedent minor's estate that was received by inheritance or will from a parent descends and is distributed to the other children of the same parent, if any, and to the offspring of any deceased child of such parent, in equal shares if all are of equal degree, and if not, then in equal shares to those in the nearest degree and by right of representation to those in a more remote degree.

5. Finally, if neither a spouse nor other kindred of any sort survives the intestate, the estate passes to the state by the process of *escheat*. Personal property *escheats* to the state of decedent's domicile at death as does real property located in that state. Real property situated outside the state of decedent's domicile escheats to the state of its location.

When a person dies intestate, any interested party, including creditors of the deceased, the government, or others, may bring a petition in probate court for the administration of the estate of the decedent.

During administration, assets of the decedent are collected and valued, and all claims, charges, and other debts owed by the estate are proved, allowed, and paid, with any asset balance left distributed to rightful takers.

If, during this procedure, it appears that no such takers (spouse or any kindred) survive the decedent to receive the residue of assets remaining in the estate after all claims against it have been satisfied, the administering probate court notifies the state attorney general and it becomes the duty of that official to protect the interests of the state in the assets of the decedent. The residue of assets is ordered by the probate court (final decree) (see page 368) to pass to the state and is transferred to the attorney general, who files a receipt-of-custody with the probate court. Personal property is taken over by the state treasurer to become part of the general fund. Real property is reported by the attorney general to be held or sold.

A problem that might arise in the procedure outline above is *erroneous escheat*. When a final decree has erroneously transferred the property of a decedent to the state on the mistaken assumption that no spouse or other kindred survived, the court may vacate such a decree (order) on petition and proof of the existence of such error (an existing valid will and/or the authenticated interests of rightful takers—blood kindred—in the estate) and enter an amended final decree assigning the previously escheated property to the appropriate successors on payment of any outstanding tax liability. If the property cannot be returned in kind because the state had sold it, the rightful successor(s) will generally receive the value of the property, at the time of the decedent's death, from the state treasury.

How property usually descends to a decedent's successors is reviewed in the Smith estate case below (page 115).

Assignment 33

Margaret is bitten by a skunk and dies of rabies. She has left a considerable estate, having materially prospered during her lifetime, but has drawn no will. Probating the estate will cost $1,900. The Hanson Funeral Parlor has submitted a $3,400 bill for services rendered. Hospital services, doctors' fees, and other medical costs stemming from attempts to save her life, total $26,000. State and federal authorities levy a $13,200 death tax claim against the estate and $15,200 is outstanding in unpaid debts which are owed solely by Margaret. The following relatives survive the deceased:

• Her husband of 43 years, Howard

• Two children, Amy and Barbara

• Six grandchildren, two each by Amy and Barbara, and two by Margaret's predeceased child, Charles

• Her mother, Patricia

- A brother and sister, Alexander and Wynn
- Four nieces, two by Alexander and two by Margaret's already dead brother, Wilbur
- Four nephews, two by Wynn and two by Veronica, Margaret's predeceased sister
- Two grandnieces, one by one of Alexander's two children, and one by one of Veronica's children
- Two grandnephews, one by one of Veronica's children, and one by one of Wilbur's children

Answer the following questions, using your own state's laws.

1. How are the charges against the intestate's estate to be handled? Who receives what amount in which order? How would the answer differ if Margaret's estate lacked sufficient funds to meet them all?

2. How would Margaret's estate descend if only her husband, Howard, were to survive her? Only her children Amy and Barbara were to survive her? Only her grandchildren were to survive her? Only her mother were to survive her? Only her brother and sister were to survive her? Only her nieces and nephews were to survive her? Only her grand-nieces and grand-nephews were to survive her?

Assignment 34

Marvin made his living traveling from city to city. He always considered Cedar Falls, Michigan, his home. Although never financially successful to any great degree, Marvin accumulated a modest-sized estate. One morning, while working in Buffalo, New York, Marvin died. At his passing Marvin owned the following items of property: (a) clothing, personal household goods, and other such effects worth $25,000; (b) $12,500 worth of tools of his trade; (c) a 1983 Ford automobile valued at $11,500; and (d) five acres of land just outside Hanover, New Hampshire, appraised value of $80,500.

Marvin also owed money at his death: $325 to a local dentist in Buffalo; $1300 in taxes on his New Hampshire acreage; $40 to a friend, Carey Brown, in Cedar Falls who had lent him that amount; $1450 to Buffalo Memorial Hospital; $2300 to the Buffalo Funeral Parlor and Burial Service; $1200 in taxes to the state and federal government.

Friend, Carey Brown, petitioned the probate court for Cedar Falls County to have Marvin's estate administered. Marvin had left no will and no surviving kindred could be found.

1. Who receives the residue of assets from Marvin's estate left for distribution after all claims owing against Marvin have been satisfied?

2. What procedure will be followed to achieve that result?

3. Would your answer to question 1 be different if three years after Marvin's estate had passed, a geographically and spiritually distant first cousin, thrice removed, Marcene, heard of Marvin's death and sought his entire estate as sole rightful successor?

4. What procedure would she follow to receive her interest?

5. What would her interest be?

Illustrating the Use of Intestate Terminology

The following situation illustrates the meaning and use of the terminology used in cases of intestacy.

The Facts

Toby Smith has died without executing a will. Surviving him are Sally Smith, Toby's present wife; Wylie Smith and Margo Smith Tyler, children by his marriage to Sally; John Smith, an adopted son; Bob Smith, his brother; Sue Smith, his sister; Doris Smith, his mother; Kay and Mary Tyler, Margo's children, Bert and Thad Smith, Wylie's illegitimate children; Rosey Thorn, Sally's daughter by a previous marriage; Tom Johnson, a foster child living with the Smiths; Jane Carson, a woman Toby had lived with, but not married; and Carol Stuart, Toby's former wife. Frank Malcolm was named administrator by the probate court to handle the affairs of Toby's estate.

Review of Terminology

Toby Smith died *intestate* because he left no will directing the distribution of his estate at his death. His situation of having died without a will is known as *intestacy,* and Toby, as the decedent, is the *intestate.* What, how, and to whom the various items of property in his estate pass on his death is controlled by *intestate succession statutes,* state laws governing the process by which intestate estates are administered. In effect, they write the "will" when the decedent fails to write one. In this case, the statutes of Toby's home state will be referred to for this purpose.

Various blood relatives, ranked in order of closeness to the intestate, in addition to the decedent's spouse, are the successors (U.P.C. § 1–201) who receive a portion of the decedent's estate. The class of individuals entitled to share in the distribution of an *intestate* estate are called *heirs* (U.P.C. § 1–201). An heir may receive either real or personal property, or both. Confusion exists in the use of the terminology describing the manner in which property passes from an intestate. The orthodox definition of heir is one entitled to inherit the decedent's real property, and a *distributee* or *next-of-kin* is one entitled to inherit decedent's personal property. However, these words are frequently used interchangeably. In order to avoid misunderstandings, we will use definitions specified in the Uniform Probate Code (U.P.C. § 1–201) for the following terms: devise, devisee, distributee, heirs, and successors (see Table 5.1, page 96).

All persons mentioned in the situation above who survived Toby, including his adopted son John, are potential *successors* or *heirs,* except Rosey Thorn, Tom Johnson, Jane Carson, and Carol Stuart, since they are not blood relatives and do not trace their relationship with Toby through *consanguinity*. His mother, Doris, is an *ascendant* possessing an interest in the estate through a direct upward blood line as an ascending *lineal ancestor*. Wylie, Margo, John, Bert, Thad, Kay and Mary, Toby's children and grandchildren, being in ·a direct blood line downward as descending lineals, are his *descendants*. Bob and Sue, his brother and sister, are not direct blood lineals, but instead trace their relationship to him through their mother, Doris, as a common ancestor. They are *collaterals* in a collateral relationship line to Toby.

Toby's adopted son, John Smith, would be entitled to share in the estate equally with Toby's natural children in virtually all states today by statute. An example of one such statute is Cal.Prob.Code § 257 (West 1956):

> An adopted child shall be deemed a descendant of one who has adopted him, the same as a natural child, for all purposes of succession by, from, or through the adopting parent the same as a natural parent. An adopted child does not succeed to the estate of a natural parent when the relationship between them has been severed by adoption, nor does such natural parent succeed to the estate of such adopted child, nor does such adopted child succeed to the estate of a relative of the natural parent, nor does any relative of the natural parent succeed to the estate of the adopted child.

Statutes such as these entitle adopted children to inherit from their adoptive parents on the same basis that natural children have for inheritance—lineal descent. At the same time, adopted children are precluded from inheritance from their natural parents. The law declares the latter relationship null and void and treats it as though it had never existed.

The inheritance rights of a child whose natural parent dies and whose surviving parent remarries, where the new spouse legally adopts the child, are sometimes delineated by statute:

> Conn. Gen. Stat. Ann. § 45–64a (West 1981)
> *Effects of Final Decree of Adoption—Surviving Rights*
>
> A final decree of adoption whether issued by a court of this state or a court of any other jurisdiction shall have the following effect in this state: . . .
> (5) Notwithstanding the provisions of subdivisions (1) and (3) when one of the natural parents of a minor child has died and the surviving parent has remarried subsequent to such parent's death, adoption of such child by the person with whom such remarriage is contracted shall not affect the rights of such child to inherit from or through the deceased parent . . ..

Assignment 35

After Louis' father died, his mother remarried; her second husband legally adopted Louis as his son. Three weeks later, the brother of Louis' natural father died intestate, leaving no surviving children. Louis wishes to claim a part of his uncle's estate. Is he entitled? Cite statutory authority from the state of Connecticut. If the above situation had occurred in your state, what statute(s) would control it?

In most states, all the successors (heirs) in the same degree of relationship to the intestate share equally through *per capita* distribution. If Toby had died leaving only his children as surviving heirs, then Wylie, Margo and John would each receive one-third of his estate per capita, a distribution equally divided among the heirs standing in the same degree of relationship to the intestate.
Example:

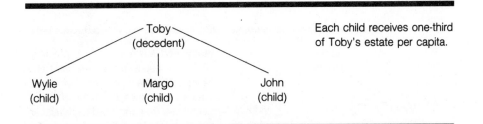

Each child receives one-third of Toby's estate per capita.

The same is true if only his grandchildren are living.
Example:

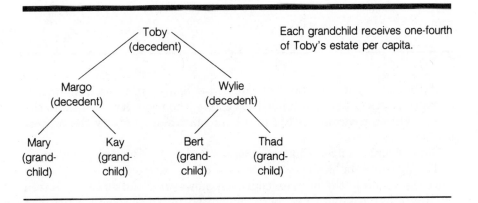

Each grandchild receives one-fourth of Toby's estate per capita.

The same is true if only his brother and sister survive his death.
Example:

Bob ———————— Toby ———————— Sue
(brother)   (decedent)   (sister)

Each sibling receives one-half of Toby's estate.

If only the grandchildren survive Toby, then Mary, Kay, Bert, and Thad each receive one-fourth of their grandfather's estate. If only Toby's brother and sister survive, Bob and Sue split their brother's estate equally.

A different result is reached when a successor (heir) predeceases the intestate decedent. If Wylie had died before her father, then when Toby died, his grandchildren through Wylie (Bert and Thad) would receive their mother's share of their grandfather's estate through the dead parent, Wylie, by right of representation (*per stirpes*) to be divided equally between them. If only Toby's natural daughter, Margo, his adopted son, John, and two of his grandchildren, Bert and Thad, survived him, this distribution per stirpes results in Margo's receiving one-third and John receiving one-third of their father's estate, and Bert and Thad each receiving one-sixth of their grandfather's estate, sharing equally the one-third interest their mother, Wylie, would have received had she survived her father, Toby.

Example:

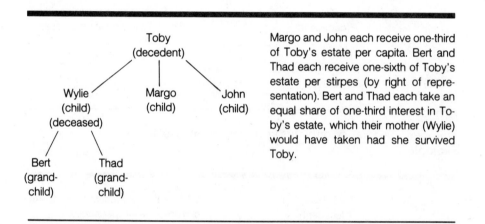

Margo and John each receive one-third of Toby's estate per capita. Bert and Thad each receive one-sixth of Toby's estate per stirpes (by right of representation). Bert and Thad each take an equal share of one-third interest in Toby's estate, which their mother (Wylie) would have taken had she survived Toby.

If Toby died without the above-named persons surviving him, or any other relatives entitled to inherit his estate, the property *escheats* to the state. The state acquires title to the intestate's property by the process of escheat.

Since Frank Malcolm has been appointed to handle the distribution of Toby's estate, he is the *administrator* of the estate functioning under the supervision of the probate court. If, however, Frank's sister, Karen (or any other woman), had been appointed by the probate court, she would be the *administratrix* of Toby's estate, performing the same duties.

Assignment 36

1. Assume that Toby Smith (see page 115) owned at his death a home valued at $150,000, $100,000 worth of stocks and bonds, $25,000 worth of household furnishings, paintings valued at $20,000, a lake cottage valued at $25,000 and jewelry valued at $5,000. On the table below, indicate all labels that apply to each person, using the list provided. Each label may apply to more than one person.

Labels

- beneficiary
- heir
- next of kin
- direct lineal bloodline (descending)
- testate
- personal representative
- legatee
- heir at law
- successor

- collateral relative
- decedent
- executor
- related by affinity
- devise
- distributee
- direct lineal bloodline (ascending)
- intestate
- administrator
- related by consanguinity

Name of Person	Orthodox Labels	U.P.C. Labels
Sally Smith		
Wylie Smith		
Margo Smith Tyler		
Rosey Thorn		
John Smith		
Tom Johnson		
Bob Smith		
Sue Smith		
Doris Smith		
Bert Smith		
Thad Smith		
Kay Tyler		
Mary Tyler		
Jane Carson		
Carol Stuart		
Frank Malcolm		
Toby Smith		

2. Indicate what portion of Toby's estate each of the persons named in 1 would receive under Minn. Stat. Ann. §§ 525.145 and 525.16 (see page 111) and N.Y.Est. Powers & Trusts 4–1.1 (see page 61).

Assignment 37

Mary Worth died without a will, leaving the following relatives surviving her: a husband, Atkinson, from her present marriage; an adopted daughter, Lana; a foster son, Thomas; two sisters, Faith and Nadine, and a brother, Thor; her mother, Theresa, and father, Lorenzo; her mother-in-law, Islodean; Atkinson's sister, Cynthia; an aunt, Rose, and an uncle, Oscar; two nephews, Donnie and Kevin, sons of her deceased brother, William; a niece, Diane, daughter of her deceased sister,

Sharon; a grandson, David, son of her deceased daughter, Denise; a granddaughter, Luella, daughter of her deceased daughter, Nancy; and Manny, a husband by a prior marriage whom she divorced.

1. Who is the intestate?

2. Who is the administrator or administratrix?

3. Name the laws that govern the passage of the decedent's estate.

4. Name the decedent's lineal relatives. Who are the ascendants of the decedent? Who are the descendants of the decedent?

5. Name the collaterals related to the decedent.

6. List all the potential successors of the decedent.

7. Name the relationship that entitles the persons in question 6 to possibly share in the decedent's estate.

8. List relatives who might be excluded from receiving any of the decedent's property.

9. How are the persons in question 8 related to the decedent?

10. Name relatives who might receive their share of the decedent's estate per capita.

11. Name relatives who might receive their share of the decedent's estate per stirpes.

12. What would happen if the decedent had no surviving relatives?

Advantages and Drawbacks of Having a Will

Advantages of a Will

The history of descent and distribution statutes proves that the individual's execution of a valid will avoids many of the legal problems that may accompany an intestate's estate.

By writing a will a person can designate how and to whom all property owned, real and personal, is to be distributed after death. Most individuals want to have a say in the distribution of their estate. When no will exists, an estate will be distributed according to the state's intestate succession statutes. The decedent's orally transmitted wishes, even if known, would not be upheld by the courts without a will. Intestate succession statutes do not take into consideration the financial status of the decedent's relatives.

Example: Harry and Sharon are the only surviving heirs of their father, Dennis. Harry is wealthy; Sharon is destitute. If Dennis dies intestate, his estate will be divided equally between his two children. A will could have provided for a larger gift to the destitute child, Sharon, and a small or no gift to the wealthy child, Harry.

Without a will, distribution of the estate under intestate succession statutes may result in the apportionment of the estate to persons to whom the decedent might not wish to devise anything, while others whom the decedent might wish to share in the estate receive nothing. **Example:** John dies intestate. During the last four years of his life, John had constantly fought over family matters with one of his brothers, Harold. John did not intend to leave any of his property to Harold, but John procrastinated in writing a will and died before executing one. John's only heirs were Harold and two other brothers, Mark and Luke. All three surviving brothers would inherit John's property in equal shares.

In the last example, John had on numerous occasions voiced his intent to leave his entire estate to his church and to the Memorial Heart Hospital. Unless John transferred his property to these recipients as *inter vivos* gifts while he lived *or* named the church and the hospital as devisees in a valid will, his intentions would be thwarted.

Many if not most decedents wish to choose the recipients of their property and to distribute the property according to the relative need or worthiness of the chosen recipients. The decedent may wish to reward faithful long-term employees or others with a testamentary gift. **Example:** For the past five years Maria has been an invalid and confined to a wheelchair. Her constant companion and friend is Sandra. If after her death, Maria wishes to leave a gift of property from her estate to Sandra, the only way she can accomplish this desire is through a will. Because Sandra is not Maria's successor (heir), Sandra will not receive any property if Maria dies intestate.

Another advantage of having a will is that the testator has the opportunity to select the person who will be the personal representative (executor or executrix). At the same time, the testator can give the named executor or executrix special powers relating to the estate, for example, the power to sell any property owned by the decedent, the authority to settle claims, and the right to distribute the residue of the estate.

A will also gives a person the opportunity to create testamentary trusts and to appoint trustees whose function it is to administer the trusts established by the will. The powers of the trustee are set forth in the will, but must conform to statutory guidelines (for discussion of trusts, see Chapters 9–11). In a will, the testate can also nominate a personal guardian (see page 181) to care for any minor children, subject to the approval of the probate court, and a property guardian (see page 181) to manage the property inherited by the minor. The personal guardian and the property guardian may or may not be the same person.

In addition, the decedent's estate may benefit from certain tax advantages when there is a will, and a will may diminish the transfer taxes levied against devisees. Skillful estate planning incorporated into the decedent's will can utilize techniques that minimize the amount of death taxes payable upon the death of a testate (see Chapter 15, page 410).

Will Substitutes

In some cases it may not be absolutely necessary to have a will, but the decision should be made only after consultation with an attorney knowledgeable about estate planning, unless the person owns no property at all. It may be possible, usually in the cases of small estates, to employ "will substitutes" instead of a will to distribute a decedent's estate. Examples of will substitutes are life insurance, joint tenancies, inter vivos trusts, and inter vivos gifts. The value and kinds of property owned by the client deserve paramount consideration in deciding whether a will should be executed.

Example: Jean and her husband, Bill, own a house in joint tenancy valued at $60,000. They have $1,200 in a joint checking account and $4,000 in a joint savings account. They own no other property. Both Jean and Bill were salaried employees during their marriage and each contributed equal sums to purchase their home and to the checking and savings accounts. Jean dies without a will. As the sole surviving joint tenant, Bill will receive all the property, which was the intent of the married couple. The tax consequences in such cases will be discussed in the tax chapter (see Chapter 15, page 413). A serious problem could result, however, if Jean and Bill were to die in a common accident and both die intestate.

Example: As another example of a will substitute, assume that Mary had only one major asset, a $100,000 life insurance policy through a group plan with premiums paid by her employer, and her husband, Mike, named as sole beneficiary. At Mary's death, Mike will receive, without a will, the proceeds of the life insurance policy (see Chapter 15, page 446).

Example: Serena owns an apartment building valued at $300,000. During her lifetime she places this property in trust (inter vivos trust), naming her brother, Reginald, trustee, and two friends, Vaughn and Renee, beneficiaries. In the trust instrument, Serena directs the trustee to pay the income from the trust res (property) to the beneficiaries, Vaughn and Renee, during their lifetimes and at the death of the last of the two to survive, to convey the apartment building and land in fee simple to the children of Renee (Christopher and Ann) as tenants-in-common. Even though Serena dies intestate, the disposition of the trust income and the trust res will be determined by the inter vivos trust instrument. Any remaining property in Serena's estate at her death will be distributed according to the state intestate succession statutes (see Chapter 9, page 258).

Example: Anyone may dispose of property during a lifetime simply by giving it away (inter vivos gift). During his lifetime, Schmidt gives to his relatives and friends $100,000 in cash, $50,000 in stocks and bonds, a pickup truck, and his collection of Chinese figurines. These gifts are executed (completed) and there are no strings attached, i.e., Schmidt retains no right to demand the return of the gifts. Gift taxes may be due and payable on the inter vivos gifts if Schmidt exceeds the $10,000 per donee annual exclusion. For complete discussion of the new gift tax laws see Chapter 15, page 423.

Checklist for Whether a Will Is Needed In order to determine whether a person needs a will, the following questions must be answered:

1. What property does the client own?

2. In what form of ownership, e.g., severalty (sole ownership), joint tenancy, or tenancy-in-common, is the property held?

3. Is the client aware of who would take his or her property if the client died without a will? Would the client be content with these persons receiving the property, or does the client desire to leave the property to someone else or to institutions such as a church or a charity?

4. Are specific items of property, real or personal, to be left to certain devisees?

5. Does the client have any special instructions for funeral and burial arrangements, or for the disposition of all or any part of the client's body for medical or educational reasons?

6. Does the client wish to establish a testamentary trust for the purpose of maintaining an income for an elderly parent, minor child, or spendthrift devisee?

7. Is there a need for a guardian to be appointed over property or the person of minor children?

8. Does the client want to appoint a personal representative (executor or executrix), to handle the administration of the estate?

9. Has the client considered the possible tax consequences to the estate with and without a will? To the devisee or heirs?

10. Does the client want any taxes owed, including inheritance taxes, to be paid out of estate assets?

11. What powers and authority does the client wish to bestow on the executor, guardian, or trustee?

12. If the client is married and the client and the spouse were to die in a common accident, have the consequences to their respective estates been considered?

Drawbacks of a Will

A person who dies leaving a will does more of a favor to his successors than a person who dies without one. Nevertheless, property transferred by will is subject to scrutiny by a probate court before it may pass to the devisees. The objective of this process is to locate all the heirs, to determine if the testate actually owns more or fewer assets than are mentioned in the will, and to satisfy creditors against the estate whose claims legally precede those of the devisees and are logical and just. The probating of a will, however, can be a time-consuming and expensive process, often causing the most inconvenience to those whom the testate intended to benefit, the successors.

Simply having a will does not remove the problems accompanying the transfer of ownership from decedent to successor. It is possible for a properly executed and published will to languish in probate until the decedent's estate has dwindled to a fraction of its original size; fees paid to the probate attorney, executor (executrix), appraiser, accountant, and other personnel the law may deem necessary all come out of the decedent's property. Not to be forgotten are the internal revenue services, the largest and most insistent "creditors." The Treasury Departments of the state and federal governments appear at all probate proceedings to claim inheritance and estate taxes; in some states, the decedents' assets are frozen for a time by order of the state inheritance tax division, so that it may collect taxes due.

Why does it take so long to probate a will? Bureaucracy, as much as expense, gives the probate process a bad name. The transfer of even a small estate may require the signing of dozens of forms, requiring perhaps hundreds of subprocesses, such as the appraisal of real estate mentioned in the will. Add to this the chronic congestion of probate court calendars (remember that an estate is not settled until a probate judge declares it so) and the miles of red tape entwining any government proceeding, and one wonders how estates survive probate at all!

Fortunately, there is a way for the testate to bypass many of the hazards of probate while still having a will. *Proper advance planning* by the property owner (estate planning) goes a long way toward eliminating snarls that may result in the devises being tied up for years while the successors wait. Estate planning might be compared to preventive medicine. Its task is to prevent future difficulties by the present application of legal expertise to the testate's wishes. A testate might wish to leave property to named beneficiaries but know nothing of the possibility of making nontestamentary (not subject to probate) dispositions such as inter vivos transactions, which could prove more advantageous to those beneficiaries. The duty of an estate planner is to make sure that the client is aware of the options available and to make the best use of them in drafting the will so that the testate's property changes ownership with a minimum of friction, expense, or delay.

Having a will enables a person to devise property in virtually any way; the testator or testatrix may give more to a favorite child or a close friend than intestate succession statutes would allow. There are, however, instances in which "the law's own estate plan" (intestate succession statutes' plan of distribution) works just as well as, or better than, a formal document, which a lawyer may charge a considerable fee to produce.

• A person who dies without a will, leaving the state to apportion the property, actually does more good to the heirs than the person who dies with a will that does not stand the test of time (becomes obsolete by the time the testator dies) or contains so many uncertainties that it may cause extensive (and expensive) contests.

• A will drafted by an attorney who has little or no experience with probate matters (e.g., a family friend who happens to be a lawyer) may turn out to be a poor instrument when the testate dies. For example, devises may be awarded to persons to whom the testate did not want to give anything.

• Persons who try to cut corners by obtaining a will at the lowest possible price may find themselves with a will that is too general; it hardly fits the testate's needs or wishes apart from some basic dispositions.

• On the other hand, a person who insists that the attorney draft a complex will should think twice if the estate is small or the devisees few. The possibility of something highly unusual happening which the complex will would take care of (e.g., the deaths of the spouse and all the devisees before the death of the testate) would hardly justify the necessity of paying an increased fee.

The point is that it is disadvantageous to have an ill-fitting, poorly drafted, or inadequate will; in such cases, having no will is better than having a defective will.

Assignment 38

1. Review section 1–201 of the U.P.C. in Appendix C on general definitions. Does your state's code have a separate section on such definitions? Note any differences from those presented in this text.

2. Does every eligible member of your family have a will? Why or why not? Should they?

3. Secure a copy of someone's will (e.g., spouse, parent) or a sample will from a law library and identify as many of the terms defined in this chapter as possible.

4. Review the difference between the orthodox (traditional) terminology for gifts made by will and that used by the U.P.C. Explain the following terms as defined by the U.P.C.: *devise, devisee, successor, heir, distributee.*

5. Roy Hallet had not made a will before he died. His survivors included a wife, Ida; three children, Nancy, Marie, and Bart; a sister, Carmela; a brother-in-law, Roger (Carmela's husband); a niece, Melanie; two second cousins, Bernie and Barbara. Roy's property included the family home, which was in his name only; several pieces of antique furniture, which he was refinishing; five U.S. savings bonds with a face value of $1,000 each; and a diamond valued at $15,000. Which of his relatives would receive Roy's property according to the intestate succession statutes of your state?

Chapter 6

Wills: Validity Requirements, Modification, Revocation, and Contests

Scope of the Chapter

Executing, modifying, and revoking wills must be done according to certain statutory guidelines.

This chapter presents the terms relating to execution, modification, and revocation and then discusses the basic requirements for the creation of a valid will. Next the ways an existing will can be changed or modified are covered, as are the procedures for demonstrating the intention of a testator or testatrix to revoke a will. The chapter concludes with a discussion of will contests—the proper persons to contest the legality of a will and the grounds for commencing a will contest.

Competencies

After completing this chapter, the paralegal should be able to:

• Use correctly the terminology associated with validity, modification, and revocation of wills

• Recognize the formal requirements for a valid will and verify that a client's will has satisfied all the requirements

• Interpret statutes and statutory language in order to apply the statute to problems presented by a client's will

• Know how to legally modify an existing will and learn good habits to avoid errors in the modifications

• Recognize what constitutes a legal revocation or rejection of a will

• Identify persons entitled to contest a will and the grounds for a will contest

Terminology Relating to Validity, Modification, Revocation, and Contests

Revocation of will
Revocation of a will is the recalling, annulling, or rendering inoperative an existing will by some subsequent act of the testator or testatrix. For example, Janet Brown has a will. She knows she can revoke her will in any of the following ways: (1) She can write a new will inconsistent with her current will and specifically revoking the earlier will; (2) she can intentionally cancel or destroy her current will by tearing, burning, or otherwise destroying it; or (3) she can dispose of the property mentioned in her will while she is living.

Revocable
Revocable means susceptible of being revoked, annulled, or made void by cancelling, rescinding, repealing, or reversing.

Operative
Operative means taking effect, e.g., when a will becomes operative, the maker of the will has died and the will is now in operation.

Execute a will
To execute a will is to write, sign, and publish the will in order to give it legal validity.

Publication of will
Publication of a will is the formal declaration made by a testator or testatrix by words, sign, or conduct at the time of signing the will that it is the maker's last will and testament.

Holographic will
A holographic will is one written entirely in the hand of the maker (the testate).

Nuncupative will
A nuncupative will is an oral will declared by the testate while suffering a last illness before a sufficient number of witnesses and later reduced to writing.

Petition for probate
The petition for probate is an application to the proper court (probate court) from the person seeking to validate a will or to administer the decedent's estate, asking the court to grant the request sought in the application. For further discussion and examples of such petitions, see Chapter 13, page 338.

Ratification
Ratification is the confirmation, approval, or sanction of a previous act done either by persons themselves or by another.

Operation of law

The phrase "operation of law" refers to the manner in which rights pass to a person by the application of the established rules of law to the particular transaction without the act, knowledge, or cooperation of the party being necessary. See previous discussion, page 91.

Example: Some states hold that if a person has an existing will and then marries, the effect of marriage on the will is to make it void—having no legal force or binding effect. This is so whether or not the testator knows or agrees with the voiding of the will by operation of law in this manner.

Prima facie   *enough info or bare essential to prove your case*

The phrase *prima facie* means at first sight, on the face of it, a fact presumed to be true unless disproved by evidence to the contrary.

Example: Gilbert makes a will in 1980. In 1982, by a valid codicil, he cancels some of its provisions. After Gilbert's death, his son contests the will, claiming the canceled provisions should be considered valid. The court decides that the codicil canceling part of the will is *prima facie* evidence of the testator's intent to revoke those parts. The effect of this decision by the court is that the codicil does cancel the provisions of the original will.

Republication

Republication is the reexecution or reestablishment by the testate of a will that had once been revoked.

Fraud

As it pertains to the creation of a will, fraud is the intentional misrepresentation of a material fact relied on by the maker of the will in determining the distribution of the estate.

Example: John tells Sheila, who is blind, that the document before her is the will she asked to be drawn. In fact, the will contains provisions distributing Sheila's estate to unintended devisees. Relying on the misrepresentations, Sheila signs the will. John has committed fraud.

Requirements for Creating a Valid Will

A will is a legally enforceable, written declaration of a person's intended distribution of property after death. The declaration is revocable during the testate's lifetime and is operative only upon death. State statutes generally control the right and power to execute a will and set the procedure that must be followed. Below are examples of state statutes concerned with the requirements for the proper execution of a will.

Minn. Stat. Ann. § 524.2–501 (West 1975), *Who May Make a Will*

Any person 18 or more years of age who is of sound mind may make a will.

Minn. Stat. Ann. § 524.2–502 (West 1975), *Execution*

Except as provided for writings within section 524.2–513 and wills within section 524.2–506, every will shall be in writing signed by the testator or in the testator's name by some other person in the testator's presence and by his direction, and shall be signed by at least two persons each of whom witnessed either the signing or the testator's acknowledgement of the signature or of the will.

Assignment 39

Mike Hasper is 17 years old. He writes his will leaving all his property to his brother, Matthew. At age 23, Mike is killed while driving a car. Mike's only other living relative is his mother, Mary. Answer the following according to your own state laws:

1. Is Mike's will valid? Explain.

2. What formal requirements for the proper execution of a will are lacking?

3. If both Mary and Matthew claim Mike's estate, who prevails?

Although testate succession statutes of the 50 states are not uniform, they are basically similar, because they require wills to comply with certain formalities in order to prevent fraud and uncertainty. The importance of the requirements for making a valid will cannot be overstated. The following required elements for properly executing a will are discussed next: (1) the capacity of the testate, (2) the form of the will, (3) the signature of the testate, and (4) witnesses.

Capacity of the Testate

Age and sanity affect the capacity of a person to create a valid will. All states require that the testator or testatrix be of majority age (18 to 21 years) and hold that an insane person lacks capacity to make a will. Sanity is the soundness of mind that enables a person to have sufficient mental capacity to understand the kinds and extent of property owned, and the effect of a will in disposing of such property. A testator or testatrix must be able to hold these facts in mind long enough to make a rational judgment. Such capacity is needed only at the time of making the will. Eccentricities of the testator or testatrix or peculiarities of the will do not establish lack of capacity to make a will.

Assignment 40

1. Suppose that Billy Budd, age 18, had inherited from his father an estate valued at $150,000 dollars. Billy wants his property to go to his dog, Snoopy. Therefore, Billy executes a formal written will leaving all his property to his dog. At age 20, while walking on the railroad tracks, Billy is killed by a train. Billy's only living relative, his mother, claimed his estate. Was Billy's will valid in your state when he died? Who would receive Billy's estate according to the law in your state?

2. Bradford is not married and has no heirs besides his sisters, Katherine and Clara, with whom he lives and who are completely dependent on him for support. Upon his death, he wills his entire estate of $100,000 to the American Lung Association, making it necessary for his sisters to live on welfare payments. Would Katherine and Clara have grounds on which to challenge the will by alleging that Bradford lacked the capacity to make a valid will? Answer the question according to your state's laws.

The Form of the Will

Generally, a will must be either written, printed, or typed. A completely handwritten, or *holographic,* will is valid, but it must meet all other formal requirements unless otherwise provided by statute. The statutes of the different states must be reviewed to determine the validity of a will drawn entirely in its maker's own hand writing (see U.P.C. § 2–503 in Appendix C).

Assignment 41

Jim Brown executed an instrument in his own handwriting, reading, "To whom it may concern. When I die, I sign everything I own over to my best friend, Sarah Williams." Signed and dated: Jim Brown, August 13, 1983. Mr. Brown was a bachelor. Two witnesses also signed the instrument. Would this document be considered a valid will? Answer the question according to your own state statutes or case law.

A few states allow oral wills under specific conditions. An oral will is called a *nuncupative* will. It is usually made during a last illness in the presence of witnesses. When allowed by statute, it generally can pass only personal property. If a nuncupative will is reduced to a writing by the testate within the statutory time period (e.g., 10 to 30 days) after it was spoken by the testator or testatrix and attested by the appropriate number of disinterested witnesses, it may be probated.

The following are examples of statutes from two states that recognize nuncupative wills under special conditions.

Cal. Prob. Code § 54 (West 1956),
Nuncupative Will; Persons Who May Make; Witnesses

A nuncupative will is not required to be in writing. It may be made by one who, at the time, is in actual military service in the field, or doing duty on shipboard at sea, and in either case in actual contemplation, fear, or peril of death, or by one who, at the time, is in expectation of immediate death from an injury received the same day. It must be proved by two witnesses who were present at the making thereof, one of whom was asked by the testator, at the time, to bear witness that such was his will, or to that effect.

Cal. Prob. Code § 55 (West 1956),
Nuncupative Will; Personal Property Disposable

A nuncupative will may dispose of personal property only, and the estate bequeathed must not exceed one thousand dollars in value.

Tex. Prob. Code Ann. § 64
(Vernon 1980), *Capacity to Make A Nuncupative Will*

Any person who is competent to make a last will and testament may dispose of his personal property by a nuncupative will made under the conditions and limitations prescribed in this Code.

Tex. Prob. Code Ann. § 65
(Vernon 1980), *Requisites of a Nuncupative Will*

No nuncupative will shall be established unless it be made in the time of the last sickness of the deceased, at his home or where he has resided for ten days or more next preceding the date of such will, except when the deceased is taken sick away from home and dies before he returns to such home; nor when the value exceeds Thirty Dollars, unless it be proved by three credible witnesses that the testator called on a person to take notice or bear testimony that such is his will, or words of like import. [For comparison, see U.P.C. § 2–502, which requires every will to be written.]

California and Texas are two states that allow nuncupative wills under specific circumstances. Notice, however, that both states allow such wills to transfer only personal, not real, property.

Assignment 42

Helen Anderson is dying of cancer at the county hospital. In the presence of her doctor and two nurses, Helen, who has no written will, announces that it is her intent to leave her entire estate to her favorite niece, Alice Marble. She asks those present to act as witnesses of her intention. Helen's only other living relative is another niece, Carla Bergen, whom Helen wishes to disinherit. Later that day, Helen dies. According to your own state statutes, would Alice be entitled to Helen's estate?

The Signature of the Testate

The signing of a will must ordinarily be done by its maker. However, because of illness or illiteracy, the mere making of a mark, e.g., an "X," can suffice in some situations. In addition, a person other than the testator or testatrix may sign the *maker's name* to the will in his or her presence, but such signing must occur at the express direction of the maker, given in a clear manner. The express direction must precede the signing. Subsequent ratification of a prior signed will is not enough. At his or her request, the hand of the testator or testatrix may be guided by another to aid in the signing.

In most cases, the maker's signature need not be at the end of the will if it can be shown that the intention to authenticate the will was present. However, some states insist that the signature appear at the end of the will. The statutes of the state that has jurisdiction over the decedent's estate must be checked (for comparison, see U.P.C. § 2–502).

Assignment 43

1. Michael Shain was 85 years old and suffered from arthritis. He asked that a will be drawn for him. The will was delivered to Michael's hospital room and in the presence of three witnesses, he said, "This is my last will. I want my property to be distributed according to its provisions." Michael did not sign nor direct another to sign the will for him. Does this document fulfill the requirements for a valid will in your state based on statute or case law?

2. Viola Carter drew a will satisfying all other statutory requirements of her state, but she signed the eight-page document on the first page only. Would her will be valid in your state? Cite the controlling law.

3. If Viola had asked Jane to sign Viola's name for her on all eight pages, would the will be valid in your state? Cite the controlling law.

Signatures of Witnesses

Statutes provide that to be valid a will must be signed in the maker's presence by two or three competent witnesses (see U.P.C. § 2–502). A will is not valid without witnesses. State statutes establish the required number of witnesses. In addition, the witnesses must be competent, i.e., capable of testifying as to the facts of execution of the will and as to the mental capacity of the testate. Various factors help determine the competency of a witness. The following seven questions must be answered in order to assess competency. The list also helps identify who is and who is not an appropriate witness.

• *Is the witness capable of testifying as to the facts of the execution of the will?* (See next example.)

- *Is the witness able, by legal standards, to testify as to the mental capacity of the testate?*

Example: Sam Jones attests (witnesses) and subscribes (signs) Greg Hartman's will. Sam is acquainted with Greg, knows the document is Greg's last will, remembers and can relate the facts of the execution of the will, i.e., declaring and signing by Greg, and can testify to Greg's mental capacity. Thus, Sam is a competent (capable) witness.

- *When is the competency of the witness required?* If the witness is incompetent at the execution of the will but later becomes competent to testify, the will is invalid.

Example: Stephen Hart is intoxicated. He is asked to witness Kevin Hanson's will. Stephen signs his name unaware of what he is signing. Later, when sober, Stephen is told he witnessed and subscribed Kevin's will. The witness' competence must exist at the time of the execution of the will. The will is not valid.

Conversely, if the witness is competent at the time a will is attested, subsequent incompetency does not invalidate the will.

Example: Stanley Novak attests and subscribes Allan Sheppard's will. Five years later Stanley becomes mentally ill and is hospitalized. Stanley's later insanity would not affect the validity of Allan's will. The purpose of the statutory requirement that a will be witnessed by a competent person is that such a person might later be required to testify that the deceased testator was of sound and disposing mind and memory at the time of the will's execution.

- *Is a devisee or successor, in U.P.C. terminology (see page 96), who is named in a will a competent witness?*

Example: In his will, Daniel Kane gives a valuable ring to Margaret Wilson. Margaret is one of the witnesses and subscribers to the execution of Daniel's will. Margaret's act of attesting a will in which she is named a devisee may cost her the ring.

A typical state statute that addresses itself to this problem is Tenn. Code Ann. § 32–1–103 (1984), *Witness—Who may act:*

> (1) Any person competent to be a witness generally in this state may act as attesting witness to a will.
>
> (2) No will is invalidated because attested by an interested witness, but any interested witness shall, unless the will is also attested by two (2) disinterested witnesses, forfeit so much of the provisions therein made for him as the aggregate exceeds in value, as of the date of the testator's death, what he would have received had the testator died intestate. . . .

This statute is typical of many in states that have not enacted the Uniform Probate Code. Here the witness is compelled to relinquish part or all of the will's devise to him or her (compare U.P.C. § 2–505).

Assignment 44

In the Daniel Kane case in the last example, determine whether a devisee who witnesses the will is a competent witness in your state.

Some states hold that a witness who has an interest in the will is disqualified as a witness and is therefore not competent. Would such a devisee-witness receive the benefit conferred by the will in your state?

• *Can the executor or trustee named in the will also act as a competent witness?* The prevailing view is that a person named executor or trustee in a will, if not a devisee of the will, is not disqualified from acting as a proper witness to a will. The basis for the rule is the opinion that an executor (or court-appointed administrator) does not have a direct interest in the will by virtue of the duty to see that the testator's wishes are carried out, even though the executor claims a representative's fee from the estate. The fact that an executor's interest is not "pecuniary, legal and immediate," as is a beneficiary's, qualifies the executor to be a witness.

Example: Fred Johnson names Robert Olson executor of his will. Robert also attests and subscribes the will. Most states consider Robert a competent witness. (Check your own state to see if it follows the majority view.)

• *Is a person disqualified as a competent witness because the testator owes him or her a debt?* Generally a creditor is competent to act as a witness so long as no devise other than the debt owed is mentioned in the will.

Example: In her will, Janet Martin provides that all her just debts, funeral expenses, and taxes should be paid out of assets of her estate. Marian Cooper is a creditor of Janet's. No other provisions in the will mention Marian. When Marian attests and subscribes the will, she does so as a competent witness.

• *According to the sample Tennessee statute quoted on page 134, can an heir, who would be entitled to inherit if the decedent died intestate, named a devisee in a will receive the devise from the decedent's estate if the heir witnesses the will?* Could such an heir and devisee validly attest to and subscribe a will *and* receive property from it?

Example: Howard is Adam's son. As Adam's heir, Howard is entitled to inherit property from Adam if Adam dies intestate. Adam, however, has a will. In it, Adam has named Howard as a devisee to receive a considerable amount of Adam's estate. Unfortunately, Howard and only one other person have attested and subscribed the will. Is Howard a competent witness? Is Howard allowed to receive any of his father's estate? Answer: In Tennessee, Howard would be a competent witness, unlike some devisee-attesters. In addition, he could receive property from his father's estate, but in an amount no greater than what he would receive according to the state statutes of intestate succession. The reason behind this and similar provisions is to enable the witness to maintain objectivity. Monetarily, it may be to the advantage of the devisee-attester to have the will admitted to probate; therefore he or she might be tempted to testify falsely about it in order to achieve this end. On the other hand, if the will is denied probate (i.e., if the testator is declared intestate), an heir would take from the estate anyway; therefore, the amount of the devise is limited in order to reduce the possibility of perjury.

Good legal practice dictates that a devisee, although competent to act as a witness, should never be a witness to a will from which the devisee benefits since the devise (gift of real or personal property) may be voided or possibly void the entire will.

Assignment 45

Answer the following according to your own state laws.

1. Can an heir of an intestate, who becomes a devisee when the intestate makes a will, be a competent witness?

2. In such a case, can the heir-devisee receive any property from the decedent testate?

3. Linda is Sara's daughter and only heir. Sara dies testate, leaving Linda through her will the following property: a diamond ring valued at $2,500; silverware worth $750; an $1,800 fur coat; and a lake cottage appraised at $25,000. The rest of Sara's estate is given to charity. The total value of the estate after deducting expenses, debts, and taxes is $100,000. Linda, and Sara's best friend, Sylvia, witness and sign the will. In Tennessee, is Linda a competent witness? In your state is Linda competent? In your state would Linda be entitled to receive any of her mother's estate? If so, how much?

4. Determine whether the following persons can act as competent witnesses in your state: (a) a minor, (b) the attorney drafting the will, (c) the spouse of the testate, (d) the executor not named a devisee, (e) a parent of the testate, (f) a creditor of the testate, (g) the probate judge, (h) a spouse of a devisee named in the will.

The witnesses to the will must sign in the conscious presence of the testator or testatrix, but not necessarily in one another's presence. In common practice, however, subscribing by witnesses is accomplished both in the presence of the maker of the will and of each other. The signatures of the witnesses attest to the act of signing by the testator or testatrix, his or her sound mind, and that they themselves signed in the presence of the will's maker. In addition, some states require that the addresses of the witnesses be given. Usually, although witnesses need not know the contents of a will, they are aware that what they have subscribed is a will. For an example of a standard attestation clause used in drafting a will, see Chapter 8, page 201.

Assignment 46

David Erickson executes a will and declares to three competent witnesses, "This is my last will and testament." In the will, Erickson leaves part of his estate to Allan Potter, who is also a witness to the will. Answer the following questions according to your state's law.

1. Must the witnesses know the contents of Erickson's will before they attest and subscribe their names to the document in order for it to be valid?

2. Can Mr. Potter receive his benefit from the will?

3. Is the will valid?

Modification of an Existing Will

The most common method of changing certain provisions in a will is a *codicil,* a separate amendment modifying parts of an existing will. A codicil may alter one clause in the will and leave the rest unchanged and enforceable, or it can replace the former will entirely. Most states require that a codicil satisfy the formalities prescribed for the execution of a valid will, such as attestation by a specified number of witnesses and the signature of the testator (see U.P.C. § 1–201[48]).

Crossing out a clause of a will and writing in a new provision (called interlineation) would not be a proper or valid codicil because such an action changes the effect of the original will but does not meet the statutory requirements of a valid codicil. In other words, the will, prior to interlineation, was executed validly in respect to attestation, signature, etc., but such validity does not apply to the will in its interlineated state. The will and codicil must meet the formal requirements of the maker's state statutes.

Drafting codicils and example clauses of wills are discussed in Chapter 8. An example of a codicil in which the testator has modified his original will by deleting one of its provisions is given in Exhibit 6.1.

Exhibit 6.1 Sample Codicil

[The facts: Henry Hamilton executed a will on June 1, 1980. One provision of the will gives his gun collection to his son, John; another gives his faithful employee, Joe Spencer, $10,000; and a third provision transfers a valuable painting to an art museum. In 1983, John lost an arm in a hunting accident. That same year, Joe Spencer died and the painting was destroyed in a fire. Henry therefore executes the following codicil to his will.]

CODICIL

I, Henry Hamilton, of River City, Cornstalk County, State of A, do make, publish, and declare this to be a codicil to my last will and testament, executed June 1, 1980.

First: Whereas in Article IV in my said last will and testament, I devised my gun collection to my son, John; and whereas my said son is no longer able to use said gun collection due to a hunting accident, I hereby give said gun collection to my son, Edwin Hamilton.

Second: Whereas in Article V, I devised $10,000 to my employee, Joseph Spencer; and whereas my said employee has died, I give said $10,000 to his wife, Renee Spencer.

Third: Whereas, I devised my original Matisse painting, "Flower Market," to the Art Museum of River City; and said painting has been destroyed, I hereby revoke said gift.

Fourth: I hereby ratify and confirm my said last will and testament, except as modified by this codicil.

IN WITNESS WHEREOF, I have hereunto set my hand to this, a Codicil to my Last Will and Testament, dated this 26th day of February, 1984.

Henry Hamilton

THIS INSTRUMENT, bearing the signature of the above-named Testator, was by him on the date thereof signed, published, and declared by him to be a Codicil to his Last Will and Testament, in our presence, who, at his request and in his presence, and in the presence of each other, we believing him to be of sound mind and disposing memory, have hereunto subscribed our names as attesting witnesses.

Mary Ann Grang ____ residing at 93 41 *Silverman Avenue*
Laverne Eskach ____ residing at 87 *Coronada Circle*

Assignment 47

On July 15, 1984, Colleen Shannon executes a will. In one of its provisions, she leaves a $50,000 diamond brooch to Susan Slade, a lifelong friend of Ms. Shannon. Sometime afterward, Susan and Colleen have a falling out. Not wanting Susan to receive the brooch, the testatrix crosses out Ms. Slade's name from the will and writes in Diane Pylkas as the new successor. A short time later, after having won $10,000 on a television quiz show, Ms. Shannon adds a page to her will giving the prize money to Patty Barron. According to your state's law, are the above changes made by the testatrix in her will valid? Draft a codicil making these changes.

Revocation and Rejection of a Will

A will is operative only after a testator or testatrix dies. Until then, it is *ambulatory*, i.e., subject to change. Revocation, terminating the existence of a will, may be accomplished in the following ways:

- Judy Wilson terminates her existing will by purposely burning it.
- Steven Burns terminates his will by tearing it in half.

• Kathy Johnson writes the word "canceled" across each page of her will, thereby terminating it.

• Jack Miles crosses out with a pen all clauses of his will, thus terminating it.

• Sally Smallwood, suffering from frostbite on both hands, asks Julie Adams to burn Sally's will. Julie, in the presence of her husband, Sam Adams, and under specific directions by Sally, burns the will.

All these acts, i.e., burning, tearing, canceling, obliterating, or otherwise destroying a will, or directing and consenting to have another person do the same, allow the maker to revoke the will. When destruction is by another person, the direction and consent of the testate and the fact of such destruction must comply with the state statute regulating the revocation of a will by destruction by a person other than the testator. Some states require such destruction to be witnessed by two persons, neither of whom is the destroyer; others require only that destruction be at the direction and with the consent of the testator. A typical state statute outlining procedures for the revocation of wills is the following Pennsylvania statute:

20 Pa.S. § 2505 (Purdon 1975), *Revocation of a Will*

No will or codicil in writing, or any part thereof, can be revoked or altered otherwise than:

(1) *Will or codicil* By some other will or codicil in writing;
(2) *Other writing* By some other writing declaring the same, executed and proved in the manner required of wills; or
(3) *Act to the document* By being burnt, torn, canceled, obliterated, or destroyed, with the intent and for the purpose of revocation, by the testator himself or by another person in his presence and by his express direction. If such act is done by any person other than the testator, the direction of the testator must be proved by the oaths or affirmations of two competent witnesses (compare U.P.C. § 2–507).

At times, statutory language, as in the above example, needs to be defined. The "intent" to terminate an existing will is apparent from the testate's acts. Clearly if one physically destroys or obliterates a will or directs others to do the same, the revocation is intentional. When the destruction is done by another person at the direction of the testate, such direction must be proved by the oaths or affirmation of two "competent" witnesses.

A will can be revoked by other than a definite act on the part of the maker or another person. For example, by operation of law (see page 129), a will is often affected by the marriage or divorce of the testator or testatrix. If the maker marries after drawing a will, it is revoked in some states by operation of law. Further, if a maker is divorced after drawing a will, all provisions in favor of the maker's former spouse are generally revoked by similar operation. This is especially true if the divorce decree contained a property settlement between the spouses. Note that although the subsequent marriage of the maker of the will voids it entirely in some states, a divorce (dissolution) after a will has been drawn voids only those provisions affecting the divorced spouse. An example of a state statute explaining the effect of marriage on an existing will is the following:

Cal. Prob. Code § 70 (West 1956),
Subsequent Marriage, Revocation as to Spouse

If a person marries after making a will, and the spouse survives the maker, the will is revoked as to the spouse, unless provision has been made for the spouse by marriage contract, or unless the spouse is provided for in the will, or in such way mentioned therein as to show an intention not to make such provision; and no other evidence to rebut the presumption of revocation can be received.

Assignment 48

Harold and Maude are close friends. Maude has drawn her will leaving half her estate to Harold and the other half to charity. If, subsequently, Harold and Maude marry, would Maude's will be voided by operation of law in California? What would your answer be according to the laws of your own state?

A state statute that addresses itself to the effect of a divorce on an existing will is the following Pennsylvania statute:

20 Pa.S. § 2507 (Purdon 1975), *Modification by Circumstances*

Wills shall be modified upon the occurrence of any of the following circumstances, among others:

.   .   .

(2) Divorce. If the testator is divorced from the bonds of matrimony after making a will, all provisions in the will in favor of or relating to his spouse so divorced shall thereby become ineffective for all purposes. . . . [Compare U.P.C. § 2–508.]

Assignment 49

Frank and Eleanor are married. Both have executed wills. The couple obtain a divorce. According to the statutes of your state, what effect would such a divorce have on the former spouses' wills?

The law is well settled that the last will or codicil (from the standpoint of time) executed with the formalities required for a written will, i.e., dated and signed by the testate and attested and subscribed by witnesses, is declared the valid will of the decedent. This is usually the decision of the courts whenever more than one will or codicil is discovered after the death of a testator or testatrix.

A revoked will should be destroyed. It may be advisable, however, to retain the former will when either the testator's testamentary capacity is questionable or there is a possibility of a will contest. The reason for such retention is that it may be found that revocation of the earlier will was dependent on the validity of the later will. Thus, if the later will is held invalid, it may be necessary to probate the earlier will. An example of a statute concerned with the retention and validity of an earlier will is 20 Pa.S. § 2506 (Purdon 1975):

> If, after the making of any will, the testator shall execute a later will which expressly or by necessary implication revokes the earlier will, the revocation of the later will shall not revive the earlier will, unless the revocation is in writing and declares the intention of the testator to revive the earlier will, or unless, after such revocation, the earlier will shall be reexecuted. Oral republication of itself shall be ineffective to revive a will (compare U.P.C. § 2–509).

Example: In 1977, Richard makes a will leaving $4,000 to his niece, Myrrha. In 1978, he revokes but does not destroy the will and writes a new one, leaving $2,000 to Myrrha and $2,000 to her sister, Melisande. Later, Melisande marries someone of whom Richard does not approve; he destroys the latter will, intending to revive the former one, but dies before accomplishing this. In the eyes of the law, Richard died intestate. Myrrha would not be entitled to the $4,000 devise, the old will having been rendered ineffective by Richard's deliberate revocation of it. The second will was itself revoked when Richard destroyed it, but this revocation does not revive the first will.

Assignment 50

1. In the previous example, would Myrrha be entitled to the $4,000 devise in your state?

2. Would Myrrha be entitled to the devise under the U.P.C.?

The current will should be kept in either a safe deposit box or another place of safekeeping maintained by the testate. Other common storage places for wills are a lawyer's safe or a bank vault. Sometimes wills are filed with the proper court, e.g., the probate court.

Will Contests

A will contest is a lawsuit that challenges the validity of an existing will. The suit is brought by a person claiming an interest, i.e., some right, in a decedent's estate.

Who Can Contest a Will

Very few wills are contested, and most contests are unsuccessful. Only a person who qualifies, i.e., someone who stands to lose a share of the decedent's estate if a will is allowed, such as a spouse, heir, or devisee of an earlier will, may make an objection to the probate court and request that a will offered for probate be rejected. Generally, creditors are not proper contestants. If the probate is denied, i.e., the will is successfully contested and declared invalid by the probate court, then the decedent's estate passes according to intestate succession laws, and all belongings are distributed as if the decedent had left no will.

Assignment 51

Harry is not mentioned in the will of his father, George. In their domiciliary state, Harry receives a share of his father's estate if George dies intestate. George's will provides that half his estate goes to his wife, Helen, and the remaining half goes to charity. As an heir, Harry contests the will and establishes his right to inherit the property in the case of intestacy. According to your state's laws, is Harry entitled to contest the will? Would this will contest succeed? If Harry wins the case, how much of his father's estate does he receive in your state?

Assignment 52

Joan is named a devisee in her Aunt Grace's will, dated April 10, 1978. In 1984 Grace executes a new will, which states that it revokes all prior wills and codicils. In the new will, Joan is not mentioned. Joan establishes that the will dated April 1978 has been properly executed while the will written in 1984 was witnessed by two persons named as devisees in the will. According to your state's laws, is Joan a proper will contestant? Would Joan's contest succeed? Explain.

Grounds for Contesting a Will

The probate court may refuse to accept a will that has been presented to it for approval for several reasons, including those cases in which the court finds legitimate grounds for a successful will contest. The following is a list of the grounds for contesting a will:

• *The will is not properly executed.*
Examples: (1) John writes but does not sign his will. (2) John writes and signs, but the will is not witnessed. (3) John writes and signs, but the witnesses are not competent (see discussion on competency, page 133).

- *The will is forged.*

Example: John's signature is copied and written by another.

- *The testate lacks capacity.*

Examples: (1) John is a minor.   (2) John is insane (mentally ill) or mentally retarded and incapable of understanding the nature of his acts.

- *The will has been revoked.*

Examples: (1) John has written a new will.   (2) John has destroyed or canceled his existing will (see page 138).   (3) John has married or been divorced since writing his will (see page 139).

- *The testate is induced by fraud to write or change the will.*

Example: John is tricked by his nephew to believe that John's only other heir is dead so that John leaves his estate to the nephew.

In order for a probate court to refuse a will on the grounds that the testate was deceived into making it, the person who contests the will before the court must prove that a beneficiary of the will actually led the testate into an erroneous belief concerning the disposing of the property (in the above example, that the testate's only other heir was dead), and that the testate, believing the false statement to be true, wrote a will accordingly.   (If John did not believe his nephew, but nevertheless wrote a will favoring the nephew over the other heir, the court would allow the will to be probated and disregard the claim of fraud.   The testate's acting on the beneficiary's willfull misrepresentation is essential.)

- *The will contains material mistakes, contradictions, or ambiguities.*

Examples: (1) John's will leaves the same items of property to different persons.   (2) John's will is written so ambiguously that it is impossible to determine his intent.

A material mistake is one that alters the substance or matter of the provision in which it appears.   If John had devised his automobile to Eugene and to Eloise in the same will, both gifts to take effect at the same time, John's mistake would be material; it would alter the devise itself.   Without further evidence to show which devisee John intended to have the automobile, the probate court would hold the devise invalid. Although a probate court does not have the power to rewrite (reform) the will in its entirety, the court may strike down individual provisions on the ground that the testator's wishes concerning the devises therein cannot be determined and admit the remaining portions of the will. Mistake may or may not invalidate a will.   If the mistake is material, e.g., a mistake as to the document signed, then the will is void.

Example: John signs a document believing it to be his will when in fact it is his wife's will.

If the mistake is a simple drafting error, e.g., it lists the address of the testate as 4711 Fair Hills Avenue instead of 4771, the will would not be declared void.

- *The testate is forced by duress or persuaded by undue influence to sign the will.*

Examples: (1) John is forced by physical threats to himself or his family to sign the will. (2) John is influenced by another with whom John had a close personal relationship to include that person in John's will while excluding his rightful successors, e.g., his spouse and children.

John might have written and executed a proper will and observed the specifications of the law of wills in his state, yet the probate court could hold it invalid because the testate was not free to dispose of the property according to his own wishes. Neither duress (threat or physical domination) nor undue influence (mental domination) is apparent from the appearance of the will, unlike a mistake; therefore, they must be proven. The presence of undue influence is especially difficult to determine, for there are as many kinds as there are personalities. The probate court must consider who the testate is, who the person exerting alleged improper influence is, and whether such influence is improper under the circumstances.

In order to create a valid will, the requisite testamentary intent must be present. A will is invalid if obtained through physical or mental influence that destroys the freedom of choice and intent of its maker. Threatening the testator or testatrix, or members of their immediate family, with violence to force the execution of a will constitutes duress and physical coercion sufficient to invalidate the will. Substituting another's wishes in place of the testator or testatrix's is another case in which coercion has been used in drawing a will. Although not physical in nature as with duress, undue or extraordinary influence on the mind of the maker can render the will invalid. In some states, a presumption of undue influence is raised if a contestant (opponent) shows (1) that a confidential relationship (doctor, attorney, clergyman, fiduciary) allowed the alleged influencer an opportunity to control the testamentary act; (2) that the maker's weakened physical and mental condition easily permitted a subversion of free will; (3) that the influencer actively participated in preparing the will; or (4) that the influencer unduly profited as a devisee under the provisions of the will.

The burden of proving undue influence is on a contestant (the person challenging the will), and the proof must be clear and convincing. Once the contestant has established sufficient evidence of the truth of the case that can be disproved only by evidence to the contrary, i.e., the contestant has established a *prima facie* case, the burden of establishing further evidence to the contrary shifts to the proponent of the will. The proponent now carries the primary responsibility for establishing the validity of the will.

Assignment 53

Suppose in the case of John Smith's will in Chapter 2, Exhibit 2.1, his son, William, had convinced his father that Mary Smith, the wife and mother, was initiating institutional commitment proceedings against John. In fact, this was not true. According to your state's laws, if

John changed his will because of this allegation, leaving everything to William, could Mary Smith have the will voided? What other rights would Mary have in the case as regards the will?

Chapter 7

Preparing to Draft a Will: Checklists and the Conference with the Client

Scope of the Chapter

This chapter is concerned with the procedures preliminary to making a will. A will must be prepared with meticulous care. Common law and state statutes prescribe standards for such preparation. Nevertheless, a drafter can fail to execute a valid and appropriate will if necessary and proper information has not been elicited from the client and certain rules of practice have not been followed.

The chapter begins by defining terms. Then it addresses the subject of gathering facts that pertain to how and to whom the client's property is to be transferred, how to minimize tax burdens, and how to provide for miscellaneous problems that arise. Examples of checklists to use with a client in preparing to draft a will are supplied. The paralegal must learn to develop checklists appropriate for each situation. Next, there is a discussion of some pitfalls in preparing the rough draft of a will. Guidelines for making the document a purposeful, legally enforceable, and unimpeachable testamentary disposition are presented.

Competencies

After completing this chapter, the paralegal should be able to:

- Collect and assimilate the relevant facts in preparation for the preliminary drafting of a will

- Identify, explain, and interpret the sources of law, e.g., common law, statutes, and the like, that determine the validity of a will

- Develop and use checklists to elicit the information necessary for the preliminary draft of a will

- Identify and understand the terminology associated with checklists
- Ensure that all necessary pertinent information is obtained accurately and completely via appropriate checklists
- Recognize when additional information is needed.

Terminology Relating to Preparing a Will

Venue
Venue is the particular place, county or city, in which a court with jurisdiction may hear and decide a case (see page 46).
Example: Harold Wickes lives in Cook County, Chicago, Illinois. He dies. The administration of his estate will be supervised by the probate court of Cook County. Thus, the venue in this instance is Cook County. "Change of venue" means transferring the location of the proceedings; a change of venue may be granted if a devisee of the will shows a good reason for the transfer to another location. If Harold's cousin, who was given a farm in Adams County, Wisconsin, could prove that Harold's actual domicile was Adams County, the venue of the probate proceedings would be changed to Adams County.

Domicile ~where you live, residence~
The domicile is that place where a person has a true, fixed, and permanent home and to which the person intends to return when absent. A temporary residence, such as a summer home, is not a domicile. A person may have only one domicile, but could have more than one residence (see page 46).

Residence
A residence is that place (locality) in which one lives or resides. Residence is not always synonymous with domicile, although they are frequently interchanged. Residence may imply a temporary dwelling, whereas domicile always denotes a permanent dwelling (see page 46).
Example: Sam's permanent home is in Dayton. He spends every winter in an apartment in Miami and two weeks each summer at a friend's cottage on Cape Cod. All three places are Sam's residences, but only Dayton is his domicile.

Advancement
An advancement is money or property given by a parent to a child in anticipation of the share that child will inherit from the parent's estate and in advance of the proper time for receipt of such property. It is intended to be deducted from the share of the parent's estate that the child eventually receives after the parent's death.
Example: Shirley Wilson has 100 shares of valuable stock. Under intestate succession laws, Shirley's only daughter would be entitled to the 100 shares. While alive, Shirley gives her daughter 50 shares. The 50 shares would be considered an advancement unless Shirley dies

testate or other evidence is presented which rebuts the advancement presumption.

Spendthrift
A spendthrift is one who spends money unwisely and wastefully.
Example: George wastes the estate left him by his father by drinking, gambling, idleness, and the like.

Life estate
A life estate is an interest in real property, e.g., land and buildings, for a lifetime, either the lifetime of the person holding the estate or of some other person. A person who holds a life estate, called the *life tenant,* possesses and is entitled to use the real property only during the lifetime of the person specified by the will that granted the life estate (see page 81).
Examples: (1) Barry receives a life estate in a lake cottage through his uncle's will. Barry may use and possess the cottage until he dies. (2) Inga receives a life estate in a tract of land for the life of Hilda. Inga may use and possess the land until Hilda dies.

Disinheritance
cut off someone from your estate

Disinheritance is the act of an owner of an estate specifically depriving another, who would otherwise be the owner's legal heir, from receiving the estate.

pretermitted heir P. 835

Example: Susan York specifically states in her will that nothing is to be given to her son, Leonard, from the assets of her estate.

Homestead
an estate homestead

A homestead is the house and the adjoining land (within statutory limits) where the head of the family lives, the family's fixed place of residence.

Fair market value
The fair market value is the monetary amount that an item of property, e.g., a house, would bring if sold on the open market. Usually, it would be the price agreed to by a willing seller and a willing buyer, neither party being compelled to offer a price above or below the average price for such an item.

legal title to the bank

Example: Fred Morley offers $60,000 to buy Sam Hacker's house. Houses of this type usually command a price of at least $60,000. The fair market value of the house is $60,000.

Mortgage
conveyance of real estate

A mortgage is a contract by which a person pledges property to another as security in order to obtain a loan.
Example: Debbie Johnson obtains a $50,000 mortgage from her bank as a loan in order to finance the purchase of a home costing $70,000.

Mortgagor ~us borrower

The mortgagor is the person who gives a mortgage to the lender.

Mortgagee bank lender

The mortgagee is the person who takes or receives a mortgage from the borrower.

Example: Debbie Johnson in the example above would be the mortgagor (borrower), and the bank would be the mortgagee (lender).

Liquidation of a life estate is an example of annuity

Annuity

An annuity is a fixed sum to be paid at regular intervals, such as annually, for either a certain or indefinite period, as for a stated number of years or for life.

Example: Sally Rudd leaves $100,000 to her nephew, Mark, to be paid to him annually in 20 equal installments of $5,000 over the next 20 years.   Each $5,000 payment is an annuity.

Promissory note

A promissory note is a promise in writing, to pay a certain sum of money at a future time to a specific person.   Exhibit 7.1 shows a typical promissory note.

general power or restrictive

Power of appointment

Power of appointment is a power or authority conferred by one person on another by deed or will, allowing the authorized person to designate or appoint the beneficiary of the property transferred by the deed or the will.[1]

rule against Perpetuities

Example: Sylvia dies.   In her will she grants a power of appointment to Henry, allowing him to select the person who will receive the residue or

---

Exhibit 7.1 Sample Promissory Note

$200.00   Date January 13, 1984

Sixty days _____ after date   I ___ promise to pay

to the order of _____ John Jones _____

Two hundred and no/100 -

Payable at First Northwestern Bank with interest at ___11___ %

Sandy Brown

---

1. Power of appointment differs considerably from power of attorney in that the former term pertains only to real property or testamentary matters, and the latter denotes the power to act as the agent (not necessarily lawyer) of another person.

remainder of her estate after she has specifically devised the majority of her assets to certain named relatives.

Receivables
Receivables are debts (such as promissory notes and the like) established in the course of business, due from others at present or due within a certain time period.

Contract for deed
A contract for deed is an agreement or contract to sell real property on an installment basis. On payment of the last installment, the title to the property is transferred by delivery of the deed to the purchaser (see Form 18).

Life insurance
Life insurance is a contract, a legally binding agreement, by which a promise is made by one party (the insurance company) to pay another (the policyholder or designated beneficiary) a certain sum of money if the policyholder sustains a specific loss (e.g., death or total disability). For this protection the policyholder makes a payment called a *premium* on a regular basis, usually annually, to the insurance company. The three kinds of life insurance mentioned in this chapter follow.

Ordinary (straight) life insurance
Ordinary, or straight, life insurance combines protection with a minimum savings feature called *cash surrender value*. Premium payments are required throughout the policyholder's lifetime. The cash value slowly increases until it equals the face amount of the policy. The policyholder may surrender the policy at any time and take out the money (cash value) for the person's own use or retain the policy until death for the benefit of the named beneficiary.
Example: Phyllis buys a $50,000 policy of straight life insurance, naming her daughter, Barbara, beneficiary. If Phyllis desires, she may at any point withdraw for her own use the savings accumulated, but she must surrender (terminate) the policy to obtain the cash value (savings). If Phyllis dies before the policy expires, Barbara would receive the proceeds ($50,000).

Term insurance
Term insurance is life insurance that is pure protection without savings (cash value). It is the cheapest insurance. It requires the insurance company to pay the face amount of insurance, i.e., the proceeds, to the beneficiary if the policyholder dies within a given time period (term).
Example: If, in the above example, Phyllis had bought instead a ten-year policy of term insurance in the amount of $50,000 and died within that period, Barbara would receive the proceeds.

Endowment insurance ~~like an annuity~~
Endowment insurance is an insurance contract in which the insurance company agrees to pay a stipulated amount when the policyholder

reaches a specified age or on the policyholder's death, if that occurs earlier.

Example: Alfred buys a policy of endownment insurance naming Matthew his beneficiary. The insurance company agrees to pay Alfred $50,000 on his sixty-fifth birthday, or to pay that amount to Matthew should Alfred die before reaching that age.

Patent

A patent is a government grant to an inventor of an exclusive right to make, use, and sell an invention for a non-renewable period of 17 years.

Copyright *prevent other people to copy your patent*

A copyright is a government grant to an author of an exclusive right to publish, reprint, and sell the manuscript for a period of the life of the author plus 50 years after the author's death for works written after January 1, 1978.

Royalty

A royalty is a payment made to an author, composer, or inventor by a company that has been licensed to either publish or manufacture the manuscript or invention of that author, composer, or inventor.

Installment purchase

An installment purchase is the purchase of goods on credit whereby the purchaser pays for them over a period of time. The purchaser (in the case of a small-loan purchase) immediately obtains the title, or ownership, of the purchase; the seller retains a security interest until the purchaser has paid the full price.

Dividend

A dividend is the share of profits or property to which the owners of a business are entitled, e.g., stockholders are entitled to dividends authorized by a corporation in proportion to the number of shares of the corporation's stock owned by each stockholder.

Premium

A premium is the sum paid or agreed to be paid by the insured person (policyholder) to the insurance company (insurer) as the consideration for the insurance contract.

Consideration

In contract terminology, consideration is the benefit requested and received by a person making a promise in return for that promise. The benefit may be an act, forbearance, or return promise given to the original promisor (the person making the promise). In sales contracts, the consideration for each party is either the price or the delivery of the goods; initially, however, the consideration is the exchange of promises.

Example: John promises to sell a hat to Andrew for $10. Andrew promises to pay the $10, i.e., he accepts John's offer. Andrew's return promise is the consideration given John for his original promise and creates a binding contract. When John delivers the hat to Andrew and

Andrew pays John the $10, the hat and the money become the consideration for the parties.

Example: John says to Andrew, "If you do not smoke or drink until age 21, I promise to pay you $100 on your 21st birthday." Andrew refrains from smoking and drinking until he is 21 years old. This forbearance, i.e., not doing something he has a right to do, constitutes consideration from Andrew to John. A contract has been formed; John must now pay Andrew.

Example: John says, "If you paint my fence, Andrew, I will pay you $30." Andrew paints the fence. By his act, Andrew has accepted John's offer and has created a contract with John. Andrew's performance of the act is the consideration given to John.

Cash surrender value

In ordinary (straight) life insurance, the cash surrender value is the cash reserve that increases (builds) each year the policy remains in force as a minimum savings feature. After the policy has been in force for a period specified by the insurer (company), the policyholder may borrow an amount not to exceed the cash value.

Primary beneficiary

The primary beneficiary is the person selected by the policyholder of a life insurance contract who is given a superior claim to the benefits of the insurance over all others.

Secondary beneficiary

The secondary beneficiary is the person selected by the policyholder as a successor to the benefits of a life insurance policy whenever the proceeds of the policy are not paid to the primary beneficiary.

Settlement option

A settlement option is one of a number of alternatives that parties to an insurance contract agree to follow to discharge their agreement.

Example: Charles Johnson, the named primary beneficiary of his deceased parent's life insurance policy, is given the option of receiving payment in a lump sum or in a monthly payment over a period of years, according to the provisions of the insurance contract. The option selected by Charles acts as a discharge of the contract.

Antenuptial contract

An antenuptial contract is a contract made by a man and woman before their marriage in contemplation of that marriage whereby the property rights of either or both the prospective husband or wife are determined. The provisions and validity of such agreements vary from state to state.

Example: John and Mary are contemplating marriage. Both are elderly, and each has two children from a prior marriage. Their first spouses are now deceased. Before their marriage, they agree in writing to retain all property that each owned separately for the benefit of their respective children.

Estate or gross estate

An estate, or gross estate, is all the property, real or personal, owned by a person.

Residue of estate

The residue of an estate is the surplus of a testator's or testatrix's estate remaining after all the debts have been discharged and specific property transferred.

Example: Jane dies testate. In her will she leaves specific gifts to named beneficiaries. After all Jane's creditors have been paid and the specific property has been transferred, the remaining assets of her estate are called the residue.

Residuary clause

A residuary clause is a clause in a will that disposes of the remaining assets (residue) of the decedent after all debts and gifts in the will are discharged (see page 190).

After-acquired property

After-acquired property is all property obtained by the maker of a will after the date of formal execution of the will.

Example: Hugh Blalock signs and executes his will on March 1, 1980. On August 10, 1982, Hugh purchases a lakeshore cottage. The cottage would be after-acquired property.

Death transfer taxes

Death transfer taxes are a government levy (rate or amount of taxation) on property transferred to others by an individual on his or her death. Such taxes include estate taxes and inheritance taxes (see below).

Estate tax

An estate tax is a tax levied on the decedent's privilege of transferring property at death and is determined by the size of the estate. The federal government and some states have this tax (see Chapter 15).

Inheritance tax

An inheritance tax is a state tax levied on the beneficiaries' privilege of receiving property from the decedent, the amount taxed to each beneficiary being determined by the amount of the property received and by the relationship of the recipient to the decedent (see Chapter 15).

Inter vivos gift

An inter vivos gift is a voluntary transfer of property by a living person, called the donor, to a recipient, called the donee. Consideration is not required of an inter vivos gift, as it would be in the case of a contract.

Gift tax

A gift tax is a tax levied by the federal government and some state governments on the making of a gift during life (see Chapter 15).

The Conference with the Client: Checklists, Preliminary Tax Advice, and Other Matters

When the attorney and paralegal meet with a client to discuss matters preliminary to the drafting of a will, they need information concerning the client's financial and family picture, e.g., who and where relatives and friends are, the extent of property holdings, the existence of creditors, and the like. In order to obtain the necessary data, checklists must be developed. In addition, the attorney should familiarize the client with the taxes imposed on a decedent's estate and give advice on how to meet them. Finally, in the conference, it should be pointed out to the client the necessity of making decisions involving how best to achieve an effective, valid distribution of the client's estate, at death, in a manner of the client's own choosing.

Using Checklists to Obtain Basic Data

The following illustrates the development and use of checklists, which are helpful in assembling the data necessary to draft a will appropriate to the individual needs of the client. Information obtained during formulation of a will is useful in determining the proper venue for probating the estate as well as in locating the devisees and the assets of the deceased. The client should be given a copy of each checklist *before* the conference so that the client has an opportunity to gather the information requested. The client should not attempt to complete the checklists alone, but instead shoud obtain the assistance of family members and the client's financial advisers. Remember, if a previously drawn will of the client exists, a copy of it must be obtained.

In Chapter 8 you will be asked to draft your own will from the sample checklists found in this chapter or from those you develop for yourself. In order to illustrate how checklists are prepared, the data necessary for their creation must first be identified. The six checklists in this chapter are created to elicit and organize information useful in preparing the preliminary draft of a will. In specific instances, additional or supplementary checklists may be needed, and the paralegal will be asked to make them.

The sample checklists in this chapter are: (1) Family Data, (2) Family Advisers, (3) Assets, (4) Liabilities, (5) Life Insurance Policies, and (6) Locations of Important Documents.

The purpose of checklists is to ensure that accurate, complete, and requisite information is obtained. Interpretation of the collected data and recognition of the need for supplementary information is a never-ending function of the paralegal's review of each checklist.

Checklist for Family Data

Complete information must be collected concerning the client, the client's family, and the devisees or successors (U.P.C. definitions) to be named in the will and should include:

- The full names, addresses and phone numbers of the participants: the maker of the will, the devisees, the executor (or executrix), the witnesses, and the trustee, if any
- The age of each participant
- The marital status of each participant
- The relationship of each participant to the client
- The mental and physical health of the client and the client's spouse
- The financial status (worth) of the client and the client's spouse and family, and the nature of any business in which the client has an interest
- Family affairs, including tensions, possible mistreatment of the client and the source of such mistreatment, debts owed by family members, advancements (property previously transferred) given to some members, spendthrifts, persons incapable of handling their own financial affairs who may need a trustee, and other pertinent matters

Using a checklist like the one in Exhibit 7.2, the paralegal can collect and organize the family data.

Exhibit 7.2 Checklist 1— Family Data

CHECKLIST: FAMILY DATA

Family Members	Name	Age	Health	Marital Status	Occupation
Client:					
Spouse:					
Children:					
Grandchildren:					
Others (Dependents):					
(Relatives):					

Domicile of Client	Address	Telephone Number	City	County	State
Home:					
Other places of residence (homes, cottages, etc.):					
Prior residences over past 10 years, if any:					

Business

Name of business:		
Business address:		

Exhibit 7.2 *(continued)*

Business	Address	Telephone Number	City	County	State
Phone number:					
Type of business (purpose):					
Form of ownership (interest):					
Sole proprietor:					
Partner:					
Corporation:					
Other:					

Family Problems

Previous marriages: _____

   Children of previous
   marriages: _____

   Settlement information: _____

Special dependency
cases: _____

   Handicapped (child,
   parent, relative: _____

   Mentally retarded: _____

   Emotional problems: _____

Trusts

Spendthrift child: _____

_____

   Life estate to be
   transferred: _____

_____

Persons to be disinherited (specific reasons listed below): _____

_____

_____

Advancements (property previously transferred before client's death): _____

_____

_____

The Need for Supplementary Data In some instances, information provided by the checklist will not be adequate to inform the attorney of all the client's needs or desires in disposing of property. The observant paralegal should note situations likely to lead to specific devises (gifts) and should further pursue these matters with the client or bring them to the attention of the supervising attorney.

Example: Suppose that George Samson, the client, indicated he had been previously married and had two children by that marriage. The paralegal would have to determine (1) whether the former spouse and children are still living; (2) whether a satisfactory property settlement has been reached by all interested parties in the prior marriage, and the terms of that agreement; and (3) whether the client intends to leave any part of his estate to his former wife and children of that marriage.

Example: Suppose the client, George, has an invalid mother who is 75 years old. He has been supporting his mother for the past 15 years and wants to continue this support for her lifetime. The original checklist has only the information that the client's mother is alive and currently an invalid. Questions put to the client by the paralegal could obtain additional information and the method by which George wishes to maintain support for his mother in case he should die first.

Example: Suppose George does not want any of his estate to go to his brother, Henry. The reasons for this decision and the manner in which George's intent can be manifested in his will must be discussed with the client under the supervision of the attorney.

Example: Suppose that in completing the checklist, George comes to the question of advancements and remembers he gave his youngest son $500 to buy a used motorbike last year. Like most people, George is not sure what constitutes an advancement. This concept must be reviewed and explained by the attorney during the conference with the client.

The checklists help the paralegal to draw out general information and to clarify the client's intentions. If additional data about specific matters and details to be incorporated into the future will must be obtained, the paralegal must perform that task.

Checklist for Family Advisers

A list of the names of the client's advisers is helpful in obtaining information about the location of the client's assets, successors, or even the previous will (see Exhibit 7.3).

Exhibit 7.3 Checklist 2—Family Advisers

CHECKLIST: FAMILY ADVISERS

	Name	Address	Telephone No.
Accountant:			
Attorney:			
Banker:			
Clergyman:			
Doctor:			

Exhibit 7.3 *(continued)*

	Name	Address	Telephone No.
Insurance agent:			
Stockbroker:			
Others:			

Checklists for Assets and Liabilities

Next, checklists reviewing all assets and liabilities of the client should be developed, and they should include the form of ownership in which the assets are held, e.g., whether each is solely owned or concurrently owned, such as a homestead in joint tenancy between a husband and wife. Such listings should include the following information:

• *Real property,* including the legal description and estimated fair market value of the homestead, all other land, and business buildings. Determine whether the property is owned individually in severalty or concurrently in joint tenancy, tenancy-in-common, or as community property (see Chapter 4). Check the location of the property. If it is outside the client's home state, ancillary administration might be necessary.

• *Tangible personal property,* including personal effects and clothing of considerable value, furniture and household goods, automobiles, boats, jewelry, antiques, art and stamp collections, and other miscellaneous items.

• Other items of personal property such as savings and checking accounts, safe deposit box, stocks and bonds, cash on hand, promissory notes receivable, mortgages, patents and copyrights.

• Insurance policies, including life, disability, health and accident, hospitalization, and annuities, must be scrutinized to determine how and to whom payments are to be made upon the client's death.

• Employee benefits like Social Security, veterans benefits, pension plans, profit-sharing plans, death benefits, stock options, and all other claims to which the client's estate or successors may be entitled.

• Business interests in a corporation, partnership, or sole proprietorship, with complete details about the client's interest, rights, and responsibilities therein.

• All debts owed by the client, including outstanding mortgages, promissory notes payable, business debts, payments owed on contracts for deeds, and accounts with a stockbroker.

• Interests and duties in trusts or estates of others, including powers of appointment (a power to dispose of property not owned by the holder of the power) which the decedent may hold by virtue of being named to this position by another's will or trust.

Using a checklist like the ones in Exhibits 7.4 and 7.5, the paralegal can collect and organize the data on the client's assets and liabilities.

Exhibit 7.4 Checklist 3—Assets

ASSETS

List below the item (by name), the estimated value of the property owned, the location and the form of ownership, e.g., single ownership by husband (H) or wife (W) or joint ownership (J) for each item.

	Item	Value	Location	Form of Ownership (H/W/J)
Cash				
Cash and checking accounts:				
Savings accounts:				
Stocks and Bonds				
Stocks (Name and no. of shares):				
Stock options:				
U.S. government bonds:				
Municipal bonds:				
Other:				
Personal Property				
Furniture and household goods:				
Furs and jewelry:				
Automobiles (type and year)				
(1)				
(2)				
Collections (art, guns, stamps, antiques, etc.):				
Other vehicles (boats, trailers, campers, snowmobiles, motorbikes, etc.):				
Wearing apparel and personal effects:				
Other:				
Real Property				
Residential (homestead):				
Business building:				
Recreational (summer cottage):				
Other:				

Exhibit 7.4 *(continued)*

	Item	Value	Location	Form of Ownership (H/W/J)

Business Interests

Sole proprietorship:

Partnership:

Corporation:

Other:

Receivables

Promissory notes
  (payable to client):

Contract for deed
  (client is seller):

Others:

Employee, Corporate and Other Benefits

Pension plan:

Stock bonus:

Profit-sharing plan:

Health insurance

  Accident and health:

  Medical and surgical:

  Hospitalization:

Social Security:

Veterans benefits:

Interests in Trusts or Other Estates:

Insurance and Annuities

Straight life or term:

Endowment or annuity:

Group life insurance :

Miscellaneous Property

Patents:

Copyrights:

Royalties:

Other:

TOTAL ASSETS (value):

Exhibit 7.5 Checklist 4—Liabilities

LIABILITIES:

List the item, its location, the estimated value of each debt, and the parties indebted, husband (H), wife (W), or both (B).

Type of Liability	Item	Value	Location	Form of Liability (H/W/B)
Promissory notes (to banks, loan companies, individuals etc.):				
Mortgages—on real property:				
Payments on contracts for deeds:				
Charge accounts and installment purchases:				
Loans on insurance policies:				
Business debts:				
Enforceable pledges to charitable and religious organizations:				
Taxes owed:				
TOTAL LIABILITIES (value):				

If the client has substantial stock holdings, a separate sheet listing the holdings should be attached to the assets checklist. Also, some of the items listed may be difficult to value, e.g., an art collection, certain clothing, business interests. The paralegal, with the client's assistance, may find it necessary to communicate with financial advisers and other experts in specific fields, e.g., an art collector and appraiser, to obtain the necessary information. If the assets of the estate include certain property, such as a patent, collections other than art, or hobby equipment, whose value may be difficult to accurately estimate, the paralegal should ask the client to suggest potential buyers or appraisers for these items. A separate list of this information should be made.

Checklist 3 (Assets) includes basic information about the existence and types of life insurance owned by the client. If necessary, a more detailed list of information about such policies must be prepared. This is an example of an instance in which the paralegal must develop a checklist within a checklist. Exhibit 7.6 shows a checklist for gathering information on the client's life insurance policies.

Assignment 54

In the John Smith case discussed in Chapter 2, John held a conference with the attorney, Ms. Brown, and the paralegal, Ms. Jones. Assume that John owned a straight life insurance policy with the Life Assurance Company of Kingstown for $50,000 as its face value. John has named Mary Smith as his primary beneficiary and William Smith as

Exhibit 7.6 Checklist 5—Life Insurance Policies

CHECKLIST: LIFE INSURANCE DATA

Insured (policyholder): _____

Insurance agent: _____ Phone: _____

Name/Policy no.	Company 1	Company 2	Company 3	Company 4	Totals
Location of policy					
Type of insurance					
Face or death value					
Dividends					
Annual premium					
Cash value					
Loan on cash value of policy					
Primary beneficiaries					
Secondary beneficiaries					
Settlement option Installment					
Annuity					
Others					

the second beneficiary. The cash value of the policy is currently $8,700. The year before John's death, be obtained a $2,500 loan on his insurance at 5 percent interest from the insurance company. When John died, a $1,200 balance, including interest, was unpaid on the loan. To whom will the life insurance be paid? How much will the beneficiary receive?

Checklist for Important Documents

The paralegal should collect all documents involving the client's property and business interests for review with the attorney. These documents may include stock certificates and options, contracts, deeds, receivables, insurance policies, income and gift tax returns for the past three years,[2] divorce decrees and alimony or child support payments or other property settlements from a previous marriage, antenuptial agreements, mortgages, inter vivos (between living persons) trust agreements in which the client is either the donor or beneficiary, and any existing will the client may have. Exhibit 7.7 is a sample checklist for gathering information about the existence and location of these important documents.

Exhibit 7.7 Checklist 6—Locations of Important Documents

CHECKLIST OF DOCUMENTS (COPIES) AND REQUESTED INFORMATION

Write in the requested information or mark with an X when the document exists and has been obtained or located.

	Location	X
Social Security number:		
Birth certificate:		
Deeds—real estate:		
Contracts for deed:		
Leases:		
Partnership agreements:		
Corporation documents:		
Charter:		
Bylaws:		
Corporation stock:		
Certificates:		
Options:		
Bonds and other debentures:		
Divorce decree:		
Antenuptial agreements:		
Trusts:		
Documents granting powers of appointment:		
Life insurance policies:		
Other insurance policies:		

---

2. The Internal Revenue Service can challenge the accuracy of a taxpayer's income tax return for the three previous taxable years, but the time period is 6 years if fraud is involved (see I.R.C. § 6531, [1939]).

Exhibit 7.7 *(continued)*

	Location	X
Income and gift tax return (last 3 years):	_____	
Federal:	_____	
State:	_____	
Current will:	_____	

Assignment 55

Using the above checklists as a guide, develop and fill in the checklists necessary for preparing a preliminary draft of your own will or some member of your family, e.g., a spouse, parent, brother or sister. Organize the data according to your checklists, taking into account assets, liabilities, family data, records location data, lists of documents needed, and advisers or sources of required information. State what additional facts, if any, are needed.

Preliminary Tax Advice and Other Matters

At the conference with the client, in addition to eliciting information by means of the checklists, the attorney or the supervised paralegal should explain the tax consequences of dying in terms understandable to the client. Resolving tax problems under the supervision of an attorney is an important function of a paralegal. Chapter 15 of this text is reserved for identifying and defining the various types of taxes (both state and federal), for applying the basic tax regulations to analytical problems, and for completing the necessary tax calculations. Therefore, Chapter 15 must be reviewed before the paralegal can perform the duties outlined below during the conference.

At the conference the following matters should be explained and discussed.

• For smaller estates, the importance of considering joint tenancy ownership to avoid a portion of administration expenses (see page 63). Guard against overemphasizing the advantages of this form of property ownership, however, since transferring property into joint tenancy may involve a gift tax and it may be impossible to sell the property later without the joint co-owner's consent (see page 425).

• How the federal estate tax can be reduced by using the marital deduction to which a client's spouse is entitled (see page 420).

• The use of certain inter vivos gifts or trusts to lower administration expenses and death taxes. The tax consequences of gifts made in contemplation of death, i.e., made within three years of the client's death, have been changed under the 1976 Tax Reform Act (see Chapter 15).

• Whether the client wants taxes on the estate paid from estate funds or whether the individual devisees are to pay taxes on their shares.

During the conference the paralegal should clarify other pertinent matters for the client and determine the client's desires in a number of situations. Particularly important are the spouse's right of election and the children's right to inherit.

Spouse's Right of Election   A married person is limited in disposing of property since one may not completely exclude a spouse. Most states offer a surviving spouse the right to renounce the will and elect a statutory share of the deceased spouse's estate, thus invalidating an exclusion from the will (see page 56). A typical state statute involving this matter is Minn. Stat. Ann. § 525.212. (West 1975), *Renunciation and election:*

> If a will make provision for a surviving spouse in lieu of the rights in the estate secured by statute, such spouse shall be deemed to have elected to take under the will, unless he shall have filed with the court . . . an instrument in writing renouncing and refusing to accept the provisions in such will. For good cause shown, the court may permit an election within such further time as the court may determine. . . . [For comparison, see U.P.C. § 2–201, *Right to elective share.*]

The language of state statutes can confuse the novice reader. The paralegal must learn how to interpret statutes correctly. For example, in the statute above, the words "in lieu of the rights in the estate secured by statute" refer to the right a surviving spouse has in the decedent spouse's estate set by the intestate succession laws (see page 108). Thus, this statute requires a surviving spouse to make a choice whenever the decedent spouse dies testate leaving property to the surviving spouse. The choice (election) must be made between taking the share of the decedent's estate as listed in the will *or* taking the intestate (statutory) share (see page 108).

Examples: John Evans dies testate and leaves his surviving spouse, Bette (1) *all* his property; (2) *some* of his property; (3) *nothing*—he disinherits Bette. In Case 1, Bette would receive through John's will all his property as his sole successor. In Case 2, Bette would have the election (statutory) right to take either through John's will or by statute. Usually, she would choose whichever was the greater. She cannot take both. In Case 3, John would fail in his attempt to disinherit his wife, since in most states she is entitled to the statutory share, which she would naturally choose.

Assignment 56

If John Evans were domiciled in your state and attempted through his will to leave all, some, or none of his property to his surviving spouse, how would your state handle each conveyance? Cite and explain your statute.

The Minnesota statute that determines the statutory share granted a surviving spouse is Minn. Stat. Ann. § 525.214 (West, 1975), *Determination of share:*

> The spouse may elect to take against any such conveyance and shall be entitled to one-third thereof if the conveyor is survived by more than one child, or by one or more children and the issue of a deceased child or children, or by the issue of more than one deceased child, and in all other circumstances one-half thereof. . . . [For comparison, see U.P.C. §§ 2–201 and 2–202.]

The statutory reference to "any such conveyance" means any testamentary disposition made by the testator or testatrix.

Assignment 57

1. Jerry and Audrey Maxwell are husband and wife. They have no children. If upon Audrey's death Jerry were to choose to take the surviving spouse's elective share according to the Minnesota statute, how much of Audrey's property would Jerry receive? Also answer this question according to your own state statute.

2. In this instance, Jerry and Audrey have had five children—Marty, Mike, Marc, Mary, and Michelle. Marc died in a childhood accident; all the other children are married and have two children of their own. Upon Jerry's death, what would be Audrey's share if she elected against the will based on the Minnesota statute? What would she receive under these circumstances according to your own state statute?

3. In a third case, Jerry and Audrey have one child, Marty, who is married and has three children. Marty dies in an industrial accident. Then Jerry dies one year later. Audrey again elects against the will. What will be her statutory share according to the Minnesota statute? According to your own state statute?

Children's Right to Inherit It is not mandatory that people leave anything to their children. Excluding children from sharing in a testate estate is best accomplished by inserting a clause in the will to the effect that testator or testatrix has intentionally made no provision for a certain named child.[3] In the event that no specific exclusion is stated in the will, the child may ultimately receive a share despite the testator's intention, as a result of an Omitted Child Statute. However,

---

3. All states except Louisiana enable parents to disinherit their children by willing their property to others (see La.Code Civ.Proc.Ann. arts. 1493, 1494, 1495 (West 1960).

a parent is responsible for the support of minor children even after death, and this obligation is entirely separate from the right to disinherit children.

Additional problems may arise whenever a testator or testatrix does not mention a child or grandchild in a will. A typical state law involving the omitted child in a will is Minn. Stat. Ann. § 525.201 (West 1975):

> If a testator omits to provide in his will for any of his children or the issue of a deceased child, they shall take the same share of his estate which they would have taken if he had died intestate unless it appears that such omission was intentional and not occasioned by accident or mistake. [For comparison, see U.P.C. § 2–302 in Appendix C.]

Assignment 58

Based on information obtained from the family data checklist illustrated earlier in this chapter, William Richardson, age 68, the prospective testator, explains that of his four adult children, Duane, James, Amy, and Beth, and one minor child, Susan, age 17, only Amy has consistently shown an interest in her father's health and welfare. Therefore, William intends to leave his entire estate to Amy. Answer the following according to your own state laws:

1. Can William disinherit his three adult children other than Amy? If so, how could this be done?

2. Can William disinherit his minor child, Susan? Explain.

3. If Duane, one of William's adult children, is physically handicapped or mentally retarded, can William disinherit him? Explain.

4. William stated in a clause in his will, "Because of their mistreatment of me, I intentionally disinherit all my other children, Duane, James, and Beth, and leave my entire estate to Amy." Susan is not mentioned, yet the words *all my other children* are included in the will. After William dies, Susan, and the other adult children, Duane, James, and Beth contest their father's will. Who prevails according to your state laws?

Guidelines for Preparing a Will

In addition to discussing with the client facts pertinent to the valid and effective drafting of a will, the paralegal must follow general rules for drafting a will to ensure its effectiveness and validity and to decrease the likelihood that persons claiming an interest in the decedent's estate might challenge it in a will contest. Following are guidelines for drafting a valid testamentary document. They provide a convenient checklist of good construction habits to develop in preparation for the execution of a will. Actual drafting assignments will be included in Chapter 8.

Guideline 1: Avoid Using Printed Forms

Printed forms are seldom useful. They may not fill the special needs of the testate and may cause problems. For instance, if part of the form is in its own print, part is typed, and part is handwritten, a will contest based on forgery could result. An alteration of any kind in a will usually casts doubt on whether the altered section is the work of the testate or of some other person who placed it in the will unknown to the testate.

Another problem is that words on printed forms are often crossed out or deleted by ink or type. Sometimes corrections or changes are written on the forms. In such cases, the question arises as to who made these changes and the reason for them. Thus, the validity of the will is in jeopardy (see page 175 for an example of such problems).

A third problem is that because printed forms are written in generalities, they do not address themselves to specific problems or objectives of the testate. Property may be inadvertently omitted, intended devisees may be excluded, and tax advantages may be overlooked.

Example: Louise Pendleton, using a printed will form, forgot to include a residuary clause leaving the residue or remainder of her estate to a named devisee. Louise had made a number of specific gifts to relatives and friends, but the bulk of her estate was in the residue. Since Louise used a printed form and no residuary clause was included, the residue of her estate would pass by intestate succession statutes.

Assignment 59

In the example above, if Louise had only two relatives, Peter, a nephew, and Clara, a grandparent, how and to whom would Louise's residuary estate be transferred according to your state laws?

Guideline 2: Use One Typewriter and Typeface

Among the good habits to develop in the construction of wills is to use the same typewriter and typeface for the entire testament. Using different typefaces makes it appear that someone other than the testate has inserted provisions. In addition, the typist should not leave blank spaces in the will, which might make possible the addition of words or names or even an entire page. Such procedures help ensure that the decedent's heirs will have a measure of protection against persons who would change the will to benefit themselves.

Example: Michael intends to leave the bulk and residue of his considerable estate to three friends—Mary Brown, Adam Korkowski and Stanley Weskoskowitz. Because of the length of Stanley's last name, the typist of the will left a long space at the end of one line of the will and started Stanley's name on the next line. Michael's residuary clause reads:

"I give and bequeath all the rest, residue and remainder of my property to Mary Brown, Adam Korkowski, _____
and Stanley Weskoskowitz share and share alike."

Joe Blitz typed his name in the empty space left on the line after Adam Korkowski's name. Unless the addition is detected and deleted before Michael's death, Joe may become a residuary devisee of Michael's will. **Example:** Paul has typed a six-page will. Before it is witnessed and signed, his brother, Robert, adds an extra page to the will in which most of Paul's estate passes to Robert. Even if Paul does not notice the additional page, he could have protected himself by signing each of the original pages and stating in the attestation clause that the will contained only six pages.

Another advantage of typing the entire will is that uncertainties so often found in holographic (handwritten) wills due to the illegible handwriting of the testate can be avoided. Typed wills are easier to read and errors are more readily identified than in handwritten wills. However, typed wills prove disadvantageous when the will is contested because of forgery, undue influence, or a question arises concerning the testate's knowledge of the contents of the will; if the testate had written a holographic will, it would defeat these contentions. **Example:** Joan is elderly and suffering from severe arthritis. She is concerned that her signature on the will may be contested as a forgery. What procedures might be followed to avert the foreseeable will contest? (1) Joan might identify her affliction within the will's provisions so all interested parties have notice of her affirmity. A will contest on the grounds of forgery requires that many persons testify to the genuineness of the writing; the testatrix's own declaration as to the reason for her unusual signature would eliminate the need for calling a great number of witnesses and provide direct evidence in the matter. (2) A better procedure is to have Joan write in her own hand the testimonium clause so that, if necessary, a handwriting expert could compare and identify the validity of Joan's signature. (3) The best procedure would be to have her personal physician witness the will so that, if called on to testify, the physician could explain the reason for the shaky signature.

Guideline 3: Word the Will Clearly

The will must be written so that the testate's intent is clear. Chapter 8 will discuss the drafting of a will and give sample clauses or provisions illustrating the step-by-step formation of a will. Our immediate concerns are the uncertainties, ambiguities, and alterations placed in the will by the testate which must be avoided. The will should be clear and understandable.

Example: Marcia's will provides: (1) I give my diamond ring to my best friend, Florence Williams. (2) I give $5,000 to my faithful employee, Steven Newell. (3) *All my personal property* I leave to my beloved son and only heir, Kevin. A conflict such as this in which the testate apparently leaves the same gifts to different persons may result in a will contest.

Guideline 4: Use Simple Language

As noted in Chapter 5, the U.P.C. has attempted to resolve the confusion surrounding the terminology used to identify gifts transferred through a will and the recipients of such gifts. Because the traditional terms "bequest," "legacy," and "devise" have been used interchangeably, much confusion has resulted. The proper way to handle this problem today is to use phrases such as, "I *give* my diamond to my daughter, Marilyn," rather than "I *bequeath* my ring, etc." Using simple, easily recognizable terms is the better practice in will construction.

Guideline 5: Consider Placing
Small Estates in Joint Tenancy

In most cases, small estates may be placed in joint tenancy so that administrative procedures and expenses can be kept to a minimum. In certain cases, a will may be unnecessary because of the nature of a joint tenancy (see discussion of will substitutes, page 122).

Guideline 6: Have All Pages of
Both the Original and Copies Signed

The original will must be signed. The copies need not be, but signing them reduces the possibility that the devisees might not receive what the testate intended to give them should the original will be lost or destroyed. Each page should be both signed and dated.

Last document you sign is will the good will.

Assignment 60

Joyce's original will cannot be found. A carbon copy, however, with Joyce's signature has been located. According to the laws of your state, would the copy be a valid testament?

Guideline 7: Include a Residuary Clause

The entire estate of the testate must be transferred. This requires employing a residuary clause (for an example of such a clause, see Chapter 8, page 190).

Guideline 8: Choose Witnesses With Care

It is good practice to have the will witnessed by individuals who are younger than the testate and who live in the same county so they will be available when the will is probated. Also, the witnesses should not be devisees of the will (see page 134). In the event the testate's mental capacity might be questioned, the testate's physician should be one of the witnesses (see previous discussion and examples of who may be a competent witness, page 134). However, some states now provide for attestation clauses which result in "self-proving" wills (see Chapter 8, p. 211).

Guideline 9: Tell Witnesses What Might Be Expected of Them

The witnesses should be informed that what they are witnessing is the testate's will and that they may be called on to testify to that fact in court. They need not read the will, however, nor be informed of its contents before they sign as witnesses.

Guideline 10: Do Not Make Additions After Execution

No words should be added after execution (writing, signing and publishing the will). Words added to the will below the testate's signature some time after execution generally do not revoke or affect the validity of the entire will. The will (above the testate's signature) is valid because the will was signed at its end at the time of execution. The maker's signature indicates that the will is complete up to the point where the signature is placed. For this reason, statutes in many states require the signature at the end or "foot" of the will. Words added after execution, whether above or below the testate's signature, may be denied execution since technically they do not form part of the will, whether or not a statute requires that the will be signed at the end. The solution would be to reexecute the will including the added provisions before the signature and to make sure the new will includes a clause revoking all previous wills and codicils.

Assignment 61

After executing and signing her will, Laura writes the following beneath her signature: "All of the provisions of my will previously mentioned shall take effect after my death unless my son, Randall, predeceases me." What effect, if any, would such an alteration have on Laura's will in your state?

Guideline 11: Use a Codicil for Minor Changes

When only a few minor changes are needed, for example, the elimination or addition of a gift, a codicil should be used.

Guideline 12: Avoid Erasures and Corrections

Great care should be taken to avoid all erasures and corrections in the drafting of a will. When a page is found to contain an error, the entire page should be retyped. Where, because of time and circumstances, it is necessary to use an altered page, the testate should approve it by signing or initialing the alteration in the margin of the page. The witnesses should also sign in the margin to indicate that the alteration was made prior to execution of the will. It is a good idea also to identify the corrections made in the attestation clause (for an example and assignment, see page 175).

Guideline 13: Word Conditions Carefully to Avoid Ambiguity

Attaching a condition to a devise may change the effect of the gift quite apart from the testate's wishes. The drafter should recognize the importance of correct wording. A conditional devise is one that takes effect, or continues in effect, according to the happening of some future event. A *condition precedent* is one in which a specified event must occur before the interest vests in (passes to) the named devisee. A *condition subsequent* is one in which an estate that is already vested in a named devisee will not continue to be vested in that devisee unless a specified event occurs. If it does not occur, the devisee will be divested of the estate, i.e., the devisee will not continue to receive the interest.

Conditions Precedent When a decedent devises property with a condition precedent attached, title (ownership) in the property does not vest until the stated event (condition) occurs. The devisee must perform some act *before* (precedent to) ownership of the devise will vest in the devisee.

Example: Andrew devises Blackacre "to Ralph when he marries Florence." Ownership of Blackacre will vest in Ralph only if and when Ralph marries Florence. If the marriage never occurs, the ownership of property will never pass to Ralph but will pass to another person named in the will, or if no one is named, will revert to the testator or his heirs by operation of law.

Example: Andrew devises a gift of $20,000 "to Renee when she receives her college degree."

Example: Andrew devises Blackacre "to Saul at such time as he comes back to Texas to live and takes possession of Blackacre." (Saul is living in California at the time the will is drafted.) The will may provide that the condition precedent be an act performed by the testator or by another person.

Example: Andrew devises "the automobile owned by me at the time of my death to my son, Chris." Andrew might buy and sell many cars prior to his death. However, only that car owned by Andrew at his death will go to Chris. If Andrew does not own a car at his death, Chris is out of luck; he will get no car.

Example: Andrew devises a gift of $30,000 "to the person who is taking care of me at death." The person taking care of Andrew at his death may be different from the one taking care of him at the time he drafts the will. The fact that Andrew may not now know the identity of his devisee does not invalidate the devise. The identity of the "person who is taking care of me at my death" is ascertainable. Whoever that person is would be entitled to the $30,000 gift.

Caution must be taken to prevent conditions that are often vague from being inserted into a will. The last example illustrates such a potential problem. At his death, Andrew may have several people caring for him, e.g., his niece, with whom he lives; a nephew who helps dress and feed Andrew; his doctor who visits him routinely; and a physical therapist who daily helps Andrew exercise.

Conditions Subsequent   A condition subsequent is one in which the non-happening of the event or a violation (breach) of a condition will terminate an estate that has already vested. If an estate vests in (passes to) the devisee when the will becomes operative but is subject to being divested on the future happening or non-happening of an event or on a breach, the condition is subsequent. If the event occurs or fails to occur, or if a specified condition is breached, the devisee will be divested of ownership of the devise (property) by "operation of law." This is also called *defeasance*.

Example: Ralph devises Blackacre "to my wife, Tina, to hold while she remains a widow." The estate vests in Tina upon the death of her husband, Ralph, and will be divested on Tina's remarriage.

Example: Sara devises her summer home "to my daughter, Rose, but if Rose fails to return to the family home within five years, then to my son, Waldo." The devise vests in Rose upon her mother's death. If Rose does not return to the family home within five years from the date of the testate's death, Rose will then be divested of the estate and it will vest in Waldo. Waldo's potential future estate is not subject to divestment (i.e., not subject to any condition) but is a *fee simple absolute* (see page 55).

In theory, the defeasance occurs by operation of law; in practice it occurs after a court action has been brought. If the devisee who has been divested of ownership in the property is in actual physical possession of the property, it will nearly always be necessary for the grantor, the grantor's heirs, or another person named by the grantor to retake or recover ownership of the property after the defeasance to (1) exercise a right of reentry (must be a positive physical act of reentering the land) and (2) bring an action in ejectment (see Glossary) in court to get the *defeased* person *dispossessed*.

Generally, the determination of whether a condition is precedent or subsequent will depend on the intention of the testator as interpreted from the language of the will in light of the circumstances. The particular expression used is not conclusive. Because the law prefers a vested estate, the presumption of courts favors a condition subsequent rather than a condition precedent. Therefore, the courts will construe ambiguous testamentary language as a condition subsequent rather than a condition precedent. The reason for this is that a vested estate is more marketable, i.e., it can be sold or conveyed more easily.

Guideline 14: Give Full Data on Devisees

The full names, addresses, and relationship to the testate of the devisees under the will must be correctly written. This avoids uncertainty as to whom the assets are to be transferred. When the devisee is a charitable corporation, the corporate name and address should be given.

Guideline 15: Give Client a Rough Draft

A rough draft of the will should be presented to the client to be scrutinized so that the client may make deletions or additions.

Assignment 62

Based on the guidelines for drafting a will, point out as many errors in the following sample will as you can.

LAST WILL AND TESTAMENT OF
Ben Brady

1.   I, Ben Brady, declare this my last will and testament.
2.   I direct that my debts be paid out of my estate.
3.   I give my son, George, my ~~two~~ *three* rings, ~~10~~ *8* guns, clothing and all my other personal property.
4.   I give my beloved wife, Sarah, my interest in our home that we own jointly; all the money (cash) I have in savings and checking at our local bank; and, if she does not remarry, my interest in the summer cottage I own with my brother.
5.   I request that no bond be required of my executor.
6.   If my wife does not survive me, I request that ~~Robert Brown~~ *Jerry Clark* be executor of this will, and he be appointed guardian of any minor children of mine.

IN WITNESS WHEREOF, I set my hand to this my last will and testament.

Date: _1/28/85_   _Ben Brady_

The will above contains many mistakes. Some of them are: No residence of the testator, Ben Brady, is given; numbers are changed in the bequest to George, e.g., two rings to three rings, 10 guns to 8 guns; the full names and addresses of the successors are not listed; conflicting benefits are bestowed, e.g., *all* my personal property to George then giving money to his wife, Sarah; no residuary clause is included; an attempt is made to pass joint tenancy property by will; there is no naming an original executor (-trix); confusion exists in the appointment of Robert Brown, whose name is apparently erased and replaced by Jerry Clark; no date is on the will; erasures are on the will; and there are no attesting signatures of witnesses.

Assignment 63

The following is an example of a printed will form. Identify at least three deficiencies the use of this form would have.

I, _____ of _____ in the County of _____ and State of _____, being of sound mind and memory, do make, publish and declare this to be my last Will and Testament.

First, I order and direct that my Execu___ hereinafter named, pay all my just debts and funeral expenses as soon after my decease as conveniently may be.

Second, after the payment of such funeral expenses and debts, I give, devise and bequeath

Lastly, I make, constitute and appoint _____ to be Execut___ of this my Last Will and Testament, hereby revoking all former wills by me made.

IN TESTIMONY WHEREOF, I have hereunto subscribed my name and affixed my seal the _____ day of _____ in the year of our Lord one thousand nine hundred and _____.

_____ [Seal]

THIS INSTRUMENT, was, on the day of the date thereof, signed, published and declared by the said Testat___ to be _____ Last Will and Testament in our presence who, at h___ request, have subscribed our names thereto as witnesses, in h___ presence and in the presence of each other.

_____ residing at _____

_____ residing at _____

Mass trust and Will
Old colony trust
update every year

Chapter 8

Drafting and Executing A Valid, Legal Will

Scope of the Chapter

This chapter covers the procedures in drafting a preliminary will, an important task of the paralegal. First, Figure 8.1 outlines the procedures in drafting a will, then important new terms are defined. Next the contents of a standard will are discussed. Sample clauses used in drafting a will, and statutes that pertain to such clauses, are included, as well as discussion of "self-proved" and "living" wills. The final section provides a sample preliminary will and a sample worksheet.

Competencies

After completing this chapter, the paralegal should be able to:

- Identify and understand the terminology used in preparing a will

- Collect and assimilate the necessary facts for drafting a will

- Analyze the data collected and make the information conform with the client's objectives in preparation for the drafting of the will

- Apply the appropriate state statutes as they affect the valid construction of a will

- Draft a preliminary will for the attorney to review, free from errors of construction that might invalidate the will or lead to a will contest

- Explain the purpose and function of a "self-proved" will and a "living" will

Figure 8.1 Events in Drafting a Will Under Attorney's Supervision

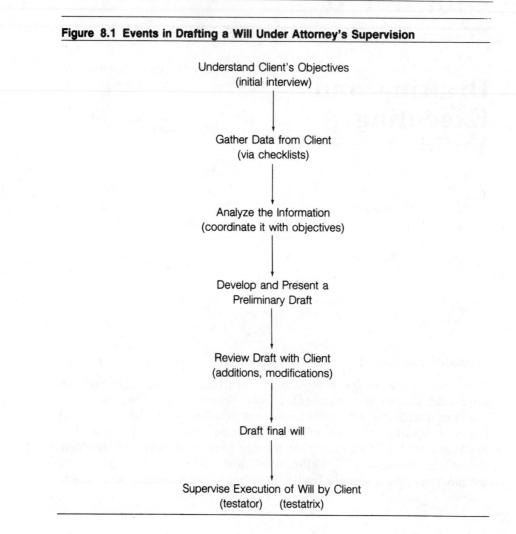

Understand Client's Objectives
(initial interview)

Gather Data from Client
(via checklists)

Analyze the Information
(coordinate it with objectives)

Develop and Present a
Preliminary Draft

Review Draft with Client
(additions, modifications)

Draft final will

Supervise Execution of Will by Client
(testator)   (testatrix)

Important New Terms

Many new terms associated with drafting wills have already been identified and defined. Testator (-trix), executor (-trix), devise, bequest, legatee, successor, and others should be familiar by now. The terms below are important additions to the reader's will vocabulary.

Marital deduction
Under the 1976 Tax Reform Act, half the decedent's adjusted gross estate could be given to the surviving spouse without becoming subject to the federal estate tax levied against the decedent's estate. The purpose of this was to equalize the impact of the federal estate tax between married persons in community property states and non-com-

munity property states.[1] The act established the amount of the estate marital deduction to be the greater of $250,000 or one-half the decedent's adjusted gross estate. The Economic Recovery Tax Act of 1981 changed this deduction; now there is an unlimited gift and estate tax marital deduction for transfers between spouses. The new law makes it possible for more than one transfer or adjustment of property interests between spouses during their marriage for tax purposes or other reasons (see page 420 for discussion of tax considerations and the marital deduction).

Adjusted gross estate

The adjusted gross estate is the value of the decedent's estate after administration expenses, funeral expenses, creditors' claims, and casualty losses have been subtracted from the value of the gross estate. The value of the adjusted gross estate was used for the purpose of computing the federal estate tax (see page 418).

Uniform Anatomical Gift Act

According to the Uniform Anatomical Gift Act, any individual who is competent and of legal age may give all or part of his or her body to any hospital, surgeon, physician, accredited medical or dental school, college or university, or any bank or storage facility for education, research, advancement of medical or dental science, therapy or transplantation, or to any specified individual for therapy or transplantation. The gift of all or part of the body may be made by a document other than a will, e.g., a "card" designed to be carried on the person which must be signed by the donor in the presence of witnesses, who in turn must sign the card in the presence of the donor (see page 185).

Exordium clause

An exordium clause is the beginning or introductory clause of a will (see sample clause on page 183).

Ademption

Ademption is revocation, recalling, or cancellation of a gift made through the will by an *act* of the testate with the intention to do so. The result is that the devisee does not receive the gift.
Example: X, in his will, conveys (devises) his farm, Blackacre, to "A and his heirs." Thereafter X sells Blackacre to B. X dies. A gets nothing. Because of his act of selling Blackacre to B, X "adempted" or "canceled' his devise to A.

Abatement

Abatement is the word used for the process of determining the order in which property in a decedent's estate will be applied to the payment of

---

1. In the eight community-property states and Puerto Rico, the surviving spouse takes, by operation of law, half the property acquired during marriage unless the parties agreed otherwise, e.g., in an antenuptial or separation agreement.

decedent's debts, taxes, and expenses. The need for abatement arises when there are insufficient assets in decedent's estate to pay all decedent's death taxes, administration and funeral expenses, and other creditors' claims. When this problem occurs, all or some of the devisees under the decedent's will will be required by state statute to contribute to the payment of the deficiency, i.e., all or some of the devisees will receive less money or property than the amount stated in the will because a portion of their respective devises will be withheld (as determined by a statutory formula) and applied to payment of the deficiency. Thus devisees might lose all or a portion of their devise. Generally, residue assets are the first to be used to pay debts, expenses, and taxes; second, the general devises, i.e., sums of money to named persons, and third, specific devises, i.e., identified property such as ten shares of stock in X Corporation or a camping trailer left to specific persons. If the personal representative distributes the testamentary devises to the named devisees and insufficient assets remain to pay debts, expenses, and taxes, the personal representative may be held personally liable for such unpaid claims (for further discussion of abatement, see page 190).

Example: Sydney makes the following testamentary gifts: $2,000 cash to Rita, a homestead valued at $45,000 to Ralph, and the residue (valued at $8,000) to Peter. Expenses, debts, and taxes amount to $12,000. The residue assets would first be applied to payment of expenses, debts, and taxes. Thus, Pete would lose all his $8,000. Second, the general gift, i.e., the sum of money left to Rita ($2,000) would be applied. Rita would lose all her $2,000. Third, Ralph would be required to pay the remaining deficiency of $2,000 or the homestead would be sold and $2,000 of the proceeds of the sale used to pay the deficiency. Ralph would get the remainder of the proceeds of the sale. If a spouse survives the decedent, however, the spouse will receive the statutory share of decedent's estate before any of the other named devisees receive their gifts through the will.

Example: Oscar dies, leaving an estate valued at $150,000 consisting of a homestead owned in his own name valued at $75,000, $30,000 in cash in a savings account, $30,000 in stocks and bonds, and $15,000 in household furnishings. Oscar leaves his home and $10,000 in cash to his spouse, Evelyn. He leaves $10,000 in cash to his nephew, Phil, and $10,000 to his niece, Trudy. The administration and funeral expenses, death taxes, and creditor's claims (debts) amount to $60,000. Thus, since these obligations must be paid first (have priority), only $90,000 remains to be distributed among the named devisees.

In the example of Oscar's will, above, the state statute on abatement will determine which devisees get what property, because not enough assets remain in decedent's estate to distribute the assets as decedent intended (specified in the will). If Oscar's estate were probated in California, it would have to adhere to the California abatement statute. This statute is typical of other state laws that determine the order of payment when the decedent's assets are insufficient:

Cal. Prob. Code § 750 (West 1956), *Payment of Debts, Expenses, or Family Allowances; Provisions by Will; Order of Resort to Estate Assets*

If the testator makes provision by his will, or designates the estate to be appropriated, for the payment of his debts, the expenses of administration, or family allowance, they must be paid according to such provision or out of the estate thus appropriated, so far as the same is sufficient. If insufficient, that portion of the estate not disposed of by the will, if any, must be appropriated for that purpose; and if that is not sufficient, the property given to residuary legatees and devisees, and thereafter all other property devised and bequeathed is liable for the same, in proportion to the value or amount of the several devises and legacies, but specific devises and legacies are exempt from such liability if it appears to the court necessary to carry into effect the intention of the testator, and there is other sufficient estate.

Personal guardian
A personal guardian is an individual or a trust institution appointed by a court to care for the person of a minor or an incompetent.

Property guardian
A property guardian is an individual or a trust institution appointed by a court to care for the property of a minor or an incompetent. The same individual can be both personal and property guardian and is then called simply the guardian.

Common disaster clause
A common disaster clause is a clause used in a will to avoid a possible undesirable result where the order of death of two or more persons cannot be established by proof. Simultaneous deaths (e.g., in an automobile accident) are deaths in a common disaster (see sample clause on page 196).

Uniform Simultaneous Death Act
The Uniform Simultaneous Death Act provides that where the inheritance of property depends on the priority of death of the decedents, and where there is no sufficient evidence that the decedents have died other than simultaneously, the property of each decedent involved shall be distributed as if he or she had survived the other (see U.P.C. § 2–104 and 20 Pa.S. § 8501 (West 1975) for comparison).

Legal description of real estate
The legal description of real estate is a description recognized by law which definitely locates real property by reference to government surveys or recorded maps.

Rule Against Perpetuities
The Rule Against Perpetuities is a rule of common law prohibiting the title to real property from settling (vesting) absolutely in a beneficiary when a certain period of time has elapsed after the making of the original grant or trust (see sample and discussion on page 198). Today, most of the states have enacted this rule into statutory law.

General devise

A general devise is a pecuniary devise payable out of the general assets of the testate.

Example: "I give Mabel Worth $10,000 for her faithful service."

Specific devise

A specific devise is a gift by will of a particular item of real or personal property.

Example: "I give Harriet Brown my Picasso painting entitled 'Woman.'"

Residual devise

A residual devise is a gift of all the testator's estate not otherwise effectively disposed of by a will.

Example: "All the rest, remainder, or residue of my property, both real and personal, I give to my daughter, Susan Miller."

Contents of a Standard Will

We now turn to the drafting of a formal will. The clauses or sections of a will are:

1. Introductory or exordium and publication clause

2. General revocatory clause

3. Provision for payment of debts and funeral expenses

4. Instructions for funeral and burial

5. Specific testamentary gifts

6. Provision for residue of estate

7. Appointment of personal representative, i.e., an executor or executrix

8. Appointment of a personal and/or property guardian

9. Simultaneous death and common disaster provision

10. Testamentary trust clause

11. Testimonium clause

12. Testator's signature

13. Attestation clause of witnesses

14. Witnesses' signatures and addresses

We will look at each of these clauses and sections in detail, along with relevant statutes and sample clauses.

Introductory or Exordium and Publication Clause

The exordium clause states that the maker of a will intends that the provisions in this written document be followed after death. In other words, to be valid, the document must appear to be a will or testamentary in nature. Other information in the introductory clause of the will might include the address, city, county, and state of its maker (helping to determine domicile for probate proceedings); any alias or other name by which the maker is known (often written "a/k/a"—also known as); and a statement of the maker's capacity and freedom from undue influence.

Sample Clause: Last Will and Testament of Rowley Morse. I, Rowley D. Morse a/k/a R. David Morse, of the City of Middleton, County of Heather, and State of Franklin, being of sound and disposing mind and memory, and not acting under undue influence of any person whomsoever, do make and publish this document to be my last will.

The purpose of the exordium clause is to declare to the public (the world) that the testate has the capacity to create a will and has the freedom and intention to do so, and understands that the document prepared is the testate's last will.

Assignment 64

Examine the following exordium clause: "Being of sound mind and body, I, D.E. Pearson, of 2914 Columba Street, Bloomington, dispose of the following property by will: . . ."

1. Is it adequate for the purposes of an exordium clause? Why or why not?

2. Could any word or phrase be misinterpreted so as to prevent the document's admission to probate?

3. Re-draft the parts of the clause likely to cause difficulty. If necessary, include information not found in the original and explain the reasons for including it.

General Revocatory Clause

Most states by statute automatically revoke prior wills on the writing, dating, and signing of a new will by the maker. The testamentary document last in time also supersedes existing codicils attached to the previous wills. If the state in which the will is offered for probate has no statute revoking prior wills, then the following clause is necessary:

Sample Clause: I hereby expressly revoke all wills and codicils heretofore made by me. See also Chapter 6, page 138, on revocation of wills.

Assignment 65

1. Henry Howard has a will. He then writes, signs, dates, and has witnessed a document changing one gift made in the will from his son, Harold, to his daughter, Helen. Answer the following according to your state statutes: Does this revision revoke Henry's original will? Is such a change legal? Is this a valid codicil?

2. In 1981, Leah Olson made a will leaving half her estate to her husband, Albert, one-fourth to their son, Lloyd, and one-fourth to their daughter, Lynda. (a) Draft such a provision for the will. If in 1984 Leah decided to change her will to leave equal shares to each of the above-named persons, how should this be done? Redraft the provision in (a) to illustrate. Does your revision legally revoke Leah's (1981) will?

Provision for Payment of Debts and Funeral Expenses

The maker of a will usually directs the named personal representative to pay all debts, administration expenses, and expenses for the funeral and for last illness out of estate funds. Such responsibility, however, is an automatic function of the personal representative of the estate and need not be embodied in a formal clause.[2]

Sample Clause: I hereby direct my executor, hereinafter named, to pay all my just debts, all administration expenses, and expenses for my last illness, funeral, and burial out of my estate.

Assignment 66

1. Check your own state statutes and determine the priority of payment of decedent's debts in your state (compare U.P.C. § 3–805 and § 3–807).

2. In writing his will, Quincy Rudd included a clause directing his executor to pay the debts owed by him at the time of his death from the *residue* of the estate. Draft a clause for his will to this effect.

Instructions for Funeral and Burial

In many states the desires of the decedent's next-of-kin legally supersede any instructions in the decedent's will concerning funeral and

---

2. Formerly (in England prior to the 19th century) personal representatives did not undertake to pay the debts of the decedent, but only to distribute the assets according to the will. Therefore it was advisable to instruct the representative to pay creditors of the estate. Today, state statutes have rendered this clause unnecessary by providing that creditors shall receive satisfaction from the decedent's debts before bequests or devises take effect (see page 190, on residuary clauses).

burial. A conflict between the wishes of the next-of-kin and the testate might arise where the testate desires to donate his or her body for medical or educational purposes (e.g., to an organ transplant bank) but the nearest relatives object. To resolve questions associated with the giving of anatomical gifts, the Uniform Anatomical Gift Act, adopted in almost all states, provides that the maker may legally determine in a will the disposition of all or any part of the body for medical or educational purposes.

If the testate wishes to make an anatomical gift, experienced will-drafters advise that such a wish be put into a letter of instruction to the family to be read before or upon the testate's death, as well as into the will. By so doing, the testate may forestall inconvenience to the family, especially if the will is read after the funeral and burial, as is usually the case. Typical state statutes concerning anatomical gifts are the following:

Fla. Stat. Ann. § 732.912 (West 1976),
Persons Who May Make an Anatomical Gift

(1) Any person who may make a will may give all or part of his body for any purpose specified . . . , the gift to take effect upon death.

(2) In the order of priority stated and in the absence of actual notice of contrary indications by the decedent or actual notice of opposition by a member of the same or a prior class, any of the following persons may give all or any part of the decedent's body for any purpose specified . . . :

    (a) The spouse;

    (b) An adult son or daughter;

    (c) Either parent;

    (d) An adult brother or sister; or

    (e) The guardian of the person of the decedent at the time of his death; but no gift shall be made by the spouse if any adult son or daughter objects.

(3) If the donee has actual notice of contrary indications by the decedent or objection by an adult son or daughter or that a gift by a member of a class is opposed by a member of the same or a prior class, the donee shall not accept the gift.

(4) The persons authorized by subsection (2) may make the gift after death or immediately before death.

(5) A gift of all or part of a body authorizes any examination necessary to assure medical acceptability of the gift for the purposes intended.

(6) The rights of the donee created by the gift are paramount to the rights of others except as provided by § 732.917.

Fla. Stat. Ann. § 732.913 (West 1976), *Persons Who May
Become Donees; Purposes for which Anatomical Gifts May Be Made*

The following persons may become donees of gifts of bodies or parts of them for the purposes stated:

(1) Any hospital, surgeon, or physician for medical or dental education or research, advancement of medical or dental science, therapy, or transplantation;

(2) Any accredited medical or dental school, college or university for education, research, advancement of medical or dental science, or therapy;

(3) Any bank or storage facility for medical or dental education, research, advancement of medical or dental science, therapy, or transplantation;

(4) Any specified individual for therapy or transplantation needed by him (compare U.P.C. § 3–701).

The Uniform Anatomical Gift Act attempts to treat comprehensively the situation of the testate who wishes to make such anatomical gifts to a recognized agency but whose state has not enacted laws dealing with the problems involved. Although the wording of the act has been modified in some states, it substantively regulates who may be a donor and a donee, the manner of executing, delivering, and amending the gift, and the rights and duties of the parties.

Sample Clause: I hereby direct my executor upon my death to see that my body be delivered to the State University Medical School to be used for educational purposes.

Assignment 67

1. Margaret is dying. She is unconscious and in a coma from which her doctors do not expect her to recover. Margaret's family is aware that another patient is seeking a kidney transplant, and the doctors have informed the family that Margaret could be a successful donor. Margaret's husband and children are in favor of donating Margaret's kidneys after her death; Margaret's parents are opposed. How would this conflict be resolved in Florida? In your state?

2. Claudia's will does not contain an anatomical gift clause. She thinks it would be a good idea to leave her eyes to the State Society for the Prevention of Blindness eye bank. Draft such a provision for the revised will she is writing.

3. Claudia realizes that her family may hold the funeral and burial before reading her will and the provision mentioned above. What should she do to prevent possible problems in this area?

Specific Testamentary Gifts

It is important to remember that under the orthodox system of terminology "legacies" are gifts of money, "bequests" are gifts of personal property, and "devises" are gifts of real property. For the purposes of this text, however, the definitions used are those of the Uniform Probate Code (U.P.C.), e.g., the disposition of both real and personal property under a will is called a devise (see Chapter 5, Table 5.1).

One of the most important functions of a will is the determination of "what goes to whom." To prevent family arguments over specific items of a decedent's estate, the will should provide for the disposition of property as its maker chooses. There may be many reasons for the maker's decision to leave specific property to certain individuals. These gifts must be made before the maker transfers the remaining assets in a residuary clause. Marital deduction provisions (discussed in

Chapter 15, page 420) must also be stated before the residue is transferred.

Sample Clause: John Harrington's will provides: "I give the sum of Two Thousand Dollars ($2,000) to my son, James L. Harrington; my diamond ring to my son, Thomas J. Harrington; and my collection of guns and rifles to my son, Harold L. Harrington. All my sons' addresses are currently the same as my own. I give the farm that I own in County of Adams, State of Franklin, legally described as follows: Lot 17, Block 8, twenty acres, known as Stonybroke, according to the plat filed with the Registrar of Titles in and for the County of Adams, State of Franklin, to my wife, Jeanine Harrington, as fee owner in severalty. Also, I give all my automobiles and all articles of personal and household goods to my wife, Jeanine Harrington, to do with as she sees fit."

An important point to remember is that, regardless of a clause like the above, because a will is ambulatory (not yet operative), its maker is free before death to destroy the will or give away or sell any property constituting a specific gift in the will. In such cases, a testamentary gift is *adeemed* (taken away by the process of ademption), and the devisee is not entitled to receive the property. Ademption has the same result as if the maker had formally canceled the gift.

Example: In the clause above, if the diamond ring left to Thomas and the gun collection left to Harold are not in John Harrington's estate at his death, then the two sons do not receive their specific devises.

The following California statute illustrates the ademption procedure:

Cal. Prob. Code § 1050 (West 1981), *Gift Before Death*

> A gift before death shall be considered as an ademption of a bequest or devise of the property given; but such gift shall not be taken as an advancement to an heir or as an ademption of a general legacy unless such intention is expressed by the testator in the grant or otherwise in writing, or unless the donee acknowledges it in writing to be such. [Compare U.P.C. §§ 2–607, 2–608, and 2–612.]

Assignment 68

1. Roger's will provides, in part: "To my daughter, Nadine, I give 100 shares of common stock in the Hopewell Corporation, if she survives me." What kind of devise is this? If Roger owns 75 shares of common stock in the Hopewell Corporation at the time of his death, would Nadine be entitled to them plus the fair market value of 25 shares? Why or why not?

2. Lillian wishes to leave her antique rosewood furniture to her daughters, Kimberly and Ellen. Draft a provision in Lillian's will for this devise.

3. At Lillian's death both Kimberly and Ellen are living in separate houses. They cannot agree on dividing the furniture. Could Lillian's will have been written so as to avoid the dispute? If necessary, redraft the provision to illustrate.

4. "To my son, Gerald, I leave 30 acres of land in Marsh County." What kind of devise is this? Is it defeasible (see Glossary)? Why or why not? If it is, redraft the provision to illustrate the testate's wishes in a valid devise.

The complications that can arise, e.g., family problems, make it necessary to draft the will carefully to satisfy the purposes and intentions of the client. Provisions for a surviving spouse must be determined and carefully written. An attempt by the testate to disinherit a spouse will generally fail, since the surviving spouse is entitled to a statutory share of the decedent testate's estate. Additional complications occur when there has been more than one marriage and two or more sets of children are potential devisees. The rule that the testate may favor or exclude anyone in the will remains, but also remaining is the rule that a spouse cannot be disinherited. Children, however, can be disinherited according to the wishes of the testate. The following illustrates a typical family problem that could affect the validity of a will.

Example: A man divorces his first wife, with whom he had two children, remarries and has a child by his second wife. His will, written during the first marriage, leaves half his estate to the wife and children of the first marriage and says nothing of the second wife or her child. Should he die without revising his will, his estate may devolve as if he had died intestate, since the will may be revoked by "operation of law" by some state statutes. For example, in states that have adopted the U.P.C. his divorce is enough to revoke (U.P.C. § 2–508); in others, remarriage or remarriage and the birth of issue revoke a will. The result of such revocation is the same as if the testator died without a will, i.e., intestate. In such a case, the second wife and *all* his children will take under the state intestate succession statutes; the first wife will be entitled to nothing.

Understanding the law of wills, and careful drafting, are necessary to resolve such problems.

Assignment 69

Harold Wilson is currently married to his second wife, Cheryl. They have two teenage children, James and Barbara. Previously, Harold was married to and later divorced from Margaret Wilson. Harold and Margaret had been married for ten years and also had two children, Wilbur and Maude. The following is an excerpt from a will written by Harold when he was married to Margaret.

Article IV

I give all my personal effects, including books, art objects, jewelry, furnishings, and other tangible items, to my wife, Margaret, and children, Wilbur and Maude, to be divided equally, as determined by my executrix.

Article V

I give the sum of two thousand dollars ($2,000) to my secretary, Jerome Davis, if he is employed by me at the time of my death.

Article VI

I give the sum of ten thousand dollars ($10,000) to my children, if they survive me, or if they do not survive me, then to my issue who survive me, per stirpes.

Article VII

I give the sum of five thousand dollars ($5,000) and all stocks, bonds, and debentures which I shall hold at the time of my death to my wife, if she survives me, or if she does not survive me, to my children who survive me in equal shares.

Answer the following questions and draft appropriate clauses to change or modify Harold's will when requested:

1. If Harold and his first wife, Margaret, as part of their divorce agreement, had a fair and complete property settlement between themselves and for the benefit of their two children, Wilbur and Maude, could Harold exclude these three members of his first family from the benefits of his current will according to your state laws? Draft the necessary provisions in Harold's will which would exclude all three members of his first family.

2. Suppose in the example above Maude is now married and has a son, Thomas, who is Harold's grandson. Thomas is physically handicapped. According to your state's laws, could Harold exclude Thomas from his will? Could Harold include Thomas, but exclude Maude? Draft sample will provisions that accomplish these purposes if allowed by your state statutes.

3. Suppose that, while married, Harold and Margaret had adopted a daughter, Marjory. At the time of the divorce, Marjory had requested that she be allowed to live with her father, Harold. The request was granted. In your state, what are the rights of an adopted child to inherit from either of the adoptive parents? Because of his affection for Marjory, Harold wants half of his entire estate to go to her with the remaining half to be split equally by his current wife, Cheryl, and his two natural minor children, James and Barbara. Would such a provision be legal in your state? If so, draft the appropriate provision(s).

4. While married to his first wife, Margaret, Harold fathered an illegitimate son, Charles. Although their relationship is known by all, Harold has never acknowledged in writing that he is Charles' father.

   a. According to your state's laws, what rights would an illegitimate child (Charles) have in his father's (Harold's) estate?

   b. Must a provision be included in Harold's will in order to exclude Charles?

   c. If Harold had acknowledged Charles as his son in writing or in any requisite statutory manner, could Charles claim a share in Harold's estate even though he (Charles) was not mentioned in the will?

d. Can any children, natural, adopted, or illegitimate, demand or claim a share of their parent's estate when not mentioned in their parent's will?

e. Can property from an estate be willed to some of the testate's children while other children are disinherited? If so, draft such a provision in Harold's will including James, Barbara, and Marjory but excluding Wilbur and Maude.

5. A different complication would result if the facts in the Harold Wilson case were changed as follows: Instead of Harold and his second wife, Cheryl, having two children, they are childless. If Harold were to die testate and leave his entire estate to Cheryl, on Cheryl's subsequent death her relatives may receive the entire estate to the exclusion of Harold's children by his first wife. Harold wants to leave his estate to Cheryl if she survives him, but he also wants to provide for his two children, Wilbur and Maude. How could this be accomplished? Draft at least two clauses, one of which includes a life estate that would allow Harold to ensure that all or part of his estate would be received by his children upon the death of either Harold or Cheryl.

6. Suppose that Harold Wilson was injured in an automobile accident, crippling him for life. He decided to leave his entire estate to his faithful nurse, Agnes, who had cared for him continuously since the year of the accident. According to your state laws, can Harold leave his estate to his nurse, excluding his wife and children?

Provision for Residue of Estate

The residuary clause allows the maker to transfer the remaining property of an estate that has not been specifically given to devisees. This includes any additional property that may come into the estate after the will has been executed or after the maker's death. Generally, the bulk of an estate falls within the residue, which is usually the source for paying all taxes, debts, and expenses of the decedent.

Sample Clause: I give all the rest, or residue of my estate, to my surviving spouse, but if she does not survive me, to my children in equal shares. I hereby direct my executor, hereinafter named, to pay out of my residuary estate, all estate, income, and inheritance taxes, all just debts, and expenses of my last illness, funeral, and burial, and those incurred in the administration of my estate (see U.P.C. §§ 3–805, 3–807, and 3–902).

When the residue is insufficient to meet priority obligations of the estate, e.g., debts, taxes, and expenses, payment must come from devises made in the will. *Abatement* is the process for determining the order in which property in the estate will be applied to the payment of such obligations and by which some gifts are lessened or totally abolished causing various named devisees to lose their benefits under a decedent's will. If estate assets needed to pay debts or prior claims are beyond those in the residuary clause, gifts usually abate, i.e., bear the loss, in the following order: (a) residual assets; (b) general devises (sums of money left by the testate to named persons); (c) specific devises (identified property, such as a work of art, left by the testate to named persons). State statutes that control the abatement process must be checked.

Some residuary clauses are simple, leaving everything to one person. Others are complex, with lengthy provisions concerning the establishment of testamentary trusts and the powers and duties of the named trustee. In either case, the will's maker must remember that if the named residuary devisee(s) should predecease the maker, there would be no one to receive the residue, so all or part of it will be distributed according to appropriate state intestate succession statutes. Thus, the residuary clause must be carefully drafted to cover potential problems caused by the sequence of deaths of named devisees.

Assignment 70

1. Suppose in the John Harrington example on page 187 in which James received $2,000, Thomas the diamond ring, and Harold the gun collection, the testator, John Harrington, added the following provision, "all the residue of my estate I leave to my wife, Jeanine Harrington." The residue is valued at $10,000. If John died and left debts and expenses amounting to $11,000, how would his testamentary gifts abate according to your state's laws?

2. In the Harrington case, if Jeanine, the residual beneficiary, predeceases John, the testator, and he has not named a successor residual beneficiary, all the assets included in the residue will pass according to the intestate succession statutes. Check to see how this problem is handled in your state.

3. Draft a residuary clause for John Harrington containing a successor residual beneficiary.

A typical state statute that determines the transfer of the decedent's residual assets is:

Cal. Prob. Code § 126 (West 1956), *Residuary Disposition*

Except as provided by Sections 1386.1 and 1386.2 of the Civil Code relating to powers of appointment, a devise of the residue of the testator's real property, or a bequest of the residue of the testator's personal property, passes all of the real or personal property, as the case may be, which he was entitled to devise or bequeath at the time of his death, not otherwise effectually devised or bequeathed by his will. [Compare U.P.C. §§ 3–902 and 3–906.]

Handwritten margin notes:
1 - Executor couldn't do
1/ no reinvest any
state loans
4/ no loans

Appointment of the Personal Representative

State statutes often enumerate the powers granted the personal representatives or trustee. The testate, however, may want to list certain specific powers and duties to help the representative facilitate the administration of the estate. Giving the representative the power to sell one's property, for instance, saves time and perhaps money; otherwise, the representative would have to obtain permission from the probate court for such a sale.[3] Such permission is called a *license to sell.* In addition, just as a contingent devisee should always be named in the event the original devisee predeceases the maker, a contingent representative should also be selected in case the original one may be unable or unwilling to serve in that capacity (for an example of statutes on executor's and administrator's powers and duties, see Wash. Rev. Code Ann. § 11.48.010 (1967) and compare U.P.C. §§ 3–701 and 3–703). **Sample Clause:** I hereby nominate and apppoint Marvin Jameson as executor of my estate and authorize him to (among other powers) sell at public or private sale any real or personal property of my estate. If Marvin Jameson predeceases me or fails to qualify or act as my executor for any reason, I appoint Myrtle B. Jameson as executrix of my estate with all powers hereinbefore mentioned.

A typical statute on the time for commencing the representative's duties is the following North Dakota law.

N.D. Cent. Code § 30.1–18–01 (1976), *Time of Accrual of Powers and Duties*

The duties and powers of a personal representative commence upon his appointment. The powers of a personal representative relate back in time to give acts by the person appointed which are beneficial to the estate occurring prior to appointment the same effect as those occurring thereafter. Prior to appointment a person named executor in a will may carry out written instructions of the decedent relating to his body, the funeral, and burial arrangements. A personal representative may ratify and accept acts on behalf of the estate done by others, where the acts would have been proper for a personal representative.

The executor or executrix appointed is responsible for collecting and preserving the estate assets, paying all allowed debts of the decedent, as well as estate expenses and taxes, and distributing the balance to devisees named in the will (see U.P.C. § 3–703).

It is important that a paralegal be able to interpret statutory language correctly. A phrase in the North Dakota statute above, "The powers of a personal representative relate back in time," refers to the fact that although representatives do not have authority to handle the administration of the estate until qualified, they do possess limited

---

3. When the estate requires detailed handling, it is best that the testate direct the executor's course of action. For example, promissory notes payable to the testate should be collected by the executor. Unless the testate mentions collection on such notes in the will, the executor might overlook this detail, with the result that the probate court might hold the representative liable.

authority (e.g., to preserve the assets of the estate before the representatives can be duly qualified), a universal though unwritten rule that several states, particularly U.P.C. states, have incorporated into their probate codes. Formal qualification of the personal representative requires a hearing before a probate judge, registrar, or clerk of the court, an order signed by the judge, and issuance of documents called Letters Testamentary or Letters of Administration (see page 326), which officially authorize the named representative to commence the administration.

Assignment 71

The following is an excerpt from Deborah Morrow's will.

Article VIII

To my executrix or her successor, should she not survive me, I give the following powers and authorities in addition to and not in limitation of the powers and authorities granted by law, to be exercised as she shall deem advisable:

(a) To sell publicly or privately, to retain, to lease, to borrow money, to mortgage or to pledge all or part of the real or personal property of my estate;

(b) To distribute the residue of my estate in cash or in kind or partly in each; for this purpose, the determination of the executor as to the value of property distributed in kind shall be conclusive.

(c) Regarding my real property: to collect rents and earnings; to keep it in tenantable repair; to make expenditures necessary to its preservation, including insuring it and employing agents and custodians of it;

(d) To determine and resolve matters and questions regarding my estate, both real and personal.

Myrna was aware that Deborah had named her executrix, and she had agreed to perform the administrative tasks. When Deborah died, Myrna took the will to the bank where Deborah's savings and checking accounts were located, showed the bank the will, and demanded that the banker close the accounts and transfer the funds to Myrna. The banker refused. Is this a proper procedure for Myrna to obtain the funds? According to your state's laws, how should Myrna obtain these assets?

Appointment of a Personal and/or Property Guardian

A parent has a statutory obligation to support children until they reach majority. Whenever the testate has minor or physically or mentally handicapped children and the other parent is deceased or unable to care for them, a personal guardian should be appointed to ensure proper care of the children after the testate's death. Otherwise, the court is left with determining who shall have custody and/or *guardianship of the person* (i.e., the child or the incompetent).

Example: Bryan dies testate. He had sole custody of his minor daughter, Kate. Bryan's wife had died several years earlier. Bryan's brother, Gerald, with whom Bryan and Kate had lived for a number of years, and Kate's maternal grandmother both claim to be a more fitting guardian for the child. The probate court must choose between the two if Bryan's will fails to name a guardian. Either Bryan or his wife could have prevented the unpleasantness resulting from this guardianship proceeding by naming in their wills a guardian of the person, and of the property, for Kate.

The testate should also appoint a *guardian of the property,* or trustee to manage property left to minor or incompetent children. If such an appointment is not made, the court must do so. The testate should empower the property guardian or trustee to hold, accumulate, and manage the funds and property for incapacitated or minor devisees or beneficiaries under a trust for the duration of their minority or incapacity (compare U.P.C. §§ 5–209 and 5–401).[4] The guardian of the person and the guardian of the property may or may not be the same person.

Sample Clause: I hereby nominate and appoint Francine E. Richter as personal and property guardian for my minor child, Debra G. Thorsby, and empower her with the right to have care, custody, and control of said minor child, and to collect, invest, and manage, without court approval, any property passing to said minor child by this will. The guardian may use the income from the property for the support, education, and well-being of said child and distribute the principal balance to her upon her 25th birthday or her marriage, whichever occurs first. In the event Francine E. Richter is unable or unwilling to act as a guardian, I hereby appoint William B. Kruger to serve in her place as personal and property guardian with all the hereinbefore mentioned powers.

A statute granting testamentary appointment of a guardian is Tex. Prob. Code Ann. § 117 (Vernon 1980), *Appointment of Guardian by Will:*

> The surviving parent of a minor may, by will or written declaration, appoint any qualified person to be guardian of the person of his or her children after the death of such parent; and, if not disqualified, such person shall be entitled to be appointed guardian of their estate after the death of such parent, upon compliance with the provisions of this Code.

A statute that treats the order of preference for the appointment of a guardian is Ind.Code, § 29–1–18–10 (West 1979), *Appointment of Guardian; Suitable persons; Requests:*

---

4. See Chapter 9 for discussion of testamentary trusts.

(a) The court shall appoint as guardian or coguardian of an incompetent the person, persons or corporate fiduciary or any combination thereof most suitable and willing to serve, having due regard to:

(1) any request made by one for whom a guardian is being appointed by reason of old age, infirmity, or other incapacity, other than insanity, mental illness, mental retardation, senility, habitual drunkenness, or excessive use of drugs;

(2) any request for the appointment contained in a will or other written instrument;

(3) any request made by a minor of the age of fourteen [14] years or over for the appointment of his guardian;

(4) any request for the appointment made by the spouse of an incompetent;

(5) the relationship by blood or marriage to the person for whom guardianship is sought;

(6) the assets or interests of the incompetent and the incompetent's estate.

Assignment 72

Rhoda's husband, Steven Clark, died testate, leaving his estate equally to Rhoda and their three-year-old adopted daughter, Karen, who has muscular dystrophy.

1. Draft a provision for Steven's will which protects Karen's interest in her father's estate.

2. If Rhoda remarries and dies intestate five years after Steven's death, would her new husband or Karen's maternal grandparents have a statutory preference to the appointment of guardian for Karen in the state of Indiana? In your own state?

Simultaneous Death and Common Disaster Provision

Inheritance and distribution problems occurred so frequently whenever a married couple died in a common disaster that nearly all states have adopted the Uniform Simultaneous Death Act (see page 181). This act provides that where the inheritance of property depends on priority of death of spouses and no sufficient evidence exists that the spouses have died other than simultaneously, the property of *each* is disposed of as if each had survived the other. Unfortunately, the act results in significant financial loss to surviving successors. For example, if a wife who died simultaneously with her husband were the *sole* successor to her husband's estate, then after his estate is taxed, debts are paid, and other disbursements made, the residue would be added to the wife's estate, where it would be taxed again.

To avoid the additional tax liability created by the act, lawyers often insert simultaneous death and common disaster clauses in wills of a husband and wife, usually in the husband's will. The clauses provide that in situations where it is impossible to determine which of a married couple died first, the husband is deemed to have predeceased his wife. Then a common devisee or devisees named in the respective wills of the spouses take the estate when both spouses die in a common accident. Besides speeding the transfer of probate assets (belonging to the decedent's estate), such a provision is also useful in resolving problems concerning how to dispose of and distribute non-probate assets, such as property held in joint tenancy, proceeds from insurance policies, and other like matters.

The presumption created by the Uniform Simultaneous Death Act has additional adverse effects. In cases where a married couple die together (in a common disaster) and the order of death of the two persons cannot be established, the act declares that each person shall be deemed to have survived the other, so that their respective estates will be treated separately. This causes delay in the ultimate settlement of the two estates, for the property of each spouse must pass through final distribution to their respective successors. The common disaster clause, by naming a devisee or devisees who would take in the event of the deaths of husband and wife at the same time, is a method commonly used to avoid the undesirable result of double administration, its expenses, and delays.

Sample Clause: In the event that my said wife, Melva A. Petersen, predeceases me or should we both die in some common accident, even though she should survive me by an appreciable length of time, such as 120 days, then I give all of the property that otherwise would have passed to her under the provision of this will to my four sons, hereinbefore (or hereinafter) named, in equal shares, share and share alike provided that they shall survive me. In the event that one or more of my said children does not survive me, then I hereby give the share of my property which that child would normally have taken under this, my Last Will and Testament, to his heirs, in equal shares, share and share alike.

A typical state statute is Conn. Gen. Stat. Ann. § 45–287 (West 1981), *Simultaneous death; Disposition of property:*

> (a) When no sufficient evidence of survivorship the title to property or the devolution thereof depends upon priority of death and there is no sufficient evidence that the persons have died otherwise than simultaneously, the property of each person shall be disposed of as if he had survived, except as provided otherwise in this section.

Assignment 73

Ruth and Edmund Barnet, husband and wife, live in Connecticut. The simultaneous death statute of the state of Connecticut appears above.

Edmund's will gives his country house to Ruth, if she should survive him, but if she does not, to his sister, Estelle. Ruth's will gives to Edmund her collection of antiques, if he should survive her, but if he does not, to her brother, Keith. Ruth and Edmund die simultaneously in an automobile collision. Answer these questions according to your own state laws:

1. Who inherits which property?

2. Would your answer differ if Ruth had died one day later than Edmund? Is there "sufficient evidence" to prevent the statute from operating?

3. If Ruth receives injuries in the accident and dies 90 days afterward, would she be entitled to receive Edmund's gift? Would Estelle?

Testamentary Trust Clause

Occasionally a person wishes to transfer ownership of property to another without giving the recipient full power over the designated property. A method generally used to accomplish this is a *trust* (see Chapters 9, 10, and 11). As previously defined, a trust is the conveyance of legal title to property to a person, the *trustee,* with the understanding that the trustee holds, manages, and controls the property for the benefit or use of another person, the beneficiary (or *cestui que trust*).

Attorneys handle the drafting of any trusts their clients wish to establish. The immediate focus here is on trusts contained in wills. The paralegal must be aware of the reasons for establishing such devises and understand the basic principles involved in their creation. This knowledge provides a foundation for intelligently and competently assisting the attorney in drafting and executing testamentary trusts.

The following characteristics common to trusts established in a will are generally essential to their validity: (1) a settlor, (2) a trustee, (3) a beneficiary, (4) a remainderman (may be the same person as the beneficiary), (5) property, (6) terms of the trust.

Trusts are useful for several purposes (see also page 222). There can be a tax saving to estates by transferring property to children and grandchildren. For example, a settlor can place property in a trust with the income therefrom paid to a child during the latter's lifetime, and the trust corpus transferred to the child's own children (settlor's grandchildren) on the child's death. The tax consequences of such a trust are discussed in Chapter 15 on page 427 under "generation-skipping" transfers.

The Rule Against Perpetuities, a common-law rule that originated in England centuries ago, affects the validity of all private non-charitable trusts. It regulates the creation of future interests and holds that no interest in property is valid unless it must vest, if at all, not later than

21 years after the death of some life in being (a living person or persons) named in the instrument (e.g., a will) that transferred the property.

The Rule Against Perpetuities has an important bearing on testamentary trusts. Because public policy, as enunciated in the rule, opposes the accumulation and monopolizing of property (restraint of its alienation by someone else), the maker of a will may not create a trust that lasts longer than 21 years after the life of a named person. The life of such a person is referred to as a "life in being" when the trust is created. To illustrate: A settlor of property presently without children cannot create a testamentary trust for grandchildren (children's children, neither of which class is yet born), since there is no "life in being" at the time of the creation of the trust. The trust is void because of the rule. On the other hand, if the settlor were to create a trust leaving property at death in trust to a daughter now living the "life in being," and on her death to the daughter's children, the trust would be legal since the duration of the trust would be measured by the life of the daughter. The trust terminates legally on her death; her child or children would receive the trust corpus. If the daughter were to die childless, the trust property would revert immediately to the settlor or the settlor's successors.

The following Georgia law exemplifies state statutes on the Rule Against Perpetuities:

Ga. Code § 44–6–1 (1982) *Perpetuities; Exceptions*

(a) Limitations of estates may extend through any number of lives in being at the time when the limitations commence, and 21 years, and the usual period of gestation added thereafter. A limitation beyond that period the law terms a perpetuity, and forbids its creation. When an attempt is made to create a perpetuity, the law gives effect to limitations not too remote, declaring the others void, and thereby vests the fee in the last taker under legal limitations.

Sample Clause: All the remainder of my estate, I devise to the Fourth Western Bank to hold in trust, invest, reinvest, and distribute the net income accruing from the date of my death, for the benefit of my son, Jeremy, and such child or children of him who reach the age of 18 years.

To avoid running afoul of the Rule Against Perpetuities in will-drafting is difficult, as evidenced by the great number of lawsuits brought by persons alleging that certain trust provisions violate the rule. For this reason, the paralegal must go over in detail the perpetuities statute of the state where the trust is to take effect to ensure that the trust harmonizes with it.

The above-quoted Georgia statute, for example, holds the effective time of a trust the remaining length of the lives of persons named in the instrument, plus 21 years, plus nine months (the "usual period of gestation"—this provision provides for persons not yet born at the time of the trust execution). The trust set up in the example clause would last for the rest of Jeremy's life and continue for 21 years and nine months. The clause, then, falls within the limits set by the Rule Against Perpetuities, but a clause entrusting property for the benefit of Jeremy's grandchildren only would not, since it is not possible for title to the property to pass to anyone in the manner specified by the rule. According to the statute, the part of the trust in violation of the rule would not be allowed to vest, i.e., pass to the grandchildren.

Testimonium Clause

The testimonium clause contains a statement by the maker of the will that it has been freely signed and a request has been made of the proper number of witnesses to do the same.

Since the testimonium clause does not contain any new information and in most instances only repeats what the testate has stated in the opening paragraphs, it would appear to be expendable. Although each state demands that the will conform to standards regarding writing, signing by the testate, and witnessing, no state statute prescribes a form for the testimonium clause. Likewise, the use of a seal to indicate the identity of the testate or the substitution of L.S. (Lieu of Seal; set in place of a seal) is largely disregarded by will-drafters, although there are adherents to the practice.

Sample Clause: In witness whereof, I have hereunto set my hand this _____ day of July, 19   , at City of Riverdale, County of Folsom, State of Jefferson, in the presence of each and all the attesting and subscribing witnesses, each of whom I have requested in the presence of the others to subscribe his name, with his address written opposite thereto, as a subscribing witness, in my presence and in the presence of all the others.

A typical statute on this matter is N.J. Stat. Ann. § 3A:3–2 (West 1953), *Formal Requisites of a Will*:

> Except as provided . . . this title, a will to be valid shall be in writing and signed by the testator, which signature shall be made by the testator or the making thereof acknowledged by him, and such writing declared to be his last will, in the presence of 2 witnesses present at the same time, who shall subscribe their names thereto, as witnesses, in the presence of the testator.

Assignment 74

After reading a copy of a will prepared for him by an attorney, Owen decides that he does not like the antiquated language of the testimonium clause. He erases it and writes the following clause in its place.

At the time this will was executed, the testator knew of and fully complied with the statutes of this state relating to the execution of wills.

/s/ _____

Witnessed this same day, April 13, 19___.

/s/ _____
(Witness)

/s/ _____
(Witness)

1. Would this clause serve in lieu of the traditionally worded testimonium clause? Why or why not?

2. Point out potential difficulties caused by this testimonium clause when the will's executor offers the document for probate. Are there any words or omissions likely to be challenged in a will contest? Why?

3. If necessary, add to or modify the clause to make it conform both to the requirements of the law and to Owen's desire to modernize its language.

Testator's Signature

For a will to be valid, its maker must sign, make a mark, or direct another to sign. In most states, the signature must be witnessed by two or more persons acting as attesting witnesses. The date, either in the beginning, within, or at the end of the will, is essential. Without it, it may be impossible to prove that the will is the last (in time) made by the testate.

A typical statute on the execution of a will is Cal. Prob. Code § 50 (West 1956), *Wills; execution; attestation.*

Every will, other than a nuncupative will, must be in writing and every will, other than a holographic will and a nuncupative will, must be executed and attested as follows:

(1) *Subscription* It must be subscribed at the end thereof by the testator himself, or some person in his presence and by his direction must subscribe his name thereto. A person who subscribes the testator's name, by his direction, should write his own name as a witness to the will, but a failure to do so will not affect the validity of the will.

(2) *Presence of witnesses* The subscription must be made, or the testator must acknowledge it to have been made by him or by his authority, in the presence of both of the attesting witnesses, present at the same time.

(3) *Testator's declaration* The testator, at the time of subscribing or acknowledging the instrument, must declare to the attesting witnesses that it is his will.

(4) *Attesting witnesses* There must be at least two attesting witnesses, each of whom must sign the instrument as a witness, at the end of the will, at the testator's request and in his presence. The witnesses should give their places of residence, but a failure to do so will not affect the validity of the will. [Compare U.P.C. § 2–502.]

Example: Walter typewrites his will. He puts his signature at the beginning of it, but types his name at the end. In California, the will is not valid for lack of a proper signature in the proper place.

Example: Dora signs her will in the presence of three witnesses. She had not said directly to them that the document was her will, but gave them to understand that the document contained her wishes for distribution of her property after death. Dora has complied with the required Declaration of Testator.

Example: Luke writes a will but neglects to date it. Previously he had made a will but had decided to discard it. He did not destroy the former will. Both documents are found after his death. The latter will does not supersede the former or prevail over it for lack of evidence that it was written at a later point in time.

Assignment 75

Edith wishes to make a will, but she is partially paralyzed and cannot write her name. Her nephew, Arthur, agrees to draw up the will and to witness the X she will make in place of her name. The clause preceding the signature follows.

I, the testatrix, Edith B. Pendergast, on this 19th day of March, 1963, subscribe my name to this will.

I, Arthur, G. Pendergast, have witnessed this mark made by Edith Pendergast, who affixed it in lieu of her signature.

1. Do these clauses fulfill your state's statutory requirements for signature by the testator? Why or why not?

2. If necessary, add to or modify the clauses to make them conform to your answer in question 1 (compare U.P.C. § 2–502).

Attestation Clause of Witnesses

Witnesses must state that they have attested the maker's signature on the will; ordinarily they sign a clause to this effect. As in the case of the testimonium clause, each state has legislation requiring subscription by witnesses, although none prescribes the words or form to be used to accomplish this. The traditional form of the attestation clause, like the familiarly worded testimonium clause, is illustrated below.

Sample Clause: The above and foregoing instrument, consisting of three (3) typewritten pages, was on the date thereof, subscribed and sealed by Alexander Littons, the testator therein named, and declared by him to be his last will and testament, in our presence, and we at his request and in his presence and in the presence of each other, have hereunto subscribed our names as witnesses thereto.

Assignment 76

"We, the undersigned, declare that Lyman Jarrett validly signed and executed this will. We sign at his request, all of us signing in each other's presence."

1. Does such a clause comply with statutory requirements? Why or why not?

2. If necessary, add to or modify the clause to make it conform to the statutory requirements.

Witnesses' Signatures and Addresses

Only the original copy of the will need be signed. However, it is advisable to sign all copies. Most states require that at least two witnesses sign the will, some states require three witnesses' signatures.
Example:

	Address
Pamela C. Hunter	*111 Wheelock Drive*
Frederick D. Burns	*2307 Ayleshire Avenue*
Marshall Jaymer	*417 Kenyon Place*

Assignment 77

Herman Sharp wrote his will, aided by Joel Prentis, a notary public. After Herman's signature, Joel wrote, "I hereby certify that this is the last will and testament of Herman Sharp. (signed) Joel A. Prentis, Notary Public. My commission expires 12/31/74. (Seal.)"

Herman had his cousin, Pearl, witness the will and intended to ask another cousin to witness it but died before accomplishing this. Is the will valid? What validates or invalidates it? What would have been a better procedure for Joel to follow?

Sample Preliminary Will

The worksheet in Exhibit 8.1 is a sample worksheet for preparing to draft a client's will. It has been completed for the hypothetical client Leona Bayn Farrell.

In our hypothetical situation, Leona Bayn Farrell wishes to make a will. She is married and has a husband, Oren, and four children, Randolph, Jonathan, Daria, and Thomas. Her estate consists of both real and personal property, all of which she acquired prior to the marriage or as testamentary gifts to her alone (i.e., it is separate property). Leona lives in Arizona, a community property state, so she may dispose of by will only half the community property acquired by herself and her husband while they are married.

Exhibit 8.1 is an example of an executed worksheet for Leona's will and a draft of the will itself drawn up from the information on the worksheet.

Exhibit 8.1 Sample Worksheet for Drafting a Will

Client's Name: <u>Leona Bayn Farrell (also known as Leona Alice Bayn)</u>

Address: <u>913 Garth Avenue,</u> City <u>Santa Maria</u>, County <u>Harkness</u>, State <u>Arizona</u>

(if more than one) <u>17 Mesa Grande,</u> Dorado, <u>New Mexico</u>.

Permanent Residence (Domicile): <u>913 Garth Avenue, Harkness County, Santa Maria.</u>

Funeral and Burial Directions: <u>I direct that my kidneys be delivered, immediately upon my death, without autopsy having been performed, to the Dorado State School of Medicine, 403 Alamoreal Street, Dorado, New Mexico, to be used for educational purposes.</u>

Method (source of payments of debts and all taxes): <u>I direct that my executor pay all my expenses, debts, and taxes from the residue of my estate.</u>

Specific Gifts

Personal Property (community property)

Beneficiary: <u>Oren Johnstone Farrell</u>   Contingent beneficiary: <u>Children</u>

Relationship: <u>Husband</u>   Relationship: <u>Sons and daughters</u>

Item: <u>Share of community property consisting of household furnishing, clothing, jewelry, books, and other personal effects.</u>

Method: <u>Devise</u>

Exhibit 8.1 *(continued)*

Personal property

Beneficiary: Randolph Bayn Farrell

Contingent beneficiary: Ella Gamble Dean

Relationship: Son

Relationship: Niece

Item: The Buick automobile which I own, serial number 70-5015-63-9229

Present location: At my permanent residence, 913 Garth Avenue

Method: Devise

Personal Property

Beneficiary: Oren Johnstone Farrell

Contingent beneficiary: Jonathan Bayn Farrell

Relationship: Husband

Relationship: Son

Item: All the farm equipment located at Siete Rios

Method: Devise

Personal Property

Beneficiary: Jonathan Bayn Farrell

Contingent beneficiary: Angela Bayn Rodgers

Relationship: Son

Relationship: Niece

Item: All the horses and riding equipment located at Vallejo Grande

Method: Devise

Real Property: Ranch—''Vallejo Grande''

Beneficiary: Jonathan Bayn Farrell

Contingent beneficiary: Angela Bayn Rodgers

Relationship: Son

Relationship: Niece

Legal description of ''Vallejo Grande'': ''The West half of Section 12, being 320 acres more or less, Township 4 North, Range 28 West of the 4th Principal Meridian, according to the United States Government survey.''

Location: County: Almedo State: New Mexico

Amount of interest: Fee simple

Method: Fee simple devise

Real Property: Farm—''Siete Rios''

Beneficiary: Oren Johnstone Farrell

Contingent beneficiary: Daria Eileen Farrell

Relationship: Husband

Relationship: Daughter

Location: County: Dorado State: New Mexico

Legal description of ''Siete Rios'': ''The Southwest Quarter of Section 13, being 160 acres more or less, Township 4 North, Range 28 West of the 4th Principal Meridian, according to the United States Government survey.''

Amount of interest: Fee simple

Exhibit 8.1 *(continued)*

Method : Fee simple devise

Residue

Beneficiary: Daria Eileen Farrell   Contingent beneficiary: Randolph Bayn Farrell

Relationship: Daughter   Relationship: Son

Interest given: Devise; if any residue remains after payment of debts, expenses and taxes

Name and Address of Executor: Randolph Bayn Farrell
119 Golden Valley Road, Santa Maria, Arizona

Contingent (Successor) Executor: Farmers National Bank, Santa Maria, Arizona

Powers of Executor: To sell publicly or privately all or part of my residual property to carry on the operations of ''Vallejo Grande'' and ''Siete Rios'' until the dispositions thereof are complete

Trusts

Trustee: Carl A. Woodward, Farmers National Bank, Santa Maria, Arizona

Property: $75,000 (cash)

Location: Farmers National Bank, Account #922160

Duration of trust (life, years, etc.): For the life of my son, Thomas Earl Farrell

Remainder: First United Methodist Church of Waco, Texas

Trustee's powers

Investment: To invest and reinvest the corpus

Management: To distribute the earned income for the benefit of Thomas Earl Farrell

Payment of income: Quarterly if possible; at least semi-annually

Payment of principal: At the trustee's discretion or at the request of Thomas Earl Farrell's natural or legal personal guardian

Power of sale: N/A

Special Provisions: Both principal and interest may be used for education, training and maintenance of Thomas Earl Farrell. If guardian and trustee disagree, guardian's opinion is to prevail.

Guardians

Guardian of person: Hal August Rodgers, husband of my niece, Angela Bayn Rodgers

Name and address: 366 Rector Avenue, County of Harkness, City of Santa Maria, Arizona

Exhibit 8.1 *(continued)*

Ward: <u>Thomas Earl Farrell</u>   Successor Guardian: <u>Randolph Bayn Farrell</u>

Bond: <u>None required</u>

Guardian of property: <u>Randolph Bayn Farrell, my son</u>

Name and address: <u>119 Golden Valley Road, County of Harkness, City of Santa Maria, Arizona</u>

Ward: <u>Thomas Earl Farrell</u> Successor Guardian: <u>Hal August Rodgers</u>

Bond: <u>None required</u>

Common Disaster Provision: <u>If any beneficiary under this will and I should die under circumstances which make it impossible to determine the order of deaths, I shall be deemed to have predeceased them. In the event that my husband and I die in a common accident, I give all the property that would otherwise have passed to him under this will to my children in equal shares.</u>

Witnesses

Names and Addresses: <u>Raymond Meador, Route 34, White Plains, Arizona</u>

<u>Philip Harston, 1661 N. 3rd Street, Santa Maria, Arizona</u>

<u>Mildred Wagoner, Route 7, Adolphus, Arizona</u>

General Notes

Location—safe deposit box: <u>Leona and Oren Farrell, joint tenants, Farmers National Bank</u>

Location where will shall be placed: <u>In the custody of Frank R. Goad, Attorney-at-Law</u>

Will prepared by: <u>Joyce Bell, paralegal assistant under supervision of attorney</u>

Date: <u>July 18, 1983</u>

LAST WILL AND TESTAMENT
OF
LEONA BAYN FARRELL

I, Leona Bayn Farrell, a/k/a (also known as) Leona Alice Bayn, residing at 913 Garth Avenue, City of Santa Maria, County of Harkness, State of Arizona, being of sound and disposing mind and memory, and not acting under undue influence of any person whomsoever, make, publish, and declare this document to be my last will and testament, and hereby expressly revoke all wills and codicils heretofore made by me.

Article I

I direct my executor hereinafter named, to pay all my just debts, and expenses for my last illness, funeral, and burial out of my estate. I further direct my executor to pay out of my residuary estate all estate, income, and inheritance taxes assessed

Exhibit 8.1 *(continued)*

against my taxable estate or the recipients thereof, whether passing by this will or by other means, without contribution or reimbursement from any person.

Article II

I direct my executor to notify the Dorado State School of Medicine, 403 Alamoreal Street, Dorado, New Mexico, of my death, so that it may receive the bequest of my kidneys to use for medical or educational purposes. I further request that no autopsy or embalming be performed upon by body unless ordered by the aforesaid school.

Article III

I direct my executor, after having completed the bequest in Article II, to deliver my body to be interred in the Paz de Christo cemetery in my family lot.

Article IV

I give that portion of our community property which I own, consisting of household furnishings, clothing, jewelry, books, and personal effects of every kind used about my home or person to my husband, Oren Johnstone Farrell, to do with as he sees fit, if he survives me; if he does not survive me, to my children that survive me in shares of substantially equal value, per stirpes.

Article V

I give the Buick automobile which I own, serial number 70–5015-63-9229, to my son, Randolph Bayn Farrell, if he survives me. If he does not survive me, I give said Buick automobile to my niece, Ella Gamble Dean.

Article VI

I give all the farming equipment located at my farm, "Siete Rios," hereinafter legally described, to my husband, Oren Johnstone Farrell, if he survives me. If he does not survive me, I give said farming equipment to my son, Jonathan Bayn Farrell.

Article VII

I give all the horses and riding equipment located at my ranch, "Vallejo Grande," to my son, Jonathan Bayn Farrell, if he survives me. If he does not survive me, I give said horses and said equipment to my niece, Angela Bayn Rodgers.

Article VIII

I give my ranch, "Vallejo Grande," in Almedo county, New Mexico, legally described: "The West half of Section 12, being 320 acres more or less, Township 4 North, Range 28 West of the 4th Principal Meridian, according to the United States Government survey," to my son, Jonathan Bayn Farrell, in fee simple if he survives me. If he does not survive me, I give said ranch in fee simple to my niece, Angela Bayn Rodgers.

Article IX

I give my farm, "Siete Rios," in Dorado County, New Mexico, legally described: "The Southwest Quarter of Section 13, being 160 acres more or less, Township 4 North, Range 28 West of the 4th Principal Meridian, according to the United States Government survey," to my husband, Oren Johnstone Farrell, in fee simple if he survives me. If he does not survive me, I give said farm in fee simple to my daughter, Daria Eileen Farrell.

Exhibit 8.1 *(continued)*

Article X

I give to Carl A. Woodward of Farmers National Bank, Santa Maria, Arizona, the sum of $75,000 to hold in trust for the life of my son, Thomas Earl Farrell. The trustee shall invest and reinvest the corpus of said trust and distribute the income earned thereby for the benefit of Thomas Earl Farrell at least semi-annually, or, if possible, quarterly. Payment of the principal shall be made at the discretion of the trustee or at the request of Thomas Earl Farrell's natural or legal personal guardian, but if the trustee and the personal guardian cannot agree on the dispensing of the principal, the personal guardian's word shall be conclusive in the situation. Upon the death of my son, Thomas Earl Farrell, the remainder of the trust property, if any, is to be given to the First United Methodist Church of Waco, Texas.

Article XI

I nominate as personal guardian to my son, Thomas Earl Farrell, Hal August Rodgers, the husband of my niece, Angela Bayn Rodgers.

I nominate as property guardian to my son, Thomas Earl Farrell, Randolph Bayn Farrell, my oldest son.

If either guardian becomes disabled or declines to serve, I nominate the other to serve in the former's capacity as well as the capacity in which he is presently serving.

I direct that bond be required of neither of said guardians for the performance of the duties of their respective offices.

Article XII

I direct my executor, hereinafter named, to pay all the just debts and expenses, including the expenses of my last illness and burial, from the residue of my estate.

Article XIII

I give the residue of my estate, after the payment of debts and expenses, as mentioned in Article XII, and after transfer of my community property mentioned in Article IV, subject to the laws of this state regarding community property, to my daughter, Daria Eileen Farrell, if she survives me. If she does not survive me, I give said residue to my son, Randolph Bayn Farrell.

Article XIV

In the event that my husband, Oren Johnstone Farrell, predeceases me or should we both die in some common accident, then I give all of the property that otherwise would have passed to him under the provisions of this will to my children, who survive me, in equal shares.

Article XV

I nominate and appoint my son, Randolph Bayn Farrell of 119 Golden Valley Road, Santa Maria, Arizona, the executor of this will, to serve without bond.

If Randolph Bayn Farrell does not survive me or does not qualify as executor, I nominate and appoint Farmers National Bank, a national banking institution located in Santa Maria, Arizona, to succeed to the executorship of this will.

My executor shall have the power to sell publicly or privately all or part of the residue of my property in the event that such sale will become necessary for the payment of debts, taxes, or expenses; to carry on the operations of "Vallejo Grande" and "Siete Rios" until the testamentary dispositions thereof are complete; and to settle all just claims against my estate.

Exhibit 8.1 *(continued)*

I subscribe my name to this will on this 18th day of July, 1983, at Santa Maria, County of Harkness, State of Arizona, in the presence of these witnesses: Raymond Meador; Philip Harston and Mildred Wagoner, each of whom I have requested to subscribe their names.

/s/ Leona Bayn Farrell

On the last date shown above, Leona Bayn Farrell, known to us to be the person whose signature appears at the end of this will, declared to us, the undersigned, that the foregoing instrument was her will. She then signed the will in our presence; at her request, we now sign our names in her presence and the presence of each other.

Names   Addresses

_____   _____

_____   _____

_____   _____

Assignment 78

Peter Rice Cochran wishes to make a will. He is presently unmarried, having been divorced from Viola Leigh after a five-year marriage during which two children, Nancy and Jean, were born. His estate consists of both real and personal property, namely, a town house; household goods; automobile; checking account of $587; certificate of deposit of $7,000; insurance policy on his life, payable to his brother, Desmond Cochran, $10,000; 100 shares of Xerox Corporation stock; savings account of $10,525.

1. Make a preliminary outline of a will for Peter Cochran using the form suggested by the Leona Farrell example. Make up facts in the testate's life (e.g., devisees who are not named above, testamentary trusts to be created) if you wish.

2. Using the will of Leona Farrell as a guide, write a will for Peter Cochran. (The testate lives in Pennsylvania. Be sure to consult the probate laws of that state before drafting the will.)

The Living Will and the Self-Proved Will

There are two other options available in some states which a drafter of a will might recommend to the testate: the Living Will and the Self-Proved Will.

The Living Will: Death with Dignity

At the present time nine states—Arkansas, California, Idaho, New Mexico, Nevada, North Carolina, Ohio, Oregon, and Texas—have adopted a Natural Death Act. This statute allows a competent person with full capacity to make intelligent decisions to execute a formal written document called a Living Will. Such a will states that in the event the person becomes physically or mentally disabled with no reasonable expectation or hope for recovery and, because of the disability the person is unable to take part in decisions, the person can request that he or she not be kept alive by artificial means. The purpose of the request is to relieve family members from the responsibility of making the decision and to alleviate guilt feelings on their part and to protect the physician and health-care institution from liability if they refrain, as requested, from using certain medical procedures.

In states that have not adopted the Natural Death Act, the person executing a Living Will cannot be assured that the request with regard to eliminating these specific medical procedures will be granted.

Exhibit 8.2 is a sample Living Will giving to a spouse the power to make decisions relating to the dying person's medical care. The Living Will can be made part of the testate's regular will.

Exhibit 8.2 Sample Living Will

LIVING WILL
OF

_____

Article I

I address this will to my family, my physician, my clergyman/rabbi, my lawyer, and to all other persons whom it may concern. If the time comes when I can no longer take part in decisions for my own future and my own medical care, I desire that this statement stand as an expression of my wishes and directions, made while I am still of sound mine.

Article II
Artificial Life Supports

If at such time there is no reasonable expectation of my recovery from extreme physical and mental disability, I direct that I be allowed to die and not be kept alive by medications, artificial means or "heroic measures." I do, however, ask that medication be administered to me to alleviate suffering, even though this may hasten the moment of death.

Article III
Location of Care

I would like to live out my last days at home, if doing so does not jeopardize the chance of my recovery to a meaningful life and if it does not impose undue burden

Exhibit 8.2 *(Continued)*

on my family. If it is not possible for me to remain at home, I would prefer to be cared for at a hospice rather than a hospital.

Article IV

Designation of Individual To Make Decisions

I have discussed my views as to life-sustaining measures with my spouse, _____, and I appoint my spouse to make binding decisions concerning my medical treatment.

I have signed this Living Will consisting of _____ pages, including this page, on _____, 19___.

_____

Signature

We certify that in our presence on the date appearing above in the State of _____, _____, signed the foregoing instrument and acknowledged it to be his Living Will, that at his request and in his presence and in the presence of each other, we have signed our names below as witnesses, and that we believe him to be of sound mind and memory.

_____ Witness Signature _____   residing at _____

_____ Witness Signature _____   residing at _____

STATE OF _____ }
                      } ss.
COUNTY OF _____ }

_____, an individual known to me, having been duly sworn, appeared before me and attested that he has read this Living Will, understands its contents and that he signed this Living Will as his own free act and deed.

_____

(Notarial Seal)

The Self-Proved Will

Some states have adopted a statute that provides for the "proving" (establishing the authenticity) of a will. This is accomplished by an acknowledgment of the testate and with affidavits (statements under oath) of the witnesses to the will. The acknowledgment and affidavits are made before an officer authorized to administer oaths by the state, e.g., a notary public, and can be signed either at the time of the execution of the will or at any subsequent date.

The form for the acknowledgment and affidavit of self-proved wills is provided in section 2–504 of the Uniform Probate Code (see Appendix C).

[handwritten margin note: notary Part People under oath]

Where to Keep the Will

It is good practice to mark carbon copies with the location of the original will and to leave the original will in one of four places: (1) in the lawyer's vault; (2) in the bank named as fiduciary in the will; (3) with the client; or (4) filed with the clerk of the appropriate probate court as is allowed in some states.   A personal safe deposit box in a bank is less accessible.   If the client puts the will in a safe deposit box, probate proceedings may be delayed.   Ordinarily a person must have permission from the state (e.g., such as is given to a county treasurer) to open the safe deposit box belonging to another.   Leaving the will with the lawyer is generally most advantageous since that allows convenient periodic review whenever necessary.

40.00 one time fee in one county

Chapter 9

Introduction to Trusts

Scope of the Chapter

The law of trusts is a difficult area of the law to master. A basic vocabulary must be developed, various kinds of trusts must be identified and their functions understood, and techniques of combining client objectives with drafting a trust agreement must be learned. Only after considerable experience working under the supervision of a trust attorney or as a trust officer or administrator of a bank will the paralegal be able to handle these matters with confidence. The purpose of this and the following chapters on trusts is to begin training the paralegal toward obtaining that confidence.

Although all states have adopted or enacted some form of probate code by statute, only a few states have trust codes. Therefore, common law is the primary source of the law on trusts. Common (case) law is judge-made law in the absence of a controlling statute. When appropriate, statutes of the states that have led in the development of trust codes will be cited in this chapter. Another major authority often cited will be the Restatement of Trusts.[1] But for the most part, the American law of trusts will be found in judicial decisions.

This chapter begins with the terminology associated with trusts. An example of how a trust works is given. The paralegal is asked to identify the terms in an actual trust instrument. The remaining units of the chapter discuss the purposes of trusts; the elements of a trust, including the participants, their interest, selection, duties, and liabilities; the trust property; the different types of trusts; and the ways in which a trust terminates.

---

1. See page 218 for definition. Restatement (Second) of Trusts, Copyright 1957 by the American Law Institute. Reprinted with the permission of the American Law Institute.

Competencies

After completing this chapter, the paralegal should be able to:

- Understand the basic terminology of trusts
- Identify and define the various kinds of trusts
- Explain the use and functions of the various trusts
- Identify the participants in the creation and operation of a trust

Terminology Relating to Trusts

Before the paralegal can prepare a preliminary draft of a trust agreement, the terminology, including the classification (types) of trusts, must be mastered.

Trust

A trust is a fiduciary relationship in which property is transferred from the creator, or settlor, of the trust to one or more persons (the trustee or trustees), who generally hold the legal title to property (the trust property) subject to equitable duties (an obligation enforceable in a court of equity) to "hold" and use the property for the benefit of another person or persons (the beneficiary or beneficiaries) who hold the equitable title (see definitions below).

Example: Barry gives Charles $30,000 to hold and invest in trust for the benefit of William.

Settlor

The settlor is the person who creates a trust, also called the donor, grantor, creator, and trustor. In the example above, Barry is the settlor.

Trustee

The trustee is the one who holds the legal title for the benefit of someone else. In the above trust, Charles is the trustee and holds legal title to the property for the benefit of William.

Beneficiary or "cestui que trust"

The beneficiary is the person having the enjoyment of property (real or personal) of which a trustee, executor, etc., has the legal title. The beneficiary is said to hold equitable title (see below) to the trust property. In the example above, William is the beneficiary (sometimes called the "cestui que trust") and holds the equitable title.

Trust property

Trust property is the property interest that the trustee holds subject to the right of someone else. The trust property in the above case is the $30,000. (Also called the *trust corpus, res, fund, estate,* or *subject matter* of the trust.)

Trust instrument

A trust instrument is any writing under which a trust is created, such as a will, trust agreement, deed of trust, declaration of trust, or court order.

Legal title

Legal title is a title enforceable in a court of law which is complete and perfect with respect to the right of ownership and possession. In the law of trusts, the trustee ordinarily holds, or is said to be *vested* with, the legal title. Vested means having the rights of absolute ownership. **Example:** John transfers by deed a lake cottage to Mary to hold in trust for the benefit of Shirley. Mary is the trustee and has legal title. Shirley is the beneficiary and holds the equitable title.

Equitable title

In the law of trusts, equitable title is a right of the beneficiary to have the legal title transferred to him or her. Another way to view equitable title is that the beneficiary of the trust is regarded as the real owner, i.e., the beneficiary is entitled to the beneficial interest of the trust property although the legal title to the property is vested in (held by) another (the trustee) (see previous example under Legal Title).

Principal

The principal is the capital or property of an estate or trust as opposed to the income, which is the fruit of capital, i.e., generated by the capital. **Example:** The $30,000 Barry gives to Charles would be the principal, and the interest earned by the principal, at say 10%, would be the income.

Income beneficiary

The income beneficiary is the beneficiary who is entitled to receive the income produced from trust property.

Fiduciary

A fiduciary is a person who owes a duty of trust and loyalty and the obligation to act in good faith for the benefit of another. An example of a person acting as a fiduciary is a trustee acting for the benefit of a trust beneficiary. Other examples are a guardian acting for a minor, or a partner acting for the other partners.

Fiduciary duty

Fiduciary duty is a duty or obligation that arises out of a position of loyalty, trust, and confidence. In the law of trusts, it is a duty that a trustee owes the beneficiary of a trust, and it requires the trustee to act with loyalty and in good faith.

Life estate

A life estate is a freehold estate (see page 78) which is held for the tenant's own lifetime or the life or lives of one or more other person(s). If the estate is for the life of a person other than the life tenant, it is known as an estate "pur autre vie."

Example: John transfers title to his farm by deed "to Mary for life." Mary has a life estate and has the right to use and possess the farm for her lifetime. Mary is the life tenant. If John had transferred the farm "to Mary during the life of Bob," he would have transferred an estate "pur autre vie."

Remainderman
The remainderman is one who is entitled to the remainder of the estate after a particular estate carved out of it has expired.
Example: In the above case, if John transferred his farm "to Mary for life, then to Sally and her heirs forever," Mary would be the life tenant and Sally would be the remainderman. When Mary died, Sally would receive the remainder of the estate in fee simple (see pages 78–81).

Dividends
Dividends are the share of money allotted to each owner (stockholder) entitled to share in a division of profits of a corporation.

Decree
A decree is the written judgment (decision) of the court.

Equity
Equity is a system of laws or judicial remedies granted by certain courts, called courts of equity (chancery), distinct from the common-law courts. Examples of such judicial remedies, granted when no adequate remedy from a court of law is available, are injunctions, reformation of contracts, and specific performance (see page 244).

Consideration
Consideration is the cause, motive, or impelling influence (i.e., something of value) which induces two or more contracting parties to enter into a contract.
Example: John agrees to mow Harold's lawn for $15. To Harold, the consideration is John's service, i.e., the mowing of the lawn; to John, the consideration is the $15 paid by Harold.

Assignment
Assignment is the transfer from one person to another of the whole of any property, real or personal, or of any estate or right therein. The person making the transfer is called the *assignor;* the person to whom the assignment (transfer) is made is the *assignee.*
Example: Abner owes Baker $50, i.e., Baker has the right to receive $50 from Abner. Baker assigns (transfers) his right to the payment to Clarence. Abner now owes Clarence $50. Baker is the assignor; Clarence is the assignee.

Court of law
A court of law is the court that administers justice according to the rules and practice of both statutory and common law. An example of a

remedy that a court of law grants is damages (money) as compensation for personal injury or breach of contract.

Court of equity

A court of equity is the court that administers justice according to the rules of equity and fairness. Examples of remedies from this court include a court order forbidding the person sued (defendant) from doing some act, i.e., an injunction, or a reforming of a contract by the court to conform the contract to the parties' intentions.

Statute of Frauds

The Statute of Frauds is a series of state laws which provide that no suit or civil action shall be maintained on certain classes of *oral* contracts unless the agreement is put in writing and signed by the party to be charged, i.e., the person being sued or an authorized agent of that person. Each state has its own Statute of Frauds patterned on the medieval English statute of the same name.

Example: Stanley has agreed orally to buy Laura's home. Their oral contract is unenforceable because of the Statute of Frauds. Therefore, in order for the contract to be legally binding and enforceable on both parties, Stanley and Laura must put their agreement in writing and both must sign.

Use

A use is the early medieval English forerunner of a trust (specifically a passive trust) based on the principle of separation of the legal title to an estate from the equitable (beneficial) title. The person who legally owned the estate (i.e., had legal title) did not have the right to gain benefits from it (a considerable right in the Middle Ages), and the person who had the right to the benefits did not legally own it. In feudal society, uses were valuable to landowners as means of assigning or avoiding the responsibilities of landowners, e.g., their obligations to their lords for military support, for payment of a portion of their crops, and the like. Consequently, many landowners abused this practice by creating uses. The Statute of Uses (see below) abolished "uses," which were equivalent to modern-day passive trusts, and put an end to the practice described above (see page 256 for a discussion of passive trusts).

Statute of Uses

The Statute of Uses is an English statute enacted in 1536 directed against the practice of creating "uses" in land and which converted the purely equitable title of persons (beneficiaries) entitled to a use into a legal title or absolute ownership with right of possession. The statute is said to "execute the use," that is, it turned equitable estates into legal estates. For example, if A transferred land to B *to the use of* C, the use would be executed and thereby B's legal estate would be vested in C, who thus became the fee simple owner. In other words, this transfer would pass the legal as well as equitable title to C, the beneficiary. Therefore C obtains not only the rights but also the responsibilities as owner of the property. This statute did not apply to certain transactions involving uses. The exemptions were (1) a use of personal property, (2) an active use, such as one in which the trustee had active duties to perform other than holding and conveying legal title, and (3) a use on a use, for example, A to B to the use of C to the use of D. These exemptions opened the way for the development of the modern law of trusts.

Parol evidence rule

Parol is a verbal contract a verbal contract has [?] contract probes you can Parol evidence rule

The parol evidence rule is a general rule of contract law that oral or written evidence (testimony) is *not* allowed to vary, change, alter, or modify any of the terms or provisions of a written contract (agreement). **Example:** After much deliberation and many changes by both parties, Lou and Bud write out and sign a contract. Later, Lou decides that the contract does not truly reflect what he and Bud had agreed. In court, neither Lou nor Bud could introduce oral or other written evidence (parol evidence) of the pre-contractual negotiations in hopes of changing the original written contract.

Restatement of Trusts

In 1935, recognizing the need to simplify and clarify the American law of trusts, a group of trust experts working for the American Law Institute set forth the existing rules of law affecting trust creation and administration and included illustrations and comments. The completed work was called the Restatement of the American Law of Trusts. In 1957, the original Restatement was revised and the revisions were incorporated into the Restatement (Second) of Trusts. Throughout the trust chapters of this book, relevant sections of the Restatement (Second) of Trust, will be cited.

Cy-pres doctrine *reform the purpose*

Cy-pres means "as near as possible." Where a testator or settlor makes a gift to a charity or for a charitable purpose and subsequently it becomes impossible or impractical to apply the gift to that particular charity, the equity court may order it applied to another charity "as near as may be possible" to the one designated by the settlor. This is known as the cy-pres doctrine.

Example: Through his will, Elmer Wilson gives the National Polio Foundation $500,000. Dr. Salk invents a vaccine that cures and prevents polio. Elmer's heirs ask the court to distribute the money to them now that the disease is preventable. The court of equity would apply the cy-pres doctrine and transfer the balance of the funds to a charity as near as possible to the testator's (Elmer's) wishes, e.g., the court may give the money to the National Crippled Children's Foundation.

Power of appointment

In the law of trusts, the power of appointment is a power or authority conferred by one person (the settlor) on another (the beneficiary) by a legal document, e.g., a deed or will, to select and nominate who shall be the successor beneficiary to receive the trust property on the termination of the original beneficiary's interest or death.

Example: Mark Henderson owns a farm in fee simple. In his will, Mark gives a life estate in the farm to his sister, Sarah, with the direction that after her life estate, Sarah appoint the remainder interest in the farm to her children as she wishes. Mark has given Sarah a power of appointment.

Cause of action
A cause of action is the right of a person to commence a lawsuit.

Necessaries
Necessaries are necessary items that supply the personal needs of an individual or family, such as food, clothing, or shelter.

Operation of law
Operation of law is the manner in which rights or liabilities pass to a person by the mere application to a particular transaction of established rules of law without the act or cooperation of the person (see pages 91 and 129).

Example: Rachel Brown transfers her shares of ABC, Inc., to Amelia Smith in trust to hold and invest for the benefit of Rachel's daughter, Janette. In the absence of a written agreement, Amelia becomes the trustee of the property by operation of law.

Condition precedent
A condition precedent is a condition that must occur before an agreement or obligation becomes binding. For example, if I state I will give you $5,000 when you graduate from college, your graduation is the condition precedent that will make me obligated (see page 173).

Condition subsequent
A condition subsequent is a condition that will continue or terminate an existing agreement once the condition does or does not occur. For example, I give you a car to use as long as you continue to go to college (see page 174).

Sovereign (governmental) immunity
Sovereign immunity is a common-law rule that exempts or frees the government from tort liability. Many states have limited or abolished this immunity.

Legal entity
A legal entity is something having legal existence, e.g., a natural or artificial person (corporation) that can sue or be sued.

Straw man
A straw man is a person used to accomplish the creation of a joint tenancy of real property between the existing owner of the property and one or more other persons by the owner transferring a deed to the straw man and the straw man immediately reconveying, by a second

deed, the property back to the original owner and the new co-owner as joint tenants.

Example: Wilbur Green owns his home in his name only. He marries and wishes to change the form of ownership of the home to a joint tenancy with his wife, Florence. In some states, in order to create the joint tenancy Wilbur is required to deed the property to another person, e.g., Mark Harper, the straw man, who then immediately signs a second deed and conveys it back to Wilbur and Florence as joint tenants. This would accomplish the change of ownership Wilbur desires.

Revocable trust

A revocable trust is a trust that the creator (the settlor) has a right or power to revoke (cancel). Generally, such a power must be expressly reserved by the settlor in the trust instrument.

Illustrating the Use of Trust Terminology

To better understand the meaning and use of trust terms, consider the following situation.

The Facts

Jack Alston Carter gives 600 shares of Successful Corp. stock to his financial adviser and best friend, Timothy Connor McEvoy, to hold in trust and to invest for the benefit of Jack's only child, Jill, and Jill's children. The provisions of this instrument (written agreement) require that Timothy pay Jill the income from the stock annually for the rest of her life and that after Jill's death the stock is to be given to Jill's children (Jack Carter's grandchildren).

THE CARTER TRUST

Trust agreement made between Jack Alston Carter, 110 Willow Street, City of Newton, County of Villerouge, State of Adams, herein referred to as Settlor, and Timothy Connor McEvoy, 1801 Lexington Avenue, City of Newton, County of Villerouge, State of Adams, herein referred to as Trustee, July 19, 1984.

Section I

Settlor hereby transfers and delivers to Trustee 600 (six hundred) shares of stock issued by Successful Corp., as described in Exhibit A, hereto attached and made a part of this document by reference, the receipt of which property is acknowledged by the trustee. Such property and any other property which may become later subject to this trust shall constitute the trust property, to be held, administered, and distributed by the trustee as herein provided.

Section II

The net income from the trust estate shall be paid to the following persons, herein referred to as income beneficiaries, in the following proportions and at the following times:

All of the net income payable to Jill Carter Hadley for her lifetime; then all of the net income payable to the children of Jill Carter Hadley who survive her until they reach the age of 21 (twenty-one).

Section III

No part of the property of this trust, except for the net income thereof, shall be distributed until the termination of this trust, as provided in Section II.

Section IV

On termination of this trust, as provided in Section II, all of the trust property, together with all its accumulated, undistributed net income, shall be transferred, conveyed, and distributed as follows:

To the surviving children of Jill Carter Hadley, share and share alike.

Section V

This agreement and the trust hereby created shall be governed by the laws of the State of Adams.

In witness whereof, the settlor and the trustee have executed this agreement on July 19, 1984 in the City of Newton, State of Adams.

Signatures

(Jack Alston Carter)

_____
                                        Settlor

(Timothy Connor McEvoy)

_____
                                        Trustee

[Exhibit A omitted here]

STATE OF ADAMS } ss.
County of Villerouge

On this 19th day of July, 1984, before me, a Notary Public within and for said County, personally appeared Jack Alston Carter and Timothy Connor McEvoy to me known to be the persons described in and who executed the foregoing instrument, and acknowledged that they executed the same as their free act and deed.

_____
                                 (Sally Madison)

My commission expires June 1, 1987.

Review of Terminology

Jack Carter, the person who creates the trust, is the *settlor,* the word being taken from the old legal language of "settling the property in trust." He may also be called the *trustor, donor, grantor,* or *creator.*

The *trustee,* the person to whom the property is tranferred in trust for the benefit of another, is Timothy McEvoy. The legal title to the property is generally held by the trustee, while the right to the use and benefit of the income from the property is enjoyed (held) by the *beneficiaries,* Jill and Jill's children. Another name for the beneficiary is *"cestui que trust"* which means "he for whom certain property in trust is held." Property held in trust (in our case the 600 shares of stock) is called the *trust corpus, trust fund, trust property, trust estate, trust res,* or the *subject matter* of the trust. A distinction is made between the *principal,* the property held in trust, and the *income,* which is earned by the principal and distributed by the trustee. In the instant case the principal would be the shares of stock, and the income would be the dividends paid by the corporation to the shareholders. According to the trust instrument's provisions, Jill is entitled to the income (dividends) from the *trust property* (stock) for the duration of her life. Jill's children are entitled to the *remainder* of the trust property, i.e, the principal (the stock) remaining after their mother dies. The children are called *remaindermen.* A trustee may also be given the power to distribute part of the *trust res* (the stock) to beneficiaries on the basis of financial need or simply the wishes of the beneficiary. In the above trust agreement, however, the trustee was not given this power. Powers are granted by the settlor when the trust is created (see Restatement [Second] of Trusts § 3 for definitions and § 37 for reservation and creation of powers).

Assignment 79

Mary Schrader gives a four-unit apartment building to her only nephew, John Simmons, to hold in trust for the benefit of his children (Mary's grand-nieces and grand-nephews). The provisions are that the monthly rents, less maintenance, etc., are to be given to the children until John's death, when ownership of the property will pass to them.

1. Who is the "cestui que trust" in the above case? What other terms are used to identify such persons?

2. Explain the difference between income and principal in reference to the above.

3. Who is the settlor? What other terms are used to identify the settlor?

4. Who is the trustee? What is the trustee's function?

Purposes of Trusts

A trust can be created for any lawful purpose but it must not contravene common or statutory law (Restatement [Second] of Trusts § 59).

Most trusts are created to distribute the income from the trust property to family members, friends, or charity and/or to preserve the trust property for later distribution to such persons on termination of the trust.   This can be accomplished during the settlor's lifetime by an *inter vivos (living) trust* or at death by a *testamentary trust.*

A trust is a practical way to transfer property for the best interests of a beneficiary. Upon the creation of a trust, the trustee assumes the duty of administering the trust, relieving, if desired, both the settlor (grantor) and the beneficiary from the responsibility of managing and conserving the property.   Numerous advantages of trusts become obvious. By means of such a device, the settlor can provide:

• Funds for the support of dependent family members, e.g., parents, spouse, children

• Funds for the college education of children

• Professional financial management for those inexperienced in handling large sums of money

• A method of sidestepping probate (court administration of a will), thus cutting costs by acting as a substitute for a will

• A preview of how well a trust works for a particular beneficiary while the settlor is still alive and able to alter or terminate the arrangement

• Savings on taxes (see Chapter 15)

Example: Clinton McBride supports his elderly mother, Martha. He realizes she is unable to handle her own financial affairs. Because of her age and frail health, Martha will most likely predecease Clinton. To transfer income-producing property by outright gift in order to have the income taxed in his mother's lower tax bracket would be illogical, since on her death the property will return to Clinton, reduced by his mother's estate and administration expenses. If Clinton places the property in trust for his mother, the income would be taxed to her without her receiving legal title to the property. (Later we shall see specifically what type of trust would be best.)

Example: Kathleen Shannon has been a homemaker and mother all her adult life. Her husband died two years ago, leaving her a substantial life insurance benefit. She wants to establish a fund for the college education of her two children. Because of inflation, she realizes that placing the money in a bank and collecting interest may not be the best way financially to achieve her purpose. Since she lacks business experience and the children are minors, the creation of a trust may be the answer.

Example: Kevin Perry, age 55, has recovered from a series of mild heart attacks. He owns property that he wants to transfer by will to his children, Abby and Kent. Since Kevin is concerned about the way the property may be used or spent by his children, he would prefer to transfer it now, while alive, in order to determine how well the property will be managed. An inter vivos trust under experienced and expert management could benefit the children now and continue after Kevin's death. The settlor may wish to create an inter vivos trust also because property placed in a living trust before the settlor's death might avoid administration delays and costs after death.

Example: Marc Livingston wants to avoid probate expense, ancillary proceedings, and the publicity of probate. He may therefore choose to create a revocable inter vivos trust to continue after his death.

Example: For income tax purposes, Shirley Held wants to transfer income-producing property to her daughter. Shirley is aware that a tax savings to her family may result. A short-term trust may be the answer (see page 295).

Example: Alfred Johnson, a 70-year-old bachelor, transfers all his stock to Expert Management Corporation to hold, invest and manage and to pay the income to him during the remaining years of his life. After his death, the trust property is to be returned to Alfred's estate to be distributed according to his will. This is an inter vivos express trust.

Example: It is possible for the settlor to achieve more than one objective by establishing an inter vivos trust continuing after death. Randy Johnson creates a trust naming himself as the beneficiary. In addition, Randy states that he wants to give the subject matter of the trust, the stock, to his nephew Charles after his death. He will thus be creating successive enjoyment of (successive interests in) the trust property—in himself before death and in Charles afterward. The income from the stock will be paid to Randy while he lives, and then the property will be transferred to Charles. If Randy is concerned that once the stock belongs to Charles, Charles will foolishly sell the stock and spend the money, Randy could empower the trustee to pay only the income to Charles until he reaches a certain age (see page 266 on spendthrift trusts).

Example: Anna wants to give a substantial amount of money to St. Mary's Hospital, but she wants to control the way the money will be used. She could establish an inter vivos trust and name herself as trustee with such powers (see page 253 for additional examples of public or charitable trusts).

Assignment 80

Jean-Luc Bernadois, a naturalized citizen, wishes to set up a trust for the benefit of his sister, Claire, who has recently arrived from Martinique and who has little knowlege of financial matters. He has government bonds valued at $25,000.

1. Assuming that Jean-Luc set up a trust, identify the settlor, the beneficiary, and the trust property.

2. Whom might the settlor appoint trustee? Why?

3. Would it be advisable to make a gift of the bonds rather than a transfer of them in trust? Why or why not?

The Elements of a Trust

Each trust has (1) a creator (settlor or grantor), (2) a trustee, and (3) a beneficiary. Since a trust differs from other legal transactions concerning property, such as the sale or gift of property, it is essential that the above participants' interest in a trust be understood. After a sale or gift of property, the entire title to it passes from seller to buyer (sale) or from donor to donee (gift). But after the creation of a trust, title to property placed in the trust passes to *two* persons. It is "split" into legal title and equitable title. The trustee receives the legal title; the beneficiary receives the equitable title. For this reason, the trustee and the beneficiary are indispensable to the existence of a trust. Once a trust is created, the settlor is not so important. Beyond furnishing property for the trust, the settlor drops out of the picture during the life of the trust unless the same person is both the settlor and either the trustee or beneficiary of the trust.

Another distinguishing feature of a trust as opposed to a sale is that *consideration,* i.e., payment to the settlor based on the trust property's reasonable value, is *not* a requirement for the creation of a trust. In other words, by placing property in trust for the beneficiary, the settlor does not require the beneficiary to pay for the transfer. A trust is a gratuitous transfer of property; consideration is not necessary (Restatement [Second] of Trusts §§ 28, 29).

Participants and Their Interests in a Trust

One person may convey property in trust to another for the benefit of a third person.

Example: Harding owns a farm, Blackacre, which he conveys by deed to Barrett in trust for the benefit of Stewart. Harding is the settlor and retains no interest. He has no further powers, duties, rights, or liabilities concerning the trust administration. Barrett is the trustee and has legal title. Stewart is the beneficiary and has equitable title. Blackacre is the trust property.

Or, one may declare himself or herself trustee for the benefit of another.

Example: Harding owns 1,000 shares of IBC, Inc., stock and declares himself trustee of the stock for the benefit of Stewart. Harding is the settlor and trustee who retains legal title. Stewart is the beneficiary and has equitable title. IBC, Inc., stock is the trust property.

Or, one person may convey property in trust to another for the benefit of himself or herself.

Example: Harding owns a farm that he conveys by deed to Barrett in trust for the benefit of himself (Harding). Harding is the settlor and beneficiary with an equitable interest in the farm. Barrett is the trustee and has legal title. The farm is the trust res.

Although customarily three parties participate in the creation of a trust, the law demands the involvement of at least two. As stated above, the same person cannot be the settlor, trustee, and beneficiary but the same person could be the settlor and trustee, or the settlor and beneficiary. The same person cannot be both sole trustee and sole beneficiary, thus holding both legal and equitable title, which would defeat the separation-of-title mechanism inherent in every trust.

The Settlor, Creator of the Trust

Provided the settlor manifests or makes a clear intent to establish a trust, no particular words are necessary to create the trust (Restatement [Second] of Trusts §§ 23, 24). A common provision is "to X, as trustee, to have and hold under the trust's provisions hereinafter set forth," but the settlor could establish a valid trust by giving property "to X for the benefit of Y." Use of the word "trust" or "trustee" is helpful but not mandatory. Also, as a review, the settlor's creation of the trust is not invalidated by its gratuitous nature, i.e., the beneficiary is not required to give the settlor consideration in return for the settlor's act of establishing the trust.

Assignment 81

Shirley gives Joanna $30,000 cash to hold and invest for the benefit of Carl. A trust is created even though the words "trust" and "trustee" were not used in its creation. The trust property is transferred as a gift. Neither Joanna nor Carl has purchased the property, so neither of them pays for receiving it.

1. Name the settlor, beneficiary, trustee, and trust corpus.
2. How does this trust differ from a sale or a gift?

"Who may be a settlor?" What qualifications or limitations exist that allow courts to enforce the trust the settlor creates? To be a settlor, a person must either own a transferable interest in property, have the right or power of disposing of a property interest, or have the ability to make a valid contract. Only those who have contractual capacity, i.e., who are not insane, intoxicated, or minors, can make an outright transfer of property into a trust (Restatement [Second] of Trusts §§ 18–22). Thus the limitations placed on persons to make contracts, wills, and other legal transactions are also limitations on settlors. Unless a person meets the qualifications, he or she cannot create a trust, and any attempt to do so is voidable. In addition, even though a person is qualified to make a trust, if the property transfer is accomplished through duress, fraud, or undue influence the settlor may avoid or cancel the trust.

Some trusts are created without a settlor. Such trusts are called *constructive trusts,* a form of an *implied trust* created (constructed) by law and enforced by the courts to prevent an injustice (see pages 263 and 259). Unlike the creation of a trust by the *intentional* acts of a settlor, a constructive trust is created by equity courts because of acts of a person or persons which are wrongful, disloyal, unconscionable, or even fraudulent.

Example: If Richard Brown steals $8,000 from his brother, William, and purchases a boat with the money, an equity court could decree (order) Richard to be a trustee of a constructive trust created by the court for the purpose of preventing an injustice. Richard would hold the boat as trustee for the benefit of William.

Once the settlor intentionally creates a trust, assuming he or she does not appoint himself or herself trustee or beneficiary, the settlor has no further rights, duties, or liabilities with respect to the trust administration. At the termination of the trust, the settlor may have the right to the return of the trust property, i.e., the settlor's reversionary interest (see page 58).

While he or she is alive, the settlor may expressly retain the power to revoke or cancel the trust and recover the trust property. When the settlor has such a power, the trust is called a *revocable trust* (Restatement [Second] of Trusts § 330). When the settlor does not reserve this power, the trust is "*irrevocable.*"

At first, the settlor may want the trust to be revocable in order to have the opportunity to see how well it works and what changes, if any, are necessary before the settlor makes the trust irrevocable. Eventually, the settlor may wish to make the trust irrevocable, since the retention of control over the trust arrangement, including the power to revoke, exposes the settlor to tax liability for the trust income and principal. Generally, the settlor must make the trust irrevocable and retain only limited powers over the trust before death; if these requirements are not met, the trust income and principal will be included in the settlor's gross estate and will be subject to estate and inheritance taxes (see Chapter 11 for further discussion on the tax consequences of trusts).

The Trustee, Fiduciary and Administrator of the Trust

The right or power to select the trustee is normally the settlor's but the right may be given to the beneficiary or to another. The trustee is the participant in a trust who holds legal title to the trust property for the benefit of another, the beneficiary. Any natural person having the legal capacity to take, hold, and own property may receive trust property as a trustee. A minor, an intoxicated individual, or an insane person has capacity to take and own property; however, such persons cannot properly administer a trust because their contracts are voidable (revocable). In other words, if such persons make contracts as part of their duties while administering the trust, they can avoid, disaffirm, or cancel their contracts because the contracts are voidable. Therefore, such trustees will ordinarily be removed and a new trustee appointed by the equity court on request of the beneficiary.

In most cases the settlor selects the trustee whose selection, if there is a question of capacity, ability, experience, or the like, the equity court either ratifies (confirms) or denies. In some instances, the settlor is considered to have only nominated a trustee; selection is the court's prerogative (Cal. Prob. Code § 1138.1[a][8] [West 1981]).

Natural or Legal Person as Trustee

Generally, the trustee selected is a person, either *natural* (e.g., a financial adviser) or *legal* (e.g., a private corporation authorized to act as a trustee by its charter and state statute, such as a trust company or bank). As a matter of practicality, settlors often choose banks as trustees because of the experience and expertise of their trust officers. The cost of hiring such trustees is always an important factor in their selection.

Example: Larry Parks, a natural person, has capacity (or ability in the legal sense) to take, hold, own, and administer property for himself; therefore he can do the same for the benefit of someone else in a trust. Before a trust is created, however, Larry becomes mentally ill (insane). Sally Parks, Larry's sister, transfers a substantial sum of money to Larry in trust to hold and invest for the benefit of their father, Samuel. If the beneficiary, Samuel, petitioned (filed an application to) the equity court and established that Larry was insane, the court would either decline to appoint Larry trustee or refuse to ratify his appointment, even though the settlor, Sally, named Larry the trustee. Here the court would do the former. In this case a trust is created, but the named trustee is incapable of administering the trust. As in this case and most other instances of failure to qualify by the trustee, fairness to the beneficiary demands that the trust be allowed to continue. Since Larry can and does hold legal title to the trust property but cannot be trustee, most states' statutes compel the transfer of the title from the incompetent (Larry) to the new trustee appointed by the court. This is accomplished by compelling Larry to transfer the trust property, i.e., the money, to the new trustee.

Example: The trust department of the Lincoln National Bank, a private corporation, is composed of persons who offer their services to the public as professional trustees. Since the bank's charter enables it to act as a trustee, it does so through these employees. Betty White transfers all her I.B.M. stock to the bank to hold and manage for the benefit of her son, Willard. The bank's trust employees would perform this service for an agreed-on fee.

Example: Ella Cunningham, age 80, transfers part of the assets of her estate in trust to her favorite niece, Paula, age 17. Ella is the beneficiary. Paula makes a contract as trustee, but she now decides not to honor her obligation, as she may do, being a minor. Since minors make voidable contracts, they may choose to avoid or cancel them. If Paula's act of avoiding the contract should dissatisfy Ella, Ella may request the court to remove Paula as trustee.

Municipality as Trustee

A municipality cannot act as trustee of a private express trust (see page 271), but it may act as trustee of a public trust, because this involves carrying out the purposes for which it was incorporated, such as the promotion of education, the relief of poverty, or the establishment of medical facilities (Restatement [Second] of Trusts § 96).

Example: Grant Morrissey left $400,000 to the City of Wakouta to establish a hospital. The City of Wakouta, acting through its elected officials, is the trustee of this money for the benefit of the public.

Federal or State Government as Trustee

The United States or an individual state may act as a trustee, but this trusteeship might present a problem in enforcement of the trust (Restatement [Second] of Trusts § 95). Because of the doctrine of sovereign immunity (a person cannot sue a government), both the national and state governments must consent to be sued when either is involved in litigation as a defendant.

Example: In 1851, the Namadji Band of Ojibwa Indians ceded land to the United States. The federal government acts as trustee to the Indians, administering the land for their benefit. Should any act of the United States (e.g., by the Bureau of Indian Affairs) cause the band to believe that the United States has violated the trusteeship, they may sue the federal government for relief in the U.S. Court of Claims. This is one instance in which sovereign immunity does not bar a beneficiary from suing a government acting as trustee.

Generally, unless a statute provides for a proceeding in court, or unless the legislature authorizes such a suit, the beneficiary cannot bring a legal action to force the federal or state government to perform the trustee's obligations. The modern trend, however, is to allow such suits.

Married Woman as Trustee

According to the old common law, a married woman could not administer a trust, could not contract, and could not convey property unless her husband joined in the conveyance. On application of the beneficiary, the court would remove the married woman as trustee and either direct her and her husband to convey the trust property to a new trustee or itself convey legal title to the trust property to a new trustee. Today a married woman has the right to act as a trustee, since modern legislation has given her the power to take, convey, and manage her property as if she were unmarried (Restatement [Second] of Trusts § 90).

Example: In 1770, Priscilla Atwood, a married woman, lived in the British Colony of Massachusetts. Priscilla could not be a trustee because her capacity to carry out the duties of trusteeship (e.g., to acquire property and hold it in her own name) was legally nonexistent. Before marriage, she had been able to exercise these rights to a limited extent but after marriage she came under the coverture (protection) of her husband, and only he could act as a trustee.

By 1870, the Massachusetts legislature enacted laws (known as Married Women's Acts) enabling Priscilla to perform many of the trustee's duties (e.g., to make a contract without her husband's consent). Such laws, however, did not cover every aspect of trusteeship duties, and a strong sentiment against women in public affairs reduced the chances that Priscilla would ever be a trustee.

By 1970, a change in social attitude toward women who engaged in business as well as enactment of equal rights laws have made commonplace the selection of a married woman as a trustee. Priscilla can be a trustee with the same rights, duties, and liabilities as her husband.

Alien as Trustee

Generally, an alien (foreigner) residing in the United States may act as a trustee (Restatement [Second] of Trusts § 93). By statute in some states, however, an alien cannot act as a trustee, and in other states, the restriction applies only to a non-resident alien.[2] In a state that has no statute on the subject, a court may remove a non-resident alien as trustee if, in the opinion of the court, the alien's serving as trustee would be detrimental to the trust. The original selection of the alien as trustee, however, will not void the trust.

Example: Graham Carmichael, born a British subject, became a citizen of the United States when he settled in Chicago years ago. His sister, Gabriella, retained her British citizenship, although she frequently visited him. On one of her visits, Graham declared his intention of making her trustee of a short-term trust for his own benefit. Gabriella is able to assume the office of trustee because the laws of Illinois (Ill. Rev. Stat., ch. 6, § 1 [1971]) permit a non-resident alien to take and hold property.

---

2. For example, California allows aliens to be trustees (see Cal. Civ. Code § 671 [West 1982]), but Louisiana does not (see La. Rev. Stat. Ann. § 9:1783 [West 1965]).

Non-resident as Trustee

A main objection to having a non-resident trustee is the difficulty the court faces in supervising the administration of the trust. The court's jurisdiction does not cross state lines. It would be impossible for anyone to serve process (papers declaring the commencement of a civil lawsuit) on such a trustee (Restatement [Second] of Trusts § 94). Although some states permit a non-resident to act as a testamentary trustee, most, by statute, require the non-resident to appoint a resident on whom process may be served if any legal problem should arise that requires court action.

Assignment 82

Below is a list of potential trustees. As a review, after first checking the statutes of your own state, place an X in the space provided according to whether the potential trustee on the list does or does not have the capacity to be a trustee of a private trust. In addition, in the column provided, place an X if the beneficiary in the trust has the right and power to apply to an equity or probate court for the removal of the original trustee because such a trustee is not permitted to serve by law.

Potential Trustee	Has Capacity	Lacks Capacity	Beneficiary Can Apply to Remove Trustee
Bank			
Municipality			
Adult man			
Adult woman			
Married woman (common law)			
Married woman (today)			
Corporation			
Minor			
Federal government			
State government			
Insane person			
Alien			
Non-state resident			

Co-Trustees

Ownership by co-trustees of trust property has always been construed as joint tenancy of that property. Under the rules of common law, a settlor could become one of the co-trustees only by transferring the property to another person (a straw man) who had agreed to receive and immediately retransfer legal title to the trust property to the group of co-trustees of which the settlor was a member. The fact that the owner of property could not confer joint tenancy on himself or herself and another (because the tenancy so created would lack the unities of time and title); see page 63, necessitated the straw man, transaction. The straw man, being a third person, could create a valid joint tenancy. In many jurisdictions today, however, a settlor may convey directly to himself or herself and the co-trustees (Restatement [Second] of Trusts § 100).

Example: Clive Yarborough plans to create a trust for the two Vietnamese war orphans adopted by his friends Laurence and Victoria Sutton, making Laurence and Victoria co-trustees with himself. The trust property is Clive's farm. In his state, Clive may make himself trustee and appoint Laurence and Victoria co-trustees at the same time without having to convey the farm to another person who would then reconvey it to the three as joint tenants.

A trust exists only when the trustee has an equitable obligation to administer the trust property for the benefit of another and when someone exists to enforce that obligation. Therefore, a sole trustee cannot be a sole beneficiary, since there would be no one to enforce the trust. If the sole trustee, who holds legal title to the trust property acquires the equitable title of the sole beneficiary as well, the legal and equitable titles merge, and the trust ends. Where the sole trustee is also one of several beneficiaries, or the sole beneficiary is also one of several trustees, the legal and equitable titles do not merge, and the trust is valid (Restatement [Second] of Trusts § 99).

Example: A settlor, Ray Norton, signs a declaration of trust naming himself trustee of four stock certificates for the benefit of himself and his wife, Vera. Because he holds complete legal title but only partial equitable title to the trust property, Ray is allowed to fill all three of these roles (settlor, trustee, and cobeneficiary) while Vera is alive. When Vera dies, however, Ray holds the entire equitable as well as legal title. The trust ends.

Acceptance or Disclaimer of Trusteeship

Normally, the settlor will name a trustee, but if the settlor does not, a trustee can be appointed by a court (Restatement [Second] of Trusts § 108). Since the trust imposes burdens on the trustee, the trustee has the right to renounce or reject (disclaim) the trust. The person named as trustee is free to choose whether to accept or reject the appointment by words or conduct. Once having rejected, however, a person does not have a second chance to accept. To avoid delay in the trust administration, the court will appoint a substitute (Restatement [Second] of Trusts §§ 35, 102).

In the absence of a definite acceptance or rejection, any positive act such as taking possession of the trust property will confirm the trustee's acceptance. Likewise, the failure of a trustee to do or say anything to indicate acceptance within a reasonable length of time will be construed as a disclaimer.

Example: Lydia Metaxis creates a testamentary trust for her grandchildren, naming her friend, Isabel Leclerc, trustee. Isabel feels that she would be unable to carry out the task of administration. Therefore she executes a disclaimer of responsibility as trustee and files it with the probate court handling Lydia's will. The disclaimer follows.

I, Isabel Andrewes Leclerc, named as trustee under the will of Lydia Metaxis, deceased, respectfully decline to act as said trustee.

In witness whereof, I have executed this instrument at the City of Puentavilla, Tarpon County, Florida.

Isabel Andrewes Leclerc

January 16, 1984

Once disclaimed, a trust cannot thereafter be accepted. The best way to eliminate any doubt of the trustee's acceptance or rejection is for the trustee to deliver to the proper person, e.g., the settlor, a signed document of the decision to accept or disclaim.

Removal or Resignation of Trustee

Trusteeship is a solemn undertaking. After accepting the duties outlined in a trust, a trustee can be relieved of the duties and office by the settlor, by death, by removal by the equity or probate court, or by resignation (Restatement [Second] of Trusts §§ 103, 104, 105, 106). Resignation is an exercise of the trustee's own discretion and must be accepted by the proper court (a court of equity or probate court). Removal of the trustee is an exercise of the court's discretion when it believes the continuation of acts by the trustee would be detrimental to the beneficiary's interests (Restatement [Second] of Trusts § 107). Grounds for the removal of a trustee include:

- Lack of capacity
- Commission of a serious breach of trust
- Refusal to give bond when bond is required
- Refusal to account for expenditures, investments, and the like
- Commission of a crime, particularly one involving dishonesty
- Long or permanent absence from the state
- Showing of favoritism to one or more beneficiaries

• Unreasonable failure to cooperate with the co-trustee if one exists (Restatement [Second] of Trusts § 107)

Mere friction between the trustee and the beneficiary is not sufficient grounds for removal.

Unless required by a state statute, by terms of the trust, or by an order of a court of equity, a trustee is *not* required to take an oath that he or she will faithfully discharge the duties, or to secure a certificate of authority from a court. Whether or not an oath is required, the trustee still has a fiduciary duty to the beneficiary. In some jurisdictions, becoming a trustee depends on performance of one or more of these acts, and failure to perform the act prevents the person initially from assuming the office. In other jurisdictions, failure of the trustee to perform a required qualifying act does not prevent assumption of the office but is considered a breach of trust allowing the court to remove the trustee at the request of a beneficiary and to appoint another trustee (Restatement [Second] of Trusts § 107).

Cost of a Trustee

Trustees perform work for the trust when they buy, sell, invest, receive income, and the like on behalf of the beneficiary, and they must be compensated. The settlor may provide a reasonable allowance for the trustee in the trust instrument; if the settlor does not, state statutes fix the amount, or in the absence of such statutes, the courts will fix a just annual compensation. There is a feeling (originating in common law principles) that the trustee should not make an unreasonable profit from the trust; therefore the actual amount of compensation is usually a small percentage of the trust's annual income.[3]

Duties of the Trustee

In general, a trust does not exist unless an active, enforceable duty is placed on the trustee, such as a duty to manage the property in some manner or to exercise discretion or judgment (Restatement [Second] of Trusts § 25). The settlor's mere order to the trustee to hold the property in trust without any direction as to its use or distribution does not suffice to create an active trust; it creates, instead, a passive trust which the law declares void (see page 256).

---

3. In a testamentary trust, the probate court may set the annual fee for a corporate trustee, such as a bank, at three-fourths of one percent of the fair market value of the trust estate. In determining whether the fee charged is reasonable, the court considers the size of the estate, the services performed, the time spent and the results achieved. In an inter vivos trust, fees are generally negotiated. State statutes may also set fees in some cases.

Example: In his will, George, the decedent, gives $100,000 to Howard expressing the hope that Howard will use the money "for religious and family purposes." Such phraseology does not indicate that George is "settling" or creating a trust. He has not indicated the duties Howard must perform as the trustee of an active trust. George might well have intended the $100,000 as a gift to Howard with "advice" on its use.

Assignment 83

Vernon Crockett drew up a trust agreement with his neighbor Benjamin Nichols, setting aside $5,000 for the first of Vernon's children who should marry. Vernon directed Benjamin to deposit the money in the Mechanic's Bank and to withdraw it at the time appointed. Is this a valid trust (i.e., does this trust impose active duties on the trustee, Benjamin)? Why or why not?

A trustee can exercise only those powers that are expressly given by the trust instrument or those that the court will construe as impliedly given by the instrument (Restatement [Second] of Trusts § 164). Modern trusts commonly give the trustee discretion to make decisions on matters that could not be foreseen by the settlor. For example, the trustee may be authorized to expend principal as well as income when, in the trustee's opinion, it is necessary for the education or medical care of a beneficiary.

Trusteeship is subject to certain rules, obligations, and guidelines.

• The trustee has the duty to carry out the terms of the trust (Restatement [Second] of Trusts § 169). The trustee is personally liable, i.e., must pay out of personal funds, for any loss sustained by failure to perform the duties of the trust unless the failure can be justified. There is no personal liability for loss sustained if the trustee has exercised the degree of care which a reasonable person would exercise under the circumstances.

• The trustee cannot delegate the performance of personal duties (Restatement [Second] of Trusts § 171).

• The trustee has a fiduciary duty to use reasonable skill, prudence, and diligence in the performance of trust duties (Restatement [Second] of Trusts § 174).

• The trustee is not permitted to profit personally from the position as trustee, other than to receive the compensation allowed by contract or by law.

• The trustee is required to invest the money or property in enterprises or transactions that will yield an income to the estate (Restatement [Second] of Trusts § 207).

- The trustee must keep accurate records so that it can be determined whether the trust has been properly administered (Restatement [Second] of Trusts § 172).

- The trustee has a duty to preserve the trust property from possible loss or damage.

- If the property includes accounts receivable or outstanding debts, the trustee has the duty to collect them.

Duty to Use Ordinary, Reasonable Skill and Prudence (Restatement [Second] of Trusts § 174)

Example: Nathan Maxwell transfers 100 shares of stock to William Mann in trust to hold and invest for the benefit of Nathan's invalid mother, Marilyn.

Whether or not a trustee, such as William Mann in the example above, receives compensation for his services, he must use at least ordinary care, skill, and diligence in the execution (performance) of the trust. The degree of ability required may be increased if William actually has greater than normal abilities or if he, as trustee, represented to the settlor that he possessed unusual capabilities before the trust was created. Therefore, professional fiduciaries, such as banks and trust companies with specialists in various areas of trust work, may be held to a higher standard because they secure a trust because of their claims of special expertise and because of the rule that more is expected of a trustee who has a special skill or knowledge of the subject. At the very least, professional fiduciaries must measure up to the standard of skill and prudence of the average, ordinary corporate trustee located in the community where the trust is created.

The law would not hold William, as trustee, responsible for every error in judgment he might make, but he is obliged to use the care and skill of an ordinary capable person who is charged with conserving a trust. If William disregards this obligation, he cannot defend himself against liability on the grounds that he acted in good faith or did not intentionally misuse the trust property. In addition, William, as trustee, cannot disclaim any personal liability on the grounds that he was simply following the practices that the settlor had always followed when ordinary skill and prudence would dictate another course.

Assignment 84

In performing the following acts, is William Mann violating his duty of reasonable care of the trust property? Why or why not?

1. William receives a dividend on one of the shares of stock in the amount of $90. He uses this to buy a birthday present for Marilyn.

2. One of the stocks William holds is performing poorly. On the advice of another executive in the corporation where William works, he sells this stock and invests in Goldbrick, Inc., which subsequently falls in value below the level of the stock formerly owned.

Duty of Loyalty (Restatement [Second] of Trusts § 170)

The loyalty duty applies to all persons in a fiduciary capacity.
Example: The will of Colin Wilcox appoints Judith Ames trustee of a $150,000 business, The Wilcox Bakery, for the benefit of his minor sons, Reynold and Richard.

Loyalty to the beneficiaries of the trust is one of the most important duties of a trustee. The duty of loyalty means that the trustee is obliged to act solely in the interests of the beneficiary. What constitutes a disloyal act would include any transaction by Judith as trustee which engenders a *conflict of interest* between herself and the beneficiaries of the trust, or between the beneficiaries and third persons. A conflict of interest is the creation of circumstances by the fiduciary (trustee) in the administration of the trust which benefits someone other than the beneficiary, thereby establishing the conflict of interest. The other party benefited is most often the trustee, but it could be any person. In the case above, a disloyal act by Judith is not automatically void. The beneficiaries may elect to disaffirm and avoid the transactions or to treat them as legal and binding. As trustee, Judith must avoid placing herself in a position where her personal interest or that of a third person might conflict with the interest of the beneficiaries.

As noted above, the trustee must act in the sole and exclusive interests of the beneficiaries. For example, buying or leasing trust property to herself, or selling her own property to the trust as an investment, would be acts of disloyalty by Judith. It does not matter that Judith acted in good faith or with honest intentions, or that the beneficiaries suffered no loss because of her disloyal acts. It is also immaterial that the trustee has made no profit for herself from her disloyal transaction, even though in most cases she does benefit in some manner. When responsible for such disloyal acts, the trustee (Judith), may be held liable for the amount of gain to herself or a third person, and the court may even remove her from the trusteeship by decree. These quite strict standards are designed not only to prevent actual unfair dealing but also to keep trustees initially from getting into positions of conflict of interest.

Assignment 85

Judith Ames performs the following acts in the course of trusteeship. Are they disloyal? Are they voidable? What additional facts, if any, would you need in order to answer these questions?

1. Judith buys a display case from the bakery, paying fair market value for it. Reynold was fully aware that she did this.

2. Colin's executor is preparing to sell some real estate as instructed by the will. Judith causes one piece of property to be withheld so that a friend may buy it. Her friend pays the amount of the property's appraised value.

3. As trustee, Judith persuades the manager to sign a contract to buy flour from the Hanrahan Co. for the next year. Hanrahan does not offer the lowest contract price for flour, nor is there any evidence that its product is better than that of other companies; however, the Ames and the Hanrahans have been friends for many years.

Duty to Take Possession of, Protect and Preserve Trust Property (Restatement [Second] of Trusts § 176)

Example: John Yeats creates an inter vivos trust consisting of stocks, bonds, and items of personal property for the benefit of his son, Roderick. He names as trustee his sister, Marcela.

In accordance with the terms of the trust instrument, Marcela has the duty to take possession of the property. If the trust property consists of money or goods and chattels, she should take immediate possession of the chattels and open a separate fiduciary bank account for the cash. Such an account should be identified as a trust account, i.e., "Marcela Yeats, Trustee for Roderick Yeats." Since Marcela handles funds for the benefit of Roderick, she has a duty to keep the trust property separate from her own individual property and from property held for other trusts. Since the trust property includes such property as promissory notes, bonds, shares of stock, and deeds to real estate, Marcela should take possession of the documents representing title (ownership) to such property and place them in a safe deposit box registered in the name of the trust. All trust property should be clearly distinguished from Marcela's own property. If it is not, Marcela will have the burden of proving which belongs to whom and might even lose her own property in the process if a court rules that the mixture of trust and personal property belongs to the trust. Possession is usually obtained from the settlor, or, if the trust was created in a will (a testamentary trust), from the named executor or representative. Failing to act promptly and reasonably in securing possession of the trust property makes the trustee personally liable for any loss caused by such negligence.

In brief, Marcela has the duty to perform whatever acts a reasonably prudent businesswoman would deem necessary in order to preserve and protect the trust property. Such acts would include placing cash in a trust account; filing legal documents such as deeds and mortgages; depositing important legal papers, documents, and valuable personal property in an appropriate place such as a safe deposit box; paying taxes on realty and maintaining that property in reasonable condition to avoid deterioration; transferring shares of stock to the appropriate person's name; maintaining adequate insurance coverage on all appropriate trust property; and the like.

Assignment 86

Are the following acts examples of a violation of the trustee's duty to preserve and protect the trust property? What additional facts must you know to assist you in answering the following?

1. Marcela withdraws a substantial part of the trust fund from its bank account and gives it to a friend to invest. Her friend is not a professional investor, and the advice proves short sighted financially. All the investments end as losses.

2. Same facts as in 1 above except the friend's advice is very lucky. The earnings on the investments suggested by Marcela's friend triple the trust account.

3. A building to which she holds title for Roderick has a defective staircase. While visiting the premises, Flora Atkinson falls down the stairs and injures herself. Was Marcela's neglecting to repair the staircase a breach of duty?

Duty to Make Trust Property Productive by Investment (Restatement [Second] of Trusts §§ 181, 227)

Example: Carmine diGrazia, a widower living in Maryland, created a trust of $100,000 and his interest in a building construction business in his will for the benefit of his two sons, Paolo and Carlo. He appoints as trustee his cousin, Catarina, his housekeeper and newly naturalized citizen. Carmine dies, and Catarina assumes trusteeship.

Catarina must invest the trust property in income-producing investments as soon as possible. Delay could constitute negligence and make her liable for any loss. Of course, Catarina's investment policies may be controlled by the authority granted her by Carmine, by the court, and by statute. Today some states set by statute a list of specific types of investments that may or must be made by the trustee. The law of the state of Maryland gives examples of the statutory investments fiduciaries may make.

Md. Code Ann. § 15–106 (1974), *Lawful Investments*

(a) *List of lawful investments*—The following investments shall be lawful investments for any person:
   (1) Debentures issued by federal intermediate banks or by banks for cooperatives;
   (2) Bonds issued by federal land banks or by the Federal Home Loan Bank Board or the Home Owners Loan Corporation;
   (3) Mortgages, bonds, or notes secured by a mortgage or deed of trust, or debentures issued by the Federal Housing Administration;

(4) Obligations of national mortgage associations;

(5) Shares, free-share accounts, certificates of deposit, or investment certificates of any insured financial institution, as defined in § 13–301(g) of this article;

(6) Bonds or other obligations issued by a housing authority pursuant to the provisions of Article 44A of the Code, or issued by any public housing authority or agency in the United States, when such bonds or other obligations are secured by a pledge of annual contributions to be paid by the United States or any agency of the United States;

(7) Obligations issued or guaranteed by the international bank for reconstruction and development.

* * *

(c) *Liability for lack of reasonable care*—This section shall not be construed as relieving any person from the duty of exercising reasonable care in selecting securities.

* * *

(e) *Other investments*—This section shall not be construed to make unlawful any investment not listed in this section.

Catarina must periodically review her investment methods and policies. If Catarina fails to examine or review at regular intervals the investments that she has made, she can be liable for the loss or lessening of the value of the trust property.

Assignment 87

Catarina makes the following investments. Do they violate her duty to make the trust property productive? What additional facts must you know to assist you in answering the following?

1. Carmine had often complained that his building construction business was unprofitable. At the time of his death, he was preparing to sell it to a business associate. Catarina, who was also named executrix of Carmine's estate, executes the sale in the name of the estate and adds the money to the trust fund.

2. Catarina buys bonds issued by the Vittore Emanuele Lodge, to which Carmine had belonged. The bonds pay 8% interest annually. Several of Catarina's neighbors and friends hold the same kind of bonds. Other kinds of debentures costing the same amount would have yielded higher rates of interest.

3. After Carmine's death, Catarina is preoccupied with details of the funeral and putting his affairs in order. She neglects to deposit part of the cash portion of the trust, i.e., $8,000, in a bank until it is too late to earn interest on the money for the quarter. Carmine kept the $8,000 in a small safe at home.

Duty to Make Payments of Income
and Principal to the Named Beneficiaries
(Restatement [Second] of Trusts § 182)

Example: Celia Brosniak, the oldest child in her family, is named
trustee of a large sum of money in the will of her aunt. The trust is for
the benefit of her brothers and sisters, who are to receive income from
the money until the youngest attains majority. Then Celia is to receive
the balance of the trust fund according to the will.

Most trusts establish two kinds of beneficiaries. There are *income
beneficiaries,* who receive the net income from the trust property for a
determined number of years or for the beneficiaries' lives; and there
are *remainder beneficiaries,* who receive the principal of the trust after
the rights of the income beneficiaries in the trust are satisfied.

If the settlor provides for separate disposition of both trust income
and trust principal, it is advisable that the trustee open two accounts,
one for the principal and one for the interest. In the example above,
this is necessary. The aunt not only designated income-receiving
beneficiaries but also chose Celia to receive the principal as a lump
sum. Celia should open a separate principal account so that she may
readily take her gift when the time comes.

It may happen that Celia will obtain money or property other than
what she was given in trust during the course of the trust administration. In such cases she must decide whether to credit the receipt of
such property to the income or principal account of the trust. Most
states have resolved this problem for the trustee by adopting the
Uniform (or Revised Uniform) Principal and Income Act (revised 1962).
These acts define in detail the duties of the trustee in regard to the
receipt of property and its disbursement into the income or principal
account. The general rule for disbursement is that money paid for the
use of the trust property and any benefit received from the employment
of that property is to be treated as trust income, while substitutes for
the original trust property, such as the proceeds from the sale of the
property, are to be considered trust principal.

Assignment 88

If the trust agreement authorized Celia in the above example to
distribute income "at best, quarterly, and at least, annually," would she
be acting within her fiduciary obligations if she withheld certain
amounts from the quarterly distributions for possible emergency expenses and thereby created a separate fund?

Duty to Account (Restatement [Second] of Trusts § 172)

Example: Nicholas Walheimer creates an inter vivos trust for the
benefit of his mentally handicapped son, David. He names Felix Basch

trustee of the fund, which consists of $65,000 worth of stock. Felix is given the power to sell and invest the stock. Nicholas thereafter dies. Frederika Wolfram is appointed David's personal and property guardian.

Felix has the duty to render an account of his administrative activities at reasonable intervals to those who are "interested" in the trust, namely the settlor, Nicholas, while alive, and the beneficiary, David, acting through his personal and property guardian, Frederika. The trustee, Felix, alone has the right to manage and control the trust property. He must retain trust documents and records, secure and file vouchers for all expenditures and disbursements, and keep an accurate and complete set of books. He is obliged to show these to Nicholas and Frederika on request. Felix has a fiduciary duty to account voluntarily (e.g., quarterly) for changes in the trust property. If the trustee fails to perform these duties, the trustee may be removed by the court, denied compensation, or even charged with the cost to the beneficiary of an accounting proceeding.

Assignment 89

Felix has been a trustee for two years. He tries to make periodic reports on the trust, but this is not always feasible, because he frequently travels while conducting business. In performing the following acts, did Felix violate his duty to account? (These are opinion questions, but you must give reasons for your answers.)

1. Felix sells some stock from the trust and buys land in the Santo Affonso Valley. Frederika asks him to account for this, so he sends her copies of the contract of sale and the deed of title.

2. At the end of the calendar year, Felix sends a balance sheet indicating the financial status of the trust property but neglects to include a dividend paid one week before the issue date of the balance sheet. Later he discovers his error. He sends to Frederika a receipt for payment of the dividend, informing her that he will rectify the error on the next annual statement.

3. Felix has the second annual statement prepared by an accountant. Having read it, Federika complains that it is too technical for her to understand. Felix replies that the statement is correct to the best of his knowledge and that he has fulfilled the duty to account required of a trustee.

Liabilities of Trustee and
Remedies of the Beneficiary and Others
(Restatement [Second] of Trusts §§ 201, 222–26)

A breach of trust by the trustee may occur in a variety of ways, which in turn determine the remedies available and the party who is entitled

to bring suit. To restore the damage committed by a trustee, the beneficiary has the right to judicial remedies at law or a suit in equity. **Example:** Joseph Connors becomes the trustee of $25,000, which he is to invest in stock and to pay any dividend to Anna Evert. When the first dividend arrives, Joseph deposits it in his personal bank account. He has violated a law by misappropriating the money. Anna should pursue an action at law for damages against him.[4]
Example: Barbara McCoy becomes the trustee of $25,000. The money is to be invested and the dividend, if any, paid to Jean Wilson. Barbara continually postpones investment of the principal. Because of her neglect and delay, Barbara is not performing her duties as a trustee. Jean should pursue an action in equity against Barbara to have her removed as trustee.

Liability of Trustee to Beneficiary

Beneficiaries have certain remedies when there has been a breach of trust by a trustee:

• The beneficiary can maintain a suit to compel the trustee to reimburse the trust for any loss or depreciation in value of the trust property caused by the trustee's breach of the trust instrument (Restatement [Second] of Trusts §§ 199, 205).
Example: Sharon has agreed to act as trustee for Joan's benefit. The trust property is a lake cottage. Sharon has obtained the deed but has not insured the property. Lightning strikes the cottage, and it is destroyed. Sharon would be personally responsible and liable for this loss.

• The beneficiary can obtain an injunction, i.e., a court order, to compel the trustee to do, or refrain from doing, an act that would constitute a breach of trust. The beneficiary can bring a civil suit in equity against the trustee asking for the court order.
Example: Stephen Adams holds shares of stock in trust for Evelyn Sandberg. According to the terms of the trust agreement, he is not authorized to sell the stock. The value of the stock has recently increased substantially. Stephen intends to sell the stock. Evelyn, on learning of the pending sale, could obtain an injunction from the equity court forbidding the sale by Stephen.

• The beneficiary can trace and recover the trust property that the trustee has wrongfully taken, unless the property has been acquired by a purchaser who, believing the trustee has a right to sell, pays an adequate price and purchases the property without having been informed of the breach of trust (Restatement [Second] of Trusts §§ 202, 284).

---

4. An action at law is a civil law suit commenced by the person, called the plaintiff, who seeks the remedy at law called damages, i.e., to be compensated monetarily.

Example: In the preceding example, Stephen sells the stock to Jane Brown, who pays full market value for the stock unaware that Stephen has no right to sell the stock or that the stock is trust property. Jane becomes the owner of the stock. Evelyn would not have a right to sue Jane, a good-faith purchaser, but she would have a right to sue Stephen for damages because of his fraud.

• The beneficiary can request the court of equity to remove the trustee for misconduct and to appoint a successor trustee (Restatement [Second] of Trusts §§ 107, 108, 109).

Example: Ronald Caster is the trustee and Vincent Price is the beneficiary of a trust. The trust agreement gives Ronald the discretion of determining the amount of income from the trust property which Vincent shall receive each year. The amount actually given to Vincent by Ronald causes a great deal of friction between them. Vincent can petition the court to remove Ronald as trustee, but the court will not do so unless Vincent can prove that the hostility causes Ronald to mismanage his trusteeship.

• The beneficiary can sue for specific performance (see page 216) to compel the trustee to perform the duties created by the terms of a private trust (Restatement [Second] of Trusts §§ 198, 199).

Example: According to the trust agreement, the trustee, Monica Murphy, is to give the trust property to the beneficiary, Julie Anderson, on Julie's attaining age 21. Six months have passed since Julie's twenty-first birthday, and Monica has not transferred the property. Julie sues Monica in the court of equity for specific performance of the agreement. If Julie succeeds in proving Monica in violation of her duty, Monica must complete the transfer.

• The beneficiary can sue for breach of the trustee's loyalty (Restatement [Second] of Trusts § 206). Breach of loyalty by the trustee includes many things. In general, breach of loyalty is any action by the trustee which upsets the trustee-beneficiary relationship. It results from the trustee's failure to administer the trust solely in the interest of the beneficiary.

Example: By will, Hollis Stately leaves his ranch, Bluelake, to Lavinia Turner in trust for his son, Francis, directing her to sell or exchange Bluelake for investment securities. Lavinia sells Bluelake for $200,000, and uses the money to buy bonds which she herself owns. Lavinia has breached the duty of loyalty by "self-dealing" with trust money (the proceeds of the sale).

Liability of Trustee to Others

The trustee also faces liability to persons outside the trust relationship (third persons) for breaching contracts or committing civil wrongs against them in the course of the administration of the trust. In such cases, the law usually holds the trustee personally liable to the third

person and disregards the fact that the trustee was acting as a representative. The trustee alone is liable. The trust estate does not have to pay damages (Restatement [Second] of Trusts §§ 262, 264, 291, 292).
Example: Christopher Doherty transfers his race horses to Lorna Sach in trust for the benefit of his niece. Lorna contracts with a feed company to provide oats for the horses, signing the contract "Lorna Sach, trustee of Bird River Stable." She neglects to pay for the grain. Lorna herself, not the trust estate, would have to pay damages if a court ordered a judgment to be entered against her because of her negligence.
Example: Lorna allows a fence on the boundary of the stable and a neighbor's farm to fall into disrepair so that some of the horses stray into the neighbor's field. Lorna would be personally liable for any damage.

Trustees of public as well as private trusts may be found guilty of breach of duty. The means by which the beneficiaries of a public trust may remedy the breach, however, are not as simple as a private trust. Only persons having a special interest in the trust, such as individuals who are beneficiaries at the time of the alleged breach, a co-trustee, or the attorney general of the state where the trust is administered, may bring suit against a trustee of a public trust. Usually, it is the attorney general or a similar public prosecutor who initiates a suit on behalf of the community that benefits from the trust (Restatement [Second] of Trusts §§ 291, 386).
Example: Ewell Bennett devised land to the city of Millville to be used as a recreation area. The recreation facility was built on the land and used for four years before a fire totally destroyed it. Thereafter, city planners decided to use the site for a school. Gwendolyn Bennett, Ewell's niece, would not be entitled to bring an action against the city, the trustee of this public trust, to enforce her uncle's wish, because she does not have the legal right to do so.

The Beneficiary, Recipient of the Trust Property or Benefits

Every valid private trust must have a beneficiary (see page 000 for discussion of private trusts.) In a private trust, the beneficiaries must either be identified by name, description, designation of class to which the beneficiaries belong, or if no beneficiary is in existence at the time the trust is created, the trustee must be able to ascertain the identity of the beneficiary within the period of the Rule Against Perpetuities (Restatement [Second] of Trusts § 112). One exception to this is a charitable trust, where it is sufficient that the beneficiaries be members of the public at large or a general class of the public (Restatement [Second] of Trusts §§ 122, 123, 364, 375).

As noted above, to create a valid private trust the settlor must name or sufficiently describe a beneficiary or co-beneficiaries to receive the equitable interest in the trust property. If the trust instrument describes the beneficiary too vaguely, a court of equity cannot validate the trust. There must be someone to enforce the trust and to ensure that the trustee will faithfully perform the previously mentioned duties. Consequently, the beneficiaries of a trust must be specifically identified. A trust established to pay the trust income to "whomever the trustee selects" without adequately describing the persons or class of persons from which the selection is to be made would be too vague and would fail. Such a trust is invalid.

Any person, including infants, insane persons in some states, and public or private corporations, may be a beneficiary in a trust, but incompetents and minors generally require guardians to act as beneficiaries for them. Trusts in which aliens, the United States, a state, a municipality, and a foreign country are beneficiaries have been upheld. In sum, the beneficiary may be any entity capable of taking title to property in the manner as a person, whether natural or created by law, e.g., a corporation, state, or nation. The beneficiary of the trust, however, need not have capacity to hold property or to make a contract, since the trustee has legal title to and control of the trust property. Many trusts are created because the beneficiary lacks legal or actual capacity to manage without assistance, e.g., a trust to benefit an insane person using a guardian appointed to act as beneficiary for the insane person (Restatement [Second] of Trusts § 117).

Example: Martha Kirk places $20,000 in trust for the benefit of the Red Cross. The Red Cross is a "corporate person." It is a definite beneficiary. This trust is as valid as if Martha had created it for the benefit of a natural person.

Example: Giovanna Bonetto belongs to a card club. The members meet once a month to play cards, amuse themselves, and perform works of charity. She dies, leaving a trust for the purpose of the club's continuing to meet and carry on its activities. This trust will fail because the card club, as such, is not a "person." The individual members are. Had Giovanna's trust named them individually as beneficiaries, the trust would have been valid.

Although it is required that the beneficiaries be definite they need not be, and frequently are not, described by name but rather by class designation. Examples of such designation are "my grandchildren" or "my issue," in which cases the identification of the beneficiaries is ascertainable, i.e., capable of being determined (Restatement [Second] of Trusts § 120). Words such as "friends," "family," and "relatives," used to designate beneficiaries, have sometimes caused trusts to fail for lack of definite beneficiaries, because such terms have broad and varied application. A trust to benefit "relatives," however, occasionally proves an exception to the rule. A court, construing "relatives" to mean those who would inherit the settlor's property according to the statutes of descent and distribution rather than those who are related to the settlor either closely or remotely by either blood or marriage, would in all likelihood uphold the trust (Restatement [Second] of Trusts § 121). Similarly, interpretation of the word "family" to mean "the settlor's spouse and issue" leads to the same result (Restatement [Second] of Trusts § 120b). Note that this requirement of definiteness of beneficiary for a private trust directly opposes the requirement of indefiniteness of beneficiary for a public (charitable) trust.

Assignment 90

1. Harding Mulholland lived at the home of his niece, Cecelia, and her husband, Edwin. He provided in his will that a trust be set up for the benefit of his nieces and nephews, Cecelia being the only one of that class at the time. Subsequently, another niece, Teresa, was born, and Cecelia died in the same year. When Harding died, Edwin petitioned the court to set aside the trust, claiming that Harding neither knew nor could have known of the current beneficiary, Teresa. Should the trust fail for lack of a definite beneficiary?

2. Willis Rokeby lives in Bangor, Maine. For five months each year, he visits his daughter in Texarkana. He hires Jacques Santin, a citizen of Canada, to take care of his house in Maine. He pays Jacques a small salary and creates a testamentary trust of the house and surrounding land for Jacques' benefit. After Willis' death, his sister, named trustee in the trust instrument, claims that Jacques cannot be beneficiary because he is not subject to the laws of either Maine or the United States. Is she correct?

Nature of the Beneficiary's Interest (Restatement [Second] of Trusts § 130)

Generally, the effect of a transfer in trust is to divide the interest in property, consisting of legal title and equitable title, so that the legal title is given to the trustee and the beneficial title or equitable title is given to the beneficiary (Restatement [Second] of Trusts § 2). The length of time the beneficiary holds the equitable interest in the trust property may be limited to a period of years, to the life of the beneficiary or that of someone else, to a condition precedent, to a condition subsequent, or to the nonoccurrence of a specified event.

Example: Patrice Avery sets aside stocks and bonds for three inter vivos trusts for each of her children: The first to be created for her son, Vinton, on condition that he return to the family home in West Virginia. This trust is based on a condition precedent. The second to her daughter, Susanna, on condition that she continue to support Patrice as she had been doing. This trust is created on a condition subsequent. The third to her daughter, Alberta, as long as she continues to study medicine at State University. This trust is created on the non-happening of a specific event, e.g., Alberta's switching to another course of study or another school.

Note that both Susanna's and Alberta's trusts begin immediately but the possibility of the premature termination of the trusts exists, whereas Vinton's does not begin until he has complied with the condition precedent.

The beneficiary's equitable interest in realty (real property) usually passes on his or her death to the beneficiary's heirs or devisees; personal property passes to the personal representative, e.g., the administrator or executor, of the beneficiary (see page 250). Another possible result is that the trust instrument itself may provide that the beneficiary's interest terminates on death, as in the case in which the beneficiary receives a life estate.

There may be more than one beneficiary to a single trust. Multiple beneficiaries usually hold the property as tenants-in-common unless the settlor expressly makes the beneficiaries joint tenants or tenants by the entireties. The doctrine of survivorship applies if the co-beneficiaries are joint tenants or tenants by the entireties (Restatement [Second] of Trusts § 113). For example, if Charles and Dennis are co-beneficiaries as joint tenants, and Charles dies, Dennis will then be the sole beneficiary and will own the entire equitable interest in the trust property, just as any joint owner with the right of survivorship succeeds to full ownership upon the death of the other joint owner.

The beneficiary of a trust is free to alienate (transfer) the interest in trust property by mortgage or devise, in the absence of any restriction imposed by statute or by the terms of the trust, to the same extent that a person who holds both equitable and legal titles is free to do so (Restatement [Second] of Trusts § 132). In some states, all transfers of beneficial interests must be in writing and signed by the beneficiary; in other states, this requirement applies only to the transfer of real property (Restatement [Second] of Trusts § 139).

Unless prohibited by statute or the trust agreement, beneficiaries may ordinarily transfer their interest in a trust by an assignment (see page 216). This legal transaction allows the beneficiary to transfer to another the benefits of the trust. This may be done to make a gift of the trust benefits or to pay the beneficiary's debts. If the beneficiary makes successive assignments of the interest in trust property (assigns the entire interest to more than one assignee, thus creating a conflict among the assignees), in some states the first assignee to notify the trustee that he or she now occupies the place of the beneficiary may compel the trustee to assent to this arrangement (Restatement [Second] of Trust § 163). In other states, assignments are effective in the order in which they are made.

Example: Greg receives an income as a beneficiary of a trust. He assigns his interest (transfers his right to receive income) to June. Thereafter, June receives the income from the trust.

Example: Barbara, the beneficiary, is entitled to receive the rents from her father's farm, Westborne. She assigns this right to the Leadenhall Co. in payment of a debt. One month later she assigns the same interest to be collected over the same period to the Montauk Kennel Club to buy a pedigreed greyhound. Only one creditor is entitled to receive the rents. Depending on the rule in her state, it would be either the first to notify her brother Miles, the trustee, or simply the Leadenhall Company, to whom Barbara first assigned the rents. In this latter case, Montauk would have no rights at all.

Creditors may attach the beneficiary's equitable interest in trust property unless statutes or trust provisions exempt the interest from creditor's claims (Restatement [Second] of Trusts § 147). If statutes exempt a legal interest from creditor's claims, a corresponding equitable interest of a beneficiary in trust property is also exempt, e.g., homestead exemptions (which apply to both legal and equitable interests). The method by which a creditor reaches an equitable interest varies from state to state. The only remedy in some states is a creditor's bill in chancery (equity) in which the creditor commences the lawsuit in an equity court. In other states, the equitable interest is subject to execution, attachment, and garnishment by the beneficiary's creditors just as if it were a legal interest.

Trust Property

The trust property is the property interest that is transferred to the trustee to hold for the benefit of another. It is sometimes called the *res, corpus, principal,* or *subject matter* of the trust. Any transferable interest in an object of ownership may become trust property. This includes ownership of real or personal property. Thus, a fee simple estate in land, a co-owner's interest (joint tenants, tenants-in-common, and the like), a mortgage, a life estate in land, a right to remove coal, a business interest, promissory notes, bonds or shares of stock (securities), a trade secret, copyright, patent, or cash could serve as trust property. Examples of non-transferable property are government pensions, existing spendthrift trusts, or tort claims of wrongful injury, i.e., the victim's right to sue a negligent party for personal injury. Non-transferable property interests may not be the subject matter of a trust.

A trust involving the transfer of personal property only may be created orally, but a settlor transferring title to real property to a trust must comply with the state statute, i.e., the Statute of Frauds, requiring a written agreement establishing the trust. The latter requirement is designed to prevent fraud and perjury (see further discussion below). The terms of the written agreement (*trust instrument*) as designated by the settlor must include the purpose of the trust, the length of time the trust will last, and a description and conveyance of the trust property. It must also include the names of the trustee and beneficiary, and the powers, duties, and rights of such parties, including how much the beneficiaries are to receive, and when they will receive it. A particular form or particular language to frame the trust is not necessary as long as the settlor makes these elements clear.

Assignment 91

Read the trust instrument on page 288 and determine whether the requirements in the preceding two paragraphs have been met.

As noted above, the English Statute of Frauds was enacted in 1677 to prevent fraud and perjury between sellers and buyers by requiring certain kinds of contracts to be written. Its American counterparts, drawn chiefly from sections 4 and 17 of the original statute, demand that a written contract, signed by the parties, be used in certain transactions. When trusts involve the transfer of land, they must conform to the state Statute of Frauds and thereby be in writing if they are to be enforced. If the trust property transferred in an inter vivos (living) trust is an interest in land, the Statute of Frauds requires that the trust be written setting forth the details of the trust (Restatement [Second] of Trusts, § 40). If a trust is created by the will of the settlor, there must be a writing that meets the requirements of a will (see Chapter 10 and the example of a trust instrument on page 288). Many U.S. states have enacted requirements similar to those of the English Statute of Frauds. Arkansas is an example.

> Ark. Stat. Ann. § 38–106 (1962). *Declarations, Creations, or Assignments of Trusts or Confidences to Be in Writing*
>
> All declarations or creations of trusts or confidences of any lands or tenements [structures built on land] shall be manifested and proven by some writing signed by the party who is or shall be by law enabled to declare such trusts, or by his last will in writing, or else they shall be void; and all grants and assignments of any trusts or confidences shall be in writing signed by the party granting or assigning the same, or by his last will in writing, or else they shall be void.

In addition to requiring a written agreement whenever transferring land in trust, the method of transfer is also strictly regulated. Land must be transferred by specific legal documents, e.g, either a deed or a will. Personal property, on the other hand, may be simply delivered to the trustee.

Example: Sharon signed a trust agreement transferring title to Greenvale, a country home, to Susan in trust for the benefit of Thomas. Sharon executed and delivered the deed to Greenvale to Susan. Sharon and Susan are parties to a trust agreement (trust instrument). Sharon is the grantor. Susan is the trustee and holds the legal title which she received from Sharon. Thomas is the beneficiary (cestui que trust) of the agreement and holds equitable title.

The agreement satisfies the state Statute of Frauds because it is written. It also complies with requirements for trusts of this nature, i.e., trusts to which real property is transferred, and is therefore, enforceable.

Assignment 92

Simon Rothstein executes a trust instrument with the Third National Bank, placing his lakeshore property in trust for the benefit of his nephew, Norman. Norman, however, does not know of the trust. Simon dies one year later. His widow, Evelyn, contends that the trust is not valid, not having been signed by Norman. Norman contends that it is valid. Who is right?

As noted above, the trust instrument must either specifically describe the trust property or clearly define the manner to be followed in identifying it. The validity of a trust depends on its enforceability. If a court is to enforce a trust, the trust property must be *in existence* (i.e., definite and certain on the *date* the trust is created, or definitely ascertainable) and *owned* by the settlor.

Example: Mary Holland is an investor and collector of art. If Mary attempts to create a trust by declaring herself trustee of the next work of art she buys, no trust is created, because the trust property is neither specifically identifiable nor owned and in existence at the time of the trust creation.

Example: Today Mike Wilson declares himself trustee of the stocks he will own on the next December 1st. No trust is created. Likewise, a trust consisting of "securities which I may purchase in 1985" or "all gas and oil leases which I may possess by next August 1st" is too vague to be enforced (Restatement [Second] of Trusts § 74).

On the other hand, a testamentary trust created in the "residue of the decedent's estate" *is* valid, even though the exact amount of the residue cannot be determined until the decedent's assets and liabilities are known. In this case, the facts needed to specifically identify the amount of the residue do exist on the date the trust is created, i.e., the date of the testate's death.

Example: In an inter vivos trust instrument, Alicia Schell states, "I give to Joan Warfield, to hold and to manage, the bulk of my savings and checking accounts for the benefit of Roberta Polenek." This instrument creates a valid trust. The trust corpus is not stated, but it is ascertainable. It is the amount of money in Alicia's checking and savings accounts on the date of the trust instrument's execution.

Assignment 93

While driving her car, Mavis Allenby struck and seriously injured Marvin Bright. Marvin now has a cause of action (right to sue in civil court) against Mavis. Can Marvin make the cause of action the subject matter of a trust? Answer the question on the basis of your own state law.

The fact that trust property may change from time to time during the trust period does not make the trust void.

Example: Alex Knight, trustee of real estate for the benefit of Letita Kruse, has the power of sale and reinvestment. He sells part of the land for cash and deposits this cash in the Citizens Bank. He buys bonds for the trust and pays for them by drawing a check on the Citizens Bank. He has effected three changes in the trust property— real estate into cash, cash into a claim on the bank (i.e., a right to withdraw the amount deposited), and the claim on the bank into bonds. The trust property has changed, but the trust is still valid.

Classification of Trusts

All trusts may be divided into two major categories, *express* and *implied*. The express trust is established by voluntary action and is represented by a written document or an oral declaration. A simple statement that the settlor intends to hold property in trust for another creates a trust by declaration. Again, no special words are necessary to create a trust, provided the intent of the settlor to establish the trust is clear. In most jurisdictions, as previously mentioned, an express trust of real property must be in writing to meet the requirements of the Statute of Frauds.

Express trusts embody deliberate acts by a settlor, either orally (i.e., a declaration) or in writing (i.e., a trust instrument). According to the purpose for which it is created, an express trust falls into the following categories: (a) private or public (charitable) trusts; (b) active or passive trusts; (c) inter vivos (living) or testamentary trusts.

Implied trusts are created not by deliberate acts but by the presumed intent of the settlor or by a decree (order) of the equity court. Implied trusts are categorized as either resulting trusts or constructive trusts (see Figure 9.1).

Figure 9.1 Classification of Trusts

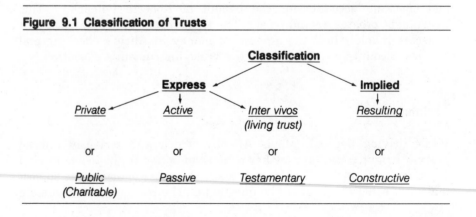

Express Trusts—Private vs. Public (Charitable)

A *private trust* is created expressly (orally or in writing) between a person who has the power to be a settlor and one who has the capacity to be a trustee for the financial benefit of a certain named beneficiary or beneficiaries. It is one of the most common types of trusts. (The following chapter will deal exclusively with the formation, required elements, and function of a private trust and will conclude with steps used in drafting a private trust.)

Example: Loraine Katz owns a one-third interest in a boutique. In her will she gives the interest to her nephew, David, to hold and manage in trust for the benefit of her niece, Tracy. Loraine, the owner of the interest, is the settlor. David, to whom she conveys the legal title to the one-third interest, is the trustee. Tracy, who is to receive the benefit of the interest (i.e., one-third of the profits of the boutique), is the beneficiary. This is a private (between two individuals) express (definitely established as a trust) testamentary (established by will) trust.

Assignment 94

Sidney Benchman transfers (assigns) the royalties to his book, to which he holds the copyright, to his business adviser, Martin Lorenz, to hold and invest for the benefit of Martitia Hughes.

1. Does the settlor intend to create a trust?

2. Is there a trustee to administer the trust?

3. Is trust property included in the instrument?

4. Is there a beneficiary or cestui que trust?

A *public* or *charitable trust* is an express trust established for the purpose of accomplishing social benefit for the public or the community (Restatement [Second] of Trusts §§ 348, 349). Although charitable trusts are public trusts, the beneficiary of the trust need not always be the *general* public. The trust fund, however, must be designated either for the benefit of the general public, e.g., a charitable trust benefiting a hospital, *or* a reasonably large, indefinite class of persons within the public who may be personally unknown to the settlor, e.g., a charitable trust benefiting the deaf in a certain city (Restatement [Second] of Trusts §§ 362, 364, 368–374). If the terms of the trust limit the distribution of its fund to named individuals rather than to an indefinite class of persons, the trust will not be classified as public. Instead, it would be a private trust. In the majority of states, the true test for creation of a valid public trust is not the indefiniteness of the persons aided by the trust but rather the amount of social benefit that accrues to the public (Restatement [Second] of Trusts § 375). Also, the purpose of the charitable trust must not include profit-making by the settlor, trustee, or other persons (Restatement [Second] of Trusts § 376). Therefore, the essential elements of an express public (charitable) trust are:

- The settlor must intend to create a public trust
- A trustee must be named to administer the trust
- Property must be transferred to the trust
- A charitable purpose must be expressly designated
- The general public must be benefited or,
- An indefinite class of persons must be named beneficiaries

Examples of charitable trusts that advance the public welfare are trusts created to maintain or propagate religion, religious education, and missionary work; further health and relieve poverty and human suffering by establishing institutions, funding research into the causes of certain diseases, or by direct aid of food, clothing, shelter, and medical care to the needy; found or maintain educational institutions, art galleries, museums, libraries, or aid students or teachers; care for and maintain public cemeteries; erect monuments to public figures or national heroes; construct and maintain public buildings or improvements, such as an irrigation system or a playground; further patriotism; conserve natural resources and scenery; or prevent cruelty to animals.

Example: Agnes Swanson died testate, providing in her will, "I give State University $100,000 to provide scholarships for mothers on welfare in the field of nurse's training." In the absence of other evidence, an express, testamentary, charitable trust is created.

Agnes is the settlor, State University is the trustee, and "mothers on welfare" are the beneficiaries. The $100,000 is the trust property. Agnes intended to create a public or charitable trust, which desire she expressed in her will. The class of persons to be benefited is smaller than "the general public" but sufficiently large and indefinite enough to enable the trust to be classified as public. For example, Verneta Baker, a mother, begins to receive welfare a year after Agnes dies; therefore, Agnes could not have named Verneta a beneficiary personally. Verneta was not a member of the class to be benefited when Agnes made her will, but now she qualifies. She and others in the same situation are indefinite beneficiaries.

The mere fact that the purpose of a trust is to give money to others does not make it a charitable trust. The settlor of a charitable trust must describe a purpose which is of substantial public benefit.

Assignment 95

Mark Nelson gives $100,000 to Luke Mellows to be distributed as Luke feels is appropriate for the benefit of Vietnam orphans formerly living in DaNang.

1. Did the settlor intend to create a trust?

2. Is there a trustee to administer the trust?

3. Is trust res (property) included?

4. Is there a charitable purpose expressly designated?

5. Will the general public be benefited?

6. Are there indefinite beneficiaries within a definite class who are the persons who actually receive the benefit?

The presence of these characteristics indicates an express, public (charitable) trust.

Where it is clear that the donor intended the trust to be performed exactly as indicated or not at all, the trust fails (terminates) when it is not possible to follow such direction. However, in the absence of this clear intent by the donor in the trust agreement, the law will *not* permit a *charitable* trust to end (fail) even though the original purpose has been accomplished or can no longer be achieved, or because the beneficiary no longer exists. Here the courts will apply the doctrine of "cy-pres" (an abbreviation of the old French words "cy pres comme possible" or "as near as possible") (Restatement [Second] of Trusts § 399).

Example: In 1955, Etta Barranger established a trust fund to provide relief to victims suffering from a particular kidney disease. In 1975, an inventor created a kidney machine that cured the disease. In order to continue the trust, it will be necessary for the court to apply the cy-pres doctrine by finding a charity whose purposes correspond "as nearly as possible" to Etta's motives in setting up the trust. For example, the court might apply the trust principal to a charity which aids the victims of a liver ailment.

The court will direct that the trust fund be held for another purpose that will be "as near as possible" to that intended by the settlor. The rationale behind the application of cy-pres is that the law tries to continue the operation of charitable trusts so as not to terminate public benefits. If a charitable trust fails for lack of foresight on the part of its settlor or simply due to modern-day advances in science, a court will review the settlor's intent in creating the trust and if possible transfer its fund to a more viable charitable use approximating that intent. The courts are anxious for the public to receive the benefits. If the court, however, is to apply the doctrine to a charitable trust, the settlor's intent must be broad and general, and it must not be restricted to one specific objective or to one particular method of accomplishing the purpose of the trust. The cy-pres doctrine applies only to charitable trusts.

Assignment 96

The will of Nehemiah Bridwell, dated 1925, created a trust for the benefit of widows of men who died while serving on whaling ships. In 1960, Jared Bridwell, Nehemiah's descendant, petitioned the court to terminate the trust and not to apply the cy-pres doctrine, alleging that the trust's purpose had become unnecessary since statistics showed that deaths "while serving on whaling ships" were negligible because of improved safety standards and the diminished whaling industry. What action should the court take?

Express Trusts—Active vs. Passive

The features that distinguish active trusts from passive trusts are the obligations of management and administration which active trusts impose on the trustee. An *active trust* is an express trust that can be either private or public (charitable). Implied trusts, such as resulting and constructive trusts (see pages 259 and 263), are *passive trusts,* as are some public trusts. A settlor who desires to create an express private *active* trust must give oral or written affirmative powers and duties to a trustee to perform discretionary acts of management or administration for the benefit of named beneficiaries or, according to the prevailing view, the trustee must be directed to convey or transfer the trust property. On the other hand, a *passive* trust commissions the trustee to perform, at most, only minor acts of a mechanical or formal nature and often creates no administrative duties at all. The trustee's mere holding of the trust property for the beneficiary with no obligations or powers to administer the trust indicates that the trust is *passive.* Modern-day passive trusts stem from the failure of the settlor to create an active trust, either accidentally, e.g. through a poor choice of words in the trust instrument, or deliberately, e.g., an attempt to evade the law for the settlor's own purposes. In order to avoid the accidental creation of a passive trust, the drafter must properly designate the active functions or duties of the trustee.

The English Statute of Uses (see page 217) has an important effect on passive but not active trusts. In feudal society the persons with legal title to land owed various duties to their lords, e.g., military support or a portion of their crops. By transferring legal title to one person for the *"use"* of a second (similar to today's passive trust), the second person could enjoy the land without being liable for the feudal duties. **Example:** Alianor conveys a fee simple estate to Baudoin for the use of Alianor, thus tranferring legal title to the fee to Baudoin. Alianor retained equitable title. Alianor would have been entitled to the use (benefits) of the land but would not have been bound to perform feudal duties.

In 1536 the Statute of Uses was passed by the English parliament with the intent to abolish such "uses" because they furnished a means of evading the duties of the landholder. The statute in effect said that the legal existence of the use would be ignored and that the person who received equitable interest (the beneficiary) of the transfer would receive the legal title as well. In the above example, after enactment of the statute, Alianor would retain legal title, and Baudoin would receive nothing, i.e., the transfer would have been ineffective. Thus the statute is said to have "executed" (liquidated) the "use" and merged the equitable title with the legal title declaring, in effect, that the two titles could not be separated. Today, U.S. statutes based on the Statute of Uses similarly affect passive trusts, i.e., trusts in which the trustee has no active duties to perform. The statute abolishes the passive trust (use) and creates legal title in the beneficiary (cestui que trust). The statute has no effect on active trusts (Restatement [Second] of Trusts §§ 67, 69). The majority of the states consider the Statute of Uses part of their common law. A few states have statutes that abolish passive trusts and declare any attempt to create them as passing the legal title directly to the beneficiary.

A contemporary example of a trust declared passive by the courts would be: Silvia appoints Arnold trustee of securities for the benefit of Harriet but neglects to give him duties to perform. Legal title to the securities should have passed to Arnold, but in such an instance it passes directly to Harriet, who holds equitable title as well. Since the legal and equitable titles are held by one person, no trust is created. Another example would be the following: If in similar circumstances Silvia had declared herself trustee for Harriet but failed to undertake active duties, the trust would have been executed also. Silvia, the holder of legal title, would have failed to pass equitable title to Harriet. Again, no trust is created. Additional examples involving resulting and constructive trusts are on pages 259–265.

Assignment 97

Neal Sanderson owns a farm, Springlake, which he conveys by deed to Rudolf Meyerling for the benefit of Barbara Jacoby. Sanderson directs Meyerling to rent the land to tenants and to use part of the income produced thereby to pay taxes and to apply the remainder for Jacoby's benefit at his own discretion. Answer the following and compare your answers with the statements in the next paragraph:

1. Is the trust express or implied?

2. Is the trust private or public?

3. Are there administrative duties that the trustee must perform?

4. Is the trust active or passive?

This trust is a private, express trust. Neal Sanderson, the settlor, conveyed his farm, the trust property, to Rudolf Meyerling, the trustee. Barbara Jacoby is the beneficiary. The trust is active because

Meyerling has the duties of renting the farm, collecting income (rent), paying taxes, and paying the remainder of the income to Jacoby.

Express Trusts—Inter Vivos vs. Testamentary

Both *inter vivos trusts* (Restatement [Second] of Trusts §§ 17, 31) and *testamentary trusts* (Restatement [Second] of Trusts §§ 33, 54) refer to express trusts either private or public in nature. As the generic names of these trusts imply, they are created at different times in the settlor's life: inter vivos (pertaining to a gift in trust made "between living persons") and testamentary (pertaining to a gift in trust made after death as a testament, i.e., as part of a last will). In the event of a question of whether a trust is inter vivos or testamentary, the criterion will be the time at which the trust became effective (for examples, see page 274, where the reasons for creating trusts, especially inter vivos trusts, are discussed). If the settlor wishes to see how well the trust operates while the settlor is alive, then an inter vivos trust must be established. Otherwise the inter vivos trust differs little from the testamentary trust. Both types of trusts are widely employed as a means of conserving property for the benefit of a surviving spouse and children.

Assignment 98

Carolyn's will dated May 1, 1984, reads, in part: "I devise the residue of my property to the Fourth State Bank as trustee, pursuant to the trust agreement of October 19, 1978, for the benefit of my daughter, Charise, to be held and managed in accordance with the terms of said agreement."

1. Has Carolyn created a valid trust by this instrument? Is it testamentary or *inter vivos*? Why?

2. How might Carolyn have created a trust of the kind opposite to your answer in 1?

Assignment 99

Herb gives Janet $40,000 to be distributed as she sees fit for the benefit of poor Amish children in Kentucky between the ages of 6 and 12. Determine whether the essential elements of an express, active, inter vivos, public trust are present:

1. Does the settlor intend to create a trust?

2. Is there a trustee to administer the trust?

3. Is trust res included?

4. Is there a charitable purpose expressly designated?

5. Is the general public benefited?

6. Are there indefinite beneficiaries within a definite class who are the persons who actually receive the benefit?

Implied Trusts—Resulting and Constructive

The second major category in the classification of trusts is the *implied trust,* subdivided into *resulting trusts* and *constructive trusts.* Both types of implied trusts are also passive trusts. Implied trusts are trusts imposed on property by the courts when trust intent is lacking. Such trusts are said to be created by "operation of law". In these trusts there is no settlor in the sense in which an express trust has a settlor. The settlor who creates an express trust does so with intent, even though the details (i.e., the language of the trust instrument or identities of the trustee or beneficiaries) might be vague enough to require court interpretation. It is impossible, however, for any person in the capacity of settlor to create an implied trust, since these, by definition, are mechanisms imposed by the equity court.

Resulting Trusts

A resulting trust is created because of inferred or presumed intent of a property owner (Restatement [Second] of Trusts §§ 404–460). There are basically three kinds of situations in the United States in which the creation of an implied, resulting trust may occur:

Situation One When one person's money has paid (supplied consideration) for an investment in land or personal property but the legal title of the property is conveyed to another person, the law presumes that a resulting trust, called a *purchase money resulting trust,* has been created for the benefit of the person who paid the consideration. That person receives equitable title to the property. The person to whom the property was conveyed, i.e., the holder of legal title to the property, is considered the trustee (Restatement [Second] of Trusts § 440).

Since a purchase money resulting trust is created by implication and operation of law, it need not be evidenced by writing. However, if there is a conflict later, it may be difficult to prove whether the conveyor intended to make a gift to the alleged trustee instead of allowing a resulting trust to be created by implication.

Courts generally require very careful proof to establish a resulting trust. The evidence must be strong and unmistakable, and the burden of proof rests on the party seeking to establish the resulting trust. Because of the difficulty in establishing the proof, the court allows parol evidence (see page 218) to be used in these cases. The grounds for the court's presuming a purchase money resulting trust are that a person who makes a gratuitous conveyance most likely intends to make a gift, but a person who furnishes consideration (pays for) a conveyance to another probably does so for reasons other than gift-giving, e.g., to facilitate resale of the property, repay a debt, obtain services of management from the transferee, or seek to avoid creditors. Seven states (Indiana, Kansas, Kentucky, Michigan, Minnesota, New York, and Wisconsin) have abolished or modified purchase money resulting trusts by statute.

Example: Aron Samuels, age 70, buys 200 shares of Honeywell, Inc., stock with money on which he needs to live. He instructs the corporation's agent to issue the certificates in the name of Miriam Slater. Miriam is not related by blood or marriage to Aron. In the absence of further evidence, Miriam holds the share as trustee in a *resulting trust* for Aron.

Situation Two When a settlor creates an express private trust gratuitously (without requiring payment of the beneficiary) and the trust fails or is declared void for any reason except that it has an illegal objective, a resulting trust arises for the benefit of the settlor or the settlor's successors (Restatement [Second] of Trusts § 411). In other words, the trust arrangement no longer exists, but the trust property does, and with it the problem of disposing of it. Should the settlor be allowed to recover the property? In general, the law deems such recovery to be the only fair solution. However, if the court rules that the private express trust was created for an illegal purpose, it generally does not decree (order) a resulting trust for the benefit of the settlor but instead declares the trust void. In such cases, the settlor of an illegal trust is generally not allowed to recover the trust property from the trustee since equity discourages such transactions and will not be a party to their enforcement.

A resulting trust also arises when a charitable trust fails in an instance where the court cannot apply the cy-pres doctrine. The trust property is held by the trustee for the benefit of the original settlor or the settlor's successors.

Example: Perrin Williams conveys his farm, Oakburne, by deed to Lee Hunter in trust for Stephen Grant. Unknown to Perrin, Stephen is dead at the time of the conveyance. The trust property now reverts to Perrin, but until Perrin takes possession of it, Lee holds Oakburne in a resulting trust for Perrin.

Example: Harmon Course, wishing to keep in the family his majority interest in the Burmingham Power Company, inserts in his will a provision that the stock will be held by the Transylvania Trust Company in trust for his grandchildren. This attempted trust is declared void by the court for contravening the state Rule Against Perpetuities (see page 181). The Trust Company does *not* hold the stock upon a resulting trust for Harmon's successors. The stock returns instead to the estate, where it will be distributed according to the will's residuary clause or, if no such clause exists, according to the statutes of descent and distribution, i.e., intestacy statutes.

Assignment 100

Allen Greenfield gratuitously transfers by deed his lakeshore cottage to Patricia Williams in trust for the benefit of Allen's son. Unknown to Patricia, Allen makes the transfer to avoid claims of his creditors. The creditors seek to have the trust set aside so that they can attach the property in payment of their claims. Patricia agrees that the trust should be declared void because of its illegal purpose, but she claims that, as an innocent party, she should be entitled to keep the property since equity should not return it to the fraudulent settlor. Who wins? Answer the question according to the laws of your own state.

Situation Three When the corpus (property) of a private express trust exceeds what is needed for the purpose intended by the settlor, or some part of the trust property remains after the trust has accomplished what its settlor had intended, the court may establish a resulting trust for the benefit of the settlor or the settlor's successors (Restatement [Second] of Trusts § 430).

Example: Regina Andrews died testate providing in her will "I give my 200 shares of Highly Successful, Inc., stock to Harriet Backer in trust to pay the income to Timothy Collins for life. After Timothy dies, there is a resulting trust for Regina's successors of the principal and future income, which remains in the trust fund, i.e., the stock.

Assignment 101

In 1980, Eustacia devises (gives) by deed all the land she owns in Pike County to the Westside State Bank for the benefit of her grandchilden and their heirs. Her grandchildren, Daniel and Dorothy, die in 1983 without leaving heirs or wills. Two months later, Eustacia dies.

1. What kind of trust, if any, did Eustacia create in 1980?

2. What kind of trust, if any, is formed in 1983?

3. Dorothy's cousin, Laverne, claims the land because she is Dorothy's next-of-kin. Is she entitled to it?

4. Who receives the equitable and the legal titles, respectively?

As noted previously, the English Statute of Frauds, which serves as the model for U.S. statutes on the same subject, required written instruments of certain important transactions. In the spirit of section 7 of the English statute, the majority of U.S. jurisdictions require, either by enacted law or by legal tradition (case law), that trust agreements concerning real estate be "reduced to writing."

A notable exception to this is the *resulting trust*. Since its creation depends not on the act of any person, but on the working of the law, it does not fall within the category of ordinary express trusts and therefore does not have to follow the requirement of written evidence as to its existence. In most circumstances, the proof of the existence of a real estate trust requires written evidence. However, the law allows resulting trusts to be proved by verbal (parol) evidence. Difficulties surrounding a purchase-money resulting trust illustrate the importance of this exception to the parol evidence rule (see page 218) (Restatement [Second] of Trusts §§ 429, 439, 460). As previously stated, a purchase-money resulting trust involves two parties: one who pays for the property but does not receive legal title to it, and one who receives legal title but does not pay for the property (see page 259). Does the person who paid (furnished) consideration hold equitable title to the property, or is the transaction a gift from the payor to the recipient? The transaction has the outward appearance of a gift; indeed, when the parties are related by blood or by marriage, there is a strong tendency, even a presumption, to regard it as a gift. A court may proceed to determine the true nature of the transaction in the following manner:

• It may presume that the transaction was intended by the parties to be a purchase money resulting trust instead of a gift. (A presumption is not an indication of how the court feels about the issue or what its ruling will be. It is simply a contention that must be proved or disproved.)

• If the party who contends that it was a gift can offer in support convincing evidence that overcomes the presumption that it was not a gift, the presumption will fail.

• But failure to present enough evidence will allow the opposing party (whom the presumption supports) to win.

Since the resulting trust is not controlled by the parol evidence rule, either party may use oral or verbal evidence to prove the case, even when such evidence contradicts the terms of a written instrument (Restatements [Second] of Trusts §§ 440, 441, 458, and generally §§ 440–460).

Example: Harold Wilkerson buys a farm with his own money from James Mason and directs James to convey the farm by deed to Harold's wife, Maude. Maude receives legal title to the farm even though Harold supplied the purchase money. Because Harold and Maude are married, it appears that the farm is a gift from husband to wife. In fact, a presumption to that effect would be made. If anything should impair the marital relationship, e.g., the spouses are divorced, causing Harold to want the farm returned to him, he must prove that the transfer to Maude was not intended as a gift and request that the equity court declare the farm in a purchase money resulting trust for his benefit.

In summary, payment for property to which the payor does not receive legal title raises the presumption of a resulting trust for the payor's benefit unless the parties involved are spouses or family members. Evidence that can be used to corroborate the presumption may include: proof of an oral agreement between the parties; acts of the parties before, at the time of, and after the transfer; or other proof which indicates that a gift or loan was not intended. For instance, if Alma's parents furnish the consideration for a transfer of property to Alma, the parents earning ability, financial status, age, health, and the like will be considered in order to determine whether the parents intended a gift to her or a resulting trust for the benefit of themselves.

Assignment 102

Upon his insolvency, Oliver Sherwood was forced to sell the building in which he conducted business. His children agreed to contribute to a fund to buy back the building. Martha Sherwood, Oliver's eldest child, presented $100,000 to the owner of the building as the repurchase price. The owner of the property re-conveyed the legal title to Oliver in return for the $100,000. According to the laws of your own state, what kind of trust is this? Why? Could Oliver again sell the building as he had previously? Could he devise (will) it to a friend or relative?

Constructive Trusts

A constructive trust is *not* created by the stated intent of a settlor. That is an express trust. Nor is a constructive trust created by the implied or presumed intent of a property owner whose acts cause the equity court to enforce a trust established by operation of law. That is a resulting trust. The point of similarity between a constructive trust and a resulting trust is that both are implied, passive trusts. Resulting trusts arise by implication of law or by an equity court decree that declares the property holder to be a trustee as a result of implied intent or because of presumed intent of the parties because of the consequences of their acts. Constructive trusts are not based on express or even implied or presumed intent. The constructive trust is exclusively a creation of the equity court established for the purpose of rectifying a wrong or preventing unjust enrichment for the wrongdoer (Restatement [Second] of Trusts § 1e; notes preceding §§ 404 and 440).

Even though both resulting and constructive trusts are passive trusts, the Statute of Uses or its similar counterpart which is adopted in the United States does not apply to these implied trusts. Such statutes *execute* passive trusts, i.e., they state that an attempt to create a passive trust results in the direct passage of the legal title to trust property to the beneficiary, thus terminating the trust. The Statute of Uses applies only to real property when it is the subject matter of a trust. In some states, statutes having an effect similar to the Statute of Uses have expanded the rule to apply to personal property. None of these statutes, however, applies to resulting or constructive trusts, even though they are passive trusts (Restatement [Second] of Trusts § 73).

When a person has acquired title to property by unlawful or unfair means or by breach of duty as trustee, the court will *construct* a trust for the benefit of the person rightfully entitled to that property. In such cases, the court declares that the person who has acquired or retained property wrongfully holds the property as "constructive trustee" for the person who has been unjustly deprived of the property. A constructive trust is therefore imposed to remedy a wrong and to prevent unjust enrichment by the person who acquired title at the expense of another. The constructive trustee receives no administrative duty other than the obligation to transfer the title and possession of the property to the proper person. The following are some circumstances in which a court of equity will establish a constructive trust (Restatement [Second] of Trusts §§ 44[1][b], 45[1][b], 44[1][a], 45[1][a], 291[d], 288[a], 291[a]).

When there is violation (breach) of an agreement between two persons on whom the law imposes a duty to exercise loyalty and good faith toward one another, such as partners in an enterprise or an agent acting for a principal, the court may impose a constructive trust.

Example: Ronald Landis and Anne Chapman agree in a formal written instrument to be business partners and to buy a motel to be operated under the partnership. They employ a real estate agent who finds a property that fits their specifications at a price of $225,000. Later Ronald learns that Anne has bought the property for her own personal use. If he so chooses, Ronald may bring a court action against Anne, charging that she used the knowledge she acquired by virtue of being a business partner to enrich herself unjustly and in violation of their agreement. If Ronald succeeds in convincing the court, it could decree Anne a constructive trustee of the property for the benefit of Ronald, thereby allowing the partnership to obtain the property at the listed price.

A court may also construct a trust when a settlor intends but fails to create an express trust.

Example: By will, Joseph Riccard devises his interest in land to Burton McKeever, because Burton had promised orally, in the presence of Virginia Moore and Joseph, to hold the property in trust for Virginia. When the will is probated, the court refuses to recognize the trust because evidence of it was not written into the will. The Statute of Frauds makes orally created trusts of real estate invalid. If Burton is allowed to keep absolute title to the land because Joseph failed to create what he intended to be a testamentary trust, Burton would be unjustly enriched. Virginia's only recourse would be to petition the equity court to "construct" a trust of Joseph's land, placing equitable title in her and leaving Burton with legal title as constructive trustee. This is within the court's power, because a constructive trust, like a resulting trust, is exempt from the parol evidence rule. The trust may be based on oral evidence which, in this case, is Burton's promise as corroborated by Virginia. The burden of proving the oral allegation (promise) would fall on Virginia.

Note that in the last two examples the persons who are made constructive trustees have violated the fiduciary relationship between themselves and another, therefore requiring intervention by a court of equity. Legally, it may appear that neither Anne nor Burton has done anything wrong; however, from the viewpoint of equity they have proceeded improperly by acting unfairly in situations that demanded fairness. In each case the wronged party generally has a choice of remedies, e.g., a choice between an action at law for damages or a suit in equity for the creation of a constructive trust. Both types of relief, however, will not be granted and therefore the wronged party must exercise a choice of remedies.

Another situation in which the court may construct a trust for the benefit of the rightful owner would be when a person obtains property by fraud or willfully converts another's personal property for the wrongdoer's own use.

Example: Clare Allison works for the Benedict Corporation. She embezzles $10,000 from the corporation and uses the money to buy a mink coat. Under these circumstances, the equity court could decree Clare to be a constructive trustee for the corporation with the duty to transfer possession and title of the coat to the company.

See Exhibit 9.1 for a summary of the types of trusts.

Exhibit 9.1 An Outline Summary of the Main Types of Trusts (Text Pages 252–265)

A. Two main types of trusts
    1. **Express trust** A trust intentionally created or declared in express terms either by oral declaration or by a written instrument. Express trusts may be—
        a. Private or public (charitable) trusts
        b. Active or passive trusts
        c. Inter vivos (living) trusts or testamentary trusts
    2. **Implied trust** A trust imposed on property by the court when trust intent is lacking but the acts of the parties make the imposition necessary. Implied trusts may be—
        a. Resulting trusts
        b. Constructive trusts

B. Express trusts (text page 253)
    1. Private or public (charitable) trusts (text pages 253–255)
        a. **Private trust** An oral or written trust created for the financial benefit of a certain named individual or individuals.
        b. **Public trust** An express trust created for the social benefit of the public, or specific groups within the public, often called a charitable trust.
    2. Active or passive trusts (text pages 256–258)
        a. **Active trust** A trust that gives the trustee the power and duty to perform discretionary acts of management or administration.

Exhibit 9.1 *(continued)*

   b.   **Passive trust**   A trust in which the trustee is a mere holder of the legal title and has no duties of administration or only minor duties that are of a mechanical or formal nature.

3.   Inter vivos or testamentary trusts (text pages 258–259)

   a.   **Inter vivos (living) trust**   An express active trust, either private or public, created during the settlor's lifetime.

   b.   **Testamentary trust**   An express active trust, either public or private, created in a decedent's will.

C.   **Implied trusts** (text pages 259–265)

1.   **Resulting trust**   An implied trust created by the equity court to carry out the true intent of a property owner or settlor in cases where the intent of such person is inadequately expressed.

2.   **Constructive trust**   An implied trust imposed by courts of equity as a means of accomplishing justice and preventing unjust enrichment. Such trusts are not based on either actual or presumed intent of the parties.

Assignment 103

1. Russell Haberman owned a tract of land which he believed to be practically worthless. His brother-in-law, Francis Holgate, offered to buy the land for one dollar an acre, knowing that it contained valuable mineral deposits of which Russell was unaware. Russell sold the land and subsequently discovered its true value. Has Francis been unjustly enriched by the transaction? Would it be advisable for Russell to ask the court to create a constructive trust for his benefit?

2. In a will dated June 6, 1970, Michelle Walker named her nephew, Clarence Wilson, beneficiary of a substantial portion of her estate. In 1982, Michelle wrote a new will in which Clarence was left nothing, and later that year Michelle died. Clarence discovered the second (1982) will but concealed its existence until the probate of the first (1970) will was completed. Then a beneficiary of the second will uncovered the truth. Some states hold that a constructive trust may be created in this case. How would your state decide this matter?

Miscellaneous Trusts

A number of special trust forms are worthy of mention. These include spendthrift, business, short-term, and Totten trusts.

Spendthrift Trusts

Spendthrift trusts are trusts created to provide a fund for the maintenance of a beneficiary while safeguarding it against the beneficiary's own improvidence or inexperience in spending money. The settlor provides that the beneficiary cannot assign (transfer) to anyone the right to receive future payments of income or principal from the trust (which the settlor believes the beneficiary would do in times of financial difficulty). At the same time, the settlor declares that creditors of the beneficiary cannot reach the trust benefits by obtaining a court order awarding them to the creditors. In this way, settlors seek to protect the beneficiary who cannot or will not handle money wisely (Restatement [Second] of Trusts §§ 152, 153, 157, 250[f], 255[a], 342[f], 343[h]).

Spendthrift trusts do not place limitations on income *received* by the beneficiary, which may be spent or given away at will or be subject to creditors' claims. Their only guarantee is that the beneficiary will not lose the income *before* receiving it. In a few states, spendthrift trusts are void. A majority of states, however, allow settlors the right to create spendthrift trusts either without qualifying that right or subjecting it to statutory restrictions, e.g., a restriction on the amount of income per year that the beneficiary may receive or the right of creditors to reach trust income in payment of "necessaries" of the beneficiary.

Example: Leo Demarest, a resident of Nevada, wishes to leave a considerable amount of property to his favorite son, Robert, although he knows Robert to be irresponsible in handling money. He fears that Robert may go into debt and pledge the income to be received from the trust to pay his creditors. Leo could enable Robert to keep the right to the trust income by inserting a "spendthrift trust" clause in his will, directing: "The beneficiary of this trust shall not have the power to alienate (transfer), pledge, or assign his interest in the principal or the income of this trust in any manner, nor shall such interest be subject to the claims of his creditors, attachment, execution or other process of law."

Assignment 104

Theodore Phelps wishes to make a gift of his utility company stocks to his daughter, Jana, who is about to be married. He knows that Jana, being inexperienced in handling securities, might very well sell them at a loss, and being headstrong, she would not listen to sound advice. Would a gift of the property be wise? Is it advisable for Theodore to establish a spendthrift trust for her?

Business Trusts

Business trusts are trusts created by settlors (usually several to one business trust) as an alternative to creating a corporation. The settlors become trustees (resembling the directors of a corporation) and hold property to be invested (as is the capital stock of a corporation before it is divided into shares) in trust for the benefit of beneficiaries (who are like shareholders in a corporation).

Example: In 1925, five independent film-producing companies decided to pool their resources by forming a business trust. Accordingly they entered into an agreement whereby the officers of each company assumed the role of trustees of the new Southwestern Film Trust. Members of the public bought certificates naming themselves beneficiaries of the trust. With the proceeds of the sale of certificates, the trustees (who were also the settlors) set up a trust fund that they administered for the benefit of the beneficiaries by investing and reinvesting it. After paying the expenses of administration (such as brokers' fees), the trustees may deduct a percentage of what is left (profit) to pay their own salaries.

Legal and business personnel use the term *Massachusetts trust* as a synonym for the business trust because that state, by making the incorporation process difficult, forced many businesses to create business trusts instead of corporations.

Short-term Trusts

Short-term trusts are trusts in which the trust property is held for a short time for the benefit of someone whose tax bracket is lower than that of the settlor and who generally pays income tax on the property for receiving its benefit during the duration of the trust. It terminates automatically after a period of time specified in the trust instrument, and it is subject to Internal Revenue regulations (see Chapter 11 for a complete discussion of such trusts).

Example: Harte Cordell earns a salary of $95,000 a year and pays a high rate of income tax. He supports his mother, Lavinia, who is 65 and pays no income tax. Harte could pay less tax by transferring part of his income-producing property to a short-term trust for Lavinia's benefit. At the end of a certain minimum number of years, set by statute, the trust property would return to him, but before that he would not pay taxes on the income property because it is in trust for Lavinia. Lavinia herself would probably pay little or no income tax because she has an old-age exemption.

Totten Trusts

Totten trusts, or savings bank trusts, are trusts in which a depositor has placed money in a bank or savings and loan association under the depositor's name but in trust for another. Commonly the trust is created by A, the depositor, in the name of "A, in trust for B," or in the name of "A, payable on death to B." Such deposits permit the depositor-trustee to withdraw the money while alive and allow the remaining balance of the funds to be transferred to the beneficiary after the depositor's death. In addition, some courts have held that the depositor in such cases may revoke the "trust" by withdrawing the entire fund or changing the form of the account. The requirements for the creation and distribution of funds in such trusts vary from state to state.

Therefore, the individual state statutes must be checked to determine how Totten trusts will be administered.

Example: Ester Brown changes a savings account in her own name to "Ester Brown, in trust for Jean Brown." Ester has converted her own account into a Totten trust, which is allowed in her state. She has the option of withdrawing as much of the money as she wishes during her lifetime because the Totten trust is revocable until the settlor's death. Upon Ester's death, Jean, the beneficiary, will own the remaining funds in the savings account.

Romanee trust beneficiaries not disclosed

Assignment 105

Matilda Beinder, age 70, would like to create a trust for the benefit of her son, Michael, who has recently experienced financial reverses. Would it be advisable for her to establish a short term trust? Why or why not?

Assignment 106

Herman Dawkins, a former member of the armed forces, is eligible to obtain a loan to buy a house under the Servicemen's Readjustment Act. His parents had seen a house and previously had wanted to buy it, but could not negotiate a loan. Herman agrees in writing to negotiate a loan, buy the house, and convey it to his parents. He buys the house but refuses to convey it as agreed. His parents petition the court to have Herman declared trustee of the house in a resulting trust for their benefit using the written agreement as proof of his wrongdoing. Would equity permit the court to declare this a resulting trust? Why or why not?

Assignment 107

Lawrence Falkner, a contractor, bought a tract of land but had the legal title transferred to his wife, Bernice, instead of himself. Bernice knew of the arrangement and did not object to it. A former client sued Lawrence and obtained a sizable judgment against him, but was not able to attach the tract of land in payment of the debt because it was in Bernice's name. Two years later the marriage of Bernice and Lawrence was legally dissolved. Lawrence claimed that the land did not belong to Bernice because he had paid for it. Would equity permit the court to declare a resulting trust for Lawrence's benefit? Why or why not?

Assignment 108

Byron Sedgewick places his most valuable property in a revocable short-term trust for the benefit of his son, Donald, because Byron has gone heavily into debt and fears that his creditors may obtain a court order to seize that property. If one of the creditors contested the trust, should the court allow the trust to stand? Why or why not (see Chapter 11)?

Termination of Trusts

A trust may be terminated:

• In accordance with its terms (Restatement [Second] of Trusts §§ 330, 334)

• Because of the illegality or impossibility of attaining the object of the trust (Restatement [Second] of Trusts § 335)

• By completely accomplishing the trust's valid purpose (Restatement [Second] of Trusts § 337)

• By revocation by the settlor when allowed by the terms of the trust (Restatement [Second] of Trusts § 330)

• By merger of all interests (legal and equitable) in the same person (Restatement [Second] of Trusts §§ 337, 341)

• On the request of all the beneficiaries when there is no express purpose that requires continuation of the trust (Restatement [Second] of Trusts § 337)

The majority of U.S. courts hold that if one or more of the settlor's purposes for creating the trust may still be achieved by the continuance of the trust, the court will not allow termination unless all the beneficiaries join in the request for termination along with the settlor.

Assignment 109

1. Define constructive trust. Under what circumstances would such a trust be created?

2. Define and give examples of a spendthrift trust, a Totten trust and a business trust.

3. In an inter vivos trust agreement, June transfers 20,000 shares of stock worth $110,000 to Mary to hold in trust for June's father. Later Mary sells the stock and replaces the stock certificates with the money from the sale as the trust property. Is the above trust void?

4. What are the grounds for the removal of the trustee?

Chapter 10

Private Express Trusts

Scope of the Chapter

This chapter illustrates the use and function of one of the most common trust forms, the private express trust. It begins with a review of trust terms and creation, the requirements for a private express trust, a discussion of private trust purposes both legitimate and prohibited, and common mistakes made by a preliminary drafter. The chapter then outlines the steps necessary for making a preliminary draft of a private express trust, including the accumulation of data through appropriate checklists. Such a draft is made from a hypothetical case, and a sample trust is included. A checklist for use in drafting a trust is at the end of the chapter.

Competencies

After completing this chapter, the paralegal should be able to:

• Identify and define a private express trust
• Explain the function and use of a private express trust
• Prepare a preliminary draft of a private express trust for review by a trust attorney or officer
• Avoid common errors in the initial draft of such trusts

Review of Terminology Relating to Trusts

The *private express trust* is a relationship in which one or more trustees hold legal title to trust property for the financial benefit of one or more

271

named or identifiable beneficiaries (Restatement [Second] of Trusts §§ 1c and 2a). It differs from a public (charitable) trust in that the settlor of a private trust devotes trust property to the use of specific, designated beneficiaries, whereas the settlor of a public trust devotes trust property to purposes beneficial to the community.

The person who creates a trust, including a private express trust, is called the *settlor, donor, maker, trustor,* or *creator.* The *beneficiary* is also called the *"cestui que trust."* The property conveyed to the trustee is called the *trust corpus,* the *subject matter* of the trust, *trust property, trust fund,* or *res.* The creating document of the trust may be a *declaration of trust, trust deed, trust instrument,* or *will;* its objectives are to vest in (transfer to) the trustee and beneficiary the property interests it describes and to establish the parties' respective rights and duties. *Testamentary trusts* are private or public express trusts created by will. *Inter vivos,* or living, trusts are trusts created during the lifetime of the settlor.

Generally the trustee has *legal title* to the trust property, and each beneficiary has an *equitable interest.* The trustee's failure to perform the terms of the trust or to act within the bounds of the law entitles the beneficiary to seek remedies from a court of equity.

Creation of a Private Express Trust

A settlor can create a private express trust in three ways (Restatement [Second] of Trusts § 17):

1. A trust can be created by inter vivos declaration (oral or written) in which the settlor is both the maker and trustee.
Example: Andrew Hamilton orally declares himself trustee of $20,000 cash, which he takes from his own bank account for the benefit of his neighbor, Joanne Iverson.

2. A trust can be created by a conveyance (inter vivos or testamentary) to a trustee in which the settlor is both maker and beneficiary with the legal title passing to the trustee and the equitable title retained by the settlor-beneficiary.
Example: Joyce gives Judy $20,000 to hold and invest for Joyce's benefit.

3. A trust can be created by a conveyance involving three people in which the settlor passes title in trust to a trustee for the benefit of another, the beneficiary. The trustee gets legal title, the beneficiary gets equitable title, and the settlor retains no interest unless the settlor retains the right to revoke or cancel the trust.
Example: Berta Englund gives Emily Wagner $20,000 to hold and invest for Ian Wagner's benefit.

In each of the previous examples, note that the requisite number of parties, i.e., settlor, beneficiary, and trustee, are present, but the number of participants in each trust varies. In the first and second examples there are two participants, and in the third there are three. This is in keeping with the motives, desires, or convenience of each settlor in creating the particular trust. The third example demonstrates a "classic" trust in which each of the three parties is a different person. The settlor may create this private trust while living or by will, which then becomes operative after death (formal requirements for creation of a private trust are covered below, page 280).

Essentials of a Private Express Trust

Every private trust must include the following elements:

- Intention of the settlor to create a trust
- A trustee to administer the trust
- A beneficiary to enforce the trust
- Trust property

The *settlor* may convey presently existing and transferable interests in real or personal property in trust, declare himself or herself *trustee* for the benefit of another, the *beneficiary,* or declare another person trustee for the settlor's own benefit or for the benefit of someone else. Commonly, the settlor places in trust land, cash, or securities, but many items may be added to this list (see page 249). The requirements for transfer of such property to a trust are similar to requirements for transfer of property where there is no trust involved:

- Land must be transferred by a deed or will executed with required formalities (see page 249). In a personal property trust, the settlor must give (deliver) the property to the trustee, who then holds legal title to it.

- The nature of the property placed in trust determines whether the declaration of trust may be oral. It may be oral if the property is personal property (such as money or securities). It must be written, however, or at least be evidenced by something written, if the property is real property (land, buildings, and the like). Each state has a statute embodying these rules, which demand written evidence to prevent fraud in certain transactions. Such statutes are derived from the English Statute of Frauds.

Example: Andy Swanson transfers $50,000 to Joe Carter to hold and invest for the benefit of Andy's son, Wilbur. All requirements of a private express trust are present.

Example: Amos Berry executes a promissory note for $5,000 payable to Grant Ogilvie in trust for Austin Berry. Ogilvie is trustee of the note for Berry. Amos, the settlor, owns a property interest in the money represented by the note and is capable of transferring it. He could not be the trustee because he could not hold himself responsible for paying the note as the trustee must do to the settlor.

Example: By signing and delivering a deed, Lora Lee Jackson gives her farm, Cottonwood, in trust for the benefit of Bill Jackson to Zeke Nunley. Furthermore, she gives Zeke the duty to pay Bill the income from Cottonwood for life and then transfer the farm to Bill's children as beneficiaries after Bill's death.

Assignment 110

Mackenzie Taylor transfers 20 shares of stock to a trust and declares himself trustee of the stock for the benefit of Lucius West.

1. Identify the settlor, trustee, and beneficiary.

2. What constitutes the trust estate?

3. What interest does Taylor have in the trust estate? Does West have an interest too?

4. Classify the trust.

Assignment 111

Louela Page owns a tract of land and conveys a deed for the land to Marlene Winston. The deed directs Marlene to hold the land in trust for Gregory Wright.

1. Identify the settlor, trustee, and beneficiary.

2. What constitutes the trust estate?

3. What interests in the estate does each of the three persons have?

4. Classify the trust. How does it differ from the Taylor trust above?

The Purposes of Private Express Trusts

A legal private trust may be used for many good purposes, especially between husband and wife or for the benefit of children (Restatement [Second] of Trusts § 59). There are several advantages of a private trust for the benefit of a spouse as an alternative to a gift outright to the spouse or giving the spouse a life estate with a remainder in the couple's descendants.

First, the settlor may carefully select the trustee to provide expert management of the property, thereby relieving the spouse of responsibility in this area, since the spouse may have no expertise in management.

Second, selection of an experienced trustee by the settlor may help ensure that the trust property will not be diminished either by poor management or by deliberate action (such as sale of the property), thereby cutting off the children's inheritance.

Third, since the possibility of death and a subsequent remarriage exists, a second husband/wife might spend the trust property income that would otherwise be the subject matter of the trust or possibly exert influence on the surviving spouse to convey the property to him or her either during the spouse's lifetime or in the spouse's will to the exclusion of the children of the first marriage. The trust ensures that the intact property will ultimately go to the children of the first marriage on their surviving parent's death. The problem of a divorce and remarriage could be resolved in a similar manner by the formation of a trust.

Example: Larry and Janet Rice are married and desire to have a substantial portion of their property transferred to their children after their respective deaths. If Larry were to die and Janet to remarry, her new husband might inherit Janet's estate or convince Janet to transfer her estate to him during her lifetime. In addition, Larry and Janet might obtain a divorce and Janet might remarry, with the same property consequences as described above. To avoid these possibilities, Janet and Larry could create a trust that would assure their children of that portion of their parents' estate which the parents intend the children to receive.

Fourth, the spouse's creation of a trust for family members gives them access to money at a time when it might be badly needed. The spouse's death may deprive the family of its greatest source of income. Even though the decedent may have been foresighted enough to execute a will, expense and delays in the probate process are not unusual. Months may pass before the persons entitled to the testate's gifts actually receive them. An inter vivos trust avoids these complications because it goes into effect before the settlor's death.

Fifth, by carefully drafting the trust instrument, the flexibility required for a family to meet changing conditions in the future may be obtained. For instance, if a settlor spouse feels the trust income may exceed the needs of the beneficiary spouse in the future, the settlor may give the trustee the power to determine the needs, distribute such income to the beneficiary, and distribute any excess income to other family members. Another example of the flexibility possible is that the trustee may be authorized to invade the principal and pay out portions of it to the beneficiary for special needs. In addition, the settlor may direct the trustee to pay portions of the trust property to the beneficiary on the beneficiary's written demand. In other words, the form and content of a trust can be tailored to fit the specific needs of the individuals involved.

Assignment 112

Charlotte died testate, giving her farm, Longacre, "to Wallace in trust for my husband, Gerard, for his lifetime, and at his death, then the property to be distributed in equal shares to our two children, Wade and Richard." At the time of Charlotte's death, all other parties mentioned were living. Does this provision of the will create a trust? Classify it. Wade and Richard are remaindermen. What does this mean?

Legal Restrictions

Generally, a trust can be created for any purpose that is legal, but the law has imposed some restrictions on what constitutes legal purposes (Restatement [Second] of Trusts §§ 59, 60). Restrictions on purposes of trusts fall into several categories. There are restrictions on purposes contrary to public policy, such as imposing total restraint on marriage or attempting to encourage divorce (Restatement [Second] of Trusts § 62).

Example: Otto Lindberg tells his son, Scott, that he will transfer his ski resort, Arrowhead, to Daniel Maulkin in trust for Scott's benefit if Scott will divorce his wife, Elizabeth. Such a restraint is against public policy and would invalidate the trust. In this case, Otto would retain the trust property (see page 279).

Some restrictions are imposed by statute. Statutes restricting trusts are usually framed in general language, e.g., N.Y. Est. Powers of Trusts Law § 7-1.4 (McKinney 1967) states: "An express trust may be created for any lawful purpose." The definition of what is "lawful" is then subject to interpretation by the New York courts. Some statutes contain further restrictions, usually in the area of real property trusts.

Example: Hermann Pfalz lives in South Dakota. As a gift to his daughter, Freida, he transfers to her in trust a part of his wheat acreage. Hermann's gift must be in writing to be valid, according to S.D. Comp. Laws Ann. § 55-1-1 (1980).

Some restrictions are against perpetuities (see page 181) and accumulations. (Restatement [Second] of Trusts § 62n and t.) The perpetuation of a trust that effectively prohibits any but members of a certain class from possessing the trust property beyond an extended statutory period contravenes public policy.

Example: In his will, Howard Engel gives $100,000 in trust to Investors, Inc., to hold and invest, to accumulate the income of the trust property for the next 100 years, and then to transfer the trust estate to the heirs of Howard equally. The trust is invalid because the rule against perpetual interests in trust property requires that the period be no greater than the continuance of lives in being at the time the trust instrument takes effect plus twenty-one years thereafter.

Another restriction is that no valid trust can be formed if it is based on an illegal contract or agreement. Where a trust is created and income is to be paid to the beneficiary on condition that the beneficiary aids in the suppression of criminal proceedings, the purpose is illegal and the trust is invalid. Any illegal purpose, such as inducing the beneficiary to live in adultery with the settlor or defrauding the settlor's creditors, will invalidate the trust. Any trust designed to induce criminal acts is invalid, e.g., a trust set up to reward a beneficiary for committing perjury or to pay legal costs and fines for a beneficiary who commits a crime (Restatement [Second] of Trusts §§ 62b, d, and 63). Any trust designed to induce tortious acts (see Tort in Glossary) is also invalid, e.g., a trust established to finance one family's feud against another.

The court is faced with difficulties not only when the entire trust is motivated by an illegal purpose but also when a legal trust contains one or more illegal provisions (Restatement [Second] of Trusts § 65). Illegal provisions rarely appear in the trust instrument, and in many cases they are not in writing at all but expressed orally in order to avoid making known the true purpose. When the trust fails for being entirely motivated by an illegal purpose, every vestige of a "trust" disappears, and the court must decide whether the trust property should be returned to the settlor by means of a "resulting trust" or be disposed of in some other manner (Restatement [Second] of Trusts §§ 422, 444). On the other hand, if the trust has several purposes, some legal and some not, the question is whether the entire trust should fail.

The court's decision depends on whether the purposes are independent or dependent. If the purposes can be easily separated, and the valid purpose enforced without violating the settlor's objective for establishing the trust, then the valid sections can be enforced and the illegal sections voided (Restatement [Second] of Trusts § 65). If the purposes are so inextricably connected that the settlor's intent cannot be achieved without executing both the valid and invalid sections, then the entire trust must fail.

The facts surrounding each case play a major role in determining the result. They must be carefully reviewed by the court before it enforces or voids a multipurpose trust containing legal as well as illegal provisions.

Example: Martin Remek transfers to a trust real and personal property that he owns, naming his sister, Sarah, trustee and his brother, Melvin, beneficiary. The true intent of this trust is to avoid payment to Martin's creditors. If the creditors petition the equity court, the court will set aside the trust and issue a decree (court order) that the trust is void and the property still belongs to the settlor, Martin. The creditors would then be entitled to satisfy (collect) their claims out of the property.

Example: Warren Hammond establishes a trust of $100,000 for the benefit of his daughter, Leslie. Warren names himself trustee and adds that income from the trust property will be given to Leslie as soon as she divorces her husband, Charles. Most courts would hold this latter condition as contrary to public policy and enforce the trust for the benefit of Leslie notwithstanding the fact that the divorce (condition) did not occur.

Assignment 113

Sherman Aldrich, retired president of a paper products firm, creates the Northwest Environmental Trust to preserve valuable forest land in the Pacific Northwest. He endows the trust with $500,000 and directs the trustees, in the trust instrument, to invest and reinvest the money for the purpose of reforesting certain tracts of land, cultivating them, and encouraging legislation favorable to the continuation of these aims.

1. Is this trust legal or illegal? Why? (Hint: See Restatement [Second] of Trusts § 65.)

2. Under what circumstances, if any, might this trust be declared invalid?

3. In the event that one of the purposes of the trust becomes or is declared to be illegal, could the remainder of the trust be enforced?

As noted in the Hammond example above, just as a trust may not violate statutory law, it may not violate public policy. A provision in a trust imposing total restraint of a marriage on a beneficiary is invalid. For instance, if the trust provides that a beneficiary will be divested of an interest if the beneficiary should *ever* marry anyone, the provision is invalid since it is against public policy to prevent a person from marrying, having children, and a normal family life (Restatement [Second] of Trusts § 62h). A trust providing income payments to a person whose spouse has died until that person remarries does not, however, oppose public policy since it restrains not marriage but remarriage. Trusts providing that a beneficiary will be divested of an interest in the following circumstances have generally been upheld as not "unduly" restraining marriage:

- The beneficiary marries a particular person
- The beneficiary marries before reaching majority
- The beneficiary marries before reaching majority without the consent of the trustee (or someone else)
- The beneficiary marries a person of a particular religious faith
- The beneficiary marries a person of a faith different from that of the beneficiary

In determining the validity or invalidity of a partially illegal trust, if the court determines that the settlor's intent was not to restrain marriage but merely to provide support to the beneficiary as long as the beneficiary remains single, it will likely declare the trust valid. The facts, in particular the settlor's intent, are crucial to the court's decision.

If a testamentary trust provides that a beneficiary will be divested for marrying without the consent of executors and trustees, and, if under provisions of the will those persons will profit by refusing to consent to the beneficiary's marriage, the provision is invalid. Provisions that are designed to prevent hasty or imprudent marriages and that subject a minor to the restraint of parents or friends during minority are allowed. The reasoning is that the law should uphold such a provision because it protects the minor from unscrupulous persons who could dissipate the proceeds established for the minor's benefit.

Likewise, a provision in a trust which divests beneficiaries of their interests if they communicate or have social relations with certain other family members is invalid as being against public policy and disruptive of family relations (Restatement [Second] of Trusts § 62g).

Another invalid provision is one that constitutes an inducement to change the religious faith of the beneficiary (Restatement [Second] of Trusts § 62i). For example, if a trust provides that Maureen Shannon is to receive her interest only if she changes her religious faith or that her interest ceases if she does not change her religious faith, the courts hold as a general rule that enforcement of such provisions restrains the religious freedom of the beneficiary by improperly inducing the beneficiary, Maureen, to change her faith.

Normally a beneficiary of a trust whose rights have been infringed by a trust may gain equitable relief from the court (Restatement [Second] of Trusts § 65d, e, f) except when the beneficiary has also been involved in the illegal bargain or arrangement, e.g., a trust created to defraud the settlor's creditors in which the beneficiary had knowledge of the fraud and agreed to the trust's formation. In such cases, courts will deny relief to the beneficiary by application of the "clean hands" doctrine (see Glossary) (Restatement [Second] of Trusts §§ 60a(3), 63). The doctrine is useful to the court in dealing with the effect that a trust with an illegal purpose will have on the validity and enforceability of the trust. The doctrine holds that the equity court refuses to be a party to help achieve and enforce such a trust. Therefore, in order to discourage others from pursuing similar schemes, the equity court leaves the parties to the illegal transaction in their present status. Thus, if a settlor transfers property to a trustee to defraud the settlor's creditors with the understanding that the trustee is ultimately to return the property to the settlor who is also the beneficiary, and the trustee does not perform to the settlor's satisfaction, the court may refuse to direct the trustee to return the property. This result would depend on whether any creditor of the settlor attacked (challenged) the trust. Various resolutions are available to the equity court. If the settlor's creditors challenge the trust, the court will generally set aside the trust as previously discussed. If the defrauded creditors of the settlor are not actually damaged by the settlor's wrongful action or can satisfy their claims against the settlor in other ways, the court may not apply the "clean hands" doctrine but instead may nullify the illegal trust and hold that an implied trust (called a resulting trust) is created in its place.

Formal Requirements for a Private Trust

A settlor's declaration of trust is the simplest method of establishing a private trust. The owner of property, i.e., the settlor, simply declares someone trustee of that property for the benefit of another person (Restatement [Second] of Trusts § 17). As mentioned previously, the settlor and the trustee or the settlor and the beneficiary may be the same person. No trust is created, however, until the declaration or the transfer of the trust property takes place. If the conveyance is a transfer of personal property to an inter vivos trust, no formalities are required for declaring the trust except that the settlor must manifest an intention to hold or place the property in trust. If the trust property is realty, the settlor must put the declaration in writing to satisfy the requirements of the Statute of Frauds (Restatement [Second] of Trusts § 40). Likewise, delivery requirements are simple. For example, if the conveyance is a gift of land, the settlor must deliver the deed to the trustee; if the gift is personal property, usually delivery of the gift itself is necessary.

Example: Carol Flexner, a widow with four children, received a large sum of money from her father's estate. In order for Carol to set up a trust of this money for her children, she need only declare orally her intention to do so and deliver the property to the trustee. If, however, Carol had received her father's resort, Edgewater, she would have no choice but to put the declaration in writing if she wished to set up a trust. She would also find it necessary to deliver the need to Edgewater to the trustee.

At common law, spouses could not transfer legal title to property to each other because husband and wife were considered "one person." Courts of equity, however, allowed a husband to declare himself trustee for his wife (Restatement [Second] of Trusts § 18a). Modern statutes allow either spouse to make a direct gift to the other. In addition, a married woman has capacity to be both a beneficiary (Restatement [Second] of Trusts § 118) or a trustee (Restatement [Second] of Trusts § 90) in her own right. No one need act for her.

A manifestation of intention to create an inter vivos trust at some later time does not create a trust at the time the settlor manifests this intent (Restatement [Second] of Trusts § 26). If a settlor declares an intention to create a trust some time in the future or makes an unenforceable promise at a subsequent time to transfer property to another person in trust, a trust does not exist. Until the settlor actually makes the transfer, a trust is not created.

Example: Cliff Reid tells Enoch Mitchell that he intends to transfer securities to Mitchell in trust for Mary Alexander Webb in the coming week. No trust arises until Reid actually transfers the securities to Mitchell in trust. Reid has not created a trust until he does so; therefore, he may change his mind and create no trust at all, or appoint someone else trustee.

If Cliff had intended himself to be both settlor and beneficiary of the trust, but had not yet acquired the trust property, he would not have created a trust simply by informing Enoch of his intention. A trust depends on the separation of the settlor's absolute title into legal and equitable titles. This cannot be done until the settlor actually owns the absolute title.

Example: Bill Taylor promises Teresa Hall that when he purchases certain shares of stock he will execute a trust instrument declaring himself trustee of the shares for Teresa's benefit. A trust is not created until Bill has both acquired the shares and declared himself trustee.

If the settlor intends to create a trust at the time of the declaration, a trust may arise at that time even if it gives the beneficiary a future interest which will not take effect until some later time (Restatement [Second] of Trusts § 26g).

Example: Luisa Harper owns 75 shares of stock in IBM and declares herself trustee of the stock for ten years for Rose Maguire's benefit. After the expiration of ten years, the income will then be paid to Tony Harper. Even though Tony's beneficial interest does not take effect until the end of the ten-year period, the trust is created at the time of Luisa's declaration.

Example: Franklin Folger's will provided in part: "To my daughter Aileen, I leave in trust the proceeds of the sale of my interest in the Great West Company, of which I am presently a partner, if the sale of such interest shall be perfected within six months of my death. If it shall not have been perfected, I leave said interest to my wife, Gladys." This provides that a trust shall begin in the future and is valid even though the sale will probably not be perfected (completed) immediately upon Franklin's death. The trust property is presently owned by the settlor. The intended trust would not take effect if Franklin did not own an interest in the company at the time he signed and dated the will.

The creation of a present trust of a promise to be performed in the future must be distingushed from the case where a settlor promises to create a trust in the future (Restatement [Second] of Trusts §§ 26n and 17e).

Example: If John Rollings, intending to create an immediate trust, makes an enforceable promise to pay money or to convey property to Clare Barrett as trustee at some time in the future, a present trust is created. Clare holds the right to be a trustee provided that John manifests an intention to create an immediate trust based on that right. Had he promised to create the trust at the time when the money is paid or the property conveyed, no trust would have resulted.

The promisor is generally not bound if the promise is made at no cost to either party, gratuitously, i.e., no consideration is given the promisor If the gratuitous promise, however, is solemnized (notarized, i.e., the promise is made under oath before a notary public), it is binding. The promisor has created a trust, and the promisee immediately becomes a trustee of the rights that the promise engenders.

Example: George Hart promises orally to give Reginald Johnston $25,000 in trust for Michael Foreman. No money is exchanged (i.e., the promise is "without consideration"), and the promise has not been otherwise solemnized. Therefore the promise does not bind George to create or Reginald to manage a trust.

Informal and Incomplete Creation of a Trust (Restatement [Second] of Trusts § 330e)

When competent legal advice is not sought, a private express trust might be drafted improperly and litigation could result. We will now take a look at some of the major mistakes made in an improperly drafted trust instrument:

• A settlor, in a hand-drawn will, indicates that he or she wants certain objectives accomplished but expresses this as a hope, desire, request, or a wish rather than as a mandate.

• The trust document does not sufficiently identify the beneficiary or fails to name a beneficiary.

• The trust instrument fails to name a trustee or fails to name a successor when the named trustee does not want to serve.

• The document names the trustee and describes the beneficiaries but does not specify the duties of the trustee.

• Although the trust instrument purports to be transferring legal title, the trust terms are not specified, or they have only been implied in an informal oral agreement.

Failure to Make Intentions Clear

It is possible to create a trust without actually using the words "trustee" or "in trust." On the other hand, in a hand-drawn instrument the use of these words is not conclusive evidence of the intent to create a trust. In order to create an express trust, the court must be satisfied that the settlor manifested an intention to impose enforceable duties on the trustee to manage the property for the benefit of others. When a testate uses precatory words such as "hope," "wish", or "recommend" to devise the property of his or her estate, the court must determine whether the testate intended an absolute gift or a trust (Restatement [Second] of Trusts § 25). It will consider all relevant factors before reaching a conclusion.

Example: Desmond Cormac's will provides, in part: "I give to my wife in the event of my death all my interest in the farm we own as tenants in common and all the stock, farm implements, etc., after my debts are paid. To have and to hold the same in fee simple and to dispose of the same among the children as she may think best." An argument could be made that the will establishes a trust in the property for the benefit of the children, but the better view is that the devisee (the wife) is given an estate in fee simple.

Example: Johan Vanderhaavn's will gives property to his wife "to be her absolute estate forever," then added the words, "it is my request that upon her death, my said wife shall give, devise, and bequeath the real property given her to persons named in the fourth clause of this will." An ambiguity is created because the testator cannot create a fee simple estate for his wife and then request that the same property be transferred on her death to others. That right belongs to the fee owner, i.e., the testator's wife. The court held that the wife took the property in fee simple and not in trust.

These examples illustrate the effects that unclear terms may have on an intended trust. In many cases, inclusion of these precatory words results in the undoing of the would-be settlor's intentions.

The early English view held that the use of such words as "request," "desire," "hope," and "wish" were a courteous means of creating duties enforceable by the courts. Today, both English and American courts hold that the use of such precatory words does *not* create a trust. The intent to create a trust containing such words must be proven by other sections of the trust instrument or by extrinsic circumstances (Restatement [Second] of Trusts § 25).

Example: Suppose a testator, Marvin Rothman, wills all his property to his wife, and then adds, "I recommend to her the care and protection of my mother and sister, and request her to make such provision for them as in her judgment will be best." Both mother and sister are invalids and in need, and the testator had supported them for some time before his death. The court would most likely hold that the wife took the property in trust with the obligation to make a reasonable provision for the testator's mother and sister. Such a testamentary trust is poorly drafted because it creates an ambiguity, i.e., a conveyance of the estate property to the testator's spouse but with a request that the spouse "care and protect" the testator's invalid mother and sister. The court chose to call this will provision a testamentary trust because of the circumstances, i.e., the fact that mother and sister were invalids, and the testator had previously cared for them.

When drafting trusts, it is best to avoid these precatory words altogether.

Failure to Name or Identify Beneficiary

When the trust instrument fails to name any beneficiary, a few cases give the trustee absolute ownership, but the general rule is that a "resulting trust" arises in favor of the decedent's estate if the trust instrument was testamentary (Restatement [Second] of Trusts §§ 44e and 45e). If the trust is inter vivos and the instrument fails to name a beneficiary, the attempt to create a trust fails.

Example: If Mel Bowles had set aside money for a trust, executed the instrument, and directed the trustee to distribute the income to persons that the trustee considered deserving, the trust would be void because

Mel did not indicate clearly who were to be the beneficiaries. Had he augmented the description, e.g., "to be distributed to my nieces and nephews" or "to the descendants of my sister, Judith," the beneficiaries would be at least discoverable.

When the trust property is in excess of the trust purposes, e.g., the settlor directs payment of such part of the income as is necessary for the support of the named beneficiary and makes no provision for the excess, the excess takes the form of a resulting trust for the benefit of the settlor or his or her successors if the settlor has died (Restatement [Second] of Trusts §§ 430–439). When the trust fails or its purpose is accomplished and the settlor is dead, the law imposes a resulting trust for the settlor's successors.

Example: Cyrus Heymann is the chief stockholder of Silver City, Inc., a retirement community. Seeking tax savings, he transfers 2,500 shares, half his holdings, to his sister, Sybil, to hold in trust for him (Cyrus being both settlor and beneficiary). Cyrus dies suddenly. The trust is therefore, terminated for lack of a beneficiary. If she continues to be trustee, Sybil holds the shares in a resulting trust for Cyrus' estate.

The presumption of a resulting trust can be rebutted if it can be shown that the settlor did not intend to create a´resulting trust, e.g., where the settlor clearly intended the trustee to retain and fully own the property or the surplus.

Example: If it appeared doubtful whether Cyrus Heymann in the above example intended a gift or a trust in transferring the stock to Sybil, evidence clarifying his intent would have to be produced. It could not, however, be verbal, such as Cyrus' bookkeeper's oral testimony on Cyrus' conversations on the subject, but would have to be written, such as a letter written by Cyrus or his tax returns, in which Cyrus makes clear that he did or did not intend to make a gift of the property to Sybil.

Failure to Name a Trustee

The trust may fail for want of a trustee as well as for want of a beneficiary. Lack of a trustee to administer the trust may come about

• If the settlor does not name a trustee in the trust instrument or fails to name a successor trustee to resolve the problem of the original trustee's death, resignation, or nonacceptance

• If the named trustee does not qualify, e.g., refuses to accept the duty, dies before the effective date of the trust, or is refused confirmation of the office by the court because of incompetence

• If the named trustee does not have legal capacity to hold property in trust, e.g., in some states an unincorporated association

• If the named trustee is removed or resigns after the effective date of the trust

If at all possible, courts try to preserve trusts. Normally, the court will not allow a trust to fail for any of the above reasons and will appoint a new trustee so long as the trust is otherwise valid (Restatement [Second] of Trusts § 108). The trust will fail only if it can be shown that the settlor intended that only the named person and no other be the trustee.

Although the laws of a few states prohibit the creation of joint tenancy, this prohibition does not apply to property held in trust. Co-trustees generally hold title to trust property as joint tenants with the right of survivorship, so if one dies, disclaims, resigns, or is removed by a court, legal title passes to the remaining co-trustee(s) by operation of law (Restatement [Second] of Trusts § 103).

Example: Curt Baird places 500 shares of Behl, Inc., in trust for the benefit of his son, Kyle, naming Curt's three brothers trustees. Later one brother resigns due to ill health. The court decides that two trustees will suffice because the settlor did not specify that there be three at all times. Therefore, the court does not appoint a new trustee. At the annual stockholder's meeting of Behl, the two trustees vote in the name of the trust. Another major stockholder objects that the Baird trust votes were invalid because they were cast by two, not three, trustees. The votes are valid. The two trustees hold the entire legal title to the trust by the right of survivorship (see page 52).

Assignment 114

Diane Welsh owns stock in several companies. On her nephew's tenth birthday she makes him beneficiary of a trust of part of her holdings, naming her friends, Amy Jones and May Ford, trustees. May dies; Amy becomes the sole trustee. Then Amy dies.

1. Who should assume legal title to the stock?

2. Eva Brown is Amy's executrix. Should she distribute income from the stock to Diane's nephew?

3. How could Diane have prevented this problem?

Drafting a Private Express Trust

A trust is a convenient device to transfer assets out of a settlor's estate. Its greatest advantage is its flexibility, its adaptability to many purposes. Therefore, before preparing a preliminary draft of a trust, the paralegal, under the attorney's supervision, must have a clear understanding of the settlor's purposes and desires in creating the trust.

The hypothetical case below describes the settlor's purposes for establishing a trust and provides a sample checklist of information the paralegal needs to prepare a preliminary draft. On the basis of the checklist data, a sample agreement is drawn, creating a private, express, irrevocable, inter vivos, active trust.

The Facts

Helen A. Flynn, age 60, lives at 1520 Holly Drive, Flowertown, Apple County, State A. Helen is a widow with two adult children, Jerry Flynn, residing at 1402 Oak Drive, Flowertown, and Janet Flynn, living at home with her mother. Helen has been a very successful businesswoman. She has also been a wise investor. Helen wants to transfer 10,000 shares of common stock of Golden Harvest, Inc., to an irrevocable trust for her son's benefit (to be designated Trust I). The annual income produced by the stock varies. Jerry has had serious business reverses, and his mother wants to help him overcome these problems. Helen wants the income produced from the stock paid to Jerry annually for the next five years. At the end of that time period, Helen instructs the trustee to transfer the trust property into two separate, equal trusts, Trust II and Trust III, for the benefit of her two children, as successor beneficiaries, for their respective lifetimes. Upon the death of Janet and Jerry, Helen wants the trusts to terminate and the principal of the trust (stock) to pass into their respective estates. Therefore Janet and Jerry will have the opportunity to determine through their individual wills to whom the stock will eventually be transferred.

Helen names her close friend and financial adviser, Betty R. White, trustee. Betty lives at 1040 Merry Lane, in Flowertown. Helen names Betty's husband, Bob, successor trustee. He would take over Betty's duties, e.g., pay trust income to the beneficiary, should Betty become legally unable to perform. Betty and Bob agree to serve without compensation. The powers and duties granted by Helen to her trustee include the trustee's right to vote the stock, to sell and reinvest in other stocks or bonds when in the best interests of the beneficiaries, and to distribute the income and principal as outlined in the trust agreement. Also, Helen wants to retain the right to remove any trustee she selects or to allow the beneficiaries, if both agree, to remove the trustee.

Using a Checklist

A checklist similar to the one in Exhibit 10.1 should be used to gather the information necessary for drafting the Flynn trust. This checklist is for illustrative purposes only. It reflects details to be included in the prospective trust instrument based on the situation previously outlined. Drafters of trust instruments would not and should not use this checklist in every situation. For example, the settlor might not want to name a successor beneficiary who would receive the benefit of the trust should the first-named beneficiary die. Exhibit 10.2 is a blank sample checklist showing information needed to draft an inter vivos trust.

Exhibit 10.1 Sample Checklist for Drafting a Private Trust

Names and Addresses of Necessary Parties

Settlor:	Helen A. Flynn	1520 Holly Drive, Flowertown, Apple County, State A
Trustee:	Betty R. White	1040 Merry Lane, Flowertown, Apple County, State A
Successor trustee:	Robert C. White	1040 Merry Lane, Flowertown, Apple County, State A
Relationship of trustee(s) to settlor:	Financial adviser and friend	

Beneficiaries

Income beneficiary:	Jerry Flynn, son	1402 Oak Drive, Flowertown, Apple County, State A
Successor beneficiary:	Jerry Flynn and	Same as above
	Janet Flynn, daughter	Same as Helen (mother)
Remainderman:	Respective estates of Jerry and Janet Flynn	
Relationship of beneficiaries to settlor:	Beneficiaries (Janet and Jerry) are the children of settlor (Helen)	

Trust Property

Stocks:	10,000 shares of common stock, Golden Harvest, Inc.
Location:	Stock shares--transferred to trustee on acceptance

Revocability of Trust   Trust is irrevocable

Trustee's Powers and Duties

Payment of income (Trust I):	Annually to Jerry for five years
Payment to successor beneficiaries (Trusts II & III):	After five years, income to be paid equally to Janet and Jerry for life
Payment (transfer) of principal:	Principal transferred in equal shares to the respective estates of Janet and Jerry on their deaths

Exhibit 10.1 *(continued)*

Investment powers:	Invest and reinvest the securities and other general powers
Term of Trustee	
Removal:	Removal may be by either settlor or both beneficiaries acting jointly
Successor in office:	Robert White, husband of proposed trustee
Trustee's Rights	
Acceptance or rejection (determine trustee's intention):	Trustees agree to serve
Compensation:	Trustees agree to serve without charge
Termination of Trust	
Duration of trust:	Settlor intends to transfer income to son for five years (Trust I); then in equal shares (Trusts II and III) to both children for life. Remainder to the children's estates
Distribution of principal of Trust I on termination of trust:	Transferred in equal shares to Trusts II and III
Distribution of principal and income of Trusts II and III on termination of said trusts:	Transferred in equal shares to respective estates of Janet and Jerry on their deaths

Assignment 115

From the completed checklist in Exhibit 10.1, draft a private, express, inter vivos, irrevocable trust with the appropriate provisions based on the facts in the Flynn case. Compare your draft with the annotated sample trust below.

ANNOTATED SAMPLE PRIVATE EXPRESS TRUST

This agreement is made June 1, 1984, between Helen A. Flynn of 1520 Holly Drive, City of Flowertown, County of Apple, State of A, hereinafter referred to as Settlor, and Betty R. White of 1040 Merry Lane, City of Flowertown, County of Apple, State of A, hereinafter referred to as Trustee.

COMMENT: The major purpose of the introductory clause in a trust is to identify the parties involved. Always include addresses to assist in proper identification.

Settlor and trustee agree to the following:

Article I

Settlor hereby transfers to trustee 10,000 shares of common corporate stock of Golden Harvest, Inc., described in Schedule A, annexed hereto and made a part thereof by this reference, the receipt of which property is hereby acknowledged by trustee, to be held in trust upon the terms herein set forth.

COMMENT: This article identifies the property of the trust. It also establishes the willingness of the person nominated to act as trustee and to accept the responsibilities outlined in later articles. Incorporation by reference, i.e., use of the words, "Schedule A, annexed hereto," enables the drafter to define the trust estate without making the trust instrument unduly long.

Article II

Trustee is authorized to receive property added to the trust estate from any person, provided such property is acceptable to the trustee.

COMMENT: If the trustee is to care for property added to the trust throughout its duration, such as stock resulting from a split, this must be stipulated. Generally, property can be added to the trust throughout its duration. If a short-term trust is desired, important tax consequences may result from such additions (see Chapter 11).

Article III

Trustee shall hold, invest, and reinvest the trust property; collect the dividends, interest, and other income thereof; and, after deducting all necessary administration expenses, dispose and distribute the net income and principal as follows:

First: The net income from the trust estate shall be placed in a trust, Trust I, and shall be paid annually to Jerry Flynn, son of the settlor, of 1402 Oak Drive, Flowertown, Apple County, State A, for five (5) years commencing from the date of this agreement.

Second: At the end of the five-year period, the trustee shall divide the trust principal and income into equal amounts and place them into two separate trusts, Trust II and Trust III. Trust II shall be established for the benefit of Jerry Flynn and Trust III for Janet Flynn, daughter of settlor, residing at settlor's address. The net incomes of Trust II and Trust III shall be paid annually to the respective beneficiaries, Jerry and Janet, until their deaths. The death of each beneficiary named herein shall terminate the respective trust created for their benefit and the principal and remaining income of the trust shall become part of the decedent beneficiary's estate and shall be distributed to the beneficiary's personal representative.

COMMENT: This article describes in detail the way income and principal of the trust estate shall be distributed. The settlor's directions for payment should be clear, specific, and complete. Ambiguities should be avoided. For example, the instrument should not recite, "The settlor wishes the trustee to manage and invest the trust estate and pay the income to Jerry Flynn for five years, and thereafter to Jerry Flynn and Janet Flynn in equal shares." Perhaps the settlor knows exactly what she intends the trust to accomplish, but the trust instrument does not convey this. The lack of definiteness leads to questions concerning the implementation of the trust, e.g., Is the trustee obliged to reinvest the trust funds? May she deduct administrative expenses? Does the trust continue indefinitely? Spelling out the powers and duties of the trustee will lessen the risk of injured feelings and litigation.

Article IV

The trustee shall have the following powers and discretions in addition to those conferred by law:

(a) To retain the property described in "Schedule A," and any other property added to the trust estate;

(b) To invest and reinvest, to sell or exchange the principal of this trust in such stocks or bonds as trustee shall in its discretion deem to be reasonable, expedient or proper regardless of whether such stocks, bonds or other property shall be legal investments for trusts under the laws of State A;

(c) To vote in person or by proxy all stocks or other securities held by trustee;

(d) To exchange the securities of any corporation or company for other securities issued by the same, or by any other corporation or company at such times and upon such terms, as trustee shall deem proper; and

(e) To exercise with respect to all stock, bonds, and other investments held by trustee, all rights, powers, and privileges as are lawfully exercised by any person owning similar property in his/her own right.

COMMENT: All powers that a settlor wishes to grant to the trustee should be included in the trust instrument and clearly defined. Limitations, if desired, should also be specifically enumerated. The settlor of this trust has definite ideas about what she wants the trustee to do. Section *b* above, for example, states that the trustee shall decide what investments shall be made on behalf of the trust, despite the statutes of State A, which declare and enumerate permissible trust investments. It is possible, and perfectly legal, for settlors to include such provisions in trust agreements. It is only when the settlor fails to mention the type of investments the trustee may make that such statutes go into effect. The intent of these statutes is benevolent rather than restrictive. They are designed to help inexperienced investors to invest prudently.

Article V

The settlor hereby declares that this agreement and the trusts hereby created shall be irrevocable and not subject to modification.

COMMENT: Placing property in trust saves income tax only if the trust is irrevocable. The income produced by the trust is always subject to tax, but savings occur when the income is taxed to a beneficiary in a lower tax bracket than to the grantor (settlor) (see I.R.C. § 676 [1939]).

Article VI

Both trustee and successor trustee have agreed to waive compensation for their services.

COMMENT: The trust instrument should provide expressly for the trustee's compensation or its waiver. In the absence of such a provision, statutes in many states fix or limit the rates of the commission. Unless the settlor indicates whether the trustee shall receive or forego compensation as agreed, the court may order the statutory amount paid from the trust income.

Article VII

The settlor hereby appoints as successor trustee, Robert C. White of 1040 Merry Lane, Flowertown, Apple County, State A. In the event that trustee or successor trustee shall die, resign, become incapacitated, or for any reason fail or refuse to act as trustee, settlor shall have the power to appoint a successor. Any successor trustee shall have all the powers and obligations of the trustee named herein.

COMMENT: It is important for the settlor to name a successor in case the original trustee is unable or unwilling to serve. Because of their fiduciary responsibilities, all trustees should be selected with care, keeping in mind the specific purposes for which the trust is created.

Article VIII

The validity of this trust and the construction of its provisions shall be governed solely by the laws of the State of A as they now exist or may exist in the future.

COMMENT: Each state may have certain restrictions on trusts which may affect the purpose of the trust. Such restrictions must be determined before a workable instrument can be drafted. A clause similar to this may prove more valuable than it would appear. For example, Helen Flynn, the settlor, lives in State A, as does Betty White, the trustee. At the inception of the trust, at least, it will be governed by the laws of A because that is the place where it is to be administered (carried out by the trustee), according to Article VIII. However, this situation can change. Suppose Betty moves to the State of N and transacts business there. The laws of N regarding trusts might be quite different from the laws of A, with the result that new limitations are placed on Betty and the trust does not achieve what Helen had intended. Or suppose that a year from now state A enacts a special tax on inter vivos trusts. Does the Flynn trust have to pay the tax, since such a law was not in existence at the time of the trust's creation? A court could resolve such problems, but the process would be both time- and money-consuming (e.g., the question involving the laws of two states, A and N, might require a federal action). It is advisable to include a clause that prevents such questions from arising.

IN WITNESS WHEREOF, settlor and trustees have executed this agreement at Flowertown, the day and year written above.

IN PRESENCE OF:

_____   _____
(Witness)   (Settlor)

_____   _____
(Witness)   (Trustee)

                                                   _____
                                                   (Successor Trustee)

STATE OF <u>A</u>   ⎫
                           ⎬ ss.
County of <u>Apple</u>   ⎭

The foregoing instrument was acknowledged before me this <u>1st</u> day of <u>June,</u> 1984, by <u>Helen A. Flynn</u> as settlor and <u>Betty White,</u> and <u>Robert White</u> as trustees. [*Notarial Seal*]

                                                   _____
                                                   Notary Public
_____

Assignment 116

George Conover decides to create an inter vivos trust for his children, Melissa and Gary, with his wife, Grace, as trustee and trust property consisting of real estate in your state which he operates as a summer residence for tourists. Using this information, and supplying more, as necessary to indicate the settlor's intention, compile checklists similar to the one in Exhibit 10.1 and, using both checklists, draft an instrument for the Conover trust.

The sample checklist in Exhibit 10.2 may be used for drafting a trust.

Exhibit 10.2 Sample Checklist for Drafting an Inter Vivos Trust

Names and Addresses of Necessary Parties

Settlor(s):   _____
                     _____

Trustee(s):   _____

Relationship, if any, to settlor: _____

Successor trustee: _____

Corporate trustee: _____

Beneficiary:

Income beneficiary: _____

Exhibit 10.2 *(continued)*

Successor beneficiary: _____

Remainderman: _____

Relationship of
  beneficiary, if any, to
  settlor: _____

Trust Property *

Real estate: _____

Stocks, bonds: _____

Cash: _____

Insurance policy: _____

Other property: _____

Trust Purpose

Description: _____
_____

Legality: _____
_____

Termination of Trust

Trust duration: _____

Distribution of principal
  upon termination: _____

Revocability of Trust

Revocable by settlor: _____

Irrevocable: _____

Trustee's Duties

Payment or withholding of
  income: _____
_____

"Sprinkling" of income
  among beneficiaries: _____
_____

Accumulation of income: _____
_____

Invasion of trust principal: _____

Payment of principal: _____

Bonding and accounting: _____

---

* An attached schedule describes the trust property in detail.   Schedule not included here.

Exhibit 10.2 *(continued)*

Trustee's Powers

Discretionary: _____

Restrictions: _____

Sale, lease or mortgage
trust property: _____

_____

Allowance or limitation on
investments: _____

Others: _____

_____

Term of Trustee

Resignation: _____

_____

Removal: _____

_____

Trustee's Rights and Liabilities

Rights: _____

Acceptance or rejection: _____

Compensation: _____

Liabilities: _____

Special Clauses in Trust

Spendthrift: _____

Others: _____

_____

_____

Termination of Trust

Death of settlor: _____

_____

Death of beneficiary: _____

_____

Distribution of trust
principal on termination
of trust: _____

_____

_____

Chapter 11

Tax Considerations
with Short-Term Trusts

Scope of the Chapter

This chapter is concerned with the uses of short-term trusts and the tax consequences of such trusts. Included are a description of the powers and duties of a grantor also acting as trustee or of another person appointed trustee, examples of typical short-term trusts, discussion of gift and estate taxes on trusts, and current federal guidelines affecting the creation and taxation of such trusts. A section on drafting a short-term trust and a sample short-term trust is provided.

Caveat: This chapter briefly summarizes tax provisions that relate to short-term trusts. In order to gain a better understanding of the subject matter, the reader is urged to study Chapter 15.

Competencies

After completing this chapter, the paralegal should be able to:

- Identify, define, and explain the use of short-term trusts

- Explain the federal guidelines affecting the creation and taxation of short-term trusts

- Begin to understand the tax consequences of the 1976 Tax Reform Act and the 1981 Economic Recovery Tax Act

- Determine, according to the Internal Revenue Code, whether the grantor, beneficiary, or trust will be taxed on the income produced by the trust

- Assist in the preliminary drafting of short-term trusts

Short-Term Trusts and Their Tax Consequences

Both the federal and state governments and some cities levy and collect taxes on income. The income subject to tax includes personal income, corporate income, and trust income, which is a form of personal income. In the law of trusts, the income produced from the property used to create the trust is taxed. The federal tax laws pertaining to trusts and trust income taxes are found in the Internal Revenue Code [I.R.C.] §§ 641–683. Either the settlor (grantor),[1] beneficiary, or in some instances the trustee must pay the taxes on income produced by trust property. Short-term trusts are frequently created to transfer the tax obligation from the settlor to the beneficiary.

It is important to delegate the drafting of the trust instrument only to counsel knowledgeable in this area. Often the paralegal will be asked to prepare a preliminary draft. The instrument must conform not only to the requirements of the Internal Revenue Code but to state law as well. For an example of a short-term trust and an exercise in drafting one, see page 316.

Duration of a Trust

Generally a trust can last for as long as the grantor wishes, but state tax laws and other statutes place limitations on the powers of the trustee and the length of time property can be held in trust. A trust cannot last indefinitely and stay within the bounds of the Rule Against Perpetuities (see page 181). *Short-term trusts* (also known as *"comeback," "give and keep," "reversionary,"* or *"Clifford" trusts*) are trusts of limited duration in which property is transferred to the trust for a stated time, after which it reverts (returns) to the grantor. The income the trust property produces is taxable to the trust, i.e., paid by the trustee, or to the beneficiary, rather than to the grantor (settlor). At the end of the trust period, the beneficiary loses equitable title to the property because of its reversion to the grantor or its passing to another beneficiary. When the grantor is in a high income bracket and the beneficiary is in a lower one, the lower rates at which the trust or low-income beneficiary pays taxes result in a tax savings. Of course, the ultimate amount of tax is an unknown since it depends on such factors as the income tax bracket of the grantor, the income tax bracket of the beneficiary, the size of the income conveyed in trust, the deductions available, and whether the trust or the beneficiary pays the tax.

In setting up a short-term trust, the law requires the grantor to give income-producing property to the trust. The trustee has legal title to the property for the duration of the trust. At the end of the trust period, the grantor gets the property back in complete ownership unless

---

1. In this chapter, the terms grantor and settlor are used interchangeably.

another beneficiary is designated. In order to qualify for tax purposes as a valid short-term trust, the duration of the trust must last for the lifetime of the beneficiary *or* for at least ten years and a day before the trust property reverts to the grantor (see I.R.C. § 673 and below, page 315). During the trust's existence, the trustee either pays the income produced by the property to the beneficiary quarterly or annually, or accumulates the income for payment to the beneficiary at or before the end of the trust. So long as the income is paid to the beneficiary and the trust lasts the required time period, the grantor is not taxed on the income (see discussion of the term "grantor-taxable" below).

Example: Mary transfers shares of stock to William to hold, invest, manage, and pay the income to her son, Robert, for ten years and a day. Then the stock is to return (revert) to Mary, if she is living, or is to be given to her successors. Mary has created a short-term trust.

Revocable and Irrevocable Trusts

Trusts may be revocable (i.e., capable of being revoked or canceled by the settlor) or irrevocable. The grantor of a revocable trust has the advantage of being able to retake or "recapture" the property placed in trust, but the disadvantage in doing so is that the income produced in the trust will be taxed to the grantor (settlor). The grantor of an irrevocable trust is at a disadvantage in that he or she cannot take back the trust property at least until the trust has ended, but at an advantage in that irrevocable trust income is not taxable to the grantor. In the terminology of trusts and tax law, a grantor who creates a revocable trust or retains control over the trust property in an irrevocable trust is said to be *grantor-taxable,* i.e., the income produced by the trust is taxed to the grantor and not to the recipient (beneficiary) (for examples of retention of control by the grantor, see pages 312–316). Remember: Income from an irrevocable short-term trust is grantor-taxable unless the trust is irrevocable for at least ten years and a day or, in some instances, the lifetime of the beneficiary.

Uses of Short-Term Trusts

Short-term trusts may be put to many uses, some of which are:

• Supporting a relative

• Financing annual gifts to children and others

• Establishing a child in a business or profession

• Financing life insurance, e.g., on a child's life for the benefit of grandchildren

Examples of such trusts will be discussed later in this chapter.

A short-term trust is most appropriate for people in middle or high income tax brackets who have some investment income to spare temporarily but who want the capital and earning power back at a later time for retirement or other needs. But short-term trusts do not bring benefits to all users. For example, in order to diminish estate and inheritance death taxes, wealthy persons may find it best to reduce their holdings by absolute gifts or by ordinary trusts in which property does *not* revert (return) to the original grantor. A trust that eventually restores the trust property to the original owner could be of little value to the wealthy settlor.

The biggest advantage of the short-term trust is that the income from the trust property is taxed at the lower-bracket rates of the trust or its beneficiaries instead of being taxed in the grantor's higher bracket. This method of attempting to shift income by means of a trust to reduce income tax is regulated by the tax laws. Only by complying with the tax rules can the grantor obtain substantial tax savings (for current federal guidelines, see page 311).

Example: In 1983, Albert Johnston is married and has three children all under the age of ten. His taxable income is $37,000, which includes $2,700 interest from U.S. bonds. Assume that Johnston's income tax is approximately $7,250 by filing a joint return and his after-tax income is $29,750. He is in a 35 percent tax bracket. Johnston sets up a temporary trust for each of his three children and puts U.S. savings bonds into each trust, creating income of $900 per year per trust. Provided none of the income from the trust is actually used for support or maintenance of the children, Johnston's tax will be $945 less. This figure represents the tax he does not have to pay on the $2,700 of trust income. Use of the income must be restricted or it will be attributed to the father, and all tax benefits will be lost (I.R.C. § 677). The three children keep the entire $2,700 bond interest, and because they earn no other income, they pay no tax on their shares. The Johnston family has a $945 increase in yearly net income. Without a trust, the tax takes 35 percent of the $2,700 bond interest; with a trust, the family keeps it all. Since the income from the trust is not being used for the support of the children, the parent does not lose the $1,000 dependency exemption for each child as long as the parent continues to furnish over half the child's support.

Albert Johnston—35% Tax Bracket		
No Trust		With Trust
Income produced by U.S. bonds $2,700		Johnston puts U.S. bonds in separate trusts for three children. Each child receives $900
Tax paid by Johnston on interest income (35%) $ 945		Tax paid by each child on the total interest income of $2,700 0
		Additional spendable income for the Johnston family $945

No matter what the client's bracket, use of a temporary trust can actually increase spendable income.

Example: Milton Ostlin, in the 50 percent tax bracket, helps support his sister with $850 a year as a gift. To do this he must earn $1,700, because he needs that much income in order to keep $850 after taxes. By putting property into a temporary trust, in an amount that would create income of $850 per year, Milton would completely remove the trust income generated ($850) from his taxable income. Milton keeps the additional $850 ($1,700 minus $850) it would have cost him to make the gift without the trust, less $425 in tax. He gains $425 spendable income. The assumption made in this case is that Milton's sister has little or no income of her own.

Milton Ostlin—50% Tax Bracket		
No Trust	**With Trust**	
Income produced by stock $1,700	Ostlin puts half the stock into trust for income to sister (sister receives)	$850
Tax paid by Ostlin on stock income (50%) 850	The other half of the stock he retains, but must pay his tax (50%)	850
	Minus tax owed	425
Amount sister receives 850	Additional spendable income for Ostlin	$425

Each trust is a separate taxable entity, and each beneficiary is taxed according to the amount of benefit (income) received. The grantor may keep the total amount of income to be derived from the principal in the lowest possible tax brackets by spreading the principal among several trusts or by setting up a separate trust for each of several beneficiaries, using either separate property or a fractional interest in a single item of property for each trust. With only one trust, more tax might have to be paid. Here again, the tax laws strictly regulate the manner in which tax savings may be achieved (I.R.C. §§ 651–652, 661–667).

The Duration Rule

The I.R.S. Code provision that the minimum period a short-term trust must run is ten years and one day from the date property is transferred to the trust *or* the lifetime of an income beneficiary, whichever turns out to be shorter (I.R.C. § 673) is called the *duration rule* (see page 315). If the beneficiary dies before the ten-year-and-a-day term expires, the trust is valid nevertheless and shifts away from the grantor whatever income is earned in the years preceding the beneficiary's death. The grantor could also set the trust to last until he or she dies or becomes disabled, if it is reasonable to expect that neither event will take place within ten years and a day. The trust instrument must be drafted, and the transfers made, so that the trust property will be reasonably certain to remain in the trust long enough to satisfy Internal Revenue's duration rule.

The duration rule applies to every part of the principal, including whatever the grantor adds after setting up the trust. Where the trust is designed to exist for 12 years, the grantor may add property to the trust principal during years 1 and 2 with no tax owed by the grantor. Income from principal added in years 3 through 12, however, is taxed to the grantor, because that part of the principal would revert in less than 10 years. The solution would be to set up a separate trust of the principal that was added during the 3 through 12-year period and to specify that this separate trust will last 10 years and a day from the date of creation.

Example: If Jack places 100 shares of stock in a short-term trust on June 1, 1975, which will end on June 2, 1985, and then added a second 100 shares on June 1, 1979, he would be liable for the income taxes on the second 100 shares, since the termination date for the trust was June 2, 1985. According to the duration rule, property added to the trust during the ten-year-and-a-day period will be taxed to the grantor.

Review, with Examples, of Uses of Short-Term Trusts

Taxes are major reducers of earned income. Consequently, almost without exception, the American consumer's spendable income, consists of after-tax dollars. The basic purpose of the short-term trust is to confer a benefit on another person by using before-tax dollars rather than after-tax dollars. The advantage is that a beneficiary who is in a lower tax bracket than the donor requires less gross income to provide a certain amount of after-tax, spendable income.

The following situations illustrate common uses of the short-term trust.

Example: Newell Canfield, in the 42 percent tax bracket, wants to have $10,000 available for his daughter's college education. One method of accumulating the money would be simply to save the income over a ten-year period but it would require all the income from a 5 percent investment of over $34,000. An alternative would be to set up a qualifying short-term trust. The same amount of money ($10,000) will be available from a 5 percent investment of only $20,000. Newell would achieve the desired result and increase his own after-tax income by $300 by using a trust.

Example: Helena, in the 50 percent bracket, wishes to give her aged father, Henry, $3,000 per year for the rest of his life. In order to make a direct gift, Helena might use the income from a 6 percent investment of $100,000. Instead, she could set up a trust to last for her father's life and put into it only $50,000 worth of property, investing this at 6 percent annually, to produce $3,000 per year for her father. Bear in mind that the donor will be taxed on the trust income if current payments from a trust are used to pay a legal obligation of support which the donor has, e.g., living expenses in the case of a minor child, or, in some states, an aged parent.

Example: Antonio Morello's 16-year-old daughter is planning to study medicine and will probably be ready to set up her own practice in about 14 years. He wants to have a fund of $25,000 ready for his daughter at that time. Without a trust, in order to reach that goal in 14 years, Antonio, who is in the 33 percent tax bracket, would have to channel into the fund the income from more than $52,000 in 5 percent securities which he owns. Another method would be for Antonio to place $35,000 of these 5 percent-yielding securities in a short-term trust for 14 years, which would accumulate $25,000 income. In addition, Antonio would have about $500 more per year of spendable income.

Example: Drew Middleton wants to help his adult son, Christopher, and his wife pay off the mortgage on their home within ten years by supplying the yearly payment of $2,500. Christopher is in the 22 percent tax bracket; Drew is in the 50 percent bracket. Without a trust, the father would have to invest $100,000 at 5 percent interest to make an annual gift of $2,500 to his son. Using a trust, he would need income-producing property worth only $64,000 at 5 percent interest to produce the $2,500 annual gift. Actually the trust would yield a larger income, but because Christopher must pay income tax on it at a rate of 22 percent, the net income would be $2,500. Drew would have $900 more spendable income per year and could avoid paying gift tax under the unified gift and estate tax law.

Powers and Duties of the Grantor–Trustee or Other Trustees

Assume that Marian Lind is the grantor throughout the discussion that follows. As grantor, she may appoint herself sole trustee and legally transfer the property from herself personally to herself as trustee, or may designate anyone else as trustee, e.g., a relative, friend, professional adviser, trust company, or bank. The trustee's powers are subject to special restrictions when either the grantor or a nonadverse party is the trustee.[2]

Where the trust property is shares of stock, Marian, the *grantor-trustee,* or some other trustee, can continue to vote it, sell it and invest in other stock, or use the stock to gain control of a corporation. The trustee controls the investment of trust funds. Where the trust proper-

---

2. A non-adverse party is defined by I.R.C. § 672 as "any person who is not an adverse party." An adverse party as defined by the Code is "any person having a substantial beneficial interest in the trust which would be adversely affected by the exercise or nonexercise of the power which he possesses respecting the trust." For further discussion, see page 313.

ty is real estate, the trustee can manage it, sell it, and buy other property for the trust. The trustee can exchange bonds for other equivalent securities or convert the property as discussed previously (see page 239).

If Marian is both grantor and trustee, she can return to herself any part of the principal, provided she replaces it with other property of equal value. She can even borrow from the trust, subject to the limitations that the loan and interest be repaid by the end of the trust's taxable year and that she provides adequate security for the loan and pays the usual amount of interest (I.R.C. § 675 [1939]).

If Marian retains overly broad powers, the tax benefits of the trust may be lost even if she never exercises these powers. The basic principle is that she will be treated as the owner of the property for income tax purposes if she keeps too much control over the property (see page 313) or makes the transfer of the property to the trust for too short a time period. She may not reclaim the property on demand (I.R.C. § 676 [1939]), use the income (I.R.C. § 677 [1939]), control the beneficial enjoyment (I.R.C. § 674 [1939]), or otherwise retain too much dominion over the property. If she does, the short-term trust will not produce the desired income tax savings since Marian, not the lower-income beneficiary, will be taxed for receiving benefits from the trust (for more on grantor-taxable trusts, see page 311).

The trustee, Marian, can be given the power to decide each year whether to distribute or accumulate the current year's income. Suppose the beneficiary receives a large amount of income from sources other than the trust. Under such circumstances, the beneficiary might pay less tax if the trust income were left to accumulate rather than being distributed to the beneficiary.

A trust over which the trustee is given the power to choose between accumulation and distribution is called a *sprinkling trust*. A *"hose and spray" power* is the trustee's power to distribute ("sprinkle") the trust income among various persons and to decide how much to distribute to each. According to the Internal Revenue Code, only someone other than the grantor can have the "hose and spray" power as trustee. If the grantor wants the trustee to have "hose and spray" powers, the appointed trustee must be someone outside the immediate family, i.e., an independent trustee who may not be a spouse, parent, brother, or sister, or in the case of multiple trustees, no more than half the trustees may be so related (I.R.C. § 674 [1939]).

The short-term trust may serve a protective purpose as well. If Marian were concerned about the responsibility of the beneficiary, she might include a *spendthrift clause* in the trust (see page 266). The trust may contain restrictions on the beneficiary's ability to transfer the trust's income to creditors or on the right of creditors to demand payment of their debts from the trust property before this property is distributed to the beneficiaries. This protection ends once the beneficiary actually receives the distribution of the income.

Gift and Estate Taxes as Related to Trusts

In recent years, tax laws have dramatically changed with the enactment of the Tax Reform Act of 1976 (TRA), the Economic Recovery Tax
Act of 1981 (ERTA), and the Tax Equity and Fiscal Responsibility Act
of 1982 (TEFRA). The Tax Reform Act and the Economic Recovery Tax
Act have made major revisions in the gift and estate tax laws. The Tax
Equity and Fiscal Responsibility Act, except for revisions concerning
pensions, has little direct effect on laws affecting gifts and estates and
will not be discussed in detail in this text.

In creating a short-term trust, the grantor is generally making a gift
to the beneficiaries and must pay tax on that gift, unless the tax is
eliminated by exclusions and the unified credit discussed below. In
addition, the grantor is keeping a "come-back" (reversionary) interest
in the trust property. The computable value of the grantor's reversionary interest in the trust property, i.e., the value of the trust property
when it reverts to the grantor, is included in the total value of the
grantor's estate if the grantor dies before the trust ends. Therefore the
grantor should consider all tax consequences before creating a trust.

Unified Gift and Estate Tax Rates

Before January 1, 1977, there were separate rate schedules for estate
taxes and gift taxes. Gift tax rates were approximately three-fourths of
the estate tax rates. The gift tax base (the amount on which the tax
was computed) was the market value of the property given as a gift; it
did not include the gift taxes paid by the donor on the gift. Therefore,
the estate was diminished by the amount of the gift taxes paid, but no
transfer (gift or estate) taxes were ever paid on that amount. The
estate tax was computed on the basis of the value of the taxable estate
(see page 418), and no deduction was permitted for the estate tax paid.
Therefore, a transfer (estate) tax was paid on the portion of the estate
used to pay estate taxes.

In the Tax Reform Act of 1976, the tax rates for estate and gift taxes
were unified into a single schedule. The rates are progressive and are
based on cumulative lifetime and deathtime transfers. One of the
purposes of the TRA was to eliminate the preferential rates in effect
prior to 1977 for lifetime transfers (three-fourths of the estate tax rates
at each corresponding bracket). Congress concluded that the lower tax
rates for lifetime gifts were unfair because so many people were not
wealthy enough to make lifetime gifts. The TRA unified tax rates
ranged from 18% for the first $10,000 in taxable transfers to a top rate
of 70% on taxable transfers in excess of $5 million. The Economic
Recovery Tax Act of 1981 amended this unified rate schedule by
significantly reducing the tax rate on transfers over $2,500,000 during a

four-year transitional period beginning in 1982. When the change is fully implemented in 1985, the maximum rate on taxable transfers over $2,500,000 will be lowered to 50%.[3] Table 11.1 reflects the annual reduction until after 1985.

Table 11.1 Unified Rate Schedule for Gift and Estate Taxes

If the Amount With Which the Tentative Tax to be Computed is:	*The Tentative Tax is:*
Not over $10,000	18% of such amount
Over $10,000 but not over $20,000	$1,800 plus 20% of the excess over $10,000
Over $20,000 but not over $40,000	$3,800 plus 22% of the excess over $20,000
Over $40,000 but not over $60,000	$8,200 plus 24% of the excess over $40,000
Over $60,000 but not over $80,000	$13,000 plus 26% of the excess over $60,000
Over $80,000 but not over $100,000	$18,200 plus 28% of the excess over $80,000
Over $100,000 but not over $150,000	$23,800 plus 30% of the excess over $100,000
Over $150,000 but not over $250,000	$38,800 plus 32% of the excess over $150,000
Over $250,000 but not over $500,000	$70,800 plus 34% of the excess over $250,000
Over $500,000 but not over $750,000	$155,800 plus 37% of the excess over $500,000
Over $750,000 but not over $1,000,000	$248,300 plus 39% of the excess over $750,000
Over $1,000,000 but not over $1,250,000	$345,800 plus 41% of the excess over $1,000,000
Over $1,250,000 but not over $1,500,000	$448,300 plus 43% of the excess over $1,250,000
Over $1,500,000 but not over $2,000,000	$555,800 plus 45% of the excess over $1,500,000
Over $2,000,000 but not over $2,500,000	$780,800 plus 49% of the excess over $2,000,000
For 1982—In the Case of Decedents Dying and Gifts Made in 1982:	
Over $2,500,000 but not over $3,000,000	$1,025,800 plus 53% of the excess over $2,500,000
Over $3,000,000 but not over $3,500,000	$1,290,800 plus 57% of the excess over $3,000,000
Over $3,500,000 but not over $4,000,000	$1,575,800 plus 61% of the excess over $3,500,000
Over $4,000,000	$1,880,800 plus 65% of the excess over $4,000,000
For 1983—In the Case of Decedents Dying and Gifts Made in 1983:	
Over $2,500,000 but not over $3,000,000	$1,025,800 plus 53% of the excess over $2,500,000
Over $3,000,000 but not over $3,500,000	$1,290,800 plus 57% of the excess over $3,000,000
Over $3,500,000	$1,575,800 plus 60% of the excess over $3,500,000

---

3. The implementation has been delayed until 1988 by the 1984 Tax Reform Act (see source note on p. 305).

Table 11.1 *(continued)*

For 1984—In the Case of Decedents Dying and Gifts Made in 1984:	
Over $2,500,000 but not over $3,000,000	$1,025,800 plus 53% of the excess over $2,500,000
Over $3,000,000	$1,290,800 plus 55% of the excess over $3,000,000
For 1985	
Over $2,500,000	50%

Source: U.S. Department of the Treasury, *I.R.S. Publication No. 448,* May 1982.
Note: This rate schedule shows that the maximum rate for the unified estate and gift tax will be reduced from 70% to 50% and that the reduction will be phased in from 1981 to 1985. However, in 1984 Congress passed the 1984 Tax Reform Act which freezes the maximum estate tax rate at 55% until 1988, when it will be reduced to 50%. The rates (percents) on taxable transfers of amounts under $2,500,000 do not change. Other important ERTA changes will be discussed in detail in Chapter 15.

Before 1977 the law provided for a "one-time gift tax specific lifetime exemption" of $30,000 for each donor. For a married couple, the exemption available was $60,000 if the spouses consented to treat the gifts as though made by both of them. In addition, an annual $3,000 per donee exclusion was permitted ($6,000 per donee if the gift-splitting provision for spouses was used). The estate tax specific exemption was $60,000 ($30,000 in the case of a decedent who was a non-resident alien). The estate tax exemption was not increased for any portion of the gift tax specific exemption which was not used against lifetime transfers (gifts). The 1976 Tax Reform Act repealed I.R.C. § 2052, which provided for the estate tax ($60,000) specific exemption, and I.R.C. § 2521, which provided for the gift tax ($30,000) specific exemption. The 1981 Economic Recovery Tax Act changed the annual $3,000 gift tax exclusion to $10,000.

Exhibit 11.1 summarizes the changes in the Gift and Estate Tax Laws.

Exhibit 11.1 Summary of Changes in Gift and Estate Tax Laws

Pre-1977

Gift Tax Laws

Exemption: $30,000—One-time gift tax lifetime exemption for each donor

Exclusion: $3,000—Annual per donee exclusion increased to $6,000 per donee if spouses consented to make gift together

Estate Tax Laws

Exemption: $60,000—One-time estate tax lifetime exemption

Changes Taking Effect in 1977 Under the Tax Reform Act of 1976

The TRA repealed both the $30,000 gift tax exemption and the $60,000 estate tax exemption and replaced them with a flat rate unified transfer tax credit that is subtracted from the tax due. A single, or as it is called, *unified credit* is subtracted from the cumulative sum of lifetime taxable gifts, with the balance available as a

Exhibit 11.1 *(continued)*

credit against estate taxes. See Ross Nygard example below. The previous separate gift and estate tax rate schedules are also combined into one unified transfer tax schedule.

The new flat rate unified transfer tax credit was phased in over a five-year period with an increase in the credit each year beginning in 1977. The yearly increase in the credit and its exemption equivalent, which replaced the old $60,000 estate tax exemption and the $30,000 gift tax exemption, is shown in the following table:

Year	Unified Credit	Exemption Equivalent
1977	$30,000	$120,667
1978	$34,000	$134,000
1979	$38,000	$147,333
1980	$42,500	$161,563
1981 & after	$47,000	$175,625

This table illustrates that a single man or woman who died in 1981 would have had to own an estate valued at more than $175,625 in order for federal estate taxes to be owed the government.

The TRA did *not* change the annual per donee $3,000 gift tax exclusion.

Changes Taking Effect in 1982 Under the Economic Recovery Tax Act of 1981

The ERTA amended the TRA and increased the amount of the unified credit from the $47,000 in 1981 as shown in the table above to the following annual changes:

Year	Unified Credit	Exemption Equivalent
1982	$ 62,800	$225,000
1983	$ 79,300	$275,000
1984	$ 96,300	$325,000
1985	$121,800	$400,000
1986	$155,800	$500,000
1987 & after	$192,800	$600,000

It is estimated that by 1987 only 0.5% of all decedents' estates will be subject to federal estate tax. As illustrated by the table here, a single person who dies in 1987 would have to have an estate valued at more than $600,000 in order for federal estate taxes to be owed the government.

The ERTA also amended the annual $3,000 gift tax exclusion. Beginning in 1982, a taxpayer may give up to $10,000 annually to any individual donee free of gift tax. If the donor's spouse consents to the gift, the annual exclusion per donee is $20,000. This consent of the spouse is called *gift-splitting*.

Gift-making, gift-splitting between spouses, and the unified credit are all means of reducing tax liability. But remember, the unified credit is allowed against lifetime gift taxes, or estate taxes, or both. However, unlike the $10,000 per donee annual exclusion, which is available to the donor each year, the unified credit once used is terminated. It can be used to diminish or eliminate the tax on lifetime gifts or to diminish or eliminate the estate tax.

Example: Ross Nygard has decided to give his son, Tim, a lifetime gift of $600,000. The table below shows the gift tax that Ross must pay, depending on the year in which he makes the gift. Assume that Ross's wife, Martha, does not agree to gift-splitting and that the $10,000 annual exclusion has already been subtracted from the total gift and that no part of Ross's unified credit has been used previously. Using the Unified Rate Schedule (Table 11.1), a $600,000 gift would have a tentative tax (tax calculated before unified credit is deducted) of $192,800.

Year Gift Made	Unified Credit	Gift Tax
1982	($192,800 – $ 62,800)	$130,000
1983	($192,800 – $ 79,300)	$113,500
1984	($192,800 – $ 96,300)	$ 96,500
1985	($192,800 – $121,800)	$ 71,000
1986	($192,800 – $155,800)	$ 37,000
1987	($192,800 – $192,800)	$ 0

By 1987 no gift tax would be owed, but the unified credit would be entirely used up. Now assume that instead of giving Tim the $600,000 outright Ross places the money in a ten-year-and-a-day (short-term) trust for Tim. This trust is established on January 1, 1982. The trust property is valued (see page 310) by the I.R.S. as follows: [4]

Trust Term	Value as Percentage of Total Value	Computed Value of $600,000 Gift
10 years	44.16%	$264,960

Gift Tax If Gift Is Given in Year	Prior to Deducting Unified Credit	After Deducting Unified Credit
1982	$75,886	$13,086 (credit—$62,800)
1983	$75,886	$ 0 (credit—$79,300, leaves $3,414 remaining)
1984	$75,886	$ 0 (credit—$96,300 with $20,414 remaining)

The tax advantages of the trust over an outright gift, which improve each year until 1987, are clear.

Assignment 117

On January 1, 1984, Marion Reese placed property valued at $650,000 in a ten-year-and-a-day short-term trust for her niece, Laurie Nelson. Using the tables on pages 416 and 417 (in Chapter 15) and page 310, compute the gift tax Marion must pay. Assume that Marion has no spouse and that she has not used up her annual $10,000 exclusion for Laurie or any part of her unified credit.

---

4. The percentage 44.16 was used before December 1983 (see page 310).

Assignment 118

In January of 1985, Reed Shapiro has decided to place $80,000 in a short-term trust for his daughter, Beth. Assume that Reed has already used his annual $10,000 exclusion for Beth in 1985 and that he has previously used $10,000 of his unified credit. Assume that Reed is not "splitting" the gift with his wife. Compute the gift tax Reed must pay.

The Gift-Splitting Provision

Gift-splitting by spouses has been retained under the new law. When married, the grantor, with the other spouse's consent, may split the lifetime gift to the donee. The gift will then be treated as though half was given by the grantor (donor) and the other half by the spouse. Thus, the spouses may give $20,000 annually to each donee tax free if each spouse consents to having the gift treated as being given half by each spouse. The result is that the married grantor can put more property into a trust while paying less gift tax than a single person would pay (I.R.C. § 2513).

Example: Using the $10,000 annual exclusion, a gift may be given free of gift tax in the following examples:

If You Are	Married	Single
and giving to one person	two $10,000 annual exclusions = $20,000	one $10,000 annual exclusion = $10,000
and giving to two persons	four $10,000 annual exclusions = $40,000	two $10,000 annual exclusions = $20,000
and giving to three persons	six $10,000 annual exclusions = $60,000	three $10,000 annual exclusions = $30,000

Assignment 119

Compute the maximum amount of a tax free gift a married couple could give to eight persons. Assume the couple has *not* previously used up any of their annual exclusions.

Perform the same computation for the year 1983 for a married couple and then a single person, assuming that the husband (in the case of the married couple) had previously given $2,000 in 1977 to his daughter, Martha, and that Martha will be one of the eight donees, and that the single person had previously given $2,800 to his mother and that his mother will be one of his eight donees.

Assignment 120

Michele and Bruce, husband and wife, decide to give a gift of $125,000 to their niece, Trudy, in December, 1984. Assuming the couple has not used either of their $10,000 exclusions for Trudy for 1984 nor the $96,300 unified credit, compute the aggregate gift tax the couple would have to pay on the gift (before the unified credit is subtracted), using the unified rate schedule shown on page 304. Now, assume that the couple chooses to reduce the gift tax as much as possible. (Remember that a *credit* is deducted *after* the tax has been computed.) How much gift tax would the couple pay?

Do the same computations, except that the amount of the gift is $570,000.

Valuation of the Short-Term (Clifford) Trust Property for Tax Purposes

The gift tax is computed not on the basis of income actually produced by the trust property but on the basis of the total value of the trust property. The total value is multiplied by a fraction supplied by Internal Revenue Service actuarial tables. These tables are based on statistical calculations to determine life expectancy. These actuarial tables reflect an attempt to value the right of the beneficiary to receive income from a given amount of property over a given period of years. The gift tax would be the same for the interest on trust property having an actual value of $10,000, no matter how much income the property produces each year.

By its decision in December 1983, the Internal Revenue Service (I.R.S.) has changed the amount a person can place into a Clifford (short term) trust without incurring a gift tax. As noted in previous discussions, the Clifford trust is a classic income-shifting device. Its major function is to divert income from the settlor, who usually is in a relatively high income tax bracket, to someone else in the family, e.g., child or aged parent, who usually is in a relatively low bracket. When the trust is established for at least ten-years and a day, its minimum period, the trust income is taxed either to the trust or to the lower income beneficiary (child or parent), depending on when this income is distributed. At the end of the term of the trust, the settlor repossesses the trust property and receives income from the trust once more.

Since inception of the Clifford trusts, an important consideration in creating them has been to assure that the current value of a gift to the trust qualified it for the annual gift tax exclusion. Provided that the income is to be paid annually to the beneficiary, that exclusion, now increased by the Economic Recovery Tax Act of 1981, is $10,000 for a single person and $20,000 for a married couple.

Under the valuation tables formerly in effect, the Internal Revenue Service used 6 percent as the annual interest rate attributable to the funds in this type of trust. Accordingly, for a ten-year period, the present value of the gift was listed at approximately 44.16% of the value of the property transferred. Therefore, the maximum amount

Table 11.2 Valuation Table

Trust Term	Percentage	Trust Term	Percentage
10 years	61.45	18 years	82.01
11 years	64.95	20 years	85.14
12 years	68.14	22 years	87.12
15 years	78.06	25 years	90.77

Source: Internal Revenue Bulletin No. 23, June 4, 1984.

that an individual could place in a Clifford trust without having the transfer be subject to a gift tax was $22,640, since $22,640 multiplied by 0.4416 is approximately $10,000. When the spouses made a gift jointly, the maximum amount doubled to $45,280.

The new valuation tables which became effective December 1, 1983 lower the amount that can be contributed without paying a gift tax (see Table 11.2). The Internal Revenue Service accomplished this change by raising the annual interest rate attributable to trust funds to 10% which is equivalent to a present value for a ten-year trust of approximately 61.45% of the amount transferred to the trust. This percentage was selected according to the Internal Revenue Service because it reflects the average annual yield rate paid on ten-year U.S. government obligations, e.g., ten-year U.S. Treasury Bonds. Consequently, the maximum that a taxpayer can put in the Clifford trust free of gift tax is now $16,275 because $16,275 multiplied by 61.45% equals $10,000, the limit on tax free gifts. If a husband and wife jointly make a gift to the trust, the maximum amount is doubled to $32,550.

For gift tax purposes, the value of the *present interest* of the trust property, i.e., the value of the trust property to its beneficiaries, varies with the length of time the trust runs and will usually be substantially less than the full (fair market) value of the property put in trust. As mentioned, the Internal Revenue Service computes the "present interest" of the property for gift tax purposes as a percentage of the full value of the trust property transferred.

Example: If after December 1, 1984, the grantor transfers property valued at $10,000 into a short-term (10-year) trust, the Internal Revenue Service would value the property for gift tax purposes at $6,145 (61.45% of $10,000). The grantor could then use his or her $10,000 annual exclusion to reduce the amount of the gift subject to tax. If the grantor, however, had previously used the $10,000 annual exclusion for that particular beneficiary and had made no prior taxable gifts, the grantor would be required to pay a gift tax on the $6,145 computed at the unified rate of 18% or $1,106.10 (see unified tax rate table, page 000). The grantor could then reduce or eliminate the gift tax by applying the unified credit (if not previously used). Therefore, if the grantor died in November, 1985, the available unified credit would be $121,800 (see table on page 306 and further discussion with examples, page 311).

The beneficiaries do not have a present interest in the income if the trust is designed to accumulate income instead of distributing it. The grantor is allowed a $10,000 annual exclusion for such trusts. Where the beneficiary is a minor, however, and the trust allows the trustee to elect between accumulating and paying out income to the beneficiary, the tax court's position is that the gift qualifies for the $10,000 exclusion under the special exclusion provision covering minors if the minor receives the accumulated income before or upon reaching the age of 21.

The right of the grantor to reclaim the trust property at the end of the trust period has a value and might subject the grantor's estate to taxation if the grantor dies during the trust period. Because of its value, this right must be included in the inventory of the decedent's estate. The value assigned to the property in trust will be less than the actual value, and since this value is added to the grantor's estate, the estate of a decedent grantor will pay less tax than that of a decedent owner whose property is valued at the fair market price (see table and examples below).

The following table shows the value of trust property which must be included in the grantor-decedent's estate. The assigned value depends on how long the trust still has to run when the grantor dies.

Trust Still to Run	Assigned Value per $100	Trust Still to Run	Assigned Value per $100
1 year	$94.34	6 years	$70.49
2 years	89.00	7 years	66.51
3 years	83.96	8 years	62.74
4 years	79.21	9 years	59.19
5 years	74.73	10 years	55.84

Example: A ten-year trust with property worth $10,000, which Norma Burch created for her aunt, still has five years to run when Norma dies. Only $7,473 of the $10,000 property would be included in Norma's estate. Any income accumulated by the trust at the time of death (but which will be distributed to the beneficiary later) will not be included in the estate. If no trust existed, all income earned from the $10,000 property after taxes, plus the $10,000 property itself, would be taxed as part of Norma's estate.

Example: Quentin Gardner, in a 32% tax bracket, sets up a short-term (ten-year) trust for his daughter with $50,000 worth of property which earns $3,000 annually. He dies two years before the end of the trust. Only $44,500 (500 × $89) is included in the estate, which is the remaining value of Quentin's right to the return of his property at the end of the trust (two years). The trust has accumulated income which will be distributed to the daughter after Quentin's death but which will not be included in the estate.

Current Federal Guidelines on Short-Term Trusts

The purpose of the short-term trust is usually to shift income tax liability from the higher income bracket of the grantor to the lower bracket of the beneficiary in order to preserve and maintain the maximum amount of the grantor's property for the benefit of family and heirs. The issue that the Internal Revenue Service and the tax court must resolve is whether (for federal income tax purposes) the grantor or the beneficiary is the owner of the trust property and thus liable for tax on its income (for current federal guidelines on short-term trusts, see I.R.C. §§ 671–677). The Internal Revenue Code and Regulations have established five rules for determining whether the grantor is the owner of the property for income tax purposes. If any one of the rules applies, the grantor is treated as the owner of all or part of the trust property. In order to avoid taxation as the owner of all or a portion of the trust property, the grantor must meet the requirements of *all five* rules: (1) the Recapture Rule (I.R.C. § 677), (2) the Enjoyment-Control Rule (I.R.C. § 674), (3) the Administrative-Control Rule (I.R.C. § 675), (4) the Premium-Payment Rule (I.R.C. § 677), and (5) the Too-Temporary Rule (Duration) (I.R.C. § 673).

Before discussing each rule individually, the definition of one essential term must be reviewed. As noted earlier, the term *grantor-taxable* means "taxable to the grantor." It is used by the guidelines to refer to any portion (all or part) of the trust property of which the grantor is treated as the owner for income tax purposes. An interest that is "grantor-taxable" is taxable to the grantor as though realized (received) by the grantor at the time it is realized (received) by the trust. In other words, if the Internal Revenue Service declares that the grantor is the owner of all or a portion of the trust property, he or she is taxed *at the time the trust receives the income* generated by the trust property. This is true even though the terms of the trust require the trustee to retain such income for distribution to the grantor at some later date or to distribute it to others, in which case the grantor will not receive it at all. The question of whether a trust is grantor-taxable depends on whether the would-be grantor has actually given up the benefit from, control of, and title to the trust property. If the answer is yes, the grantor is not taxed (the trust is not grantor-taxable); if no, the grantor is taxed (the trust is grantor-taxable).

Rule One: The Recapture Rule

The Recapture Rule makes the grantor liable for the tax if the income from the trust *may* be used for the benefit of the grantor or the grantor's spouse (I.R.C. § 677).

If the income of an interest in a trust *may* be paid to the grantor during any time period of the trust, i.e., may be recaptured by the grantor, that income is grantor-taxable. It is not necessary that the income of the trust be distributed immediately. Even if income were accumulated over the entire length of the trust, it would still be taxed to the grantor if he or she is to receive it at *some* time. However, only that part of the income payable to the grantor is taxed to the grantor.

Example: Ryan Jarrett creates a trust lasting ten years and one day and names Phillip Henslow income beneficiary and Karl Hauser to receive the remainder (principal and income) at the end of the trust. Dana Hopkins, the trustee, is given the discretionary power to pay the income to Ryan instead of to Phillip at any time during the trust. Ryan will be taxed for the amount of income he receives, if any, because of the Recapture Rule.

Associated with the tax consequences of the Recapture Rule is another legal concept involving an *adverse party*. An adverse party is any person having a substantial beneficial interest in a trust, e.g., a beneficiary who would lose that interest if the grantor revoked the trust. A grantor who cannot revoke a trust without the consent of an adverse party will not be taxed as the owner of the trust property (see I.R.C. § 672).

Under the Internal Revenue Code and the terms of the trust, if any person as an adverse party has the power to prevent payments to the grantor, the Recapture Rule does not apply, and the grantor is not taxed.

Example: If, in the Jarrett trust above, Ryan had provided that Karl, the remainderman, must consent to the trustee's discretionary decision to pay income to Ryan, Karl would be considered an "adverse party." Since Karl has this power, Ryan will not be taxed even if Karl does not exercise it. In other words, because Karl has the power to allow Ryan to receive or prevent him from receiving the trust income, Ryan is not grantor-taxable. Ryan will be taxed only on the trust income he actually receives, not on *all* the income the trust generates.

Rule Two: The Enjoyment-Control Rule

The Enjoyment-Control Rule makes the grantor liable for the tax if the grantor retains the power to control the beneficial enjoyment of the trust income or corpus (I.R.C. § 674).

The retention of the power to control or influence the enjoyment of the income or principal from the trust subjects the grantor to taxation, even though the trust property may never again directly benefit the grantor personally, e.g., may never return to the grantor. The income of a trust which is subject to control by the grantor without the consent of an adverse party is grantor-taxable. To avoid taxation, therefore, the grantor must deliberately have no say in how the benefits are to be distributed after the trust instrument is created. Examples of the kinds of powers that create tax liability for the grantor under the Enjoyment-Control Rule would be the power to "sprinkle" trust income among several beneficiaries, the power to accumulate or distribute trust income, or the power to add or delete a beneficiary to the trust.

Example: If Amy establishes a trust, names Betty as income beneficiary, and states that on Betty's death the principal is to be distributed to such of Amy's descendants as Amy, if alive, shall designate, then the remainder interest, i.e., the principal, alone of the entire trust is grantor-taxable under the Enjoyment-Control Rule because the trust gives Amy some kind of control over the remainder portion.

If the trust had provided that Betty designate the remaindermen or that Amy designate them with Betty's approval, then Betty would be an "adverse party," and the trust would not have violated the rule. Notice that Betty's income interest during Betty's lifetime is not within the rule and would not be taxed to the grantor, Amy, during that period.

Numerous exceptions to the Enjoyment-Control Rule enable the grantor to exercise moderate control of the enjoyment of a trust without being taxed for it. A few of the more common exceptions to the rule are permissible powers to add beneficiaries, such as after-born children (see Glossary), to name the particular recipients of charitable contributions, and to appoint the remainder interest in the grantor's will.

Rule Three: The Administrative-Control Rule

The Administrative-Control Rule make the grantor liable for the tax if the grantor retains control that may be exercised primarily for the grantor's own benefit (I.R.C. § 675).

Even if the grantor stays within the limits of Rules One and Two above by not recapturing the trust property or exercising control of its beneficial enjoyment, the grantor may be taxable by retaining certain administrative powers. The trustee is the fiduciary of the trust, whose duties include carrying on its business; the grantor is not a fiduciary (unless he or she is also the trustee) and does not have the power to administer (conduct business for) the trust. In most cases, unless also the trustee, the grantor has nothing to do with the trust apart from setting it up. This is especially true of a short-term trust where tax consequences are of the essence. If the grantor attempts to invade the province of the trustee's duties, e.g., to buy, sell, or invest trust property, or the grantor attempts to remove or reacquire property from the trust and substitute other property of equal value, such administrative action will cause the Internal Revenue Service to label the trust "grantor-taxable." It is of no consequence that the grantor has paid full market value for the substituted property (I.R.C. § 675).

Example: Carol White delivers stock certificates valued at $75,000 to Sara Newell to hold, sell, and reinvest for the benefit of Carol's son, Samuel. Immediately the stock increases in value by 10 percent. After a few months, Carol wants the property back and persuades Sara to return the stock in exchange for $75,000 in cash. If the original purpose of establishing the short-term trust was to avoid or diminish taxes, the attempt will not succeed, because the income will be considered grantor-taxable due to the violation of the administrative-control rule.

Rule Four: The Premium-Payment Rule

The Premium-Payment Rule makes the grantor liable for the tax if the trust income may be used for the benefit of the grantor (I.R.C. § 677).

The grantor may not use the income from a trust to pay premiums of insurance policies on the grantor's or the grantor's spouse's life, nor may any other person have a power to make the trust pay such premiums without the consent of an adverse party. If this happens, the income is grantor-taxable. One exception to the premium-payment rule is the situation in which the beneficiary of the trust *voluntarily* elects to use income distributed from the trust to pay the premiums on the grantor's life, the income being in the control of the beneficiary, not of the grantor. This income is not considered the property of the grantor; therefore it is not taxed to the grantor (I.R.C. § 677).

Example: William Benedix transfers $150,000 in trust to Jeremy Wilson to hold and invest for the benefit of William's elderly mother, Hanna. The trust instrument includes a provision that part of the annual income produced by the trust is to be used to pay life insurance premiums on William's life. Such a provision makes William grantor-taxable on the trust income.

Rule Five: The Too-Temporary (Duration) Rule

The Too-Temporary Rule, or Duration Rule see page 296, makes the grantor liable for the tax if the grantor retains a reversionary interest to take effect in less than ten years and a day (I.R.C. § 673).

The concern behind the Too-Temporary Rule is whether the grantor has conveyed the interest in the trust property for too short a time period. In general, the Internal Revenue Code requires that the property be transferred to the trustee for a period of at least ten years and one day. During this time, the transfer must be irrevocable to the grantor, i.e., the grantor cannot take back the trust property under any pretext. Once property has been placed in a short-term trust, it cannot be touched by the grantor for ten years and a day in order for the grantor to avoid paying tax on it (I.R.C. § 673).

There are two exceptions to the Too-Temporary Rule. The Too-Temporary Rule will *not* apply if the grantor's life expectancy is greater than ten years and the trust is established to terminate on the grantor's death, at which time the trust property is to revert to the grantor's estate.

Example: Mark creates a ten-year-and-a-day trust, transfers the trust property, i.e., 10,000 shares of Clayton Corporation stock, to Patricia for the benefit of Carl, and also provides that, if he (Mark) should die before the end of the trust, the trust property is to be returned to Mark's estate. Mark might have to pay income tax generated by the trust property if, at the time of the transfer, his life expectancy is less than ten years. If less than ten years, the rule applies; if greater, the grantor avoids the income tax.

The Too-Temporary Rule will also *not* apply if the remainder interest in the trust property does not revert to the grantor before the end of ten years and a day or before the death of the income beneficiary, even if the beneficiary's life expectancy is less than ten years.

Example: In the above case, if Mark creates a trust to last for ten years and one day or to last for Carl's lifetime, and transfers property in trust to Patricia for the benefit of Carl, the income from the trust property payable to Carl would not be grantor-taxable, even if Carl's life expectancy is only one year.

As long as the trust lasts for ten years and a day or the income beneficiary's life, the Too-Temporary Rule does not apply regardless of the actual or expected period of duration.

These exceptions to the Too-Temporary Rule will allow the grantor to regain the property in less than ten years and a day but still avoid the payment of income tax during the trust's existence where the duration of the trust is the lifetime of either the grantor or the beneficiary. Generally, however, once the property returns to the grantor or his or her successor, the grantor becomes income-taxable under the Recapture Rule.

Each of the five rules must be satisfactorily complied with if the grantor is to successfully create a short-term trust for the purpose of personally avoiding the payment of taxes on the income earned by the property transferred to the trust. If any one of the five previously described rules applies, the grantor becomes the owner of the conveyed property for tax purposes and is taxed on the income of the trust.

Drafting a Short-Term Trust

It is important to enlist the services of competent counsel when creating a trust and drafting the trust instrument, which must conform to Internal Revenue Service requirements and to state laws. I.R.S. regulations change constantly, to ensure that any income which should be taxable does not escape taxation.

The particular purpose of the trust, the type of trust property, the needs of the beneficiary, and the qualifications and abilities of the appointed trustee will determine the actual wording of the trust instrument. Under the supervision of an attorney, the paralegal may assist in making a preliminary draft of a trust. Below is an example to illustrate the drafting procedures in creating a short-term trust.

Assignment 121

Based on the facts below, draft a short-term trust. Compare your draft with the annotated sample draft below. Before attempting your draft, review form books, i.e., books containing sample trust forms, in your local law library. Use a checklist similar to those in Chapter 10.

Facts:

Rodger and Adele Sinclair of 1010 South Shore Drive, Happytown, Carver County, State X, are married and are in a middle income bracket. Adele's mother, Frieda Wendt, age 65, is a widow, lives alone in her own modest home at 10 North Holmes Street, Pleasantown, Olson County, State Y, and receives, as her only income, Social Security benefits. Rodger and Adele want to create a short-term trust to last for either Frieda's lifetime or for the statutory ten years and one day and then revert to the settlors or their estates. The subject matter of the trust is 100 shares of preferred stock in the Boston Gas Light Co., a corporation. The stock is owned by Adele and Rodger in joint tenancy. The annual income and interest created by the stock amounts to $3,000 a year. Rodger and Adele have asked their close friend and financial adviser, Claude Arlen Brown, of 1425 Pleasure Lane, Happytown, to act as trustee, and they direct him to pay annually the $3,000 income from the trust property to Frieda. If Claude refuses to serve, the Sinclairs intend to appoint Samuel Adams as successor trustee. The date of the trust is March 1, 1984.

ANNOTATED SAMPLE SHORT-TERM TRUST

This trust agreement is made and executed this 1st day of March, 1984 by and between Rodger Sinclair and Adele Sinclair, husband and wife, of 1010 South Shore Drive, Happytown, Carver County, State X, hereinafter called the "settlors," and Claude Arlen Brown, of 1425 Pleasure Lane, Happytown, Carver County, State X, hereinafter called the "trustee."

In consideration of the mutual covenants and promises set forth herein, settlors and trustee agree to the following terms and provisions:

Article I

Settlors hereby transfer and deliver to trustee and trustee hereby acknowledges receipt of the trust property consisting of 100 shares of preferred stock in the Boston Gas Light Co., a corporation. Such property together with any other property that may be added to this trust, shall constitute the trust property and shall be held, managed, and distributed by the trustee as provided herein.

COMMENT: This article identifies the subject matter of the trust, passes title of the property to the trustee, and, when accepted, establishes the trustee's fiduciary duties. Any trust property added to the trust estate after the original date creating the trust must held in the trust for ten years and a day from the date of acquisition, or until the named beneficiary's death, in order for the settlor to avoid being taxed on the income from the added property. The tax savings are created not because any income escapes taxation but because the income is taxed at the beneficiary's lower rate.

Article II

The trustee shall pay the entire net income of the trust property annually to Frieda Wendt, 10 North Holmes Street, Pleasantown, Olson County, State Y, the mother of settlor, Adele Sinclair, herein called the beneficiary. Such payments shall continue until the beneficiary's death or until ten years and one day after the date of execution of this trust agreement, whichever shall occur first. On the death of the beneficiary or the expiration of the hereinbefore mentioned time period, the trust shall terminate. Upon termination, all undistributed income shall be paid to the beneficiary, or if the beneficiary is deceased, to the personal representative of the beneficiary's estate. The trust principal shal be returned and delivered to the settlors, or if the settlors are deceased, to the personal representative of the estate of the settlors.

COMMENT: The settlors may successfully create a tax saving trust in the above manner, but they must give up the right to the income from the trust property for at least ten years and a day or until the beneficiary dies. They also must give up the right to use and control the trust principal for their own benefit during that time period. Once the trust terminates, the remaining *income* for the year of termination is distributed to the beneficiary or to the beneficiary's personal representative in order to shift the income tax to the beneficiary. This procedure, if followed, prevents the settlors from receiving a reversionary interest in the undistributed income. See page 315 for problem created by I.R.C. § 673. The trust principal can and, in the above case, will return to the original settlors.

Article III

This trust agreement is irrevocable and shall not be amended, altered, or changed.

COMMENT: Throughout the term of the trust, if the settler has the power or right to reacquire the title to the trust property, the settlor, not the beneficiary, will be taxed on the income of the trust. (I.R.C. § 676.) Therefore, the settlors in the above case resolve this problem by making the trust irrevocable.

Article IV

In addition to the powers otherwise granted to the trustee by the laws of this state, the trustee shall have the following powers:

1. To receive, hold, and retain any property transferred to the trust, or to refuse to accept such property if acceptance would in any way violate the best interests of the beneficiary;
2. To invest and reinvest the trust property in notes, stocks, bonds, and securities of any kind at the discretion of the trustee;
3. To undertake any acts which are necessary for the proper administration of the trust in the judgment of the trustee.

COMMENT: The specific powers of the trustee granted by the settlors are enumerated in this article. The trustee may be given broad powers or specific ones with expressed limitations on such powers. Any powers granted by the settlor must conform to state laws.

Article V

The trustee shall render an annual accounting to the settlors, or, if the settlors are deceased, to the personal representatives of their estates.

COMMENT: The accounting required of the trustee ensures the performance of an important fiduciary duty and enables the settlors or their designated representatives to review the accuracy and honesty of the trustee's administration.

Article VI

The trustee shall be entitled as compensation for his services the sum of *One hundred fifty dollars ($150)* per year.

COMMENT: Fair compensation for the trustee's services should be expressly provided in the trust agreement. In the absence of such a provision, state statutes may fix or limit the amount of the compensation, but the majority of statutes on this subject are so vague (allowing the trustee "reasonable compensation," for example) that the better practice would be to define the trustee's compensation in the instrument. If no compensation is to be paid or the trustee is willing to waive compensation, an appropriate provision expressing this intent should be included in the trust agreement. The cost of employing a corporate trustee, e.g., a bank's trust officer, is a factor that the grantor must consider before establishing a trust.

Article VII

The trustee may resign at any time the trust agreement shall be in force. If death, disability, or resignation of the trustee occurs, Samuel Adams shall be the successor trustee with all powers, rights, and duties hereunder conferred on the trustee.

COMMENT: To cover the possible death, disability, or resignation of the original trustee, a successor trustee should always be named. This prevents the necessity of applying to the court for the appointment of another trustee.

IN WITNESS WHEREOF, the parties have hereunto set their hands this 1st day of March, 1984.

_____
Settlor

_____
Settlor

_____
Trustee

STATE OF _____ } ss
County of Carver _____ }

The foregoing instrument was acknowledged before me this 1st day of March, 1984 by Adele Sinclair, Rodger Sinclair, and Claude Brown.

[Notarial Seal]

_____

Chapter 12

Personal Representatives

Scope of the Chapter

This chapter provides a more in-depth review of previously discussed law governing estate or personal representatives. It identifies and defines them and reviews their duties in preparation for the administration of a decedent's estate. It discusses only those functions that must be performed after the decedent's death, i.e., duties the personal representative should be ready to perform when the probate court confirms his or her appointment. Because the paralegal is often asked to assist in performing some of the responsibilities of the personal representative, especially in cases where an attorney is the representative, knowledge of the representative's duties is essential.

The chapter begins by defining the types of representatives, describing the mechanics of their appointment, and citing sample statutes that outline appointment procedures. Then the basic powers and duties of the personal representative in preparing for formal proceedings are explained, along with the role of the paralegal in assisting with these duties. For an overview of the duties of the representative, see also page 40.

Competencies

After completing this chapter, the paralegal should be able to:

• Identify and define the various types of personal representatives involved in the administration of decedents' estates

• Understand the procedures for appointing the personal representative in formal probate proceedings

- Explain the basic functions performed by the personal representative in preparation for the probate administration
- Recognize the paralegal's role in assisting the personal representative in the performance of the required duties of estate administration

Types of Representatives and How They Are Appointed

The term "personal representative" refers to anyone empowered or authorized to administer the estate of the deceased, whether the deceased died testate or intestate. The personal representative of a testate decedent is the executor or executrix named in a will. If the decedent dies intestate, the personal representative is an administrator or administratrix. The personal representative, in either testate or intestate cases, may also be any one of the following:

- A special administrator or administratrix
- An administrator or administratrix *cum testamento annexo* (also known as administrator C.T.A.)
- An administrator or administratrix *de bonis non* (also called administrator D.B.N.)
- An ancillary administrator or administratrix

Each of these will be reviewed in this chapter. The Uniform Probate Code dispenses with the use of the above terms and simply identifies *all* persons charged with the administration of a decedent's estate as personal representatives.

The role of the representative may be performed by a private individual, an attorney, or a trust officer of a business such as a bank. In intestacy cases, the personal representative is selected from the order of preference for appointment set by statute. One state statute illustrating the order or preference is 20 Pa.S. § 3155 (Purdon 1975):

(a) *Letters testamentary*—Letters testamentary shall be granted by the registrar to the executor designated in the will, whether or not he has declined a trust under the will.

(b) *Letters of administration*—Letters of administration shall be granted by the registrar, in such form as the case shall require, to one or more of those hereinafter mentioned and, except for good cause, in the following order:

    (1) Those entitled to the residuary estate under the will.

    (2) The surviving spouse.

    (3) Those entitled under the intestate law as the register, in his discretion, shall judge will best administer the estate, giving preference, however, according to the sizes of the shares of those in this class.

    (4) The principal creditors of the decedent at the time of his death.

    (5) Other fit persons.

    (6) If anyone of the foregoing shall renounce his right to letters of administration, the register, in his discretion, may appoint a nominee of

the person so renouncing in preference to the persons set forth in any succeeding clause.

(c) *Time limitation*—Except with the consent of those enumerated in clauses (1), (2) and (3), no letters shall be issued to those enumerated in clauses (4) and (5) of subsection (b) until seven days after the decedent's death. [For comparison see U.P.C. § 3–203 in Appendix C.]

Executor or Executrix

The executor (the man) or executrix (the woman) is the person designated by a will when the decedent dies testate to see that all its testamentary provisions are fulfilled and to handle the affairs of the decedent's estate (see U.P.C. § 1–201[30]).

General Administrator or Administratrix

The general administrator or administratrix is the general representative, either man or woman, selected and appointed by a probate court to administer the estate of an intestate.

Special Administrator or Administratrix

The special administrator or administratrix is the personal representative, either man or woman, appointed temporarily by a probate court to handle certain immediate needs of an estate, such as managing a business in the capacity of the decedent, until a general administrator or executor can be appointed. This representative usually handles Summary Proceedings (see Chapter 13, page 370).

Administrator or Administratrix Cum Testamento Annexo

The administrator or administratrix cum testamento annexo, also called administrator C.T.A. (means administrator with the will annexed), is the personal representative appointed by the court in two situations: (1) where the maker of the will does not name an executor or executrix or (2) where the maker of the will does name an executor or executrix but the latter cannot serve because of deficiency in qualification or competency. The following state statutes identify the position of administrator C.T.A.

20 Pa.S. § 3325 (Purdon 1975), *Administrator C.T.A.*

An administrator with a will annexed shall have all the powers given by the will to the executor, unless otherwise provided by the will. When he has been required to give bond, no proceeds of real estate shall be paid to him until the court has made an order excusing him from entering additional security or requiring additional security, and in the latter event, only after he has entered the additional security.

Cal. Prob. Code § 409 (West 1956), *Administrators With Will Annexed; Authority; Discretionary Power; Priority of Appointment*

Administrators with the will annexed have the same authority over estates which executors named in the will would have, and their acts are as effectual for all purposes; but if a power or authority conferred upon an executor is discretionary, and is not conferred by law, it shall not be deemed to be conferred upon an administrator with the will annexed. Persons are entitled to appointment as administrators with the will annexed in the same order of priority as in the appointment of administrators, except that, one who takes under the will has priority over one who does not, and need not be entitled to succeed to the estate or some portion thereof under the law of succession. Administration may be granted to one or more competent persons who are not otherwise entitled to appointment as a matter of priority, upon the written request filed with the court by a resident of the United States who takes more than 50 percent of the value of the estate under the will.

Administrator or Administratrix De Bonis Non

The administrator or administratrix *de bonis non,* also called administrator D.B.N. (means administrator of goods not administered), is a court-appointed personal representative who replaces a previous administrator who has begun but failed to complete the administration of an intestate estate for any reason, including death. Below is a sample statute that creates the administrator D.B.N. position.

20 Pa.S. § 3326 (Purdon 1975), *Administrator D.B.N. and D.B.N.C.T.A.*

An administrator de bonis non, with or without a will annexed, shall have the power to recover the assets of the estate from his predecessor in administration or from the personal representative of such predecessor and, except as the will shall provide otherwise, shall stand in his predecessor's stead for all purposes, except that he shall not be personally liable for the acts of his predecessor. When he has been required to give bond, no proceeds of real estate shall be paid to him until the court has made an order excusing him from entering additional security or requiring additional security, and in the latter event, only after he has entered the additional security.

Example: Frazier is the executor of Eleanor's will. While he is in the process of settling her estate, he dies suddenly. The probate court will appoint a replacement who will bear the title of administrator D.B.N. **Example:** Geraldine writes and executes a will, but she neglects to name an executor. On her death, the probate court will decide if the document is admissible to probate and if so will appoint an administrator C.T.A. for Geraldine's estate.

Ancillary (Foreign) Administrator or Administratrix

The ancillary administrator or administratrix is the personal representative appointed by the court overseeing the distribution of that part of a decedent's estate located in a jurisdiction (state) different from the one of the main administration which is the decedent's domicile at the time of death (see U.P.C. § 1–201[14]). See further discussion in Chapter 13, page 339.
Example: Bernice, a legal resident of California, dies in Oregon at the summer residence she owns. Her will is admitted to probate in

Maricopa County, California, where she had been domiciled. The court will have to appoint an ancillary administrator to see that Bernice's Oregon estate is distributed according to the will and the laws of Oregon.

Exhibit 12.1 summarizes the different types of personal representatives.

Exhibit 12.1 Types of Personal Representatives: Summary Chart

- The personal representative of a *testate* decedent is called *executor* (if a man) or executrix (if a woman).

- The personal representative of an *intestate* decedent is called *general administrator* (if a man) or general *administratrix* (if a woman).

- In special cases the personal representative for either a testate decedent or an intestate decedent may be called *special administrator (-trix), administrator (-trix) C.T.A., administrator (-trix) D.B.N., ancillary administrator (-trix)*.

- The general administrator (-trix) is often called simply the administrator (-trix).

- The special administrator (-trix) is appointed by the probate court to handle estate problems that arise before it has appointed a general administrator (-trix).

Assignment 122

Suppose in Joshua Foley's will, his son, William, the named executor, had refused to serve after Joshua's death and no contingent (successor) executor was named in the will.

1. If his wife, Ethel, were appointed as personal representative by the probate court, what title would she have?

2. If instead William had commenced probate proceedings but became unable to complete them due to illness, and Ethel was then appointed by the court as his replacement, what would her title be?

3. If Ethel were appointed by a probate court to handle the administration of the estate of her brother, George Clark, who lived and died in another state, what would her title be?

4. If Joshua had forgotten to name an executor, what would the court most likely do?

5. If Joshua had been in the process of completing a transfer of the majority interest in a corporation when he died and the court named a person to continue the transfer before a regular probate proceeding could be held, what would be the title of that person?

Assignment 123

Harriet died intestate. Her only heirs were her son, Henry, and her mother, Maude. Harriet's only debt outstanding was to her best friend, Sally, valued at $2,000. Explain who would have priority of appointment as personal representative in Minnesota, Pennsylvania, and your own state.

Appointment Procedure

The mechanics for appointing a representative, either confirming an executor in a testamentary case or appointing an administrator in an intestate proceeding, are similar but not identical. The appointment and responsibilities of the personal representative in formal and informal probate proceedings will be discussed in Chapters 13 and 14 respectively.

In most states it is the Petition to Prove a Will that forms the basis for the appointment of an executor or executrix, while the Petition for Administration serves the same purpose for an administrator or administratrix (see page 339). Both petitions contain the facts establishing jurisdiction in a specific probate court. Facts necessary to establish that a certain court has jurisdiction of the matter include the date and place of death, the domicile of the decedent, the names, ages, and addresses of heirs or successors, the value and the nature of decedent's real and personal property, debts, and the names and addresses of the petitioners.

In both cases, the probate court sets a time and place for a hearing on the petition. At the hearing, after the witnesses testify, the court appoints the representative (executor or administrator), who must file an oath of office and in some cases post a bond, which constitutes an expense of the estate and may be deducted on the death tax forms. Procedural matters will be discussed in greater detail in subsequent chapters. An example of a statute requiring a bond is 20 Pa.S. § 3175, *Requiring or changing amount of bond:* "The court, upon cause shown and after such notice, if any, as it shall direct, may require a surety bond, or increase or decrease the amount of an existing bond, or require more or less security therefore" (see also U.P.C. §§ 3–603 and 3–604).

Assignment 124

Determine whether your own state has bond requirements. If so, state briefly what they are. Cite all relevant statutes.

By the granting of Letters Testamentary an executor or executrix is appointed; by the granting of Letters of Administration an administrator or administratrix is appointed. Both Letters Testamentary and Letters of Administration are conclusive proof and evidence that the person named therein is the duly appointed, qualified, and acting personal representative of the decedent's estate with the powers, rights, duties, and obligations conferred by law. The person who applies for either Letters Testamentary or Letters of Administration must be competent to discharge the representative's obligations.

The decision on competency is an exercise in discretion by the court. An executor is named by the will, so the court cannot arbitrarily appoint someone else to fill the position. This does not mean, however, that the court is compelled to appoint the named executor or that the appointee must be the most suitable and competent of all possibilities. For example, a minor named as executor would not be appointed by the court even though selected by the testate. If the minor, however, had attained majority at the time of the testate's death or subsequently at the time for admission or proof of the will, the minor could be competent to act as representative and could be appointed by the court.

The appointment of an administrator calls for greater discretion on the part of the court. Where the decedent has left no indication of who is to supervise the distribution of the estate, the court must decide who, of all the applicants, would be appropriate. In most states the order of preference is set by statute. Again, the court cannot overrule a preference with or without cause unless the state statutes grant the court this power, but the court may use its discretion to appoint one who occupies a lower position in the statutory order (see page 322).

Example: Ridgely names his wife, Yvonne, executrix. Following his death, she will become the executrix of his estate unless the court finds her mentally incompetent or otherwise subject to disqualification. Ridgely's sister, Loretta, is an accountant and more experienced in business than Yvonne, but the court will not replace Yvonne with Loretta or anyone else unless it finds Yvonne unqualified to act as executrix. Similarly, if Ridgely had died intestate, Yvonne, being his wife, would be the first in most states to be considered by the court when it names the administrator or administratrix.

If, in intestacy, an administrator or administratrix has been appointed, but then a will naming a personal representative is discovered and admitted by petition to probate, the court will terminate the powers of the intestate representative (administrator) and approve the appointment of the executor or executrix, who will continue the probate of the estate. The following statute illustrates the basis for the termination of an intestate appointment and the appointment of a new representative.

20 Pa.S. § 3181 (Purdon 1975), *Revocation of Letters*

(a) When no will—The register may revoke letters of administration granted by him whenever it appears that the person to whom the letters were granted is not entitled thereto.

(b) When a will—The register may amend or revoke letters testamentary or of administration granted by him not in conformity with the provisions of a will admitted to probate. [compare U.P.C. § 3–612.]

Example: Roxanne Bridges dies. According to state law, her husband, Neil, is appointed administrator since no will can be found. After being appointed administrator and Letters of Administration are issued, Neil discovers a will drawn by Roxanne in an old shoe box in the family home. Roxanne names her father, Harold Jensen, executor in the will. On the basis of this discovery, Neil's administration terminates, and Harold will be appointed executor in order to continue the probate administration.

The specific procedures of administration and the representative's duties after appointment are discussed in succeeding chapters.

Assignment 125

Juliana was in her last illness when she made a will naming her brother, Roland, executor. Unknown to her, Roland had been declared legally insane the previous year. A month after Juliana's death, Roland is declared sane and applies for Letters Testamentary. Juliana's sister, Clarissa, contests Roland's application, stating that his insanity disqualifies him from acting as executor. In your state, is she correct?

Preparing for Formal Proceedings

With respect to the assets of the estate, the representative has a fiduciary obligation, a duty to utilize the highest degree of care and integrity in handling property. Following appointment by the court, the personal representative's general responsibilities are:

1. To discover and collect all assets of any value and manage the estate of the decedent

2. To settle all just claims against the estate and see that they are paid

3. To distribute the remainder of the estate as required by will or by law

The mechanics of administering an estate are complex and varied. The specific obligations facing a representative are determined by statutes and by the will, if one exists, such as the representative's duty to pay an allowance to the surviving family. Statutes vary from state to state. Therefore, the list of duties presented below is not intended to be all-inclusive or exhaustive, but to provide a basis for understanding the major duties in any given administration.

Immediate Concerns After the Death and Burial of the Decedent

Death of the testate requires immediate preparations for probate. The needs of the family take priority on the death of one of its members, especially when the decedent was the family breadwinner. The paralegal acting for the law firm selected by the representative of the deceased to assist in administering the estate aids in seeing that the family needs are satisfied. An initial conference with members of the decedent's family should be called promptly, since many of the needs should be met within a few weeks after the decedent's death. The paralegal may be asked to help search for and obtain the will, notify appropriate parties of the decedent's death, obtain certified copies of the death certificate, and set a date for the family conference.

Search for and Obtain the Will

One of the first responsibilities of the representative in formal proceedings is to obtain, review, and make copies of the will, if one exists. A paralegal performing this investigative function should not neglect to look in the office of the decedent's attorney, in the vault where the decedent banked, in a safe deposit box, or in a place in the decedent's home considered secure. Family, friends. and business advisers must be contacted for information about the will's existence and location. If the search is successful and the will is found, copies and a summary of the contents of the will are made.

Assignment 126

To test your investigatory abilities, make a list of as many places as possible where a will could be kept. Then select members of your family, e.g., spouse, parents, brothers, or sisters, who have made wills and determine if your list would help you find their wills. If your list does not locate their wills, what additional steps would you follow in order to discover whether a will exists and its location?

Notify Appropriate Parties of the Decedent's Death

After finding the will, the paralegal summarizes it and sends copies to persons named in the will. The paralegal may be asked to notify other appropriate parties, such as banks, depositories, and loan associations, of the decedent's death so these financial institutions may meet certain legal obligations including:

• Prevent persons (holders of joint accounts with the decedent) from withdrawing money from the accounts in an attempt to avoid death taxes levied on the transfer of assets at the time of death

• Provide for the safekeeping of any safe deposit box contents

• Close all demand (checking) accounts

Obtain Certified Copies of the Death Certificate

Seldom is the attorney contacted to assist in sorting out a decedent's estate before the funeral arrangements are complete. The funeral director obtains the necessary burial permits and the death certificate, which is the document executed by a physician listing the name of the decedent and the place, time, date, and cause of death. The funeral director gives the death certificate to the family, and they in turn give it to their attorney. When necessary, additional certified copies of the death certificate may be obtained from the City Health Department, the Bureau of Vital Statistics, the Clerk of District Court, or a state Registrar. Copies must accompany applications for filing claims, obtaining insurance benefits, collecting benefits from Social Security or the Veterans Administration, and filing deeds transferring title to real estate with the county recorder's office or the Register of Deeds office (see Death Certificate, Form 33).

Set a Date for the Family Conference

Shortly after decedent's death, the paralegal may also be asked to schedule a family conference for the immediate future. All persons named in the will should be asked to attend this conference. A convenient time for this meeting would be on the day of the opening of the safe deposit box, if one is owned by the decedent.

Example: Maxine has a will. Her husband, Malcolm, knows of its existence since he has been appointed executor. Maxine dies, but her will cannot be found. Malcolm believes the will is located in Maxine's safe deposit box. Although a bank must seal the box upon learning of the owner's death, generally an officer of the bank will be allowed to determine whether the owner's (decedent's) will is kept in the safe deposit box. If it is, the bank will forward the will to the probate court, thereby avoiding unnecessary delays in locating the will and commencing the decedent's estate administration.

The Family Conference

At the family conference, the paralegal must obtain information pertinent to future administrative duties. The attorney or experienced paralegal acting under the attorney's supervision and assisting the personal representative should:

1. *Explain the provisions of the will* if the original or a copy is available. The attorney and paralegal also review the general nature of probate administration, including the appointment of the personal representative, the preparation of the inventory and appraisal, the various tax returns, and the final account and decree of distribution. The times within which these steps must be taken are explained and the use of a "tickler" system in order to avoid overlooking dates involving important procedural matters is reviewed (see 13, below). If possible, an estimate is made for the length of time the administration will take.

2. *Obtain information about the general size and nature of the decedent's estate* using checklists similar to those in Chapter 7. Determine whether formal or informal probate proceedings should be followed or whether it is possible to settle the estate by a method other than the normal probate proceeding.[1]

3. *Inquire about and obtain list of known debts and obligations* both personal and those relating to any business interest of the decedent.

4. *Obtain the facts necessary for the preparation of the Petition to Prove the Will,* if the decedent died testate, or Petition for General Administration, if decedent died intestate (see page 339). Be sure to use the appropriate state or county forms for these petitions (see examples of such forms in Appendix A, Forms 1 and 19).

5. *If the deceased owed any members of the family a debt, explain to the creditor the need to file a claim.* The time limits for procedures to approve such claims will be discussed in subsequent chapters.

6. *Discuss the election rights of the surviving spouse.* Explain that if the decedent has made a provision in the will for the surviving spouse, the spouse has the right to elect to take the statutory amount of decedent's estate (as determined by the state in which the estate is probated instead of the amount in the will). Typical state statutes on the right of election are 20 Pa.S. § 2508 (Purdon 1975) and Minn. Stat. Ann. § 525.212 (West 1975). Prepare for the spouse's signature a document renouncing the provisions of the will, should the choice be to reject the will and to take the statutory share, and arrange to have it witnessed according to the statute. Note on the "tickler" form (Exhibit 2.2) that it must be filed with the probate court within a statutory time period, e.g., six months after the will has been accepted by the court. For each state, the time limit and the possibility of having it extended must be determined.

7. *Explain disclaimer,* its procedures and effects. Some state statutes provide that a devisee may disclaim any interest in whole or in part, which the devisee would receive from the will by filing a disclaimer in probate court (see Form 20). If they determine it to be in the best interest of such devisee, the personal representatives of a devisee, e.g., a guardian of a minor or of an incompetent, or an executor or administrator of the estate of a deceased devisee, may execute and file a disclaimer on behalf of the devisee. A devisee may empower an agent or attorney to disclaim on his or her behalf. If the statutory requirements are

---

1. In certain situations it is not necessary to probate the estate of a decedent. No administration is necessary if the decedent did not own solely any property at the time of death. If everything was owned with another person in joint tenancy, special probate proceedings will probably be followed. Upon death of the decedent, the surviving joint tenant will automatically take the decedent's share under the joint ownership agreement. In these instances, a special administrator may be appointed and a statutory procedure called "Summary Distribution" followed to distribute by order of the probate court whatever the decedent may have owned at the time of death, but without the elaborate probate process. (See Chapter 13 on handling the above situations.)

satisfied, a devisee who waives an interest may have the right to transfer or assign the interest to anyone. Otherwise, the interest disclaimed will be distributed according to the directives of the will or by intestate succession, and it will be disposed of just as if the disclaimant had died immediately before the decedent (compare U.P.C § 2–801). **Example:** Mathilda dies leaving her summer home to her brother, Jeremiah, age 70. Jeremiah has no need of the home and does not wish to pay inheritance tax on the gift. He executes and files a disclaimer of the home.

8. *Determine the wishes of the devisees* of your decedent client's will and prepare the necessary documents and forms to implement their wishes. Explain that whether the decedent died with or without a will, the surviving spouse and minor children are entitled to reasonable maintenance during administration of the decedent's estate for a statutory time period, e.g., twelve to eighteen months, as determined by the probate court. A typical state statute on maintenance is Md. Code 1974, art. 93, § 3–201 (1957) *Family allowance:*

> **(a)** *Amount of allowance*—The surviving spouse is entitled to receive an allowance of $2,000 for his personal use, and an additional allowance of $1,000 for the use of each unmarried child of the decedent who has not attained the age of 18 years at the time of the death of the decedent. Upon receipt of an allowance for an unmarried child under 18 years of age of the decedent who is not also a child of the surviving spouse, the surviving spouse shall distribute that allowance as provided in § 1–3501 of this article.
>
> **(b)** *Tax exemption*—The allowance, which is available in both testate and intestate estates, is exempt from the Maryland inheritance tax.

When maintenance is necessary, forms known as *petitions for maintenance* (Form 68) are completed and presented to the probate court. Property belonging to the surviving spouse, the income of the family, the size of the decedent's estate and the socioeconomic status of the family are considered in determining the amount of maintenance. State statutes setting the amount of maintenance are worded vaguely enough to give the court and the personal representative leeway to accommodate these factors (e.g., the representative is to allow a "reasonable" amount, which the court may modify at its discretion). Find the statutory requirements of your state and plan accordingly. Have family members decide the amount necessary to support themselves adequately for the time period allowed. If the estate is insolvent, an effort should be made to obtain the largest family maintenance possible so that the decedent's limited assets are used primarily for the family.

In some states a surviving spouse (or if there be none, then minor children) is entitled, in addition to maintenance, to all the decedent's wearing apparel plus household goods and furniture not exceeding in value a statutory dollar amount, e.g., $2,000 (compare U.P.C. § 2–403 on family allowances). The spouse may select (receive) this property before the estate is liable for debts, including the decedent's funeral costs (see page 110). The form employed is usually called "Petition to Set Apart Personal Property" (see Form 66).

If a spouse survives, he or she is the petitioner, and if not, the guardian of the minor children signs the petition. No notice need be given within the petition and order. The spouse, under certain circumstances, is also allowed the decedent's automobile.

9. *Discuss whether there is any particular item of property the family wishes to retain* whenever the size of the debts of the decedent may require the sale of property. If the personal representative has been given the power of sale by the will, it is conceivable that he or she may sell an item of property, e.g., a painting, which the family regards as sentimentally valuable and prefers not to sell.

10. *Check the estate plans of the surviving spouse* and make arrangements to amend his or her will. If there is no surviving spouse and the decedent was the last occupant in a home, the post office should be notified to forward mail to the next of kin or representative of the estate.

11. *Discuss or inquire about any other documents that may have a direct or indirect bearing* on the status or transfer of the decedent's estate, such as marital agreements, records of any gifts made before death, or transactions such as trust agreements.

12. *Obtain names and addresses of decedent's advisers,* including the tax adviser, accountant, trust officer, insurance agent or broker, or stockbroker.

13. *In preparation for the probate procedure,* prepare a calendar checklist (tickler) of important tax dates and deadlines (Exhibit 2.2) and a checklist of probate procedures (page 40). After obtaining the necessary information, explaining the probate process, and answering the questions of the family members, the conference is concluded. The duties of the representative and the paralegal, however, are just beginning.

Assignment 127

Assume some married member of your family has died. Perform the following tasks. (To preserve confidentiality, you can change the names of all parties concerned.)

1. Determine whether the decedent left a will.

2. If a will exists, locate it.

3. Using the sample from this text, prepare a "tickler" system.

4. Using the text's checklist or your own, determine the assets and liabilities of the "decedent's" estate.

5. Obtain the facts necessary for the Petition to Prove the Will or, if no will exists, the Petition for General Administration. Then fill out the appropriate form.

6. Assume the decedent owed you a $5,000 debt based on a promissory note and you are willing to cancel the debt. How might this be done?

7. Determine whether your state grants an election right to a surviving spouse. Cite the statute and determine whether the decedent's spouse would receive a greater share under the will or under the statute.

8. Assume you are named as a devisee in the will. Fill out the disclaimer form and assign the interest to your best friend.

9. Cite your state statute on maintenance and family allowance. Fill out the forms.

10. Check to see if the "decedent's" spouse has a will.

Chapter 13

Formal Probate
Administration

Scope of the Chapter

The probate procedures in administering an intestate's or testate's estate are the concerns of the next two chapters. There are two types of probate proceedings: formal (supervised) and informal (unsupervised). Formal probate proceedings are discussed in this chapter. After a brief explanation of the difference between formal and informal probate, the chapter discusses the initial steps required for formal probate. Included are procedures, sample forms used in probating a typical estate, the statutes of various states illustrating similarities and differences in the procedures, special proceedings in formal probate, and the liability of the representative. The chapter ends with an illustrated case problem, one with accompanying executed forms and one with an assignment asking the student to complete a similar case problem.

Competencies

After completing this chapter, the paralegal should be able to:

• Recognize the circumstances under which formal probate procedures are appropriate

• Identify and explain the formal probate procedures for administering a decedent's estate whether death occurred testate or intestate

• Recognize the need for special proceedings in formal probate under appropriate circumstances

• Explain the potential liability of the personal representative

• Apply the procedures and prepare the legal forms used in formal probate administration for a set of facts involving a decedent's estate

Formal Versus Informal Probate Proceedings

When a person dies leaving a will (testate) the will must be accepted and recorded as valid through formal or informal probate proceedings.

Formal (supervised) probate is the more widely accepted type of probate proceedings. As the name indicates, it follows a form. Formal probate requires the petitioner (proponent) of a will to give notice to all parties with an interest, e.g., heirs, devisees, creditors, so they may be present at an initial hearing to contest the validity of the will if they so desire. (In formal probate practices, the notice requirement and formal proceedings are mandatory in the administration of intestate estates as well as testate estates, so that estates of every kind come under the supervision of the probate courts.) At the hearing, all persons who received notice of the initial hearing or who appear without notice must file their objections, if any, to the admission of the will to probate or to appointment of the personal representative. If such objections are not timely filed, the objectors may thereafter be precluded from contesting the will or the appointment.

Informal (unsupervised) probate requires the proponent of the will to produce the will along with living witnesses to the testator's signature before the appropriate representative of the court (judge, registrar, or clerk). After the witnesses or the proponent have given testimony under oath, the will is "proved" (U.P.C. §§ 3–301, 3–302, 3–303). Generally, informal probate does not require that notice be given to devisees, successors, creditors, or other interested parties (but compare U.P.C. §§ 3–306, 1–401, 3–204). If a party wants to contest the validity of the will or the appointment of a personal representative, affirmative action must be taken to acquire a formal hearing. Such action would transfer the proceeding from an informal to a formal one. This must be done within the defined statutory time periods (U.P.C. § 3–401). Informal probate creates an optional system of probate practices unsupervised by the court which can expedite proceedings when that is the wish of all interested parties. It works especially well for small and moderate-sized estates, where administrative costs such as fees for recording various documents would appreciably reduce the decedent's assets.

In this chapter we will be concerned solely with formal probate. Chapter 14 will cover informal probate proceedings.

Formal Probate Administration and Procedures, With or Without a Will

The word "estate" includes the interest in every type of property, real and personal, owned by the decedent at the time of death. When death occurs, everything the decedent owns becomes part of the deceased's *estate*. The decedent's personal representative holds and manages the assets of the estate until those who are entitled to them (devisees, if the decedent left a will; heirs, if the decedent died without a will) can assume ownership. In either instance, the personal representative's work is termed *administration*. The decedent's estate, also called the gross estate, is subject to taxes, both federal and state, when the owner dies. The gross estate includes probate as well as non-probate property. The probate property consists of solely owned assets (assets that are in the decedent's name only) and property held as a tenant-in-common. These assets are the ones handled by the probate court whether a will exists or not. A decedent's will gives the court specific instructions as to what is to be done with the decedent's solely owned property and that which is owned in tenancy-in-common. It has no effect on jointly owned property, insurance policies payable to a named beneficiary other than the decedent's estate, and some kinds of inter vivos trusts (see page 90), which are the non-probate assets. If there is no will, the court follows the probate procedures under the laws of intestate succession (see page 100).

This chapter deals with the actual probate procedures for handling an estate when the decedent dies either testate or intestate. Included in the discussion are references to the various forms (see Appendix A) that must be completed. It is the personal representative's duty to see that these procedures are properly and timely executed. The attorney, retained by the representative, and the paralegal help the representative perform this duty.

The Choice of Formal or Informal Probate

In the majority of cases, whenever the decedent has made a will and owns property subject to probate at the time of death, the personal representative selects formal probate proceedings for handling the administration of the estate. Formal probate commences with a petition and the filing of the will with the probate court or a petition for appointment of an administrator. Such proceedings may be unnecessary in a number of cases however. First, for example, in states that have adopted the Uniform Probate Code the estate may be handled by informal probate, in which the representative completes transfer of the decedent's assets without court's supervision (see Chapter 14). Second, if the decedent's assets are limited so that the estate will be depleted in the process of administration, the representative can petition the court for appointment of a "special administrator" to settle the estate, without the complexity of the formal probate procedures, under "summary proceedings" (see page 370). Third, formal probate (or any kind of probate procedure) is unnecessary when the decedent's estate consists exclusively of non-probate assets (such as jointly owned securities, which pass automatically to the surviving joint owner when the decedent dies). In any of these circumstances, the custodian of the will, if a will exists, is still required to deliver the will to the probate court.

Commencing Formal Probate Proceedings

Assuming all the preliminary work and correspondence has been accomplished by the representative with the assistance of the attorney and the paralegal (e.g., discovering the will, if one exists, holding the family conference) probate proceedings can begin.

In matters relating to commencing formal probate, the paralegal may play a role in:

- Petitioning to prove the will
- Petitioning for administration when no will exists
- Petitioning for probate of an out-of-state will
- Arranging for publication of Order for Hearing and Affidavit of Publication
- Mailing the notice of Order for Hearing and Affidavit
- Establishing a checking account for the estate
- Paying funeral bills
- Mailing notice of rights to spouse and minor children, and affidavit
- Reviewing ancillary matters prior to the hearing to prove will or for general administration
- Arranging for appearance of witness(es)
- Miscellaneous duties before hearing
- Obtaining an order for hearing either the Petition to Prove Will or for general administration

The paralegal who is assisting the personal representative must be familiar with these procedures, the contents of the related documents, and the time limits for filing them. The paralegal should also be aware that the procedures detailed below will vary from state to state.

Petitioning to Prove a Will

Any person having an interest in the estate, such as a named executor, devisee, or creditor of the decedent, may file a petition with the court to have a will proven (admitted to probate) (see Form 1). A petition is a written document addressed to a court or judicial official requesting that the court order certain legal actions. The petition is essential for determining that the court has jurisdiction over the decedent's estate. To establish jurisdiction in a state probate court, the petition to prove a will generally must allege:

- The death and place of death of the decedent
- The domicile of the decedent in the state at the time of death, or the presence of property left by the decedent subject to administration in that state

- The existence of the will [1]
- Names, ages, and addresses of the decedent's named devisees
- That notice has been given to the named devisees
- The estimated value of the real and personal property
- The amount of debts, if known
- The name and address of the personal representative, e.g., the executor or executrix, named in the will

Petitioning for Administration When No Will Exists

A Petition for Administration in case of intestacy sets forth facts similar to the Petition to Prove the Will. It should contain the names, addresses, and ages of all heirs of the decedent so far as they are known to the petitioner, a fair estimate of the value of the decedent's real and personal property, the amount and general character of the decedent's debts, and the name and address of the person who is requesting Letters of Administration (see Form 19). As a general rule, the surviving spouse has first priority to the appointment as general administrator, then the next-of-kin, or both, in the discretion of the court. If the surviving spouse or next-of-kin so choose, they may nominate another person to serve as administrator. If any of the possible administrators are incompetent, unsuitable, or unwilling to act, or if no petition has been filed within a statutory number of days, e.g., 45 days after the decedent's death, administration may be granted to one or more creditors of the decedent or to the creditors' nominee. The petition must be accompanied, however, by an itemized and verified statement of the creditor's claim.

Minors, mentally incompetent persons (as adjudged by a court), and non-residents of the state usually cannot act as personal representatives.

Petitioning for Probate of a Foreign Will

As a rule, any will admitted to probate in the decedent's domiciliary (home) state may also be admitted to probate in a county in another state of the United States in which the decedent left property subject to probate administration. The representative appointed to administer this property in the other (foreign) state is called the *ancillary administrator.*

If the decedent was born in or has left heirs in another country and if no petition has been filed within a statutory number of days, e.g., 30 days after the decedent's death, administration may be granted to the consul or other representative of that country or their nominee, but only if the person appointed resides in the state and files a copy of the appointment with the state's Secretary of State. Finally, administra-

---

1. The will usually accompanies the petition, unless it has previously been forwarded to the court.

tion may be granted to any suitable and competent person, whether interested in the estate or not, provided the court considers it in the best interests of the estate and heirs.

Generally, along with the petition to prove or admit to probate a will in a foreign state (Form 21), the representative must send:

- An authentic copy of the will
- A certificate from the clerk of the court in the domiciliary state affirming the will's correctness
- A certificate from the probate judge reinforcing the clerk's certificate
- A certificate affirming the court's authority to admit the will
- A copy of the order admitting the will to probate

Note, however, that requirements may vary from state to state.

Arranging Publication of Order for Hearing and Affidavit of Publication

The next task for the paralegal acting for the attorney and client is to contact a legal newspaper (one that specializes in printing legal concerns), or at least a newspaper that is generally circulated in the county in which the proceedings are pending, and arrange for publication of the Order for Hearing (see Form 22). For an example of such publication, see Form 55. The states may vary in their publication requirements. In many states, the order must be published once a week for three consecutive weeks. The first publication must occur within a statutory time period, e.g., two weeks after the date of the court order fixing the time and place for hearing. An Affidavit of Proof of Publication must be filed with the probate court within a statutory number of days prior to the hearing. Sometimes the county clerk of the probate court makes the arrangements for publication, but the paralegal must check to be sure it is done within the time allotted by court rule and must check the accuracy of the court's order for hearing. In some counties, the publisher sends the Affidavit of Publication directly to the court, in others the publisher fills out the affidavit, which the representative, attorney, or paralegal, files with the probate court.

Mailing the Notice of Order for Hearing and Affidavit

Within a statutory number of days prior to the hearing, a copy of the order for a hearing on the petition must be mailed to all persons named in the petition whose names and addresses are known. This notice is necessary to establish the court's jurisdiction over the decedent's estate, and the proceedings will become invalid if it is not sent. If there are no heirs or devisees, i.e., persons entitled to the estate, the property will escheat (pass) to the state and the notice should then be sent to the attorney general. If the decedent was born in a foreign country, notice must also be mailed to the consul or other representative of that country if such consul resides in the state and has filed a copy of his or her appointment with the state's secretary of state (see Form 3 and 56). The representative must submit an affidavit, attesting to the mailing of the notices, to be filed with the court (see Form 55).

Establishing a Checking Account for the Estate

At the close of probate, the representative must account to the court for the financial and physical status of the estate. This account must show the court the results of management of the estate, including property received, increases or decreases in inventory, and all disbursements made. The records must be complete and accurate. Therefore, the representative of the estate must open an estate checking account. The paralegal may be asked to do this for the client. In a bank account used only for the estate, the check imprint should read as in Exhibit 2.3, page 31. Monies may be deposited in the account immediately (from such sources as savings or checking accounts), but withdrawals may be made only after the representative has been appointed by the probate court. The representative should keep accurate account records and make copies of all vouchers (canceled checks, receipts, and the like), since they must be approved by the probate court in the final accounting.

Paying Funeral Bills

The funeral bill is a debt for which a claim can be filed by the funeral director. The representative need not pay it until the claim period expires; however, it may be possible to obtain a discount by paying the bill promptly. By statute, the funeral bill, up to a stipulated amount, is generally a preferred claim. (On priority of debts, see page 361.) Prompt payment is important to an estate where there are few assets, since failure to pay this bill and other priority debts before distributing the assets can lead to personal liability for the representative.

Mailing Notice of Rights to Spouse and Minor Children and Affidavit

In most states, if a decedent has left a spouse or minor children, a notice of right to allowances must be mailed to each such person within a period of time set by statute, e.g., 14 days prior to the date set for hearing on the petition (see Form 7). Also, if the spouse has not already contested the will, notice of rights dealing with renunciation and election (see page 166) must be mailed to the spouse. The representative must file an affidavit with the court showing the mailing of both notices (see Form 3 and 56). An explanatory letter accompanying these notices is helpful to avoid confusion. A child of the testate does not have the right to elect against the will. Only the surviving spouse has the right of election.

Reviewing Ancillary Matters Prior to the Hearing to Prove the Will or for General Administration

When the decedent owns real estate or tangible personal property located in another state, it is necessary to make arrangements with a representative in that state for holding ancillary administration proceedings there. According to provisions in the will or the statutes, the ancillary administrator (representative) collects assets and pays debts and taxes due in the state where the property is located and remits the residue to the personal representative of the principal (domicile) state for final settlement. The estate cannot be closed until the ancillary administration is completed, since the determination of estate tax cannot be settled until the property, debts, and claims in all states are known. Even before the hearing to prove the will, one should make preliminary arrangements for any needed representative in another state.

Arranging for Appearance of Witnesses

If anyone with an interest in the estate raises objections to the will, he or she must file them with the court before the hearing. (Some of the most common objections are by a spouse dissatisfied with the amount received in the will, by a child who has been disinherited, or by any devisee who claims that the will was signed under fraud or undue influence, or that the testate was incompetent.) If there are any objections to the will, the witnesses to the will must appear in court to testify that the testate knew the document to be a will and signed it in accordance with state statutes. If a witness lives more than 100 miles away from the place of the hearing, a written statement that the witness affirms to be true (a deposition) may serve in lieu of testimony in open court (see Forms 61 and 23). A few states provide for a "self-proved" will, which makes the testimony of subscribing witnesses unnecessary (for an example of such a statute, see Minn. Stat. Ann. § 524.2–504 [West 1975] or U.P.C. § 2–504).

Miscellaneous Duties Before Hearing

Other duties of the paralegal, under the supervision of an attorney, before the hearing may be the following:

• Send copies of the will and a preliminary estimate of the estate to the appropriate devisees and/or heirs

• Collect all available pertinent information for final income tax returns and prepare a "tickler" form (Exhibit 2.2)

• If the decedent was the sole proprietor of a business, determine if there are outstanding obligations to employees, such as federal and state taxes not withheld or Social Security contributions that have not been deducted from their salaries

• Assemble data on non-probate property (see page 357)

• If the decedent has owned real property jointly with another, inquire of the state department of taxation whether an affidavit of survivorship will be necessary (see Form 24). Since the title to the property will now be in the name of the survivor, check the state public record division to find what changes must be made to transfer the title. Frequently, the survivorship affidavit must be cleared with the proper county tax official and filed with the county real estate recorder. Your own state procedure must be followed

• Inquire into all substantial gifts made by decedent and all transfers made in trust. Such items have special tax considerations and are discussed further in Chapter 15.

Obtaining an Order for Hearing the Petition Either to Prove the Will or for General Administration

As soon as possible after the filing of the petition either to have the will admitted to probate or for administration of the intestate estate, the court will make and enter its order fixing a time and place for hearing the petition. The date of the order signals the beginning of the statutory period for creditors of the estate to file their claims against the estate (on claims, see page 360).

A court officer, such as the clerk, will prepare the order, but the paralegal should check to make sure this is done (see Forms 25 and 26).

Probate Court Procedure

The next steps in the continuation of formal probate proceedings include:

• The hearing to prove the will or for general appointment
• Selection of the personal representative
• The order admitting the will or granting administration
• The issuing of Letters Testamentary or Letters of Administration
• Appointment of trustees and guardians
• The order admitting foreign wills to probate

Hearing to Prove the Will or for General Appointment

On the date set for the hearing to prove the will or for general appointment, the personal representative, either the executor named in the will or the petitioner seeking appointment, and at least one subscribing witness, if necessary, should accompany the attorney to the court.[2] Any person who has an interest in the estate and who wishes to

---

2. No testimony from a subscribing witness is necessary, for example, if the will is self-proved.

contest the validity of the will or the appointment of the petitioner as administrator must file the objection with the court and should appear at the hearing. For the purpose of hearing the will contest, the court will then set a different date and time. If no interested person raises an objection, the petitioner, i.e., either the person who petitions to have the will admitted to probate or the person seeking appointment as administrator, testifies to the facts of the will or intestacy. Usually this testimony will suffice to prove the will or to appoint the administrator (-trix) (but compare U.P.C. § 3–405). If the petitioner is unable to testify to the facts, another person who can give such evidence must be present at the hearing. This person testifies under oath and answers questions that elicit such information as the date of the decedent's birth, death, and will, the domicile of the decedent, the probable value of the decedent's estate and debts, and the names of devisees, executors, and other interested parties (any person entitled to receive a share of the decedent's assets). Then, if necessary when the hearing is to prove a will, one or both of the subscribing witnesses are also sworn and testify as to the execution of the will and the capacity (age and sanity) of the testate. In addition, they verify the testimony of the first witness, the petitioner, insofar as possible. Exhibit 13.1 is an example of a typical transcript at a hearing to prove a will. Note that the questions are asked from the information requested on the petition itself in a manner that requires a simple yes or no answer (see Form 1).

Exhibit 13.1 Transcript of Hearing to Prove a Will

1. Are you the petitioner _____ as named in the petition for the probate of the estate of _____, the deceased?

2. And you reside at _____?

3. And have an interest in the proceeding as _____?

4. And to your knowledge decedent was born _____ at _____?

5. And that the decedent died on _____ at _____?

6. And the decedent at the time of his death resided at _____ in the city of _____, county of _____, state of _____?

7. And that the names and addresses of decedent's spouse, children, heirs and devisees and other persons interested in this proceeding and the ages of any who are minors so far known or ascertainable with reasonable diligence by you are: _____? Is that correct?

8. And that no personal representative of the decedent has been appointed in this state or elsewhere whose appointment has not been terminated?

9. And that the original of decedent's last will duly executed on _____, 19__, is in the possession of the court, and there are no codicil or codicils to the will?

10. And that to the best of your knowledge, you believe the will has been validly executed. Is that correct?

11. And that you are unaware of any instrument revoking the will?

Exhibit 13.1 *(continued)*

12. And that you are entitled to priority and appointment as personal representative because you are nominated in the last will of the decedent as personal representative with no bond required. Correct?

Finally, that you request the Court enter a judicial order formally:

1. Finding that the testator is dead

2. Finding that venue is proper

3. Finding that the proceeding was commenced within the time limitations prescribed by the laws of this state

4. Determining decedent's domicile at death

5. Determining decedent's heirs

6. Determining decedent's state of testacy

7. Probating the valid and unrevoked last will of decedent including any valid and unrevoked codicil thereto

8. Determining that petitioner is entitled to appointment as personal representative under the laws of this state

9. Appointing petitioner as the executor of the estate of decedent with no bond in a(n) (formal) (informal) administration

10. Authorizing issuance of letters testamentary to petitioner upon qualification and acceptance

11. Granting such other and further relief as may be proper

Proof of publication and mailing of notice of the hearing to all interested parties should also be offered in evidence at this hearing. Finally, after the hearing, the testimony of the subscribing witness(es) should be signed before and delivered to the judge unless the signature(s) may be waived.

If the will is contested and a date is set for the contest hearing, all witnesses to the will's execution should be present at the hearing to testify. A witness living more than 100 miles away or an ill or disabled witness may testify by deposition, as mentioned above. If the party contesting the will is successful, the probate court may set aside part or all of the will and declare it void. The decedent's estate will then pass by the state's intestate succession statute.

Selection of the Personal Representative

As discussed in Chapter 12, the kind of representative the court appoints at the hearing depends on the action, or lack of action, taken by the decedent. If the decedent names a representative in the will, the court appoints that individual *executor* (or *executrix*) to carry out the direction and request of the testate. If decedent dies intestate, the court appoints a *general administrator* (or *general administratrix*) to handle the estate.

Order Admitting Will or Granting General Administration

At testate proceedings, after the witness(es) testify and the will has been proved, the court makes its order admitting the will to probate. In intestate proceedings, the court issues an order granting general administration of the estate (see Form 27). A copy of the Certificate of Probate also appears in Appendix A (Form 5). In both cases, the court appoints a personal representative (i.e., executor or administrator) and fixes the representative's bond, if one is needed, based on the value of the estate, the type of assets, the relationship of the representative to the decedent, and other relevant facts.

Although the bond may be prepared by a surety (bonding) company or others, the representative or the attorney is responsible for the preparation of the form(s) of both bond and oath. Usually one form contains the bond and oath (see Form 28). To facilitate this process, an employee of a bonding company may be present in court on hearing days with appropriate bond forms, and therefore the bond and oath can be completed and filed with the court immediately after the hearing. In the case of a corporate representative or bank, the order will require the filing of an acceptance of the position of representative of the estate (see Form 59). No bond is required, however, in the case of the corporate representative, and bond may not be required of a personal representative.[3] The court will consider a request[4] for a minimum bond or no bond when the request is made in a decedent's will or is signed by all persons interested in the estate and submitted at or before the time of the hearing (see Form 29).

Issuance of Letters Testamentary or Letters of Administration

After the representative has filed an oath of office and the court has approved the bond if one is required, the court issues the appropriate documents conferring authority. In most states these documents, for the executor or executrix, are called Letters Testamentary; for the administrator or administratrix, they are called Letters of Administration.

The authority conferred by these letters is the same. The letters are certified (accompanied by a certificate from the clerk of probate court stating they are in full force). The representative is then qualified to act for the decedent's estate (see Forms 63 and 105). After the appointment, one of the first duties of the personal representative, if the estate contains probate assets, is to file for a federal identification number and a Notice of Fiduciary Relationship as required by the I.R.C. § 6903 (1954) (see Forms 62 and 64). These forms must be filed because the decedent's estate is an entity in itself and will be taxed as such (see Chapter 15 page 438).

---

3. The testate in the will may specifically request that the probate court require no bond of the named personal representative.

4. In addition to the testate, the personal representative will normally make the request for the benefit of interested parties.

Appointment of Trustees and Guardians

While alive the testate has the opportunity to establish testamentary trusts in the will to take effect upon death. This allows the testate to appoint a trustee whose function it is to administer the trust created in the will. Since the will and therefore the trust become effective only upon the death of the testate, technically, the trustee is appointed at that time. The trustee's powers must conform to statutory guidelines whether or not the testate sets them forth in the trust agreement incorporated into the will (for full information on trusts and trustees, refer to Chapter 9).

Generally, there are two types of guardianships—guardianship of the property or estate and guardianship of the person for the benefit of an individual lacking legal capacity such as a minor or incompetent (see page 181). The guardian of the person of a minor is responsible for the custody and care of the minor. It is the responsibility of the guardian of the property to manage the ward's property, invest, when appropriate, the assets, and make disbursements in accordance with the laws of the state. Both guardians should be named in the will and may be same person, but like the executor they must be approved and appointed by the probate court. Once appointed, the guardians are accountable to the court (see Form 30). The guardian's duties and powers are set by statute or the will's provisions. When acting in the name of the ward, the guardian should always sign legal documents listing the ward's name followed by the words "by _____, guardian."

If the decedent fails to name either type of guardian or dies intestate, the court will appoint a suitable guardian(s) for the benefit of the minor children. Guardians may also be appointed for persons who may or may not be minors but who are physically or mentally handicapped. The testate, in choosing a trustee to administer a trust set up by will or a guardian of the property, should select a person who is competent and experienced in the management of property and investments.

Usually a parent will act as guardian of both the child's person and the child's property, but in some states parents are specifically prevented by law from acting as guardian of their children's property. In all states, the court has the final word in the appointment of guardians. State laws that allow a parent to act as guardian of the child's property or to act as guardian of both the child's person and property are permissive rather than mandatory.

Order Admitting Foreign Wills to Probate

The decedent may die leaving property in another state as well as in the state of domicile (residence). All property must be distributed to interested parties, e.g., successors, heirs, or creditors. Disposing of property in the state of residence is comparatively easy; disposing of property in the foreign (non-residential or non-domiciliary) state requires a separate procedure.

If a will has been admitted to probate by a proper court in the state where the decedent was domiciled, this will may thereafter be admitted to probate as a foreign will in another state. The probate court of such other state will make its order admitting the "foreign" will and appointing an *ancillary administrator*. Generally, the qualifications required by the probate court for a person to be appointed ancillary administrator are the same as those required for a domiciliary administrator (see Form 31).

Table 13.1 is a summary comparison of the procedures to follow in formal probate administration for testate and intestate cases. Note

Table 13.1 Comparison of Formal Testate and Intestate Procedures

Testate Procedures	Intestate Procedures
1. File will (and codicils if any)	1. File petition for administration
2. File petition to prove will and for appointment of representative (or petition for probate of foreign will)	2. Order for hearing
3. Order for hearing	3. See to publication of order for hearing (in some counties the clerk attends to this)
4. See to publication of order for hearing (in some counties the clerk attends to this)	4. File affidavit of publication (in some counties the publisher attends to this)*
5. File affidavit of publication (in some counties the publisher attends to this) *	5. Mail notices to persons entitled to them
6. Mail notices to persons entitled to them	6. File affidavit of mailing notices
7. File affidavit of mailing notices	7. Establish checking accounts for estate
8. Establish checking accounts for estate	8. Mail notices of rights of spouse and minor children, if required
9. Mail notices of rights of spouse and minor children, if required	9. Review ancillary administration matters
10. Review ancillary administration matters	10. Ensure appearance of petitioner
11. Ensure appearance of petitioner and witness(es) to will at hearing	11. File request for reduced bond, if appropriate
12. File request for reduced bond, if appropriate	12. Hearing for administration
13. Hearing to prove will	13. Selection of the administrator
14. Order admitting will to probate and appointing representative (in some counties this is prepared by the clerk), certificate of probate	14. Order granting administrator
15. Issuance of Letters Testamentary	15. Issuance of Letters of Administration
16. Apply for federal identification number	16. Apply for federal identification number
17. Send notice of fiduciary to I.R.S.	17. Send notice of fiduciary to I.R.S.
18. Appointment of guardians or trustees if any	18. Appointment of guardians or trustees if any
19. Prepare and file bond and oath (if representative is an individual)	19. Prepare and file bond and oath (if representative is an individual)
20. Prepare and file acceptance (if representative is a corporation)	20. Prepare and file acceptance (if representative is a corporation)

* Some publishers send the affidavit directly to probate court; others fill out the affidavit form, but the representative must file it with the court.

that there are some differences between the two procedures (testate and intestate) up to the point of appointment and acceptance. Hereafter, the procedures for both are quite similar.

Procedures Before Estate Distribution

We have covered probate procedures up to and including the order appointing the personal representative and the establishment of the representative's authority by issuance of the letters. In both testacy and intestacy, before the estate is distributed, the representative must be concerned with:

- Opening the safe deposit box
- Collecting and preserving the decedent's assets
- Preparing the inventory
- Preparing an appraisal (same form used as inventory)
- Preparing a schedule of non-probate assets
- Filing the original inventory and appraisal, the schedule of non-probate assets, and the state inheritance tax return, if required, with the court and appropriate tax officer

It is essential that the representative, with the assistance of an attorney and a paralegal, carefully and expeditiously accomplish these tasks, since complete information as to the value of the decedent's gross estate, including the probate and non-probate assets, is necessary for the determination of death taxes. Thus the representative must not only take possession of all property when required to do so but must also inventory (list) all probate assets accurately and report all non-probate assets, making certain that these assets are properly valued.

Opening the Safe Deposit Box

Most statutes require that once the bank learns of the decedent's death it must seal any box leased by the decedent (whether the decedent held the box solely or in joint tenancy with another person) until an examination of the contents of the box has been made by the county treasurer's office or a representative thereof. If the decedent's will is in the safe deposit box, the bank usually takes it out and forwards it to the probate court before sealing the box. It is the responsibility of the bank to prevent anyone from removing any other contents of the box until the arrival of (a) the personal representative with the appointment papers, either Letters Testamentary or Letters of Appointment; and (b) the representative from the county treasurer's office.

The box should be opened only when the estate's attorney or paralegal, the representatives of the family, the county treasurer or deputy, and the representatives of the bank are present together. After the bank's representatives unseal the box, they are permitted to distribute the contents to either the surviving joint tenant (if the decedent had owned the box in joint tenancy) or to the personal representative (if the decedent had owned the box solely).

Proper disposition of the contents may present problems. If it happens that the box had been owned jointly, the surviving owner would be apparently entitled to its contents. If the contents, however, were not also jointly owned, the survivor is not entitled to them and may have to relinquish possession if the will or intestacy statute gives them to others.

Often, life insurance policies are kept in safe deposit boxes. When the named beneficiary is someone other than the estate of the decedent, the policies may be handed over to the appropriate beneficiary, but only after photocopies have been made so that they can be used in the calculation of possible state and/or federal death taxes (for more on life insurance policies, see page 351). If a federal estate tax return must be filed, U.S. Treasury Form 712 must be obtained from the insurance company for each policy and filed with the return (see Form 32). This form gives the names of the beneficiary, the decedent, and the insurance company, the face amount of the policy, the premium cost, and the like.

Collecting and Preserving the Decedent's Assets

Apart from personal property set aside as family allowances for the surviving spouse and minor children, all personal property owned solely by the decedent comes under the care of the personal representative. The court holds the representative responsible for collecting and preserving existing assets. The representative's duties in this area are:

• *To take possession of all the decedent's probate personal property.* Non-probate assets, including jointly owned property, life insurance benefits, and the like, are not subject to the marshaling (collection) authority of the representative. Title to the decedent's *personal property* passes to (vests in) the personal representative when appointed by the probate court. This passage of title is retroactive to the decedent's death. In other words, title vests in the representative as if the representative had assumed title as soon as the decedent died. After payment of all debts, the representative transfers title in such property to those who are entitled to it (successors). Title to the decedent's *real property,* however, vests immediately upon the decedent's death in the devisees of a testate estate or the heirs of an intestate estate. In appropriate instances, however, the personal representative may obtain possession of real property (by entering onto the land with a court order) and convey (sell) it in order to meet creditor's claims. A typical state statute on this matter is Pennsylvania's:

20 Pa.S. § 3311 (Purdon 1975), *Possession of*

Real and Personal Estate; Exception

A personal representative shall have the right to and shall take possession of, maintain and administer all the real and personal estate of the decedent, except real estate occupied at the time of death by an heir or devisee with the consent of the decedent. He shall collect the rents and income from each asset in his possession until it is sold or distributed, and, during the administration of the estate, shall have the right to maintain any action with respect to it and shall make all reasonable expenditures necessary to preserve it. The court may direct the personal representative to take possession of, administer and maintain real estate so occupied by an heir or a devisee if this is necessary to protect the rights of claimants or other parties. Nothing in this section shall affect the personal representative's power to sell real estate occupied by an heir or devisee (compare U.P.C. § 3–709).

- *To keep all real property (e.g., houses and other buildings) in reasonably good repair.* The property should be adequately insured, and no taxes should be allowed to become delinquent. Tenants in possession of any real property owned by the decedent should be notified immediately that rent is to be paid to the representative of the estate. All such payments are then included in the estate account.

- *To locate the decedent's real and personal property.* It will be necessary for the representative to contact many people: relatives, friends, business associates, banking officials, stockbrokers, attorneys, insurance agents, employers, and persons handling the decedent's claims within the Social Security Administration and the Veterans Administration.

- *To search for important documents and papers* that might contain information on the location of unknown assets. These include stocks, bonds, checkbooks, saving account passbooks, insurance policies, charge account cards, credit cards, canceled checks, old tax returns, deeds, contract for deeds, trust documents, bills of sale for personal property, title cards or certificates for automobile ownership transfer, and cards for membership in various agencies and fraternal organizations. Records filed with various county and city departments should also be reviewed for this purpose.

- *To protect certain items of value in the estate,* once they are collected, including stocks, bonds, insurance policies, promissory notes, mortgages, jewelry, and stamp or coin collections. It is desirable to rent a safe deposit box for their safekeeping.

- *To check all insurance policies* (life, hospitalization, car and home) for coverage and expiration dates. It might be advisable to terminate, continue, or transfer the benefits under the policies to the appropriate parties or to transfer ownership to the "Estate of John Doe" account.

Collecting estate assets can be complex work, depending on the number and diversity of the assets. The representative of a typical estate will be dealing with such assets as bank accounts, securities, debts owed the decedent, causes of action, jointly owned property, insurance benefits, death benefits, and automobiles.

Bank Accounts Accounts solely in the name of the decedent will be released only to the representative of the estate. After determining the location of the decedent's bank accounts (savings, checking, and credit union), the representative must withdraw the funds using the decedent's passbook and certified copies of the Letters Testamentary or Letters of Administration.   The representative may wait to withdraw these funds until after the quarterly interest has been earned.   The withdrawn funds are to be placed in the "Estate of John Doe" account.

Joint accounts must also be located, although these accounts go to the surviving joint tenant, e.g., a spouse.   The date on which the joint account was established, the source from which the account was created, and the amounts must be obtained and reported on the inheritance (death) tax form.   The amount of the joint account may be included in the decedent's gross estate for tax purposes.   For further discussion on tax consequences of joint ownership, see page 414.

"Totten trusts" (savings account trusts in the decedent's name for the benefit of another) are payable directly to the named beneficiary in many but not all states.   Information on Totten trusts and the state's treatment of them must be obtained for tax purposes.

Securities   A search must be undertaken to discover all the decedent's securities (stocks, bonds) including accounts with brokers or stocks held in the broker's name.   Securities are often found either among the decedent's possessions or in a safe deposit box.   Generally, securities remain registered in the decedent's name and are transferred to the proper successors after administration of the estate is completed.   Determination must be made as to whether the decedent, before death, effectively transferred ownership of the stock to another.   Transfer of securities is discussed in detail on page 365.

Debts Owed the Decedent   Inquiries should be made into all outstanding debts owed *to* the decedent.   Check to determine whether the decedent held any mortgages, contracts for deed, promissory notes or similar evidences of indebtedness to the decedent.   Such debtors may include devisees or heirs.   Because they must repay the estate, their debts might cancel out the benefits they receive from it unless their debts are forgiven in the will.

Arrange for the continued collection of loans, rents, interest, dividends, royalties, and income tax refunds and attempt to collect delinquent obligations.   These monies are to be transferred into the estate account.   A collection agency may be hired to collect delinquent debts.   The probate court will approve a reasonable compromise settlement of a disputed debt owed to the decedent so long as it appears to be in the best interest of the estate.

Causes of Action   A legal wrong for which a civil suit for damages (see Glossary) can be brought creates for the wronged or injured party a "cause of action," i.e., a right to sue.   If the person suing, dies while in the process of litigation, the claim or "cause of action" may also die (end).   When by statute, the personal representative is allowed to pursue the "cause of action" for the benefit of the decedent's estate or heirs, any recovery in damages becomes an asset of the estate.   State statutes on the subject of "causes of action" as assets of the estate allow or bar such lawsuits depending on the circumstances surrounding death, the nature of the action, and many other factors. A paralegal must carefully read the state statutes and commentaries on them to determine if a particular decedent's "cause of action" survives and should be continued. The findings must be discussed with the supervising attorney for final resolution.

Example: Sally Simmons negligently backs her car into her neighbor's yard striking a supporting beam of the neighbor's porch, which causes the roof of the porch to collapse. Considerable property damage results. Susan Swanson, the neighbor, sues Sally in civil court, but after commencing the lawsuit, Susan dies. The personal representative of Susan's estate must continue the suit if no settlement is reached. Any recovery becomes an asset of Susan's estate.

Example: Tom Jensen is struck by a car driven negligently by Michael Howard. Although Tom is seriously injured, causing him to be hospitalized, his doctors assure him that he will completely recover in time. While convalescing two months after the accident and after commencing a lawsuit against Michael, Tom has a heart attack and dies. Medical experts establish that the heart attack is totally unrelated to the previous accident. Under these circumstances in some states, Tom's "cause of action" dies with him. The personal representative of Tom's estate would not be allowed to continue Tom's lawsuit except to recover "special damages," i.e., the medical and hospital expenses and loss of wages incurred by Tom because of the automobile accident. "Pain and suffering" damages are not recoverable.

Jointly Owned Property Property of any kind, real or personal, held in the form of ownership known as joint tenancy does not become a probate asset of the decedent's estate. If the decedent held such property with another person as joint tenants, the property would automatically become the surviving joint tenant's upon the decedent's death. In order to clear title to real property held in joint tenancy by the decedent, the representative must:

1. Execute in duplicate an Affidavit of Survivorship if the property is the homestead and the surviving joint tenant is the decedent's spouse (see Form 24)

2. File a certified copy of the death certificate of the decedent and one copy of the Affidavit of Survivorship with the proper section of the county land office, i.e., the county recorder or registrar (see Form 33)

3. Send one copy of the Affidavit of Survivorship to the office of the commissioner of taxation or the appropriate state tax officer.

In some states, when the value of the homestead does not exceed a statutory amount, e.g., $75,000, and the homestead is inherited by the spouse or minor children, the above three procedures may cancel the state inheritance tax lien (claim) on the homestead which would otherwise exist. In order to cancel an inheritance tax lien on all other jointly held real property, the surviving joint tenant must file with the county land office the following:

• An Affidavit of Survivorship on which there is certification by the commissioner of taxation that no inheritance tax is due or that the tax has been paid

• A certified copy of the decedent's death certificate

Insurance benefits If the decedent had held insurance policies payable either to the estate or to named beneficiaries the representative should obtain U.S. Treasury Department Form 712 (Life Insurance Statement for a Decedent Insured) for each policy (see Form 32 in Appendix A). These forms must be filed with the federal estate tax return, and they must contain information needed in order to prepare the death tax returns (see Form 119 and Chapter 15, page 447).

If the decedent had retained the rights of a policy owner, called incidents of ownership (e.g., the right to change the beneficiary, to convert the policy to another form of insurance, or to cancel it altogether), the Internal Revenue Service considers that the decedent had held enough control over the policy for it to be considered an asset of the estate. As such, it is subject to both state and federal death taxes. Death benefits will go directly to the named beneficiary without being taxed, only if the insurance company is informed that the insured person gives up these rights (incidents of ownership) at least three years before death (see page 32). There are no death taxes due on an insurance policy taken out on decedent's life by another person so long as the beneficiary is not the decedent's estate.

When the decedent's estate is the beneficiary of the policy, the personal representative must determine and execute the proper procedure for filing the claim. The insurance company frequently requires that the beneficiary file the claim on the company's own claim form in order to receive proceeds from the policy. Therefore, notice of the date of decedent's death should be given to the insurance company and all other documents required by the company should be prepared. These generally include the death certificate, the return of the original life insurance policy, and, if required, a copy of the Letters Testamentary or Letters of Administration. If any premium has been paid by the decedent in advance, the representative must request that the company return the unearned portion of this premium to the decedent's estate.

Hospitalization and disability insurance companies must be notified, especially where the decedent was hospitalized for any length of time before death. Payments from these policies may be made directly to those who provided care during the last illness; otherwise, they are paid directly into the decedent's estate. Cancellation of life, auto, home, and other types of insurance premiums, when appropriate, must be made, and refunds received should be paid into the estate account.

The representative is responsible for maintaining adequate insurance coverage on the estate assets. When existing policies are sufficient, they should be transferred from the decedent's name to the representative's name. Purchases of additional coverage must be made when necessary.

Death Benefits Other death benefits, payable to the decedent's estate, which must be collected include employee benefit plans, Social Security, and Veterans Administration benefits. If the decedent was entitled to accrued earned pay, accrued vacation pay, sick leave, terminal pay, pension or profit-sharing plans, deferred compensation plans, group insurance plans, stock options, year-end bonus or back pay uncollected, and labor or credit union benefit plans, such compensation should go into the estate account.

If the benefits are a form of employee compensation such as pension or profiting-sharing plans, the representative must seek them out and determine to whom these benefits are to paid. If they are payable to a named beneficiary and not to the estate, and the decedent did not contribute to the plan the entire proceeds from said plan are exempt from both state and federal death taxes. If the decedent did contribute to the plan, a proportion of the proceeds would be subject to tax. If payable to decedent's estate, employee benefits are subject to federal tax and are usually subject to state death taxes as well.

If the decedent was a veteran of any war, including the Korean and Vietnam wars, the decedent's successors may be entitled to such benefits as insurance, pensions, burial expenses, and other benefits, according to the rules of the Veterans Administration or state law. (See page 159.) Death benefits under Social Security and veterans benefits are generally either paid directly to the surviving spouse or applied to the payment of funeral and burial expenses. A Social Security lump sum death benefit, a maximum of $255, may be available to the decedent's estate. The form used to apply for this benefit is Social Security Form SSA–8. Funeral directors have the forms, which authorize applying such benefits toward the settlement of the funeral bill. This is often the procedure followed.

A union or fraternal lodge to which the decedent may have belonged should be checked to see if any benefits are due the decedent or the successors. In addition, the surviving spouse and minor children of a decedent covered under Social Security benefits may have the right to a claim for monthly benefits given to survivors of the decedent. The local Social Security office must be contacted.

Automobiles As owner of the decedent's automobile(s), the estate or the personal representative could become legally liable for injuries or damage caused by improper and negligent use. Therefore, the automobile(s) should be transferred to the persons entitled to them as soon as possible after the death of the decedent or, if a state statute demands, within a certain number of days. The ways of transferring title to the decedent's car to the appropriate person vary from state to state. State statutes or regulations control the transfer of title to the car. The appropriate person to whom title is transferred could be a surviving spouse who elects to take the car (see Minn. Stat. Ann. § 525.15 [West 1975] for a typical state statute), a surviving joint tenant owner, a devisee in the decedent's will, or a purchaser who pays the market value to the personal representative. The statutory requirements or regulations for title transfer must be checked.

Preparing an Inventory of the Assets

An inventory should be made jointly by the personal representative and the attorney or paralegal. In practice, this becomes one of the more important paralegal tasks. The inventory amounts to a complete physical check of all the assets of the decedent and a listing of said assets and their value at the time of decedent's death on the forms provided for the inventory (see Form 65). The organization of the inventory and the degree of particularity with which items should be listed are matters of judgment. The inventory should be well organized, complete, and accurate. The appraisers hired by the personal representative and appointed by the court (if required by state law or on demand by an interested party) can then expeditiously appraise the assets. Also, this inventory must be completed to make available all data necessary for the preparation of the federal estate tax return (see page 444 on this.) The time limit for filing the inventory is determined by state statute. As previously mentioned, the value of securities for purposes of the inventory are generally computed as of the date of decedent's death (see page 445 for alternate valuation date), as are all the other assets, and must include the following often forgotten items: (1) interest and rent accrued at the date of death and (2) any dividends declared before death (see Form 65). A preliminary or partial inventory can be made if it is necessary to sell assets before the inventory and appraisal can be completed.

Preparing an Appraisal

Once the inventory is completed and the representative has signed an oath stating that all known property of the decedent has been inventoried, the court-appointed appraisers, if any, should be contacted. Generally, the appraisers are real estate agents or brokers selected from the local real estate association. An appraiser must not have any interest in the estate or property therein.

In states that require appointment of appraisers, the probate judge generally appoints qualified persons, often at the original hearing and without the necessity of filing a petition, to determine the value of the particular type of property of the estate (see Form 6). Even in those states in which appointment of appraisers is not required, the representative, the court, or any interested party may request a professional appraisal.

Before the appraisers begin their work, they should sign the oath of appraisers (see Form 34). Then, accompanied by the attorney or more often the paralegal, they should complete their work. There is usually nothing to be gained by trying to minimize the value of the estate for state inheritance tax purposes, since this valuation is the basis for determining the income tax upon resale, and inheritance tax rates on small estates are much lower than income taxes.

After the appraisal, the representative files this inventory with the probate court and pays the appraisers' fee. The normal fee for each appraiser is generally set by statute (either a percentage of the estate or whatever the court determines to be fair and reasonable). Some states set minimum and/or maximum appraisal fees depending on the size of the estates. Other states no longer permit percentage fees. Fees charged by the appraisers can be deducted as a proper administration expense on both federal and state, if any, estate tax returns.

Preparing a Schedule of Non-Probate Assets

After collection of the decedent's assets and the inventory and appraisal have been completed, assets that are not part of the probate estate but that are included in the gross estate of the decedent must be identified. The form used to list these assets of the estate is an affidavit called the Schedule of Non-Probate Assets (see Form 70). Property that qualifies as non-probate assets would include:

• Life insurance proceeds and annuities not payable to the estate

• Real or personal property held in joint tenancy

• Contracts, such as employment contracts, which contain pension plans, profit-sharing, or group health insurance

• Certain forms of trusts, e.g., Totten trusts, established by the decedent in favor of another person

All such assets are exempt from creditor's claims, since only probate assets are subject to the debts of the decedent.

It is the responsibility of the surviving joint tenant or tenants to transfer the title to jointly owned property into their own name(s). Generally, if real estate is jointly owned and is to be transferred, the representative must obtain a certified copy of the death certificate (Form 33) and an Affidavit of Survivorship (Form 24) on which the state tax officer, e.g., the commissioner of taxation, has certified that any state inheritance tax due has been paid. These documents must be filed with the proper county officer for recording real property. Accompanying the forms must be a copy of the state inheritance tax return (see Form 71). The paralegal must see that these forms are properly completed and executed before submitting them to the supervising attorney for final approval.

Insurance on the life of the decedent payable to a named individual (not to the estate) is a non-probate asset. Life insurance that benefits the estate of the decedent is deemed an asset of the estate and is therefore subject to federal estate taxation. If the policy names an individual beneficiary (e.g., a relative, friend, or business partner), the responsibility of claiming benefits from the insurance company falls on that beneficiary. The attorney or paralegal should verify that the beneficiary has presented the claim to the company. The beneficiary should use the company's own form and present the original policy and a copy of the death certificate to the company. Whether the proceeds are payable to an individual or to the estate, the representative must submit a Life Insurance Statement for a Decedent Insured (U.S. Treasury Form 712) when paying the federal estate tax (see Form 32 in Appendix A).

Since a number of settlement options are available from the insurance policies, familiarity with these options and their tax consequences to the named beneficiaries of the policy is essential. For example, if the insured decedent had authorized a lump sum payment of the face amount of the policy in order to utilize the marital deduction for tax purposes, the spouse of the policyholder must have been named beneficiary (see Chapter 15). In the case of an annuity option, in which a specific amount of the principal of the proceeds from the insurance is paid to the beneficiary at determined intervals until the full amount is dissipated, a portion of these annual payments will be considered a return of principal and will not be subject to income tax. The remaining portion of these annual annuity payments will be considered interest subject to income taxation. According to I.R.C. § 101 (1954), however, the first $1,000 of such interest on insurance principal payable to the surviving spouse of the decedent is exempt annually from personal income tax.

Example: If the decedent, Sam MacGregor, chooses an annuity settlement option, his wife, Elizabeth, will receive the proceeds in the form of annual payments that will continue until she has received the entire amount. A fraction of each payment, i.e., the interest, will be subject to tax as a return on Sam's investment; another fraction, i.e., the return of principal, will be exempt. In Elizabeth's case, she may exempt from her federal income tax the first $1,000 of the interest received per year because she is the surviving spouse.

The paralegal must contact the decedent's former employers to determine whether employment contracts containing pension plans, profit-sharing, group insurance, or other employment benefits were in force at the time of the decedent's death. Benefits from such contracts distributed according to the terms set forth in the contracts are not considered part of the decedent's probate estate, but they may be included in the decedent's gross estate for tax purposes if the decedent paid all or part of the contributions (see Chapter 15).

Trusts established by the decedent may be either probate or non-probate assets. One example of a trust classified as a non-probate asset is a Totten trust. This trust is established by the decedent's deposit of money in a savings account in the decedent's own name as trustee for the benefit of another. (In most states the words "trustee for" or "in trust for" must appear in the name of the account.) The depositor-trustee retains all power over such a trust, including the right to revoke it at any time or for any reason before death. Upon the death of the depositor, the trust account becomes the sole property of the named beneficiary without the necessity of any probate proceeding. If a savings account, however, is not truly a Totten trust, it will be subject to death taxes, attachment by creditors, or family allowances to the surviving spouse and/or minor children.

Filing the Inventory and Appraisal, Schedule of Non-Probate Assets, and Inheritance Tax Return With the Court and Appropriate Tax Officer

Once the Schedule of Non-Probate Assets has been completed, it is attached to the Inventory and Appraisal form and filed with the probate court. Copies of these two forms are then mailed to the commissioner of taxation or the appropriate state officer in charge of the state's inheritance and gift tax division. A copy of the Petition to Prove the Will with the copy of the will attached or the Petition for General Administration is also sent to this office, e.g., the state office of taxation. These copies must conform to those filed with the probate court.

Next, the form used for the state inheritance tax return should be completed (see Form 71). This return lists the value of property contained in the Inventory and Appraisal and in the Schedule of Non-Probate Assets, and includes the deductions and exemptions claimed by the personal representative of the estate (see page 463). From this information, the amount of tax due the state can be computed and paid. This inheritance tax return is then filed with the state office of taxation, and a copy is filed with the probate court. When no probate is necessary, a Schedule of Non-Probate Assets and the inheritance tax return are filed with the state office of taxation and any tax due is paid.

Distribution of the Estate and Payment of Claims

The following procedures are essential for the distribution of a decedent's estate:

- Distribution of family allowances to surviving spouse and/or minor children
- Filing and hearing of creditor claims and payment of allowed claims
- Transfer of assets—real and personal property

Distribution of Family Allowances to Surviving Spouse and/or Minor Children

After the property is appraised, and the Inventory and Appraisal filed, the surviving spouse or minor children, or the guardian of minor children, may submit a Petition to Set Apart the Personal Property of the decedent allowed by statute whether the decedent died testate or intestate (see Form 66). After approving the petition, the court will issue an order "setting apart" said property (see Form 67). In some states, separate petitions and orders are used, one for the homestead, another for the personal property.

We have already discussed the types and value of the property that can be set aside according to one state's (Minnesota's) law (see page 110). If by state statute the homestead passes directly to the surviving spouse and/or to the minor children, the state will often exempt the homestead (up to a statutory amount) from inheritance taxation. If the spouse receives ownership greater than a life estate in the homestead, federal tax law will allow the homestead as part of the marital deduction. A homestead may qualify as part of the marital deduction for federal estate tax purposes if it passes directly to the surviving spouse. It would not qualify for the marital deduction if the spouse receives only a life estate in the homestead (I.R.C. § 2056). Concerning the decedent's personal property set apart as family allowances, it should be noted (1) that states generally hold that such property is not subject to state inheritance tax but instead is allowed as a deduction on the inheritance tax return and that there is no federal estate tax deduction granted for such property (see I.R.C. §§ 2056, and generally, 2053–2057, 2106).

Until final settlement of the estate, the surviving spouse and/or minor children may receive reasonable maintenance from the assets of the estate. The amount is determined by the value of the estate and the socioeconomic status of the decedent. State statutes determine the length of time that the family may receive maintenance (e.g., 12 to 18 months). The court, at its discretion, may lengthen this period. In most states, maintenance and the statutory family allowances are exempt from the claims of all creditors, including claims for administration of the estate and funeral expenses. The Petition for an Order Allowing Maintenance and the order from the court granting it to the decedent's family are found on Forms 68 and 69. For state inheritance tax purposes, the amount of maintenance established and allowed by the court for one year is a proper deduction and therefore is not taxed by the state on the inheritance tax return. State statutes, however, should be consulted to determine the monetary limit allowed as a tax deduction.

Filing and Hearing of Creditor Claims and Payment of Allowed Claims

Before any of the decedent's assets can be distributed to the devisees or heirs of the estate, and after setting apart the family allowances and maintenance, the decedents' just debts must be paid. Those to whom the decedent owed money are given notice through publication (see page 340) that their debtor has died and that they must file their claims with the decedent's personal representative.

Statutes have established a definite procedure for the filing and hearing of creditors' claims. The court's order setting the date for the hearing of either the Petition to Prove the Will or the Petition for General Administration also establishes the time limits for creditors to file their claims. For this purpose, creditors should use the Proof of Claim form containing the claimant's address and signature and the affirmation of a notary public (see Form 35). If the claim is based on any written instrument, such as a contract, promissory note, or bank draft, the claimant must attach a copy of the instrument to the Proof of Claim.

The time period set by most state statutes during which creditors have to file their claims is generally two to six months from the date of the probate court's above-mentioned order to hear the petition. If the claimant does not act within the time allowed, the right to present it at any other time is lost. If, however, the claimant can demonstrate a good reason for requesting an extension, the court may extend the period by giving notice to the personal representative of the estate.

During and after the time period for filing claims, it is necessary to check with the personal representative to determine whether any of the claims should be contested. If the decision is made to contest a claim, then the representative must, before or on the date of the hearing, file all objections to a claim or file claims against those claims (counterclaims) to which the decedent was entitled. The document used to file this objection or counterclaim is called the Objection to Claims and is served on the claimant and filed with the probate court (see Form 15). Contested claims are not heard on the date set for hearing allowed claims, but on another hearing date, for which arrangements must be made. Notice of this second date for contested claims must be given to the creditors. The representative of the estate, in writing, can admit the claims that are just and proper debts of the decedent. All other contested claims must be proven legitimate at this hearing in order to be allowed (approved) by the court. Also, claims of the representative or claims in which the representative has an interest are allowed only if proven by evidence satisfactory to the court. Once the claims are allowed, it is the duty of the representative to pay them and to file receipts or vouchers (canceled checks) when the final account (Form 72) is presented to the probate court.

The laws that regulate probate procedures have given certain kinds of debts priority. In the event that assets of the decedent's estate are insufficient to pay all debts in full, the priority of payment of debts, after first paying, in most states, the family allowances, is set by statute.

A typical list of the priority of debts is the following Pennsylvania statute.

20 Pa.S. § 3392 (Purdon 1975), *Classification and Order of Payment*

If the applicable assets of the estate are insufficient to pay all proper charges and claims in full, the personal representative, subject to any preference given by law to claims due the United States, shall pay them in the following order, without priority as between claims of the same class:

(1) The costs of administration.
(2) The family exemption.

(3) The costs of the decedent's funeral and burial, and the costs of medicines furnished to him within six months of his death, of medical or nursing services performed for him within that time, of hospital services including maintenance provided him within that time, and of services performed for him by any of his employes within that time.

(4) The cost of a gravemarker.

(5) Rents for the occupancy of the decedent's residence for six months immediately prior to his death.

(6) All other claims, including claims by the Commonwealth (compare U.P.C. § 3–805).

Notice that the Pennsylvania statute lists the costs of administration before the amount of the family exemption granted in Pennsylvania.

Generally, only probate assets of the decedent's estate are subject to creditors' claims. Therefore, the following would be exempt from creditors' claims: non-probate assets such as jointly owned real or personal property (including joint savings or checking accounts); proceeds from life insurance policies payable to named beneficiaries; death benefits, including employee benefits, retirement benefits, and benefits under annuity contracts; and U.S. Savings Bonds payable on death to a beneficiary other than decedent's estate.

Since parties who hold these debts have a prior claim to the assets of the decedent's estate, the heirs or named devisees of the decedent may find themselves receiving nothing from the estate. It is quite possible that there may not be any assets remaining in the estate after all the creditors have been paid.

Assignment 128

Erma Gledig, recently deceased, left the bills listed below. According to your own state law, in what order are the following to be paid, if at all, by her executor, Sherwin Gledig, her husband?

1. Salary payable to Erma's nurse-companion for a week prior to Erma's death

2. State inheritance tax due on a devise to Erma from her brother, who predeceased her

3. Attorney's fee payable to a lawyer who advised Erma during a real estate transaction

4. Claim for services rendered by the Cahill Funeral Home

5. Claim from the U.S. Commissioner of Internal Revenue for income tax unpaid in the previous year

6. Sherwin's executor's bond

7. Unpaid installment on an automobile owned jointly by Erma and Sherwin

Transfer of Assets: Real and Personal Property

Transfer of Real Estate   If the decedent's personal property is sufficient to pay the allowances, expenses, taxes, and the rest of the debts, all real estate will pass free and clear to the named devisees in the will or to heirs by intestate succession. In such cases, the personal representative is usually not obliged to take possession of the real estate. But if the personal property assets of the decedent are insufficient to pay the debts, the representative is obligated to take possession of the real estate for the purpose of selling it to satisfy these obligations (see page 350). In addition, the court may decide that the sale of the real estate is in the best interests of the persons with an interest in the realty and order such a sale. The homestead, however, may not be sold without written consent of the surviving spouse, which must be filed with the court.

The sale of real estate can be accomplished in one of two ways: (1) If the decedent's will gives the personal representative (executor) the power to sell the estate's real estate, the representative needs no court order to proceed; (2) if the decedent had no will or failed to include in the will a power of sale, the representative may not proceed without a court order, which may authorize either a private or public sale of the real property. In either instance, the personal representative must execute numerous legal forms.

If the representative (executor) is granted power-of-sale by the decedent's will, it is possible to sell real estate without a court order, but it is still advisable to obtain such an order. To sell real estate, the representative will also need a certified copy of the will, a certified copy of the order admitting a will to probate and a certified copy of the Letters Testamentary, and a Probate Deed (see Form 36).

If the decedent's will does not contain a power of sale or if the decedent dies intestate and the representative of the estate deems it wise to sell, mortgage, or lease real estate owned by the decedent, the probate court may authorize a *private sale* as requested. To accomplish this, the following steps are necessary:

• The representative must prepare and file a Petition to Sell—Mortgage—Lease Real Estate to be presented to the court after the inventory and appraisal has been filed. This document is necessary only if the will does *not* give the power of sale to the executor or if there is no will (see Form 37).

• The probate judge then signs the Order for Hearing Petition to Sell—Mortgage—Lease Real Estate requested by the representative (see Form 38). The order sets the date, place, and time for the hearing and must be published and printed in the same manner as the hearing to prove the will (see page 340). Notice of this hearing in the form of the publication or a copy of the Order for Hearing must be sent to the devisees or heirs in order to comply with the general probate notice requirements.

• At the Hearing on the Petition to Sell—Mortgage—Lease, the representative of the estate presents a certified copy of the will, a certified copy of the order admitting a will to probate, and a certified copy of the Letters Testamentary, and a Probate Deed, along with the probate judge's order. Oral testimony of the representative as to the facts set forth in the petition is presented. If satisfied as to the need to sell the real estate, the judge signs the Order for Sale—Mortgage—Lease of Real Estate at Private Sale (see Form 39).

• If required by the court, the real estate must be reappraised by two or more disinterested persons where a considerable period of time has elapsed since issuance of the order. This is necessary because of the possible substantial increase or decrease in the property's value. The form used is the Warrant to Appraisers at Private Sale and Oath of Appraisers (see Form 40). Generally, the appraisers are the same persons who made the original inventory and appraisal for the estate. Once the market value of the realty has been determined, the property cannot be sold at private sale for less than that price. The appraisers sign the Oath of Appraisers and Appraisal of Lands Under Order for Sale (see Form 34).

• The court may require, at its discretion, that the representative post an additional bond (see Form 101).

• Once the private sale is completed, the representative must file the Report of Sale of Land at Private Sale Under Order for Sale with the court (see Form 41). (Delete those parts of the form applicable only to a public sale.)

• After the representative has filed the report of sale and complied with the terms of the order for sale, the court will approve the sale and enter its Order Confirming Private Sale of Real Estate. With only a few modifications, it can be used to confirm a public sale as well (see Form 42). The court authorizes the representative to execute and deliver the proper deed (see Form 36).

• In order to complete the sale and to ensure that the buyer will have clear and marketable title to the land, the representative must file in the county recorder's office certified copies of: the Letters of Administration or Letters Testamentary, the Order for Sale of Real Estate at Private Sale, the Order Confirming Private Sale of Real Estate, and the Probate Deed issued by the representative, called either the administrator's deed or the executor's deed.

Public sale of real estate may also be authorized by the court. The representative executes the same documents as those used in a private sale, including the Petition and Order for Hearing to Sell Real Estate; the Order for Sale of Real Estate at Public Auction; the Report of Sale of Land at Public Auction; and the Order Confirming Sale of Real Estate at Public Auction. The representative must gather these documents, file an additional bond if necessary, and obtain and file certified copies of the same instruments used in the private sale covered previously. The only additional requirement for the public auction is that if such a sale is authorized by the court, published notice of the time and place of the sale are often required for a specific statutory notice period. Proof of such publication must be filed with the court before the court will formally confirm the sale.

Transfer of Securities (Corporate Stock) As a general rule, stocks need not be transferred to the name of the personal representative of the estate. They may be left in the name of the decedent and sold or transferred to the persons entitled to them at the conclusion of the administration of the estate. Whenever stock is transferred from one person to another, whether by sale, gift, devise, or inheritance, the transfer is handled by a transfer agent [5] or corporation. When the transfer of decedent's stock is to be made to a devisee under the will or an heir under intestacy proceedings, the transfer agent must be given:

• The stock certificate representing the number of shares to be transferred, endorsed (signed) by the personal representative, and the signature guaranteed by a bank or a member firm of the New York Stock Exchange

• A certified copy of the Letters Testamentary or Letters of Administration

• A certified copy of the Decree of Distribution (see page 368 and Form 14)

• The address and Social Security number of the devisee or heir receiving the stock

If the securities are registered in the name of the decedent and another person as joint tenants, a transfer from joint tenancy to sole ownership requires, in addition to the documents and data mentioned above, that the transfer agent receive a death certificate of the decedent, an affidavit of survivorship (see Form 24), and a state inheritance tax waiver for those states that require a stock transfer tax to be paid (see Form 43). After obtaining the required materials, the transfer agent changes the registry on the corporate books by writing in the new owner's name and address and issues new stock certificates to the new owner. Questions about procedures in accomplishing the transfer of corporate stock can best be answered by contacting the appropriate stock transfer agent.

If the decedent lived in a rural area, the representative should make inquiries concerning the decedent's ownership of stock in a grain-elevator, creamery, or other farmer cooperatives. It is possible that the decedent kept no records of such stock ownership in obvious locations such as the safe deposit box or at home; consequently, a thorough check of outside sources (e.g., the associations themselves) is necessary.

If the decedent owned any U.S. savings bonds of Series A, B, C, D, F, or G that were not redeemed before death, they should be presented

---

5. A transfer agent is the party designated by the corporation as the one to be contacted whenever a stock transfer, e.g., a sale or gift of stock, is performed.

immediately for payment because they have matured and no longer bear interest.

The Final Account and Closing the Estate

The final steps before the probate court can discharge the personal representative from obligations to the decedent's estate, devisees, or heirs at law are:

• Filing the Final Account and Petition for Settlement and Distribution

• Requesting an Order for a hearing on the Petition for Final Account, which sets a time and place for the hearing and requires publication

• Giving notice of the hearing on the final account to all parties with an interest in the estate

• Attending the hearing

• Before a final settlement and Decree of Distribution is granted, preparing and filing copies of all federal and state death tax and income tax returns

• Requesting an order allowing the Final Account to be granted

• Computing and filing state inheritance tax return or waiver

• Once the inheritance tax is paid or waived, requesting that the Decree of Distribution be signed, thereby allowing assets to be transferred

• Collecting receipts for all property distributed

• Filing the Petition for Discharge of Representative (executor or administrator) with the receipts

• Requesting that the probate court sign the Order Discharging Executor or Administrator and the Sureties

• Sending a copy of the Order Discharging the Representative to the surety.

Filing the Final Account and Petition for Settlement and Distribution

Once all just claims have been paid and receipts for such payments collected, the representative must file a verified (notarized) account of the administration and petition the court for settlement of the estate (see Form 16). Beginning with the original inventory (see page 356), the representative's account must show all changes in the assets of the estate, including debits and credits of cash and any interest that may have accrued during administration of the estate. This accounting should fully disclose the balance of property available for distribution to named devisees under the will or heirs after the payment of creditors.

Property remaining on hand for distribution should be identifed in such a way that the representative may readily determine the persons entitled to receive such property. The representative should keep vouchers in the form of canceled checks or receipts to substantiate the payments for any and all disbursements or for assets distributed during administration of the estate including the representative's own fees and claims against the estate.

The final account must be filed within the time allotted by statute for settlement of the estate, in some states one year from the date of the representative's appointment. For good cause, the probate court may grant an extended time for settlement.

The form for the final account lists the steps and information that must be included for the court's review. Incidental expenses (for miscellaneous items such as copies of the final decree and filing fees) necessarily occur after the final decree has been granted and can only be estimated.

Order for Hearing Final Account

The probate court issues an order for a hearing on the Petition for Final Account, setting the time and place for the hearing (see Form 72). Notice of the hearing must be published in conformity with statutory requirements of the state, e.g., publication of the notice once a week for three weeks in a legal newspaper in the county of the court's jurisdiction. The newspaper publishing the notice may be required to file with the probate court an affidavit proving that the notice was published and to send a copy of this proof to the representative (see Form 3).

Notice of the Hearing to Interested Parties

The representative gives notice of the hearing to interested parties by mailing a copy of the court's order for a hearing to each devisee or heir within a statutory time period, e.g., at least 14 days before the hearing. The representative then submits an affidavit to the court verifying that notice has been mailed to these persons and also to the state's tax official, e.g., the state officer of taxation (see Form 56).

Hearing on the Petition for Final Account

The hearing on the Petition for Final Account gives all parties with an interest in the estate of the decedent the opportunity to appear and examine the representative's accounting. Explanations and corrections of the account and intended distribution should be discussed and resolved at this time. Then the representative requests that the court accept the final account.

Federal and State Estate and Income Tax Returns

Before the final account is allowed and the Decree of Distribution is issued, federal and state death and income tax returns must be completed and filed with the final account (see Chapter 15).

Order Allowing Final Account

After all taxes have been paid and the final account has been accepted, the court signs an order allowing the account (see Form 75).

State Inheritance Tax Return or Waiver

In states that have an inheritance tax, a copy of the order allowing the Final Account generally must be filed with the state's official tax collector. If an inheritance tax is due, the representative must pay the tax and obtain a receipt from the state officer of taxation to be filed with the probate court. In some states, the probate court computes the inheritance tax after the final account has been allowed. In such cases, the representative does not make the tax payment or prepare the tax waiver (if no tax is due) until this time (see Forms 71 and 43). Within a specified time after the filing of the tax return, objections to the amount of tax may be made. After such time period expires, the state inheritance tax return becomes final.

Decree of Distribution Entered by the Court

After the determination and payment of the inheritance tax, or its waiver, when no tax is owed, the court enters a Decree of Distribution (see Form 14). In its decree, the court determines the persons entitled to the estate, names the heirs or devisees, states their relationship to the decedent, describes the property, and determines the property to which each person is entitled. This decree also states (a) that notice for the final hearing was duly given; (b) that the deceased died testate or intestate, including the date of death and the residency of the decedent; (c) that the estate has been fully administered, including the payment of all allowed claims, and administration, funeral, and last illness expenses; (d) that the final account has been approved and settled; and (e) that all inheritance, estate, and income taxes have been paid.

Once the final decree is entered, the assets of the decedent's estate can be transferred. Title to personal property passes immediately to the appropriate heirs or devisees. In some states, real property passes differently. The right to possess the decedent's real property may vest in the heirs or devisees immediately after the Decree of Distribution, but legal title may remain with the representative until a certified copy of the decree has been filed with the county recorder or other official in the county where the land is located. The statutes of the individual states must be checked to determine the exact procedure.

The passing of title to real property held in joint tenancy by the decedent necessitates filing with the county recorder an Affidavit of Survivorship that has been certified by the state department of taxation (see page 343), a certified copy of the death certificate, and a certified copy of the Decree of Distribution in order to transfer legal title of the real property to the surviving joint tenant or tenants.

Collecting Receipts for All Property Distributed   After all distributions have been made, the representative must collect receipts for all property distributed, real or personal, from each person to whom property has been distributed.   The representative must file these receipts in order to account for all the assets transferred.

Petitioning for Discharge of the Representative   When the distributions have been made and the receipts obtained from the heirs or devisees, the representative (executor or administrator) files the Petition for Discharge of the Representative (see Form 78).

Order for Discharge of the Representative   After having presented the Petition for Discharge, the representative will request an Order for Discharge from the probate court.   Local custom determines whether the attorney for the estate or the probate court prepares this order allowing the representative to close the estate (see Form 79).

Cancellation of Representative's Bond

A copy of the Order Discharging the Representative is sent to the bonding company (surety) in order to cancel the representative's bond. Usually the representative requests the return of any unused premium for the bond.   This act terminates the administration of a decedent's estate.

Special Proceedings in Formal Probate

Some of the special probate proceedings used in unique circumstances are: special administration, summary distribution or assignment, and administration of omitted property.

Special Administration

Special administration is a procedure used by the probate court to administer the estate of a decedent under specific circumstances.   It has limited purposes and is commenced only when a good reason for it exists.   Reasons for appointing a special administrator are; (1) to preserve the decedent's estate until an executor or general administrator is appointed, e.g., in cases where a will or the appointment of an executor or general administrator is being contested; (2) to handle the collection and distribution of small estates, where there is no need to appoint a representative but in which administration cannot be done solely by a summary distribution and; (3) to give immediate attention, when necessary, to the management of a business left by the decedent.

Special administration is accomplished in the following manner:

1. A person having an interest in the estate files a Petition for Appointment of a Special Administrator (see Form 44). This includes an itemized listing of the estate's real and personal property and a valid reason why it is necessary and expedient to have a special administrator appointed.

2. The judge signs the Order Granting Special Administration and appoints the special administrator (see Form 45).

3. The special administrator files the *oath and bond* (see Forms 59 and 101). The amount of the bond is fixed by the court. The paralegal must check individual state statutes to see if a bond is required.

4. The court issues Letters of Special Administration conferring appropriate powers on the special administrator (see Form 46).

5. The special administrator files an Inventory and Appraisal of the personal property of the decedent (see Form 65). As a rule, if another person is to act as general administrator, the special administrator does not take possession or control of real property. If there is to be a summary distribution without general administration, then the special administrator must include real estate in the inventory and may take possession of it, as does the general administrator.

6. The powers of the special administrator officially cease when the executor or general administrator is appointed and the Letters Testamentary or Letters of General Administration are issued. Before being discharged, the special administrator must file a Final Account and Report of Special Administration, including vouchers and receipts for all disbursements (see Form 47). This final account will also provide for the deliverance of all remaining assets of the estate into the hands of the new representative (executor or general administrator).

7. The probate judge then signs the Order Approving the Final Account and Report of the Special Administrator (see Form 48). The order allows the final account and discharges the special administrator and the sureties. When the special administrator and the executor or general administrator are the same person, only one inventory and one final account need be filed.

Summary Distribution or Assignment

In some states, if the size of the estate of a decedent is so small that it is exempt from debts, or so moderate that after all allowances, priority expenses, just claims, and taxes have been paid, the gross probate estate, exclusive of any homestead, does not exceed a statutory value, e.g., $50,000, then the estate may be closed by abbreviated (summary) proceedings and the property transferred to the proper persons (see Chapter 14). The form used to accomplish this procedure is the

Petition for Summary Distribution or Assignment (see Form 49). The court in such cases may conclude that there is no need for the appointment of a representative. In such summary proceedings, however, the court may require the petitioner to file a bond for an amount approved by the court to protect any interested party from misrepresentation or negligence on the part of the petitioner as to the facts presented in the petition requesting the summary distribution of the decedent's property. If the probate court grants the petition for summary distribution, it will enter its Final Decree and assign the property to the appropriate parties (see Form 50). If the decedent died testate, however, no decree would be entered until a hearing to admit the will to probate has been held.

Administration of Omitted Property

When property has been omitted from a final decree of the probate court, a petition may be filed by any person claiming an interest in the omitted property (see Form 51). At a hearing, the court will determine to whom the omitted property will be distributed. The court can then, without notice, summarily decree the distribution of the property once all tax liability has been paid (see Form 52).

Limitations on and Liability of the Personal Representative

In collecting and managing the assets of an estate, the representative cannot personally profit because profit-taking would violate the fiduciary duty to the estate. The personal representative is also not allowed to purchase claims against the estate or to sell property to the estate while retaining a personal interest in the estate (compare U.P.C. § 3–712).

Example: Paulina Neven, the administratrix of Charlotte Neven's estate, obtained an order from the probate court allowing her to rent out land belonging to Charlotte while the estate was being settled. Paulina rents it to herself. If one of Charlotte's heirs objects to this apparent self-dealing, Paulina would have to prove that she had paid as much or more rent than anyone else renting the land would have been charged.

The representative who acts reasonably and in good faith faces no personal liability for decreases in the value of estate assets during administration. If decreases occur due to negligence or delay, however, the court will impose damages on the representative to compensate the estate for the loss. The compensation, often called a "surcharge," is paid by the representative out of personal funds (compare U.P.C. § 3–808).

Example: If in the above example the court had found Paulina guilty of self-dealing with the estate's assets, it would require her to compensate the estate, e.g., by paying, from her own funds, the amount of loss she had caused the estate.

When total assets of an estate are not sufficient to pay all just debts and other charges against it, the law provides an order of priority for payments. The representative is personally liable for placing a less preferred creditor in a more favorable position than is appropriate and thus causing improper payment.

Example: Charlotte died leaving bills for her last illness, federal taxes payable for the previous year and a bill from a local grocery. Paulina pays the grocer's bill before the federal tax lien. Because the grocer is a "less preferred creditor," Paulina must pay the amount due the federal government from her own funds if the estate cannot pay it.

Case Problems

Problem 1

Jane M. Doe of 1005 Easy Street, St. Paul, Minnesota, died testate (with a will) on September 20, 1982. She was married to John C. Doe, age 76, and had one child, Sandy R. Doe, age 45. Mrs. Doe was born on November 6, 1900, in the state of Michigan. Her parents moved to Minnesota that year. On September 4, 1931, she married John C. Doe in St. Paul, Minnesota. Mrs. Doe was a retired real estate broker and her legal residence (domicile) at the time of her death was St. Paul, Minnesota. Mrs. Doe died in the Porta Veta Hospital in St. Paul after suffering from cancer for approximately nine months. Her attending physician was Dr. Norma J. Dennison, 2067 Doctor's Exchange Building, St. Paul, Minnesota. Her attorneys were Cranwall and Schuster, 999 St. Paul Trust Company Building, St. Paul, Minnesota.

Beneficiaries under Mrs. Doe's will are her husband, John C. Doe; daughter, Sandy R. Doe; the American Cancer Society; Girl's Clubs of America; and the Newark Institute of Higher Learning. Beneficiaries under insurance contracts (not taking under the will) are her brother, Jay A. Dee; husband, John C. Doe; and the estate.

Exhibit 13.2 shows the assets that Mrs. Doe individually owned or in which she owned an interest as specified at her death. Exhibit 13.3 shows liabilities and debts owed by Mrs. Doe at her death. Exhibit 13.4 shows costs incurred after Mrs. Doe's death. Exhibit 13.5 shows the beneficiaries of Mrs. Doe's estate and the maintenance of the family during administration.

Exhibit 13.2 Assets of Jane M. Doe

Cash *

Traveler's checks (not cashed)	$ 1,000
Checking Account—First National City Bank of St. Paul no. 55–5555	50,000
Savings deposit—American National Bank of St. Paul no. 44–4444	15,000

Stocks and Bonds

American Telephone and Telegraph, 100 shares (6 months after Mrs. Doe's death decreased in value to $4,800)	5,000
Minnesota Co-op, 1,000 shares	4,500
American National Slide Rule, 1,000 shares (joint tenancy with husband)	75,000
Minnesota Company, 100 shares (joint tenancy with daughter)	5,000

U.S. Government Bonds

Bond No. R4502363E	$ 74
Bond No. R4502364E	$ 74

Personal Property

Clothing—personal effects	$ 500
Furs—mink coat	$ 1,500
Automobile—1978 Chevrolet Nova	$ 2,000
Furniture and household goods	$ 2,000

Real Property

Residential (homestead) 1005 Easy Street St. Paul, MN	$50,000

Legal description: Lot 615, Block 42, Reiser's Addition to St. Paul

Mortgage $30,000 at St. Paul Bank and Trust Company

Rental Property

Duplex 776 Noname Road St. Paul, MN	$91,000

Exhibit 13.2 *(continued)*

Legal description: Lots 16 & 17, Block 20

Lovey's Addition to St. Paul (¼ interest: $22,750; Mortgage— $40,000: ¼ interest of debt is $10,000 at St. Paul Bank and Trust Company

Receivables

Forrest Furriers—Promissory Note (accrued interest = $350	$10,350
Judgment against Forrest R. Redding	$20,000

Interests in Trusts and Other Estates

St. Paul Trust Co.—annual income to Mrs. Doe until her death, then to her daughter, Sandy R. Doe until her death. Established by Mrs. Doe's uncle.	$ 6,000 annual
Power of Appointment (general; unexercised)—To distribute income or corpus (500 shares Green Giant). Established by Mrs. Doe's father.	$50,000

Insurance and Annuities

Prudential Life Insurance Company—No dividends. Beneficiary: Jay A. Dee (brother)	$10,000
Minnesota Life Insurance Company—Dividends. Beneficiary: Estate	$20,000
Accumulated Dividends	$ 100
Ecko Life Insurance Company (premiums of $50 per month paid by Order of the Doves). $100 per month to Mrs. Doe for life; then $100 per month to her husband for his life.	$ 100 per month
Life expectancy of 4 years.	$ 4,800 ($100 per month times 48 months)

---

* Note: Five months prior to her death, Mrs. Doe transferred funds from her checking account to her husband ($20,000) and to her daughter ($30,000). Mrs. Doe obtained this cash by selling Airco Corporation stock which she owned and she then placed the cash in her checking account.

Exhibit 13.3 Liabilities and Debts of Jane M. Doe

Liabilities

Mortgage on homestead, 1005 Easy Street, St. Paul Bank and Trust Company	$30,000
Mortgage on duplex, 776 Noname Rd., St. Paul Bank and Trust Company ($40,000; ¼ interest = $10,000).	$10,000
Total	$40,000

Debts

Approved claims against the estate

Ace's Plumbing Co. (company claims *$480* is owed; Mrs. Doe's personal representative claims *$230* is owed) (contested claim)	$ 480
St. Paul Telephone Company	$ 50
St. Paul Electric Company	$ 100
Harvey's Garbage Pickup	$ 50
Dr. Norma J. Dennison	$ 600
St. Paul Rents (rental of wheelchair)	$ 50
Total	$ 1,330

Exhibit 13.4 Costs Incurred After Jane Doe's Death

Funeral Expenses

Newark and Newark Funeral Home	$ 2,500
Morningside Florists	100
Happy Acres Cemetery	1,000
Stone Monument Company—gravestone	500
Rev. B. Stone	25
Total	$ 4,125

Administration Expenses

Philip Masterson Co., Inc., appraisals	$ 500
Smith & Smith, Inc., preparation of tax returns	$ 250
Attorney's fees	$15,000
Compensation of representative	$10,000
Publication of orders	$ 50
Certified copies	$ 5
Bond premiums (none)	$ 0
Miscellaneous expenses	$ 450
Expenses of last illness unpaid at death (Porta Veta Hospital)	$ 850
Total	$27,105

Exhibit 13.5 Those Who Receive Benefits from the Estate of Jane M. Doe

Individuals

John C. Doe (husband)

Under will—Any interest in real property, and residue after specific gifts (bequests)	$187,205
Joint tenancy—Stock	$ 75,000
Gift—Cash	$ 20,000

Sandy R. Doe (daughter)

Joint tenancy—Stock	$ 5,000
Gift—Cash	$ 30,000

Jay A. Dee (brother)

Life insurance policy	$ 10,000

American Cancer Society

Under will	$ 10,000

Girl's Clubs of America

Under will	$ 5,000

Newark Institute for Higher Learning

Under will	$ 1,000
Estate—Life insurance policy (part of residue, see above)	$ 20,000

Family Maintenance During Administration

$400 per month for 12 months	$ 4,800

Forms must be completed (executed) for the formal probate of the Jane M. Doe estate. From the information given in the above exhibits, the following sample forms (found in Appendix A) have been executed.

1. Petition for Formal Probate of Will and for Appointment of the Personal Representative (Executor) (Form 53)

2. Order and Notice of Formal Appointment of Personal Representative, Notice of Hearing for formal Probate of Will, and Notice to Creditors (Form 54)

3. Affidavit of Publication (Form 55)

4. Affidavit of Mailing Order or Notice of Hearing (Form 56)

5. Statutory notice of rights of surviving spouse and/or minor children (reverse side of Form 56)

6. Proof of Placing Order for Publication (Form 57)

7. Order of Formal Probate of Will and Formal Appointment of Executor (Form 58)

8. Acceptance of Appointment and Oath by Individual (Form 59)

9. Bond, if required, or waiver (Form 60)

10. Testimony of Witnesses (Form 61)

11. Application for federal identification number (Form 62)

12. Letters Testamentary (Form 63)

13. Notice of Fiduciary Relationship (Form 64)

14. Inventory and Appraisal (Form 65)

15. Petition for Allowance of Selection of Personal Property (Form 66)

16. Order Allowing Selection of Personal Property (Form 67)

17. Petition for Family Maintenance (Form 68)

18. Order for Family Maintenance (Form 69)

19. Schedule of Non-Probate Assets (Form 70)

20. State inheritance tax return (Form 71)

21. Final Account (Form 72)

22. Order for Hearing on Final Account and Petition for Distribution and for Mailed Notice (Form 73)

23. Affidavit of Mailing Order or Notice of Hearing on Final Account (Form 74)

24. Federal and state death and income tax returns (see Chapter 15)

25. Order Allowing Final Account (Form 75)

26. Petition for Order of Complete Settlement of the Estate and Decree of Distribution (Form 76)

27. Order of Complete Settlement of Estate and Decree of Distribution (Form 77)

28. Receipt for Assets (Form 97)

29. Petition for Discharge of Personal Representative (Form 78)

30. Order Discharging Personal Representative (Form 79)

31. Copy of order discharging personal representative sent to surety, if any.

Situation 2

Harvey R. Horwell of 999 Okinawa Street, St. Paul, Minnesota, 55101, died intestate on June 3, 1978. He was married to Harriet O. Horwell and had seven children, all minors, named Larry H., Harry O., Gary R., Sherrie E., Mary A., Terry R., and Jerry I. Horwell. Mr. Horwell was born on September 9, 1930, in the State of Hawaii. His parents moved to Minnesota in 1932. On December 12, 1950, Mr. Horwell married Harriet O. Narriet in Watertown, South Dakota. Mr. Horwell was a funeral director and his legal residence at the time of his death was Ramsey County, St. Paul, Minnesota. Mr. Horwell died in St. Paul Ramsey Hospital in St. Paul, Minnesota. His attending physician was Dr. May B. Baad, 2113 Medical Center, St. Paul, Minnesota, 55104. His attorneys were Peterson, Peterson, Wojtowicz and Peteroni, 906 First State Bank Building, St. Paul, Minnesota 55101.

Assignment 129

1. Develop checklists and add to your checklists data necessary to fill in the required forms for the formal probate of an intestate's estate in your state. If your state has not adopted the U.P.C.'s formal probate procedure, follow the probate procedures and execute the forms used by your state.

2. Obtain and complete the forms for the formal probate of Mr. Horwell's estate as though he were a resident of your state.

Chapter 14

Informal Probate Administration Under the Uniform Probate Code

Scope of the Chapter

This chapter outlines the proceedings involved in informal probate according to the Uniform Probate Code (U.P.C.). The procedures are listed and the relevant U.P.C. sections are cited. Sample forms are identified and listed in Appendix A. Next a case study of an estate that would appropriately be administered by informal probate procedures is presented. The paralegal is taken step by step through the informal proceeding in order to become familiar with the procedures. Then case problems involving testate and intestate situations are presented to illustrate estate administration using informal probate procedures. Executed forms required for informal probate administration serve as illustrations for the student.

Competencies

After completing this chapter, the paralegal should be able to:

• Identify and explain the different methods of administering decedents' estates under the Uniform Probate Code

• Recognize the circumstances under which the use of informal probate procedures are appropriate

• Explain the steps in informal probate administration of a decedent's estate

• Apply the procedures and prepare the legal forms used in informal probate administration for a set of facts involving a decedent's estate

The Choice of Formal or Informal Probate

The administration of a decedent's estate may be initiated by any of several procedures under the Uniform Probate Code:

• Formal appointment of the representative and formal proceedings thereafter, in testacy and intestacy (U.P.C. §§ 3–401 through 3–414)

• Informal appointment of the representative and informal proceedings thereafter, in testacy and intestacy (U.P.C. §§ 3–301 through 3–311)

• Collection of the decedent's personal property by affidavit and summary proceedings thereafter for small or moderate-sized estates (U.P.C. §§ 3–1201 through 3–1204)

Some states require the representative to follow a formal (solemn) procedure in the course of administration. Others combine the U.P.C. procedures, noted above, with local practices such as elimination or lowering of the requirement for a representative's bond. Those states which have adopted all or part of the U.P.C. are able to offer all the above-mentioned procedures. Noteworthy contributions of the U.P.C. are introduction of (1) procedures that are unsupervised or only partially supervised by the court (informal or common probate) and (2) simplified summary procedures that reduce the expenses of administration and make the transfer of small estates to the heirs or devisees much easier. In view of the great diversity among state practices, even among those that have enacted the U.P.C., the paralegal's wisest course is to become familiar with the laws of the state in which the paralegal lives and works.

When one applies for the position of personal representative of an estate that exceeds the limits for summary proceedings (see page 370), the applicant may select a formal or informal method of settling the estate. The U.P.C. defines formal proceedings as "those conducted before a judge with notice to interested persons" (U.P.C. § 1–201[15]) and informal proceedings as "those conducted without notice to interested persons by an officer of the court acting as a registrar for probate of a will or appointment of a personal representative" (U.P.C. § 1–201[19]). A court-appointed officer (registrar, clerk, or referee) skilled in overseeing decedents' estates takes the place of the judge in informal procedure. That officer has the power to do everything the judge would do (e.g., appoint the personal representative and make findings of fact in relation to the will).

The U.P.C. allows a unique "in and out" method of settling estates— partly "in" the probate court even though most of the administration takes place "out" of it (informally). In informal proceedings, the personal representative or any person interested in the estate, as defined by (U.P.C. § 1–201[20]), may petition the court to adjudicate a disputed issue (e.g., the amount of a creditor's claim). After settlement of the dispute, the representative may resume informal procedures.

This flexible use of formal proceedings within informal probate proves advantageous to the representative who prefers the freedom of informal probate but who may encounter a complexity that the court is better suited to handle.

Example: Reginald Canby died testate leaving all his property to his son, Damon. Reginald's wife predeceased him. Vanessa, Reginald's daughter, contends that Damon used undue influence on their father in his last illness to persuade him to write this will. Although the executor of Reginald's estate had elected to follow informal probate procedures, Vanessa may petition the probate court to settle this question. After the court has made its decision, it may allow the estate to resume informal probate or order it to continue formal, supervised probate (U.P.C. §§ 3–501, 3–502).

Informal probate has its advantages, but before selecting it the petitioner seeking to be appointed representative should consider the merits of informal probate in regard to the particular estate. In some cases informal probate will not decrease the amount of time required for probate, although it does in a majority of cases. The representative of an estate enmeshed in tax-law difficulties will probably not find informal probate advantageous. The representative of the average estate, however, may find it preferable.

Informal probate generally reduces the amount of time between the beginning and end of administration. It involves fewer steps and less-complicted procedures (e.g., the filing of fewer papers) than formal probate. The estate can be more easily distributed since the representative does not have to give notice of hearings, or obtain court approval for every item distributed, and may not be required to obtain a bond or submit an account at the end, depending on the circumstances.

The representative may request court supervision at any time; however, informal probate does not demand that the court supervise even the representative's closing of the estate after administering it. Because the purpose of informal probate is in part to help relieve congestion in the probate court, the greater part of informal probate transactions are carried out without the court's direct involvement. Not infrequently a hearing to prove the will and to appoint a representative is the only in-court proceeding. Of course, this is not always the case, since any person interested in the estate (e.g., a creditor or devisee) may petition the court to determine a matter using formal proceedings.

Example: Fred McManus dies intestate, survived by a son, Bruce, and a brother, Paul. The registrar of probate court, who is empowered to conduct informal probate proceedings, appoints Paul personal representative of Fred's estate. Bruce challenges the informal appointment of his uncle, Paul, to administer the estate. The court will then appoint a personal representative in a formal proceeding, according to the order of priority (see page 339).

The U.P.C. does away with required appraisal of estate assets unless demanded by the representative, another interested party, or the court. The value of real estate and closely held businesses should be appraised by an independent expert. The representative is entitled to hire and pay the appraiser(s) out of estate assets (U.P.C. § 3–707).

Example: Tillie's (decedent) estate, according to her will, is to be divided equally among her two sisters, Sherie and Noreen, and one brother, Waldo. Included in her estate are valuable paintings. Waldo, who was informally appointed to administer the estate, set the value of the paintings at $5,000. The other property in the estate was sold at public auction for $10,000 cash. Waldo decided to keep the paintings for himself and give Sherie and Noreen $5,000 in cash each. The two sisters, who believe the art collection is worth much more, can demand that it be appraised by an art expert.

The availability of informal proceedings for probating a will and settling the estate is one of the chief advantages of the Uniform Probate Code. Since it is designed to be adopted by state legislatures, and in fact has been adopted by many either wholly or partially, informal probate is available to a great number of persons.

Priority of Persons Seeking Appointment as Personal Representatives

In both formal and informal proceedings, persons who could qualify as representatives of the estate are considered in the following order of priority:

1. The person named personal representative (executor) by the will, if there is one

2. The surviving spouse of the decedent when the spouse is a devisee of the decedent (in testacy)

3. Other devisees of the decedent

4. The surviving spouse of the decedent when not a devisee

5. Other heirs of the decedent

6. Any creditor of the decedent, provided that no one with a higher priority standing has applied for appointment within 45 days of the death of the decedent (U.P.C. § 3–203[a]).

The person who has the highest standing in this order and who is willing to serve does not always become the representative. The court or the registrar must appoint the representative and will not appoint a person who is under the age of 18 or otherwise unsuitable for the position. This latter decision must be made by the court at the petition of an interested person.

In some instances, persons having priority fail to apply or are in some way disqualified. If that happens, the court, in a formal proceeding, will consider the nominees of persons having priority and try to arrive at a solution beneficial to the estate and satisfactory to those interested in it (U.P.C. § 3–203[b]).

Application for Informal Probate
and Appointment of Representative

The application for informal probate or informal appointment must be verified (i.e., made under oath) by the applicant as accurate and complete to the best of the applicant's knowledge. It is filed with the registrar or clerk of the probate court (U.P.C. § 3–301 and Form 87).

1. The following general information is required on all applications for informal probate of a will or for informal appointment:
  • Relation of the applicant to the estate (e.g., named executor)
  • Name, age, date of death of decedent, county and state of decedent's domicile at time of death; names and addresses of spouse, children, heirs, devisees, and ages of those who are minors
  • A statement indicating the county or city where the proceedings are to take place, if decedent was not domiciled at the date of death in the state where the application for informal probate has been filed
  • The name and address of any personal representative of the decedent who has been appointed in this state or elsewhere whose appointment has not been terminated
  • A statement that the applicant has not received nor is aware of any "demand for notice of any probate or appointment proceeding concerning the decedent that may have been filed in this state or elsewhere"
  • A statement indicating whether the applicant has received a demand for notice, or is aware of any demand for notice of any probate or appointment concerning the decedent that may have been filed in this state or elsewhere
  • A statement that the time limit for informal probate or appointment has not expired either because three years or less have passed since the decedent's death, or, if more than three years from death have passed, circumstances as described by Section 3–108 authorizing tardy probate or appointment have occurred.

2. If the application is for informal probate of a will it must, in addition to giving the information and statements listed under 1 above, affirm:
  • That the court has possession of the original last will, or that the original will or an authenticated copy probated in an ancillary proceeding in another jurisdiction is included with the application
  • That the applicant believes the will to have been validly executed
  • That the applicant is unaware of any instrument revoking the will and believes the submitted instrument is the decedent's last will
  • A statement that the time limit for informal probate or appointment has not expired either because three years or less have passed since the decedent's death or, if more than three years from death have passed, circumstances as described by section 3–108 authorizing tardy probate or appointment have occurred.

3. An application for informal appointment of a personal representative (e.g., an executor) to administer an estate under a will sets forth the following in addition to the general information referred to in 1 above:
- A description of the will by date and place of execution
- The time and place of probate or the pending application or petition for probate
- The name, address, and standing of the applicant among those who are entitled to be personal representative under U.P.C. § 3–203.

4. An application for informal appointment of an administrator when the decedent died intestate states, in addition to the statements listed above in 1:
- That the applicant is not aware of any unrevoked testamentary instrument relating to property located in the state, or if the applicant is aware of any such instrument, the reason for its not being probated (U.P.C. § 3–301[4]). (If the registrar learns of the existence of a later will, probate of the earlier one will be denied because a valid will supersedes those predating it.)
- The priority of the applicant, and the names of any other persons who have a prior or equal right to the appointment under U.P.C. § 3–203 (see Form 99).

Example: Martha Engle, whose mother died testate, naming Martha executrix, desires to be appointed informally and to have the will probated informally. She must complete data discussed in 1, 2, and 3 above.

Example: Corey Davis desires to be named personal representative to the estate of his father who died intestate. Corey's mother predeceased his father. Corey must complete the data discussed in 1 and 4 above.

In the example of Martha Engle, suppose that when Martha's mother had died no will could be found, and Maria Engle, Martha's sister, had been informally appointed personal representative in intestacy. Subsequently the will was discovered and Martha sought the appointment. Martha would then have to complete, in addition to the data discussed in 1, 2, and 3, a "change of testacy status" form, requesting that she replace Maria (U.P.C. § 3–301[5]) (see Form 80).

In the example of Corey Davis, suppose that when Corey's father died, Corey's brother, Alton, produced an instrument resembling a will under which Alton was named executor and that he was appointed representative by the court. Subsequently, the document was proved not to be a will, and Corey sought appointment as personal representative. Corey would also have to complete a "change of testacy status" form, because the decedent, formerly considered testate, is now intestate.

By definition, informal probate of a will and informal appointment are proceedings conducted "without notice to interested persons" (U.P.C. § 1–201[19]). A person applying for informal appointment and/or informal probate of a will does not have to notify persons interested in the estate unless those persons have filed a written demand to be notified, in accordance with U.P.C. § 3–204 (see also U.P.C. § 3–306 and page 387). The applicant must, however, notify anyone having a superior right to be personal representative, e.g., a person who has been previously appointed personal representative or a person who stands higher in the order of priority for appointment.

Example: Ernest Falcott wants to be informally appointed representative to his father's estate and have the will informally probated. No representative has been previously appointed. His cousin, Julia, files a demand to be notified. Ernest must therefore notify Julia of his applications for informal probate of a will and informal appointment as well as his mother, Letitia, who has a superior right to be representative.

Persons applying for informal proceedings must verify under oath the statements of their applications (e.g. Form 81). The registrar is required to make "proofs and findings" for informal probate and informal appointment applications to check the truth and accuracy of statements therein and has the power to disqualify or decline applications if not satisfied (U.P.C. §§ 3–303, 3–305, 3–308, 3–309). Unintentional mistakes made by the applicant are correctable, but deliberate falsification that injures someone interested in the estate will give the injured person a cause of action against the applicant (U.P.C. §§ 1–106 and 3–301(6)).

Acceptance by the Registrar

Having completed the forms necessary for informal proceedings, the applicant submits them to the registrar, who scrutinizes them for errors or omissions that might invalidate the application. The registrar must be satisfied

• That the applicant has carried out the requirements of the U.P.C.

• That the applicant has solemnly affirmed the statements made in the application to be true to the best of the applicant's knowledge

• That the applicant is an interested person as defined by U.P.C. § 1–201(20) (see Appendix C)

• That the applicant has chosen the proper venue (location) for having the will probated or for being appointed representative

• That persons who have demanded notice of proceedings (U.P.C. § 3–204) have been notified of this proceeding

• That 120 hours have elapsed since the decedent's death

In addition, the registrar will check each application for particular requirements. For example, for informal probate, the registrar must possess the original of a properly executed will which has not been revoked, the statutory time limit for probate must not have expired, and the will must be the kind which may be probated informally.[1] For informal appointment, the person seeking appointment must be entitled to do so by the order of priority, and the will to which the appointment relates must have been probated either formally or informally (U.P.C. § 3–203).

It may be that the registrar will not be satisfied with the contents of the application for any of several reasons. Some of which are illustrated below.

Example: The registrar denies Joceyln Galbreth's application for informal probate of her brother's will because another sister, Elin Galbreth, had applied for probate earlier.

Example: The registrar denies Gilbert Havlicek's application for informal probate of his mother's will because the will is written on two apparently unconnected papers and it is not clear if one revokes the other.

Example: The registrar denies Conrad Marquart's application for informal appointment as representative of his sister's estate because another representative had been appointed and has not died or resigned.

Example: The registrar denies Marina Yladak's application for informal appointment as representative of her father's estate because she indicated on her application that her father might have had another will which is still in existence (U.P.C. §§ 3–305, 3–309).

Informal probate is available only for uncomplicated wills or estates. The registrar's denial of an application usually results in the commencement of formal probate proceedings.

If satisfied with the information contained in the application for informal proceedings, and after 120 hours have elapsed since the decedent's death, the registrar signifies acceptance of the application by issuing a Written Statement of Informal Probate (Form 88) and/or appoints the applicant the representative of the estate by issuing Letters Testamentary or Letters of Administration (see Forms 63 and 105). The Letters empower the applicant to assume the powers and duties of the office of representative but do not take effect until the applicant has filed a statement of acceptance of these powers and duties and has paid the necessary fees (Form 59). At this time, the representative's bond, if required, must be filed with the court (Form 101). Any person who has an interest in the estate worth more than $1,000, incuding creditors with claims greater than $1,000 may demand that the representative be required to post a bond, or the court may require it (U.P.C. §§ 3–603 and 3–605).

Assignment 130

Laurel Shepard, the granddaughter of Maryanna Means, who died intestate, has applied to be informally appointed representative (admin-

---

1. Informal probate of certain wills may not be advisable. The registrar has a duty to decline informal probate of alleged copies of lost or destroyed wills, of wills consisting of a series of testamentary instruments (rather than a single one), and of other irregular instruments.

istratrix) of her grandmother's estate. Before submitting the application, she brings it to you as the assistant of the attorney who is representing the estate to be checked. Comment on the following queries that you must bring to the attention of the attorney:

1. Laurel is not sure that she qualifies as an "interested person" because she had seen her grandmother only two or three times before her death.

2. Laurel believes that her priority may be inferior to that of Florence Kingsley, Maryanna's nurse for seventeen years, who had lived with and cared for Maryanna.

3. Laurel has not given notice to Georgina Means, Maryanna's daughter, because she does not know Georgina's address and has not been in contact with her for a long time.

4. Maryanna had resided and died in Lafayette County, Indiana, but had left a farm and a bank account in Merced County, California. Laurel does not know if Lafayette County, where she is applying, is the proper place for administration.

5. Laurel is not sure that her uncle, Jason Means, who lives in Merced County, has not been appointed representative which might present a challenge to her own application.

6. Laurel does not believe that she can affirm the truth of her statements in the application because of the uncertainties stated above.

Notice Requirements

Persons having an interest in the estate may file a demand to be notified (Demand for Notice) of the petitioner's application for informal probate or informal appointment (U.P.C. § 3–204). An interested person might be one who has a financial interest in the estate, a previously appointed representative who is still acting in that capacity, or someone who occupies a place in the order of priority for appointment (U.P.C. §§ 1–201 [20] and 3–203).

Once a demand has been filed, the registrar will notify the representative to keep the demandant informed of proceedings related to the estate. If the demandant believes that the applicant is not qualified to be the representative, is using a revoked will, or otherwise objects to informal proceedings, the demand for notice ensures an opportunity to request formal or supervised administration when necessary. If the demandant is not given notice of a subsequent order or proceeding, it remains effective. However, the personal representative will be liable for damages caused the demandant resulting from the omission of notice (U.P.C. § 3–204) (see Form 82).

Notice of Application for Informal Probate

The petitioner seeking informal probate must give notice as required by U.P.C. § 1–401 of the application for informal probate to any person demanding it pursuant to U.P.C. § 3–204 and to any personal representative of the decedent whose appointment has not been terminated (U.P.C. § 3–306 and Form 89). No other notice of informal probate is required.

If an informal probate is granted, within 30 days thereafter the applicant shall give written information of the probate to the heirs and devisees. The information shall include the name and address of the applicant, the name and location of the court granting the informal probate, and the date of the probate. The information shall be delivered or sent by ordinary mail to each of the heirs and devisees whose address is reasonably available to the applicant. No duty to give information is incurred if a personal representative is appointed who is obligated to give the written information required by section 3–705. An applicant's failure to give information as required by this section is a breach of the duty to the heirs and devisees but does not affect the validity of the probate (U.P.C. § 3–306[6]).

Notice of Application for Informal Appointment

The petitioner seeking informal appointment must give notice as required by U.P.C. § 1–401 of the intention to seek an informal appointment to any person demanding it pursuant to U.P.C. § 3–204 and to any person having a prior or equal right to appointment not waived in writing and filed with the court (U.P.C. § 3–310 and Form 83). No other notice of an informal appointment proceeding is required.

Demand for Notice of Order or Filing

Any person who has a financial or property interest in a decedent's estate may file a demand with the court for notice of any order or filing relating to that estate, at any time after the death of the decedent (see U.P.C. §§ 3–204, 5–406, 3–603). The demand for notice must state the name of the decedent, the nature of the demandant's (person making the demand) interest in the estate, and the person's address or that of the attorney representing the person (see Form 82). The clerk will mail a copy of such demand to the personal representative, if any. After such a demand is filed, no order or filing to which the demand relates can be made or accepted without notice as required in U.P.C. § 1–401 to the demandant or his or her attorney. If such notice is not given, the order or filing is still valid, but the person receiving the order or making the filing may be liable for any damage caused by the omission of notice.

The notice requirement arising from a demand may be waived in writing by the demandant and will cease when the demandant's interest in the estate terminates. Interested persons are protected by their right to demand prior notice of informal proceedings (see U.P.C. § 2–204), to contest a requested appointment by use of a formal testacy proceeding, or by use of a formal proceeding seeking the appointment of another person. Interested persons also have available to them the remedies provided in U.P.C. § 3–605 (demand for bond by interested persons) and § 3–607 (order restraining personal representative).

Although not obligated to do so unless a demand has been filed, since publication under U.P.C. § 3–801 is sufficient, the representative should give personal notice to creditors. The U.P.C. allows creditors four months from the date of the first publication of notice to file claims (see U.P.C. §§ 3–801, 3–802, and 3–803). The court has the discretion to allow late claims if the estate is still open, but the court can refuse such claims unless good cause is shown. Once the account of the representative is settled, the court cannot allow the claim (see Forms 84, 89, and 95).

Method and Time for Giving Notice

If notice of a hearing on any petition, application, order, or filing is required (except for specific notice requirements as otherwise provided in the U.P.C.), the petitioner or applicant must give notice of the time and place of hearing of any petition, application, order, or filing to any interested person or to his or her attorney (U.P.C. § 1–401). Such notice must be given one of three ways:

• By mailing a copy of the notice at least 14 days *before the time set* for the hearing by certified, registered, or ordinary first class mail addressed to the person being notified at the post office address given in the demand for notice, or at the person's office or place of residence

• By delivering a copy of the notice to the person being notified personally at least 14 days before the time set for the hearing

• If the address, or identity of any person is not known and cannot be ascertained with reasonable diligence, by publishing at least once a week for three consecutive weeks a copy of the notice in a newspaper having general circulation in the county where the hearing is to be held, the last publication of which is to be at least 10 days before the time set for the hearing.

For good cause, the court may provide a different method or time of giving notice for any hearing. Prior to or at the hearing, proof of giving the notice must be made and filed. (See U.P.C. § 1–401.) Any person, including a *guardian ad litem,* conservator, or other fiduciary, (see Glossary), may waive notice by a writing signed by the person or his or her attorney and filed in the proceeding (see U.P.C. § 1–402).

Notice must be given to every interested person or to one who can bind an interested person, as described in U.P.C. § 1–403. U.P.C. § 1–403 also describes pleading and notice requirements when parties are bound by others.

Duties and Powers of the Personal Representative in Informal Probate

The greatest responsibility of the representative is proper distribution of the decedent's estate. In a testate administration, the representative distributes according to the will and within the bounds of law (e.g., the representative pays priority family allowances and debts first). In an intestate administration, the representative distributes according to the state statutes of descent and distribution.

The duties and powers of the personal representative in informal probate are outlined generally in the U.P.C. §§ 3–701 to 3–721.

As a fiduciary, the personal representative must observe the standards of care applicable to fiduciaries (see page 215). Since it is necessary for the representative to hold temporary title to assets that belong to others (the devisees or heirs), the personal representative is liable to successors for damage resulting from improper use of power or mishandling estate assets (e.g., selling an asset where there was no need to do so) (U.P.C. §§ 3–703, 3–712).

An informally appointed representative possessing Letters Testamentary or Letters of Administration needs no further approval before beginning distribution. Only when the representative or another interested person requests court supervision of heretofore unsupervised proceedings (the "in and out" feature) does the representative have to obtain the court's order to proceed (U.P.C. § 3–704).

Notification of Devisees or Heirs and Creditors

Not later than 30 days following appointment, the representative must notify the decedent's devisees or heirs of the appointment (see page 387) (U.P.C. § 3–705). The notice is sent by ordinary mail and must include the name and address of the personal representative, indicate that it is being sent to all persons who have or may have some interest in the estate, indicate whether bond has been filed, and describe the court where papers relating to the estate are on file. This notice is part of the fiduciary obligation, but the representative's neglect to give notice will not invalidate the appointment or powers of the office. If it causes loss or damage to a devisee or heir, however, that person has a cause of action for damages against the representative for breach of the fiduciary duty (U.P.C. §§ 3–204 and 3–712).

Example: Eula Gribben died intestate in Virginia leaving a small estate. All of her heirs live in Virginia except her son, Lewis, who lives in Delaware. Her brother, Lloyd Adcock, was informally appointed administrator and gave notice to all of the heirs except Lewis. Should Lloyd omit Lewis in the distribution of the estate, Lewis would have a cause of action against Lloyd for the omitted share and possibly for damages if Lloyd's mistake caused him harm (e.g., needless expense of court fees).

The representative must also notify creditors of the estate of the appointment by publishing in a general-circulation county newspaper the announcement of the representative's appointment (see page 389). The notice must appear once a week for three successive weeks. Creditors have four months after the date of the first publication to present their claims or else the claims are barred (U.P.C. § 3–801).

Payment of Creditors' Claims

After the four-month period, the representative must pay creditors' claims which are determined to be just (i.e., are allowed). The order in which just claims are to be paid is found in U.P.C. § 3–805. The representative has the power to disallow or disqualify claims that creditors have made fraudulently or otherwise unjustly against the estate (U.P.C. § 3–803). The creditors can appeal the representative's decision in court.

Example: Bertrand Dorn had a credit account with the National Oil Company. Before his death, the company sent him a bill for $48.79. Bertrand disputed this, claiming that he owed only $18.79 according to service station receipts. His representative may refuse to pay the $48.79 claim by following U.P.C. procedures for "allowance of claims" (U.P.C. § 3–806).

Inventory Property

Within three months of appointment, the personal representative must prepare an inventory of property owned by the decedent at the time of death and mail it to all interested persons who request it. The personal representative may also file the original copy of the inventory with the court (U.P.C. § 3–706). The inventory must list the assets of the estate with sufficient description for accurate identification, value the assets at fair market value, and include the kind of mortgage or other encumbrance on each item and the amount of that encumbrance (see Form 65).

The estate assets may be of such a kind that the representative is unfamiliar with their fair market value or the court may order that a third person who has no interest in the estate appraise the estate assets. In either case, the representative has permission to hire independent appraisers to assist in valuation, but if they do perform appraisals, the representative must list on the inventory their names, their addresses and the items they valued (U.P.C. § 3–707).

Hold and Manage the Estate

Until discharged or released from the appointment, the representative has the same power over the title to the decedent's property as the decedent. The representative holds title in a similar manner to that of a trustee in an express trust (see page 253). Both a trustee and the representative are given powers and duties that require the exercise of the prudence and restraint expected of a fiduciary for the benefit of others: the trustee for beneficiaries; the representative for devisees, heirs, or creditors. The personal representative is liable for loss or damage caused to such persons by improper exercise of these powers. In other words, the representative is liable as is a trustee who misuses the power given by the settlor and causes harm to those whom the power was intended to benefit (U.P.C. § 3–712).

Example: Merle Hendricks, the informally appointed representative for his father's estate, was given the power of sale by the will. He sells an antique lamp from the estate to his wife at a lower price than he would have asked of a stranger. Merle has violated his fiduciary duty by self-dealing with estate assets (U.P.C. § 3–713).

Duties of a Special Administrator

If, during administration, the representative dies, becomes unable to carry out the duties, or resigns, a special administrator assumes the duties until the registrar can appoint another general representative (U.P.C. §§ 3–609, 3–613, 3–614).

The procedure by which a special administrator is appointed differs from that of a general representative. An interested person applies to the registrar for his or her own or another person's appointment to the position. The registrar considers the relation of this nominee to the estate and other factors that have a bearing on the nominee's fitness to administer the estate temporarily (U.P.C. § 3–615), but the registrar need not make the extensive inquiry pursuant to U.P.C. § 3–308 or adhere to the order of priority of U.P.C. § 3–203.

An informally appointed special administrator has the same powers and duties as those of a general representative, including collecting, preserving, managing, and accounting for the estate assets (U.P.C. § 3–616). If the general representative had previously performed a specific duty satisfactorily, such as filing the inventory, the special administrator need not repeat the task. Furthermore, the special administrator must deliver title to the assets to the person appointed the new general personal representative (U.P.C. § 3–616), at which time the special administrator's authority terminates (U.P.C. § 3–618).

Example: Serena Gunther's will named her brother, Cyrus, executor. He was subsequently appointed informally to that position. Adelaide Gunther, the decedent's cousin and devisee, petitioned the court to remove Cyrus for having failed to file a fiduciary income tax return for the estate. Upon Cyrus's removal, Adelaide requested and received the position of special administratrix. She must now continue the affairs of the estate, including filing the delinquent return.

Closing the Estate

When the representative has completed administration of the estate, including distribution of assets to creditors (U.P.C. Article 3, Part 8) and to devisees or heirs (U.P.C. Article 3, Part 9), the representative must close the estate (wind up its affairs) and seek a discharge from office (termination) (see Form 98).

An informally appointed representative may choose to close the estate informally by signing a sworn statement to the effect that the representative believes the estate's assets to have been distributed correctly and its business transacted. The representative may use this method if the administration has not been totally supervised by the court. In the case of continuous supervision, the U.P.C. demands *formal closing* by either of the methods described in U.P.C. §§ 3–1001 and 3–505 or 3–1002.

The representative's sworn statement informally closing an estate must verify:

• That a notice to creditors was published more than six months before the date of the present statement.

• That the representative has fully administered the estate, paying all taxes due on it and claims against it (including creditors' and successors' claims), and that the assets of the estate have been distributed to the persons entitled. If the representative has not completed distribution, the reasons for partial distribution must be explained in the statement.

• That the representative has sent a copy of the statement to all of the claimants who have made themselves known and to all distributees of the estate (U.P.C. § 3–1003).

The time periods creditors have to assert and present claims include the following:

• Under U.P.C. § 3–803, all claims against a decedent's estate which arose before the decedent's death are barred against the estate, the personal representative, and the heirs and devisees of the decedent unless presented within four months after the date of the first publication of notice to creditors if notice is given in compliance with U.P.C. § 3–801, or within three years after the decedent's death, if notice to creditors has not been published.

- Under U.P.C. § 3–1005, the rights of all creditors whose claims have not been previously barred against the personal representative for breach of fiduciary duty (see U.P.C. § 3–803 above) are barred unless a proceeding to assert the claim is commenced within six months after the filing of the representative's *closing statement.* Creditors do, however, have the right to recover from a personal representative for fraud or inadequate disclosure related to the settlement of the decedent's estate.

- Under U.P.C. § 3–1006, the claim of a creditor, heir, or devisee of a decedent for recovery of property or the property's value from a distributee of improperly distributed property is forever barred at the later of three years after the decedent's death or one year after the time of distribution of the property. This section does not bar an action to recover property or its value due to fraud.

If a personal representative has distributed the assets of the estate to other claimants, e.g., devisees, heirs, or other creditors, a creditor with a valid but undischarged claim must press the claim in a judicial proceeding against one or more of those who received the assets (U.P.C. § 3–1004).

Example: Annelise Frechette closes her mother's estate informally by filing a sworn statement with the probate court. Two months afterward, the owner of a gift shop who had not been given notice presents a bill for some items that Mrs. Frechette had bought on credit. Annelise is personally liable to the creditor for not having given him notice as she had to the other creditors. The creditor can obtain payment of the bill by initiating a judicial proceeding against Annelise or any distributee, but the creditor cannot collect from both. If the creditor obtains a judgment and payment from Corinee Mays, one of the five distributees, then Corinee may demand of the other four distributees, who were given notice of the creditor's claim and pending litigation, four-fifths of the amount which she had to pay so that all will bear the burden equally.

If no proceedings involving the representative are pending in the court one year after the closing statement is filed, the representative's authority is terminated (U.P.C. § 3–1003). Termination does not automatically accompany closing. The authority of the representative remains active for this one year. Once terminated, the representative has no power to conduct affairs in the name of the estate. The U.P.C. provides the one-year grace period between closing and termination for the resolution of unforeseen business, such as that in the preceding example.

It is important that the representative obtain receipts or evidence of payment for everything distributed from the estate whether or not the representative has decided to close the estate under one of the methods described in U.P.C. § 3–1001 through § 3–1003. (Note: it is legitimate but impractical not to close the estate at all but simply to rely on the receipts collected to show that the estate has been fully distributed. Relying on receipts affords no protection to the representative should complications arise.) Collecting and retaining receipts enables the representative to reinforce the closing statement or the request that the court formally close the estate. Alternatively, the representative may obtain from each distributee an affidavit reciting that each received the correct amount.

After the estate has been closed and the representative discharged, someone may discover additional property belonging to the decedent which had not been administered (e.g., rare books, to which the will referred but which could not be located during administration). Proper disposition of the assets will necessitate reopening the estate. The court that has jurisdiction of the recently discovered assets will, upon petition by an interested person, appoint a representative, the same as had been previously appointed, if possible (U.P.C. § 3–1008). Reopening the estate and subsequent administration are both court-supervised proceedings. The court, however, may permit them to be conducted formally (with notice) or informally (without notice).

Administration of Small Estates

A noticeable percentage of decedent's estates fall into the category of "small or moderate-sized," meaning that they have a gross value of less than $5,000. For such estates, the procedures described above (giving notice to creditors, etc.) may prove too complicated to be helpful. U.P.C. § 3, Part 12, provides alternate methods of handling estates that are too small for regular administration. For example, when the value of the estate is less than $5,000 any successor of the decedent (devisee or heir) may collect debts owed to the decedent by others 30 days after the decedent's death. To accomplish this, the successor must present the debtor with an *affidavit* stating that:

• The value of the entire estate, less liens and encumbrances, does not exceed $5,000

• Thirty days have elapsed since the death of the decedent

• No application or petition for the appointment of a personal representative is pending or has been granted in any jurisdiction

• The claiming successor is entitled to payment or delivery of the property (U.P.C. § 3–1201) (see Form 85).

Successors who collect in this manner act in the capacity of the decedent's representative; debtors who pay successors are discharged of the debt as if they had paid the representative (U.P.C. § 3–1202).

Having collected the decedent's credits by this method and having located and collected the remainder of the estate's personal property assets, the successor must deliver them to those entitled. A representative, if one has been appointed, is entitled to receive the assets for distribution. If the estate is so small that nothing remains after the homestead allowance, the family allowance, exempt property (personal belongings, etc.), and priority debts are taken care of, the successor distributes it and files a closing statement. This is called the *summary administrative procedure* (U.P.C. §§ 3–1203 and 3–1204). In New York State, the successor who performs these duties is called a *voluntary administrator* because he or she "administers" the estate without compensation when the size of the estate does not warrant the appointment of a representative. New York statutes do not apply to states other than New York, of course, but they do indicate some of the details of the procedure outlined in U.P.C. § 3, Part 12.

Example: Paula Kent died intestate, leaving no estate except $375 in salary payable to her by her employer, a bank account of $2,095 owned jointly with her brother, Glenn, a homestead owned jointly with her sister, Rosemary, and personal belongings valued at $495. Her sister, Rosemary, obtains an affidavit from the probate court of the county in which she and Paula had resided and collects the $375 from Paula's employer. The personal belongings are in the home that she and Paula had jointly owned and occupied; Rosemary has no difficulty locating them. Her next action is to notify the probate court of her collection of the assets and wait for its direction. In Rosemary's county, the registrar oversees collection by affidavit and informal distribution of small estates. The bank account passes immediately to Glenn and the house to Rosemary, these being non-probate assets to which the survivor has the right of ownership. Paula had no spouse or dependent children, so there is no need for family allowances or property to be exempted from the estate. She had no debts, except $20 she owes to a doctor, but not because of a last illness so it is not a priority debt. Rosemary must subtract this $20 from the $870 total of Paula's estate before dividing the remainder equally between herself and Glenn, Paula's only heirs. Each of them will receive $425. To close the estate, Rosemary files a closing statement similar to the one previously discussed on page 393, according to U.P.C. § 3–1204 (see Form 86).

Alternatively, the heir or devisee of a decedent could have the court supervise the entire administration.

Step-by-Step Procedures in Informal Probate

The following case study describes a small estate that could conveniently be administered through the use of the U.P.C. informal probate procedures by an informally appointed personal representative. Follow the personal representative step by step through the informal procedures. As a further review of informal probate procedures, three Case Problems, with appropriate forms and/or questions, are included.

Case Study

Elvira Krueger died testate on February 4, 1983, in a state that has adopted the Uniform Probate Code (U.P.C.). Elvira left a son, Ralph, a daughter, Sara, and a daughter, Christa, none of whom are minors. Elvira's husband predeceased her. Elvira owned property valued at $9,000 at the time of her death: household furniture and goods valued at $5,000, a few pieces of antique furniture valued at $2,000, an automobile valued at $1,400, and a tent trailer for camping valued at $600. In her will, Elvira appointed her daughter, Sara, executrix of her estate and directed that the estate assets be distributed as follows: "the automobile and tent trailer to my son, Ralph; the antique furniture to my daughter, Sara; and the household furniture and goods to be sold and the proceeds to be distributed to my three children, Ralph, Sara, and Christa so that each of them will receive an amount of my property equal to that of the others." Sara later sells the household furniture and goods for $5,000.

Under the terms of the will, Sara must distribute the antique furniture (valued at $2,000) and $1,000 cash to herself (total—$3,000), $3,000 cash to Christa, and the automobile (valued at $1,400), the tent trailer (valued at $600), and $1,000 cash to Ralph. These devises, however, will be reduced by expenses and debts that must first be paid out of the estate assets.

Informal Procedures to Be Utilized by Sara

Sara will file an application with the registrar requesting both informal probate of her mother's will and informal appointment of herself as personal representative. She must verify that the application is accurate and complete to the best of her knowledge and belief. The application must set forth information regarding Sara's interest in the estate and identifying the decedent (U.P.C. § 3–301). Since Elvira resided in the state in which Sara is applying for informal appointment, Sara must wait 120 hours (five days) after Elvira's death before the registrar will finalize her appointment. Had Elvira been domiciled in a different state, Sara would have to wait 30 days for finalization in this state.

Sara must give notice of the application for informal probate and appointment by one of the methods specified by U.P.C. § 1–401 to (1) any interested person who has filed written demand with the clerk pursuant to U.P.C. § 3–204; (2) any personal representative of the decedent whose appointment has not been terminated; and (3) any interested person who has a prior or equal right to appointment which has not been waived in writing and filed with the court (U.P.C. §§ 3–306 and 3–310).

Both Ralph and Christa have filed written demands for notice with the court. Therefore, Sara must give notice of the application to her sister and brother. The validity of an order which is issued or a filing which is accepted without notice to Ralph or Christa will not be affected by the lack of notice, but Sara may be liable for any damage caused to either of them by the absence of notice (U.P.C. § 3–204).

Example: Christa filed with the court a demand for notice according to U.P.C. § 3–204, stating her interest in Elvira's estate (devisee) and her own name and address. Sara, the personal representative, finds it necessary to use the money from the sale of Elvira's household goods to pay creditors and obtains a court order permitting her to do this. Christa's share in the proceeds of the sale is therefore reduced, but in anticipation of the share of cash she was to receive originally, she had negotiated a bank loan. If Sara fails to notify her of the order permitting payment of creditors so that Christa is damaged by not being able to repay the loan, Christa will have a cause of action against Sara.

The registrar, on receiving Sara's application and making the findings required by U.P.C. § 3–303, will issue a Written Statement of Informal Probate. The informal probate will be conclusive on all persons unless the probate court, upon petition of an interested party, issues a superseding order changing the estate administration to a formal testacy proceeding. Defects in Sara's application or in procedures followed in informally probating her mother's will do not by themselves render the probate void (U.P.C. § 3–302).

When the registrar approves Sara's application for informal probate and appointment, she must qualify and file her acceptance pursuant to U.P.C. §§ 3–307, 3–601 and 3–602. Once the registrar issues the Letters of Appointment [2] (U.P.C. § 1–305), Sara will have all the powers and be entitled to perform all the duties pertaining to her office pursuant to U.P.C. Article 3, Part 7.

As an informally appointed general representative, Sara will not have to file a bond. She would be required to post a bond if it is demanded by any interested party, e.g., a creditor or devisee, having an interest in the estate exceeding $1,000, or if the will had required her to file a bond, or if she had been appointed special administratrix (see page 323) (U.P.C. §§ 3–603, 3–605). The person who demands a bond must write the request and file it with the court (U.P.C. §§ 3–603, 3–604, 3–605, and 3–606). For example, if Ralph files a written demand for a bond with the court, the registrar will mail a copy of the demand for a bond to Sara. Sara must then obtain a bond and file it with the court unless the court determines in formal proceedings that a bond is unnecessary or that Sara had deposited cash or collateral with an agency of the state to secure performance of her duties (U.P.C. §§ 3–603, 3–605).

If the registrar is satisfied that Elvira had complied with the requirements for executing a will pursuant to U.P.C. § 2–502, e.g., that the will contains the required signatures of two witnesses and attestation clause, the registrar will allow the proceedings to continue without further proof. The registrar may assume execution if the will appears to have been properly executed or may accept an affidavit (sworn statement) of any person having knowledge of the circumstances of execution, whether or not that person actually witnessed the will (U.P.C. § 3–303[c]).

Elvira's will contained signatures of two competent witnesses (her brother and aunt) and a proper attestation clause. The registrar approved Sara's application for informal probate and appointment. If

---

2. Letters Testamentary or Letters of Administration (see pages 322 and 346).

for any reason the registrar had decided that the will should not be admitted to probate or that the informal appointment should be denied, the application would have been denied. In that case, Sara would be required, if the estate is to be administered, to initiate formal probate proceedings (U.P.C. §§ 3–305 and 3–309).

Sara is now officially Elvira's personal representative, possessing the powers (e.g., to distribute the assets according to the will) and duties (e.g., to pay creditors before devisees) of a general representative (U.P.C. § 3–307[b]). Her appointment can be terminated, either voluntarily or by court order, at any time during administration of the estate. Sara's death, disability (such as being declared legally insane), or resignation would terminate her office. She might be removed by court order after a hearing initiated by a person interested in the estate (U.P.C. §§ 3–608 through 3–612).

Example: Marston Keefe, a creditor of Elvira, believes that Sara should be removed from office for failing to pay his claim against the estate. He files with the court, pursuant to U.P.C. § 3–611, a petition for a hearing seeking her removal. The court arranges a hearing at which Sara must appear to defend her action. If the court decides that she has abused the power of personal representative, it may direct that Sara be removed and someone else appointed to the position. If it so decides, the court may also regulate the disposition of assets remaining in the estate until the successor in office takes charge.

Sara must inform the heirs and devisees, Ralph and Christa, of her appointment by personal delivery or first class mail not later than 30 days after the appointment. Her failure to do this constitutes a breach of fiduciary duty but does not render invalid her acts as personal representative (U.P.C. § 3–705).

Within three months after her appointment, Sara must prepare and file with the court either by mail or in person an inventory of all property owned by Elvira at the time of her death. The inventory must list all assets with reasonable detail and indicate, as to each listed item, its fair market value at the date of her mother's death and the type and amount of all encumbrances against any item (U.P.C. § 3–706). Sara herself is allowed to appoint appraisers without the approval of the court, but that appointment may be challenged by an interested party as provided by U.P.C. § 3–607. Sara must send a copy of the inventory to interested persons who have requested it (U.P.C. § 3–706). She may also file the original with the court.

A personal representative owes a fiduciary duty to the devisees comparable to that of a trustee and is not permitted to engage in "self-dealing," i.e., dealing for one's own benefit (U.P.C. § 3–713).

Example: Sara appraised the fair market value of a grand piano at $500 and decided that she would purchase it from the estate. Ralph and Christa objected, asserting the fair market value of the piano to be at least $1,200. Ralph petitioned the probate court to issue an order restraining Sara from purchasing the piano and ordering an independent appraisal, pursuant to U.P.C. § 3–607. The court issued an order temporarily prohibiting Sara from proceeding with the purchase and notified both of them of a hearing on the matter to take place within ten days. At the hearing, the court will decide if Sara's course of action is unfair to the interests of the petitioner or the estate, as it might be if, for example, the independent appraiser had valued the piano substantially above $500. If so, the court will then issue an order permanently restraining Sara's action.

Sara would be liable to Ralph and Christa for any damage or loss resulting from any breach of her fiduciary duty to the same extent as a trustee of an express trust.

If Sara had bought the piano from the estate for $500 instead of its fair market value, i.e., $1,200, the estate would suffer because less money would result from the sale of the household goods and furnishings and therefore less would be available to pay Elvira's creditors or to be distributed to her devisees. According to law, creditors are the first to be paid from non-specific or general devises, e.g., the sale proceeds (money). If Elvira had left a good many expenses, these expenses might consume much of the general devise, leaving little for Ralph or Christa (U.P.C. § 3–712).

Example: Suppose the sale of household goods brings $3,500 to the estate. If Elvira's bills total $3,600, all of which must be paid from the estate's assets, the $3,500 will have to be apportioned among the creditors. They will receive a percentage of what Elvira had owed them. Any of the creditors would have a cause of action against Sara, who caused the total to be smaller by undervaluing the piano.

Elvira specified in her will that Sara would not receive any compensation for her services as personal representative, but nothing was mentioned about payment of creditor's claims, funeral expenses, and the like. Elvira had hospitalization and medical insurance that paid all the expenses of Elvira's last illness except for $60 to her doctor and $30 to the hospital. She also owed $90 to a local department store for clothing she had purchased. There was no provision in the will for payment of these obligations or for payment of funeral expenses ($1,800) or expenses of administration, such as filing fees ($75). Sara must pay the funeral and administration expenses before the other debts since those have priority (U.P.C. § 3–805).

Since none of Elvira's three children are minors or dependent children, U.P.C. § 2–401 (homestead allowance) and U.P.C. § 2–403 (family allowance) are not applicable to her estate. The three children, however, are entitled to share the $3,500 exempt property allowance (U.P.C. § 2–402). Together they are entitled to a sum not exceeding $3,500 in the form of household furniture, automobiles, furnishings, appliances, and personal effects, except for the portion of these chattels owned by creditors with security interests, e.g., an unpaid car dealer who sold the decedent a car on an installment payment plan.

Example: Two months prior to her death, Elvira had bought a $900 stove from an appliance dealer. She agreed to make a down payment and pay $25 per month plus interest. The dealer was to retain title to the stove as a security interest until Elvira had finished paying for it. At the time of her death, she had paid $150 toward the purchase price. Under the terms of the contract, the dealer would be able to repossess the stove if Elvira died before completing the payments. Therefore, the stove is not available as part of the exempt property. The children's rights to the exempt property have priority over all claims against the estate except for homestead and family allowances, which are not applicable here because there is no surviving spouse or minor or dependent children. Elvira's estate has sufficient assets, after distributing the exempt property ($3,500) to Sara, Ralph, and Christa, to pay debts, expenses of a last illness, and expenses of administration. Therefore, Sara will distribute the assets of her mother's estate as follows:

Exempt property (to be shared by Sara, Ralph, and Christa)	$3,500
Funeral expenses	1,800
Administration expenses	75
Doctor	60
Hospital	30
Department store	90
Total prior obligations	$5,555
Value of all estate assets	9,000
Less prior obligations	5,555
	$3,445

After prior obligations are accounted for, $3,445 in estate assets remain. Sara will add that amount to the $3,500 exempt property to determine the shares of the three children.

$$\begin{array}{r} \$3,500 \\ +\ 3,445 \\ \hline \$6,945 \end{array} \div\ 3\ =\ \$2,315$$

Each child is entitled to estate assets valued at $2,315. The children will receive less than Sara had determined prior to consideration of debts and expenses. Originally, each child would have received estate assets and/or cash valued at $3,000 (see page 397). After payment of debts and expenses, each child is entitled to receive estate assets and/or cash valued at $2,315.

Therefore, Sara may distribute the assets of Elvira's estate to Ralph, Christa and herself as follows:

Sara		Ralph		Christa	
Antique furniture	$2,000	Automobile	$1,400	Cash	$2,315
Cash	315	Tent trailer	600		
Total	$2,315	Cash	315	Total	$2,315
		Total	$2,315		

Sara must make the distribution expeditiously and may do so without order by the court (U.P.C. § 3–704). Ralph, Christa, Sara (the distributees of the estate), and Elvira's creditors take the property subject to the proviso that they return it to the personal representative should some unexpected event occur (U.P.C. § 3–909). This section of the U.P.C. protects the personal representative from unjustified litigation by distributees. The representative is liable, however, for improper distribution or payment of claims (U.P.C. §§ 3–703, 3–712 and 3–808).

Example: If Sara had overlooked the hospital bill ($30) and therefore paid $10 more to each devisee, each devisee (including herself) would be responsible for returning his or her share of the money improperly paid plus one-third of the interest that would have accrued on $30 from the date of distribution to the present date. The reason for the payment of interest is that the creditor does not have the use of the money until later (when it would be supposedly less valuable than earlier), so interest is added.

Persons who purchase from the distributees are also protected (U.P.C. § 3–910). Sara will execute instruments or deeds of distribution transferring or releasing the antique furniture, automobile, and the tent trailer to Ralph and herself as evidence of their respective titles to these assets (U.P.C. § 3–907).

Having completed the distribution of estate assets, Sara's last duty is to close the estate (wind up its affairs) in one of two ways:

- Formally, by petitioning the court to declare that the estate has been settled fully in regard to all persons interested in it. This method protects the estate against potential danger from details overlooked by the personal representative, e.g., the payment of inheritance taxes, because it avails the estate of the court's experience (U.P.C. § 3–1001).

- Informally, by filing a sworn closing statement with the court in which Sara gives her word that she had completed every detail of the administration.

If Sara chooses to close her administration by filing a closing statement with the court, she need not file a formal accounting with the court. She must, however, furnish Ralph and Christa and other interested parties with a full account in writing, together with a copy of the closing statement filed with the court (U.P.C. §§ 3–1001, 3–1002, and 3–1003).

Sara chose to close the estate by filing a closing statement with the court pursuant to U.P.C. § 3–1003. No earlier than six months after the date of her original appointment, she must file a verified statement asserting that she has (1) published notice to creditors and that the first publication occurred more than six months prior to the date of the present statement; (2) fully administered her mother's estate by making payment, settlement, or other disposition of all claims presented, paying expenses of administration and estate and inheritance and other death taxes, except as specified in the statement, and distributing the assets of the estate to the persons entitled; and (3) sent a copy of the closing statement to all the distributees of the estate and to all creditors or other claimants of whom she is aware whose claims are neither paid nor barred, and has furnished a full account in writing of her administration to the distributees (U.P.C. § 3–1003).

If no proceedings involving Sara are pending in court one year after the closing statement is filed, her authority (appointment) terminates.

An order closing an estate under U.P.C. § 3–1001 or 3–1002 would terminate Sara's appointment. Her closing statement under U.P.C. § 3–1003, however, would not terminate it, since it is an affirmation by Sara that she believes the affairs of the estate are completed. Any creditor not paid whose claim has not been barred by the time limit can assert that claim against the distributees, i.e., Sara, Ralph, and Christa (U.P.C. § 3–1004).

Example: When Sara was appointed, she published a notice to creditors in accordance with U.P.C. § 3–801. Several creditors presented claims within the period allowed for presentation, and Sara paid all except the $90 clothing bill from a local store. The store may obtain payment, even though Sara has filed a closing statement, by demanding $90 from one of the three distributees. That distributee is then entitled to demand $30 from each of the other distributees so that each will have contributed an equal amount. Sara can also be sued pursuant to U.P.C. § 3–608 for actions that she performed before the termination of her appointment. Under U.P.C. § 3–610(a), her authority ends one year after she has filed the closing statement. Even after termination, Sara remains liable to suit unless the applicable statute of limitations has run or unless her administration has been terminated by an adjudication settling her accounts (U.P.C. § 3–1005).

Example: Before giving the automobile to Ralph as Elvira had directed in her will, Sara used it for her personal convenience. She was involved in a collision resulting in $1,000 damage to the automobile. Because this occurred while Sara was the personal representative of the estate, Ralph may sue her for having failed to exercise due care with respect to one of the estate's assets during or within six months after the termination of her administration.

Suits against Sara by successors of the will and creditors for breach of her fiduciary duty are barred unless begun within six months after Sara filed the closing statement. Rights of successors and creditors to recover for fraud, misrepresentation, or inadequate disclosure are not barred by the six-month limitation (U.P.C. §§ 3–1005, 3–807, 3–808).

Using a closing statement offers Sara more protection than if she had relied merely on the receipts collected to show that the estate has been fully distributed.

Sections 3–1001 and 3–1002 of the U.P.C. provide for judicial proceedings for closing by which Sara could gain protection from all interested persons or from Ralph and Christa, the other devisees (successors), only. Section 3–703 of the U.P.C. provides very limited protection for a personal representative who relies only on receipts. These sections afford protection to the representative for acts or distributions that were authorized when done but that became doubtful because of a later change in testacy status. There is no protection against later claims of breach of fiduciary obligation except for those arising from consent or waiver of individual distributees who may have bound themselves by receipts given to the personal representative. In addition, the closing statement method provides notice to third persons that Sara's authority has terminated, whereas reliance on receipts alone does not. The closing statement method provides a useful means of closing small, non-complex estates where the distributees are all members of the family and when disputes are unlikely.

Assignment 132

1. Make a list of and obtain all the forms Sara would use in administering her mother's estate according to the Uniform Probate Code. Fill in the forms after reviewing Case Problem 2 (see page 406).

2. Suppose that six months before Sara had filed the closing statement Christa found a will executed by her mother with a date later than the probated will and which devised all Elvira's property to Christa. What should Christa do?

3. Would distribution of the assets of Elvira's estate have been different if Christa had been a minor at the time of her mother's death? If so, how? Suppose Elvira in her will had appointed neither a personal guardian nor a property guardian for Christa. How would the guardianship be determined?

4. Ralph claims that he, not Sara, should be appointed representative because he is the oldest of the children and thus has a higher priority. Should he petition the court to remove Sara and appoint himself on these grounds?

5. In her inventory, Sara omits a living-room chair valued at $50. If she discovers the error but neglects to file an amended inventory, what might be the consequence?

6. Before her death, Elvira had begun to negotiate the sale of the automobile to Moira Byrne, but they had not agreed on a purchase price. Sara completes the sale at a price of $1,350 intending to give the money, instead of the automobile, to Ralph. Has Sara breached her fiduciary duty?

7. Sara discovers a policy of insurance on Elvira's life which Elvira had taken out 25 years ago and which was not mentioned in the will. Should Sara record the value of this policy in her inventory of estate assets? May she use the proceeds to pay Elvira's creditors? The beneficiary of the policy is Elvira's estate.

8. Elvira had opened a charge account at a local department store. Prior to her death she had charged but had not yet paid for $50 worth of merchandise. The credit manager of the store wants to be sure that Sara will not overlook or disallow the claim. Could he demand that Sara be bonded to ensure against loss to the store?

9. The registrar declines to issue an order of informal probate because the registrar doubts that Elvira's signature on the will is genuine. One of the witnesses to the will is deceased and the other cannot be located. How could Sara have the will admitted to probate? Could she still follow informal procedures as planned?

Case Problems

Problem 1

Carl Bergmeister dies intestate on September 19, 1981, leaving outstanding assets valued at $272,800:

Homestead	$48,000
Furniture and household items	16,000
Shares of stock in Alcoa Aluminum	62,000
One-half interest in an apartment building held in tenancy-in-common (building valued at $250,000)	125,000
Two Miro paintings	18,000
1975 automobile	3,800
Total	$272,800

Several relatives survive Carl: Jenneille Bergmeister, wife; Naomi Bergmeister, daughter; Scott Bergmeister, son, who is a minor; David Bergmeister, son from a previous marriage; Carolyn Bergmeister, mother; Gustaf Bergmeister, father; Nora Stark, sister; Robin Stark, niece (daughter of Nora); Jarod Harrison, brother-in-law (wife's brother); and Verlayne Sather, first cousin.

Suppose that Naomi Bergmeister, Carl's daughter, makes an application for informal appointment of herself in intestacy pursuant to U.P.C. § 3–301.

1. Who has priority for such an appointment?

2. If someone else having priority over Naomi is an invalid and does not feel capable of assuming the duties of administering Carl's estate, could that person decline the appointment? How can the priority be waived?

3. What steps must Naomi take to assure her own informal appointment? What forms would she use?

Assume that Naomi is appointed personal representative.

1. Describe the steps she will take in administering, distributing, and closing her father's estate. Use the informal methods you think most appropriate.

2. Make a list of and fill in all forms Naomi will use. Assume that up to his death on September 19, 1981, Carl earned $30,000 from his employment and $8,000 from dividends on his stock and that accrued but unpaid dividends amounted to $1,000. Assume also that a $10,000 mortgage exists on the homestead; funeral expenses were $3,500, expenses for Carl's last illness were $270 to his doctor and $420 to the hospital, and that Carl owed $4,200 to a contractor for repairs on the homestead.

3. It must also be determined whether federal or state estate and/or inheritance taxes must be paid. Read Chapter 15 and obtain and complete the necessary tax forms for the Bergmeister estate, including decedent's final income tax return and the fiduciary income tax return for income earned by the estate.

With regard to handling the real property owned by Carl at his death, Naomi should consider U.P.C. § 3–715, especially subparagraphs 3, 6, 7, 8, 9, 10, 11, 15, 18, and 23, which discuss the transactions authorized for a personal representative especially those relating to land transactions. She must also consult the probate court of the county where Carl's land is located (if different from the county of his domicile) to see if there are local laws pertaining to real estate transactions (e.g., that the personal representative must obtain the court's permission to sell, mortgage, or lease real estate, and that the personal representative must wait a certain number of days before finalizing such transactions).

How will Naomi convey real property to heirs entitled to it—by deed or otherwise?

Assume that David Bergmeister, Carl's son by a previous marriage, files a petition with the probate court for *formal* appointment of a personal representative because he is dissatisfied with Naomi's appointment. What will be the result? Could Naomi still exercise her powers while the formal proceeding is pending (see U.P.C. § 3–401)?

What documents, if any, should Naomi file in order to convey a clear marketable title to the successors?

Problem 2

Cheryl Ann Kennedy died testate on August 1, 1982, at 1010 Willow Street in Hennepin County, Minneapolis, Minnesota 55409. She was born January 13, 1949, in Minneapolis, Minnesota.

The successors of Cheryl included her husband, Charles; two twin daughters, Cherry and Cindy; three sons, Carl, Corey, and Christopher; her mother, Catherine Kelly; and one sister, Karen Kelly. The ages of the family members are Charles, 34, Cherry and Cindy, the twins, age 3, Carl is 5, Corey is 9, Christopher is 10, Catherine Kelly is 60, and Karen Kelly is 38. All members of the family live at 1010 Willow Street.

Cheryl's estate included the following assets:

• A home, the family residence, owned by Cheryl before her marriage and still recorded in her name only, valued at $65,000

• A summer cottage in joint tenancy with Charles, given to Cheryl and Charles by Cheryl's father, valued at $25,000

• A savings and a checking account in joint tenancy with Charles with a total value of $10,000

• One thousand shares of Execo stock in joint tenancy with Charles worth $12,000

• Fifty shares of Users, Inc., stock left to Cheryl by her father, worth $2,000 in her name only

• A car (1979 Ford Granada) worth $3,500 in her name

- A life insurance policy payable to Charles with a face value of $5,000
- A diamond ring worth $1,500
- A mink coat worth $4,000
- Household goods worth $5,000
- Other personal property worth $300
- Clothing worth $200

The only debt Cheryl owed was $110 for two wigs purchased from Beauty Products, Inc.

Except for the diamond ring, which was left to her sister, Karen, Cheryl's will stated that all of her estate should go to her husband, Charles, if he survived her, and if not, to her children in equal shares. The will names Charles executor and was executed on November 21, 1980. Charles hires an attorney, Susan Brown, 1400 Main Street, Minneapolis, Minnesota 55455, to help with the estate administration.

For the informal, unsupervised probate administration of Cheryl's will, the following forms must be executed. Review them in Appendix A.

1. Application for Informal Probate of Will and for Informal Appointment of Personal Representative (Form 87)

2. Testimony of Subscribing Witness (Form 61)

3. Statement of Informal Probate of Will and Appointment of Personal Representative (Form 88)

4. Notice of Informal Probate of Will and Appointment of Personal Representative and Notice to Creditors (Form 89)

5. Proof of Placing of Order for Publication (Form 90)

6. Affidavit of Mailing Order of Informal Appointment or Notice of Hearing (Form 91)

7. Acceptance of Appointment and Oath by Individual (Form 92)

8. Letters Testamentary (Form 93)

9. Proof (Affidavit) of Publication, often provided to registrar by publisher (not executed; see sample Form 3)

10. Inventory and Appraisement (Form 94)

11. Schedule of Non-Probate Assets (not executed; see sample Form 70)

12. Self-Assessed State Inheritance Tax Return (not executed; see Sample Form 71)

13. Written Statement of Claim (Claims) (Form 95)

14. Final Account (not executed; see sample Form 72)

15. Informal Deed of Distribution (Form 96)

16. Receipt for Assets by Distributee (Successor) (Form 97)

17. Informal Administration: Personal Representative's Statement to Close Estate (Closing Statement) (Form 98)

Problem 3

All the facts in the Cheryl Kennedy case, including the assets and liabilities listed, are the same, except in this instance Cheryl died intestate. The forms that must be executed for the informal probate administration of Cheryl's estate in Minnesota are the following:

1. Application for Informal Appointment of Administrator (Form 99)

2. Order and Notice of Informal Appointment of Personal Representative (Administrator) and Notice to Creditors (Form 100)

3. Bond, if required (Form 101)

4. Acceptance of Appointment and Oath of Administrator (Form 102)

5. Proof of Placing Order for Publication (Form 103)

6. Affidavit of Mailing of Notice of Appointment and Notice to Creditors (Form 104)

7. Letters of General Administration (Form 105)

8. Proof (Affidavit) of Publication, often provided to registrar by publisher (not executed, see sample Form 3)

9. Inventory and Appraisement (Form 106)

10. Schedule of Non-Probate Assets (not executed; see sample Form 70)

11. Self-Assessed State Inheritance Tax Return (not executed; see sample Form 71)

12. Written Statement of Claim (Form 107)

13. Final Account (not executed; see sample Form 72)

14. Informal Deed of Distribution by Personal Representative (Form 108)

15. Closing Receipt for Assets by Distributee (Form 109)

16. Informal Administration: Personal Representative's Statement to Close Estate (closing statement) (Form 110)

17. Application for Certificate from Registrar—Application for Release of Bond (Form 111)

18. Certificate of Registrar—Release of Bond (Form 112)

Assignment 133

Review the forms that must be executed in the Cheryl Ann Kennedy intestate case problem 3. If Cheryl had died intestate in your state, identify and complete the forms required for the probate administration of her estate. Compare your executed forms with those in Appendix A.

Chapter 15

Tax Considerations In the Administration of Estates

Scope of the Chapter

Although the personal representative and the attorney have the ultimate responsibility for proper and prompt probating of an estate, the paralegal assisting the attorney must also be knowledgeable about legal and procedural matters applicable to estate administration, including the tax consequences to the estate of the decedent. The paralegal who intends to specialize in estate administration will need to acquire an extensive knowledge of tax laws and procedures. Appropriate steps must be taken to ensure familiarity with all currently applicable federal and state tax laws. Federal and state statutes must be checked to see if they have been repealed or amended, or if new statutes have been enacted. Two good sources for current federal tax laws are the Prentice-Hall and the Commerce Clearing House (CCH) looseleaf tax services (Exhibit 15.1).

This chapter provides a foundation for understanding tax considerations in the administration of estates. For purposes of illustration, the basic materials used in the preparation of the federal death tax returns and some of the returns prepared for the State of Minnesota are incorporated. State tax forms vary substantially. Paralegals must familiarize themselves with their own state's forms and tax law. The forms mentioned appear in Appendix A.

The first part of this chapter consists of an introduction to tax concerns, an overview of the tax changes brought about by the 1976 Tax Reform Act and the 1981 Economic Recovery Tax Act, and such tax considerations as the unified transfer tax credit, the unified gift and estate tax, the marital deduction, trusts, lifetime gifts, and generation-skipping transfers. Then the tax returns themselves are discussed, including the decedent's final income tax returns, federal and state; the fiduciary's income tax returns, federal and state; the U.S. (federal)

Exhibit 15.1   Sources for Current Federal Tax Laws

estate tax return; the state estate tax return; and the state inheritance tax return. A hypothetical case is worked through all these forms.

Competencies

After completing this chapter, the paralegal should be able to:

• Distinguish and identify the different kinds of income and death taxes that must be paid

• Understand and explain various ways to transfer assets while alive in order to lessen the amount of taxes owed to the state and federal governments by a decedent's estate

• Understand the tax consequences on gifts and estates created by the 1976 Tax Reform Act and substantially amended by the 1981 Economic Recovery Tax Act

• Prepare the tax returns of a decedent's estate

Introduction to Tax Concerns

The federal government and many state governments levy and collect taxes on income. The income subject to such tax includes personal income, corporate income, and trust income, which is a form of personal income. It is the duty of the personal representative of the decedent's estate to file the *income tax* returns for the estate and to see that any income tax owed the federal or state government is paid out of estate assets. In addition, the personal representative must file federal and state income tax returns for any income that accrues or is earned after the decedent's death until the close of the taxable year or until the date of final distribution of the estate. These tax returns are called U.S. or state fiduciary income tax returns.

Death taxes are measured by the amount of property transferred at death. There are two kinds of death taxes: estate taxes and inheritance taxes.

The *federal estate tax* is a tax levied on the privilege of transferring property at death. The rate and amount of the tax is determined by the size of the estate, and like the income tax it is a progressive tax, i.e., the larger the estate the higher the tax rate. By 1985, the rate will range from 18 percent to 50 percent. This is a tax on the estate itself, not on the successors.

A *state inheritance or succession tax* is the tax levied on the privilege of receiving property from a decedent at death. The rate or amount of this tax is determined by state law and depends on the amount of the share of the decedent's estate received by a particular successor and on the relationship of the successor to the decedent. It also is a progressive tax. Some states do not impose an inheritance tax on successors. Individual state statutes must be checked.

The federal government imposes an estate tax but no inheritance tax. States usually have either an estate tax or an inheritance tax or both. The federal and state estate and inheritance tax statutes require the personal representative to file, by a prescribed time, the appropriate tax returns or, alternatively, a report of assets, deductions, exemptions, and credits so that the amount of the tax or taxes can be determined by the Internal Revenue Service or the state Department of Taxation. These statutes also require the representative to pay the tax due within the prescribed time. Failure to make timely payment makes the representative personally liable for any interest charged or penalties resulting from this neglect, except when the representative has filed an Application for Extension of Time with the appropriate agencies.

In summary, the personal representative of the decedent's estate may have to file some or all of the following returns: U.S. individual income tax return, state individual income tax return, U.S. fiduciary income tax return, state fiduciary income tax return, U.S. estate tax return, state estate tax return, and state inheritance tax return. Each of these will be discussed in detail in this chapter.

The personal representative is responsible for paying all taxes out of the estate assets. These include income, fiduciary, estate, and inheritance taxes, unless the will specifies that the devisees pay the inheritance tax out of their devise. If prior to distribution of the estate the personal representative proves that the estate does not have enough cash (or assets to be sold) to pay the taxes without fault on the part of the representative, the representative is free from personal liability to pay the taxes. If the representative distributes the estate, however, and then does not have enough assets left to pay the taxes, the representative must pay the taxes out of his or her own pocket. Therefore, it is imperative that the representative make sure that sufficient assets remain for the payment of all taxes and debts before distributing any of the estate assets. Certain preferred claims have priority for payment before taxes are paid, e.g., administrative expenses, funeral expenses, and expenses of the last illness (see an example of a priority of debts statute, page 361, but compare U.P.C. § 3–805).

An Overview of the Tax Changes of 1976 and 1981

In 1976 and 1981, Congress extensively overhauled federal estate and gift tax laws, making the first major changes in these laws since 1942, with the exception of a law providing for a marital deduction in 1948. The two new acts, the 1976 Tax Reform Act (TRA) and the 1981 Economic Recovery Tax Act (ERTA), contain more than 250 separate provisions. Both individuals and businesses are affected by these new and complex tax laws.

The 1976 Tax Reform Act and the 1981 Economic Recovery Tax Act have and will continue to have a tremendous impact on estate planning and administration as well as on income tax considerations for grantors, testators, and beneficiaries. Many of the new provisions are complex and will require numerous qualifying regulations and rulings. Attorneys, paralegals, and others who specialize in estate planning and administration must be well versed on these comprehensive changes and their effects. Under the new laws, death tax revenues will not increase for the next few years. Generally, tax payments will be assessed only against the wealthy and the moderately wealthy. The changes will benefit smaller estates; the vast majority of estates which were previously required to file federal estate tax returns and pay estate taxes will now be required to do neither.

The following is a summary of some of the major changes in federal estate and gift tax laws included in the Tax Reform Act of 1976 and the Economic Recovery Tax Act of 1981. Refer to Chapter 11 (specifically Exhibit 11.1 on p. 305) for another review of these important changes.

• The TRA combined the previously separate gift and estate tax rate schedules into one unified transfer tax system, and the ERTA extended the time from 1981 to 1987 for implementation and increased the amount of the unified credit (see Table 15.2). The ERTA also reduced the maximum unified gift and estate tax bracket from 70% to 50%, to be phased in over a four-year period (1982–85).

• Pre-1977 laws provided for a $60,000 federal estate tax exemption, a $30,000 one-time specific lifetime gift tax exemption, and a $3,000 annual gift tax exclusion. The TRA eliminated both the estate tax and the gift exemptions and replaced them with a flat rate unified transfer tax credit phased in over a five-year period (1977–81) and was extended by the ERTA for the years 1981–87. In 1987 and thereafter, the credit will amount to $192,800. This $192,800 flat-rate unified credit is equivalent to an exemption of $600,000. The $3,000 annual gift tax exclusion was retained by the 1976 act but amended by the ERTA in 1981 and increased to $10,000 per donee per year beginning in 1982.

• Under the TRA, all gifts made within three years of the death of the decedent, together with the applicable gift tax paid or payable on such gifts, were added back into the decedent's gross estate. All such gifts made beginning January 1, 1977, were automatically included in the decedent's estate regardless of the donor's intent. This was to prevent appreciation of such transferred property from escaping taxation. The ERTA reverses this policy. In general, under the ERTA, gifts made within three years of death are *not* considered in the computation of the taxable estate. As an exception, however, gifts of life insurance in which the insured policyholder retains the "incidents or rights of ownership" in the policy and which are made within three years of death are still included in the gross estate. In addition, certain incomplete transfers, e.g., retained life estates or revocable transfers, will continue to be included in the decedent's gross estate regardless of when made.

• For federal estate tax purposes, the allowable marital deduction was increased by the TRA to the greater of $250,000 or half the Adjusted Gross Estate (see Glossary and page 179). The marital deduction, however, could not exceed that amount actually left to the surviving spouse. For gift tax purposes under the TRA, a spouse could give up to $100,000 to his or her spouse free of gift tax; the second $100,000 gift was taxable; and 50 percent of gifts that exceed $200,000 were free of gift tax. The ERTA completely changed the marital deduction for both gift and estate tax purposes. Under the ERTA, the gift and estate tax marital deduction for transfers between spouses is *unlimited.*

• Nontaxable generation-skipping transfers are limited to the amount of $250,000 for such transfers to the decedent's grandchildren (see page 427). The amount by which any such transfer exceeds $250,000 is subject to a newly created special tax called the *generation-skipping tax.* This law, however, imposes no limitation on direct transfers, i.e, a gift or bequest made directly to a grandchild or great-grandchild. Such outright transfers are exempt from the generation-skipping tax.

• Under the TRA, the system for filing the quarterly gift tax return was simplified, and a return was required only when the aggregate taxable gifts for a particular year were in excess of $25,000. The ERTA now requires only an annual gift tax return on April 15 following the year of the gift, except in the case of a deceased donor. In that case, the representative must file the gift tax return no later than the filing of the estate tax return, e.g., generally nine months after the date of death.

• Under the TRA, property held in joint tenancy by a husband and wife was to be treated as belonging one-half to each spouse for estate tax purposes. (This provision applies only to joint tenancy between spouses.) To qualify, however, the joint interest must have been created by one or both of the spouses (see page 447 for further discussion). The ERTA changed and simplified the rules relating to jointly held property by providing that when spouses jointly owned property with the right of survivorship, the gross estate of the first spouse to die includes half the property's value regardless of which spouse furnished the funds to purchase the property and also regardless of how the joint tenancy was created.

• The TRA provided for an orphan's exclusion for minors (natural or adopted children under 21 having no surviving parent). The exclusion for estate tax purposes amounted to $5,000 multiplied by the difference between 21 and the child's age. ERTA repealed the orphan's exclusion beginning in 1982.

General Tax Considerations

Before turning to the various tax returns that usually must be completed as part of the administration of a decedent's estate, certain general tax considerations need to be considered. One should remember that the estate, after the decedent's death, is a new legal being; the legal existence of the decedent has terminated. The estate has rights and obligations, and it is a taxpayer.

Everybody wants to reduce the death taxes owed the government or, if possible, to avoid them entirely whenever legally possible. There are numerous ways to accomplish tax savings on a decedent's estate. The most frequently used methods include: (1) making use of the increased unified credit and the reduced Unified Rate Schedule for federal estate and gift taxes; (2) making use of the marital deduction; (3) creating trusts; and (4) making gifts during the decedent's lifetime.

Unified Transfer Tax Credit and Unified Gift and Estate Tax Rates

The 1976 Tax Reform Act not only created a unified transfer tax credit for gifts and estates, but also unified federal gift and estate tax rates into a single schedule. The unified rate will be applied to *all* tranfers of assets subject to tax, whether the transfers occur during life by inter vivos gift or after death by will or intestate succession.[1]

Unified Transfer Tax Credit

The TRA, which took effect on January 1, 1977, substituted the new unified credit, which was subtracted from the tax due. The unified credit was phased in over a five-year period with an increase each year.

---

1. The provisions of the TRA were applicable to gifts made subsequent to December 31, 1976, and to estates of persons who died after that date until the enactment of the ERTA in 1981.

Table 15.1. Phase-in of New Unified Credit with Exemption Equivalents Under 1976 Tax Reform Act

Year	Unified Credit	Exemption Equivalent
1977	$30,000	$120,667
1978	$34,000	$134,000
1979	$38,000	$147,333
1980	$42,500	$161,563
1981	$47,000	$175,625

The yearly increase in the unified credit and its exemption equivalent [2] are shown in Table 15.1. Table 15.2 shows how the ERTA continued the annual increase. Because of this credit increase, a person who dies unmarried in 1987 can have a gross estate valued at $600,000 before any federal estate tax will be owed the government. When the ERTA is fully implemented in 1987, less than 0.5% of all decedents' estates will be subject to federal estate taxes. Table 15.2 shows that the estate tax savings is considerable if the decedent does not die until after 1987.

Unified Gift and Estate Tax Rates

The federal gift and tax rates in the 1976 Unified Rate Schedule, Table 15.3, ranged from 18% on the first $10,000 of taxable transfers up to 70% of taxable transfers above $5,000,000. After the tax was computed, the credit was applied (subtracted) from the tax owed, e.g., a credit of $30,000 was applied in 1977 for persons who died that year, which is the equivalent of an exemption of $120,667. As a result, an estate did not pay a tax in 1977 unless it was in a 30% or above tax bracket. In other words, the lowest applicable rate at which the computed tax owed was not canceled out by the unified credit was 30% in 1977.
Example: Jody Carter died in November 1977, leaving a taxable estate of $120,667. The formula for computing the federal estate tax is

Table 15.2 Annual Increases in the Unified Credit with Exemption Equivalents Under the 1981 Economic Recovery Act

Year	Unified Credit	Exemption Equivalent
1982	$62,800	$225,000
1983	$79,300	$275,000
1984	$96,300	$325,000
1985	121,800	$400,000
1986	155,800	$500,000
1987 and thereafter	192,800	$600,000

2. In lieu of the old $30,000 gift tax exemption and the old $60,000 Federal Estate tax exemption, the unified credit is now equivalent to the yearly exemption equivalents shown in Tables 15.1 and 15.2. The year of death and the corresponding exemption equivalent determine the federal estate tax liabilty of the decedent's estate if the decedent died unmarried.

Table 15.3 Unified Rate Schedule for Gift and Estate Taxes

If the amount with which the tentative tax to be computed is:	*The tentative tax is:*
Not over $10,000	18% of such amount
Over $10,000 but not over $20,000	$1,800 plus 20% of the excess over $10,000
Over $20,000 but not over $40,000	$3,800 plus 22% of the excess over $20,000
Over $40,000 but not over $60,000	$8,200 plus 24% of the excess over $40,000
Over $60,000 but not over $80,000	$13,000 plus 26% of the excess over $60,000
Over $80,000 but not over $100,000	$18,200 plus 28% of the excess over $80,000
Over $100,000 but not over $150,000	$23,800 plus 30% of the excess over $100,000
Over $150,000 but not over $250,000	$38,800 plus 32% of the excess over $150,000
Over $250,000 but not over $500,000	$70,800 plus 34% of the excess over $250,000
Over $500,000 but not over $750,000	$155,800 plus 37% of the excess over $500,000
Over $750,000 but not over $1,000,000	$248,300 plus 39% of the excess over $750,000
Over $1,000,000 but not over $1,250,000	$345,800 plus 41% of the excess over $1,000,000
Over $1,250,000 but not over $1,500,000	$448,300 plus 43% of the excess over $1,250,000
Over $1,500,000 but not over $2,000,000	$555,800 plus 45% of the excess over $1,500,000
Over $2,000,000 but not over $2,500,000	$780,800 plus 49% of the excess over $2,000,000

For 1982—In the case of decedents dying and gifts made in 1982:	
Over $2,500,000 but not over $3,000,000	$1,025,800 plus 53% of the excess over $2,500,000
Over $3,000,000 but not over $3,500,000	$1,290,800 plus 57% of the excess over $3,000,000
Over $3,500,000 but not over $4,000,000	$1,575,800 plus 61% of the excess over $3,500,000
Over $4,000,000	$1,880,800 plus 65% of the excess over $4,000,000

For 1983—In the case of decedents dying and gifts made in 1983:	
Over $2,500,000 but not over $3,000,000	$1,025,800 plus 53% of the excess over $2,500,000
Over $3,000,000 but not over $3,500,000	$1,290,800 plus 57% of the excess over $3,000,000
Over $3,500,000	$1,575,800 plus 60% of the excess over $3,500,000

For 1984—In the case of decedents dying and gifts made in 1984:	
Over $2,500,000 but not over $3,000,000	$1,025,800 plus 53% of the excess over $2,500,000
Over $3,000,000	$1,290,800 plus 55% of the excess over $3,000,000

Table 15.3 *(continued)*

For 1985

Over $2,500,000	50%

Source: U.S. Department of the Treasury, *I.R.S. Publication No. 448*, May 1982.
Note: In the Tax Reform Act of 1984, Congress froze the maximum estate tax rate at 55% until 1988 when it will be reduced to 50%.

$23,800, plus 30% of the excess of such amount over $100,000 (see 1976 TRA § 2001). Therefore, this estate was in the 30% tax bracket. The tentative federal estate tax (before subtracting the unified credit) was $30,000. In 1977 a unified credit of $30,000 was allowed (1976 TRA § 2010), which canceled out the $30,000 tentative tax (see Exhibit 15.2 for calculations).

Thus, for estates of decedents who died in 1977, if the estate was larger than $120,667 the tentative tax was greater than $30,000. It was therefore not canceled out by the $30,000 unified credit. The tax payable is the difference between the tentative tax and the amount of the available unified credit. (Caveat: All or a portion of the unified credit may previously have been used up by applying the credit to previous lifetime taxable gifts.)

When the credit has been fully phased in by 1987, the lowest applicable rate will be 37%, with a unified credit of $192,800 and exemption equivalent of $600,000 (see Table 15.2).

Assume that seven different individuals own exactly the same assets and each one died in a different year beginning in 1977. None of the seven had made taxable lifetime gifts. All seven left a taxable estate of $250,000. Table 15.4 illustrates the tentative tax, the unified credit, and the estate tax due after applying (subtracting) the unified credit.

Therefore, any taxpayer who is single and dies leaving a taxable estate of the value of the exemption equivalent or less would not be

---

Exhibits 15.2 Calculating the Federal Estate Tax on Jody Carter's Estate

Taxable estate (value) $120,667

Tax computation from Unified Rate Schedule ($23,800, plus 30% of the excess over $100,000 from the 1977 tax schedule)

Calculation:

Taxable estate over $100,000 times 30%	$ 20,667
	× .30
	$6,200.10
	23,800
	+6,200 (rounded)
	$ 30,000
Tentative tax	$30,000
Less unified credit for 1977	30,000
Tax owed	$ 0

Table 15.4 Decline in Federal Estate Tax Due to Unified Credit

	Year	Taxable Estate	Tentative Tax	Credit	Federal Estate Tax Due
A dies	1977	$250,000	$70,800	$30,000	$40,800
B dies	1978	250,000	70,800	34,000	36,800
C dies	1979	250,000	70,800	38,000	32,800
D dies	1980	250,000	70,800	42,500	28,300
E dies	1981	250,000	70,800	47,000	23,800
F dies	1982	250,000	70,800	62,800	8,000
G dies	1983	250,000	70,800	79,300	0

Using the Unified Rate Schedule (Table 15.3), the tentative tax and the tax due are computed as follows: The taxable estate is $250,000, therefore the tentative tax is $70,800 plus 34% of the excess of such amount over $250,000 as shown on the rate schedule. The tentative tax is exactly $70,800, from which is subtracted the unified credit for the appropriate year to determine the estate tax due.

liable for any federal estate tax. For example, if Tom Draxton dies in 1984 with his taxable estate valued at $325,000 or less, his estate pays no tax. Likewise, if Shirley Baxter dies in 1986 and her taxable estate is $500,000 or less, her estate would owe no federal estate tax.

Under the new laws, gift taxes are computed by applying the Unified Rate Schedule to cumulative lifetime taxable transfers and subtracting the taxes payable for prior taxable periods. Federal estate taxes are computed by applying the Unified Rate Schedule to cumulative lifetime and deathtime transfers, then subtracting the gift taxes payable. In some circumstances, adjustments must be made for taxes on lifetime transfers in the decedent's estate (see page 425). In general, any portion of the unified credit which is used against gift taxes will reduce the credit available to be used against the federal estate tax. The amount of the unified credit allowed cannot be greater than the amount of the computed transfer tax.

Calculating the Federal Estate Tax

The method for computing the amount of the federal estate tax under the new law is to apply the unified rates to the decedent's cumulative lifetime transfers and transfers made at death, then subtract the taxes payable on the lifetime transfers (the gift tax, as computed by applying the unified rate, would have previously been paid at the time assets were transferred during decedent's life). Computation of the federal estate tax is outlined in Exhibit 15.3. Review the outline carefully for future computation examples. See other discussion with examples, pages 421 and 422.

The tax credits listed in Exhibit 15.3 include the previously discussed unified credit and the credits for state death taxes (see Exhibit 15.5), i.e., the decedent's estate is allowed a federal credit for the state death taxes actually paid up to specific limits; for foreign death taxes, i.e., property subject to tax in a foreign country; and for estate taxes paid

Exhibit 15.3 Method for Computing Federal Estate Tax

Gross Estate (all property owned at decedent's death) $_____

Less:
Funeral expenses   _____
Administration expenses   _____
Debts   _____
Taxes   _____
Total deductions   _____   _____

Equals:
Adjusted Gross Estate   _____

Less:
Marital deduction *   _____
Charitable deduction **   _____
Total deductions   _____

Equals:
Taxable Estate   _____

Plus:
Adjusted taxable gifts (post-1976 lifetime taxable
  transfers not included in gross estate)   _____

Equals:
Tentative Tax Base (Taxable Amount)   _____

Compute:
Tentative tax (using Unified Rate Schedule in
  Table 15.3)   _____

Less:
Gift taxes paid on post-1976 gifts   _____

Equals:
Tax Payable Before Credits   _____

Less:
Tax credits:
  Unified credit   _____
  Credit for state death taxes   _____
  Credit for foreign death taxes   _____
  Credit for estate taxes on prior transfers   _____
                    Total Credit Reduction   _____   _____

Equals:
Federal Estate Tax Owed   _____

Note: When a decedent leaves everything to his or her spouse, there would be no estate tax
because of the unlimited marital deduction.
* See page 420.
** See page 458.

Table 15.5 Declining Credit for Tax on Prior Transfers

Years After 1st Death	Credit (Percent of Amount Transferred)
1 and 2	100%
3 and 4	80
5 and 6	60
7 and 8	40
9 and 10	20
After 10	No credit

by the estates of other decedents for assets included in the current decedent's estate. This is called the "credit for tax on prior transfers" and is allowed only if the two deaths occur within a short time of each other, e.g., within ten years. The purpose of this credit was to prevent the same property from being taxed too often. The credit is limited to the smaller of the following amounts:

1. The amount of the federal estate tax attributable to the transferred property in the first decedent's (transferrer's) estate

2. The amount of the federal estate tax attributed to the transferred property in the second or current decedent's estate

The credit is allowed in a declining percentage of the smaller amount mentioned above over the ten-year period (see Table 15.5).

Example: Mary Perkins dies, leaving her daughter, Molly, property worth $400,000. Mary's estate paid $80,000 in federal estate taxes on the property transferred to Molly. Now Molly dies. The amount of the credit available to Molly's estate would be as follows:

Year of Molly's Death After Mary's Death	Credit to Molly's Estate
1 year	$80,000 (100%)
2 years	$80,000 (100%)
3 years	$64,000 (80%)
4 years	$64,000 (80%)
5 years	$48,000 (60%)
6 years	$48,000 (60%)
7 years	$32,000 (40%)
8 years	$32,000 (40%)
9 years	$16,000 (20%)
10 years	$16,000 (20%)
After 10th year	No credit

The Marital Deduction

Estates

The marital deduction can be a substantial tax-saving device for an estate (see also pages 452–458). Under the Tax Reform Act of 1976, the maximum marital deduction for property passing from a decedent to a surviving spouse was the greater of $250,000 or half the decedent's

Adjusted Gross Estate.   However, only the amount actually left to the spouse could be deducted, even though it was less than half the decedent's adjusted estate gross.

To obtain the *Adjusted Gross Estate,* subtract administration and other expenses, creditors' claims, and casualty losses (property losses by theft, fire, storm, and the like not covered by insurance) from the gross estate (i.e., the total assets of the decedent).

Gross Estate (Total Assets)	*Minus*	Administration and Other Expenses, Creditors' Claims, Casualty Losses	*Equals*	Adjusted Gross Estate

Example: Suppose in the John Smith administration discussed in Chapter 2 the total value of John's gross estate is $275,000 and his administration expenses and creditors' claims amount to $25,000.   He has no casualty losses or other expenses.   His adjusted gross estate is $250,000.
Example: Fred Brown died in 1981.   The total value of his gross estate is $800,000.   Fred left his entire estate to his wife, Sally, and he had made no lifetime taxable gifts.   Fred's federal estate tax is computed as shown in Exhibit 15.4.

If Fred Brown had died in 1982 or thereafter, there would be no federal estate tax since Fred left his entire estate to his surviving spouse, Sally.   The Economic Recovery Tax Act of 1981 provides for an *unlimited federal estate tax marital deduction* for transfers between spouses.   A testate's estate is entitled to the marital deduction if there is a surviving spouse and if the decedent leaves all or a portion of his or her estate to the surviving spouse.   If the decedent spouse dies intestate, the surviving spouse is entitled to a statutory share of the decedent's estate.   The amount of the statutory share of the surviving spouse is the amount of the marital deduction in such cases.   Therefore, if Fred had died in 1982 there would be no tax owed by his estate after his death because he left everything to Sally and because of the unlimited marital deduction.

The ERTA of 1981 also added language to I.R.C. § 2056, pertaining to the estate tax marital deduction and to I.R.C. § 2523, pertaining to the gift tax marital deduction (see page 423).   The 1981 law contains a "terminable interest rule," which would allow certain property to qualify for the estate and gift tax marital deduction which previously did not qualify.   The eligible property is called "qualified terminal interest property" (QTIP), i.e., property that passes from the decedent spouse and in which the surviving spouse has a qualified income interest for life.   Examples of QTIP property that qualify for marital deduction treatment are (1) trusts with a life interest to the surviving spouse, the remainder to the children, and (2) a legal life estate to the surviving spouse and the remainder to others, e.g., their children.

The qualifying of QTIP property for the marital deduction becomes an important estate-planning tool.   The reason is that when one person (A) creates a life estate in property for another person (B) and the owner of the life estate (B) dies, the property in which B had the life

---

Exhibit 15.4 Computation of Fred Brown's Federal Estate Tax

Gross Estate	$800,000
Less:	
Administration expenses and debts	$200,000
Equals:	
Adjusted Gross Estate	$600,000
Less:	
Marital deduction	$300,000
Equals:	
Taxable Estate	$300,000
Plus:	
Adjusted taxable gifts	$ 0
Equals:	
Taxable Amount	$300,000
Compute tentative tax on Taxable Amount (using Unified Rate Schedule in Table 15.3)	$ 87,800
Less:	
Tax payable on gifts made after 1976	$ 0
Equals:	
Gross Estate Tax	$ 87,800
Less:	
Unified credit (for 1981)	$ 47,000
Equals:	
Estate Tax After Unified Credit	$ 40,800
Less:	
State death tax * credit (based on adjusted taxable estate of $240,000)	$ 3,600
Equals:	
Federal Estate Tax Owed	$ 37,200

* See page 459.

---

estate interest is *not* estate taxed on B's federal estate tax return. The only estate tax exception is the generation-skipping tax (see page 427).

In order to qualify as QTIP property for marital deduction treatment:

1. The surviving spouse life tenant must have a "qualifying income interest for life" in the property. The surviving spouse has a qualified income interest for life if (a) the surviving spouse is entitled to all the income from the property, payable annually or at more frequent intervals, and (b) no person during the surviving spouse's lifetime has the power to appoint any part of the property to any person other than the surviving spouse. However, a power exercisable only at or after the death of the surviving spouse is allowed.

2. The executor of the decedent spouse's estate must *elect* to treat the property as QTIP property on the decedent's estate tax return. If the election is made by the executor, then the property will qualify for the marital deduction.

The use of trusts with a life interest to a surviving spouse is one method of substantially reducing the tax consequences to a decedent's estate. Examples of such trusts are included in Appendix C.

Gifts

The marital deduction can also be used when there is a transfer by gift of any property between spouses. Under the 1976 Tax Reform Act, the gift tax marital deduction was changed. It provided for:

• An unlimited marital deduction for the first $100,000 interspousal gift

• Taxation of the second $100,000 given to the spouse

• A 50% maximum marital deduction on all gifts to a spouse of over $200,000.

Example: In November 1977, Sally gives her husband, Bill, $153,000. Sally first deducts her $3,000 annual exclusion, then deducts $100,000 (the first $100,000 is free of gift tax), leaving a remainder of $50,000 subject to gift tax. (Recall that the 1976 law eliminated the $30,000 lifetime exemption.)

Gift value	$153,000
Deduct annual exclusion	3,000
	$150,000
Deduct first $100,000 free from gift tax	100,000
	$ 50,000
Since second $100,000 or less is subject to gift tax	$ 50,000 is subject to the gift tax.

Example: In January 1978, Bruce Paulson places property valued at $500,000 in a ten-year short-term trust for his wife, Wilma. The trust instrument provides that upon Bruce's death, prior to the termination of the trust, the trust property will pass to Wilma. Applying the 1976 marital deduction, the first $100,000 is tax free, the second $100,000 is taxed, and 50 percent of the gift valued at over $200,000 is taxed. The Internal Revenue Service will value the trust property at $220,800 ($500,000 × 44.16%) (see page 307).

Value of trust property	$220,800
First $100,000 (not taxed)	− 100,000
Remainder	120,800
Second $100,000 (taxed—see calculations below)	− 100,000
Remainder (50% of this will be taxed)	20,800
(Second $100,000 and 50% of amount over $200,000 is taxed)	$100,000
	+ 10,400
	110,400

The amount to be taxed is $110,400, before subtracting the unified credit. The gift tax on $110,400 would be $26,920. Assuming that Bruce had made no prior taxable gifts, that he had not previously used his unified credit, but that he had used his $3,000 annual exclusion for Wilma, the tax would be computed as follows:

Taxable amount	$110,400
Tax computation:	
(from Table 15.3)	
$23,800, *plus* 30% of the excess of such amount over	
$100,000	$ 26,920 (gift tax)
Subtract Unified Credit for 1978	34,000
Tax owed	0

Bruce would still have $7,080 (i.e., $34,000 less $26,920) of his unified credit left to be used to reduce gift taxes on gifts he may give in the future or to reduce federal estate tax if Bruce died in 1978.

The Economic Recovery Tax Act of 1981 changed the result of both examples given above. Beginning in 1982, the annual gift tax exclusion (see page 425 and examples page 426) was increased from $3,000 per donee per year to $10,000 per donee per year. At the same time, the marital deduction on gift taxes for lifetime transfers (gifts) of any property between spouses became unlimited. In the above examples, Sally's and Bruce's annual exclusions would be $10,000 instead of $3,000, and neither would owe any gift taxes because they made their gifts to their spouses and because after 1982 such gifts are not taxed.

Thus, the Economic Recovery Tax Act of 1981 completely changed the gift tax marital deduction. It allows for an *unlimited marital deduction* for gift transfers between spouses. Therefore, if John gives his spouse, Mary, $10,000, $100,000 or $1,000,000, none of the property or cash is subject to gift tax. There is no upper limit on how much John can give his spouse. However, gift tax returns showing the marital deduction must be filed annually on April 15 following the year of the interspousal transfer.

Creation of Trusts

Another method used to diminish death taxes is the creation of trusts (see Chapters 9–11). It is possible to leave property in a testamentary trust for beneficiaries named by the settlor (testator) so that additional estate taxes are not due at the death of the beneficiary. One such trust, combined with the marital deduction, can result in substantial savings to the estate of a decedent over the course of two generations if properly planned and executed (see pages 454–458).

Lifetime Gifts

A person who makes a gift is called a *donor,* and a person who receives a gift is called a *donee.* Gifts made during the lifetime (inter vivos) of the decedent can in some cases result in tax advantages. The new tax laws (the TRA and the ERTA) have unified the gift and estate tax rates into a single rate schedule with progressive rates that are computed on the basis of cumulative transfers made both during lifetime and at death.

Under the TRA, any gift made within three years of the decedent's death was automatically included in the decedent's gross estate at death. The presumption was that the gift was made in contemplation of death. Moreover, the gift tax paid on the gift at the time it was given was also included in the decedent's gross estate at death. The ERTA reversed this rule, so that today gifts made within three years of death (except life insurance gifts; see page 354) are *not* included in the decedent's gross estate.

But some incentives for inter vivos gift-giving remain under the new laws. The $3,000 per donee annual exclusion has been increased by the ERTA to $10,000 per donee. Any appreciation in value of a lifetime gift which may accrue between the date the gift is made and the date of the donor's death is not subject to a transfer tax. Also, income taxes may be reduced when the gift property produces income and the property is transferred during life to a donee who is in a lower income tax bracket than the donor (see page 298).

The laws governing gifts and taxes on such gifts provide that:

- A gift must be intended and delivered by the donor.

- Any person can give a gift tax-free up to $10,000 per year to each donee, plus, if the donor's spouse joins in the gift, the exclusions of both spouses may be used, resulting in an exclusion of $20,000. This is called *gift-splitting.*

- The federal unified gift and estate tax rate is a progressive tax.

- When the gift is to the donor's spouse, there is an unlimited gift tax marital deduction.

Before one becomes too enthusiastic about transferring property by gift, it is well to remember that, once transferred, the property can no longer be controlled by the donor. The property passes to the new owner, the donee, and that person alone has title to it. Also, one must guard against giving gifts with strings attached. In most cases, when the donor retains control over the gift, income from the gift property will be taxed to the donor and the property will be included in the donor's gross estate for federal estate tax purposes upon the donor's death (I.R.C. §§ 2036–2038).

Example: In 1980, Janet Brown made a gift to her niece, Sue, of property valued at $173,625. Janet had made no previous taxable gifts. The unified credit for 1980 is $42,500. Janet computes her gift tax for 1980 as follows:

Total taxable gifts for 1980	$173,625
Annual exclusion	− 3,000
Taxable gifts	$170,625
Prior taxable gifts	+ 0
Total Taxable Gifts	$170,625
Tentative tax on total taxable gifts [4]	$ 45,400
Tentative tax on prior taxable gifts	− 0
Gift tax before unified credit	$ 45,400
Allowable unified credit	− 42,500
Net Gift Tax	$ 2,900

In 1983, Janet makes another gift to Sue of $100,000. The gift tax annual exclusion is now $10,000 instead of $3,000, and the unified credit for 1983 is $79,300. Janet computes her gift tax for 1983 as follows:

Total taxable gifts for 1983	$100,000
Annual exclusion	− 10,000
Taxable Gifts	$ 90,000
Prior taxable gifts (1980 gift)	+$173,625
Total Taxable Gifts	$263,625
Tentative tax on total taxable gifts (rounded) [5]	$ 75,433
Tentative tax on prior taxable gifts	− 45,400
Gift tax before unified credit	$ 30,033
Allowable unified credit ($79,300−$42,500)	− 36,800
Net Gift Tax	$ 0

In order to avoid any gift tax for 1983, Janet would use only $30,033 of the $36,800 remaining credit for that year and thereby have no gift tax liability. *Note*: If Janet died in 1983 and she had made no other taxable gifts that year, her *estate* would have, from the unified gift and estate tax schedule, $6,767 ($36,800 − $30,033) remaining as her unified credit that could be subtracted from any estate tax liability she may have at the time of her death.

---

4. Determined from Unified Rate Schedule using the over $150,000 but not over $250,000 line gives the tentative tax of $38,800 plus 32% of the excess over $150,000. This becomes $38,800 *plus* $6,600, which equals $45,400 (see Exhibit 15.2).

5. From the Unified Rate Schedule (Table 15.3) the tentative tax is $70,800 plus 34% of the excess over $250,000. This becomes $70,800 plus $4,633, which equals $75,433.

Assignment 134

1. If Janet Brown had made the same gift to Sue in 1981 instead of 1980, would Janet have to pay any gift tax?

2. If Janet Brown made the 1983 gift to her nephew, Mike, instead of to Sue, would the gift tax computation and gift tax due be any different?

Generation-Skipping Transfers

What are known as generation-skipping transfers (trusts) have been used in the past as a means of avoiding taxes, but they are now taxed. To understand this newly enacted area of tax law, the following terms must be mastered.

Terminology Relating to Generation-Skipping Transfers

Grantor
The grantor is the testator or donor who creates a generation-skipping trust.

Generation-skipping trust
A generation-skipping trust is a trust whereby property or benefits transferred by a grantor are split between persons (beneficiaries) from two or more generations younger than the generation of the grantor of the trust.
Example: Malcolm establishes a trust with the income payable to his only daughter, Shirley, for life, and the remainder of the trust property to Shirley's children. The beneficiaries of the trust are Shirley and Shirley's children. These two generations have a present or future right to receive trust income or trust property. The trust is a generation-skipping trust because there are two or more generations of younger-generation beneficiaries (see below) than the generation of the grantor (Malcolm).
Example: Malcolm establishes a trust with the income payable to his wife, Irene, for life, and the remainder of the trust property to his grandchildren. This is *not* a generation-skipping trust because there are not two or more generations of beneficiaries who are "younger" than the grantor (Malcolm).

Younger-generation beneficiary
A younger-generation beneficiary is any beneficiary who is assigned to a generation younger than the grantor's generation.
Example: In the first example under generation-skipping trust, Malcolm is the grantor. His daughter, Shirley, is a member and beneficiary of the *first* "younger generation" and his grandchildren (Shirley's

children) are members and beneficiaries of the *second* "younger generation." A grantor's generation includes his or her spouse and the
grantor's sisters, brothers, first cousins, and their spouses. The first
"younger generation" would include the grantor's children, nieces,
nephews, first cousins once removed and their respective spouses.

Deemed transferor

The deemed transferor is an ancestor of the beneficiary of a generation-
skipping transfer who is of a generation younger than the grantor and
whose taxable estate at death forms the basis for the generation-
skipping transfer tax.

Example: In the first example above, Shirley is the "deemed transfer-
or" with respect to the transfer of the trust property to Shirley's
children, i.e., the grantor's grandchildren. Shirley's taxable estate on
her death will form the basis for determining the generation-skipping
transfer tax.

Taxation on generation-skipping transfers

Taxation on generation-skipping transfers is the tax on the combined
total value of the deemed transferor's taxable estate and that of the
generation-skipping transfer, minus the tax on the deemed transferor's
own estate.

Taxable estate

The taxable estate is the gross estate less funeral expenses, administration expenses, claims against the estate, unpaid mortgages, encumbrances, and losses incurred during administration.

Taxable termination

Taxable termination is termination of a property interest of a beneficiary of a generation younger than the grantor and its passing to a
beneficiary of a still younger generation.

Example: Jack Wallace creates a trust with the income payable to his
daughter, Bernice, for life and the remainder to his grandchild, Gregory
(Bernice's son). When Bernice dies, there is a taxable termination of
her interest, and her taxable estate forms the basis for the generation-
skipping transfer tax. Bernice is the deemed transferor.

Taxable distribution

Taxable distribution is a payment other than from income from a
generation-skipping trust to a younger-generation beneficiary prior to
termination of the interest of an older-generation beneficiary.

Example: Sandra Harlow creates a trust with the income payable to
her son, Glen, for life and the remainder to her grandchild, Susan
(Glen's daughter.) The trustee is given the discretionary power to
distribute trust property to Susan. If a distribution of trust property is
made to Susan while Glen is alive, the distribution is taxable (see page
433).

Grandchildren-of-grantor exclusion

An exclusion up to $250,000 from the generation-skipping transfer tax is allowed to the grantor's grandchildren with respect to a deemed transferor where the grandchildren are the beneficiaries of a generation-skipping transfer.

Example: Judy Carlson creates a trust with the income from the trust property payable for life to her son, Donald, and the remainder to Donald's two children (Judy's grandchildren). Regardless of the number of grandchildren entitled to the remainder interest or the value of the trust at Donald's death, the maximum exclusion from the generation-skipping transfer tax for the benefit of the grandchildren can be no more than $250,000.

The amount of the exclusion does not depend on the number of grandchildren benefited, but rather on the number of deemed transferors through whom the grandchildren receive their benefits.

Example: Charles Atkins creates two trusts. The first trust makes the income from the trust payable to his daughter, Beverly, for life and the remainder to Beverly's three children (Charles' grandchildren). Beverly is the deemed transferor. The second trust makes the income from the trust payable to Charles' son, Henry, for life and the remainder to Henry's two children (Charles' grandchildren). Henry is the deemed transferor. Since the exclusion is based on the number of deemed transferors and not on the number of grandchildren, Charles' three grandchildren (Beverly's children) will be entitled to a $250,000 exclusion from the generation-skipping transfer tax when Beverly dies, and Charles' two grandchildren (Henry's children) will also be entitled to a $250,000 exclusion from the tax when Henry dies.

Distributee

The distributee is a beneficiary of a trust to whom trust property, including income, has been distributed.

Power of appointment

Power of appointment is a power given by the donor to the donee to appoint the property to donee's estate, creditors, or the creditors of the estate or to any person during the donee's lifetime.

Introduction to Generation-Skipping Transfers

When reading the following discussion of generation-skipping transfers, keep in mind these basic principles:

- Generation-skipping transfers (trusts) are now taxed.

- There must be two or more generations of beneficiaries who belong to generations younger than the generation of the grantor in order for tax consequences to result.

- The generation-skipping tax is imposed on each generation-skipping transfer that is either a taxable termination or a taxable distribution.

- The taxable estate at death of the person identified as the deemed transferor forms the basis for the generation-skipping transfer tax.

- The deemed transferor's estate has no liability for payment of the generation-skipping tax. The trustee or the distributee of the generation-skipping trust is responsible and liable for payment of the tax.

Before 1977, termination of the interest of a trust beneficiary, a life tenant, and the like was not taxable except when the person whose interest terminated had a general power of appointment or was also the grantor. Therefore, families, through the use of generation-skipping transfers, might pay transfer taxes only once every several generations. **Example** (pre-1977 law): Joann established a trust that provided for a life interest to her daughter, Colleen, then a life interest to Colleen's son, Buford (Joann's grandson), with the remainder to Timmy, Buford's son (Joann's great-grandson). As long as the child's (Colleen's) and grandchild's (Buford's) interest in the trust was limited to a right to income, a discretionary right to principal distributions, or a limited power of appointment over the trust, the trust property would not be included in their gross estates for federal estate tax purposes. Transfer taxes would be paid only on the original transfer [6] (life interest from Joann to Colleen) and on the last transfer [7] (remainder to Timmy). The tax on two generation-skipping transfers was avoided: (1) termination of Colleen's (grantor's child) life interest and transfer of the life interest to Buford (grantor's grandchild) and (2) termination of Buford's life interest and transfer of the remainder interest to Timmy (grantor's great-grandchild). Therefore, two generations were given current beneficial enjoyment over the trust property with no transfer tax costs.

The key to this tax avoidance was the rule that a life interest in property left to one person (A) by someone else (X) would not be taxed as part of A's gross estate when A, the life tenant (page 55) dies. Thus, if successive life estates, e.g., to A for life, then to B for life, then to C for life, then the remainder to D, are created, estate taxes are avoided when A, B, and C die. The Rule Against Perpetuities (page 181) was the only limit placed on the use of successive life estates, but if the grantor had two or three generations of living descendants, e.g., children, grandchildren, and great-grandchildren, the grantor could establish successive life estates for these descendants and thereby avoid that rule. The grantor could create a life estate for a spouse, then a child, then a grandchild, then a great-grandchild, with the remainder to a great-great-grandchild. In such a case the only estate tax would be on the death of the original grantor, and then none would be due until the death of the great-great-grandchild.

To eliminate this method of tax avoidance, Congress added an entire new chapter 13 to the Internal Revenue Code and established a new tax

---

6. A gift tax, based on the fair market value of the property on the date of original transfer, payable at the time of the initial gift.

7. An estate tax payable on the death of the ultimate beneficiary, who receives outright distribution of the remainder of the trust property.

called the *generation-skipping transfer tax.* Its purpose is to assure that no generation is absolved from tax on property transferred from a prior generation. The new tax does not prevent or tax all life estates, but it imposes the new tax when a succession of life estates is created to attempt to avoid tax. The provisions of chapter 13 apply to all transfers that divide up the beneficial enjoyment of the transferred assets among two or more generations, such as trusts (page 214), life estates (page 81), estates for years (page 84), and insurance and annuity contracts (page 150). The transfer tax on the transfer to each successive generation will now be roughly the same as if the original grantor had made an outright gift to each generation and the property was subject to estate tax at the donee's death. The tax, however, is paid out of the proceeds of the trust property by the trustee or the distributee of the generation-skipping trust (see 1976 Tax Reform Act § 2006, adding §§ 2601–2603, 2611–2614, 2621, and 2622; generally applicable to generation-skipping transfers occurring after April 30, 1976).

In a generation-skipping trust, two or more generations of beneficiaries are members of generations that are "younger" than the generation of the grantor of the trust. A "generation" is determined with reference to the family line. Adopted children are treated the same as natural children. The grantor, the grantor's spouse, and the grantor's brothers and sisters are all in the same generation regardless of their ages. The children of the grantor are members of the first "younger generation," and the grantor's grandchildren are members of the second "younger generation." Where beneficiaries of generation-skipping transfers are not members of the grantor's family, the generation is determined by measuring the difference between the age of the grantor and the age of the beneficiary as follows: beneficiaries who are not more than $12\frac{1}{2}$ years younger than the grantor are members of the grantor's generation; beneficiaries who are more than $12\frac{1}{2}$ but not more than $37\frac{1}{2}$ years younger than the grantor are members of the first younger generation (i.e., equivalent to the grantor's children's generation).

A "beneficiary" is a person who has either a present or a future interest or power of appointment in a generation-skipping trust. An interest includes (1) the right to receive income or property from the trust during its duration; (2) the right to receive a distribution on the termination of the trust, or (3) the contingent interest of one who is a permissible recipient of income or property under a power exercisable by himself or herself or another. One who has a power of appointment with respect to a trust is treated as a beneficiary if he or she can establish or alter the beneficial enjoyment of the property or income of the trust. One who merely manages the trust property is not treated as a beneficiary. Generally, even one who has only a limited power of appointment is treated as a beneficiary under the generation-skipping provisions. There is, however, one exception: when the holder of the power has the sole discretion to allocate income or property of the trust among lineal descendants of the grantor who are members of a generation or generations younger than that of the person who holds the right of allocation.

Example: Irene established a trust for the benefit of her grandchildren, Todd and Melinda. The trust instrument provided for a power of appointment to the children's father, Merve, to allocate (distribute) trust income or property between them.

Here the father is not treated as a beneficiary (because of the applicable exception). Therefore, this is not treated as a generation-skipping trust and the generation-skipping tax is not imposed at the time Merve allocates trust income or property to his children. Of course, the establishment of the trust may be subject to a gift tax or to an estate tax if established pursuant to a will.

Example: Chad established a trust which provided that trust income would be paid to Chad's daughter, Beth, for life and that the trustee would have the power after Beth's death to distribute trust income or property to Chad's grandchildren, with the remainder over to Chad's great-grandchildren. Chad's child, Beth, his grandchildren, and his great-grandchildren all are beneficiaries because all have a present or future interest. Since there are two or more generations of younger-generation beneficiaries, this is a generation-skipping trust.

A "special" tax, i.e., the generation-skipping tax, is imposed on each generation-skipping transfer which is either a "taxable termination" or a "taxable distribution."

Taxable Termination A taxable termination is the termination of an interest or power of a younger-generation beneficiary who is older than any other younger-generation beneficiary. It occurs when *all* of the following conditions are present:

• The interest or power in the generation-skipping trust has terminated

• The interest belonged to a younger-generation beneficiary who at one time had more than a future interest or power

• There is in existence a still younger generation beneficiary who is entitled to an interest in the trust

Example: Becky (the grantor) creates a trust with income for life to her son, Ralph, with the remainder over to Becky's grandchild, Anna, upon Ralph's death. When Ralph dies, there is a taxable termination of his interest because his death terminates the interest of a younger-generation beneficiary who is older than any other younger-generation beneficiary (Anna) of the trust.

The same rule applies if the trust had provided income to Ralph for 20 years with the remainder to Anna. The taxable termination would occur at the end of 20 years.

Ralph belongs to a generation younger than Becky's (mother-grantor) generation, and an older generation than Anna's (grandchild) generation. When two or more trust beneficiaries are members of the same generation, the taxable termination occurs when the last of the interests of that generation terminates. At that time a tax will be imposed based on the value of the assets for all the beneficiaries of that particular generation. There is no taxable termination, however, when the interest which terminates is a future interest.

Example: Bradford establishes a trust with income to his son, Steven, for life, then income to Bradford's grandchild, Deanna, for life, with the remainder over to Bradford's great-grandchild, Keith. If Deanna (grandchild) dies first, there is no taxable termination on her death because she never held a "present" income interest. This provision avoids the gross inequity of imposing a tax based on an interest that was never realized.

The generation-skipping tax is imposed only once each generation with respect to the same property. Where members of several different generations have a present interest or power in the same trust, and the interest of a younger-generation beneficiary terminates first, the generation-skipping tax will be postponed until the interest of the older generation terminates. The tax is also postponed when the trust is a "sprinkling" (discretionary) trust since it is difficult to determine the value of the terminated interest until the interests of all members of intervening generation beneficiaries have terminated. Any one group may receive all or any part of the trust property or none of it. Postponement of the tax may be allowed in certain other instances that are defined by the applicable statutes and Internal Revenue Service regulations. Also, the U.S. Treasury Department has been given authority to promulgate "separate share" rules, which will determine whether a trust in which there are several interests will be treated as one trust or as two or more separate trusts.

A taxable termination does not occur when a beneficiary assigns the beneficiary's interest. The taxable termination occurs upon the death of the assignor (see Glossary), however, if termination would have occurred had the assignor retained the interest.

Taxable Distribution   A taxable distribution occurs when a distribution is made from a generation-skipping trust to a younger-generation beneficiary whenever there are one or more younger-generation beneficiaries who are members of a generation older than the recipient's generation. However, if only current income (i.e., income under I.R.C. § 643[b]) is distributed there is no taxable distribution. The income distribution may, of course, be subject to payment of income tax by the income beneficiary. In other words, a taxable distribution from a trust occurs when *all* of the following conditions are present:

• The distribution is made from a generation-skipping trust

• The distribution is not made from income

• The distribution is made to a younger-generation beneficiary

• There is at least one other younger-generation beneficiary who (a) is assigned to a generation older than the distributee's generation and (b) has more than a mere future interest or power in the trust (I.R.C. § 2613[a][1])

Example: Neil Rollins established a testamentary trust which provided that trust income be paid to his daughter, Sophie, for life with the remainder over to Neil's grandchild, Betty. The trustee was given the power to distribute the trust property to Sophie or Betty. If the trustee distributes any of the trust property to Betty during Sophie's lifetime, the distribution is taxable. This is so because, although both Sophie (Neil's child) and Betty (Neil's grandchild) are younger than Neil (grantor), the distribution was made to Neil's grandchild, who is younger than Neil's child. A distribution was made to a younger-generation beneficiary (younger than the grantor), Betty, but there was a younger-generation beneficiary (Sophie) who was a member of a generation older than Betty's generation.

In no case will a taxable termination or taxable distribution be subject to both the estate or gift tax *and* the generation-skipping tax. Therefore, if a gift or estate tax is paid on a termination or distribution, the generation-skipping tax will not be imposed.

Example: Lauren Provo established a testamentary trust with income to her son, Larry, for life, then to her grandchild, Carrie, for life. The trust also provided Carrie with a general power of appointment. This means that Carrie may, by will, determine to whom the property will be distributed after Carrie's death. In addition, the trust stated that if Carrie does not exercise her power of appointment the remainder will go to Lauren's great-grandchild, Garrett. Because of Carrie's general power of appointment, at her death the trust property is subject to estate tax. Therefore, if Carrie dies without having exercised her general power of appointment, there is no taxable termination, i.e., generation-skipping tax, at her death.

As previously stated, the generation-skipping tax is substantially equivalent to the gift or estate tax that would have been imposed if the property had been transferred outright to each generation. The value of the property subject to the generation-skipping tax is added to the other taxable transfers of the "deemed transferor." This results in the generation-skipping transfer being taxed at the transfer tax rate of the deemed transferor. The deemed transferor of a generation-skipping transfer is the parent of the transferee (beneficiary) who has the closer relationship to the grantor of the trust than the other parent of the transferee. Relationship by blood or adoption is considered to be closer than relationship by marriage. The deemed transferor is *always* the parent of the transferee (beneficiary) who is more closely related to the grantor, whether or not the parent is living at the time of the generation-skipping transfer, *except* in the case where that parent will never be a younger-generation beneficiary of the trust *and* there is some other ancestor (grandparent, great-grandparent, and the like) who is related by blood or adoption, but not by marriage, to the grantor of the trust, who is a younger-generation beneficiary of the trust (I.R.C. § 2612[a][2]). If both these conditions are met and the ancestor is also a younger-generation beneficiary of the trust, then that ancestor will be the deemed transferor (rather than the parent of the transferee who is more closely related to the grantor).

Example: Rodney Allison established a trust for his grandchild, Alicia, for life, with the remainder over to Rodney's great-grandchild, Terry. Rodney's son, Howard, Alicia's father, is alive but not mentioned in the trust. Alicia (the parent of Terry) and not Howard, her father, is the deemed transferor when the trust property passes to Terry. Although Howard is the parent (ancestor) more closely related to the grantor (Rodney) and is of a younger generation, he is not a beneficiary of the trust. Therefore, Alicia qualifies as the deemed transferor.

Example: Rodney Allison establishes a trust for Robert, the husband of his grandchild (Alicia) for life, with the remainder over to Rodney's great-grandchild, Terry. Rodney's grandchild, Alicia (and not Alicia's husband, Robert), is the deemed transferor because Alicia is the parent of the transferee (Terry, Rodney's great-grandchild) more closely related to the grantor (Rodney). When Robert (grandchild's husband) dies, the value of the trust property will be added to Alicia's (grandchild) taxable transfers for the purpose of determining the applicable tax rate. If Alicia (grandchild) is still living, the deemed transfer will be taken into account for the purpose of determining the transfer tax rate to be applied for any later deemed transfers attributable to the grandchild (Alicia). However, the deemed transfer will not be taken into account in determining transfer tax rates to be applied to Alicia's gifts or estate.

Example: Lois Bellois established a trust for the benefit of Lois' child, Roy, for life, with the remainder over to Lois' great-grandchild, Anna. In this case, Roy is the deemed transferor when the property passes to Anna because Anna's parent is not a younger-generation beneficiary of the trust.

Example: Frank Nelson established a trust for the benefit of his niece, Denise, for life, then to Denise's son, David, for life, with the remainder to Frank's great-grandchild, Gregory. Denise (grantor's niece) would be the deemed transferor upon her death when the life interest passes to David (Denise's son). Upon the death of David, when the property passes to Gregory, however, Frank's grandchild, Blake (the great-grandchild's parent), will be the deemed transferor. This is so because no ancestor of Gregory (great-grandchild) was a younger-generation beneficiary of the trust.

Example: Helen Jorgens established a discretionary trust, the trustee being given the power to allocate income between Helen's grandchild, Rita, and Helen's niece's daughter, Susan, with the remainder over to Helen's great-grandchild, Jordan. Here Rita (Helen's grandchild) is the deemed transferor when the property passes to Jordan (Helen's great-grandchild) because Rita is the parent of Jordan (transferee) and she is also one of the younger-generation beneficiaries of the trust.

In the case where a trust is established for the benefit of persons who are not related to the grantor (e.g., friends), the deemed transferor is the parent of the transferee having the closest "affinity" or relationship with the grantor. In most cases, this will be the person named in the will or trust instrument, or the lineal descendant of that person who has an intervening interest or power in the trust.

Example: Maurey Peterson established a trust for the benefit of his friend, Jack (who is 15 years younger than Maurey), for life, then to Jack's issue per stirpes (page 102) for life, with the remainder over to their issue. Jack is the deemed transferor upon his death. Each of Jack's children will be deemed transferors upon their deaths, assuming that each of Jack's children is more than 37½ years younger than Maurey (the grantor).

When a will or trust instrument does not state clearly in what manner the trust property should be allocated, it is presumed that the property will pass to each beneficiary in proportion to the amount each would have received under a maximum exercise of discretion in the beneficiary's favor. It is also presumed that discretion will always be exercised per stirpes, in the absence of an express contrary intention in the will or trust instrument.

Computation of the Generation-Skipping Tax

To compute the generation-skipping tax, the following method is used. The value of the property subject to the generation-skipping transfer tax is added to other taxable transfers, i.e., gifts or estate, of the deemed transferor. The unified tax rate is determined from the Unified Rate Schedule, (Table 15.3; see also I.R.C. § 2001), and a tentative tax is computed on the total value of all the transfers. Next the tax on all transfers other than the generation-skipping transfer in question is subtracted from the tentative tax. Information regarding the tax bracket of the deemed transferor for the purpose of computing the tax can be obtained from the Internal Revenue Service. The tax is paid out of the proceeds of the trust property. In no case is either the deemed transferor or his or her estate liable for the tax. However, a trustee is personally liable for the tax in the case of a taxable termination, and distributees of a taxable distribution are personally liable for the tax to the extent of the value of the property distributed to them. The property is subject to a tax lien until the tax is paid.

If the deemed transferor is no longer living at the time of the taxable event (termination of an intervening interest or distribution of trust property), the tax will be determined by the hypothetical effect of adding the "deemed transfer" back into the "deemed transferor's" estate.

Step One   To compute the generation-skipping tax, the appropriate rate from the Unified Rate Schedule (Table 15.3) is applied to the following amounts:

1. The fair market value of the property passing pursuant to the generation-skipping transfer in question

2. The fair market value of any previous generation-skipping transfers from the same deemed transferor

3. All previous adjusted taxable gifts made by the deemed transferor

4. The taxable estate at the death of the deemed transferor

Step Two Applying the Unified Rate Schedule, a tentative tax is then computed on the sum of the value of items 2, 3, and 4 above and subtracting that amount from the tax computed under Step One. In a case where the deemed transferor is still living at the time of the generation-skipping transfer, the same computations are made as shown in Steps One and Two, except that item 4 is omitted.

Other Concerns With Generation-Skipping Transfers

Property that passes pursuant to a trust is entitled to many of the benefits available under gift and estate tax laws applicable where property is transferred outright, but only to the extent that property which passes pursuant to the trust is subject to the generation-skipping tax.

When the deemed transferor dies prior to or at the same time that the generation-skipping transfer occurs, the trust is entitled to any available (unused) portion of the deemed transferor's unified credit, the charitable deduction, and the credit for any taxes paid on previous transfers. The trust is also entitled to subtract the credit for state death taxes paid and deductions for losses and expenses of administration. In addition when the generation-skipping transfer occurs within three years and nine months after the death of the deemed transferor, the trust is entitled to any reduced rate that results from the increased marital deduction.

Generation-skipping transfers to grandchildren of the grantor are exempt from the generation-skipping tax to the extent that total transfers do not exceed $250,000 through each deemed transferor, i.e., through each child of the grantor who is also the parent of the grandchild-transferee. For example, if the grantor has three children and each of the three children has children, up to $750,000 can be transferred to the grantor's grandchildren free of any generation-skipping tax. Where the grantor leaves life interests to the grantor's children, with remainders to grandchildren, the maximum amount that can be excluded from the tax is limited by the number of children not by the number of grandchildren.

Applicable tax regulations issued by the Internal Revenue Service prescribe who must file returns for the generation-skipping tax (see I.R.C. § 2603). The distributee files in the case of a taxable distribution. The trustee files in the case of a taxable termination. Regulations may also require a trustee to furnish information that the Internal Revenue Service considers necessary. If the generation-skipping transfer occurs before the death of the deemed transferor, a return must be filed before the 90th day after the close of the taxable year of the trust. If the generation-skipping transfer occurs at the same time as or after the deemed transferor's death, the return must be filed on or before the 90th day after the last day for filing a return for the deemed transferor's estate (i.e., the estate tax return).

Procedures for reporting are similar to those required for gift and estate taxes. There is no minimum filing amount, however. A return for the generation-skipping transfer is required even when no tax is due as a result of the exclusion for transfers to grandchildren.

The law concerning generation-skipping transfers,[8] is applicable generally to transfers occurring after June 11, 1976. It does not apply to transfers under irrevocable trusts that were in existence on June 11, 1976, or in cases of decedents who died prior to January 1, 1983, pursuant to a will or revocable trust which existed on June 11, 1976, and which was not amended after that date. Amendments which occurred after June 11, 1976, but which did not create or increase the amount of generation-skipping transfers are disregarded. In cases where the testator or grantor is incompetent to change the will or trust, the January 1, 1983, date is extended for two years after the disability is removed. For persons dying after January 1, 1983, the generation-skipping tax will be assessed against generation-skipping transfers made in wills or revocable trusts no matter when they are made.

Tax Returns

It is the responsibility of the personal representative (the fiduciary) of the decedent's estate to file income tax returns for the estate and to pay any taxes owed out of estate assets. Depending on the situation, the representative may have to file some or all of the following returns:

- U.S. Individual Income Tax Return
- State Individual Income Tax Return
- U.S. Fiduciary Income Tax Return
- State Fiduciary Income Tax Return
- U.S. Estate Tax Return
- State Estate Tax Return
- State Inheritance Tax Return

Decedent's Final Income Tax Returns, Federal and State

The representative, also called the fiduciary, of the decedent's estate has the obligation to file all required income tax returns for the estate both federal and state. (I.R.C. § 6012[b], and Minn. Stat. Ann. § 290.37, 1[i] and [j] [West 1962]). The filing and payment of the income tax due must be completed within the time period determined by law, e.g., on or before the 15th day of the fourth month following the close of the taxable year in which the decedent died. Failure to do this

---

8. 1976 Tax Reform Act § 2006 adding I.R.C. §§ 2601, 2602, 2603, 2611, 2612, 2613, 2614, 2621, 2622, and amending I.R.C. §§ 691 and 2013.

may make the representative personally liable for any interest and penalties assessed.

The Internal Revenue Code § 6109 requires that an identification number be included on tax returns and other documents. On the decedent's final federal income tax return, this number is usually the decedent's Social Security number. This number is not used by the representative on the federal Fiduciary Income Tax Return. Instead, the number the representative uses is a separate identification number. To obtain this number, a Form SS–4 is completed and filed with the U.S. Internal Revenue Service Center for the district where the decedent lived (see Form 62 and instructions on back of the form).

Federal Individual Income Tax Return

The instructions for a 1983 final Form 1040, U.S. Individual Income Tax Return, list standard deductions called "zero bracket amounts" that apply to all individuals, whether single or married, regardless of income. The standard deduction or zero bracket amount for a single person and an unmarried head of a household amounts to $2,300. For married persons filing jointly, the zero bracket amount is $3,400. If a married person files separately, the deduction or amount is $1,700. These changes affect the income levels at which a person must file a tax return. There are exceptions, but in general a federal income tax return for 1983 must be filed for someone who is:

- Single and under age 65, earning at least $3,300 in 1983
- Single, over 65, and earning at least $4,300
- Married, filing jointly, both under 65, and earning at least $5,400
- Married, filing jointly, and one spouse is 65 or older, earning at least $6,400
- Married, both 65 or older, with a combined income of $7,400 or more
- A dependent who has dividends, interest, or other unearned income of $1,000 or more
- A widow or widower, under 65, earning at least $4,400 with a dependent child, or if 65 or older, earning at least $5,400
- Self-employed, with net earnings of at least $400

Examples of income that must be reported include income from self-employment, dividends, profits from partnerships, and interest on deposits, bonds or notes. Whenever the decedent during the year of his or her death earned income exceeding the amounts and under the circumstances described above, the decedent's personal representative must file the tax return (see Form 9). If income of the decedent was withheld during the past year for which a refund is due, the personal representative must file a Statement of Claimant to Refund Due—Deceased Taxpayer along with the federal income tax return (see Form 113).

When preparing the decedent's final federal income tax return, there are special considerations.

First, if the decedent is survived by a spouse, a joint return can be filed if the surviving spouse agrees and if the surviving spouse has not remarried before the close of the taxable year. A joint federal return includes the income of the decedent to the date of death and the income of the surviving spouse for the entire year. With a state return, it may be advisable to file separate returns. For the client's benefit, both federal and state tax returns should be computed separately and jointly to determine which method results in the lesser tax and whether prompt filing or requesting an extension would be more advantageous. If the decedent's final federal income tax return is filed as a separate return, it may be advantageous to file the return as soon as possible and to request early audits by the Internal Revenue Service. This prevents the discovery at some later date of a large unplanned tax deficiency. With a joint federal return, the proportion of the total tax due to be paid by each spouse is determined by the percentage of the total income each earned during the year.

Second, the Internal Revenue Code § 213(d) permits the representative to treat the decedent's medical expenses, which are paid from the estate within one year after death, as deductions on the income tax return for the year. If the representative decides on this election, a Medical Expenses Deduction Waiver must be filed, waiving the right to claim the medical expenses as an estate tax deduction (see I.R.C. § 2053) (see Form 1040, Schedules A & B, Itemized Deductions, in Appendix A as Form 117). The representative has the option of using the medical expenses either as a deduction for the final income tax return or as an expense of the decedent's last illness on the estate tax return. Generally, the choice should be made on the basis of which offers the greater tax saving, e.g., if the decedent's income was small for that year but he or she dies leaving a large estate, it would be more advantageous to use medical costs as an expense for estate tax purposes because this deduction will reduce the taxable estate. This election may not be available on a state return. Note: Beginning in 1983, only that part of medical and dental expenses that is more than 5% of the adjusted gross income may be deducted.

Third, on the decedent's final federal income tax return a personal exemption is allowed for each taxpayer. An additional exemption is allowed for persons who are or will attain age 65 by the close of the taxable year. Another exemption is allowed for legal blindness. The blindness exemption must be supported by a statement from an optometrist, ophthalmologist, or another licensed physician stating the extent of blindness.

Finally, income "in respect of the decedent" is the gross income that the decedent had a right to receive or could have received had he or she continued to live and should properly be included in the decedent's final return. The interest on stocks, bonds, income from sales of assets on an installment basis, and the like are examples of continuing income that should be included in the decedent's final return. For various reasons, certain income may be omitted from the decedent's final return, e.g., where the decedent's final return is filed before such income is received by the executor. Income "in respect of the decedent" which has been omitted from the decedent's final income tax return would then be included in the fiduciary's income tax return for the year in which the income is received. For example, if decedent had died in January 1983, interest on bonds received in July 1983 (which would have been omitted from decedent's final income tax return filed by April 15, 1983) would be included in the fiduciary's income tax return. Tax may be saved on certain bonds, e.g., U.S. Series E savings bonds, by electing not to pay the tax on the interest earned until they are cashed (I.R.C. § 454). If the decedent died in January 1983, he or she would probably have little income for the year 1983; therefore it may be a good idea to declare the interest income from all previous years on the decedent's final income tax return for 1983.

State Individual Income Tax Return

On the state level, a final individual income tax return is also required. The following states do *not* have a state income tax: Florida, Nevada, South Dakota, Connecticut, Texas, Washington, and Wyoming. In Minnesota, the representative of the estate of a decedent who was a resident, a non-resident, or a person who moved into or out of Minnesota during the year must file a return if the decedent earned enough income in Minnesota to require a filing (Minn. Stat. Ann. § 290.37 [West 1962]). A form called the Minnesota Individual Income Tax Return (Form M–1) is used for this purpose (see Form 10). The representative may also file a claim for a state refund on behalf of the decedent's estate if a refund is due (see Form 114).

Both the federal Form 1040 and Minnesota's M–1 form are due on or before the 15th day of April following the close of the decedent's tax year, unless that day falls on a weekend. These returns must include all the decedent's income from the first day of the taxable year until the date of death.[9] The opportunity to request an extension of time to file these final returns is allowed at both the federal and state levels.

Extensions for Federal and State Returns

An Application for Automatic Extension of Time to File U.S. Individual Income Tax Return (U.S. Treasury Form 4868; Form 115 in Appendix A) may be filed, *except* in cases where the Internal Revenue Service is requested to compute the tax, there is a court order to file the return by the original due date, or a six-month extension while traveling abroad has been given previously. This application must be filed on or before April 15 or the normal due date of the return.

---

9. The federal Individual Income Tax Return must be filed with the Internal Revenue Service Center for the district in which the decedent was domiciled at the date of death.

The extension of time for filing usually does *not* extend the time for payment of the tax due. With a payment equal to the estimated tax, the form is completed in duplicate, signed by the representative, and sent to the District Director of Internal Revenue. If the tax is not paid at this time, interest accrues from the regular due date of the return until the tax is paid. In addition, for each month the return is late, the law provides a 5% penalty of the tax due per month, not to exceed a maximum of 25%. If the taxpayer intends to request an extension to file both federal and state income tax returns, a copy of the federal automatic extension form (see Form 115) must accompany the *state* return when that return is filed.

If no federal extension to file the federal income tax return is made but a state income tax extension is requested, Minnesota residents may ask for the extension by filing Form M–522E, Application for Extension of Time to File Minnesota Income Tax Return—Other Than Corporation (Minn. Stat. Ann. § 290.45[2] [West 1962]) (see Form 116). As with the federal form, it must be submitted on or before the due date for filing the return. The form is filled out in duplicate and sent to the Minnesota Department of Revenue. No payment is required with this filing, but interest accrues at the rate of 11% per year on any tax due for the year from the regular due date of the return until the tax is paid.

Assignment 135

Find out how a taxpayer in your state seeks an extension of time to file the state income tax return. Is there a form? If so, what is it called and what is its number? Check your state statutory code and/or your state tax regulations on this. If an extension is permitted in your state, for how long and under what conditions can it be obtained? Is there an interest assessment? Any penalty?

Fiduciary's Income Tax Returns, Federal and State

Federal Fiduciary Income Tax Return

In addition to filing the decedent's final federal Individual Income Tax Return, the personal representative of the estate must also file the federal Fiduciary Income Tax Return (I.R.C. § 6012). This return includes accrued income and income earned after the decedent's death which is not included on the decedent's final individual income tax return. The representative is obligated to prepare and file such an income tax return for the estate for the period from the date of the decedent's death to the date of final distribution. Any tax due the federal government for that time period must be paid by the representative out of estate assets.

Within a statutory number of days of one's appointment (e.g., 30 days), the representative must file a Notice of Fiduciary Relationship with the Internal Revenue Service (I.R.C. § 6903) (see Form 64). Accompanying the form must be satisfactory evidence that the personal representative has the authority to act as a fiduciary, such as a certified copy of the court order appointing the representative.

Form 1041, U.S. Fiduciary Income Tax Return (see Form 11) must be filed for all domestic decedent estates with gross income for the taxable year of $600 or more, or for estates that have a beneficiary who is a non-resident alien; and for some domestic trusts (I.R.C. § 6012). The return must be filed on or before the 15th day of the fourth month following the close of the taxable year of the estate or trust. The forms are sent to the address listed for the state where the fiduciary resides in the instructions for filing Form 1041. If an extension of time is needed, the representative can file an Application for Extension of Time to File U.S. Fiduciary or Partnership Return (see Form 118). Once the tax payment is due, interest will accrue on the tax due from the due date until total payment is made. Prior to distribution of the estate assets, the fiduciary pays the tax on income earned; after distribution, the successors (heirs or devisees) pay tax on income earned from assets that were distributed to them.

Example: Jean Carlton died on February 3, 1983. Stocks that Jean owned earned dividends of $5,000 between the date of Jean's death and October 19, 1983, the date of distribution of estate assets to heirs and devisees. The $5,000 will be included in the federal fiduciary income tax return. All dividends earned by the stock after October 19, 1983 will be income of the heirs or devisees to whom the stocks were distributed. For instance, if the stock was distributed to Karen and earned $2,000 in dividends from October 19, 1983, through December 31, 1983, Karen would report the $2,000 on her own income tax return for the year 1983, which she will file on or before April 15, 1984.

When the federal return is filed, a copy of the will, if any, must be filed with it if the gross income of the estate is $5,000 or more for any taxable year (Reg. § 1.6012–3[a][2]). In cases that require a copy of the will, the personal representative must attach to the copy a written declaration that it is a true and complete copy, and include a statement that the will, in the representative's opinion, determines the extent to which the income of the estate is taxable to the estate and the beneficiaries, respectively.

State Fiduciary Income Tax Return

On the state level, using Minnesota as an example, the representative of every estate must file a Form M–2, Minnesota Fiduciary Income Tax Return (see Form 12) if the taxable net income of the decedent's estate exceeds the fiduciary credit allowed, i.e., if the value of the estate's gross income for the year is $2,550 or more. The return covers the period from the date of the decedent's death to the close of the taxable year.

Important considerations for fiduciary income taxes are determination of distributable net income, distribution deductions, the character of distributed income, simple or complex trusts, and the like. If the decedent reported the sale of certain assets on the installment basis when living, this installment reporting continues not only after the decedent's death on the fiduciary income tax return but also after the distribution of the property to the successors on the successors' returns.

As with the federal form, the state fiduciary income tax return is due on or before the 15th day of the fourth month following the close of the taxable year of the estate or trust for the period from the date of the decedent's death to the date of final distribution. The return is submitted to the state fiduciary income tax division at the State Department of Revenue. Some states require that a copy of the will be filed with their state returns in all cases, in addition to a statement similar to that required by the federal government.

Assignment 136

1. Whose obligation is it to complete and file income tax returns for a decedent's estate in your state?

2. How much interest, if any, is charged in your state for filing a late income tax return? Are there any penalties? Who is liable for interest and penalties in your state?

3. What constitutes sufficient income to require filing of a decedent's final income tax and fiduciary income tax returns—state and federal?

4. What are the conditions under which a joint tax return can be filed by the surviving spouse?

5. Describe the content and purposes of the federal Fiduciary Income Tax Return. Where is this explained in the Internal Revenue Code?

Assignment 137

John Jones died in June. Following his death, his representative received checks from the A & M Mining Co. ($350), Bester Power & Light ($50), Social Security ($400), and Pronot Can Co. ($100). Will the representative have to file a federal Fiduciary Income Tax Return? Assume that the estate earned no other income after John's death.

U.S. (Federal) Estate Tax Return

U.S. Treasury Form 706, U.S. Estate Tax Return (Form 119 in Appendix A) must be filed within nine months of the decedent's death for the estate of every citizen or resident of the United States whose gross estate on the date of the person's death is greater than the amounts shown in the table below:

Death During	Gross Estate
1982	$225,000 +
1983	$275,000 +
1984	$325,000 +
1985	$400,000 +
1986	$500,000 +
1987 and thereafter	$600,000 +

The federal government imposes a tax on the total value of a decedent's estate, i.e., the value of all property, real or personal, tangible or intangible, wherever situated, to the extent of the decedent's interest therein at the time of death. (I.R.C. §§ 2031, 2033.) However, any personalty,[10] that a surviving spouse claims belongs to said spouse is not included in the deceased person's total estate for estate tax purposes if such a claim can be reasonably supported. The value of the decedent's property transferred under circumstances subject to the tax is called the *gross estate*.

Determining the Gross Estate

The gross estate includes all assets owned by the decedent at death and the value of any interest the decedent held in any property, e.g., the entire interest in a home less the mortgage balance. The gross estate will also include lifetime gifts of property in which the decedent retained "incidents of ownership" (see page 32).

For estate tax purposes, the property owned by a decedent which is included in the gross estate is valued in one of two ways. The assets may be valued on the basis of their fair market value on the date of the decedent's death. This date-of-death rule is established by statute. (I.R.C. § 2031.) Or the representative of the decedent's estate may elect an *alternate valuation date* in order to determine the fair market value of decedent's property. (I.R.C. § 2032.) (But note, that while the alternate valuation date is allowed for federal estate tax purposes, it is usually not allowed for a state's inheritance tax calculations.) The purpose of the alternate valuation date is to prevent an unreasonable tax liability on the decedent's estate whenever, shortly after decedent's death, the value of this property takes a drastic plunge. For example, if the decedent owned a large number of shares of stock and the stock's value on the market decreased substantially shortly after death, the estate could have an enormous tax burden if the property was valued at the date of death for estate tax purposes. Therefore the I.R.C. provides that property included in the gross estate which has not been distribut-

---

10. Personalty is any property that is not real property, e.g., household furnishings, stocks and bonds, an automobile.

ed, disposed of, sold, or exchanged as of the alternate valuation date, a date six months after the decedent's death, may be valued as of that date if the representative so elects instead of assigning the value that prevailed at the date of death (I.R.C. § 2032). The election of the alternate evaluation date by the representative on the decedent's estate tax return must be made during the statutory time period allotted for filing such a return, e.g., nine months after the date of the decedent's death unless an extension of time has been properly requested and granted; otherwise the right to the election is lost.

Example: Ben died on July 2, 1983. On that date, 100 shares of stock which he owned in Benville Mining Company was valued at $10,000. Six months later, the value of the stock had dropped to $7,500 (a $2,500 loss). In determining the value of Ben's gross estate, the personal representative has the option of assigning the value to the stock (and all other estate assets) which prevailed on July 2, 1983, i.e., the stock would be valued at $10,000; or assigning the value to the stock (and all other estate assets) which prevailed on January 2, 1984, six months after Ben's death, i.e., the stock would be valued at $7,500.

In the example above, assuming the value of other estate assets had not increased sufficiently to offset the $2,500 loss on the stock, it would be advantageous to the estate to choose the alternate valuation date. Because the gross estate would therefore be reduced by $2,500, no estate tax would be paid on that amount.

The problem of taxing the proceeds from life insurance policies is also resolved by the I.R.C. Obviously, if the decedent's estate or executor is the named beneficiary of the life insurance policy, the proceeds of the policy are part of the decedent's gross estate for tax purposes. Under I.R.C. § 2042, the gross estate will also include the proceeds of all life insurance policies payable to all other beneficiaries in which the decedent possessed at his or her death any of the "incidents of ownership," as defined by the I.R.C. "Incidents of ownership" refers to the right of the insured (decedent) or the estate to the economic benefits of the policy. Therefore, it includes the right to change the beneficiary.

These assets comprising the decedent's gross estate and other items affecting the amount of tax owed must be listed in separate sections, called schedules, and identified as Schedules A through Q in the U.S. Estate Tax Return. The schedules require careful preparation and must include values and claims, e.g., debts owed by decedent to creditors, substantiated by documents and affidavits. Some of the basic data to be included on each schedule are shown in Exhibit 15.5. For more complete information on the individual schedules, see instructions for Form 706, U.S. Estate Tax Return, printed each year by the Internal Revenue Service.

Exhibit 15.6 shows a gross estate as an example of some of the kinds of property found in Schedules A through I.

According to common law dower or curtesy rights or their statutory substitutes, a surviving spouse is entitled to receive a percentage of the value of the gross estate. By will, the decedent may leave a greater

Exhibit 15.5 Basic Data for Schedules A–Q in U.S. Estate Tax Return

Schedule A—Real Estate

Regardless of its location, all interest in real property (except a joint tenancy interest) owned by the decedent at the time of death must be listed in Schedule A. This includes all land, buildings, fixtures attached to the real estate, growing crops, and mineral rights. An interest in real property that terminates on the decedent's death, such as a life estate, is not included. Property owned in joint tenancy is not included in Schedule A but is listed in Schedule E.

Schedule B—Stocks and Bonds

All stocks and bonds owned by the decedent are listed in Schedule B. The name of the corporation, the number of shares, the class of shares (common or preferred), and the par value, if any, are some of the data listed in reference to stocks. The principal stock exchange on which the stock is listed and traded should be given. For unlisted stock, the state and date of incorporation and the location of the principal place of business must be given.

The data on bonds must include the number held, the principal amount, the name of the obligor, the date of maturity, the rate of interest, the dates on which interest is payable, the series number if more than one issue, and the principal exchange on which the bonds are listed. Also, interest accrued on bonds to the date of the decedent's death must be shown.

Schedule C—Mortgages, Notes, and Cash

Information on Schedule C should include:

- Mortgages owned by the decedent (original face value and unpaid balance, date of mortgage, date of maturity, name of maker, property mortgaged, interest dates, and rate of interest)
- Promissory notes owned by the decedent
- Contracts to sell land (description of interest owned by the decedent, name of buyer, date of contract, description of property, sale price, initial payment, amounts of installment payments, unpaid balance of principal and accrued interest, interest rate, last date to which interest has been paid, and termination date of the contract)
- Cash and its location, whether in possession of the decedent, bank, other person, safe deposit box, etc.
- All bank accounts except accounts in joint tenancy (name and address of depositor, amount on deposit, whether checking, savings, or time deposit account, rate of interest, and amount of interest accrued and payable).

Schedule D—Insurance on Decedent's Life

Included in Schedule D are proceeds of insurance on the decedent's life received or receivable by or for the benefit of the decedent's estate or representative; insurance on the decedent's life receivable by any other beneficiary if the decedent at death possessed any incidents of ownership in the policy (see page 32); benefits received under fraternal benefit societies operating under a lodge system, group insurance, accidental death benefits, double indemnity, provisions of life insurance, and war risk insurance, but not annuities (annuities are included in Schedule I).

Schedule E—Jointly Owned Property

Schedule E includes the value of any interest in property held by the decedent and any other person in joint tenancy. The full value of jointly owned property must be included in decedent's gross estate, except where a surviving joint tenant can prove

Exhibit 15.5 *(continued)*

he or she provided all or a portion of the consideration for the property or that the property or a fractional share therein was acquired by gift, bequest, devise or inheritance.

Schedule F—Miscellaneous Property

Schedule F is a catch-all schedule for probate assets owned by the decedent but not reportable in other schedules. It includes debts due the decedent, interests in business (sole proprietorship or partnership), patents and royalties, insurance on the life of another, household goods and personal effects, farm products and crops that have been severed from the land, and numerous other items.

Schedule G—Transfers During Decedent's Life

Transfers made by the decedent during life, by trust or otherwise, except for bona fide sales for an adequate and full consideration in money or money's worth, are subject to tax and are included in Schedule G.

Schedule H—Powers of Appointment

Included in the gross estate under Schedule H is the value of certain property with respect to which the decedent possessed a general power of appointment at the time of death (page 150) or once possessed a general power of appointment and exercised or released that power prior to death.

Schedule I—Annuities

Annuities (periodic payments for a specified period of time) are included in Schedule I. These include annuities or other payments receivable by any beneficiary by reason of surviving the decedent under any form of contract or agreement (other than life insurance) entered into after March 3, 1931. The amount to be included is only that portion of the value of the annuity receivable by the surviving beneficiary which the decedent's contribution to the purchase price of the annuity or agreement bears to the total purchase price.

Schedule J—Funeral Expenses and Expenses Incurred in Administering Property Subject to Claims

All deductible funeral expenses are included in Schedule J. Funeral expenses must be reasonable, as judged by the size of the decedent's estate. Other deductible expenses are the personal representative's commission, attorney's fees, and miscellaneous administration expenses.

Schedule K—Debts of Decedent and Mortgages and Liens

Under Schedule K, only valid debts owed by the decedent at the time of death can be included. Any debt that is disputed or the subject of litigation cannot be deducted unless the estate concedes it to be a valid claim. Property tax deductions are limited to taxes that accrued prior to the date of the decedent's death. Federal taxes on income during the decedent's lifetime are deductible, but taxes on income received after death are not deductible. Notes unsecured by a mortgage or another lien are also included in this schedule. "Mortgages and liens" are those obligations secured on property which are included in the gross estate at the full values and are deductible only to the extent that the liability was contracted for an adequate and full consideration in money or money's worth.

Exhibit 15.5 *(continued)*

Schedule L—Net Losses During Administration and Expenses Incurred in Administering Property Not Subject to Claims

Included in Schedule L are losses limited strictly to those that occur during the settlement of the estate from fire, storm, shipwreck, or other casualty, or from theft to the extent that such losses are not compensated for by insurance or otherwise. Expenses incurred in administering property not subject to claims are usually expenses resulting from the administration of trusts established by the decedent before death or the collection of other assets or the clearance of title to other property included in the decedent's gross estate for estate tax purposes but not included in the decedent's probate estate.

Schedule M—Bequests, etc., to Surviving Spouse (Marital Deduction)

Schedule M lists any property that passes to the surviving spouse. The marital deduction is authorized for certain property interests passing from decedent to the surviving spouse. It includes property interests that are part of the decedent's gross estate. The deduction is generally not available if the gross estate consists exclusively of the decedent's interest in property held by the decedent and surviving spouse under community property laws (see page 452 on the marital deduction).

Schedule N—Section 2032A Valuation

Included in Schedule N are the names of the parties who received any interest in specially valued property. With respect to qualified real property interests that are included in the decedent's gross estate, the executor of the estate may elect to value the real property, e.g., farm or property used in a closely held business, on the basis of its actual use rather than on its market value. The total decrease in the value of such property for the estate of a person who dies after 1982 is limited to $750,000.

Schedule O—Charitable, Public, and Similar Gifts and Bequests

Included in Schedule O are charitable transfers made by will or other written instruments.

Schedule P—Credit for Foreign Death Taxes

Schedule P includes credit for foreign death taxes, which is allowable only in case the decedent was a citizen or resident of the United States. In some cases, non-citizens who are residents may claim credit if the President has issued a proclamation granting the credit to citizens of a foreign country of which the resident was a citizen and if that country allows a similar credit to decedents who were citizens of the United States residing in that country.

Schedule Q—Credit for Tax on Prior Transfers

Included in Schedule Q is property received by the transferee (the decedent) from a transferor who died within ten years before or two years after the decedent (see discussion on page 459). Credit is allowable for all or a part of the federal estate tax paid by the transferor's estate with respect to the transfer as long as the specified period of time has not elapsed. Where the transferee was the transferor's surviving spouse, no credit is given to the extent that a marital deduction was allowed the transferor's estate. Also, no credit is authorized for federal gift taxes paid in connection with the transfer of the property to the transferee.

Exhibit 15.6 Sample Gross Estate

1.	Home	$ 40,000
	Household furniture	10,000
	IT&T Stocks	50,000
2.	Joint tenancy in an apartment building which, when established, was not subject to a gift tax. One-half of the value is included in decedent's gross estate.	$150,000
3.	100 shares of Nelson Manufacturing Co. stock. Decedent devised the income (dividends) from the stock to his son for life, the stock itself to be transferred to the decedent's daughter upon his son's death.	$ 25,000
4.	*Office building* Decedent had placed the building in a trust for his niece—the income to be paid to himself for ten years, then the building to be transferred to the niece. The decedent, however, had retained the right to change the beneficiary of the trust and to revoke it.	$100,000
5.	*Cash gift* * Decedent made a gift of $20,000 to a friend two years prior to decedent's death.	$ 20,000
6.	*Annuity* Decedent made deductible payments of $1,500 each for five years to an individual retirement account. In addition, nondeductible payments of $1,000 each for five years were made. The surviving spouse is eligible to receive the benefits of this account as an annuity having a value of $18,000. The amount of the annuity to be included is arrived at as follows:	$ 7,200

$$\frac{\text{Non-deductible payments}}{\text{Total payments}} \quad \frac{1{,}000 \times 5}{2{,}500 \times 5} = \frac{5{,}000}{12{,}500} = 40\% \text{ of } 18{,}000 = 7{,}200$$

7.	Sam established a trust in which he placed $100,000 worth of various stocks. The trust named the decedent the trustee and gave the decedent a general power of appointment over the trust income and the trust property.	$100,000
8.	Accumulated, undistributed income from trust.	10,000
9.	Life insurance policy naming the executor as beneficiary.	$ 10,000
10.	Life insurance policy naming the estate as beneficiary.	5,000
	TOTAL ASSETS (gross estate)	$527,200

* The Economic Recovery Tax Act of 1981 reverses the policy of the 1976 law, which required that all gifts made within three years of the date of death be included in the decedent's gross estate. This change in the law applies to all estates of decedents who died on or after January 1, 1982.

portion of the estate to the surviving spouse, but the decedent cannot defeat the common law or statutory share to which the spouse is entitled.

Determining the Taxable Estate

After all the decedent's property subject to the federal estate tax has been determined, the various exemptions, deductions, and claims allowed by statute are subtracted from the gross estate to determine the *taxable estate,* which is the estate on which the tax is imposed (see I.R.C. § 2051 and pages 415–420). The estate tax is computed using the Unified Rate Schedule (Table 15.3), and the unified credit is subtracted to obtain the *gross tax due.* Any additional credits allowed against the tax are then subtracted from the gross tax, and the difference is the final *net tax due.*

In determining the taxable estate and computing the tax, the deductions, claims, and credits allowed by statute include:

- Specific deductible items (expenses, liens, encumbrances, debts, and taxes)
- Losses during the handling of the estate
- Marital deduction
- Charitable deductions
- Unified credit (and other allowable credits, e.g., foreign death taxes)

These deductions, excluding the marital deduction and unified credit, generally average from 5% to 10% of the gross estate. Of course, the liabilities of the decedent must also be determined before taxing the remaining assets.

Deductible Items I.R.C. § 2053 gives deductible expenses and liabilities. The expenses that are deductible from the gross estate include funeral and administration expenses. If administration expenses are used as a deduction on the federal estate tax return, they cannot be used again as a deduction on the federal income tax return. The same is true of medical expenses for the last illness. Examples of proper administration expenses are a representative's compensation, attorney's fees, and such miscellaneous items as court costs, surrogate's (judge's) fees, accountant's fees, appraiser's fees, storing costs, and other expenses necessary for preserving and distributing the assets of the estate. The rule regarding funeral expenses is that "a reasonable amount may be spent." What is reasonable must be considered in light of the size of the estate and the amount of indebtedness. Objections usually come from other successors, not from the Internal Revenue Service. If one successor spends too much out of the residuary estate for funeral or other expenses, other successors can object. If the court determines that such expenditure was unreasonable, it may order the spender to reimburse the estate. When the estate is small after obligations are paid, the court is concerned that enough will be left to support the family and will not allow excessive funeral expenses.

Expenses incurred by the decedent for estate planning, including fees paid to the estate planner (attorney or other adviser) regarding tax matters, investment, and setting up a revocable funded living trust, are deductible. Fees incurred for planning for disposition of property by will or inter vivos gift are among the expenses that are not deductible.

The lifetime debts of the decedent are proper deductions. Debts incurred after death as part of the administration of the estate are not deductible as debts of the decedent, but they may be deductible as administration expenses. All allowed debts, including unpaid mortgages, are proper deductions.

The deduction for taxes is limited to taxes that accrued against the decedent while alive. It does not extend to taxes accruing after death. Thus, the final federal income tax paid by the representative for the decedent's own income is deductible, but, the income tax on the estate's income is not. Federal estate and state inheritance taxes paid for the privilege of transferring the estate are not deductible. Certain credits, however, are allowed for state and foreign death taxes which must be paid (see below).

Losses   The next deduction subtracted from the gross estate is for losses sustained during the administration of the decedent's estate (see I.R.C. § 2054). Such losses do not include the lessening of the value of assets of the estate, e.g., a drop in the value of stock or the loss in the sale of some property. Losses that are deductible are theft and casualty losses that occur during the administration of the estate. Casualty losses include losses due to fires, storms, shipwrecks, and the like. When such losses are recovered from insurance policies or from a suit for damages, they are not deductible. In addition, if the casualty or theft loss has already been deducted from the decedent's or the estate's income tax, such losses cannot be deducted from the gross estate for tax purposes.

When the above expenses, losses, and debts have been subtracted from the gross estate, what remains is the figure called the *adjusted gross estate* (I.R.C. § 2056[c]2).

Marital Deduction   The next and potentially most valuable deduction, the marital deduction, is then calculated. The marital deduction was first enacted into federal law in 1948 and amended in 1976 by the Tax Reform Act and in 1981 by the Economic Recovery Tax Act (ERTA). In effect, the current statute gives each spouse the right to leave to the surviving spouse an unlimited amount of the decedent spouse's estate free from estate tax.

For example, suppose a decedent's gross estate is $1,000,000. The total amount of deductions allowed for expenses, liens, debts, taxes, and losses is $300,000. The decedent has left $100,000 to various charitable organizations, with the balance of the estate going to the decedent's surviving spouse. The *adjusted gross estate* is the gross estate minus the deductions for expenses, encumbrances, indebtedness, taxes, estate-planning expenses, and losses previously mentioned. Therefore, the adjusted gross estate in our example is $1,000,000 less the $300,000—or $700,000. Note that the charitable deduction is not involved in determining the adjusted gross estate. It is a proper deduction in determining the *taxable estate,* but it is deducted only after the amount of the marital deduction has been determined and deducted.

The marital deduction allowed in this illustration would then be $700,000, since the decedent has left the entire estate to his or her spouse. If a decedent had left the surviving spouse less than $700,000, e.g., had given the spouse $400,000, the amount of the marital deduction would be limited to the amount passing to the spouse outright, the $400,000.

Note that in every state a surviving spouse is entitled to common law dower or curtesy rights, or statutory rights in lieu thereof. If a decedent devises less to the surviving spouse than the amount to which he or she is entitled under applicable state law, the spouse may elect to receive the amount to which he or she is entitled under the above rights (usually the larger amount). The amount received by the spouse pursuant to such election then becomes the amount of the marital deduction up to the statutory maximum.

The marital deduction applies to either the husband's estate or the wife's estate when one dies and the other spouse survives. Because of its tax-saving advantages, the marital deduction is an important tax consideration in estate planning. However, indiscriminate use of the marital deduction without regard for other methods of disposition, such as successive estates to avoid a second tax upon the death of the surviving spouse, may actually increase rather than decrease the tax liability of the two estates. Such overuse of the marital deduction may needlessly subject too much property to taxation when the surviving spouse dies. Thus, when one spouse considers giving property to the other spouse in order to qualify for the marital deduction, the donor spouse faces the dilemma of choosing between this method of possible tax saving to his or her estate or choosing successive estates, which do not qualify for the marital deduction but would not incur a second tax at the surviving spouse's death, as in the case of the marital deduction. **Example:** Suppose a husband has an adjusted gross estate valued at $1,200,000. Assuming he dies in 1987, having made no taxable lifetime gifts, he could leave his entire estate to his wife outright and, with the unlimited marital deduction, no tax would be due from his estate upon his death. However, his wife now has the entire estate, and assuming her adjusted gross estate totals the same $1,200,000 at her death, her estate is taxed on the entire $1,200,000. The tax is $427,800 less the $192,800 unified credit, or $235,000.

From a tax-saving viewpoint, it is more economical for the husband to leave $600,000 of his estate to his wife outright or in a so-called "marital trust." This trust could provide for investment advice or management protection, but it makes the property available to the spouse (wife) on her request. The other $600,000 is placed in a "family" or non-marital trust, with all income from the trust payable to the spouse (wife) for her lifetime; the remainder goes to their children at the death of the wife. Using this method, there is no tax on the husband's estate at his death because of the marital deduction and the unified credit. There is also no estate tax on the wife's estate at her death because the $600,000 in the family trust in which she has only a life estate is not taxable to her estate on her death. It passes free of tax to the remaindermen (the children). Her taxable estate, therefore, is only the $600,000 from the marital deduction trust on which the tax is $192,800, from which the $192,800 unified credit will be subtracted, leaving a tax payable of zero. The tax saving (to the wife's estate) which results from using the second method rather than the first is $235,000.

Therefore, a principal means of reducing the tax impact is the creation of two testamentary trusts when there is a surviving spouse. It is very important in this case to follow the requirements laid out in the Internal Revenue Code. For example, assuming the *wife* is the decedent, her estate may be divided into two testamentary trusts. One trust is called the "marital deduction trust" (Trust A), representing an amount equal to half the adjusted gross estate, which the husband receives tax-free, as previously discussed. The husband has the right to use the income from this trust (and as much of the principal as he desires, if this provision is included in the trust instrument), and he can dispose of Trust A property at his death according to his own wishes. Only the property the husband disposes of at his death is taxable against his estate, i.e., the value of his adjusted gross estate. The husband's estate will be entitled to subtract the available unified credit from the tax payable. None of the property in Trust A is taxable against his deceased wife's estate.

The second half of the decedent wife's estate is put into a second trust (Trust B). Trustees will pay to the surviving spouse, the husband in this case, the income from this trust for his life and as much of the principal as they in their discretion deem necessary. Upon the death of the widower, the balance of the property remaining in Trust B goes to the children or other named beneficiaries. Therefore, the property in Trust B is not subject to estate tax when the widower dies (I.R.C. § 2033). However, Trust B property may be subject to the estate tax upon the death of the decedent wife. The wife's estate is entitled to subtract the available unified credit for the year of her death from the tax payable.

To avoid subjecting Trust A property to estate tax upon the death of the decedent wife, the surviving husband, in addition to being entitled to all the income from the trust, must be given a general power of appointment over the assets of this trust, including the right to direct how and to whom the property in Trust A is to be distributed during his lifetime and after his death through his will. The income from Trust A is distributed at least annually to the widower. Trust B is responsible for all debts, taxes, and expenses of the decedent wife's estate. All the income and as much of the principal of Trust B as the trustees deem necessary go to the widower during his life, the remainder to their children upon his death.

In this way, only that portion of the decedent wife's estate which is placed in Trust B (i.e. one-half) is subject to tax at her death, and only the amount still remaining of that portion of her estate which is placed in Trust A is taxed at the subsequent death of the widower. A substantial tax saving is therefore possible. Other factors, such as the value of the surviving husband's property prior to the wife's death, may limit the tax advantages of the "marital deduction trust" (see sample trust provisions and explanations, pages 288–292).

Concerning the use of such testamentary trusts to reduce taxes owed, there are two concerns. First, the ERTA, which established the unlimited marital deduction, does not allow wills drawn before September 1981 to qualify the decedent's estate for the new deduction. In such earlier wills, the estate's marital deduction follows the 1976 (TRA) law, which limited the marital deduction to the greater of $250,000 or half the decedent's adjusted gross estate. Therefore, a review of wills drawn before September 1981 is essential for sound estate planning.

Second, many spouses were reluctant to take advantage of the marital deduction because they did not want to give their spouses the general power of appointment that allowed the surviving spouse to determine to whom the trust property would be given on that spouse's death. They wanted to be sure that the assets acquired during their first marriage eventually went to the children of that marriage. Granting a general power of appointment made property eligible for the marital deduction tax advantages, but it also created the problem of inheritance to the children if for example, the surviving spouse remarried. The ERTA resolved this problem with the creation of the "qualified terminal interest property" (QTIP) and its QTIP trust. This trust allows property to qualify for the marital deduction *and* ensures the right of the children to receive the assets when the second spouse (and parent) dies. The requirements for property with its "qualifying income interest" to be used in a QTIP trust are discussed on page 421 and must be reviewed. The essential difference between the standard marital deduction trust with the power of appointment and the QTIP trust is the executor's election on the decedent spouse's estate tax return to specifically elect QTIP status for that trust. In other words, in our example above, the QTIP trust, like Trust B, would give income to the husband for life, then the remainder to their children, but the husband has no power to dispose of the principal at his death. The executor would elect to have this trust become a QTIP trust, and the property would then be transferred to the children when the husband (father) dies. The one disadvantage is that the executor's election causes the QTIP trust property to be taxed in the second spouse's (the husband's in our case) estate when he dies even though he does not get the property or have the right to determine to whom it will go.

The following three methods of disposing of one testatrix's estate at death make it possible to compare the different tax consequences. The facts in this hypothetical case are: Alyssa dies on March 4, 1982, leaving an adjusted gross estate of $600,000. She was married to Clarence, who survived her, and the couple had two children. Clarence dies in an accident on December 28, 1982. Assume that neither Alyssa nor Clarence had made any taxable lifetime gifts and that the *only* allowable credit is the unified credit.[11]

Method 1: Alyssa left the entire adjusted gross estate, $600,000, to Clarence outright. Because of the unlimited marital deduction, the

---

11. Disregard the credit for tax on prior transfers for these examples (see discussion on page 420).

estate tax payable at Alyssa's death is zero. The estate tax payable at Clarence's death (on $600,000 adjusted gross estate) is $130,000—a total tax of $130,000 on the two estates (see Unified Rate Schedule, Table 15.3).

On Alyssa's death	
$600,000 passes to Clarence tax free because of the marital deduction	No Tax
Tax payable on Alyssa's adjusted gross estate	$ 0
On Clarence's death	
Tax on $600,000	$192,800
Unified Credit for 1982	62,800
Tax payable on Clarence's adjusted gross estate	$130,000
Tax payable on Alyssa's death	$ 0
Tax payable on Clarence's death	$130,000
Total tax payable on two estates	$130,000

Note that if Clarence had lived until 1987, the unified credit would have increased to $192,800 and the tax payable on his death in that year would be zero.

Method 2: Alyssa left $300,000 outright to Clarence, which passes tax free because of the marital deduction. She placed $300,000 in trust with the income to be paid to Clarence for his life and the remainder over to the couple's two children on Clarence's death. "Remainder over" means that the trust property is distributed in equal shares to the two children on Clarence's death. The $300,000 in trust is not taxed to Clarence's estate at his death, because a life estate by definition ends upon the death of the life beneficiary and therefore is not taxable to the life beneficiary's estate (I.R.C. § 2033). There is a tax payable of $25,000 at Alyssa's death. There is a tax payable of $25,000 on Clarence's death.

On Alyssa's death	
$300,000 passes to Clarence tax free because of the marital deduction	No Tax
Tax on $300,000 placed in trust with income for life to Clarence and remainder over to children on Clarence's death	$ 87,800
Unified credit for 1982	62,800
Tax payable on $300,000 remaining of Alyssa's adjusted gross estate (taxable estate less amount of marital deduction)	$ 25,000
On Clarence's death	
$300,000 in trust distributed to children	No Tax
Tax on $300,000 (Clarence's adjusted gross estate)	$ 87,800
Unified credit for 1982	62,800
Tax payable on Clarence's adjusted gross estate	$ 25,000
Tax payable on Alyssa's death	$ 25,000
Tax payable on Clarence's death	$ 25,000
Total tax payable on two estates	$ 50,000

Method 3: Alyssa left $225,000 to Clarence outright, which passes free of tax because of the marital deduction. She placed $375,000 in trust with the income to be paid to Clarence for his life and the remainder over to the two children at Clarence's death. The $375,000 in trust is not taxed to Clarence's estate at his death (see Method 2 for explanation). No tax is due on Clarence's adjusted gross estate ($225,000) at his death because the amount of the tax is wiped out by the $62,800 unified credit. The tax payable on Alyssa's estate at her death is $50,500.

On Alyssa's death	
$225,000 passes tax free to Clarence because of the marital deduction	No Tax
$375,000 placed in trust with income for life to Clarence and remainder over to children on Clarence's death	$113,300
Unified credit for 1982	62,800
Tax payable on $375,000 remaining of Alyssa's adjusted gross estate (taxable estate less amount of marital deduction)	$ 50,500
On Clarence's death	
$375,000 in trust distributed to children	No Tax
Tax on $225,000 (Clarence's adjusted gross estate)	$ 62,800
Unified credit for 1982	$ 62,800
Tax payable on Clarence's adjusted gross estate	0
Tax payable on Alyssa's death	$ 50,500
Tax payable on Clarence's death	0
Total tax payable on two estates	$ 50,500

It is extremely unlikely that Clarence's adjusted gross estate would neither increase nor decrease during his life and after the death of Alyssa. The same is true of the value of the trust property. In order to simplify the computations, however, we have allowed these amounts to remain stable.

In Method 1, the total tax on the two estates was $130,000. In Method 2, the total tax was only $50,000, a tax saving over the first method of $80,000. In Method 3, the total tax was $50,500, a tax saving of $79,500 over the first method. However, the tax was $500 more than the second method.[12] Obviously, skilled estate planning is very important.

In the above example, the income from the trust paid to Clarence during his life would be subject to payment of *income tax* by Clarence.

The amounts left to the surviving spouse outright in the three methods could also have been placed in a trust for the surviving spouse pursuant to the rules described on page 453, in which case the tax consequences would have been the same as if such amounts had been

---

12. Depending on the year of the second spouse's (Clarence's) death in our examples, the credit for tax on prior transfers would affect the amount of tax payable under Method 2 (see discussion page 420).

devised outright (i.e., not in trust).   An example of a "marital deduction trust" is in Appendix B.

Charitable Deductions   The final federal estate tax deduction allowed by statute is the charitable deduction (see I.R.C. § 2055).   After the adjusted gross estate has been computed, the marital deduction and charitable deductions are subtracted to arrive at the net taxable estate. The charitable deduction includes any transfer of estate assets for public, charitable, and religious purposes.   There are no limits on the charitable deduction except that it cannot exceed the value of the transferred property required to be included in the gross estate (I.R.C. § 2055[d]).   If all assets of the decedent are left to charity and do not exceed the limits of the statute, the entire transfer is non-taxable.   The kinds of transfers that qualify for the charitable deduction are described in I.R.C. § 2055 and include:

(a) *In general.*—For purposes of the tax imposed by section 2001, the value of the taxable estate shall be determined by deducting from the value of the gross estate the amount of all bequests, legacies, devises, or transfers.—

(1)   to or for the use of the United States, any State, any political subdivision thereof, or the District of Columbia, for exclusively public purposes;
(2)   to or for the use of any corporation organized and operated exclusively for religious, charitable, scientific, literary, or educational purposes, including the encouragement of art, or to foster national or international amateur sports competition (but only if no part of its activities involve the provision of athletic facilities or equipment), and the prevention of cruelty to children or animals, no part of the net earnings of which inures to the benefit of any private stockholder or individual, which is not disqualified for tax exemption under section 501(c)(3) by reason of attempting to influence legislation, and which does not participate in, or intervene in (including the publishing or distributing of statements), any political campaign on behalf of any candidate for public office;
(3)   to a trustee or trustees, or a fraternal society, order, or association operating under the lodge system, but only if such contributions or gifts are to be used by such trustee or trustees, or by such fraternal society, order, or association, exclusively for religious, charitable, scientific, literary, or educational purposes, or for the prevention of cruelty to children or animals, such trust, fraternal society, order, or association would not be disqualified for tax exemption under section 501(c)(3) by reason of attempting to influence legislation, and such trustee or trustees, or such fraternal society, order, or association, does not participate in, or intervene in (including the publishing or distributing of statements), any political campaign on behalf of any candidate for public office; or
(4)   to or for the use of any veterans' organization incorporated by Act of Congress, or of its departments or local chapters or posts, no part of the net earnings of which inures to the benefit of any private shareholder or individual.
For purposes of this subsection, the complete termination before the date prescribed for the filing of the estate tax return of a power to consume, invade, or appropriate property for the benefit of an individual before such power has been exercised by reason of the death of such individual or for any other reason shall be considered and deemed to be a qualified disclaimer

with the same full force and effect as though he had filed such qualified disclaimer.

Since charities may have similar names, it is important that the charity be designated in the will or trust by its full and correct name. It is also possible that another charity may have the same name. It is wise to consider this possibility and make sure the charity is properly identified to prevent later conflicts. The testator or testatrix may limit the use of the gift if he or she wishes. Gifts made to individuals are not deductible under the charitable deduction provision.

After the marital and charitable deductions are subtracted from the adjusted gross estate, the tax is computed using the appropriate rate from the Unified Rate Schedule (Table 15.3) (I.R.C. § 2001). Then the available (unused) unified credit (and other allowable credits, if any) are subtracted from the tentative tax to arrive at the net tax payable (see estate tax computation method Exhibit 15.3 on page 419).

Credits After determining the adjusted gross estate and subtracting the allowed deductions from it in order to determine the taxable estate, the final calculations to ascertain the amount of the federal estate tax can be made. This involves multiplying the taxable estate by the appropriate unified tax rate to get the tentative tax, and then subtracting the unused unified credit and any other available credits from the tentative tax to find the *net tax*, the amount of tax actually due the government. The credits against the tax included under I.R.C. §§ 2010–2015 are:

• The unified estate and gift tax credit.

• The credit for state death taxes that have actually been paid to the decedent's state.

• The credit for any federal gift tax paid on transfers made during the lifetime by the decedent which are also subject to the federal estate tax because the decedent had made an incomplete gift (retained incidents of ownership or a gift in contemplation of death). It does not include state or foreign gift taxes.

• The credit for foreign death taxes (to help alleviate the burden of double taxation on the decedent's estate from two or more nations).

• The credit for estate taxes paid on the estate of the spouse of the decedent when the spouse died ten years or less prior to the death of the decedent. The amount of the credit is computed on the basis of a percentage of the estate tax paid on the estate of the first spouse to die; the amount of the credit decreases as the length of time increases between the deaths of the first spouse and the decedent.

Once the allowable credits are determined and subtracted from the gross tax, the remaining figure, called the net tax, is the tax due the federal government. The tax is paid at the same time the federal estate tax return is due. Federal estate, state estate, and state inheritance taxes must be paid either out of the estate assets or by the persons to whom the estate assets are distributed. The will may contain a provision that requires such persons to pay estate and/or inheritance taxes due on a devise; otherwise, these taxes are generally paid out of the residue of the estate. Sometime after the representative files the estate tax return, the I.R.S. sends an "estate tax closing letter" or notifies the representative that the return is not acceptable. If not acceptable, the I.R.S. will determine the proper tax and request prompt payment.

Assignment 138

1. Review the section in the Internal Revenue Code dealing with alternate valuation. How does it work? What is its purpose?

2. Define "incidents of ownership." On what tax form does this phrase appear?

3. List examples of property subject to federal estate tax. Give imaginary figures for said examples (i.e., $10,000 to Mary Doe as provided in paragraph of decedent's will). Using the examples, create a fact situation from which a sample federal estate tax return can be completed.

4. Explain the marital deduction and its use. Review the section of the Internal Revenue Code where it is discussed.

5. List the expenses, claims (debts), deductions, and credits allowed by the federal government when computing federal estate tax.

6. Describe the marital deduction trust and its tax-saving function.

7. Give examples of charitable deductions.

State Estate Tax Return

A state's estate tax is imposed on the decedent's privilege of transferring property and is measured by the value of the property transferred. Only the state of the decedent's domicile has power to impose an estate or inheritance tax on the decedent's estate. The exception to this general rule is that property located in a state other than the decedent's domicile is taxable in such other state. Often a state estate tax is imposed on estates of residents in addition to the state inheritance tax (see discussion below). All the states, except Nevada, have an inheritance tax or an estate tax or both. For an example of a state estate tax form, see Form 8.

In states that have both estate and inheritance taxes, the estate tax is due and payable 12 months after the decedent's death and is recovered from the credit for state death taxes given in the determination of the federal estate tax. In other words, the state estate tax assessed is the amount by which the maximum credit allowable on the

Form 706 U.S. Estate Tax Return exceeds the amount of state inheritance taxes assessed and paid. For example:

Federal credit for state death taxes allowed from Form 706	$ 187,280
State inheritance tax assessed and paid	−$185,000
State estate tax	$ 2,280

If the inheritance tax paid is greater than the federal credit, then no state estate tax is owed.

This tax is assessed by the probate court and computed by the state Commissioner of Revenue. In cases where an estate is not probated, the tax is determined and computed only by the Commissioner of Revenue.

The state estate tax return is filed with the Commissioner of Taxation by the representative after final settlement with the federal taxing authorities if a federal estate tax is due under the provisions of the law. The representative must include with this return a copy of the federal estate tax return and a copy of the federal audit report or closing letter accepting the federal return as filed. Within 90 days, the state Commissioner of Revenue shall make an order determining the tax due and mail one copy to the appropriate probate court and two copies to the representative. The representative returns one of these copies and the remittance due to the Commissioner of Revenue.

State Inheritance Tax Return

A number of states impose an inheritance tax on the recipients of both real and personal property transferred to them from the estate of a decedent resident of the state. It is a tax on inherited property, i.e., a tax on your beneficiaries' right to receive your property, and the rate of tax varies with the relationship of the heir or devisee to the decedent and the value of the property received. The tax must be computed separately for every successor. The separate computations are then added to determine the total tax.

The surviving spouse and minor children are taxed at the minimum rate. This tax differs from the federal and state estate taxes, where the tax rate remains the same for all estates of the same size no matter to whom the property is distributed. In cases of probate, the Commissioner of Revenue requires that the representative file within one year from the date of the decedent's death copies of the following:

• The Schedule of Non-Probate Assets
• The Inventory and Appraisal
• The Petition to Prove the Will, if any
• The Final Account
• The State Inheritance Tax Return (see Form 71)

• The U.S. Estate Tax Return (if one was filed). (This must be filed at the time of filing the original.)

In cases of non-probate, a Schedule of Non-Probate Assets and the Inheritance Tax Return are filed separately. The primary source of information regarding the inheritance tax is usually a state statute.

The property taxed by the state is generally the same as that listed on the U.S. Estate Tax Return Form 706. Initially, the precise information is listed on the Inventory and Appraisal and/or the Schedule of Non-Probate Assets, and these forms are then the basis for proper execution of the Inheritance Tax Return. A discussion of these forms follows.

Inventory and Appraisal of Probate Assets

The Inventory and Appraisal form contains the same items included on the U.S. Estate Tax Return, including a listing of the decedent's real estate, furniture and household goods, wearing apparel and ornaments, corporate stocks, mortgages, bonds, notes with encumbrances, and all other personal property. This form may contain the oath, verification, and certification of appraisers (see pages 356–357 and Form 65).

Schedule of Non-Probate Assets

The filing of the Schedule of Non-Probate Assets is generally required under state law. This schedule covers all transfers from deceased persons to heirs or devisees and transfers made during a decedent's lifetime over which he or she had rights of ownership or control which are not listed in the inventory in a state's probate proceeding (see Form 70). Items included consist of property held in joint ownership, insurance policies, annuities, and transfers by the decedent (see pages 357–359).

Jointly Owned Property   All real or personal property in which the decedent had an interest as a joint owner at the time of his or her death must be included on this schedule. An affidavit giving such details as the source, nature, amount, and proportion of the survivor's interest must be filed by the surviving joint owner. For property held in joint tenancy, a satisfaction of waiver of the inheritance tax lien can be obtained by filing with this schedule an Affidavit of Survivorship, Joint Tenancy or Remainderman (see Form 24).

Insurance   All life insurance and accident insurance policies must be reported where the proceeds are payable to a named beneficiary other than the estate or the executor. When the named beneficiary is the estate or the executor, the proceeds are recorded on the Inventory and Appraisal rather than on the Schedule of Non-Probate Assets. If the decedent held any "incidents of ownership" in any insurance policy, the proceeds are taxable and must be included on the Inventory and Appraisal. This control is defined under federal law as (a) the right to change the beneficiaries directly or indirectly, (b) the right to the cash surrender value, (c) the right to assign, revoke, or pledge the policy, (d) the right to obtain loans against the policy, or (e) reversionary interests. War Risk Insurance policies issued by the United States are exempt from taxes only if the policy benefits are not payable to the estate or executor.

Annuities and Deposits On this schedule, all annuities, pension and/or retirement funds, supplemental contracts, or deposits are listed. In relation to annuities, if the payments or a lump sum are to be transferred to a beneficiary, they are subject to tax, except in those cases where the benefits are supplied in their entirety by the employer.

Transfers by the Decedent As on the federal estate tax return, transfers of property interests made by the decedent intended to take effect in possession or enjoyment after the decedent's death are taxable. Under such transfers, copies of trust instruments, if any exist, are to be attached.

Miscellaneous Any transfer of property belonging to the decedent which has not been otherwise included is listed under this heading.

The values shown on the Inheritance Tax Return contained in the Schedule of Non-Probate Assets and Inventory and Appraisal are conclusive. However, the Commissioner of Revenue or any person owing the tax has 90 days from the filing of the return to file objections to the return. If an objection is made, the probate court will set a time for a hearing on the objection. A 30-day notice of the hearing must be sent to the Commissioner of Revenue, the representative of the estate, and every person owing a portion of the tax. In the case of non-probate proceedings, each person owing a share of the total tax is required to file a Schedule of Non-Probate Assets with the Commissioner of Revenue.

Deductions, Exemptions, and Credits

As with the federal law, states may allow deductions for funeral expenses, administration expenses, expenses of the last illness, claims allowed by the probate court, accrued taxes or liens, and attorney's fees. In contrast to the federal marital deduction, there may be a marital exemption that is (for example) 50% but not more than $250,000 of the net taxable value passing to the surviving spouse of a decedent domiciled in the state at the time of death, reduced by the value of real property outside of the state and tangible personal property permanently located outside the state. Also, the charitable exemption in the state may be more limited than for federal purposes in that an exemption may be allowed only if the charity is operating within the state. On the other hand, the state may allow a deduction of a portion of the federal estate tax, for example, a direct deduction for the family maintenance allowance not to exceed $500 per month for one year if the estate is insolvent, or 18 months if the estate is solvent, and not to exceed in any event $9,000, and personal property to be set apart as in previous probate proceedings.

The exemptions under state law also may include charitable exemptions if they meet the requirements for exemption as set by state law, homestead property to a specific value, railroad retirement funds or Social Security death benefits, war risk policies, personal exemptions based on the recipient's relationship to the decedent, property previously taxed if it qualifies for an exemption, and certain qualified annuities and other death benefits.

In computing the amount of the inheritance tax, the rates are graduated according to the relationship to the heir or devisee to the decedent. For example, the decedent's widow or widower may be allowed a specific exemption of $60,000, whereas a brother or sister may be exempt for only $1,500.

Final Note. The importance of obtaining correct information for the tax returns cannot be overstated. It is in this area that the most precise work of the paralegal will be done.

Assignment 139

1. Return to the Jane Doe case in Chapter 13, page 372. After reading the case, review the executed federal and state tax forms found in Appendix A (Forms 71 and 119.) Assume you have been appointed personal representative of your own estate (even though impossible) and now must file all death tax returns required by the federal and your state government. Develop appropriate checklists for your own set of circumstances, e.g., assets, liabilities, forms of ownership, etc., and execute all required federal and state tax returns.

2. Review the law in your own state pertaining to the establishment of state estate and/or inheritance taxes, if any. Cite the authority. States may have amended their estate and/or inheritance tax laws after Congress enacted the 1976 Tax Reform Act. Check for changes.

3. Describe the types of property that are to be included on an inheritance tax return, if any, in your state. Give imaginary monetary figures with each.

4. Describe and list the deductions, exemptions, and credits allowed by your state on an inheritance tax return. Cite the authority and give figures for each.

5. Using the information in questions 3 and 4, create your own fact situation and complete the following forms according to the laws of your state: Inventory and Appraisal, Schedule of Non-Probate Assets, Inheritance Tax Return.

APPENDIX   A

Sample Forms

Form *

465

* These forms are for purposes of illustration only. They represent the types of documents that might be used in particular situations and jurisdictions.

Form *

33. Death Certificate
34. Oath of Appraisers and Appraisal of Lands Under Order for Sale
35. Proof of Claim
36. Probate Deed
37. Petition to Sell-Mortgage-Lease Real Estate
38. Order for Hearing Petition to Sell-Mortgage=Lease Real Estate
39. Order for Sale, Mortgage, or Lease of Real Estate at Private Sale
40. Warrant to Appraisers at Private Sale and Oath of Appraisers
41. Report of Sale of Land at Private Sale under Order for Sale
42. Order Confirming Private Sale of Real Estate
43. State Inheritance Tax Waiver
44. Petition for Appointment of a Special Administrator
45. Order Granting Special Administration
46. Letters of Special Administration
47. Final Account and Report of Special Administration
48. Order Approving the Final Account and Report of the Special Administrator
49. Petition for Summary Distribution or Assignment
50. Final Decree Summary Assignment or Distribution
51. Petition Claiming Interest in Omitted Property (Petition for Determination of Descent)
52. Decree of Distribution (Descent) of Omitted Property
53. Petition for Formal Probate of Will and for Formal Appointment of Personal Representative
54. Order and Notice of Formal Appointment, Notice of Hearing for Formal Probate of Will and Notice to Creditors
55. Proof (Affidavit) of Publication
56. Affidavit of Notice of Hearing Final Account
    Statutory Notice of Rights of Surviving Spouse and/or Minor Children (Reverse Side of Form)
57. Proof of Placing Order for Publication
58. Order of Formal Probate of Will and Formal Appointment
59. Acceptance of Appointment and Oath by Individual
60. Bond, if Required, or Waiver
61. Testimony of Witnesses
62. Federal Identification Number (Form SS–4)
63. Letters Testamentary
64. Notice of Fiduciary Relationship
65. Inventory and Appraisement
66. Petition for Allowance of Selection of Personal Property
67. Order Setting Apart (Allowing Selection of) Personal Property
68. Petition for Family Maintenance
69. Order for Family Maintenance
70. Schedule of Non-Probate Assets
71. Minnesota Inheritance Tax Return
72. Final Account
73. Order for Hearing on Final Account and Petition for Distribution and for Mailed Notice
74. Affidavit of Mailing Order or Notice of Hearing on Final Account
75. Order Allowing Final Account
76. Petition for Order of Complete Settlement of the Estate and Decree of Distribution
77. Order of Complete Settlement of the Estate and Decree of Distribution
78. Petition for Discharge of Personal Representative
79. Order for Discharge of Personal Representative
80. Change of Testacy Status-Application for Informal Appointment of Successor
81. Verification
82. Demand for Notice
83. Notice of Informal Appointment
84. Allowance of Disallowance of Claim
85. Affidavit for Collection of Personal Property
86. Statement Closing Small Estate by Sworn Statement of Personal Representative
87. Application for Informal Probate and Informal Appointment of Representative
88. Statement of Informal Probate of Will and Order of Informal Appointment
89. Notice of Informal Probate of Will and Appointment of Personal Representative and Notice to Creditors

Form *

Form 1 Petition to Prove a Will (Petition for Probate of Will)

Form 4351 Rev. 6-76

524.3-401 #1   UPC 29

STATE OF MINNESOTA

COUNTY OF _____

PROBATE COURT
COUNTY COURT-PROBATE DIVISION

In Re: Estate of

Court File No. _____

**PETITION FOR
PROBATE OF WILL**

_____
Deceased

TO THE HONORABLE JUDGE OF THE ABOVE NAMED COURT:

Petitioner, _____ , respectfully states:

1. Petitioner resides at _____ ;

2. Petitioner has an interest herein as _____ ,
   and is, therefore, an interested person as defined by the laws of this State;

3. Decedent was born _____ , 19 ___ , at _____ ;

4. Decedent died on _____ , 19 ___ , at _____ ;

5. Decedent at the time of his death resided at _____ ,
   City of _____ , County of _____ , State of _____ ;

6. That the names and addresses of decedent's spouse, children, heirs and devisees and other persons
   interested in this proceeding and the ages of any who are minors so far as known or ascertainable
   with reasonable diligence by the petitioner are:
   NOTE—Classify the heirs and others entitled to take per stirpes and give the name, date of
   death, relationship/interest and address, if known, of their predeceased ancestor. Give
   the birthdate of any heir or devisee taking a life interest.

Name	Age	Relationship/Interest	Address

7. That venue for this proceeding is in the above named County of the State of Minnesota, because
   the decedent was domiciled in such County at the time of his death, and was the owner of property
   located in the State of Minnesota, or because, though not domiciled in the State of Minnesota, the
   decedent was the owner of property located in the above named County at the time of his death.
   (See back*)

Form 2 Proof of Publication of Notice (Placing Order for Publication)

STATE OF MINNESOTA

COUNTY OF HENNEPIN

PROBATE COURT

COURT FILE NO._____

In Re: Estate of

PROOF OF PLACING ORDER
FOR PUBLICATION

_____
Deceased

_____
_____

TO THE CLERK OF PROBATE COURT:

This is to verify that _____

_____

_____

_____, applicant(s)

has (have) made arrangements for the publication of:

☐   NOTICE OF INFORMAL APPOINTMENT OF PERSONAL
REPRESENTATIVE(S) AND NOTICE TO CREDITORS

☐   NOTICE OF INFORMAL PROBATE OF WILL AND APPOINTMENT OF
PERSONAL REPRESENTATIVE(S) AND NOTICE TO CREDITORS

☐

once a week for two consecutive weeks in the **FINANCE AND COMMERCE Daily**

Newspaper
_____

and this is to confirm that the same will be published accordingly commencing
in the next available issue, and that arrangements for payment of the cost of
said publication have been made.

Dated: _____

FINANCE AND COMMERCE Daily Newspaper
Publisher

By: _____

Form 3 Proof of Publication and Mailing (Affidavit of Mailing Order or Notice of Hearing)

Form 5—2m—7-78

AFFIDAVIT OF PUBLICATION

STATE OF MINNESOTA)
                (SS.
COUNTY OF HENNEPIN)

...., being duly sworn on oath says he is and

during all the times herein stated has been the......................publisher and printer of the newspaper known as

FINANCE AND COMMERCE

and has full knowledge of the facts herein stated as follows: (1) Said newspaper is printed in the English language in newspaper format and in column and sheet form equivalent in printed space to at least 900 square inches. (2) Said newspaper is a daily and is distributed at least five (5) days each week, or four (4) days in a week in which a legal holiday is included. (3) Said newspaper has 25 percent of its news columns devoted to news of local interest to the community which it purports to serve and does not wholly duplicate any other publication and is not made up entirely of patents, plate matter and advertisements. (4) Said newspaper is circulated in and near the municipality which it purports to serve, has at least 500 copies regularly delivered to paying subscribers, has an average of at least 75 percent of its total circulation currently paid or no more than three months in arrears and has entry as second-class matter in its local post-office. (5) Said newspaper purports to serve the City of Minneapolis in the County of Hennepin, and it has its known office of issue in the City of Minneapolis in said county, established and open during its regular business hours for the gathering of news, sale of advertisements and sale of subscriptions and maintained by the managing officer of said newspaper or persons in its employ and subject to his direction and control during all such regular business hours and at which said newspaper is printed. (6) Said newspaper files a copy of each issue immediately with the State Historical Society. (7) Said newspaper has complied with all the foregoing conditions for at least two years preceding the day or dates of publication mentioned below. (8) Said newspaper has filed with the Secretary of State of Minnesota prior to January 1, 1966 and each January 1 thereafter an affidavit in the form prescribed by the Secretary of State and signed by the managing officer of said newspaper and sworn to before a notary public stating that the newspaper is a legal newspaper.

He further states on oath that the printed

PROBATE NOTICE

hereto attached as a part hereof was cut from the columns of said newspaper, and was printed and published therein in the English language, once each week, for two (2) successive weeks; that it was first so published on

......................the..............day of........................., 19.....

and was thereafter printed and published on every..............................
to and including

......................the..............day of........................., 19.....

and that the following is a printed copy of the lower case alphabet from A to Z, both inclusive, and is hereby acknowledged as being the size and kind of type used in the composition and publication of said notice, to wit:

abcdefghijklmnopqrstuvwxyz

....

Subscribed and
sworn to before me this..............day of........................., 19.....

....
Notary Public, Hennepin County, Minnesota

Form 4 Order Admitting Will to Probate

No. 3541—Order Admitting Will to Probate. (Revision of 1906.)

State of Minnesota,

County of_____ }

IN PROBATE COURT

IN THE MATTER OF THE ESTATE OF

_____

Decedent. }

Order Admitting Will to Probate.

The above entitled matter came on to be heard, on the_____day of_____

_____19   upon the petition of

for the allowance of an instrument filed therewith purporting to be the last will and testament of the

above named decedent; and the court having duly heard the same and all the evidence produced in

support thereof, and having duly considered the same, finds as follows:

FIRST—That the citation of this court, dated the_____day of_____.

19 ___, has been duly served and published as directed therein and required by law.

SECOND—That said decedent died on the_____day of_____

19 ___, and at the time of his death was a resident of_____

in the County of_____State of_____,

and left estate in the County of_____State of Minnesota.

THIRD—That the subscribing witness___to said purported last will and testament of said dece-

dent, to-wit:_____

and_____duly sworn and examined, and_____

testimony reduced to writing, subscribed by_____and filed herein.

FOURTH—That said instrument presented for probate as aforesaid, was duly executed by said

decedent as his last will and testament, according to law; and that said decedent, at the time he exe-

cuted the said instrument, was of sound mind and free from undue influence, of lawful age, and

under no restraint_____

_____

_____

IT IS THEREFORE ORDERED, ADJUDGED AND DECREED, that the said instrument pre-

sented and proved as aforsaid be, and the same hereby is, established and allowed as the last will and

testament of the above named decedent, and is hereby admitted to probate.

Dated_____19 ___

_____

Judge of Probate.

Form 5 Certificate of Probate

No. 3554—Certificate of Probate of Will. (Revision of 1906.)

IN COUNTY COURT
PROBATE DIVISION
CERTIFICATE OF PROBATE

State of Minnesota,

County of _____

In the Matter of the Estate of

_____, Decedent

Be it Remembered. That on the day of the date hereof at a _____ Term

of said County Court, pursuant to the notice duly given, the last will and testament of _____

_____, Decedent, late of said County of _____

bearing date the _____ day of _____, 19 _____, and being the

annexed written instrument, was duly proved before the County Court, in and for the County of

_____ aforesaid; and was duly allowed and admitted to probate by said Court

according to law; as and for the last Will and Testament of said

_____ deceased, which said last Will and Testament is recorded and the exam-

ination taken thereon filed in this office.

In Testimony Whereof, The Judge of the County Court of

said County has hereunto set his hand and affixed the seal

of said Court at _____ in said County,

this _____ day of _____, 19 _____

_____
Judge

Court Seal

Form 6 Order Appointing Appraisers

525.51 #8   UPC --

STATE OF MINNESOTA

COUNTY OF _____

PROBATE COURT
COUNTY COURT-PROBATE DIVISION

In Re: Estate of

Court File No. _____

ORDER APPOINTING APPRAISERS

_____
Deceased

The petition of _____ dated _____, 19 ___,
for an order appointing appraisers in the estate of the above named decedent having duly come on for
hearing before the above named court, the undersigned Judge having heard and considered such
petition, being fully advised in the premises, makes the following findings and determinations:

1. That the petition for an order appointing appraisers is complete.

2. That the time for any notice has expired and any notice as required by the laws of this state has
   been given and proved.

3. That the petitioner has declared or affirmed that the representations contained in the petition are
   true, correct and complete to the best of his knowledge or information.

4. That the petitioner appears from the petition to be an interested person as defined by the laws of
   this state.

5. That appraisers should be appointed in the estate of the above named decedent because:
   _____
   _____

6. The following named persons are qualified to be appraisers herein: _____
   _____
   _____

Now, therefore, it is ORDERED, ADJUDGED, and DECREED by the court as follows:

1. That the petition is hereby granted.

2. That the above named persons are hereby appointed appraisers.

Dated: _____

(COURT SEAL)

_____
Judge

Form 7 Notice of Right to Allowances and Right of Election

Form 3654½ — Probate Court Rules 2.4 and 2.5 (Rev. 1955)

State of Minnesota,

County of_____ } 88.

IN THE MATTER OF THE ESTATE OF)

_____ {
Decedent)

IN COUNTY COURT
PROBATE DIVISION

Notice to Spouse or Minor Children

Pursuant to Probate Court Rules you are hereby advised of rights under the Minnesota statutes as hereinafter set forth.

ALLOWANCES TO SPOUSE OR MINOR CHILDREN

When a decedent dies with or without a will the allowances to the spouse or minor children are as follows:

525.15 ALLOWANCES TO SPOUSE. When any person dies testate, or intestate,

(1) The surviving spouse shall be allowed from the personal property of which the decedent was possessed or to which he was entitled at the time of his death, the wearing apparel, and, as selected by him, furniture and household goods not exceeding $2,000 in value, and other personal property not exceeding $1,000 in value;

(2) When, except for one automobile, all of the personal estate of the decedent is allowed to the surviving spouse by clause (1), the surviving spouse shall also be allowed such automobile.

(3) If there be no surviving spouse, the minor children shall receive the property specified in clause (1) as selected in their behalf;

(4) During administration, but not exceeding 18 months, unless an extension shall have been granted by the court, or, if the estate be insolvent, not exceeding 12 months, the spouse or children, or both, constituting the family of the decedent shall be allowed such reasonable maintenance as the court may determine;

(5) In the administration of an estate of a non-resident decedent, the allowances received in the domiciliary administration shall be deducted from the allowances under this section.

In all estates where there is a will the following rule applies to the spouse who has not consented to the will:

525.212 RENUNCIATION AND ELECTION. If a will make provision for a surviving spouse in lieu of the rights in the estate secured by statute, such spouse shall be deemed to have elected to take under the will, unless he shall have filed an instrument in writing renouncing and refusing to accept the provisions of such will within six months after the filing of the certificate of probate. For good cause shown, the court may permit an election within such further time as the court may determine. No devise or bequest to a surviving spouse shall be considered as adding to the rights in the estate secured by sections 525.145 and 525.16 to such spouse, unless it clearly appears from the contents of the will that such was the testator's intent.

DATED _____

_____
Judge

_____
Attorney   for Estate

_____

Form 8 State Estate Tax Return

IG Form 13 (Rev. 4/75)

MINNESOTA ESTATE TAX RETURN
AND
ORDER DETERMINING ESTATE TAX

Mail to:

Minnesota Department of Revenue
INHERITANCE AND GIFT TAX DIVISION
Centennial Office Building
St. Paul, Minnesota 55145

SEE INSTRUCTIONS ON REVERSE SIDE

Name of Decedent	Social Security No.	Date of Death	County of Residence	Probate Court File No. (If no probate, say NONE)

COMPUTATION OF TAX

Total federal estate tax paid . . . . $ _____

Maximum Credit for State Death Taxes as finally determined . . . . $ _____

DEDUCTIONS: Inheritance tax paid other States $ _____

Inheritance tax paid State of Minnesota $ _____ $ _____

Net Estate Tax Due State of Minnesota $ _____

I, _____The Execut _____, Administrat _____, Transferee, Custodian, Trustee of the above estate, or authorized person do hereby declare that copies of the initial Petition, Will (if any), Inventory and Appraisal and Schedule of Non-Probate-Assets disclosing all property known to affiant as belonging to decedent and required to be shown therein, Final Account, Minnesota Inheritance Tax Return, Federal Estate Tax Return, and Federal Audit Report and/or Federal Closing Letter, have been filed with the Commissioner of Revenue: that I have carefully examined this return and that it is, to the best of my knowledge and belief, true, correct, and complete.

The undersigned, therefore, prays the Commissioner of Revenue for a determination of the estate tax due from said estate under the provisions of Minnesota Statutes, Sections 291.34 to 291.40 inclusive.

Signature _____

Address _____

Date _____ , 19____

_____

ORDER DETERMINING ESTATE TAX

FOR OFFICIAL USE ONLY

FILE ONLY IF ESTATE TAX IS DUE

Form 9 Federal (U.S.) Individual Income Tax Return

Form **1040** U.S. Individual Income Tax Return	Department of the Treasury—Internal Revenue Service	**1983**	(0)	

For the year January 1-December 31, 1983, or other tax year beginning	, 1983, ending	, 19	OMB No. 1545-0074

Use IRS label. Otherwise, please print or type.	Your first name and initial (if joint return, also give spouse's name and initial)	Last name	Your social security number
	Present home address (Number and street, including apartment number, or rural route)		Spouse's social security number
	City, town or post office, State, and ZIP code	Your occupation	
		Spouse's occupation	

Presidential Election Campaign
Do you want $1 to go to this fund? . . . . Yes ☐ No ☐
If joint return, does your spouse want $1 to go to this fund? Yes ☐ No ☐
Note: *Checking "Yes" will not increase your tax or reduce your refund.*

For Privacy Act and Paperwork Reduction Act Notice, see Instructions.

Filing Status

Check only one box.

1 ☐ Single
2 ☐ Married filing joint return (even if only one had income)
3 ☐ Married filing separate return. Enter spouse's social security no. above and full name here. _____
4 ☐ Head of household (with qualifying person). (See page 6 of Instructions.) If the qualifying person is your unmarried child but not your dependent, write child's name here. _____
5 ☐ Qualifying widow(er) with dependent child (Year spouse died ▶ 19___). (See page 6 of Instructions.)

Exemptions

Always check the box labeled Yourself. Check other boxes if they apply.

6a ☐ Yourself ☐ 65 or over ☐ Blind
b ☐ Spouse ☐ 65 or over ☐ Blind

Enter number of boxes checked on 6a and b ▶ ☐

c First names of your dependent children who lived with you _____

Enter number of children listed on 6c ▶ ☐

d Other dependents: (1) Name	(2) Relationship	(3) Number of months lived in your home	(4) Did dependent have income of $1,000 or more?	(5) Did you provide more than one-half of dependent's support?

Enter number of other dependents ▶ ☐

e Total number of exemptions claimed . . . .

Add numbers entered in boxes above ▶ ☐

Income

Please attach Copy B of your Forms W-2, W-2G, and W-2P here.

If you do not have a W-2, see page 5 of Instructions.

7 Wages, salaries, tips, etc. **7**
8 Interest income *(also attach Schedule B if over $400 or you have any All-Savers interest)* . . . **8**
9a Dividends *(also attach Schedule B if over $400)* _____ , 9b Exclusion _____
c Subtract line 9b from line 9a and enter the result **9c**
10 Refunds of State and local income taxes, from worksheet on page 10 of Instructions *(do not enter an amount unless you deducted those taxes in an earlier year—see page 10 of Instructions)* **10**
11 Alimony received **11**
12 Business income or (loss) *(attach Schedule C)* . . . . ▶ **12**
13 Capital gain or (loss) *(attach Schedule D)* **13**
14 40% capital gain distributions not reported on line 13 (See page 10 of Instructions) **14**
15 Supplemental gains or (losses) *(attach Form 4797)* **15**
16 Fully taxable pensions, IRA distributions, and annuities not reported on line 17 . . . . **16**
17a Other pensions and annuities, including rollovers. Total received | 17a |
b Taxable amount, if any, from worksheet on page 10 of Instructions **17b**
18 Rents, royalties, partnerships, estates, trusts, etc. *(attach Schedule E)* **18**
19 Farm income or (loss) *(attach Schedule F)* . . . . ▶ **19**
20a Unemployment compensation (insurance). Total received | 20a |
b Taxable amount, if any, from worksheet on page 11 of Instructions **20b**
21 Other income (state nature and source—see page 11 of Instructions) _____ **21**

Please attach check or money order here.

22 **Total income.** Add amounts in column for lines 7 through 21 . . . . ▶ **22**

Adjustments to Income

(See Instructions on page 11)

23 Moving expense *(attach Form 3903 or 3903F)* **23**
24 Employee business expenses *(attach Form 2106)* **24**
25a IRA deduction, from the worksheet on page 12 . . . . **25a**
b Enter here IRA payments you made in 1984 that are included in line 25a above ▶ _____
26 Payments to a Keogh (H.R. 10) retirement plan **26**
27 Penalty on early withdrawal of savings **27**
28 Alimony paid **28**
29 Deduction for a married couple when both work *(attach Schedule W)* **29**
30 Disability income exclusion *(attach Form 2440)* **30**
31 **Total adjustments.** Add lines 23 through 30 . . . . ▶ **31**

Adjusted Gross Income

32 **Adjusted gross income.** Subtract line 31 from line 22. *If this line is less than $10,000, see "Earned Income Credit" (line 59) on page 16 of Instructions. If you want IRS to figure your tax, see page 3 of Instructions* . . . . ▶ **32**

Form 10 State (Minnesota as Example) Income Tax Return

Form M-1

MINNESOTA Income Tax Return 1983

Before you begin, read "Use of Information" in the Instructions.

Please print or type

Your first name and initial	Last name(s)	Your social security number	Check box and fill in name of Minnesota city or township where you lived in 1983 ☐ City ☐ Township
Spouse's first name and initial		Spouse's social security number	County
Present home address (number and street, apartment number, or rural route)			Occupation number from page 25 of the instructions ___ You ___ Spouse
City, town or post office	State	Zip code	If your name, address or marital status changed since you sent in your 1982 return, fill in date of change:

7 ☐ Check this box if you are married   8 ☐ Check this box if your spouse is filing a separate form   Check only if one of these applies: 9 ☐ Nonresident full year   10 ☐ Resident part year

State Elections Campaign Fund — Check a box for you and a box for your spouse. Dependents 18 and older not filing their own forms may also contribute by checking a box and signing below. This will not increase your tax or reduce your refund.

	Independent-Republican	Democratic-Farmer-Labor	Minor Party		General State Campaign Fund	No Contribution
You	11 ☐	14 ☐	17 ___	(Fill in the number from page 4 of the instructions)	20 ☐	23 ☐
Spouse	12 ☐	15 ☐	18 ___		21 ☐	24 ☐
Dependents 18 or older	13 ☐	16 ☐	19 ___		22 ☐	25 ☐

Does your Minnesota income (line 6) include any wages or compensation for personal services performed in Wisconsin while a Minnesota resident (read instructions, page 4)? 26 ☐ Yes 27 ☐ No   If yes, fill in amount of Wisconsin income: You $_____   Spouse $_____

Staple a copy of your W-2 form(s) here. Place your check here — please do not staple check.

		A Wife Only	B Husband, Joint Return or Single Person
1	Federal adjusted gross income (from line 32 of federal Form 1040 or line 14 of Form 1040A or line 3 of Form 1040EZ) 1		
2	Federal deduction for a married couple when both work (from line 29 of federal Form 1040 or line 12 of Form 1040A) 2		
3	Additions (read instructions, page 5). 3		
4	Total (add lines 1, 2 and 3) 4		
5	Subtractions (read instructions, page 7) 5		
6	Minnesota gross income (subtract line 5 from line 4) 6		
7	Federal income tax deduction (attach Schedule M-1B) 7		
8	Minnesota adjusted gross income (subtract line 7 from line 6) 8		
9	Total deductions (choose one method and check the box) ☐ Standard deduction (read instructions, page 11). . . . . 9 ☐ Itemized deductions (from line 30 on the back of this form)		
10	Minnesota taxable income (subtract line 9 from line 8) 10		
11	Tax from table on pages 23 and 24 of the instructions 11		
12	Total (add the amounts in columns A and B, line 11) 12		
13	Credits before tax (from line 41 on the back of this form). 13		
14	1983 income tax (subtract line 13 from line 12. Fill in this result or the amount from line 42 on the back of this form, whichever is smaller. If 13 is greater than 12, write "none.") 14		
15	Surtax (multiply the amount on line 14 by 0.10 (10%)) 15		
16	**Total 1983 income tax** (add lines 14 and 15). 16		
17	If you wish to donate to the Minnesota Nongame Wildlife Fund, fill in the amount ($1 or more) here. This will reduce your refund or increase the amount you owe 17		
18	Total (add lines 16 and 17) 18		
19	Credits after tax (from line 47 on the back of this form) 19		
20	If line 19 is greater than line 18, subtract 18 from 19 and fill in the amount of your **Refund** 20		
21	If you pay estimated tax, fill in the amount of refund from line 20 you want credited to 1984 Estimated Tax, if any . 21 _____		
22	If line 18 is greater than line 19, subtract 19 from 18 and fill in the **Amount You Owe** 22		

(Make your check or money order out to Commissioner of Revenue Put your social security number on your check)

Check ☐ if Schedule M-429I is attached (read instructions, page 22) _____

Taxpayer — I declare under the penalties of criminal liability for willfully making a false return, that this return is true, correct and complete to the best of my knowledge and belief. I hereby confess judgment to the State of Minnesota for the amount of the tax shown due hereon, to the extent not timely paid. **Preparer** — This return is true, correct and complete to the best of my knowledge and belief.

Sign Here

| Your signature | Spouse's signature (if joint or combined return) | Date | ( ) Daytime telephone no. |
| Signature of preparer if not taxpayer | Minn. I.D. or soc. sec. no. | Date | ( ) Daytime telephone no. |

Mail to: Minn. Individual Income Tax   St. Paul, Minn. 55145

Form 11 Federal (U.S.) Fiduciary Income Tax Return

Form **1041** Department of the Treasury Internal Revenue Service	**U.S. Fiduciary Income Tax Return** For the calendar year 1983 or fiscal year beginning.........................., 1983, and ending........................., 19......	OMB No. 1545-0092 **1983**

Check applicable boxes:
- ☐ Decedent's estate
- ☐ Simple trust ($300)
- ☐ Complex trust ($100)
- ☐ Complex trust ($300)
- ☐ Grantor type trust
- ☐ Ancillary return
- ☐ Bankruptcy estate
- ☐ Generation-skipping trust
- ☐ Testamentary trust
- ☐ Family estate trust
- ☐ Pooled income fund

Name of estate or trust (Grantor type trust, see instructions)

Name and title of fiduciary

Address of fiduciary (number and street)

City, State, and ZIP code

☐ First return   ☐ Final return   ☐ Amended return

Change in fiduciary's ▶   ☐ Name or   ☐ Address

Employer identification number

Nonexempt charitable and split-interest trusts check applicable boxes (See instructions):
- ☐ Described in section 4947(a)(1)
  - ☐ Not treated as a private foundation
- ☐ Described in section 4947(a)(2)

For Paperwork Reduction Act Notice, see page 1 of the instructions.

Income

1	Dividends (Enter full amount before exclusion)	1
2	Interest income (Enter full amount before exclusion)	2
3	Partnership income or (loss)	3
4	Income from another estate or trust	4
5a	Gross rent and royalty income ....; **b** Less total expenses (Attach schedule)	
c	Net rent and royalty income or (loss)	5c
6	Net business and farm income or (loss) (Attach Schedules C and F (Form 1040))	6
7	Capital gain or (loss) (Attach Schedule D (Form 1041))	7
8	Ordinary gain or (loss) (Attach Form 4797)	8
9	Other income (State nature of income)	9
10	**Total** income (Add lines 1 through 9) ▶	10

Deductions

11	Interest	11	
12	Taxes	12	
13	Charitable deduction (from Schedule A, line 11)	13	
14	Fiduciary fees	14	
15	Attorney, accountant, and return preparer fees	15	
16	Other deductions (Attach a separate sheet listing deductions)	16	
17	**Total** (Add lines 11 through 16) ▶		17
18	Subtract line 17 from line 10		18
19	Income distribution deduction (from Schedule B, line 19) (See instructions) (Attach Schedule K-1 (Form 1041))		19
20	Dividend and interest exclusion (See instructions)		20
21	Estate tax deduction (Attach computation)		21
22	Long-term capital gain deduction from Schedule D (Form 1041) (☐ Charity—See instructions)		22
23	Exemption		23
24	**Total** (Add lines 19 through 23) ▶		24
25	Taxable income of fiduciary (Subtract line 24 from line 18) ▶		25

Computation of Tax

26	**Tax: a** Tax rate schedule ....; **b** Other tax....................; Total ▶	26c
27	**Credits: a** Foreign tax....................; **b** Investment....................; **c** Jobs....................; Total ▶	27d
28	**Credits: a** Alcohol fuel....................; **b** Nonconventional fuel..............; **c** Research ....; Total ▶	28d
29	**Total** (Add lines 27d and 28d)	29
30	**Balance** (Subtract line 29 from line 26c)	30
31	Tax from recomputing prior year investment credit (Attach Form 4255)	31
32	Alternative minimum tax (Attach Form 6251)	32
33	**Total** (Add lines 30 through 32) ▶	33
34	**Credits: a** Form 2439....................; **b** Form 4136....................; **c** Form 6249 ....; Total ▶	34d
35	**Federal income tax: a** Previously paid ▶ ....; **b** Withheld ▶ ....; Total ▶	35c
36	**Total** (Add lines 34d and 35c) ▶	36
37	**Balance of tax due** (Subtract line 36 from line 33) (See instructions)	37
38	Overpayment (Subtract line 33 from line 36)	38

Please Sign Here

Under penalties of perjury, I declare that I have examined this return, including accompanying schedules and statements, and to the best of my knowledge and belief, it is true, correct, and complete. Declaration of preparer (other than fiduciary) is based on all information of which preparer has any knowledge.

▶

Signature of fiduciary or officer representing fiduciary   Date

Paid Preparer's Use Only

Preparer's signature ▶	Date	Check if self-employed ▶ ☐	Preparer's social security no.
Firm's name (or yours, if self-employed) and address ▶		E.I. No. ▶ ZIP code ▶	

Form 12 State (Minnesota as Example) Fiduciary Income Tax Return

Form **M-2** Minnesota Fiduciary Income Tax Return **1983**

Print or type   For calendar year 1983 or fiscal year beginning _____, 1983, ending _____, 19 ___

Name of estate or trust	Decedent's social security number	If return is for an estate, fill in decedent's last address and date of death
Name and title of fiduciary	Federal identification number	
Address of fiduciary (number and street) County	Minnesota identification number	
City, town or post office State Zip code	Amount of interest from Minnesota state, county, local or municipal obligations $	

Computation of Taxable Income

1 Taxable income (line 25 of federal Form 1041. Attach a copy) 1
2 Exemption claimed (line 23 of federal Form 1041) 2
3 Fiduciary's expenses, interest, taxes, depreciation or depletion and other deductions not allowed by Minnesota 3
4 Fiduciary's losses not allowed by Minnesota 4
5 Federal income tax refunds (read instructions) 5
6 Adjustment **Increase** (line 56, column E) 6
7 Excluded gain realized by a trust (applicable only to trusts) 7
8 Total (add lines 1 through 7) 8
9 Modification relating to gains allocated to principal (attach schedule) . . . 9
10 Adjustment **Decrease** (line 56, column E) 10
11 Fiduciary's net income not assignable to Minnesota 11
12 Total (add lines 9 through 11) 12
13 Balance (subtract line 12 from line 8) 13
14 Federal income tax deduction (read instructions) 14
15 Taxable income (subtract line 14 from line 13. Read instructions) 15

Computation of Tax

16 Taxable income of fiduciary 16
17 Tax from table on pages 5 and 6 of instructions 17
18 Tax on a lump-sum distribution (attach Schedule M-1LS) 18
19 Total (add lines 17 and 18) 19
20 Fiduciary credit: (a) for a trust $5 (b) for an estate $68 20
21 Energy credit (read instructions) 21
22 Research and development credit (attach Schedule RD) 22
23 Total (add lines 20 through 22) 23
24 1983 income tax (subtract line 23 from line 19. If line 23 is greater than line 19, fill in zero) 24
25 Minimum tax on items of tax preference (attach Schedule M-1MT) 25
26 Total tax (add lines 24 and 25) 26
27 Surtax (multiply the amount on line 26 by 0.10 (10%)) 27
28 **Total 1983 income tax** (add lines 26 and 27) 28
29 Gasoline and special fuel tax credit (attach Schedule GTC) 29
30 Tax previously paid 30
31 Minnesota income tax withheld 31
32 Total (add lines 29 through 31) 32
33 If line 28 is greater than line 32, subtract 32 from 28 and fill in **Amount You Owe** . . . 33
34 Amount **paid** with return (make your check or money order out to Commissioner of Revenue) . 34
35 If line 32 is greater than line 28, subtract 28 from 32 and fill in your **Refund** 35

Fiduciary — I declare under penalties of criminal liability for willfully making a false return, that this return is true, correct and complete to the best of my knowledge and belief. I confess judgment to the State of Minnesota for the amount of tax shown due, to the extent not timely paid. **Preparer** — This return is true, correct and complete to the best of my knowledge and belief.

Sign Here

Signature of fiduciary or officer representing fiduciary   Minn. I.D. or soc. sec. no.   Date   ( ) Telephone number

Signature of preparer other than fiduciary   Minn. I.D. or soc. sec. no.   Date   ( ) Telephone number

Mail to: Minn. Fiduciary Income Tax   Centennial Office Building   St. Paul, Minnesota 55146

Form 13 Registration Card or Certificate of Title

STATE OF MINNESOTA
CERTIFICATE OF TITLE
TO A MOTOR VEHICLE
THIS TITLE IS PRIMA FACIE PROOF OF OWNERSHIP
KEEP IN A SAFE PLACE — ANY ALTERATION OR ERASURE VOIDS THIS TITLE

VEHICLE IDENTIFICATION NUMBER   MAKE   YEAR   TYPE

TITLE NUMBER   DATE ISSUED   NEW OR USED   IF NEW, DATE OF FIRST SALE   FOR CENTRAL OFFICE USE ONLY

FIRST SECURED PARTY'S INTEREST RELEASED BY: SECOND SECURED PARTY'S INTEREST RELEASED BY:

AUTHORIZED SIGNATURE **X**   AUTHORIZED SIGNATURE

ASSIGNMENT BY RECORDED OWNER(S): I (WE), CERTIFY THIS VEHICLE IS FREE FROM ALL SECURITY INTERESTS , WARRANT TITLE, AND ASSIGN THE VEHICLE TO:

PRINT BUYER'S NAME(S)   OWNER'S SIGNATURE(S) ALL OWNERS MUST SIGN   DATE OF SALE

X

APPLICATION FOR TITLE BY BUYER(S)   COMPLETE FRONT AND BACK   PLEASE PRINT (DARK INK)

PRINT BUYER'S NAME(S) LAST, FIRST, AND MIDDLE   DATE OF BIRTH

STREET ADDRESS   CITY   COUNTY   STATE   ZIP CODE

IS THIS VEHICLE SUBJECT TO SECURITY AGREEMENT(S)?   YES ☐   NO ☐   IF YES, COMPLETE SECTION BELOW

FIRST SECURED PARTY (PRINT NAME)   DATE OF SECURITY AGREEMENT

STREET ADDRESS   CITY   STATE   ZIP CODE

SECOND SECURED PARTY (PRINT NAME)   DATE OF SECURITY AGREEMENT

STREET ADDRESS   CITY   STATE   ZIP CODE

IF THERE IS AN ADDITIONAL SECURITY AGREEMENT(S) COMPLETE AND ATTACH DPS2017.   NAME OF INSURANCE COMPANY   POLICY NUMBER

BUYER SUBSCRIBED AND SWORN TO BEFORE ME:

X

NOTARY SIGNATURE   DATE

I (we), certify I (we) am (are) of legal age, have bought this vehicle subject to liens shown and no others, this vehicle is and will continue to be insured while operating upon the public streets and highways, and all of my (our) declarations are true and correct.

X

COUNTY   DATE MY COMMISSION EXPIRES   BUYER'S SIGNATURE(S) ALL BUYERS SIGN.

DETACH THIS PORTION   **DO NOT SEPARATE UNTIL SOLD**

MINNESOTA MOTOR VEHICLE REGISTRATION CARD   **RECORDED OWNER(S) RECORD OF SALE**

PLATE NUMBER   TITLE NUMBER   PLATE NUMBER

PLATES EXPIRE   TAX   TAX BASE   TITLE NUMBER

MAKE   MODEL YEAR   TYPE   V.I.N.

V.I.N.   STICKER NUMBER

RECORDED OWNER(S)

BUYER'S SIGNATURE(S)   SALE DATE

STREET ADDRESS

CITY   STATE   ZIP CODE

Form 14 Decree of Distribution (Descent)

Form 4492

525.312 #8   UPC –

STATE OF MINNESOTA

PROBATE COURT
COUNTY OF _____   **COUNTY COURT-PROBATE DIVISION**

In Re: Estate of   Court File No. _____

_____   **DECREE OF DESCENT**
                    Deceased

    The petition of _____, dated _____, 19____, for determination of descent in the estate of the above named decedent having duly come on for hearing before the above named Court, the undersigned Judge having heard and considered such petition, being fully advised in the premises, makes the following findings and determinations:

1. That the petition for determination of descent is complete.

2. That the time for any notice has expired and any notice as required by the laws of this State has been given and proved.

3. That the petitioner has declared or affirmed that the representations contained in the petition are true, correct and complete to the best of his knowledge or information.

4. That the petitioner appears from the petition to be an interested person as defined by the laws of this State.

5. That decedent died testate at the age of _____ on _____, 19____, at _____ and that more than three years have elapsed since the death of said decedent and it appears from the petition that the time limit for original appointment proceedings has expired.

6. That, on the basis of the statements in the petition, this Court has jurisdiction of this estate, proceedings and subject matter.

7. That venue for this proceeding is in the above named County of the State of Minnesota, because the decedent was domiciled in such County at the time of his death, and was the owner of property located in the State of Minnesota, or because, though not domiciled in the State of Minnesota, the decedent was the owner of property located in the above named County at the time of his death.

8. That all decedent's heirs are as identified in the petition commencing this proceeding.

9. That no will or authenticated copy of a will of decedent probated outside of this State in accordance with the laws in force in the place where probated has been admitted to probate nor administration had in this state.

10. That the original, duly executed and apparently unrevoked last will, if any, and codicil or codicils thereto, if any, of the decedent or authenticated copy thereof and statement probating the same is in the Court's possession.

11. That the petition does not indicate that existence of a possible unrevoked testamentary instrument which may relate to property subject to the laws of this State, and which is not filed for probate in this Court.

12. That in and by decedent's last will, if any, the decedent devised the hereinafter described property to the following named beneficiaries in the following proportions or parts: (State actual legal relationship of each to decedent)

Form 15 Objection to Claims

No. 3656—Objections and Offsets of Representative to Claims Filed.

State of Minnesota,

County of_____ } 88.

IN COUNTY COURT PROBATE DIVISION

IN THE MATTER OF THE ESTATE OF }

_____

Objections and Offsets to Claim of

_____

Now comes the representative of the above named decedent and makes and files the following

_____*(1) to the claim of*

_____*above named, and to the allowance thereof, to-wit:*

_____*(2)*

Form 16 Petition for Settlement and Distribution
HC 4721

STATE OF MINNESOTA
COUNTY OF HENNEPIN

PROBATE COURT

FILE NO. _____

In the Matter of the Estate of

* FINAL ACCOUNT AND
PETITION FOR SETTLEMENT
AND DISTRIBUTION

_____
Decedent

READ INSTRUCTIONS AT END OF FORM

	DEBITS	CREDITS
DEBITS		
Personal Estate described in Inventory.............$ _____		
Increase on same:		
Interest ....$ _____		
Dividends ....$ _____		
Refunds ....$ _____		
Other _____$ _____		
_____$ _____		
Personal Estate Omitted in Inventory_____$ _____		
$ _____		
Received from Sale of Real Estate:		
Cash ....$ _____		
Contract for Deed ....$ _____ $ _____		
Received Rent of Real Estate ....$ _____		
Gain on Sale of Personal Property ....$ _____		
Advanced to Estate ....$ _____		
TOTAL DEBITS	$ _____	
CREDITS-DISBURSEMENTS		
Decrease in Personal Estate:		
Loss on Sale of		
Personal Property......$ _____		
Other_____$ _____		
TOTAL Decrease		$ _____
EXPENSES OF ADMINISTRATION		
Fees Probate Court Voucher No. ...$ _____		
Certified Copies Voucher No. ...$ _____		
Appraisers Fees Voucher No. ..$ _____		
Printing Fees Voucher No. ....$ _____		
Compensation of Representative Voucher No. ....$ _____		
Attorneys Fees (If over Minimum,		
attach Schedule) Voucher No. ....$ _____		
Maintenance by Order of Court Voucher No. ...$ _____		
Amount Set Aside by Order of Court Voucher No. ....$ _____		
Bond Premiums Voucher No. ....$ _____		
$ _____		
$ _____		
TOTAL Expenses of Administration		$ _____
FUNERAL EXPENSES		
Mortician Voucher No. ....$ _____		
Marker Voucher No. ....$ _____		
Flowers Voucher No. ....$ _____		
Cemetery Voucher No. ..$ _____		
$ _____		
$ _____		
TOTAL Funeral Expenses		$ _____
EXPENSES OF LAST ILLNESS		
Medical Attendance Voucher No. ...$ _____		
Medicine, etc. Voucher No. ....$ _____		
Nursing Voucher No. ....$ _____		
Hospital Voucher No. ....$ _____		
$ _____		
$ _____		
TOTAL Expenses of Last Illness		$ _____

Form 17 Deed

Warranty Deed
Individual to Joint Tenants   Form No. 5-M

This Indenture, *Made this..................day of.., 19.........,*
between...

of the County of...and State of.., part..........
of the first part, and..
.., of the County of..............
...........................and State of..., parties of the second part,

Witnesseth, *That the said part......... of the first part, in consideration of the sum of.................*
...DOLLARS,
to.......................in hand paid by the said parties of the second part, the receipt whereof is hereby acknowl-
edged, do.........hereby Grant, Bargain, Sell, and Convey unto the said parties of the second part as joint
tenants and not as tenants in common, their assigns, the survivor of said parties, and the heirs and
assigns of the survivor, Forever, all the tract...... or parcel...... of land lying and being in the County of
..and State of Minnesota, described as follows, to-wit:

To Have and to Hold the Same, *Together with all the hereditaments and appurtenances there-*
unto belonging or in anywise appertaining, to the said parties of the second part, their assigns, the sur-
vivor of said parties, and the heirs and assigns of the survivor, Forever, the said parties of the second part
taking as joint tenants and not as tenants in common.
And the said...

part........ of the first part, for..heirs, executors and administrators do..........
covenant with the said parties of the second part, their assigns, the survivor of said parties, and the heirs
and assigns of the survivor, that..............................well seized in fee of the lands and premises aforesaid and
ha.........good right to sell and convey the same in manner and form aforesaid, and that the same are
free from all incumbrances,

And the above bargained and granted lands and premises, in the quiet and peaceable possession of the
said parties of the second part, their assigns, the survivor of said parties, and the heirs and assigns of the
survivor, against all persons lawfully claiming or to claim the whole or any part thereof, subject to
incumbrances, if any, hereinbefore mentioned, the said part......... of the first part will Warrant and
Defend.

In Testimony Whereof, *The said part......... of the first part ha......... hereunto set...............*
hand...... the day and year first above written.

In Presence of

Form 18 Contract for Deed

Contract for Deed
Individual Vendor

Form No. 54-M

This Agreement, *Made and entered into this* .... *day of* ...., 19........., *by and between* ....

part .... *of the first part, and* ....

.... *, part* .... *of the second part,*

Witnesseth, *That the said part* .... *of the first part in consideration of the covenants and agreements of said part* .... *of the second part, hereinafter contained, hereby sell* .... *and agree* .... *to convey unto said part* .... *of the second part,* .... *and assigns, by a* .... *Deed, accompanied by an abstract evidencing good title in part* .... *of the first part at the date hereof, or by an owner's duplicate certificate of title, upon the prompt and full performance by said part* .... *of the second part, of* .... *part of this agreement, the tract* .... *of land, lying and being in the County of* .... *and State of Minnesota, described as follows, to-wit:*

And said part .... *of the second part, in consideration of the premises, hereby agree* .... *to pay said part* .... *of the first part, at* .... *as and for the purchase price of said premises, the sum of* .... *Dollars, in manner and at times following, to-wit:*

Said part............ of the second part further covenant...... and agree...... as follows: to pay, before penalty attaches thereto, all taxes due and payable in the year 19........, and in subsequent years, and all special assessments heretofore or hereafter levied, ...;

also that any buildings and improvements now on said land, or which shall hereafter be erected, placed, or made thereon, shall not be removed therefrom, but shall be and remain the property of the part............ of the first part until this contract shall be fully performed by the part............ of the second part; and at............................own expense, to keep the buildings on said premises at all times insured in some reliable insurance company or companies, to be approved by the part............ of the first part, against loss by fire for at least the sum of..Dollars

and against loss by windstorm for at least the sum of.. ....Dollars, payable to said part............ of the first part, ...heirs or assigns, and, in case of loss, should there be any surplus over and above the amount then owing said part............ of the first part, ...heirs, or assigns, the balance shall be paid over to the said part............ of the second part as..interest shall appear, and to deposit with the part............ of the first part policies of said insurance. But should the second part............ fail to pay any item to be paid by said part............ under the terms hereof, same may be paid by first part............ and shall be forthwith payable, with interest thereon, as an additional amount due first part............ under this contract.

Form 19 Petition for General Administration

STATE OF MINNESOTA   IN PROBATE COURT   HC 4755

COUNTY OF HENNEPIN

Re Estate of

_____

              Decedent.   **PETITION FOR GENERAL ADMINISTRATION**

_____ _respectfully represent_ _____ ;

1. Petitioner_____ reside _____ at _____ ;

2. Petitioner_____ ba ____ an interest herein as _____ ;

3. Diligent search has been made for a Will of decedent and none has been found;

4. Decedent was born_____ , 1 _____ , at _____ ;

5. Decedent died intestate on _____ , 19 _____ , at

_____ ;

6. Decedent at the time of h _____ death resided at _____ ,

_____ , Hennepin County, Minnesota;

7. Decedent's estate consists of:

    (A) $ _____ Real Estate in Minnesota:

           (1) $ _____ Homestead

           (2) $ _____ Other real estate

    (B) $ _____ Personal Property:

           (1) $ _____ Household goods

           (2) $ _____ Wearing apparel

           (3) $ _____ Money (Cash)

           (4) $ _____ Investments

           (5) $ _____ Other Personal

                   Property and Nature:

8. Estimate Non-Probate Assets $ _____ ;

9. Probable amount of decedent's debts is $ _____ ;

10. Decedent was survived by the following named persons who are all of the decedent's heirs at law:

(SEE NOTE ON BACK)

NAME	AGE	RELATIONSHIP	ADDRESS
1.			
2.			
3.			
4.			
5.			
6.			
7.			
8.			
9.			
10.			

Form 20 Disclaimer

STATE OF MINNESOTA

COUNTY OF _____

PROBATE COURT

FILE NO. _____

DISCLAIMER

WHEREAS, the undersigned, _____ is the surviving _____ of _____, who died on _____, a resident of and domiciled in _____ County, Minnesota, leaving a Last Will and Testament dated _____ _____; and

WHEREAS, Article _____ of said Last Will and Testament provides in part as follows:

WHEREAS, at the time of said decedent's death, said decedent owned:

WHEREAS, the undersigned wishes to disclaim and refuse to accept any interest to which—he is or may be entitled under the terms of said Will in said _____;

NOW, THEREFORE, in consideration of the foregoing, and pursuant to the provisions of Chapter 552, Session Laws for Minnesota of 1967 (Section 525.532, Minnesota Statutes 1967), and all other applicable law, the undersigned beneficiary hereby declines, refuses, releases, renounces, and disclaims forever any interest in said _____.

STATE OF MINNESOTA   )

) ss.

COUNTY OF _____)

On this _____ day of _____, before me, a Notary Public, within and for said County, personally appeared _____ _____, to me known to be the person described in and who executed the foregoing instrument and acknowledged that she executed the same as her free act and deed.

_____

(NOTARIAL SEAL)

Form 21 Petition for Probate of Foreign Will

No. 3665 — Petition for Probate of Foreign Will. (Revised and adopted by Probate Judges Ass'n. 1925.)

State of Minnesota,   **COUNTY COURT**
County of.......................................   **PROBATE DIVISION**

IN THE MATTER OF THE ESTATE OF   PETITION FOR PROBATE OF

....   FOREIGN WILL.

Your petitioner respectfully represents and states to the Court:

First—That he is a resident of the...........................*of*.......................
in the County of.......................*State of*.......................*and has*
an interest in the estate of the above named decedent, in this to-wit:.......................
....

Second—That the above named decedent then being a citizen of the Country of...........
died on the.......................*day of*.......................*19*..........,
at.......................*in the County of*.......................
State of......................., *leaving a last will and testament; and that in and by said*
will.......................*was named and appointed to be the*
executor.......*thereof,*...*(1)*

Third—That said last will and testament of said decedent was duly proved, allowed and admitted to
probate in and by the.......................*court in and for the County of*
.......................*State of*......................., *on the*.......................
day of.......................*19*......., *and that letters*.......................
....
.......................*thereon were duly issued to*.......................
.......................*on the*.......................*day of*.......................*19*.......
....*(1)*

Fourth—That said decedent died seized and possessed of certain.......................*property*
and estate lying and being in the County of.......................*State of Minnesota, de-*
scribed and of the estimated value as follows, to-wit:.......................

Fifth—That your petitioner herewith presents duly authenticated copies of said will and of the pro-
bate thereof in the court above named, and represents that said court above named was a court having
jurisdiction to admit said will to probate, and that its order and decree admitting said will to probate is
still in force.

Form 22 Order and Notice of Hearing for Foreign Will

No. 3669 (Revised 1972)

State of Minnesota, } 88.

County of................

IN COUNTY COURT
PROBATE DIVISION

IN RE ESTATE OF

....
Decedent.

Order for Hearing on Petition for Probate of Foreign Will, Limiting Time to File Claims and for Hearing Thereon

Authenticated copies of the last Will of said decedent and of the instrument admitting it to probate in the.............................Court in the County of.............................

and the State of.............................having been filed with the Petition of.............................praying for the allowance of said Will in this Court and for the appointment of.............................

as.............................

It is Ordered, *That the hearing thereof be had on............................., 19.......,*

at.............................o'clock.............................M., before this Court in the probate court room in the court house in............................., Minnesota; that the time within which creditors of said decedent may file their claims be limited to 60 days from the date hereof, and that the claims so filed be heard on.............................19......., at.............................o'clock.............................M., before this Court in the probate court room in the court house in............................., Minnesota, and that notice hereof be given by publication of this order in the.............................and by mailed notice as provided by law.

Dated............................., 19.......

....
Judge.

(Court Seal)

....
Attorney for Petitioner.

Form 23 Deposition of Witness

Form JPR64—

STATE OF MINNESOTA
COUNTY OF HENNEPIN

PROBATE COURT

File No..............................

Re Estate of

....
.... Decedent.

**Commission to Take Deposition
of Witness to Will
and Deposition**

To ....

....Street.., Greeting:

You are hereby appointed commissioner to take the deposition of.......................................
.... subscribing witness...... to the last will of the above named decedent, which will is transmitted herewith. You will cause the said witness...... to come before you at a time and place designated by you and examine .....h...., on oath or affirmation, respecting the due execution of said will, and immediately thereafter return such deposition signed by such witness...... and certified by you, together with this commission and such will, by registered mail in a sealed envelope addressed to the Clerk of the Probate Court at Minneapolis 15, Minnesota.

Dated.., 19..........

.... Probate Judge.

(Court Seal)

DEPOSITION

residing at ....Street, ...

respectively being duly sworn depose...... and say...... that .....h ....of legal age, that .....h w.............. present at the execution of the instrument now before .....h...., bearing date.................................., 19.........., and referred to in the foregoing commission; that .....h........... subscribed .....h........... name........... thereto as witness......, at the request of the testat......, in h........... presence and in the presence of the other subscribing witness; that all the subscribing witnesses signed in the presence of each other and of the testat.......; that .....h..... saw the testat...... sign said instrument at the end thereof and heard h..... acknowledge the same to be h..... last will, and that said testat....... at the time of such execution was of legal age, of sound mind and memory, and not under any restraint.

COMMISSIONER'S CERTIFICATE

State of..

County of..

BE IT KNOWN that I took the annexed deposition pursuant to the annexed commission; that I was then and there..(state title and office); that I exercised the power of that office in taking such deposition; that by virtue thereof I was then and there authorized to administer an oath; that each witness, before testifying, was duly sworn to testify the whole truth and nothing but the truth relative to the cause specified in the annexed commission; that the testimony of each witness was carefully read over to him by me before he signed the same; that the examination was conducted on behalf of the petitioner by..............................
.........................and on behalf of........................... by ....;

Witness my hand and seal this................... day of.., 19..........

(Seal)

.... Commissioner.

Form 24 Affidavit of Survivorship

Form 3816—Affidavit of Survivorship—Joint Tenancy or Remainderman and Certified Copy of Death.
Department of Taxation, Form IG-10, (Revised 1976)

State of Minnesota,

County of_____ } *ss.*

AFFIDAVIT OF SURVIVORSHIP— JOINT TENANCY OR REMAINDERMAN

Estate of_____, *deceased.*

_____, *of*_____,

Minnesota, being duly sworn, on oath says that   he is the surviving joint tenant-remainderman of the decedent named herein.

*That*_____*died on the*_____*day of*

(Decedent)

_____, 19____, *at the age of*_____*years at*_____,

*State of*_____, *with residence at*_____, *County*

(Address)

*of*_____, *State of*_____. *That a duly certified copy of*

the record of h_____ death as contained herein or attached hereto is made a part hereof.

That said decedent at and prior to death was the owner of an interest as joint tenant—life tenant in the hereinafter described property in which the following named person(s) is — are — surviving joint tenant or remainderman.

Name	Age	Relationship to Decedent	Residence

*That the respective interests of decedent and survivor(s) as joint tenants — life tenant and remainderman — were created by an instrument of conveyance dated*_____, 19____, **and filed for record*_____, 19____, *and recorded in the office of the Register of Deeds of*_____*County, Minnesota, in Book*_____*of*_____, *page*_____,* in the following described property, to-wit:*

That no part of the above property was the homestead of decedent unless so specified in the description. That affiant has disclosed to the Commissioner of Taxation all transfers of property from the decedent to any beneficiary of which affiant has knowledge or information, which transfers may be subject to Minnesota inheritance tax.

That affiant makes this affidavit and files said certified copy of record of death as evidence of the death of said joint tenant—life tenant—and the termination of said joint tenancy and all such estate, title interest and lien as was or is limited upon the life of said decedent.

_____

*Subscribed and sworn to before me this*_____

*day of*_____, 19____

_____

*Notary Public,*_____*County , Minn.*

*My commission expires*_____, 19____

*Statement between asterisks applies if property is an interest in land.

Form 25 Order for Hearing Petition for Probate of Will

No. 3845 (Revised J. of P. Ass'n 1939.)

State of Minnesota,

County of _____

}ss.

IN PROBATE COURT

IN RE ESTATE OF

_____
Decedent

Order for Hearing on Petition for Probate of Will, Limiting Time to File Claims and for Hearing Thereon

_____ having filed a petition for the probate of the _____ as Will of said decedent and for the appointment of _____ , which Will is on file in this Court and open to inspection;

It is Ordered, That the hearing thereof be had on _____ , 19____, at _____ o'clock _____ M., before this Court in the probate court room in the court house in _____ , Minnesota, and that objections to the allowance of said will, if any, be filed before said time of hearing; that the time within which creditors of said decedent may file their claims be limited to four months from the date hereof, and that the claims so filed be heard on _____ , 19____, at _____ o'clock _____ M., before this Court in the probate court room in the court house in _____ , Minnesota, and that notice hereof be given by publication of this order in the _____ and by mailed notice as provided by law.

Dated _____ , 19____

(Probate Court Seal)

_____
Probate Judge

_____
Attorney   for Petitioner

Form 26 Order and Notice of Hearing Petition for Administration

Form 4562

524.3-105 #4   UPC

STATE OF MINNESOTA

COUNTY OF _____

PROBATE COURT
COUNTY COURT-PROBATE DIVISION

In Re: Estate of

Court File No. _____

ORDER AND NOTICE OF HEARING
PETITION FOR ADMINISTRATION

_____
Deceased

        NOTICE IS HEREBY GIVEN that a petition dated _____ ,19 __ ,
has been filed herein for a judicial order formally _____
_____
and any objections thereto must be filed with the Court.

        IT IS ORDERED and notice is hereby given that the petition will be heard on the ___ day of
_____ ,19 __ , at _____ o'clock ___ .M. by the above named Court at
_____ , Minnesota. That, if proper, and no objections are filed, the petition will be
granted.

        IT IS FURTHER ORDERED That the petitioner give notice of said hearing by _____
_____
_____ .

Dated: _____

_____
Judge

_____
Clerk

_____
Attorney for Petitioner

_____
Address/Phone

Form 27 Order Granting Administration

No. 3542—Order Granting Administration. (Revised 1940)

State of Minnesota,

County of ....

IN COUNTY COURT

PROBATE DIVISION

IN THE MATTER OF THE ESTATE OF .... Decedent:

The petition of .... praying that letters of administration upon said estate be granted to ....

.... came duly on for hearing at a .... Term of this Court, held on the

.... day of .... 19........ Said petitioner appeared in person

and no one appeared in opposition.

The Court having duly considered said petition and the evidence adduced in support thereof, finds as follows:

First: That notice of said hearing has been given and served by the publication of the order for said hearing issued herein in the .... and by mailed notice as by law and the order of this Court provided.

Second: That the said decedent died intestate on the........................ day of .... 19........

Third: That said decedent was a resident of...

at the time of h............death and left estate within the County of .... and State of Minnesota, to be administered upon.

Fourth: That... is by law entitled, a suitable and competent person, to administer upon said estate.

Therefore, It is ordered that said petition be granted and ....

be and hereby is appointed.. of the estate of said decedent, and that letters of administration issue to .... upon.................... filing.........................the oath by law required and a bond in this Court in the penal sum of .... Dollars, with sureties to be approved by the Judge of this Court conditioned according to law.

Dated.................................... 19........   By the Court,

....

.... Attorney.

.... Judge

COURT
SEAL

Form 28 Bond and Oath

HC 4777

Bond and Oath of Executor; Special Administrator; Administrator; Administrator C.T.A.; D.B.N.; D.B. N.C.T.A.; Guardian

STATE OF MINNESOTA } ss.
COUNTY OF HENNEPIN

IN THE MATTER OF THE { GUARDIANSHIP
ESTATE OF

IN PROBATE COURT

File No. _____

BOND

KNOW ALL MEN BY THESE PRESENTS, That _____

_____ of _____

in the County of Hennepin, State of Minnesota, as principal and _____

_____ of said County and State, as surety _____, are

held and firmly bound to HON. MELVIN J. PETERSON, Judge of Probate of the County of Hennepin, Minnesota, in the

sum of _____ DOLLARS,

lawful money of the United States, to be paid to the said Judge of Probate or his successors in office; for which payment well and truly to be made, we bind ourselves, our and each of our heirs, executors and administrators, jointly and severally firmly by these presents.

The condition of this obligation is such that if the above bounden _____

_____ who has been appointed _____

of the estate of the above named _____ shall

well and faithfully discharge all the duties of _____ trust as such representative of said estate according to law then this obligation shall be void otherwise it shall be and remain in full force and virtue.

WITNESS, Our hands and seals this _____ day of _____ , 19 _____

_____ (Seal)

_____ (Seal)

_____ (Seal)

STATE OF MINNESOTA } ss.
COUNTY OF HENNEPIN

ACKNOWLEDGMENT

BE IT KNOWN, That on this _____ day of _____ , 19 ____, personally appeared before me

_____ , to me well known

to be the person who executed the foregoing bond, and _____ acknowledged the same to be _____

own free act and deed, and that _____ executed the same for the uses and purposes therein expressed.

SEAL

_____
Notary Public, Hennepin County, Minn.
My Commission expires _____ , 19 _____

STATE OF MINNESOTA } ss.
COUNTY OF HENNEPIN

ACKNOWLEDGMENT OF SURETY

On this _____ day of _____ , 19 ____, before me appeared, _____

_____ , to me personally known, who

being duly sworn did say that he is the Attorney-in-Fact of _____

_____ that the seal affixed to the foregoing instrument is the corporate

seal of that corporation and that said instrument was executed in behalf of the corporation by authority of its Board of Directors; he acknowledged said instrument to be the free act and deed of said corporation.

SEAL

_____
Notary Public, Hennepin County, Minn.
My Commission expires _____ , 19 _____

APPROVAL

I do hereby approve the within Bond, this _____ day of _____ , A. D. 19 _____

_____
Judge.

STATE OF MINNESOTA } ss.
COUNTY OF HENNEPIN

OATH

I _____

of _____

(Number), (Street or Avenue) _____ (City or Town)

in the County of _____ State of _____

do swear that I will faithfully and justly perform all duties of the office and trust which I now assume as

_____ of the person and estate of _____

(Guardian; Executor; Special Administrator; Administrator; Administrator C.T.A.; D.B. N.; D.B.N. C.T.A.)

_____
(Deceased, Minor, Mentally Ill, Incompetent, or Mentally Deficient)

late of _____ to the best of my ability. So help me God.
(County and State)

Subscribed and sworn to before

me this _____ day of _____ , 19 _____

_____
Notary Public, Hennepin County, Minn.
My Commission expires _____
SEAL

Form 29 Request for Minimum Bond

HC 4796

STATE OF MINNESOTA
COUNTY OF HENNEPIN

RE ESTATE OF

_____
Decedent.

IN PROBATE COURT

File No..............

REQUEST FOR
MINIMUM BOND

The undersigned, being all of the persons interested in said estate as heirs, devisees or legatees, do hereby request the Court to fix the bond of the representative in an amount not to exceed $ _____.

Dated _____, 19____.

Form 30 Order Appointing Guardian

STATE OF MINNESOTA

COUNTY OF _____

PROBATE COURT
COUNTY COURT-PROBATE DIVISION

In Re: Guardianship of

Court File No. _____

ORDER APPOINTING
GENERAL GUARDIAN

_____
Ward _____

A petition for the appointment of a general guardian of the above named ward _____ having been duly heard and considered and it being necessary and expedient to appoint a general guardian because of minority ____ old age ____ imperfection, deterioration of mentality-excessive intoxication, gambling, idleness, debauchery.

Now, therefore, it is ORDERED, ADJUDGED, and DECREED by the court as follows:

1. That the petition is hereby granted.

2. That upon the approval and filing of a bond in the amount of $ _____, and of an oath, _____ be appointed general guardian ____ of the person ____ and estate ____ of the above named ward ____ and that letters issue.

Dated: _____

(COURT SEAL)   _____
                                            Judge

Form 31 Order Admitting Foreign Will

No. 3664—Order Admitting Foreign Will to Probate.

State of Minnesota, }ss.

County of...

**IN COUNTY COURT
PROBATE DIVISION**

In the Matter of the Estate of

....

.... *Decedent*

}

**Order Admitting Foreign Will
to Probate**

The above entitled matter came on to be heard by the Court, on the...day of

...., 19........., upon the petition of..

....praying for the admittance and allowance of the

will of said decedent to probate; and the Court, having heard the said petition and the evidence in support

thereof, and examined the said will and the authentication thereof and the files and records in said

matter, finds the following facts:

First—That notice of said hearing has been given by the publication in...

....

of the order of this court for said hearing issued on the.................day of.............................., 19.........,

as required by law...

....

....

....

Second—That said decedent died on the.........................day of.............................., 19........., at

....in the County of...

State of ....leaving a last will and testament, in which

named and appointed to be executor..... thereof...(1)

....

....

Third—That said will of said decedent was duly proved, allowed and admitted to probate in and by

the..Court in and for the County of...

State of...on the.................day of.............................., 19.........,

and letters..thereon

issued to..on the

....day of.............................., 19........., ...(2)

....

Fourth—That the..Court above named, in which the

said will was proved, allowed and admitted to probate, was a court of competent jurisdiction to allow said

will and admit it to probate, and that it appears that the order and decree of said Court allowing said

will and admitting the same to probate is still in force.

Form 32 U.S. Treasury Form 712 (Life Insurance Statement)

FORM 712 (REV. MAY 1966)	U.S. TREASURY DEPARTMENT—INTERNAL REVENUE SERVICE **LIFE INSURANCE STATEMENT** *(To be filed by Executor with Federal Estate Tax Return, Form 706)*	
	1. NAME OF INSURANCE COMPANY	
	2. NAME OF DECEDENT (*Insured*)	
	3. KIND OF POLICY	4. NO. OF POLICY
	5A. NAMES OF BENEFICIARIES	5B.
Enter these items on Schedule D, Form 706	5C.	5D.
	6. FACE AMOUNT OF POLICY $	7. PRINCIPAL OF ANY INDEBTEDNESS TO THE COMPANY DEDUCTIBLE IN DETERMINING NET PROCEEDS
	8. INTEREST ON INDEBTEDNESS (*Item 7*) ACCRUED TO DATE OF DEATH $	$
	9. AMOUNT OF ACCUMULATED DIVIDENDS $	10. AMOUNT OF POST-MORTEM DIVIDENDS $
	11. AMOUNT OF RETURNED PREMIUM $	
	12. AMOUNT OF PROCEEDS IF PAYABLE IN ONE SUM $	13. VALUE OF PROCEEDS AS OF DATE OF DEATH (*If not payable in one sum*) $

14. DATE OF DEATH OF INSURED	15. DATE OF ISSUE OF POLICY	16. AMOUNT OF PREMIUM

17A. PROVISIONS OF POLICY WITH RESPECT TO THE DEFERRED PAYMENTS OR TO THE INSTALLMENTS (*NOTE: Where marital deduction under Code section 2056 is involved, if other than lump sum settlement authorized, copy of insurance policy should be attached.*)

17B. AMOUNT OF INSTALLMENTS $	17C. DATE OF BIRTH AND NAME OF ANY PERSON THE DURATION OF WHOSE LIFE MAY MEASURE THE NUMBER OF PAYMENTS	17D. AMOUNT APPLIED BY THE INSURANCE COMPANY AS A SINGLE PREMIUM REPRESENTING THE PURCHASE OF INSTALLMENT BENEFITS $

17E. BASIS (*Mortality table and rate of interest*) USED BY INSURER IN VALUING INSTALLMENT BENEFITS

18. WAS THE INSURED THE ANNUITANT OR BENEFICIARY OF ANY ANNUITY CONTRACT ISSUED BY THE COMPANY?

☐ YES   ☐ NO

19. NAMES OF COMPANIES WITH WHICH DECEDENT CARRIED OTHER POLICIES AND AMOUNT OF SUCH POLICIES IF THIS INFORMATION IS DISCLOSED BY YOUR RECORDS

The undersigned officer of the above-named insurance company hereby certifies that this statement sets forth correct and true information.

DATE OF CERTIFICATION	SIGNATURE	TITLE

INSTRUCTIONS

PURPOSE OF STATEMENT.—The information shown by this statement is required for the purpose of determining the statutory gross estate of the insured for Federal estate tax purposes.

STATEMENT OF INSURER.—This statement must be made, on behalf of the insurance company which issued the policy, by an officer of the company having access to the records of the company. For purposes of this statement, a facsimile signature may be used in lieu of a manual signature and, if used, shall be binding as a manual signature.

DUTY TO FILE.—It is the duty of the executor to procure this statement from the insurance company and file it with the return. However, if specifically requested, the insurance company should file this statement direct with the official of the Internal Revenue Service making the request.

SEPARATE STATEMENTS.—A separate statement must be filed for each policy listed on the return.

Form 33 Death Certificate

This becomes a permanent legal record when properly executed. Please type, or use permanent ink.

MINNESOTA DEPARTMENT OF HEALTH
Section of Vital Statistics
CERTIFICATE OF DEATH

LOCAL FILE NUMBER

STATE FILE NUMBER

1. DECEASED — NAME	FIRST	MIDDLE	LAST	2. SEX	3. DATE OF DEATH	MONTH	DAY	YEAR

| 4a. AGE (IN YEARS LAST BIRTHDAY) | 4b. UNDER ONE YEAR MONTHS DAYS | 4c. UNDER ONE DAY HOURS MINUTES | 5. DATE OF BIRTH | MONTH DAY YEAR | 6. RACE SPECIFY | 7a. COUNTY OF DEATH |

| 7b. LOCATION OF DEATH (CITY, VILLAGE OR TOWNSHIP) | 7c. INSIDE CORPORATE LIMITS SPECIFY YES OR NO | 7d. HOSPITAL OR OTHER INSTITUTION — NAME (IF NOT IN EITHER, GIVE STREET AND NUMBER) |

| 8. BIRTHPLACE (STATE OR FOREIGN COUNTRY) | 9. CITIZEN OF WHAT COUNTRY | 10. MARRIED, NEVER MARRIED, WIDOWED, DIVORCED SPECIFY | 11. SPOUSE — NAME |

| 12. WAS DECEASED EVER IN U.S. ARMED FORCES SPECIFY YES OR NO | 13. SOCIAL SECURITY NUMBER | 14a. USUAL OCCUPATION (GIVE KIND OF WORK DURING MOST OF WORKING LIFE, EVEN IF RETIRED) | 14b. KIND OF BUSINESS OR INDUSTRY |

| 15a. RESIDENCE — STATE | 15b. COUNTY | 15c. CITY, VILLAGE OR TOWNSHIP | 15d. INSIDE CORPORATE LIMITS SPECIFY YES OR NO |

| 16a. FATHER — NAME | 16b. BIRTHPLACE (STATE OR FOREIGN COUNTRY) | 17. ADDRESS OF DECEDENT | STREET AND NUMBER | POST OFFICE |

| 18a. MOTHER — MAIDEN NAME | 18b. BIRTHPLACE (STATE OR FOREIGN COUNTRY) | 19. INFORMANT — NAME | ADDRESS |

MEDICAL CERTIFICATION

20. PART I — DEATH WAS CAUSED BY (ENTER ONLY ONE CAUSE PER LINE (A), (B) AND (C))	IF DIAGNOSIS DEFERRED CHECK BOX	APPROXIMATE INTERVAL BETWEEN ONSET AND DEATH
A. IMMEDIATE CAUSE		
B. DUE TO, OR AS A CONSEQUENCE OF		
C. DUE TO, OR AS A CONSEQUENCE OF		

SAMPLE

| PART II OTHER SIGNIFICANT CONDITIONS | 21a. AUTOPSY SPECIFY YES OR NO | 21b. IF YES, WERE FINDINGS CONSIDERED IN DETERMINING CAUSE OF DEATH |

| 22a. ACCIDENT, SUICIDE, HOMICIDE OR UNDETERMINED SPECIFY IF DEFERRED CHECK | 22b. DATE OF INJURY MONTH DAY YEAR HOUR | 22c. INJURY AT WORK SPECIFY YES OR NO |

| 22d. PLACE OF INJURY (AT HOME, FARM, STREET, FACTORY, OFFICE BUILDING ETC.) | 22e. LOCATION STREET OR RFD NUMBER CITY, VILLAGE OR TOWNSHIP COUNTY STATE |

| 22f. HOW INJURY OCCURRED | (ENTER NATURE OF INJURY IN PART I OR PART II, ITEM 20) |

23a. CERTIFICATION — PHYSICIAN MONTH DAY YEAR MONTH DAY YEAR	23b. CERTIFICATION — MEDICAL EXAMINER OR CORONER
I attended the deceased from _____ to _____ and last saw him/her alive on _____ . I (did, did not view the body after death. Death occurred at _____ M at the place and time and on the date stated above and to the best of my knowledge due to the causes stated.	On the basis of the examination of the body and/or the investigation, in my opinion death occurred at _____ M, on the date and due to the causes stated above. The decedent was pronounced dead on _____ MONTH DAY YEAR at _____ M.
23c. PHYSICIAN — SIGNATURE	23d. MEDICAL EXAMINER OR CORONER — SIGNATURE
23e. PHYSICIAN — NAME (TYPE OR PRINT)	23f. MEDICAL EXAMINER OR CORONER — NAME (TYPE OR PRINT)
23g. MAILING ADDRESS PHYSICIAN, MEDICAL EXAMINER OR CORONER	23h. DATE SIGNED MONTH DAY YEAR

| 24a. BURIAL, CREMATION, REMOVAL SPECIFY | 24b. CEMETERY OR CREMATORY — NAME | 24c. LOCATION (CITY, VILLAGE OR COUNTY) (STATE) |

| 24d. DATE OF BURIAL, CREMATION OR REMOVAL MONTH DAY YEAR | 25a. FUNERAL HOME — NAME | 25b. FUNERAL HOME — ADDRESS |

| 26a. DATE FILED BY LOCAL REGISTRAR MONTH DAY YEAR | 26b. LOCAL REGISTRAR — SIGNATURE | 27. MORTICIAN OR FUNERAL DIRECTOR — SIGNATURE |

SIGNATURE OF SUB REGISTRAR

19___

BURIAL OR REMOVAL PERMIT ISSUED

Form 34 Oath of Appraisers and Appraisal of Lands Under Oath for Sale

No. 3606—Oath of Appraisers of Lands Under Order for Sale. (Revised J. of P. Assn. 1937)

State of Minnesota, } ss.

County of...............................

IN PROBATE COURT

In the Matter of the Estate of

....
Decedent—*Ward*

Oath of Appraisers and Appraisal
of Lands Under Order for Sale

OATH OF APPRAISERS

State of Minnesota, }

County of...............................

I, ...

and I, ..., *do swear that I will faithfully and*

justly perform all the duties of the office and trust which I now assume as appraiser of the lands of the

above named ....*under and pursuant*

to that certain order for sale of said lands at private sale, made by the above named Court on the

.....................day of..., 19............, and that I will appraise

the said land described in said order for sale at its true and full value, So Help Me God.

Subscribed and sworn to before me this

.................................day of..........................., 19..........   ....

....
Notary Public

....*County, Minn.*

My commission expires....................................., 19..........

APPRAISAL

We, the undersigned appraisers appointed by the above named Court in and by its certain order for

sale to ....to sell certain lands

belonging to the above named..., dated

the.............................day of..., 19.........., do hereby certify and report:

That we did first and before making said appraisal take and subscribe the foregoing oath as by law

required and thereafter did appraise at their true and full value in cash those certain tracts or parcels of

land lying and being in the County of.., State of Minnesota, described

in said order for sale, as follows, to-wit:

Form 35 Proof of Claim

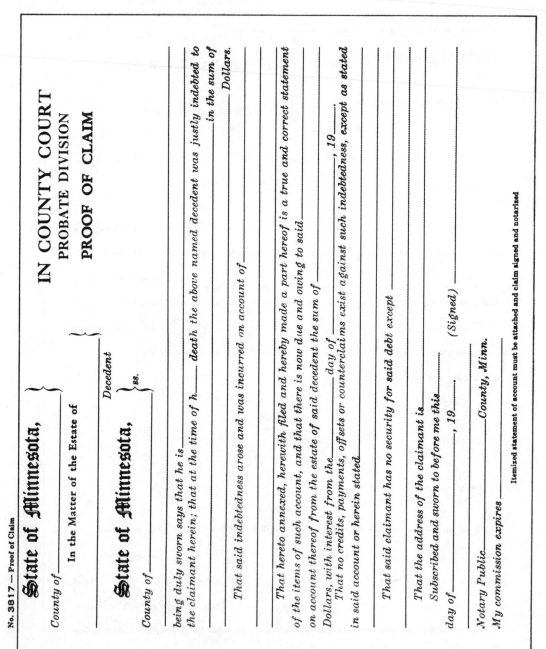

No. 3817 — Proof of Claim

State of Minnesota,

County of _____

In the Matter of the Estate of _____

_____ Decedent

IN COUNTY COURT

PROBATE DIVISION

PROOF OF CLAIM

State of Minnesota,

County of _____ } ss.

_____ being duly sworn says that he is the claimant herein; that at the time of h_____ death the above named decedent was justly indebted to _____ in the sum of _____ Dollars.

That said indebtedness arose and was incurred on account of _____

That hereto annexed, herewith filed and hereby made a part hereof is a true and correct statement of the items of such account, and that there is now due and owing to said _____ on account thereof from the estate of said decedent the sum of _____ Dollars, with interest from the _____ day of _____, 19_____. That no credits, payments, offsets or counterclaims exist against such indebtedness, except as stated in said account or herein stated.

That said claimant has no security for said debt except _____

That the address of the claimant is _____

Subscribed and sworn to before me this _____ day of _____, 19_____.

_____ (Signed) _____

_____ Notary Public.

My commission expires _____ County, Minn.

Itemized statement of account must be attached and claim signed and notarized

Form 36 Probate Deed

Form 4570

PROBATE DEED OF SALE INDIVIDUAL PERSONAL REPRESENTATIVE TO INDIVIDUAL

THIS INDENTURE, Made this _____ day of _____ , 19 _____ ,
between _____ ,
as Personal Representative _____ of the Estate of _____ , deceased,

part _____ of the first part, and _____

of the County of _____ and State of _____ ,
part _____ of the second part,

WITNESSETH, that whereas _____a (single) (married) person of
the County of _____ and State of _____ died on
_____ , 19 _____ , and the _____ Court of _____ County,
Minnesota did appoint _____
_____ Personal Representative _____
of the estate, and whereas by the laws of the State of Minnesota, said Personal Representative _____
(is) (are) empowered to make and execute a conveyance of real estate.

NOW, THEREFORE, the said part _____ of the first part, in consideration of the sum
of _____ DOLLARS,
to _____ in hand paid by the said part _____ of the second part, the
receipt whereof is hereby acknowledged, do _____ hereby Grant, Bargain, Sell, and Convey
unto the said part _____ of the second part, _____ heirs and assigns, Forever, all
the tract _____ or parcel _____ of land lying and being in the County of
_____ and State of Minnesota, described as follows, to-wit:

TO HAVE AND TO HOLD AND SAME, Together with all the hereditaments and appurtenances
thereunto belonging or in anywise appertaining, to the said part _____ of the second part, _____
heirs and assigns, Forever.

IN TESTIMONY WHEREOF, The said part _____ of the first part ha_____ hereunto set _____
hand _____ the day and year first above written.

_____

_____

_____
as personal representative _____ of the Estate of

_____
Deceased.

I, _____ , spouse of the above named
decedent, do hereby consent to the within conveyance.

_____

Form 37 Petition to Sell-Mortgage-Lease Real Estate

No. 3882 — Petition of Representative to Sell-Mortgage-Lease Land. (Revised by J. of P. Assn., 1964.)

State of Minnesota, }ss

County of..

IN PROBATE COURT

File No.............................

In the Matter of the Estate of:

....

Ward Decedent

**Petition of Representative
to Sell-Mortgage-Lease Land**

YOUR PETITIONER respectfully represents and shows to the Court:

That he is the duly appointed representative in the above entitled matter, with LETTERS in full force and effect.

That it is expedient to sell-mortgage-lease the land hereinafter described for the best interest of the estate and for the benefit of the heirs thereof, viz: (state reasons)

*(A) HOMESTEAD: That tract of land lying and being in the County of..,
State of Minnesota described as follows, viz:*

(1) The terms and conditions of the mortgage, or the lease, proposed herein on the above homestead, are as follows:

Form 38 Order for Hearing Petition to Sell-Mortgage-Lease Real Estate

No. 3847 (Revised J. of P. Ass'n 1969.)

State of Minnesota, } ss.

IN PROBATE COURT

County of ....

IN RE ESTATE OF

....
Decedent - Ward

Order for Hearing on Petition to .... Sell .... Real Estate

The representative of said estate having filed herein a petition to ....

certain real estate described in said petition;

It is Ordered, That the hearing thereof be had on ....

19 ...., at .... o'clock........ M., before this Court in the probate court room in the court house in

..................., Minnesota, and that notice hereof be given by mail as

provided by law.

Dated ...., 19 ....

....
Probate Judge.

(Probate Court Seal)

....
Attorney for Petitioner.

Form 39 Order for Sale, Mortgage, or Lease of Real Estate at Private Sale

No. 3875—Order for Sale of Real Estate at Private Sale. (Revision—J. of P. Ass'n, 1936)

State of Minnesota, } ss.

County of..

In the Matter of the Estate of

....

IN PROBATE COURT

File No...

Order For Sale of Real Estate
at Private Sale

The above entitled matter came on to be heard by the Court on the...
day of.., 19........., upon the petition of...
....as representative in the above entitled matter,
praying for an order to sell certain real estate described in said petition; and the Court having heard the
said petition and all the evidence adduced in support thereof, and having duly considered the same and
examined the files and records in said matter, finds the following facts:

FIRST—That notice of said hearing has been given and served as required by law and the order of
this Court for said hearing.

SECOND—That the said representative appeared at said hearing in person and by attorney
....and was duly examined relative to said matter by the Court
and that ....appeared in opposition to said petition.

THIRD—That it would be for the best interest of said estate and the persons interested therein that
the property hereinafter described, be sold.

It is Therefore Ordered, FIRST—That the said representative of said estate be, and hereby is,
authorized and directed to sell at private sale the real estate hereinafter described, situate and being in
the County of.., State of Minnesota, to-wit:

Form 40 Warrant to Appraisers at Private Sale and Oath of Appraisers

No. 3605—Warrant to Appraisers at Private Sale and Oath of Appraisers

State of Minnesota, } ss.

County of ....

IN PROBATE COURT

IN THE MATTER OF

.... }

....

The STATE OF MINNESOTA To ....

.... of said County, GREETING:

Whereas, *License to sell real estate at private sale was issued and granted to* ....

....

....

on the .... day of .... 19........

And Whereas, *We are desirous that the said real estate be duly appraised, pursuant to the statute in such case made and provided;*

Therefore, *Trusting in your integrity and disinterestedness, we have appointed and do by these presents, appoint you appraisers of the following described real estate, situate and being in the County of* .... *and State of Minnesota, to-wit:*

and being severally duly sworn, to the faithful execution of said trust, you are hereby required faithfully and honestly to appraise the same, at its full cash value, as by you determined; and the said appraisal so made, you will certify and subscribe, and together with this Warrant deliver without delay to the said

.... *Hereof fail not.*

In Testimony Whereof, *We have caused the seal of the Probate Court of said County to be hereunto affixed.*

WITNESS: The Honorable ....

(L. S.) *Judge of Probate, at* .... *in said County,*

this .... *day of* .... 19........

....

Judge of Probate.

Form 41 Report of Sale of Land at Private Sale under Order for Sale

No. 3641—Report of Sale of Land at Private Sale Under Order For Sale. (Revised J. of P. Ass'n, 1937)

𝕾tate of 𝕸innesota,

County of_____ }

In the Matter of the Estate of

_____

_____ Decedent—Ward }

IN PROBATE COURT

REPORT OF SALE OF LAND AT PRIVATE SALE UNDER ORDER FOR SALE

Your petitioner respectfully reports to the court his proceedings under that certain order for sale granted to him in the above entitled matter on the_____day of_____, 19____, to sell at private sale the lands of said_____ hereinafter described, as follows, to-wit:

First—That before making sale of the real estate hereinafter described under said order for sale, he executed and filed in this court his bond required by the said order for sale.

Second—That before making sale of said real estate under said order for sale, he caused the same to be re-appraised by_____ the appraisers appointed in said order for sale to appraise the same, and the appraisement thereof to be filed in this court_____(1)

Third—That on the_____day of_____, 19____, he, pursuant to said order for sale, sold to_____ _____of_____ th____tract____ or parcel____ of land, described in said order for sale, and lying and being in the County of_____, State of Minnesota, described as follows, to-wit:_____

for the sum of_____Dollars,

Form 42 Order Confirming Private Sale of Real Estate

No. 3876—Order Confirming Private Sale of Real Estate (Revised—J. of P. Assn., 1936)

State of Minnesota, }ss.

County of..}

In the Matter of the Estate of

....

....

IN PROBATE COURT

File No...

Order Confirming Private Sale of Real Estate

The above entitled matter came on to be heard on the..day of

...., 19........., upon the report of..

....as representative in the above entitled matter of the sale of certain real estate pursuant to the order of this court for sale thereof granted therefor, and on petition for the confirmation of said sale; and the court having considered the said report, and having been advised relative to the same, and having examined the files and records in said matter, finds herein the following facts, to-wit:

FIRST—That pursuant to a petition duly made and filed in this court, and the order of this court duly issued for hearing on said petition, and notice of said hearing duly given as provided by law, and a hearing duly had by this court on said petition, an order for sale in said above entitled matter was duly made and filed in this court whereby the said representative of said estate was authorized and directed to sell at private sale the real estate hereinafter described.

SECOND—That pursuant to said order for sale, the said representative before making the sale of real estate specified in said report and hereinafter referred to, complied with all the conditions and provisions in said order contained.

THIRD—That the said representative, before making said sale, did cause the real estate hereinafter and in said order for sale described to be re-appraised by the persons appointed for that purpose in said order for sale, and their re-appraisal thereof to be filed in this court..

FOURTH—That on the..day of.., 19........., the said representative, pursuant to said order for sale, did sell, at private sale, to..

....

for the sum of..DOLLARS, the tract...... of land, described in said order for sale, lying and being in the County of..

...., State of Minnesota, described as follows, to-wit:

Form 43 State Inheritance Tax Waiver

Form 4009 (Rev. J. of P. Assn. 12-64)

State of Minnesota,

County of ....

Re Estate of

....

Died...................................., 19........

PROBATE COURT

File No...

**PETITION FOR
INHERITANCE TAX RETURN
WAIVER**

(Decree of descent)

(Summary distribution)

(Administration)

....*respectfully represents that he is the (petitioner-
representative) in these proceedings and knows of no omission from his (petition-inventory and appraisal)
and schedule of non-probate assets; that there is no inheritance tax due the State of Minnesota by reason
of any transfer of property caused by decedent's death; and that the required filing of any self assessed
inheritance tax return should be waived by the Court pursuant to Minnesota Statutes Sec. 291.09 Subdivision 1. (e).*

SUMMARY OF ASSETS

Probate:

Homestead - - - - $ ....

Other real estate - - - ....

Personal property - - - ....

Non-probate:		*Survivor-Beneficiary*	*Relation*
Joint homestead - - - - - $...............		....	....
		....	....
		....	....
Joint other real estate - - -		....	....
		....	....
Joint personal property - - -		....	....
		....	....
Insurance - - - - - -		....	....
		....	....
Annuities and Deposits - - -		....	....
		....	....
Transfers by decedent - - -		....	....
		....	....
Miscellaneous - - - - -		....	....
		....	....

   *Wherefore petitioner prays that the Court issue a waiver of the filing of any self assessed inheritance
tax return herein.*

Dated.., 19..........   ....

*NOTE: Make proper deletions within the parentheses so that the Commissioner of Taxation can know the
       type of Court proceedings.*

Form 44 Petition for Appointment of a Special Administrator

No. 3885—Petition for Appointment of Special Administrator. (Revised by J. of P. Assn. 1936)

State of Minnesota,

County of_____

IN PROBATE COURT

IN THE MATTER OF THE ESTATE OF

_____
                    Decedent.

Petition for Appointment of Special
Administrator

Your petitioner respectfully represents and states to the court:

First—That he is a resident of_____in the County of_____

State of Minnesota, and is interested in the said estate of decedent as_____

_____

Second—That said decedent died _____testate on the_____day of_____

19___, at_____in the County of_____State of

_____, and at the time of his death was a resident of the County of

_____State of_____, citizen of_____,

and left estate in the County of_____State of Minnesota, of the character and

estimated value following, to-wit:

PERSONAL PROPERTY

(1st)   Household goods of the estimated value of   -   -   -   -   - $_____

(2nd)   Wearing apparel of the estimated value of   -   -   -   - $_____

(3rd)   Capital stock of the estimated value of   -   -   -   - $_____

(4th)   Notes, bonds, mortgages and other evidences of indebtedness of the esti-
          mated value of   -   -   -   -   -   -   -   - $_____

_____ $_____

_____ $_____

          Total personal property   -   -   -   -   -   - $_____

1. Homestead in_____County, Minnesota, as follows:

   A. City Property_____

   _____ $_____
                         (Give Area)

   (or)
   B. Rural Property_____

   _____ $_____
                         (Give Area)

2. Real Estate other than Homestead:

   A. City Property_____Lots without Buildings $_____

      City Property_____Lots with Buildings $_____

   B. Rural Property_____Acres Improved Land $_____

      Rural Property_____Acres Unimproved Land $_____

   Third—That it is necessary and expedient that a special administrator of said estate be appointed,

for the following reasons:_____

_____

   Fourth—That_____who is a resident of_____

County, Minnesota, and whose post office address is_____is a suitable

person to act as special administrator of said estate_____

Form 45 Order Granting Special Administration

No. 3655—Order Granting Special Administration (Rev. 1944)

State of Minnesota,

County of_____

IN PROBATE COURT

IN THE MATTER OF THE ESTATE OF

_____

Decedent.

Order Granting Special Administration

On reading and filing the petition of_____

praying that special administration of the estate of the above named decedent be granted to

_____,

and upon due consideration of said petition and the evidence adduced in support thereof, the court finds:

FIRST—That said decedent died on the_____day of_____, 19____,

and at the time of_____death was a resident of the County of_____

State of_____, and at time of_____death left estate in the

County of_____, State of Minnesota.

SECOND—THAT_____

(Here state the facts necessitating special administration)

THIRD—That it is necessary and expedient, for the preservation and best interests of said estate,
that special administration of said estate be granted.

Now Therefore, it is Ordered, That special administration of said estate be, and the same
hereby is, granted; and that_____be, and_____hereby is
appointed such special administrat_____ of said estate, to administer the same according to law until
the further order of this court or the appointment and qualification of a general representative of said
estate according to law; and that before letters of special administration are to_____issued, _____
shall take and file_____oath as required by law, and file_____bond in the penal sum of
_____Dollars, with sufficient sureties as
provided by law, to be approved by the Judge of this court and conditioned as by law required.

Dated_____, 19____

_____
Judge of Probate

Form 46 Letters of Special Administration

Form 4555

524.3-614 #7   UPC

STATE OF MINNESOTA

COUNTY OF _____

In Re: Estate of

_____
Deceased

PROBATE COURT
COUNTY COURT-PROBATE DIVISION

Court File No. _____

LETTERS OF
SPECIAL ADMINISTRATION

The above named decedent having died on _____ , 19 ___ , having been appointed and qualified, _____
is hereby authorized to act as special administrator according to law.

Dated: _____

_____
Judge/Registrar

(COURT SEAL)

Form 47 Final Account and Report of Special Administration

No. 3653—Final Account and Report of Special Administrator. (Revision of 1906)

State of Minnesota,

County of..

IN PROBATE COURT

IN THE MATTER OF THE ESTATE OF

....

....

Decedent.

Final Account and Report of Special Administrator

Your petitioner...*respectfully represents and shows to the court:*

FIRST—*That letters of special administration of the above named estate were to him issued on the*

....*day of*.., 19............

SECOND—*That he has collected all the personal property of said decedent,*..

and preserved all the property of said decedent for the general representative of said estate; and made and filed in this court on the..*day of*.., 19............

a true inventory of all the goods, chattels, rights, credits and effects of said decedent.

THIRD—..*(1)*

....

....

FOURTH—*That under and by leave of the court, he has sold the following described personal property of said decedent and collected and received therefor the following sums, to-wit:*

.... $..

.... $..

.... $..

.... $..

.... $..

.... $..

.... $..

Total receipts from sales $..

FIFTH—*That he has collected and received other sums due said decedent from other sources as follows:*

.... $..

.... $..

.... $..

.... $..

.... $..

Total amount collected other than from sales $..

Total of all receipts - - - - - - $..

SIXTH — *That he has necessarily paid out and expended in administrating said estate and caring for the same, the following amounts for the following purposes:*

Form 48 Order Approving the Final Account and Report of the Special Administrator

No. 3652.—Order Approving Account of Special Administrator. Revision of 1906.

State of Minnesota,

County of...

IN PROBATE COURT

IN THE MATTER OF THE ESTATE OF

_____

Decedent.

Order Approving Account and Report of Special Administrator.

The report and final account of...as special administrator of the estate of the above named decedent having been made and filed in this court on the...........................day of.........................19....., and the court having read and considered the same, and having heard and considered the evidence adduced in support thereof, and examined the files and records in said matter, finds as follows:

FIRST—That the said special administrator has collected all the personal property of said decedent, cared for, gathered and secured all the crops belonging to his said estate, preserved all the property of said decedent and cared for the same, has sold all the personal property of said decedent he was authorized to sell by leave of this court and accounted for the proceeds of the same, has taken charge of the real property of said decedent as he was authorized to do by leave of this court, and cared for the same and reported his doings thereon to this court, has made and filed in this court a true inventory of all said property of said decedent, has in all things obeyed the orders of this court in said matter, and is ready to turn over and deliver to the general representative of said estate all the property of said decedent.

SECOND—That said special administrator has made and filed in this court a full account of all his receipts and disbursements in said special administration of said estate, a summary statement of which is as follows, to-wit:

Total receipts from sales of personal property
     under leave of court, - - - $...
Total collections from other sources; - - $...
Total expenditures and expenses, - - $...
Balance, - - - - - - $............................. $...

THIRD—That...has been appointed general representative of said decedent, and that letters...
have been to him issued

Therefore it is Hereby Ordered, That the report and account of said special administrator, as adjusted and settled by the court herein, be, and the same hereby is, approved and allowed; and that said special administrator be, and he hereby is, authorized and directed, to forthwith turn over and deliver to said general representative of said estate all of the property of said decedent in his possession and under his control, and that upon the filing in this court of the receipt of said general representative therefor, the said special administrator, together with the sureties on his bond, be discharged from all further liabilities and duties in said matter.

Dated...19.......

....
Judge of Probate.

Form 49 Petition for Summary Distribution or Assignment

525.51 #1   UPC —

STATE OF MINNESOTA

PROBATE COURT
COUNTY COURT-PROBATE DIVISION

COUNTY OF _____

In Re: Estate of

Court File No. _____

PETITION FOR
SUMMARY ASSIGNMENT OR
DISTRIBUTION
(Testate) (Intestate)

_____
Deceased

TO THE HONORABLE JUDGE OF THE ABOVE NAMED COURT:

Petitioner, _____ , respectfully states:

1. Petitioner resides at _____ ;

2. Petitioner has an interest herein as _____ ,
and is, therefore, an interested person as defined by the laws of this State;

3. Decedent was born _____ , 19 ___ , at _____ ;

4. Decedent died _____ testate at the age of _____ on _____ , 19 ___ ,
at _____ .

5. Decedent at the time of his death resided at _____ ,
City of _____ , County of _____ , State of _____ ;

6. That the names and addresses of decedent's spouse, children, heirs and devisees and other persons interested in this proceeding and the ages of any who are minors so far as known or ascertainable with reasonable diligence by the petitioner are:
NOTE - Classify the heirs and others entitled to take per stirpes and give the name, date of death, relationship/interest and address, if known, of their predeceased ancestor. Give the birthdate of any heir or devisee taking a life interest.

Name	Age	Relationship/Interest	Address

7. That venue for this proceeding is in the above named County of the State of Minnesota, because the decedent was domiciled in such County at the time of his death, and was the owner of property located in the State of Minnesota, or because, though not domiciled in the State of Minnesota, the decedent was the owner of property located in the above named County at the time of his death.

8. That no personal representative of the decedent has been appointed in this State or elsewhere whose appointment has not been terminated.

9. That petitioner has not received a demand for notice and is not aware of any demand for notice of any probate or appointment proceeding concerning the decedent that may have been filed in this State or elsewhere or proper notice has been given.

Form 50 Final Decree Summary Assignment or Distribution

525.51 #13   UPC —

STATE OF MINNESOTA

PROBATE COURT
COUNTY OF _____   COUNTY COURT-PROBATE DIVISION

In Re: Estate of

Court File No. _____

FINAL DECREE
SUMMARY ASSIGNMENT
DISTRIBUTION

_____
                    Deceased

The petition of _____ dated _____ , 19 ____ , for summary assignment or distribution of the estate of the above named decedent having duly come on for hearing before the above named Court, the undersigned Judge having heard and considered such petition, being fully advised in the premises, makes the following findings and determinations:

1. That the petition for summary assignment or distribution is complete.

2. That the time for any notice has expired and any notice as required by the laws of this state has been given and proved.

3. That the petitioner has declared or affirmed that the representations contained in the petition are true, correct and complete to the best of his knowledge or information.

4. That the petitioner appears from the petition to be an interested person as defined by the laws of this state.

5. That the above named decedent testator herein is dead having died testate at the age of _____ years on _____ , 19 ____ , at _____ .

6. That venue for this proceeding is in the above named County of the State of Minnesota, because the decedent was domiciled in such county at the time of his death, and was the owner of property located in the State of Minnesota, or because, though not domiciled in the State of Minnesota, the decedent was the owner of property located in the above named county at the time of his death.

7. That this Court has jurisdiction of this estate, proceeding and subject matter.

8. That the estate of said decedent consists of the following property, to-wit:

(A) Personal property of the value of $ _____ comprising the following items, viz.:

Form 51 Petition Claiming Interest in Omitted Property
(Petition for Determination of Descent)

Form 4573

524.3-413 #5   UPC

STATE OF MINNESOTA

COUNTY OF _____

In Re: Estate of

_____
Deceased

PROBATE COURT
COUNTY COURT-PROBATE DIVISION

Court File No. _____

PETITION FOR
DETERMINATION OF DESCENT
(Omitted property)
(Incorrectly described property)

TO THE HONORABLE JUDGE OF THE ABOVE NAMED COURT:

Petitioner, _____ , respectfully states:
1. Petitioner resides at _____ ;

2. Petitioner has an interest herein as _____ ;
and is, therefore, an interested person as defined by the laws of this State;

3. Decedent was born _____ , 19 ___ , at _____ ;

4. Decedent died ____testate at the age of ____ on _____ , 19 ___ , at ____
_____ ;

5. Decedent at the time of his death resided at _____ ,
City of _____ County of _____ , State of _____ ;

6. That the names and addresses of decedent's spouse, children, heirs and devisees and other persons
interested in this proceeding and the ages of any who are minors so far as known or ascertainable
with reasonable diligence by the applicant are:
NOTE — Classify the heirs and others entitled to take per stirpes and give the name, date of
death, relationship/interest and address, if known, of their predeceased ancestor.
Give the birthdate of any heir or devisee taking a life interest.

Name	Age	Relationship/Interest	Address

Form 52 Decree of Distribution (Descent) of Omitted Property

Form 4574

	524.3-413 #6	UPC

STATE OF MINNESOTA

COUNTY OF _____

In Re: Estate of

_____
Deceased

PROBATE COURT
COUNTY COURT-PROBATE DIVISION

Court File No. _____

DECREE OF DESCENT
(Omitted property)
(Incorrectly described property)

The petition of _____ , dated _____ , 19 ___ , for determination of descent in the estate of the above named decedent having duly come on for hearing before the above named Court, the undersigned Judge having heard and considered such petition, being fully advised in the premises, makes the following findings and determinations:

1. That the petition for determination of descent is complete.

2. That the time for any notice has expired and any notice as required by the laws of this State has been given and proved.

3. That the petitioner has declared or affirmed that the representations contained in the petition are true, correct and complete to the best of his knowledge or information.

4. That the petitioner appears from the petition to be an interested person as defined by the laws of this State.

5. That decedent died testate at the age of _____ on _____ , 19___ , at _____ .

6. That, on the basis of the statements in the petition, this Court has jurisdiction of this estate, proceedings and subject matter.

7. That venue for this proceeding is in the above named County of the State of Minnesota, because the decedent was domiciled in such County at the time of his death, and was the owner of property located in the State of Minnesota, or because, though not domiciled in the State of Minnesota, the decedent was the owner of property located in the above named County at the time of his death.

8. That all decedent's heirs are as identified in the petition commencing this proceeding.

9. That no will or authenticated copy of a will of decedent probated outside of this State in accordance with the laws in force in the place where probated has been admitted to probate nor administration had in this state-except in the _____ Court of_____ County under file number _____ in which proceedings the (Order) (Decree) of Distribution was entered on _____ , 19 ___ , wherein the hereinafter described real and/or personal property was (omitted) (incorrectly described) as follows, to-wit:

Form 53 Petition for Formal Probate of Will and for Formal Appointment of Personal Representative

FORM 4353

Form 524.3-401 #3
Form 524.3-502 #2   UPC 33

STATE OF MINNESOTA   PROBATE COURT
                                     COUNTY COURT-PROBATE DIVISION
COUNTY OF Ramsey

In Re: Estate of   Court File No. __999999__

                                     PETITION FOR FORMAL PROBATE
___Jane M. Doe___   OF WILL AND FOR FORMAL
              Deceased   APPOINTMENT OF EXECUTOR

TO THE HONORABLE JUDGE OF THE ABOVE NAMED COURT:

Petitioner, ___John C. Doe___, respectfully states:

1. Petitioner resides at 1005 Easy Street , St. Paul, MN 07102   ;

2. Petitioner has an interest herein as **Named personal representative and devisee** ;
   and is, therefore, an interested person as defined by the laws of this state;

3. Decedent was born ___November 6___, 19_00_, at_Detroit, Michigan_   ;

4. Decedent died on ___September 20___, 19_77_, at __St. Paul, MN 07102__   ;

5. Decedent at the time of her death resided at _1005 Easy Street,_   ,
   City of_St. Paul_, County of _Ramsey_, State of _Minnesota_   ;

6. That the names and addresses of decedent's spouse, children, heirs and devisees and other
   persons interested in this proceeding and the ages of any who are minors so far known or
   ascertainable with reasonable diligence by the petitioner are:

Note: Classify the heirs and others entitled to take per stirpes and give the name, date of death,
relationship/interest and address, if known, of their predeceased ancestors. Give the birth date of any
heir or devisee taking a life interest.

Name	Age	Relationship/Interest		Address
John C. Doe	76	husband	devisee, heir personal rep.	1005 Easy Street St. Paul, MN 07102
Sandy R. Doe	45	daughter	devisee, heir	1005 Easy Street St. Paul, MN 07102
American Cancer Society		Devisee		222 Glen Acre Dr. St. Paul, MN 55102
Girl's Clubs of America		Devisee		111 Cookie Lane St. Paul, MN, 55102
Newark Institute of Higher Learning		Devisee		444 Brilliant Drive St. Paul, MN 55102

7. That venue for this proceeding is in the above named County of the State of Minnesota, because
   the decedent was domiciled in such county at the time of his death, and was the owner of property
   located in the State of Minnesota XXXXXXXXXXXXXXXXXXXXXXXXXXXXXXXXXXXXXXXXXXXXXX,
   XXXXXXXXXXXXXXXXXXXXXXXXXXXXXXXXXXXXXXXXXXXXXXXXXXXXXXXXXXXXXXXXXXXXXXXXXXXXX.

Form 53 continued

8. That no personal representative of the decedent has been appointed in this state or elsewhere ~~XXXXXXXXXXXXXXXXXXXXXXXXXXXXXXXXXX~~.

9. That petitioner has not received a demand for notice and is not aware of any demand for notice of any probate or appointment preceeding concerning the decedent that may have been filed in this state or elsewhere or proper notice has been given.

10. That the original of decedent's last will duly executed on ___June 2___ , 19 45 ~~XXX~~ ~~XXXXXXXXXXXXXXXXXXXXXXXXXXXXXXXXXXXXXXXXXXXXXXXXXXXXXXXXXXXXXXXXXXXXXXXXXX~~ ~~XXXXXXXXXXXXXXXXXXXXXXXXXXXXXXXXXXXXXXXXXXXXXXXXXXXXXXXXXXXXXXXXXXXXXXXXXX~~ ~~XXXXXXXXXXXXXXXXXXXXXXXXXXXXXXXXXXXXX~~

11. That the petitioner, to the best of his knowledge, believes the will ~~XXXXXXXXXXXXXXXXXXXXXX~~ t~~XXXXXXhas XXXXXX~~e been validly executed.

12. That after the exercise of reasonable diligence, the petitioner is unaware of any instrument revoking the will, and the petitioner believes that the instrument which is the subject of this petition is the decedent's last will.

13. That the time limit for formal probate and appointment as provided by the laws of this state has not expired because three years or less have passed since the decedent's death.

14. That the petitioner ~~or~~ ___John C. Doe___ is entitled to priority and appointment as personal representative because petitioner ~~XXXXXXXXXXXXXXXXXXXXXXX~~ is nominated in the last will of the decedent as personal representative, with (no) ~~XXXXXXXXXXXXXXXXXXXXXXXXXXXXXXXXX~~ bond, in an ~~XXXXXXXXXXXXXXXXXX~~ (undesignated) administration; ~~XXXXXXXXXXXXXXXX~~ ~~XXXXXXXXXXXXXXXXXXXXXXXXXXXXXXXXXXXXXXXXXXXXXXXXXXXXXXXXXXXXXXXXXXXXXXXXXX~~ ~~XXXXXXXXXXXXXXXXXXXXXXXXXXXXXXXXXXXXXXXXXXXXXXXXXXXXXXXXXXXXXXXXXXXXXXXXXX~~ ~~XXXXXXXXXXXXXXXXXXXXXX~~

WHEREFORE, your petitioner requests the order of this Court fixing a time and place for hearing on this petition, and that after the time for any notice has expired, upon proof of notice, and hearing, the Court enter a judicial order formally;

1. Finding that the Testator is dead;

2. Finding that venue is proper;

3. Finding that the proceeding was commenced within the time limitations prescribed by the laws of this state;

4. Determining decedent's domicile at death;

5. Determining decedent's heirs;

6. Determining decedent's state of testacy;

7. Probating the valid and unrevoked last will of decedent including any valid and unrevoked codicil thereto;

8. Determining that petitioner ~~XX~~ _____ is entitled to appointment as personal representative under the laws of this state;

9. Appointing petitioner ~~OX~~_____ as the executor of the estate of decedent with no ~~XX~~ _____ bond, in a ~~XXXXXXXXXXXX~~ (supervised) administration;

10. Authorizing issuance of letters testamentary to petitioner ~~OX~~ _____ upon qualification and acceptance.

11. Granting such other and further relief as may be proper.

FURTHER, under penalties for perjury for deliberate falsification therein; I declare or affirm that I have read the foregoing petition and to the best of my knowledge or information, its representations are true, correct and complete.

Dated: ___September 25, 1977___

Probate Assets
      Homestead - $20,000 **(Net)**
      Other Real Estate - $12,750 **(Net)**
      Personal Property - $185,498

/S/ John C. Doe
Petitioner

/S/ John Cranwall
Attorney for Petitioner
1st Trust Bldg.
St. Paul, Mn. 55101
Address/Phone
(612) 111-0011

Form 54 Order and Notice of Formal Appointment, Notice of Hearing for Formal Probate of Will and Notice to Creditors

Form 524.3-310 #3
524.3-403 #8
524.3-801 #4

OS150 (Rev. 7/76)   UPC——

STATE OF MINNESOTA   **PROBATE COURT**
                                        COUNTY COURT—PROBATE DIVISION

COUNTY OF Ramsey

In Re: Estate of   Court File No. 999999

____Jane M. Doe____
                Deceased

ORDER AND NOTICE OF FORMAL
APPOINTMENT OF PERSONAL
REPRESENTATIVE, NOTICE OF HEARING
FOR FORMAL PROBATE OF WILL AND
NOTICE TO CREDITORS

TO ALL INTERESTED PERSONS AND CREDITORS:

It is Ordered and
Notice is hereby given that informal appointment of ____John C. Doe____

whose address is 1005 Easy Street, St. Paul, MN 55102

as personal representative of the estate of the above named decedent, has been made. Any heir, devisee or other interested person may be entitled to appointment as personal representative or may object to the appointment of the personal representative and the personal representative is empowered to fully administer the estate including, after 30 days from the date of issuance of his letters, the power to sell, encumber, lease or distribute real estate, unless objections thereto are filed with the Court (pursuant to Section 524.3-607) and the Court otherwise orders.

Notice is hereby given that on the ____30th____ day of ____October____ , 19 77 , at ____10:00____ o'clock _A_.M., a hearing will be held in this Court at _St. Paul_ Minnesota, for the formal probate of an instrument purporting to be the will of the above named decedent, dated ____June 2____ , 1945 , _____

and that any objections thereto must be filed with the Court.

Notice is further given that ALL CREDITORS having claims against said estate are required to present the same to said personal representative or to the Clerk of the Court within four months after the date of this notice or said claims will be barred.

Dated: ____September 30, 1977____

                              /S/ I. M. Honest
                           X̶e̶g̶i̶s̶t̶e̶r̶ Judge

                              /S/ Thomas Malone
                           Clerk

____/S/ John Cranwall____
Attorney

____1st Trust Bldg., St. Paul, MN 55101____
Address (612) 111-0011

NOTE: If notice to creditors has been previously given, delete the Notice to Creditors herein.

Form 55 Proof (Affidavit) of Publication

Form 5—3m—9—77

STATE OF MINNESOTA

COUNTY OF Ramsey

} SS.

AFFIDAVIT OF PUBLICATION

Warren E. Maul, being duly sworn on oath says he is and during all the times herein stated has been the...........
publisher of the newspaper known as

FINANCE AND COMMERCE

and has full knowledge of the facts herein stated as follows: (1) Said newspaper is printed in the English language in newspaper format and in column and sheet form equivalent in printed space to at least 900 square inches. (2) Said newspaper is a daily and is distributed at least five (5) days each week, or four (4) days in a week in which a legal holiday is included. (3) Said newspaper has 25 percent of its news columns devoted to news of local interest to the community which it purports to serve and does not wholly duplicate any other publication and is not made up entirely of patents, plate matter and advertisements. (4) Said newspaper is circulated in and near the municipality which it purports to serve, has at least 500 copies regularly delivered to paying subscribers, has an average of at least 75 percent of its total circulation currently paid or no more than three months in arrears and has entry as second-class matter in its local post-office. (5) Said newspaper purports to serve the City of Minneapolis in the County of Hennepin, and it has its known office of issue in the City of Minneapolis in said county, established and open during its regular business hours for the gathering of news, sale of advertisements and sale of subscriptions and maintained by the managing officer of said newspaper or persons in its employ and subject to his direction and control during all such regular business hours and at which said newspaper is printed. (6) Said newspaper files a copy of each issue immediately with the State Historical Society. (7) Said newspaper has complied with all the foregoing conditions for at least two years preceding the day or dates of publication mentioned below. (8) Said newspaper has filed with the Secretary of State of Minnesota prior to January 1, 1966 and each January 1 thereafter an affidavit in the form prescribed by the Secretary of State and signed by the managing officer of said newspaper and sworn to before a notary public stating that the newspaper is a legal newspaper.

He further states on oath that the printed

PROBATE NOTICE

hereto attached as a part hereof was cut from the columns of said newspaper, and was printed and published therein in the English language, once each week, for two (2) successive weeks; that it was first so published on Wednesday the 30th day of September, 1977 and was thereafter printed and published on ....
Wednesday the 20th day of October, 1977 and that the following is a printed copy of the lower case alphabet from A to Z, both inclusive, and is hereby acknowledged as being the size and kind of type used in the composition and publication of said notice, to wit:

abcdefghijklmnopqrstuvwxyz

Subscribed and
sworn to before me, this 30th day of September, 1977.

....
Notary Public, Ramsey County, Minnesota

DOROTHY V. WOLF
NOTARY PUBLIC—MINNESOTA
RAMSEY COUNTY
My Commission Expires Sep. 23, 1984.

COURT FILE NO. 999999

ORDER AND NOTICE OF
HEARING ON PETITION FOR
PROBATE OF WILL
, AND
APPOINTMENT OF
PERSONAL REPRESENTATIVES IN
SUPERVISED ADMINISTRATION
AND NOTICE TO CREDITORS

STATE OF MINNESOTA
COUNTY OF Ramsey

PROBATE COURT

In Re: Estate of
Jane M. Doe,
Deceased.

TO ALL INTERESTED PERSONS AND CREDITORS:

It is ordered and notice is hereby given that on Monday, the 30th day of October, 1977, at ten o'clock A.M., a hearing will be held in the above named Court at C-4 Ramsey County Court House, St. Paul, Minnesota, for the probate of an instrument purporting to be the Will of the above decedent and for the appointment of John C. Doe, whose address is 1005 Easy St., St. Paul, Minnesota 07102.

, as personal representative of the estate of the above named decedent in supervised administration. That, if proper, and no objections are filed, said personal representatives will be appointed to administer the estate, to collect all assets, pay all legal debts, claims, taxes, and expenses, and sell real and personal property, and do all necessary acts for the estate. Upon completion of the administration, the representatives shall file a final account for allowance and shall distribute the estate to the persons thereunto entitled as ordered by the Court, and close the estate.

Notice is further given that ALL CREDITORS having claims against said estate are required to present the same to said personal representatives or to the Clerk of Probate Court within four months after the date of this notice or said claims will be barred.

Dated: October   th, 1977.
HON. I. M. Honest,
Judge of Probate Court.
Thomas Maloney,
Clerk of Probate Court.

(COURT SEAL)

By: John Cranwall,
Attorney,
1st Trust Bldg.
St. Paul, MN 55101

Form 56 Affidavit of Notice of Hearing Final Account

OS107 (Rev. 7/76)

Form 524.1—401 #2
525.83

UPC—

STATE OF MINNESOTA

COUNTY OF ___Ramsey___

PROBATE COURT
COUNTY COURT—PROBATE DIVISION

Court File No. ___999999___

In Re:

(ESTATE
(~~CONSERVATORSHIP~~
(~~GUARDIANSHIP~~

OF ___Jane M. Doe___

Deceased ~~~~

AFFIDAVIT OF MAILING ORDER OR NOTICE
OF HEARING Formal appointment of Personal
Representative Notice of
Hearing for Formal Probate
of Will and Notice to Creditors.

ATTACH COPY OF NOTICE OR ORDER HERE

(A clipping of newspaper publication
is attached here.)

STATE OF MINNESOTA
COUNTY OF ___Ramsey___ } ss

___I.M. Truthful___
being first duly sworn on oath deposes and says that on
the ___5th___ day of ___October___,
19 _77_ , at _St. Paul, MN_ in said
County and State __he mailed a copy of the Order or
Notice hereto attached to each _heir, devisee &_
personal representative

whose name and address are known to affiant, after exercising due diligence in ascertaining the correctness of said name and address, by placing a true and correct copy thereof in a sealed envelope, postage prepaid and depositing the same in the U. S. Mails at _St. Paul, MN._

and addressed to the following named persons:
NOTE: (Instructions at bottom of page)

NAME	Street or Post Office	CITY	STATE
John C. Doe	1005 Easy Street	St. Paul	MN 07102
Sandy R. Doe	1005 Easy Street	St. Paul	MN 07102
American Cancer Society	222 Glen Acre Drive	St. Paul	MN 55102
Girl's Clubs of America	111 Cookie Lane	St. Paul	MN 55102
Newark Institute of Higher Learning	444 Brilliant Drive	St. Paul	MN 55102

Subscribed and sworn to before me this ___5th___ day of
___October___ , 19 _77_

/S/ Judith Harris

Notary Public, ___Ramsey___ County, Minn.
My Commission expires ___March 7___ , 19 _81_ .

/S/ I.M. Truthful

SEAL

NOTED INSTRUCTION: <u>In Estates</u> To each heir, devisee, personal representative, the foreign consul pursuant to M.S. 524.3—306 and 524.3—403, and the Minnesota Attorney General, if a devisee is the trustee of a charitable trust or if the decedent left no devisees or heirs. <u>In Conservatorships and Guardianships</u> To each of persons as directed by the Court.

(Over)

Form 56 Statutory Notice of Rights of Surviving Spouse and/or Minor Children (Reverse Side of Form)

<u>AFFIDAVIT OF MAILING</u>
ALLOWANCES TO SPOUSE AND/OR CHILDREN

When a decedent dies with or without a will the allowances to the spouse or children are as follows:

525.15 ALLOWANCES TO SPOUSE. When any person dies testate, or intestate,
(1) The surviving spouse shall be allowed from the personal property of which the decedent was possessed or to which he was entitled at the time of his death, the wearing apparel, and, as selected by him, furniture and household goods not exceeding $2,000 in value, and other personal property not exceeding $1,000 in value;

(2) When, except for one automobile, all of the personal estate of the decedent is allowed to the surviving spouse by clause (1), the surviving spouse shall also be allowed such automobile.

(3) If there be no surviving spouse, the minor children shall receive the property specified in clause (1) as selected in their behalf;

(4) During administration, but not exceeding 18 months, unless an extension shall have been granted by the court, or, if the estate be insolvent, not exceeding 12 months, the spouse or children, or both, constituting the family of the decedent shall be allowed reasonable maintenance.

(5) In the administration of an estate of a non-resident decedent, the allowances received in the domiciliary administration shall be deducted from the allowances under this section.

In all estates where there is a will the following rule applies to the spouse who has not consented to the will:

525.212 RENUNCIATION AND ELECTION. If a will make provision for a surviving spouse in lieu of the rights in the estate secured by statute, such spouse shall be deemed to have elected to take under the will, unless he shall have filed with the court and mailed or delivered to the personal representative, if any, within nine months after the date of death, or within six months after the probate of the decedent's will, whichever limitation last expires, an instrument in writing renouncing and refusing to accept the provisions in such will. For good cause shown, the court may permit an election within such further time as the court may determine. No devise to a surviving spouse shall be considered as adding to the rights in the estate secured by sections 525.145 and 525.16 to such spouse, unless it clearly appears from the contents of the will that such was the testator's intent.

STATE OF MINNESOTA
COUNTY OF __Ramsey__ } ss

_____I. M. Truthful_____ being first duly sworn on oath deposes and says that on
the ___5th___ day of ____October____, 19 _77_, at __St. Paul, MN__
in said County and State, he mailed a copy of Sections 525.15 and 525.212 of Minnesota Statutes as hereinbefore set out to decedent's spouse and children constituting the family of decedent at their last known address after exercising due diligence and ascertaining the correctness of said addresses by placing a true and correct copy thereof in a sealed envelope, postage pre-paid and depositing the same in the U. S. Mails at __St. Paul__
_____, Minnesota, and addressed to the following:

NAME	STREET OR POST OFFICE	CITY	STATE
John C. Doe	1005 Easy Street	St. Paul	MN

/S/ I.M. Truthful

Subscribed and sworn to before me this ___5th___ day of
_____October_____, 19 _77_.

/S/ Judith Harris

Notary Public, _____Ramsey_____ County, Minn.
My Commission expires _March 7_____, 19 _81_.   SEAL

Form 57 Proof of Placing Order for Publication

STATE OF MINNESOTA   PROBATE COURT

COUNTY OF RAMSEY   COURT FILE NO. 999999

In Re: Estate of   PROOF OF PLACING ORDER
                                               FOR PUBLICATION

Jane M. Doe
                Deceased

TO THE CLERK OF PROBATE COURT:

This is to verify that   John C. Doe, whose address is 1005 Easy St., St. Paul,
  Mn 07102   , applicant(X)

has XXXXXX made arrangements for the publication of:

    NOTICE OF INFORMAL APPOINTMENT OF PERSONAL
                         REPRESENTATIVE(S) AND NOTICE TO CREDITORS

 X   NOTICE OF FORMAL PROBATE OF WILL AND APPOINTMENT OF
                         PERSONAL REPRESENTATIVE(S) AND NOTICE TO CREDITORS

once a week for two consecutive weeks in the FINANCE AND COMMERCE Daily
                                                             Newspaper

and this is to confirm that the same will be published accordingly commencing

in the next available issue, and that arrangements for payment of the cost of

said publication have been made.

Dated: September 30, 1977

                                       FINANCE AND COMMERCE Daily Newspaper
                                                             Publisher

                              By: /S/ Dorothy V. Wolf

Form 58 Order of Formal Probate of Will and Formal Appointment

FORM 4376

Form 524.3-409 # 2
Form 524.3-414 # 4
Form 524.3-502 # 11   UPC 34

STATE OF MINNESOTA

COUNTY OF RAMSEY

PROBATE COURT
COUNTY COURT-PROBATE DIVISION

In Re: Estate of

Court File No. ___999999___

ORDER OF FORMAL PROBATE
OF WILL AND FORMAL
APPOINTMENT OF EXECUTOR

_____Jane M. Doe_____
Deceased

The petition of ___John C. Doe___ dated ___September 25___, 19_77_, for the formal probate of the last will and for formal appointment of executor of the above named decedent having duly come on for hearing before the Judge of the above named court, the undersigned Judge having heard and considered such petition, being fully advised in the premises, makes the following findings and determination:

1. That the petition for formal probate of will and for formal appointment of a personal representative is complete.

2. That the time for any notice has expired and any notice as required by the laws of this state has been given and proved.

3. That the petitioner has declared or affirmed that the representations contained in the petition are true, correct and complete to the best of his knowledge or information.

4. That the petitioner appears from the petition to be an interested person as defined by the laws of this state.

5. That the above named decedent testator herein is dead having died on ___September 20___, 19 77_, at ___St. Paul, MN 55102___.

6. That, on the basis of the statements in the petition, this court has jurisdiction of this estate, proceeding and subject matter.

7. That venue for this proceeding is in the above named County of the State of Minnesota, because the decedent was domiciled in such county at the time of his death, and was the owner of property located in the State of Minnesota, or because, though not domiciled in the State of Minnesota, the decedent was the owner of property located in the above named county at the time of his death.

8. That decedent's heirs are as identified in the petition commencing this proceeding.

9. That decedent died testate.

10. That the original, duly executed and apparently unrevoked last will of the decedent or, if previously probated elsewhere, an authenticated copy thereof and statement probating the same is in the court's possession, and therefore, that any will to which the requested appointment relates has been or will be formally probated upon the entry of this order.

11. That the petition does not indicate the existence of a possible unrevoked testamentary instrument which may relate to property subject to the laws of this state, and which is not filed for probate in this court.

12. That it appears from the petition that the time limit for original probate and appointment proceedings has not expired.

Form 58 continued

13. That from the statements in the petition, petitioner ~~XXXXXXXXXXXXXXXXXXXXXXXXXXXXXXXXXXXXXXXX~~ has priority entitling appointment because petitioner ~~XXXXXXXXXXXXXXXXXXXXXXXXXXXXXXXXXX~~ is nominated in the last will of the decedent as executor, with (no) ~~XXXXXXXXXXXXXXXXXXXXXXXXXXXX~~ bond, in an ~~XXXXXXXXXXXXXXXXXXXXXXXXXX~~ (undesignated) administration, ~~XXXXXXXXXXXXXXXX~~

   and is not disqualified to serve as a personal representative of the decedent;

14. That the petition does not indicate that a personal representative has been appointed in this or another county of this state whose appointment has not been terminated.

15. That this proceeding is uncontested, the petition being unopposed, no objections having been filed.

   Now, therefore, it is ORDERED, ADJUDGED and DECREED by the court as follows:

1. That the petition is hereby granted.

2. That the last will duly executed _____June 2_____, 19_45_, and codicil or codicils thereto, if any, of the decedent is hereby formally probated.

3. That _____John C. Doe_____ is hereby formally appointed as the executor of the estate of _____Jane M. Doe_____, deceased, with _____no_____ bond, in an (~~unsupervised~~) (supervised) administration.

4. That upon qualification and acceptance, letters testamentary be issued to John C. Doe _____

Dated: ___October 30, 1977___

                                        ____/S/ I. M. Honest____
                                              Judge

   (COURT SEAL)

Form 59 Acceptance of Appointment and Oath by Individual

FORM 4401

Form 524.3-601 #1   UPC 43

STATE OF MINNESOTA

COUNTY OF __Ramsey__

In Re: Estate of

__Jane M. Doe_____
                    Deceased

PROBATE COURT
COUNTY COURT-PROBATE DIVISION

Court File No. _____999999_____

ACCEPTANCE OF APPOINTMENT
AND OATH BY INDIVIDUAL

TO THE ABOVE NAMED COURT:

STATE OF MINNESOTA   )
) ss
COUNTY OF ____Ramsey_____   )

I, __John C. Doe_____, residing at __1005 Easy Street__

in the City of __St. Paul_____, County of __Ramsey_____, State of __MN_____
as a condition to receiving letters as ___Personal Representative_____
in the above entitled matter, hereby accept the duties of the office, agree to be bound by the provisions
of the statutes relating thereto and hereby submit to the jurisdiction of the Court in any proceeding
relating to the said matter that may be instituted by any person interested therein; and swear that I
will faithfully and justly perform all duties of the office and trust that I now assume as _____
_personal representative_____
in the above entitled matter to the best of my ability.

                                        __/S/ John C. Doe_____
                                        Personal Representative

Subscribed and sworn to before me this
30th day of __October_____, 19 __77__

__/S/ Judith Jones_____
Notary Public, _____County, Minn.   SEAL
My Commission Expires __March 7_____, 19__81__

Form 60 Bond, if Required, or Waiver

FORM 4405

Form 524.3-603   UPC — —

STATE OF MINNESOTA

COUNTY OF _Ramsey_

In Re: Estate of

_____
Jane M. Doe
Deceased

PROBATE COURT
COUNTY COURT-PROBATE DIVISION

Court File No. _____ 999999 _____

REQUEST FOR WAIVER OF BOND

   The undersigned, being all interested persons with an apparent interest in excess of $1,000.00, other than creditors, hereby request that no bond be required of _____ **John C. Doe** _____, the nominated or appointed personal representative in the above estate.

Dated: _October 30, 1977_

                       /S/   John C. Doe
                       Personal Representative

Form 61 Testimony of Witnesses

OS140 (Rev. 7/76)

Form 524.3—303
524.3—405 #1

UPC——

STATE OF MINNESOTA

COUNTY OF Ramsey

In Re: Estate of

Jane M. Doe

Deceased

PROBATE COURT
COUNTY COURT—PROBATE DIVISION

Court File No. 999999

TESTIMONY OF
SUBSCRIBING WITNESS TO WILL

STATE OF MINNESOTA

COUNTY OF Ramsey

ss

TESTIMONY

Harvey Horwell _____, residing at
662 Hepner St., St. Paul, MN 55105 _____,
being first duly sworn on behalf of the proponent of decedent's will states that I am one of the subscribing witnesses to the instrument now shown me dated the ___2nd___ day of ___June___ , 19 45 , and purporting to be (the xxxxxxxxxxxxxxxxxxxxxxxxxxxxxxxxxxxxxxxCodicil to) the Last Will and Testament of Jane M. Doe
now here petitioned for probate; that on the day of the date thereof, said instrument was to me published by said decedent and declared by him that he had signed the same as (this xxxxxxxxxxxxxxxxxxxxxxxxxxxCodicil to) her Last Will and Testament; that at decedent's request, I did then and there sign my name as a subscribing witness thereto in the presence of decedent.

That to the best of my knowledge and belief, decedent at the time of the execution of said instrument as aforesaid was of sound and disposing mind, memory and understanding, of lawful age and under no constraint or undue influence.

/S/ Harvey R. Horwell _____
Subscribing Witness

Subscribed and sworn to before me this 3rd
day of October , 19 77 .

/S/ I. M. Honest _____
~~Notary Public~~/Judge/~~Register~~

(NOTARIAL SEAL)

Form 62 Federal Identification Number (Form SS–4)

Form **SS–4** (Rev. 8–76)
Department of the Treasury
Internal Revenue Service

Application for Employer Identification Number

(For use by employers and others as explained in the Instructions)

1 Name (True name as distinguished from trade name. If partnership, see Instructions on page 4)

Estate of Jane M. Doe

2 Trade name, if any (Enter name under which business is operated, if different from item 1)

John C. Doe, personal representative

4 Address of principal place of business (Number and street)

1st Trust Bldg.

6 City and State

St. Paul, MN

7 ZIP code   **55101**

9 Type of organization
- [ ] Individual
- [ ] Partnership
- [ ] Corporation
- [ ] Nonprofit organization (See Instr. on page 4)
- [ ] Governmental (See Instr. on page 4)
- [X] Other (specify)   **Estate**

11 Reason for applying
- [ ] Started new business
- [ ] Purchased going business
- [X] Other (specify)   **Fiduciary**

13 Nature of business (See Instructions on page 4)

N/A

15 Peak number of employees expected in next 12 months (If none, enter "0") ▶ **N/A**
- [ ] Nonagricultural
- [ ] Agricultural
- [ ] Household

17 To whom do you sell most of your products or services?
- [ ] Business establishments
- [ ] General public
- [ ] Other (specify)   **N/A**

18 Have you ever applied for an identification number for this or any other business? [ ] Yes [X] No
If "Yes," enter name and trade name (if any). Also enter the approximate date, city, and State where you first applied and previous number if known. ▶ **N/A**

Date **10/24/77**

Signature and title   **Personal Representative**

3 Social security number, if sole proprietor

000 : 00 : 0000

5 Ending month of accounting year   **undecided**

8 County of business location   **Ramsey**

10 Date you acquired or started this business (Mo., day, year)   **Sept. 20, 1977**

12 First date you paid or will pay wages for this business (Mo., day, year)   **N/A**

14 Do you operate more than one place of business? **N/A** [ ] Yes [X] No

16 If nature of business is manufacturing, state principal product and raw material used   **N/A**

Telephone number

Please leave blank ▶ | Geo. | Ind. | Class | Size | Reas. for appl. | Part I

Form 63 Letters Testamentary

Form 4403 Rev. 6-76

524.3-601 #3   UPC 43

STATE OF MINNESOTA

COUNTY OF __Ramsey__

In Re: Estate of

    __Jane M. Doe__
          Deceased

**PROBATE COURT
COUNTY COURT-PROBATE DIVISION**

Court File No. __999999__

LETTERS TESTAMENTARY

    The above named decedent having died on __September 20__ , 19 __77__ , and

__John C. Doe__

having been appointed and qualified, (is⟩   hereby authorized to act as personal representative
according to law.

Dated: __Oct. 30, 1977__

                                          /S/ I. M. Honest
                                          Judge XXXXXXXX

            (COURT SEAL)

Form 64 Notice of Fiduciary Relationship

Form **56** (Rev. Sept. 1976) Department of the Treasury Internal Revenue Service	**Notice of Fiduciary Relationship** (Under section 6903 of the Internal Revenue Code)

PART I—In General. (All fiduciaries complete this part.)

Fiduciary's name
   John C. Doe

Fiduciary's address (Number and street)
   1st Trust Building,

City, State, and ZIP code
   St. Paul, MN 55101

Name of person for whom you are acting (as will be shown on the tax return)	Identifying number (See Instr. D.)
Estate of Jane M. Doe	236-246975

Address of person for whom you are acting (Number and street)
   1005 Easy Street

City, State, and ZIP code
   St. Paul, MN 07102

If you are acting for a decedent, show date of death	Decedent's social security number
September 20, 1977	000-00-0000

Description of evidence of authority to act as a fiduciary (Check the applicable boxes.)

☐ Certified copy of will attached
☐ Certified copy of court order appointing the fiduciary attached
☐ Certified copy of trust instrument attached
☐ Specimen form of "Illinois type" land trust agreement attached
☐ Specimen form of "Illinois type" land trust agreement filed previously with Internal Revenue Service (Specify location and date _____)
☒ Other (describe)

    Conformed copy of will

PART II—Nature of Liabilities. (All fiduciaries except "Illinois type" land trust fiduciaries complete this part.)

Specific liabilities of the person for whom you are acting known to you:

☐ Income tax for period(s) ▶ _____
☐ Gift tax for period(s) ▶ _____
☒ Estate tax
☐ Other (specify) ▶ _____
☐ Liability of person for whom you are acting
☐ Transferee liability of person for whom you are acting
☐ Fiduciary liability of person for whom you are acting under section 3467 of the Revised Statutes as amended (31 U.S.C. 192) concerning payment of tax from a decedent's estate

PART III—"Illinois type" Land Trusts. ("Illinois type" land trusts fiduciaries complete this part.)

Beneficiary's name	Identifying number (See Instr. D.)
Beneficiary's address (Number and street)	Percentage (or fraction) owned

City, State, and ZIP code

Sign here ▶ I have examined this notice and to the best of my knowledge it is correct.

/s/ John C. Doe   Personal Representative   10/30/77
Fiduciary's signature   Title   Date

Form 64 continued

Instructions

A. Who may file.—A fiduciary may use Form 56 to provide the written notice under section 301.6903–1 of the regulations.

B. When to file.—File Form 56 within 30 days after becoming the fiduciary.

C. Where to file.—File Form 56 with Internal Revenue Service where the return of the person for whom you are acting is filed.

D. Identifying number.—If you are acting for an individual, enter the individual's social security number; for all others, including an estate or a trust, enter the employer identification number.

E. Termination notice.—The written notice of termination required in 26 C.F.R. 301.6903–1 accompanied by satisfactory evidence of the termination, should include the name and address of the person, if any, who has been substituted as fiduciary.

F. Signature.—You must sign Form 56 and show a descriptive title, such as guardian, trustee, deceased's personal representative, receiver, or conservator.

Supplemental Instructions for "Illinois type" Land Trusts

G. Who may file.—You may use Form 56 for each original and each later beneficiary as well as for each assignment or transfer of a beneficial interest for security purposes. Under an "Illinois type" land trust (in the few states permitting its use) the fiduciary holds title subject to the obligation to make conveyances as the beneficiary may direct, and the beneficiary holds all rights to the possession, management, and income of the trust property. "Illinois type" land trusts may be held to convert the interest of the beneficiary to personal property and may permit recording the trust by number only without disclosing the names of the trust beneficiaries.

H. When to file.—File Form 56 within 30 days after becoming the fiduciary or after transfer of a beneficial interest in the trust.

I. Where to file.—File Form 56 with Internal Revenue Service where a return would be filed for the location where you are acting.

J. Name of trust for which you are acting.—If the trust is known only by a number, enter that number for the name of the trust.

U.S. GOVERNMENT PRINTING OFFICE : 1976—O–575–305

K. Termination notice.—A written notice may be filed for any termination of a beneficial interest in the trust.

Privacy Act Notice.—The written notice is mandatory under section 6903 of the Internal Revenue Code and 26 C.F.R. 301.6903–1 if you wish to receive notices of tax liability for the person for whom you are acting. Form 56 is furnished as a convenience and the use of this particular form therefore is not mandatory. The principal purpose of the notice is to inform Internal Revenue Service that you are a fiduciary. Other routine uses may include computer programs. If you do not notify the Internal Revenue, notices of tax liability sent to the last known address of the taxpayer, transferee, or other person subject to liability will be considered sufficient compliance with the requirements of the code.

Disclosure of the identifying number for the person for whom you are acting is mandatory under section 6109 of the Code and 26 C.F.R. 301.6109–1. The principal purpose is to properly identify the person for whom you are acting. Other routine uses may include computer programs. If you do not furnish the identifying number, the Internal Revenue Service may suspend processing the notice of fiduciary relationship until the number is received.

Form 65 Inventory and Appraisement

FORM 4428

Form 524.3-706   UPC 54

STATE OF MINNESOTA   **PROBATE COURT**
COUNTY OF ___RAMSEY___   **COUNTY COURT-PROBATE DIVISION**

In Re: Estate of   Court File No. ___999999___

___Jane M. Doe___   **INVENTORY AND APPRAISEMENT**

     Deceased   Date of Death ___September 20___, 19__77__
                                Social Security No. ___000-00-0000___

TO THE HONORABLE JUDGE AND/OR REGISTRAR OF THE ABOVE NAMED COURT:

___John C. Doe___, the undersigned personal representative, respectfully
states:

1. That the following is a true and correct inventory and appraisement, at date of death values,
   of all the property of the above named estate, both real and personal, which has come into
   the possession of said representative and of which said representative has knowledge after
   diligent search and inquiry concerning the same, classified as follows, to-wit: (See instructions at end of last page.)

SCHEDULE A — Real Estate

Item number	Legal Description (Specify street address of city realty; acreage of rural land; and liens, if any)	Assessor's Estimated Market Value (Do not use "Green Acres" Value or Assessor's Limited Market Value)	GROSS APPRAISED VALUE
1.	Homestead, being in the County of ___Ramsey___, State of Minnesota: 1005 Easy Street, St. Paul, MN Legally described as follows, to wit: Lot 615, Block 42, Reiser's Addition to St. Paul (Plat #22760 Parcel #7600) Balance of Mortgage at St. Paul Bank & Trust Co. $30,000.00	$37,500.00	$50,000.00
2.	Other Real Estate, being in the County of ___Ramsey___ State of Minnesota: an undivided 1/4 interest in Duplex located at 776 Noname Road St. Paul, Minnesota Legally described as follows, to wit: Lots 16 & 17, Block 20 Lovey's Addition to St. Paul (Plat #32689 Parcel #5562) 1/4 of Mortgage Balance of $40,000 at St. Paul Bank & Trust $10,000.00	68,250.00 Total 17,062.50 (1/4)	91,000.00 Total 22,750.00 (1/4)

Form 65 continued

Real Estate SCHEDULE A — TOTAL $ 72,750.00

SCHEDULE B — Stocks and Bonds

Item number	Description (Specify face amount of bonds or number of shares and par value where needed for identification; and liens, if any)	GROSS APPRAISED VALUE
	STOCK	
1.	100 Shares American Telephone and Telegraph, Common, Cert. # C068927 dated 12/3/62, at $50.00/share	5,000.00
2.	1,000 Shares Minnesota Co-op, Common, Cert. # D2289663 dated 12/3/62, at $4.50/share	4,500.00
	UNITED STATES SAVINGS BONDS	
3.	$50.00 U.S. Savings Bond Series E, Bond # R 4502363E Purchased April 1963	74.00
	$50.00 U.S. Savings Bond Series E, Bond # R 4502364E Purchased April 1963	74.00

Personal Property SCHEDULE B — TOTAL $ 9,648.00

SCHEDULE C — Mortgages, Notes, and Cash

Item number	Description (Specify recording data; bank and account numbers; accrued interest; location of actual cash; and liens, if any)	GROSS APPRAISED
1.	American Express Traveler's Checks #10008 - 10017 for $100 each	1,000.00
2.	1st National City Bank of St. Paul - checking account $55-555	50,000.00
3.	American National Bank of St. Paul - passbook savings certificate #44-444, rate: 5.5% per annum	15,000.00
4.	$10,000 - Forrest Furriers Promissory Note dated 3/20/74 payable 3/20/79 with interest payable at 7% per annum.	10,000.00
	Accrued interest from 3/20/77 to 9/20/77	350.00

Personal Property SCHEDULE C — TOTAL $ 76,350.00

Form 65 continued

SCHEDULE D — Other Miscellaneous Property

Item number	Description (Specify location of property and liens, if any)	GROSS APPRAISED VALUE
	Furniture and Household goods:	2,000.00
	Wearing apparel and Ornaments:	
1.	Furs - Mink Coat	1,500.00
2.	Clothing and personal effects	500.00
	All other personal property (including partnership and business interests, insurance and annuities payable to estate, other receivables, farm crops, machinery, etc.):	
3.	1973 Chevrolet - Nova, Vehicle Identification Number 6778899926	2,000.00
4.	Judgement - dated February 19, 1973 for personal injuries in auto accident against Forrest A. Redding collected in full on Dec. 20, 1977	20,000.00
5.	Minnesota Life Insurance Company Policy # J666221 Face Amount $20,000 Accumulated Dividends 100	20,100.00
6.	* SEE BELOW	50,000.00

Personal Property SCHEDULE D — TOTAL $ 96,100.00

SUMMARY

Total Gross Value of Real Estate	$ 72,750.00	
Less Liens	$ 40,000.00	
Net Value of Real Estate		$ 32,750.00
Total Gross Value of Personal Property	$	
Less Liens	$	
Net Value of Personal Property		$ 182,098.00
TOTAL NET APPRAISEMENT		$ 214,848.00

2. That a copy hereof has been mailed to the surviving spouse if there be one, and to all residuary distributees of the above named decedent and to interested persons or creditors who have requested the same.

* Trust created under agreement dated 12/2/50 by father of decedent for decedent's benefit under which decedent had a general power of appointment (to distribute income and/or principal) which power had not been exercised during decedent's lieftime, but which decedent exercised under her will. The assets remaining in this trust and subject to this power are 500 shares of Green Giant common stock and undistributed earnings (dividends) thereon.

Form 65 continued

FURTHER, under penalties for perjury for deliberate falsification therein, I declare or affirm that I have read the foregoing and to the best of my knowledge or information, its representations are true, correct and complete.

Dated: ____1/20/78_____

                                              /S/   John C. Doe
                                              ‾‾‾‾‾John C. Doe‾‾‾‾‾‾‾‾‾‾‾‾‾
                                              Personal Representative

/S/ John Cranwall
‾‾‾‾‾‾‾‾‾‾‾‾‾‾‾‾‾‾‾‾‾‾‾‾‾‾‾‾‾‾‾
Attorney
         John Cranwall
         First Trust Building
         St. Paul, Minnesota 55101
Address/Phone   000-0000

INSTRUCTIONS:

(1) The classification of assets herein is intended for them to be comparable to the Federal Estate Tax Return Form 706 with the exception of Schedule D herein which includes insurance and annuities payable to the estate and which are otherwise includable under separate Schedules of said Form 706.

(2) It is to be noted that the GROSS APPRAISED VALUE is requested of each asset without reduction by any lien requested to be specified as a part of its description. The reduction for liens is later taken under the Summary of Assets.

(3) It is also to be noted that each asset of a Schedule is to be given its "Item number" to facilitate a ready reference similar to the Estate Tax Form 706.

(4) Finally, it is to be noted that the Assessor's Estimated Market Value is requested. This information is always available to the Department of Revenue upon its request. The accurate furnishing of the information can result in better servicing of the inheritance tax returns.

(5) It is recommended that the appraisal report of any independent appraiser should be properly referenced and attached as an Exhibit including the name and address of any such appraisers.

Form 66 Petition for Allowance of Selection of Personal Property

Form 4481

525.151 #1   UPC --

STATE OF MINNESOTA

COUNTY OF ___Ramsey___

PROBATE COURT
COUNTY COURT-PROBATE DIVISION

In Re: Estate of

Court File No. ___999999___

PETITION FOR ALLOWANCE OF
___Jane M. Doe___   **SELECTION OF PERSONAL**
                          Deceased   **PROPERTY**

TO THE HONORABLE JUDGE OF THE ABOVE NAMED COURT:

Petitioner, ___John C. Doe_____, respectfully states:

1. Petitioner resides at ___1005 Easy Street, St. Paul, MN 07102_____ ;

2. Petitioner has an interest herein as ___named personal representative, spouse and___
   ___devisee_____and is, therefore, an interested person
   as defined by the laws of this state;

3. The above named decedent was survived by ___John C. Doe_____, h ___er___
   spouse and the following minor children whose names and ages are:

   _____

   _____

   _____

4. Petitioner hereby selects the following items of personal property listed and described in the
   inventory of decedent's estate, to-wit:

Description	Value	Description	Value
1973 Chevrolet - Nova	$ 1000.00		$
		TOTAL VALUE	$1000.00

   WHEREFORE, your petitioner requests the Order of this Court fixing a time and place for
hearing on this petition, and that after the time for any notice has expired, upon proof of notice, and
hearing, and/or the Court enter a judicial order allowing the selection of said property to
___John C. Doe_____ according to law, and granting such
other and further relief as may be proper.

   FURTHER, under penalties for perjury for deliberate falsification therein, I declare or affirm thát
I have read the foregoing petition and to the best of my knowledge or information, its representations
are true, correct and complete.

Dated: ___October 1, 1977___

                                                    ___/S/ John C. Doe_____
                                                    Petitioner

___/S/ John C. Cranwall_____
Attorney for Petitioner
   999 St. Paul Trust Company Building
   St. Paul, MN 55101
Address/Phone **(612) 111-0011**

Form 67 Order Setting Apart (Allowing Selection of) Personal Property

Form 4482

525.151 #2   UPC —

STATE OF MINNESOTA

COUNTY OF ___Ramsey___

PROBATE COURT
COUNTY COURT-PROBATE DIVISION

In Re: Estate of

Court File No. ___999999___

ORDER ALLOWING SELECTION OF
PERSONAL PROPERTY

___Jane M. Doe___
Deceased

The petition of ___John C. Doe___ dated _October 1_, 19 _77_, for allowance of selection of personal property in the estate of the above named decedent having duly come on for hearing before the above named court, the undersigned Judge having heard and considered such petition, being fully advised in the premises, makes the following findings and determinations:

1. That the petition for allowance of selection of personal property is complete.

2. That the time for any notice has expired and any notice as required by the laws of this state has been given and proved.

3. That the petitioner has declared or affirmed that the representations contained in the petition are true, correct and complete to the best of his knowledge or information.

4. That the petitioner appears from the petition to be an interested person as defined by the laws of this state.

5. That the above named decedent was survived by ___John C. Doe___, h _er_ spouse and the following minor children whose names and ages are:

___

___

___

6. That the petitioner has selected certain items of personal property listed and described in the inventory of decedent's estate.

Now, therefore, it is ORDERED, ADJUDGED, and DECREED by the court as follows:

1. That the petition is hereby granted.

2. That the selection of the following personal property to-wit:

Description	Value	Description	Value
1973 Chevrolet - Nova	$1000.00		$
		Total Value	$1000.00

Form 67 continued

be, and the same is hereby allowed and that the personal representative of said estate immediately transfer and make delivery of said personal property to _____John C. Doe_____

_____

_____

    IT IS FURTHER ORDERED that the lien of Minnesota inheritance taxes on said described property is hereby waived.

Dated: _____October 30, 1977_____

        (COURT SEAL)

                                  /s/ I. M. Honest_____

                                             Judge

Form 68 Petition for Family Maintenance

Form 4483

525.151 #3   UPC 7

STATE OF MINNESOTA

COUNTY OF _Ramsey_

PROBATE COURT
COUNTY COURT-PROBATE DIVISION

In Re: Estate of

Court File No. _999999_

PETITION FOR
FAMILY MAINTENANCE

Jane M. Doe
      Deceased

TO THE HONORABLE JUDGE OF THE ABOVE NAMED COURT:

Petitioner, _John C. Doe_ , respectfully states:

1. Petitioner resides at _1005 Easy Street, St. Paul, MN 07102_ ;

2. Petitioner has an interest herein as _named personal representative, spouse and devisee_ and is, therefore, an interested person as defined by the laws of this state;

3. The above named decedent was survived by _John C. Doe_ , h<u>er</u> spouse and the following minor and/or dependent children whose names and ages are:

4. That decedent's estate is (solvent) (insolvent).

5. That a reasonable and necessary family allowance of $ _4800.00_ should be paid to and for the use and benefit of decedent's surviving spouse and minor and/or dependent children constituting the family of decedent.

WHEREFORE, your petitioner requests the Order of this Court fixing a time and place for hearing on this petition, and that after the time for any notice has expired, upon proof of notice, and hearing, and/or the Court enter a judicial order directing the payment of a family allowance in the amount of $ _4800.00_ to be paid in periodic installments of $ _400.00_ per month, and granting such other and further relief as may be proper.

FURTHER, under penalties for perjury for deliberate falsification therein, I declare or affirm that I have read the foregoing petition and to the best of my knowledge or information, its representations are true, correct and complete.

Dated: _October 1, 1977_

/S/ **John C. Doe**
Petitioner

/S/ _John C. Cranwall_
Attorney for Petitioner
  999 St. Paul Trust Company Building
  St. Paul, MN 55101
Address/Phone **(612) 111-0011**

Form 69 Order for Family Maintenance

Form 4484

525.151 #4   UPC 8

STATE OF MINNESOTA

COUNTY OF __Ramsey__

                                                     PROBATE COURT
                                                     COUNTY COURT-PROBATE DIVISION

In Re: Estate of   Court File No. __999999__

                                                     ORDER FOR FAMILY MAINTENANCE

    __Jane M. Doe__
                Deceased

The petition of __John C. Doe__ dated __October 1__, 19 __77__, for an order for family maintenance in the estate of the above named decedent having duly come on for hearing before the above named court, the undersigned Judge having heard and considered such petition, being fully advised in the premises, makes the following findings and determinations:

1. That the petition for an order for family maintenance is complete.

2. That the time for any notice has expired and any notice as required by the laws of this state has been given and proved.

3. That the petitioner has declared or affirmed that the representations contained in the petition are true, correct and complete to the best of his knowledge or information.

4. That the petitioner appears from the petition to be an interested person as defined by the laws of this state.

5. That the above named decedent was survived by __John C. Doe__,
__her__ spouse and the following minor and/or dependent children whose names and ages are:

6. That decedent's estate is (solvent) (insolvent).

7. That a family allowance of $ __4800.00__ is reasonable and necessary for the use and benefit of decedent's surviving spouse and minor and/or dependent children constituting the family of decedent to be paid in periodic installments of $ __400.00__ per month.

Now, therefore, it is ORDERED, ADJUDGED, and DECREED by the court as follows:

1. That the petition is hereby granted.

2. That the personal representative be and is hereby directed to pay as family allowance the sum of $ __4800.00__ in installments of $ __400.00__ per month to __John C. Doe__, surviving spouse of __Jane M. Doe__, deceased, for the use and benefit of said spouse and minor and/or dependent children constituting the family of decedent.

Dated: __October 30, 1977__

                                                   __/S/ I. M. Honest__
                                                                   Judge

        (COURT SEAL)

Form 70 Schedule of Non-Probate Assets

Form IG-2 (Rev. 6-76)
Form 10BR Walter S. Booth & Son, Minneapolis

STATE OF MINNESOTA
SCHEDULE OF NON-PROBATE ASSETS

NAME OF DECEDENT____Jane M. Doe____

DATE OF DEATH ____September 20, 1977____

SOCIAL SECURITY NUMBER ___000-00-0000___

GENERAL INFORMATION

List on this Schedule the transfer of all assets in which the decedent had an interest and were not reported on an Inventory and Appraisal filed in a probate proceeding. Assets must be recorded at their fair market value on the date of death. If Federal alternate values were used, make appropriate adjustments on Minnesota Inheritance Tax Return, Form IG-1.

Decedent's residence at death (street, city, state)				
1005 Easy Street, St. Paul, Minnesota				
Place of death (city & state only)	Cause of death		Age at death	Length of last illness
St. Paul, Minnesota	Cancer		76	9 months
Business or occupation	If retired, former business or occupation			Marital status at death
Retired	Real Estate Broker			Married
Will there be Minnesota probate proceedings?	If yes, designate county and probate file number if proceedings have commenced.			
YES ☒ NO ☐	Ramsey 999999			

Name, relationship and birthdate of surviving spouse, children, or issue of deceased children of decedent. Leave blank if information appears on Application or Petition for Probate.

NAME   RELATIONSHIP   DATE OF BIRTH

See petition to prove will

	Yes	No
Did the decedent have access to a safe deposit box or other place of safekeeping at the time of death? If "Yes," enter the name and address of the bank or depository.		X
Was any jointly held property acquired by the decedent and surviving joint tenant by gift or inheritance from a third person?		X
Does any surviving joint tenant claim to have furnished any consideration in money or property for the purchase or acquisition of joint tenancy property?		X
Did the undersigned make a diligent and careful search for all property left by the decedent and conduct an inquiry regarding any transfers of his property during his lifetime, including transfers for less than adequate or full consideration in money or money's worth?	X	

NON-PROBATE DEDUCTIONS

MAKE NO ENTRIES IF PROBATE PROCEEDINGS HAVE COMMENCED

Deductions for certain items are allowed to the survivor who paid the expenses. These deductions are to be entered on Schedule A, B, or C under "SHARE OF NON-PROBATE DEDUCTIONS." List here: (a) Funeral expenses $____ (b) Last illness expenses paid after death $____ (c) Attorney's fees $____ (d) Other (attach supplement) $____ Enter total dollar amount of a, b, c, and $____ include no power schedule. (These items are explained in instructions.)

SUMMARY OF NON-PROBATE ASSETS

1. Property held in joint tenancy (from Part I, page 2) . . . . $ _80,000.00_
2. Insurance (from Part II, page 3) . . . . _10,000.00_
3. Pensions, annuities, retirement accounts (from Part III, page 3) . . . . _4,800.00_
4. Transfers by decedent (from Part IV, page 4) . . . . _50,000.00_
5. Miscellaneous assets/Collections by Affidavit (from Part V, page 4) . . . . _NONE_
6. Total Non-Probate Assets. Add lines 1 through 5 . . . . $
   THIS AMOUNT IS TO BE ENTERED ON LINE 1, PAGE 1, FORM IG-1   144,800.00

I,____John C. Doe____, in my capacity as__personal representative__
(personal representative, transferee, custodian, trustee or other authorized capacity) declare under penalty of perjury that I have carefully examined this return and accompanying schedules, and they are to the best of my knowledge true, correct and complete.

Signature _/s/ John C. Doe_   Address _1005 Easy Street_

Date ____February 21, 1978____   St. Paul, MN   07102

MAIL TO: Department of Revenue, Inheritance & Gift Tax Division, Centennial Office Building, St. Paul, Minnesota 55145

Page 1

Form 70 continued

Page 2

PART I — PROPERTY HELD IN JOINT TENANCY

List all property in which the decedent held an interest at the time of his death as joint tenant or as co-owner with right of survivorship. This includes real estate, personal property, bank accounts, U.S. Savings Bonds, etc. Property must be listed at its fair market value at the date of death. For real estate enter the Assessor's Estimated Market Value in Column (C) from the real estate tax statement dated closest to the decedent's death. This value is to be used ONLY as a GUIDE in determining the fair market value of the real estate. Do not use the Assessor's Limited Market Value from the real estate tax statement.

(A) Description of property. If real estate, give the legal description and acreage. If city real estate, also show the street address. Give the fair market value of all property. Specify and subtract the liens and encumbrances and enter the net fair market value in Column (D). If the real property constituted the homestead of the decedent at death, enter "homestead."	(B) Surviving Joint Tenant. Name and relationship to decedent.	(C) Assessor's Estimated Market Value of real estate from real estate tax statement. Per share value of stock.	(D) Net fair market value of property.
1 - 1000 Shares American National Slide Rule Company, Common, Certificate #NC022 January 5, 1961 Unit Value	John C. Doe (husband)	$75.00	$75,000.00
2 - 100 Shares Minnesota Company, Common, Certificate #AB221 January 5, 1961 Unit Value	Sandy R. Doe (daughter)	$50.00	5,000.00

1. Total net fair market value of joint tenancy property (from Column D) . . . . $ | 80,000.00

2. Enter the dollar value of the joint property that is exempt from inheritance tax to surviving joint tenants. See explanation* . . . . | 0

3. Taxable joint tenancy property (line 1 minus line 2). Enter here and on page 1, line 1 . . . . ▶ | 80,000.00

*Under Minnesota law, the net fair market value of jointly held property is taxable to the survivor, unless it can be shown that all or part of the cost of the property was furnished by the survivor, or that such survivor received a part of the property as an inheritance or gift from a third party. If this can be demonstrated to the satisfaction of the Inheritance and Gift Tax Division, the survivor's percentage of the original cost multiplied by the fair market value will be exempt from tax. Proof of the amount claimed exempt must be presented. This proof should be in the form of a sworn statement of facts, accompanied by appropriate documentary evidence attached to this schedule.

Form 70 continued

Page 3

PART II – INSURANCE

List all life and accident insurance proceeds payable on the death of the decedent, to named beneficiaries. War risk insurance and service-man's group life insurance are exempt from inheritance tax. If the decedent held any of the incidents of ownership in the policy, the proceeds of the policy are entirely subject to tax to the named beneficiary. Examples of the term "incidents of ownership" include: the power to change beneficiaries, to surrender the policy, to assign the policy, to revoke an assignment, to pledge the policy for a loan or to obtain from the insurer a loan against the surrender value of the policy. If policy was assigned or surrendered, give assignment or surrender date in Column (A).

(A) Name of company and policy number, and assignment or surrender date.	(B) Beneficiary and relationship to decedent. Give full name and address.	(C) Did decedent possess any of the incidents of ownership at death? If "No," attach proof of other ownership.		(D) Amount paid or payable at death.
		Yes	No	
Prudential Life Insurance Company Policy #11-1111-123	Jay A. Dee (brother)			10,000.00

1. Total of policies (from Column D) . . . . $	10,000.00
2. Less exempt amount	-0-
3. Taxable insurance (line 1 less line 2). Enter here and on page 1, line 2 . . . . ►	10,000.00

PART III – PENSIONS, ANNUITIES, RETIREMENT ACCOUNTS

List all proceeds from any pension, annuity (include U.S. Civil Service Retirement) or retirement account (I.R.A. or Keogh) paid or payable to any survivor as a result of the decedent's death. If the annuity or pension plan is qualified under the Internal Revenue Code, attach proof. Generally, the representative of a public service plan or private retirement plan will furnish information as to the value of the plan and exempt amount, if any.

(A) Pension or Annuity. Name of company or payer.	(B) Enter the amount of a lump sum payment or, if to be paid periodically, enter the amount to be paid and the length of the term of such payment in months, years or for life.	(C) Beneficiary or transferee. Name, address and relationship to decedent.	(D) If taxable, enter the taxable amount.
Ecko Life Insurance Company Policy #99-9999	$100 per month for Life (value based upon life expectancy of male, age 77, is approximately 4,000 x 1,200/year)	John C. Doe (husband 1005 Easy Street St. Paul, MN	$4,800.00
Taxable pensions, annuities, retirement accounts (from Column D). Enter here and on Part I, page 1, line 3 ►		$	4,800.00

Form 70 continued

PART IV — TRANSFERS BY DECEDENT

List gifts of a value of $3,000 or more made by the decedent during his lifetime. Any outright gift made by the decedent within 3 years before his death is presumed to have been made in contemplation of death and may be subject to inheritance tax. Report transfers intended to take effect at decedent's death such as: accounts held in trust for another; transfers where the decedent retained a life or income interest; transfers where the deed or instrument of title is delivered or recorded at or after the decedent's death. Where the decedent held a general power of appointment which was exercised by will, the assets subject to the power should be reported on the Inventory and Appraisal. Where the power was exercised by the decedent during his lifetime or was relinquished by the decedent, the assets subject to such general power should be reported here.

(A) Date of transfer.	(B) Description of property. If real estate, give legal description, acreage, and street address if city property. Show the fair market value and specify and subtract any liens and encumbrances. Enter the net value in Column (E).	(C) Transferee name and relationship to decedent.	(D) Assessor's Estimated Market Value of real estate from real estate tax statement dated closest to decedent's death. List per share value of stock.	(E) Net fair market value of property.
4/20/77	Cash Transferred within three years of death	John C. Doe (husband)		20,000.00
4/20/77	Cash Transferred within three years of death	Sandy R. Doe (daughter)		30.000.00

Total transfers (from Column E). Enter here and on page 1, line 4. . . . . ►$ 50,000.00

PART V — MISCELLANEOUS ASSETS/COLLECTIONS BY AFFIDAVIT

List the transfer of any property belonging to the decedent which has not been otherwise reported either on this Schedule or on an Inventory and Appraisal. If no probate proceeding has been started, include automobiles, household goods, personal effects, assets collected by affidavit, and other tangible or intangible property.

(A) Description of property.	(B) Transferee, heir or beneficiary relationship to decedent.	(C) Market value of whole property.
NONE		

Total miscellaneous (from Column C). Enter here and on page 1, line 5 . . . . ►$ NONE

Form 71 Minnesota Inheritance Tax Return

Form IG-1 (Rev. 6-76)   P969   *For Department Use Only*

MINNESOTA INHERITANCE TAX RETURN

Decedent's County of Residence	Name of Decedent		
Ramsey	Jane M. Doe		
County of Probate and Probate File Number, if any	Social Security Number	Date of Death	
Ramsey 999999	000-00-0000	September 20, 1977	

SUMMARY OF NON-PROBATE ASSETS

1. Total of Non-Probate Assets, page 1, Form IG-2. If no probate, do not complete lines 2-9. Adjust for federal alternate values. Enter amount here and on line 10. . . . . $ 144,800.00

PROBATE ASSETS FROM INVENTORY FILED IN PROBATE COURT

2. Real estate . . . . $ 32,750.00

3. Personal property 182,098.00

4. Plus adjustments:

    4a. Omitted assets (see instructions) . . . .
    4b. Other adjustments (attach explanation) . . . .

5. Enter total adjustments. Add lines 4a and 4b . . . . $

6. Total probate assets. Add lines 2, 3 and 5 . . . . $ 214,848.00

PROBATE DEDUCTIONS & ADJUSTMENTS

7. The following deductions and adjustments are allowed against taxable probate assets:

    7a. Adjustments (attach explanation) . . . . $
    7b. Living allowance (maintenance of family 4,800.00
    7c. Personal effects (statutory selection) 3,500.00
    7d. Appraiser fees, bond premiums, publications 550.00
    7e. Compensation of representative 10,000.00
    7f. Attorney fees 15,000.00
    7g. Funeral expenses 4,125.00
    7h. Expenses of last illness unpaid at death 850.00
    7i. Individual income taxes unpaid at death, Federal $ _ _ _ _ _ _ _ _ _ _ _ _
        Minnesota $ _ _ _ _ _ _ _ _ _ _ _ _ _ _ _ _ _
    7j. Valid claims against the estate . (debts. of. decedent) 1,760.00
    7k. Miscellaneous deductions (attach explanation) 705.00
    7l. Federal Estate Tax ($ _ _ _ _ _ _ _ _ _ _ _ _). Deduct only if a liability
        of estate per Will or Trust. Otherwise apportion . . . .

8. Enter total deductions and adjustments. Total lines 7a through 7l . . . . $ 41,290.00

9. Net probate assets for distribution. Line 6 minus line 8 . . . . $ 173,558.00

10. Total assets for distribution. Line 1 and line 9 . . . . $ 318,358.00

TAX

11. Tax due. From Schedule A, B or C . . . . $ 4,908.00

12. Previous payments . . . .   -0-

13. Balance due or refund due. Line 11 less line 12 . . . . $ 4,908.00
    There may be penalty and interest — see instructions

SPECIAL EXTENSIONS OF TIME FOR PAYMENT (TWO YEARS FOR HARDSHIP AND FIVE YEAR INSTALLMENT PLAN ON TAX OVER $5,000) MAY BE AVAILABLE. SEE INSTRUCTIONS

I, John C. Doe _____ , in my capacity as _____ personal representative _____
(personal representative, transferee, custodian, trustee or other authorized capacity) declare under penalty of perjury that I have carefully examined this return and accompanying schedules, and they are to the best of my knowledge true, correct, and complete.

Signature _____ /s/ John C. Doe _____   Address _____ 1005 Easy Street _____

Date _____ June 6, 1978 _____   St. Paul, Minnesota   07102

FILE this return within one year of decedent's death, unless an extension is granted PRIOR TO THAT TIME. MAIL TO: Department of Revenue, Inheritance and Gift Tax Division, Centennial Office Building, St. Paul, Minnesota 56145. Make CHECKS payable to "Commissioner of Revenue."

Form 71 continued

Form IG-1   Page 2

TAX TABLES AND PERSONAL EXEMPTION TABLE

The Tax Tables and Personal Exemption Table are to be used with Schedules A and B to compute the inheritance tax due from any survivor of any Minnesota resident dying on or after July 1, 1959, and to compute the tax for survivors of non-residents dying between July 1, 1959 and December 31, 1972.

To compute the tax due from survivors of decedents dying before July 1, 1959 refer to the appropriate Minnesota Statutes or contact the Inheritance Tax Division.

The personal exemption must be subtracted from the "Total Assets" before arriving at "Amount Subject to Tax." The Personal Exemption Table below gives the survivor's exemption, based upon the date of death of the decedent, and notes which Tax Table to use. Determine the tax due and enter on the appropriate line on Schedule A or B.

SURVIVOR'S PERSONAL EXEMPTION TABLE

WIFE
Death between 7-1-59 and 6-30-76, $30,000 exemption. Use Table 2.
Death on and after 7-1-76, $60,000 exemption. Use Table 1.

HUSBAND
Death between 7-1-59 and 6-30-76, $6,000 exemption. Use Table 4.
Death on and after 7-1-76, $60,000 exemption. Use Table 1.

MINOR CHILD* (NATURAL OR ADOPTED), DEPENDENT CHILD (ADULT OR MINOR)
Death between 7-1-59 and 6-30-76, $15,000 exemption. Use Table 3.
Death on and after 7-1-76, $30,000 exemption. Use Table 2.

ADULT CHILD* (NATURAL OR ADOPTED), GRANDCHILD OR DESCENDANT OF A GRANDCHILD, MUTUALLY ACKNOWLEDGED CHILD, MOTHER OR FATHER, GRANDPARENT AND LINEAL ANCESTOR
Death on and after 7-1-59, $6,000 exemption. Use Table 4.

*As of 6-1-73, the age of majority in Minnesota is 18 years.

STEP-CHILD
Death between 7-1-59 and 7-31-73, $500 exemption. Use Table 6. Death on and after 8-1-73, $6,000 exemption. Use Table 4.

BROTHER OR SISTER, NEPHEW OR NIECE, HALF-BROTHER, HALF-SISTER, DESCENDANT OF BROTHER OR SISTER, WIFE OR WIDOW OF A SON, HUSBAND OF A DAUGHTER
Death on and after 7-1-59, $1,500 exemption. Use Table 5.

HUSBAND OF A DECEASED DAUGHTER OF DECEDENT
Death between 7-1-59 and 6-30-76, $500 exemption. Use Table 6. Death on and after 7-1-76, $1,500 exemption. Use Table 5.

ALL OTHERS, INCLUDING BUT NOT LIMITED TO: EX-SPOUSE, UNCLE, AUNT, COUSIN, DESCENDANT OF A STEP-CHILD, BROTHER-IN-LAW, SISTER-IN-LAW, NON-RELATIVE
Death on and after 7-1-59, $500 exemption. Use Table 6.

TABLE 1.
($60,000 Exemption)

If the Amount Subject to Tax Is:

Over —	But Not Over —	The Tax Due Is —	Of the Amt. Over —
$ 0	$ 40,000	$ 0 + 3%	$ 0
40,000	90,000	1,200 + 4%	40,000
90,000	140,000	3,200 + 5%	90,000
140,000	240,000	5,700 + 6%	140,000
240,000	340,000	11,700 + 7%	240,000
340,000	440,000	18,700 + 8%	340,000
440,000	940,000	26,700 + 9%	440,000
940,000	-------	71,700 + 10%	940,000

TABLE 2.
($30,000 Exemption)

If the Amount Subject to Tax Is:

Over —	But Not Over —	The Tax Due Is —	Of the Amt. Over —
$ 0	$ 20,000	$ 0 + 2%	$ 0
20,000	70,000	400 + 3%	20,000
70,000	120,000	1,900 + 4%	70,000
120,000	170,000	3,900 + 5%	120,000
170,000	270,000	6,400 + 6%	170,000
270,000	370,000	12,400 + 7%	270,000
370,000	470,000	19,400 + 8%	370,000
470,000	970,000	27,400 + 9%	470,000
970,000	-------	72,400 + 10%	970,000

TABLE 3.
($15,000 Exemption)

If the Amount Subject to Tax Is:

Over —	But Not Over —	The Tax Due Is —	Of the Amt. Over —
$ 0	$ 10,000	$ 0 + 1½%	$ 0
10,000	35,000	150 + 2%	10,000
35,000	85,000	650 + 3%	35,000
85,000	135,000	2,150 + 4%	85,000
135,000	185,000	4,150 + 5%	135,000
185,000	285,000	6,650 + 6%	185,000
285,000	385,000	12,650 + 7%	285,000
385,000	485,000	19,650 + 8%	385,000
485,000	985,000	27,650 + 9%	485,000
985,000	-------	72,650 + 10%	985,000

TABLE 4.
($6,000 Exemption)

If the Amount Subject to Tax Is:

Over —	But Not Over—	The Tax Due Is —	Of the Amt. Over —
$ 0	$ 19,000	$ 0 + 2%	$ 0
19,000	44,000	380 + 4%	19,000
44,000	94,000	1,380 + 6%	44,000
94,000	144,000	4,380 + 7%	94,000
144,000	194,000	7,880 + 7%	144,000
194,000	294,000	11,380 + 8%	194,000
294,000	394,000	19,380 + 8%	294,000
394,000	494,000	27,380 + 9%	394,000
494,000	994,000	36,380 + 9%	494,000
994,000	-------	81,380 + 10%	994,000

TABLE 5.
($1,500 Exemption)

If the Amount Subject to Tax Is:

Over —	But Not Over —	The Tax Due Is —	Of the Amt. Over —
$ 0	$ 23,500	$ 0 + 6%	$ 0
23,500	48,500	1,410 + 8%	23,500
48,500	98,500	3,410 + 10%	48,500
98,500	148,500	8,410 + 12%	98,500
148,500	198,500	14,410 + 14%	148,500
198,500	298,500	21,410 + 16%	198,500
298,500	398,500	37,410 + 18%	298,500
398,500	498,500	55,410 + 20%	398,500
498,500	998,500	75,410 + 22%	498,500
998,500	-------	185,410 + 25%	998,500

TABLE 6.
($500 Exemption)

If the Amount Subject to Tax Is:

Over —	But Not Over —	The Tax Due Is —	Of the Amt. Over —
$ 0	$ 24,500	$ 0 + 8%	$ 0
24,500	49,500	1,960 + 10%	24,500
49,500	99,500	4,460 + 12%	49,500
99,500	149,500	10,460 + 14%	99,500
149,500	199,500	17,460 + 16%	149,500
199,500	299,500	25,460 + 18%	199,500
299,500	399,500	43,460 + 20%	299,500
399,500	499,500	63,460 + 22%	399,500
499,500	999,500	85,460 + 26%	499,500
999,500	-------	215,460 + 30%	999,500

Form 71 continued

Form IG-1 Sched. A

SCHEDULE A
COMPUTATION OF INHERITANCE TAX
MINNESOTA RESIDENT WHO DIED ON OR AFTER JULY 1, 1976

Name of decedent as on Form IG-1	Date of death	Social Security Number
Jane M. Doe	September 20, 1977	00-000-0000

USE THIS SPACE ONLY FOR SURVIVING HUSBAND OR WIFE

Name (of surviving spouse)	Actual Relationship	Date of Birth
John C. Doe	(Husband) ☒ (Wife) ☐	12/12/1900

INHERITANCE TAX

1. Surviving spouse's share of non-probate assets. From Form IG-1, line 1 . . . . $ 99,800.00
2. Excess living allowance. Amount from Form IG-1, line 7b, minus $9,000 . . . . ---
3. Enter surviving spouse's share of net probate assets. Form IG-1, line 9 . . . . 157,558.00
4. Total assets. Add lines 1, 2 and 3 . . . . $ 257,358.00
5. Exemptions and additional allowable deductions
   - 5a Personal exemption 60,000.00
   - 5b Homestead exemption. Share of net value up to $45,000 . . . . 20,000.00
   - 5c Substitute homestead exemption (see instructions) . . . . ---
   - 5d Share of non-probate deductions, if paid by surviving spouse . . . . ---
   - 5e Share of Federal Estate Tax, if apportioned. (see instructions) . . . . ---
   - 5f Other. Attach explanation . . . . ---
6. Total deductions and exemptions. Total, lines 5a through 5f . . . . $ 80,000.00
7. Amount subject to tax. Line 4 minus line 6 . . . . $ 177,358.00
8. Tentative tax. From Table #1, Form IG-1, page 2 . . . . $ 7,941.48
9. Maintenance credit. $9,000 (minus amount on Form IG-1, line 7b) x 3% 9000-4800=4200X3% 126.00
10. Inheritance tax. Line 8 minus line 9. If more than zero, complete lines 11-20 . . . . $ 7,815.48

ALTERNATIVE MARITAL EXEMPTION TAX COMPUTATION

> NOTE: Do not use personal, homestead or substitute homestead exemptions for the computation below.

11. Total assets from line 4, above, less line 2 . . . . $ 257,358.00
12. Living allowance of family. Enter amount from Form IG-1, line 7b 4,800.00
13. Assets available for marital exemption. Add lines 11 and 12 . . . . $ 262,158.00
14. Additional allowable deductions
    - 14a Share of non-probate deductions (Form IG-2, page 1) . . . . -0-
    - 14b Share of Federal Estate Tax, if apportioned . . . . -0-
    - 14c Other. Attach explanation . . . . ---
15. Total additional deductions. Total lines 14a through 14c . . . . ---
16. Net assets available for marital exemption. Line 13 minus line 15 . . . . $ 262,158.00
17. Marital exemption. $250,000 or one-half of line 16, whichever is less 131,079.00
18. Amount subject to tax. Line 16 minus line 17 . . . . 131,079.00
19. Marital exemption tax. From marital exemption tax table below . . . . $ 3,618.16
20. Alternate inheritance tax. Enter here the tax on line 10 or on line 19, whichever is less . . . (Round) . . . . $ 3,618.00

> INHERITANCE TAX FOR ALL SURVIVORS LISTED ON SCHEDULE A, PAGE 1 AND 2 MUST BE ADDED TOGETHER, AND TOTAL LISTED ON FORM IG 1, LINE 11.

MARITAL EXEMPTION TAX TABLE
If the Amount Subject to Tax on Line 18 is:

Over -	But Not Over -	The Tax Due Is -	Of the Amount Over -
$ 0	$ 25,000	$ 0 + 1½%	$ 0
25,000	50,000	375 + 2%	25,000
50,000	100,000	875 + 3%	50,000
100,000	150,000	2,375 + 4%	100,000
150,000	200,000	4,375 + 5%	150,000
200,000	300,000	6,875 + 6%	200,000
300,000	400,000	12,875 + 7%	300,000
400,000	500,000	19,875 + 8%	400,000
500,000	1,000,000	27,875 + 9%	500,000
1,000,000	- - -	72,875 + 10%	1,000,000

Page 1

Form 71 continued

Page 2

SCHEDULE A

USE THIS SPACE ONLY FOR MINOR OR DEPENDENT CHILD

Name of minor or dependent child	Actual relationship	Date of Birth

1. Share of non-probate assets. From Form IG-1, line 1 . . . . $ _ _ _ _ _ _ _ _

2. Share of net probate assets. From Form IG-1, line 9 . . . . _ _ _ _ _

3. Total assets. Add lines 1 and 2 . . . . $ _____

4. Exemptions and additional allowable deductions
   4a Personal exemption . . . . 30,000.00 _
   4b Homestead exemption. Share of net value up to $45,000 . . . . _ _ _ _ _
   4c Substitute homestead exemption.(see instructions) . . . . _ _ _ _ _
   4d Share of non-probate deductions, Form IG-2, page 1 . . . . _ _ _ _ _
   4e Share of Federal Estate Tax, if apportioned . . . . _ _ _ _ _
   4f Other. Attach explanation . . . . _ _ _ _ _

5. Total deductions and exemptions. Total, lines 4a through 4f . . . . $ _____

6. Amount subject to tax. Line 3 minus line 5 . . . . $ _____

7. Tax due from this survivor. See Table #2, Form IG-1, page 2 . . . . |$

USE THE FOLLOWING SPACES FOR ADDITIONAL TAX COMPUTATIONS FOR ALL OTHER SURVIVORS AND ADDITIONAL MINOR OR DEPENDENT CHILDREN

Name of survivor	Actual relationship	Date of Birth
Sandy R. Doe	Daughter	April 12, 1932

1. Share of non-probate assets. From Form IG-1, line 1 . . . . $ 35,000.00 _

2. Share of net probate assets. From Form IG-1, line 9 . . . . -0- _ _ _

3. Total assets. Add lines 1 and 2 . . . . $ 35,000.00

4. Exemptions and additional allowable deductions
   4a Personal exemption. From Personal Exemption Table . . . . 6,000.00 _
   4b _ _ _ _ _ _ _ _
   4c _ _ _ _ _ _ _ _
   4d _ _ _ _ _ _ _ _

5. Total deductions and exemptions. Total, lines 4a through 4d . . . . $ 6,000.00

6. Amount subject to tax. Line 3 minus line 5 . . . . $ 29,000.00

7. Tax due from this survivor. See Tax Tables, Form IG-1, page 2 . . . . |$ 780.00

Name of survivor	Actual relationship	Date of Birth
Jay A. Dee	Brother	12/2/1906

1. Share of non-probate assets. From Form IG-1, line 1 . . . . $ 10,000.00 _

2. Share of net probate assets. From Form IG-1, line 9 . . . . -0- _ _

3. Total assets. Add lines 1 and 2 . . . . $ 10,000.00

4. Exemptions and additional allowable deductions
   4a Personal exemption. From Personal Exemption Table . . . . 1,500.00 _ _
   4b _ _ _ _ _ _ _ _
   4c _ _ _ _ _ _ _ _
   4d _ _ _ _ _ _ _ _

5. Total deductions and exemptions. Total, lines 4a through 4d . . . . $ 1,500.00

6. Amount subject to tax. Line 3 minus line 5 . . . . $ 8,500.00

7. Tax due from this survivor. See Tax Tables, Form IG-1, page 2 . . . . |$ 510.00

Form 71 continued

P994 — Form IG-1A (Rev. 6-77)

COMPUTATION OF TAX FOR ADDITIONAL BENEFICIARIES

Name of survivor	Actual relationship	Date of birth
Minnesota Cancer Society	Medical Research (Scientific)	

1. Share of non-probate assets. From Form IG-1, line 1 .... $
2. Share of net probate assets. From Form IG-1, line 9 .... 10,000.00

3. Total assets. Add lines 1 and 2 .... $ 10,000.00
4. Exemptions and additional allowable deductions
   - 4a Personal exemption. From Personal Exemption Table ....
   - 4b Exempt under MS291.05 (1)   10,000.00
   - 4c _____
   - 4d _____

5. Total deductions and exemptions. Total, lines 4a through 4d .... $ 10,000.00

6. Amount subject to tax. Line 3 minus line 5 .... $ ---

7. Tax due from this survivor. From Tax Tables, Form IG-1, page 2 .... $ NONE

Name of survivor	Actual relationship	Date of birth
Girls Club of America	Charitable	

1. Share of non-probate assets. From Form IG-1, line 1 .... $
2. Share of net probate assets. From Form IG-1, line 9 .... 5,000.00

3. Total assets. Add lines 1 and 2 .... $ 5,000.00
4. Exemptions and additional allowable deductions
   - 4a Personal exemption. From Personal Exemption Table ....
   - 4b Exempt under MS 291.05 (1)   5,000.00
   - 4c _____
   - 4d _____

5. Total deductions and exemptions. Total, lines 4a through 4d .... $ 5,000.00

6. Amount subject to tax. Line 3 minus line 5 .... $ ---

7. Tax due from this survivor. From Tax Tables, Form IG-1, page 2 .... $ NONE

Name of survivor	Actual relationship	Date of birth
Newark Institute for Higher Learning	Educational Research	

1. Share of non-probate assets. From Form IG-1, line 1 .... $
2. Share of net probate assets. From Form IG-1, line 9 .... 1,000.00

3. Total assets. Add lines 1 and 2 .... $ 1,000.00
4. Exemptions and additional allowable deductions
   - 4a Personal exemption. From Personal Exemption Table ....
   - 4b Exempt under MS 291.05 (1)   1,000.00
   - 4c _____
   - 4d _____

5. Total deductions and exemptions. Total, lines 4a through 4d .... $ 1,000.00

6. Amount subject to tax. Line 3 minus line 5 .... $

7. Tax due from this survivor. From Tax Tables, Form IG-1, page 2 .... $ NONE

Name of survivor	Actual relationship	Date of birth

1. Share of non-probate assets. From Form IG-1, line 1 .... $
2. Share of net probate assets. From Form IG-1, line 9 ....

3. Total assets. Add lines 1 and 2 .... $
4. Exemptions and additional allowable deductions
   - 4a Personal exemption. From Personal Exemption Table ....
   - 4b _____
   - 4c _____
   - 4d _____

5. Total deductions and exemptions. Total, lines 4a through 4d .... $

6. Amount subject to tax. Line 3 minus 5 .... $

7. Tax due from this survivor. From Tax Tables, Form IG-1, page 2 ....

Form 71 continued

P994 — Form IG-1A (Rev. 6-77)

COMPUTATION OF TAX FOR ADDITIONAL BENEFICIARIES

Name of survivor	Actual relationship	Date of birth

1. Share of non-probate assets. From Form IG-1, line 1 . . . . $_ _ _ _ _ _ _ _ _ _
2. Share of net probate assets. From Form IG-1, line 9 . . . . _ _ _ _ _ _ _ _ _ _

3. Total assets. Add lines 1 and 2 . . . . $_
4. Exemptions and additional allowable deductions
    4a Personal exemption. From Personal Exemption Table . . . . _ _ _ _ _ _ _ _ _ _
    4b _____ _ _ _ _ _ _ _ _ _ _
    4c _____ _ _ _ _ _ _ _ _ _ _
    4d _____ _ _ _ _ _ _ _ _ _ _

5. Total deductions and exemptions. Total, lines 4a through 4d. . . . . $_
6. Amount subject to tax. Line 3 minus line 5 . . . . $_
7. Tax due from this survivor. From Tax Tables, Form IG-1, page 2 . . . . |$

Name of survivor	Actual relationship	Date of birth

1. Share of non-probate assets. From Form IG-1, line 1 . . . . $_ _ _ _ _ _ _ _ _ _
2. Share of net probate assets. From Form IG-1, line 9 . . . . _ _ _ _ _ _ _ _ _ _

3. Total assets. Add lines 1 and 2 . . . . $_
4. Exemptions and additional allowable deductions
    4a Personal exemption. From Personal Exemption Table . . . . _ _ _ _ _ _ _ _ _ _
    4b _____ _ _ _ _ _ _ _ _ _ _
    4c _____ _ _ _ _ _ _ _ _ _ _
    4d _____ _ _ _ _ _ _ _ _ _ _

5. Total deductions and exemptions. Total, lines 4a through 4d. . . . . $_
6. Amount subject to tax. Line 3 minus line 5 . . . . $_
7. Tax due from this survivor. From Tax Tables, Form IG-1, page 2 . . . . |$

Name of survivor	Actual relationship	Date of birth

1. Share of non-probate assets. From Form IG-1, line 1 . . . . $_ _ _ _ _ _ _ _ _ _
2. Share of net probate assets. From Form IG-1, line 9 . . . . _ _ _ _ _ _ _ _ _ _

3. Total assets. Add lines 1 and 2 . . . . $_
4. Exemptions and additional allowable deductions
    4a Personal exemption. From Personal Exemption Table . . . . _ _ _ _ _ _ _ _ _ _
    4b _____ _ _ _ _ _ _ _ _ _ _
    4c _____ _ _ _ _ _ _ _ _ _ _
    4d _____ _ _ _ _ _ _ _ _ _ _

5. Total deductions and exemptions. Total, lines 4a through 4d . . . . $_
6. Amount subject to tax. Line 3 minus line 5 . . . . $_
7. Tax due from this survivor. From Tax Tables, Form IG-1, page 2 . . . . |$

Name of survivor	Actual relationship	Date of birth

1. Share of non-probate assets. From Form IG-1, line 1 . . . . $_ _ _ _ _ _ _ _ _ _
2. Share of net probate assets. From Form IG-1, line 9 . . . . _ _ _ _ _ _ _ _ _ _

3. Total assets. Add lines 1 and 2 . . . . $_
4. Exemptions and additional allowable deductions
    4a Personal exemption. From Personal Exemption Table . . . . _ _ _ _ _ _ _ _ _ _
    4b _____ _ _ _ _ _ _ _ _ _ _
    4c _____ _ _ _ _ _ _ _ _ _ _
    4d _____ _ _ _ _ _ _ _ _ _ _

5. Total deductions and exemptions. Total, lines 4a through 4d. . . . . $_
6. Amount subject to tax. Line 3 minus 5 . . . . $_
7. Tax due from this survivor. From Tax Tables, Form IG-1, page 2 . . . .

Form 72 Final Account

OS263 (Rev. 7/76)

Form 524.3—1001 # 1
524.3—1002 # 1
524.3—1003 #2

UPC 82

STATE OF MINNESOTA

COUNTY OF __Ramsey__

In Re: Estate of

__Jane M. Doe__
Deceased

Social Security Number: __000-00-0000__

PROBATE COURT
COUNTY COURT—PROBATE DIVISION

Court File No. __999999__

FINAL ACCOUNT

READ INSTRUCTIONS AT END OF FORM

	DEBITS	CREDITS
DEBITS		
Personal Estate Described in Inventory . . . . $ 182,098.00		
Increase on same:		
Interest . . . . $ 3,230.00		
Dividends . . . . $ 2,460.00		
Refunds . . . . $ -o-		
Other _____ $ -o-		
_____ $		
Personal Estate Omitted in Inventory _____$ -o-		
_____ $		
Received from Sale of Real Estate:		
Cash. . . . . $ -o-		
Contract for Deed . . . . $ -o- ___$		
Received Rent of Real Estate. . . . . * . $ 1,100.00		
Gain on Sale of Personal Property . . . . $ -o-		
Advanced to Estate . . . . $ -o-		
TOTAL DEBITS.	$ 188,888 00	
* Assume rent is net of expenses		
CREDITS - DISBURSEMENTS		
Decrease in Personal Estate:		
Loss on Sale of		
Personal Property . . . . $ -o-		
Other _____ $ -o-		
TOTAL Decrease	. . . .	$ -o-
EXPENSES OF ADMINISTRATION		
Fees Probate Court. . . . . $ 2.00		
Certified Copies. . . . . $ 5.00		
Appraisers Fees . . . . $ 500.00		
Printing Fees. .Publication. of. orders. . . . . $ 50.00		
Compensation of Representative. . . . . $ 10,000.00		
Attorneys Fees to Date Hereof . . . . $ 15,000.00		
Estimated Future Fees to be Charged. . . . . $ -o-		
Maintenance of Family. . . . . $ 4,800.00		
Statutory Selection . . . . $ 3,500.00		
Bond Premiums . . . . $ -o-		
Principal and interest pd.on mortg.$ 3,850.00		
Miscellaneous _____ $ 698.00		
TOTAL Expenses of Administration	. . . .	$ 38,405 00
FUNERAL EXPENSES		
Mortician. . . . . $ 2,500.00		
Marker. . . . . $ 500.00		
Flowers . . . . $ 100.00		
Cemetery. . . . . $ 1,000.00		
Rev. B. Stone _____ $ 25.00		
_____ $		
TOTAL Funeral Expenses.	. . . .	$ 4,125 00
EXPENSES OF LAST ILLNESS		
Medical Attendance . . . . $		
Medicine, etc. . . . . $		
Nursing . . . . $		
Hospital. . . . . $ 850.00		
_____ $		
_____ $		
TOTAL Expenses of Last Illness	. . . .	$ 850 00

Form 72 continued

	DEBITS	CREDITS

<u>TAXES</u>

Real Estate Taxes:
Homestead .... $ 650.00
Other Real Estate .... $ 250.00 $ 900.00
Income Taxes of Decedent:
Minnesota .... $_____
Federal .... $_____ $ -o-
Fiduciary Income Taxes:
Minnesota .... $_____
Federal .... $_____ $ -o-

Personal Property Tax .... $_____
Minnesota Gift Tax for 1977 $ 680.00
*Minnesota Inheritance Tax $ 4,908.00
              TOTAL Taxes .... $ 6,488.00
* Assume Tax Clause in will
      OTHER CLAIMS ALLOWED AND PAID (See Instruction J.)

Ace's Plumbing Co. $ 230.00
St. Paul Telephone Company $ 50.00
St. Paul Electric Company $ 100.00
Harvey's Garbage Pick-Up $ 50.00
Dr. Norma J. Dennison $ 600.00
St. Paul Rents $ 50.00
_____ $_____
_____ $_____
_____ $_____
_____ $_____
_____ $_____
_____ $_____
_____ $_____
_____ $_____
_____ $_____
              TOTAL Claims Paid .... $ 1,080.00

DEVISES PAID AND DISTRIBUTED (See Instruction H.)

_____ $_____
_____ $_____
_____ $_____
_____ $_____
_____ $_____
_____ $_____
_____ $_____
_____ $_____
_____ $_____
              TOTAL Devises Paid and Distributed .... $ _____

TOTAL DEBITS AND CREDITS .... $ 188,888.00 $ 50,948.00
*BALANCE OF PERSONAL PROPERTY ON HAND
      FOR DISTRIBUTION $ 137,940.00

PERSONAL PROPERTY ON HAND FOR DISTRIBUTION
(Attach Schedules Where Necessary)

Household Goods and Wearing Apparel _____ $ None
Corporation Stock 100 Shares American Telephone and Telegraph
                      Certificate #CO68927   5,000.00
1000 Shares Minnesota Co-op Certificate #D2289663   4,500.00
$50.00 U.S. Savings Bond #R4502363E   74.00
$50.00 U.S. Savings Bond #R4502364E   74.00

Mortgages, Bonds, Notes, Contracts for Deed, Etc. _____
Forrest Furriers Promissory Note dated 3/20/74 due 3/20/79   10,000.00

Cash on Hand _____   64,792.00
All Other Personal Property (Describe): __1973 Nova__   2,000.00
Fur - Mink Coat   1,500.00
Power of Appointment Trust   50,000.00

TOTAL (Must agree with *Balance shown above) $ 137,940.00

Form 72 continued

REAL ESTATE ON HAND FOR DISTRIBUTION

Homestead: being in the County of Ramsey, State of Minnesota:

Legally described as follows, to wit:
Lot 615, Block 42, Reiser's Addition
to St. Paul (Plat #22760 Parcel #7600)

Balance of Mortgage at St.Paul Bank & Trust Co. $30,000.00

Other Real Estate in the County of ___Ramsey___, State of Minnesota:
An undivided 1/4 interest in Duplex located in the following described property:
Lots 16 & 17, Block 20
Lovey's Addition to St. Paul
(Plat #32689 Parcel #5562)

One Fourth of:
Mortgage balance of $40,000 at St. Paul Bank & Trust $10,000.00

Under penalties for perjury for deliberate falsification therein, I declare or affirm that I have read the foregoing account and to the best of my knowledge or information, its representations are true, correct and complete.

Dated ___August 31, 1978___

/s/ John C. Doe
John C. Doe,
Personal Representative

/s/ John Cranwall
Attorney John Cranwall
999 St. Paul Trust Co. Bldg.
St. Paul, Minnesota 55105

Address/Phone

Form 73 Order for Hearing on Final Account and Petition for Distribution and for Mailed Notice

Form 4465

524.3-1001 #4   UPC --

STATE OF MINNESOTA

COUNTY OF <u>RAMSEY</u>

PROBATE COURT
COUNTY COURT-PROBATE DIVISION

In Re: Estate of

Court File No. <u>999999</u>

ORDER FOR HEARING ON FINAL
ACCOUNT AND PETITION FOR
DISTRIBUTION AND FOR
MAILED NOTICE

<u>Jane M. Doe</u>
Deceased

    The personal representative of the above named estate having filed his final account and petition for order of settlement of estate and distribution and allowance thereof and for decree or order of distribution to the persons thereunto entitled;

    IT IS ORDERED, That the hearing thereof be had on <u>September 18</u>, 19<u>78</u>, at <u>10</u> o'clock <u>A</u>.M., before the above named Court at <u>St. Paul</u> _____, Minnesota, and that all persons having an interest in said estate present objections, if any they have, why said petition should not be granted.

    This Order shall be served at least 14 days prior to such date of hearing by mailing copies hereof to all distributees according to law.

Dated: <u>August 3, 1978</u>

(COURT SEAL)

<u>/S/ I. M. Honest</u>
Judge

By <u>/S/ Thomas Malone</u>
Clerk

<u>/S/ John Cranwall</u>
Attorney for Personal Representative

<u>1st Trust Bldg., St. Paul, MN 55101</u>
Address/Phone **(612) 111-0011**

Form 74 Affidavit of Mailing Order or Notice of Hearing On Final Account

FORM 4307

Form 524.1-401 #2
525.83   UPC — —

STATE OF MINNESOTA

COUNTY OF ___Ramsey___

IN RE: (ESTATE
                          (CONSERVATORSHIP
                          (GUARDIANSHIP
OF ____Jane M. Doe____

Deceased — ~~Conservatee~~ — ~~Ward~~

ATTACH COPY OF ORDER
OR NOTICE HERE

**PROBATE COURT
COUNTY COURT-PROBATE DIVISION**

Court File No. _999999_

**AFFIDAVIT OF MAILING ORDER
OR NOTICE OF HEARING** on
Final Account and Petition for
Distribution and for Mailed Notice

STATE OF MINNESOTA
COUNTY OF _Ramsey_   ss.
___I.M. Truthful___

being first duly sworn on oath deposes and
says that on the __4th__ day of _August_,
19_78_, at _St. Paul_ in said
County and State __he mailed a copy of the
Order or Notice hereto attached to each
heir, devisee, beneficiary of trust and
the personal representative

whose name and address are known to affiant,
after exercising due diligence in ascertaining
the correctness of said name and address, by
placing a true and correct copy thereof in a
sealed envelope, postage prepaid and depositing the same in the U.S. Mails at
St. Paul, Minnesota

and addressed to the following named persons:
NOTE: (Instructions at bottom of page)

NAME	STREET or POST OFFICE	CITY	STATE
John C. Doe	1005 Easy Street	St. Paul	Minn. 55102
Sandy R. Doe	1005 Easy Street	St. Paul	Minn. 55102
American Cancer Society	222 Glen Acre Drive	St. Paul	Minn. 55102
Girl's Club of America	111 Cookie Lane	St. Paul	Minn. 55102
Newark Institute of Higher Learning	444 Brilliant Drive	St. Paul	Minn. 55102

/S/ I.M. Truthful

Subscribed and sworn to before me this __4th__
day of _August_, 19_78_.

___/s/ Judith Harris___   (SEAL)
Notary Public, _Ramsey_ County, Minn.
My Commission expires _January 15_ 19_81_.

NOTED INSTRUCTION: In Estates To each heir, devisee, personal representative, the foreign
consul pursuant to M.S.524.3-306 and 524.3-403, and the Minnesota
Attorney General, if a devisee is the trustee of a charitable trust or if
the decedent left no devisees or heirs.
In Conservatorships and Guardianships To each of persons as directed
by the Court.

Form 74 continued

AFFIDAVIT OF MAILING
ALLOWANCES TO SPOUSE AND/OR CHILDREN

When a decedent dies with or without a will the allowances to the spouse or children are as follows:

525.15 ALLOWANCES TO SPOUSE. When any person dies testate, or intestate,
(1) The surviving spouse shall be allowed from the personal property of which the decedent was possessed or to which he was entitled at the time of his death, the wearing apparel, and, as selected by him, furniture and household goods not exceeding $2,000 in value, and other personal property not exceeding $1,000 in value;

(2) When, except for one automobile, all of the personal estate of the decedent is allowed to the surviving spouse by clause (1), the surviving spouse shall also be allowed such automobile.

(3) If there be no surviving spouse, the minor children shall receive the property specified in clause (1) as selected in their behalf;

(4) During administration, but not exceeding 18 months, unless an extension shall have been granted by the court, or, if the estate be insolvent, not exceeding 12 months, the spouse or children, or both, constituting the family of the decedent shall be allowed reasonable maintenance.

(5) In the administration of an estate of a non-resident decedent, the allowances received in the domiciliary administration shall be deducted from the allowances under this section.

In all estates where there is a will the following rule applies to the spouse who has not consented to the will:

525.212 RENUNCIATION AND ELECTION. If a will make provision for a surviving spouse in lieu of the rights in the estate secured by statute, such spouse shall be deemed to have elected to take under the will, unless he shall have filed with the court and mailed or delivered to the personal representative, if any, within nine months after the date of death, or within six months after the probate of the decedent's will, whichever limitation last expires, an instrument in writing renouncing and refusing to accept the provisions in such will. For good cause shown, the court may permit an election within such further time as the court may determine. No devise to a surviving spouse shall be considered as adding to the rights in the estate secured by sections 525.145 and 525.16 to such spouse, unless it clearly appears from the contents of the will that such was the testator's intent.

STATE OF MINNESOTA
COUNTY OF_Ramsey_____   ss.
____I.M. Truthful_____ being first duly sworn on oath deposes and says that on the_4th_ day of_August____, 19_78_, at_ St. Paul _____ in said County and State, he mailed a copy of Sections 525.15 and 525.212 of Minnesota Statutes as hereinbefore set out to decedent's spouse and children constituting the family of the decedent at their last known address after exercising due diligence and ascertaining the correctness of said addresses by placing a true and correct copy thereof in a sealed envelope, postage pre-paid and depositing the same in the U.S. mails at_____, Minnesota, and addressed to the following:

NAME	STREET or POST OFFICE	CITY	STATE
John C. Doe	1005 Easy Street	St. Paul	MN 07102

_____/s/ I.M. Truthful_____

Subscribed and sworn to be before me this
4th__ day of_August_____, 1978_.

___/s/ Judith Harris_____   (SEAL)
Notary Public_Ramsey_____ County, Minn.
My Commission expires_Jan 15____, 19_81_.

Form 75 Order Allowing Final Account

Form 4467

524.3-1001 #6
524.3-1002 #5

UPC 85

STATE OF MINNESOTA

COUNTY OF ___Ramsey___

PROBATE COURT
COUNTY COURT-PROBATE DIVISION

In Re: Estate of

Court File No. ___999999___

ORDER ALLOWING FINAL ACCOUNT

___Jane M. Doe___
Deceased

The _____personal_____ representative having accounted for every part of the estate of decedent according to law, and a summary statement of the accounts being as follows:

Debits .... $___188,888.00___

Credits .... $___50,948.00___

Balance .... $___137,940.00___

IT IS ORDERED, that said accounts are hereby finally settled and allowed.

Dated: ___September 18, 1978___

(COURT SEAL)

_____/s/ I.M. Honest___
Judge

Form 76 Petition for Order of Complete Settlement of the Estate and Decree of Distribution

OS264 (Rev. 7/76)   Form 524.3-1001 #2   **UPC 82**

STATE OF MINNESOTA   **PROBATE COURT**
COUNTY COURT—PROBATE DIVISION
COUNTY OF _Ramsey_   Court File No. _999999_

In Re: Estate of   **PETITION FOR ORDER OF COMPLETE**
SETTLEMENT OF THE ESTATE
Jane M. Doe   **AND DECREE OF DISTRIBUTION**
         Deceased

TO THE HONORABLE JUDGE OF THE ABOVE NAMED COURT:

Petitioner, _John C. Doe_ , respectfully states:

1. Petitioner resides at _1005 Easy Street, St. Paul, MN 55102_ ;

2. Petitioner has an interest herein as _named personal representative and devisee_ , and is, therefore, an interested person as defined by the laws of this State;

3. Decedent was born _November 6_ , 19_00_ , at _Detroit, Michigan_ ;

4. Decedent died testate at the age of _76_ years on _September 20_ , 19 _77_ , at _St. Paul, MN 55102_

5. Decedent at the time of ~~his~~ her death resided at _1005 Easy Street_ , City of _St. Paul_ , County of _Ramsey_ , State of _Minn._ .

6. That the names and addresses of decedent's spouse, children, heirs and devisees and other persons interested in this proceeding and the ages of any who are minors so far known or ascertainable with reasonable diligence by the petitioner are:

   NOTE: Classify the heirs and others entitled to take per stirpes and give the name, date of death, relationship/interest and address, if known, of their predeceased ancestor. Give the birthdate of any heir or devisee taking a life interest.

Name	Age	Relationship/Interest		Address
John C. Doe	76	husband	devisee, heir personal rep.	1005 Easy St. St. Paul, MN 55102
Sandy R. Doe	45	daughter	devisee, heir	1005 Easy St. St. Paul, MN 55102
American Cancer Society		devisee		222 Glen Acre Dr. St. Paul, MN 55102
Girl's Clubs of America		devisee		111 Cookie Lane St. Paul, MN 55102
Newark Institute of Higher Learning		devisee		444 Brilliant Dr. St. Paul, MN 55102

Form 76 continued

7. That venue for this proceeding is in the above named County of the State of Minnesota, because the decedent was domiciled in such County at the time of his death, and was the owner of property located in the State of Minnesota, or because, though not domiciled in the State of Minnesota, the decedent was the owner of property located in the above named County at the time of his death. (See below*)

8. That petitioner has not received a demand for notice and is not aware of any demand for notice of any probate or appointment proceeding concerning the decedent that may have been filed in this State or elsewhere or proper notice has been given.

9. That the estate of the above named decedent has been fully administered and all expenses, debts, valid charges and claims allowed have been fully paid.

10. That a final account has been or herewith is duly filed and presented for consideration and approval or should be completed.

11. That the original of decedent's will, if any, duly executed on _____ June 2 _____ , 19 45 , and any codicil or codicils thereto was formally probated by this Court's order dated _Octrober 30_ _____ , 19 77 .

12. That the time for presenting claims which arose prior to the death of the decedent has expired.

WHEREFORE, your petitioner requests the order of this Court fixing a time and place for hearing on this petition, and that after the time for any notice has expired, upon proof of notice, and hearing, the Court enter a judicial order formally:

1. Determining decedent's state of testacy if not previously determined.
2. Considering the final account herein or compelling an accounting and distribution or approving the accounting and distribution made herein. _____ June 2 _____ , 19 45 , and
3. Construing decedent's will, if any, duly executed on _____ , 19 ____ , and any codicil or codicils thereto probated by this Court's order dated _October 30_ _____ , 19 77 .
4. Determining decedent's heirs.
5. Adjudicating the final settlement and distribution of the estate.
6. Determining the persons entitled to distribution of the estate.
7. As circumstances require, approving settlement and directing or approving distribution of the estate and/or issuing a decree of distribution determining the persons entitled to the estate and assigning the same to them in lieu of ordering the assignment.
8. Waiving the lien of inheritance taxes or finding that taxes have been satisfied by payment or decree the property subject to lien.
9. Determining testacy as it affects any previously omitted or unnotified persons and other interested parties and confirming any previous order of testacy as it affects all interested persons.
10. Granting such other and further relief as may be proper.

FURTHER, under penalties for perjury for deliberate falsification therein, I declare or affirm that I have read the foregoing petition and to the best of my knowledge or information, its representations are true, correct and complete.

Dated: ___August 10, 1978___

/S/   John C. Doe
_____
Petitioner

/S/   John Cranwall
_____
Attorney for Petitioner

1st Trust Bldg.
St. Paul, MN 55101   (612) 111-0011
Address/Phone

*ASSETS

Homestead $___20,000___ (net)

Other Real Estate $___12,750___ (net)

Personal Property $__185,498__

Form 77 Order of Complete Settlement of the Estate and Decree of Distribution

Form 4469

524.3-1001 #8
524.3-1002 #7

UPC 85

STATE OF MINNESOTA

COUNTY OF _____Ramsey_____

PROBATE COURT
COUNTY COURT-PROBATE DIVISION

In Re: Estate of

Court File No. _____999999_____

ORDER OF COMPLETE SETTLEMENT
OF THE ESTATE AND DECREE OF
DISTRIBUTION

_____Jane M. Doe_____
Deceased

The petition of _____John C. Doe_____, dated __August 10__, 19 _78_, for an order of complete settlement of the estate and order of distribution in the estate of the above named decedent having duly come on for hearing before the above named court, the undersigned Judge having heard and considered such petition, being fully advised in the premises, makes the following findings and determinations:

1. That the petition for order of complete settlement of the estate and order of distribution is complete.

2. That the time for any notice has expired and any notice as required by the laws of this state has been given and proved.

3. That the petitioner has declared or affirmed that the representations contained in the petition are true, correct and complete to the best of his knowledge or information.

4. That the petitioner appears from the petition to be an interested person as defined by the laws of this state.

5. That decedent died _____ testate at the age of _76_ years on __September 20,__ 19 _77_, at _____Saint Paul, MN 07102_____.

6. That venue for this proceeding is in the above named County of the State of Minnesota, because the decedent was domiciled in such county at the time of his death, and was the owner of property located in the State of Minnesota, or because, though not domiciled in the State of Minnesota, the decedent was the owner of property located in the above named county at the time of his death.

7. That this court has jurisdiction of this estate, proceedings and subject matter.

8. That the said estate has been in all respects fully administered, and all expenses, debts, valid charges and all claims allowed against said estate have been paid.

9. That the personal representative has filed a final account herein for consideration and approval.

10. That decedent's will, if any, duly executed on _____June 2_____, 19 _45_, and any codicil or codicils thereto, was probated by the order of this Court dated __October 30__, 19 _77_, and should be construed to provide that under the provisions thereof, decedent devised his estate as follows: (State actual legal relationship of each devisee to decedent)

```
American Cancer Society                Charitable Devisee   $10,000.00
Girl's Clubs of America                Charitable Devisee   $ 5,000.00
Newark Institute of Higher Learning    Charitable Devisee   $ 1,000.00

John C. Doe  Husband  all the rest, residue and remainder of
                      the real and personal property of the
                      decedent's estate.
```

Form 77 continued

11. That the following named persons are all the heirs of the decedent and their actual legal relationship is as stated, except if decedent died testate, no heirs are named unless all heirs are ascertained.

John C. Doe   husband,

Sandy R. Doe   daughter,

12. That the title to the hereinafter described real and personal estate has passed to and should be conveyed or transferred to the following named persons who are entitled thereto as all the distributees of the decedent whose actual legal relationship to the decedent is as stated in the following proportions or parts:

The whole thereof to decedent's husband, John C. Doe.

13. That the residue of the estate of decedent for distribution consists of the following described property:

(A) Personal property of the value of $ 137,940.00 _____ comprising the following items:

1. Under decedent's will, the following is specifically given to John C. Doe:

Stock and Bonds
100 Shares American Telephone and Telegraph....$ 5,000.00
$1000 Shares Minnesota Co-op................... 4,500.00
$50.00 U.S. Savings Bond.......................   74.00
$50.00 U.S. Savings Bond.......................   74.00

Mortgages and Notes
Forrest Furriers Promissory Note dated 3/20/74
    due 3/20/79............................... 10,000.00

Cash.. 64,792.00

Other Personal Property
1973 Nova...................................... 2,000.00
Fur - Mink Coat................................ 1,500.00
Power of Appointment Trust..................... 50,000.00

                              Total.......$137,940.00

Form 77 continued

(B) Real property described as follows:

(1) The homestead of decedent situate in the County of _____ Ramsey _____,
State of Minnesota, described as follows:

    Lot 615, Block 42, Reiser's Addition to St. Paul

(2) Other real estate in the County of _____ Ramsey _____,
State of Minnesota, described as follows:

    An undivided 1/4 interest in Duplex located in the follow-
ing described property:

        Lots 16 & 17, Block 20
        Lovey's Addition to St. Paul

14. That the lien of inheritance taxes on the above described property should be waived.

15. That any previous order determining testacy should be confirmed as it affects any previously omitted or unnotified persons and other interested persons.

Now, therefore, it is ORDERED, ADJUDGED, and DECREED by the court as follows:

1. That the petition is hereby granted.
2. That decedent died ____ testate.
3. That the final account of the personal representative herein is hereby approved.
4. That decedent's will, if any, duly executed on ___ June 2 ___, 19 45 , and any codicil or codicils thereto are construed as above stated.
5. That the heirs of the decedent are determined to be as set forth above.
6. That the residue of the estate of decedent is as above stated.
7. That the personal representative herein is directed to make good and sufficient conveyance of title to the real and personal estate described herein to the persons named herein who are the persons entitled to distribution of the estate in the portions or parts as above stated to have and to hold the same, together with all the hereditaments and appurtenances thereunto belonging or in anywise appertaining, their heirs, successors and assigns, without prejudice, however, to any lawful conveyance of said property or any part thereof by said persons, or any of them, heretofore made.
8. That the lien of inheritance taxes, if any, on the above described property is hereby waived.
9. That any previous order determining testacy is hereby confirmed as it affects any previously omitted or unnotified persons and other interested persons.

Dated: ___ September 18, 1978 ___

                                    /s/ I.M. Honest
(COURT SEAL)   Judge

Form 78 Petition for Discharge of Personal Representative

Form 4470

524.3-1001 #9
524.3-1002 #8   UPC—

STATE OF MINNESOTA

COUNTY OF ___Ramsey___

PROBATE COURT
COUNTY COURT-PROBATE DIVISION

In Re: Estate of

Court File No. ___999999___

PETITION FOR DISCHARGE OF
PERSONAL REPRESENTATIVE

___Jane M. Doe___
        Deceased

TO THE HONORABLE JUDGE OF THE ABOVE NAMED COURT:

Petitioner, ___John C. Doe___, respectfully states:

1. Petitioner resides at ___1005 Easy Street, St. Paul, MN 07102___;

2. Petitioner has an interest herein as ___personal representative and devisee___, and is, therefore, an interested person as defined by the laws of this state;

3. That petitioner has fully administered upon the estate of said decedent, and has paid all expenses, debts and charges chargeable upon the same;

4. That petitioner's final account as such personal representative has been heretofore presented to and allowed by said Court, and the decree or order of distribution made therein, and that petitioner has paid all taxes required to be paid by the personal representative and filed proper receipts therefor.

5. That the balance of the said estate remaining in petitioner's hands for distribution as per said order allowing said final account, has been paid out and distributed in accordance with said decree or order of distribution, as follows, to-wit:

LEGACIES AND/OR DISTRIBUTIVE SHARES	SHARE VALUE
1. John C. Doe 1005 Easy Street St. Paul, MN Surviving Spouse	$ 137,940.00
2.	$
3.	$
4.	$
5.	$
6.	$
7.	$
8.	$
9.	$
10.	$
11.	$
12.	$

and has filed in said Court proper receipts from all parties above named for their respective legacies and/or distributive shares.

WHEREFORE, your petitioner requests the Order of this court fixing a time and place for hearing on this petition, and that after the time for any notice has expired, upon proof of notice, and hearing, the Court enter a judicial order formally discharging the personal representative and releasing and discharging the sureties upon the personal representative's bond and granting such other and further relief as may be proper.

FURTHER, under penalties for perjury for deliberate falsification therein, I declare or affirm that I have read the foregoing petition and to the best of my knowledge or information, its representations are true, correct and complete.

Dated: ___September 29, 1978___

                    ___/s/ John C. Doe___
                    Petitioner

___/s/ John Cranwall___
Attorney for Petitioner
   First Trust Building
   St. Paul, MN 55101
Address/Phone
   (612) 111-0011

Form 79 Order for Discharge of Personal Representative

Form 44:.

524.3-1001 #10
524.3-1002 #9   UPC --

STATE OF MINNESOTA

COUNTY OF RAMSEY

PROBATE COURT
COUNTY COURT-PROBATE DIVISION

In Re: Estate of

Court File No. 999999

ORDER DISCHARGING
PERSONAL REPRESENTATIVE

Jane M. Doe
Deceased

The petition of ____John C. Doe____, dated ____Sept. 29, 19 78__, for an order discharging personal representative in the estate of the above named decedent having duly come on for hearing before the above named court, the undersigned Judge having heard and considered such petition, being fully advised in the premises, makes the following findings and determinations:

1. That the petition for an order discharging personal representative is complete.

2. That the time for any notice has expired and any notice as required by the laws of this state has been given and proved.

3. That the petitioner has declared or affirmed that the representations contained in the petition are true, correct and complete to the best of his knowledge or information.

4. That the petitioner appears from the petition to be an interested person as defined by the laws of this state.

5. That the personal representative herein, having paid or transferred all of the property of the estate of decedent to the persons entitled thereto, paid all taxes required to be paid by said representative and filed proof thereof, complied with all the orders and decree of the Court and with the provisions of law, and fully discharged the personal representative's trust,

Now, therefore, it is ORDERED, ADJUDGED, and DECREED by the court as follows:

1. That the petition is hereby granted.

2. That the personal representative and the sureties on said representative's bond, if any, are hereby finally discharged.

Dated: October 13, 1978

(COURT SEAL)

/S/ I. M. Honest
Judge

Form 80 Change of Testacy Status—Application for Informal Appointment of Successor

FORM 4336

Form 524.3-301 (5)   UPC — —

STATE OF MINNESOTA

COUNTY OF_____

In Re: Estate of

_____
Deceased

**PROBATE COURT
COUNTY COURT-PROBATE DIVISION**

Court File No. _____

**APPLICATION FOR INFORMAL
APPOINTMENT OF SUCCESSOR
PERSONAL REPRESENTATIVE
APPOINTED UNDER DIFFERENT
TESTACY STATUS**

TO THE HONORABLE REGISTRAR OF THE ABOVE NAMED COURT:

Applicant, _____, respectfully states:

1. Applicant resides at _____;

2. Applicant has an interest herein as _____,
and is, therefore, an interested person as defined by the laws of this state.

3. That on _____, 19___, _____ was
appointed the personal representative of the above named decedent under a different testacy
status by order of the above named court upon the application or petition filed in said matter
by _____, dated _____, 19___.

4. That the applicant or _____ has priority for appointment as personal representative of the estate of the decedent because: _____
_____
_____

   WHEREFORE, your applicant requests that applicant or _____ be informally
appointed as successor personal representative, with no or _____ bond, in an unsupervised administration; that letters testamentary be issued to applicant or _____;
and such other and further relief as may be proper.

   FURTHER, under penalties for perjury for deliberate falsification therein, I declare or affirm
that I have read the foregoing application and to the best of my knowledge or information, its
representations are true, correct and complete.

Dated: _____

_____
Applicant

_____
Attorney for Applicant

_____
Address/Phone

Form 81 Verification

FORM 4305

Form 524.1-310   UPC — —

STATE OF MINNESOTA	**PROBATE COURT**
COUNTY OF_____	**COUNTY COURT-PROBATE DIVISION**

In Re: Estate of   Court File No. _____

                                                              VERIFICATION

_____
                  Deceased

STATE OF MINNESOTA
                                                    ss.
COUNTY OF_____

I, _____, being duly sworn state that I am the_____
herein; that I have read the foregoing _____ and know the contents thereof; that the
same is true of my own knowledge, except as to those matters therein stated on information and
belief, and as to those matters I believe them to be true, and I know and am informed that the
penalties for perjury may follow from deliberate falsification therein.

Dated: _____

Subscribed and sworn to before me this_____
day of_____, 19___.

_____Notary Public,

_____ County, Minnesota   (SEAL)

My Commission expires_____, 19___

_____
Attorney

_____
Address/Phone

Form 82 Demand for Notice

FORM 4329

Form 524.3-204 #1   UPC — —

STATE OF MINNESOTA

COUNTY OF_____

In Re: Estate of

_____
                . Deceased

PROBATE COURT
COUNTY COURT-PROBATE DIVISION

Court File No. _____

DEMAND FOR NOTICE

TO THE CLERK OF THE ABOVE NAMED COURT:

Demandant, _____, respectfully states:

1. The Demandant resides at _____;

2. The Demandant has financial or property interest in the estate of the above named decedent, and is, therefore, an interested person as defined by the laws of this state by reason of the following facts: _____

WHEREFORE, the undersigned hereby demands notice of all orders and filings pertaining to decedent's estate. Notice may be served upon the undersigned at his above stated address, or upon his attorney, _____.

FURTHER, under penalties for perjury for deliberate falsification therein, I declare or affirm that I have read the foregoing demand and to the best of my knowledge or information, its representations are true, correct and complete.

Dated: _____

_____
Demandant

_____
Attorney for Demandant

_____
Address/Phone

Form 83 Notice of Informal Appointment

<table>
<tr><td>OS150 (Rev. 7/76)</td><td>Form 524.3-310 #3
524.3-403 #8
524.3-801 #4</td><td>UPC--</td></tr>
</table>

STATE OF MINNESOTA

COUNTY OF _____

In Re: Estate of

_____
Deceased

PROBATE COURT
COUNTY COURT—PROBATE DIVISION

Court File No. _____

**NOTICE OF INFORMAL APPOINTMENT OF
PERSONAL REPRESENTATIVE, NOTICE
OF HEARING FOR FORMAL PROBATE
OF WILL AND NOTICE TO CREDITORS**

TO ALL INTERESTED PERSONS AND CREDITORS:

Notice is hereby given that informal appointment of _____
_____ ,
whose address is _____
_____ ,
as personal representative of the estate of the above named decedent, has been made. Any heir, devisee or other interested person may be entitled to appointment as personal representative or may object to the appointment of the personal representative and the personal representative is empowered to fully administer the estate including, after 30 days from the date of issuance of his letters, the power to sell, encumber, lease or distribute real estate, unless objections thereto are filed with the Court (pursuant to Section 524.3-607) and the Court otherwise orders.

Notice is hereby given that on the _____ day of _____ , 19 ____ , at _____ o'clock ____.M., a hearing will be held in this Court at _____ , Minnesota, for the formal probate of an instrument purporting to be the will of the above named decedent, dated _____ , 19 ____ , _____
_____ ,
and that any objections thereto must be filed with the Court.

Notice is further given that ALL CREDITORS having claims against said estate are required to present the same to said personal representative or to the Clerk of the Court within four months after the date of this notice or said claims will be barred.

Dated: _____

_____
Registrar

_____
Clerk

_____
Attorney

_____
Address

NOTE: If notice to creditors has been previously given, delete the Notice to Creditors herein.

Form 84 Allowance or Disallowance of Claim

Form 4446

524.3-806(b) #6   UPC --

STATE OF MINNESOTA
                                        PROBATE COURT
COUNTY OF _____   **COUNTY COURT-PROBATE DIVISION**

In Re: Estate of   Court File No. _____

                                         ORDER FOR DISALLOWANCE
                                         OF CLAIM

_____
          Deceased

     The petition of _____dated _____, 19 ___,
for an order for disallowance of claim in the estate of the above named decedent having duly come on
for hearing before the above named court, the undersigned Judge having heard and considered such
petition, being fully advised in the premises, makes the following findings and determinations:

1. That the petition for an order for disallowance of claim is complete.

2. That the time for any notice has expired and any notice as required by the laws of this state has
   been given and proved.

3. That the petitioner has declared or affirmed that the representations contained in the petition are
   true, correct and complete to the best of his knowledge or information.

4. That the petitioner appears from the petition to be an interested person as defined by the laws of
   this state.

5. That _____, Claimant, presented a claim on _____
   _____in the amount of $ _____.

6. That the claim should be disallowed for the reason that _____
   _____

7. That no notice of disallowance was mailed to claimant within two months of the presentment of
   said claim.

8. That payment of said claim has not been made.

     Now, therefore, it is ORDERED, ADJUDGED, and DECREED by the court as follows:

1. That the petition is hereby granted.

2. That the claim of _____, presented on _____, 19 ___,
   in the amount of $ _____, is hereby formally disallowed.

Dated: _____

                                         _____
                                                    Judge
     (COURT SEAL)

Form 85 Affidavit for Collection of Personal Property

FORM 4476   524.3 - 1201

STATE OF MINNESOTA   )   **AFFIDAVIT FOR COLLECTION**
) ss.   **OF PERSONAL PROPERTY**
COUNTY OF _____)

Affiant, _____, being first duly sworn,
deposes and states:

1. Affiant resides at _____ ;

2. _____ died at the age of _____ on _____ ,
   19 _____ , and at the time of death, resided at _____,
   City of _____, County of _____ State of _____ ,
   having Social Security Number _____ ;

3. Affiant as _____is the successor of the above identified
   decedent;

4. The value of the entire estate, wherever located, less liens and encumbrances, does not exceed
   $5,000.00;

5. Thirty (30) days have elapsed since the death of the decedent;

6. No application or petition for the appointment of a personal representative is pending or has been
   granted in any jurisdiction;

7. Affiant, the claiming successor, is entitled to payment or delivery of the following described
   property, to-wit: _____
   _____
   _____

   FURTHER AFFIANT SAYETH NOT.

Dated: _____

                                                    _____

Subscribed and sworn to before me this
_____ day of _____, 19 _____

_____
Notary Public, _____ County, Minn.
My Commission Expires _____   (SEAL)

Form 86 Statement Closing Small Estate by Sworn Statement of Personal Representative

Form 4477

524.3-1204   UPC --

STATE OF MINNESOTA

COUNTY OF _____

PROBATE COURT
COUNTY COURT-PROBATE DIVISION

In Re: Estate of

Court File No. _____

**STATEMENT CLOSING SMALL
ESTATE BY SWORN STATEMENT OF
PERSONAL REPRESENTATIVE**

_____
Deceased

TO THE HONORABLE JUDGE OF THE ABOVE NAMED COURT:

The undersigned, _____, respectfully states:

1. The undersigned resides at _____;

2. The undersigned is the personal representative in the above named estate.

3. That disbursement and distribution of the entire estate of the above named estate has been made.

4. That to the best of the knowledge of the undersigned personal representative, the entire estate, less leins and encumbrances, did not exceed an exempt homestead as provided for in Section 525.145, the allowances provided for in Section 525.15, costs and expenses of administration, reasonable funeral expenses, and reasonable, necessary medical and hospital expenses of the last illness of the decedent.

5. That the undersigned personal representative has fully administered the estate by disbursing and distributing it to the persons entitled thereto.

6. That the undersigned personal representative has sent a copy of the closing statement to all distributees of the estate and to all creditors or other claimants of whom he is aware whose claims are neither paid nor barred and has furnished a full account in writing of his administration to the distributees whose interests are affected.

FURTHER, under penalties for perjury for deliberate falsification therein, I declare or affirm that I have read the foregoing statement and to the best of my knowledge or information, its representations are true, correct and complete.

Dated: _____

_____
Personal Representative

_____
Attorney for Personal Representative

_____
Address/Phone

Form 87 Application for Informal Probate and Informal Appointment of Representative

FORM 4334

Form 524.3-301 #3   UPC 21

STATE OF MINNESOTA   **PROBATE COURT**
                                          COUNTY COURT-PROBATE DIVISION
COUNTY OF Hennepin

In Re: Estate of   Court File No. __198540__

Cheryl Ann Kennedy   **APPLICATION FOR INFORMAL**
_____   **PROBATE OF WILL AND FOR**
            Deceased   **INFORMAL APPOINTMENT**
                                          OF EXECUTOR

TO THE HONORABLE REGISTRAR OF THE ABOVE NAMED COURT:

   Applicant, __Charles Kennedy__ , respectfully states:

1. Applicant resides at __1010 Willow Street, Minneapolis MN   55409__ ;

2. Applicant has an interest herein as __named executor and husband__ ,
   and is, therefore, an interested person as defined by the laws of this state.

3. Decedent was born __January 13__ , 19__44__ , at __Minneapolis, MN__ ;

4. Decedent died on __August 1__ , 19__77__ at __Minneapolis, MN__ ;

5. Decedent at the time of his death resided at __1010 Willow Street__
   City of __Minneapolis__ , County of __Hennepin__ , State of __Minnesota__ ;

6. That the names and addresses of decedent's spouse, children, heirs and devisees and other
   persons interested in this proceeding and the ages of any who are minors so far known or
   ascertainable with reasonable diligence by the applicant are:

Note: Classify the heirs and others entitled to take per stirpes and give the name, date of death,
relationship/interest and address, if known, of their predeceased ancestors. Give the birth date of any
heir or devisee taking a life interest.

Name	Age	Relationship/Interest	Address
Charles Kennedy	34	husband/devisee/ named executor	1010 Willow Street Minneapolis, MN
Cherry Kennedy	3	daughter/devisee/heir	same
Cindy Kennedy	3	daughter/devisee/heir	same
Carl Kennedy	5	son/devisee/heir	same
Corey Kennedy	9	son/devisee/heir	same
Christopher Kennedy	10	son/devisee/heir	same
Catherine Kelly	60	mother/heir	same
Karen Kelly	38	sister/devisee/heir	same

That decedent left no surviving children other than herein named and

no issue of deceased children

7. That venue for this proceeding is in the above named County of the State of Minnesota, because
   the decedent was domiciled in such county at the time of his death, and was the owner of property
   located in the State of Minnesota, or because, though not domiciled in the State of Minnesota,
   the decedent was the owner of property located in the above named county at the time of his death.

Form 87 continued

8. That no personal representative of the decedent has been appointed in this state or elsewhere whose appointment has not been terminated.

9. That applicant has not received a demand for notice and is not aware of any demand for notice of any probate or appointment proceeding concerning the decedent that may have been filed in this state or elsewhere ~~or prior proceeding concerning the decedent~~.

10. That the original of decedent's last will duly executed on ___November 21___, 19 __75__, ~~and codicils or codicils thereto executed on xxxxxxxxxxxxxxxx19xxxxxx xif previously probated elsewhere, an authenticated copy thereof and statement probating the same is in the possession of the court or accompanies this application~~

                                                                                                                                                                                  *

11. That the applicant, to the best of his knowledge, believes the will ~~and codicils or codicils thereto, if any,~~ has ~~or have~~ been validly executed.

12. That after the exercise of reasonable diligence, the applicant is unaware of any instrument revoking the will ~~and codicils or codicils thereto~~, and the applicant believes that the instrument which is the subject of this application is the decedent's last will.

13. That the time limit for informal probate and appointment as provided by the laws of this state has not expired because three years or less have passed since the decedent's death.

14. That the applicant ~~or~~ _____ is entitled to priority and appointment as executor because applicant ~~xx~~ _____ is nominated in the last will of the decedent as executor, with (no) ~~(minimum xx~~ (mention of _____) bond, in an ~~unsupervised~~ ~~xxxx~~) (undesignated) administration; ~~xx because~~ _____

    and is not disqualified to serve as a personal representative of the decedent.

15. That at least 120 hours have elapsed since decedent's death.

    WHEREFORE, your applicant requests that said will, ~~including any valid and unrevoked codicil or codicils thereto~~ be informally probated; that applicant ~~or~~ _____ be informally appointed as executor, with no ~~xx~~ _____ bond, in an unsupervised administration, that upon qualification and acceptance, letters testamentary be issued to applicant ~~xx~~ _____; and granting such other and further relief as may be proper.

    FURTHER, under penalties for perjury for deliberate falsification therein, I declare or affirm that I have read the foregoing application and to the best of my knowledge or information, its representations are true, correct and complete.

Dated: __August 30, 1977__

                                    __/S/ Charles Kennedy__
                                    Applicant

__Susan G. Browning__
Attorney for Applicant

__1400 Main Street, Mpls., MN 55455__
Address/Phone
     338-2905

                         * ASSETS

Personal property		Homestead	$ 65,000.00
Stock	$ 2,000.00		
Automobile	3,500.00	Other Real Estate	$ -0-
Clothing & Misc.	13,500.00		
Total	$19,000.00	Personal Property	$ 19,000.00
		Total Assets	$ 84,000.00

Form 88 Statement of Informal Probate of Will and Order of Informal Appointment

FORM 4339

Form 524.3-302 #2   UPC 22

STATE OF MINNESOTA	**PROBATE COURT**
	COUNTY COURT-PROBATE DIVISION
COUNTY OF__Hennepin__	
In Re: Estate of	Court File No. __198540__
	STATEMENT OF INFORMAL PROBATE
__Cheryl Ann Kennedy__	**OF WILL AND ORDER OF INFORMAL**
Deceased	**APPOINTMENT OF EXECUTOR**

The application of _Charles Kennedy_____dated
____August 30_____, 19 77 , for the informal probate of the last will and for informal appointment of executor of the above named decedent having come before the undersigned Registrar of the above named court, the undersigned Registrar having considered such application makes the following determinations:

1. That the application for informal probate of will and for informal appointment of a personal representative is complete.

2. That the applicant has declared or affirmed that the representations contained in the application are true, correct and complete to the best of his knowledge or information.

3. That the applicant appears from the application to be an interested person as defined by the laws of this state.

4. That, on the basis of the statement in the application, jurisdiction of this estate, proceeding and subject matter is proper.

5. That, on the basis of the statements in the application, venue is proper because the decedent's domicile at the time of his death was in the above named County of the State of Minnesota and was the owner of property located in the State of Minnesota; ~~or because, though not domiciled in the State of Minnesota, the decedent was owner of property located in the above named county at the time of his death.~~

6. That the original, duly executed and apparently unrevoked last will of the decedent ~~or, if previously probated elsewhere, an authenticated copy thereof and statement probating the same, is~~ in the Registrar's possession, and therefore, that any will to which the requested appointment relates ~~has been~~ or will be informally probated upon the entry of this order.

7. That any notice as required by the laws of this state has been given.

8. That the application does not indicate the existence of a possible unrevoked testementary instrument which may relate to property subject to the laws of this state, and which is not filed for probate in this court.

9. That it appears from the application that the time limit for original probate and appointment proceedings has not expired.

10. That from the statements in the application, the person whose appointment is sought has priority entitling appointment because he is nominated in the last will of the decedent as executor, with no ~~oox~~_____ bond, in an (~~unsupervised~~) (undesignated) administration, ~~or because~~ _____

and is not disqualified to serve as a personal representative of the decedent.

11. That the application does not indicate that a personal representative has been appointed in this or another county of this state whose appointment has not been terminated.

Form 88 continued

12. That at least 120 hours have elapsed since the decedent's death.

Now, therefore, it is ORDERED by the Registrar as follows:

1. That the last will last executed ___November 21___, 19__75__, of the decedent, including any codicil or codicils thereto is hereby informally probated.

2. That ___Charles Kennedy___ is hereby informally appointed as the executor of the estate of ___Cheryl Ann Kennedy___, deceased, with ___no___ bond, in an unsupervised administration.

3. That upon qualification and acceptance letters testamentary be issued to _____
Charles Kennedy

Dated: _September 7, 1977_

                                    /s/ Lorina B. Arneson
                                    Registrar

Form 89 Notice of Informal Probate of Will and Appointment of Personal Representative and Notice to Creditors

OS143 (Rev. 7/76)

Form 524.3-310 #2
524.3-801 #2

UPC—

STATE OF MINNESOTA

COUNTY OF __Hennepin__

In Re: Estate of

__Cheryl Ann Kennedy__

Deceased

PROBATE COURT
COUNTY COURT—PROBATE DIVISION
Court File No. 198540

NOTICE OF INFORMAL PROBATE OF WILL
AND APPOINTMENT OF PERSONAL
REPRESENTATIVE AND NOTICE TO CREDITORS

TO ALL INTERESTED PERSONS AND CREDITORS:

Notice is hereby given, that an application for informal probate of the above named decedent's last will, dated __November Twenty-first__, 19 75 ,

has been filed with the Registrar herein, and the application has been granted in formally probating such will. Any objections may be filed in the above named Court, and the same will be heard by the Court upon notice of hearing fixed for such purpose.

Notice is hereby further given that informal appointment of __Charles Kennedy__

whose address is __1010 Willow Street, Minneapolis MN   55409__ ,

as personal representative of the estate of the above named decedent, has been made. Any heir, devisee or other interested person may be entitled to appointment as personal representative or may object to the appointment of the personal representative and the personal representative is empowered to fully administer the estate including, after 30 days from the date of issuance of his letters, the power to sell, encumber, lease or distribute real estate, unless objections thereto are filed with the Court (pursuant to Section 524.3-607) and the Court otherwise orders.

Notice is further given that ALL CREDITORS having claims against said estate are required to present the same to said personal representative or to the Clerk of the Court within four months after the date of this notice or said claims will be barred.

Dated: __September 7, 1977__

__/S/ Lorina B. Arneson__
Registrar

__/S/ Bradford R. Mitlar__
Clerk

__Susan G. Browning__
Attorney

__1400 Main St. Minneapolis, MN   55455__
Address

NOTE: If notice to creditors has been previously given, delete the Notice to Creditors herein.

Form 90 Proof of Placing Order for Publication

STATE OF MINNESOTA

COUNTY OF HENNEPIN

PROBATE COURT - UNSUPERVISED

COURT FILE NO. __198540__

In Re: Estate of

__Cheryl Ann Kennedy__
Deceased

PROOF OF PLACING ORDER
FOR PUBLICATION

TO THE CLERK OF PROBATE COURT:

This is to verify that ___Susan G. Browning___

_____ Attorney for ___, applicant(ꭤ)

has (ꜰꜰꜰꜰꜰ) made arrangements for the publication of:

☐ NOTICE OF INFORMAL APPOINTMENT OF PERSONAL
REPRESENTATIVE(S) AND NOTICE TO CREDITORS

[X] NOTICE OF INFORMAL PROBATE OF WILL AND APPOINTMENT OF
PERSONAL REPRESENTATIVES(S) AND NOTICE TO CREDITORS

☐

once a week for two consecutive weeks in the ___Legal Newsweekly___

and this is to confirm that the same will be published accordingly commencing

in the next available issue, and that arrangements for payment of the cost of

said publication have been made.

Dated: September 8, 1977

/S/ D.C. Morrison
Publisher

Form 91 Affidavit of Mailing Order of Informal Appointment or Notice of Hearing

OS107 (Rev. 7/76)

Form 524.1—401 #2
525.83

UPC--

STATE OF MINNESOTA

COUNTY OF HENNEPIN

PROBATE COURT
COUNTY COURT—PROBATE DIVISION

Court File No. 198540

In Re: (ESTATE
          (~~CONSERVATORSHIP~~
          (~~GUARDIANSHIP~~

OF _____

Cheryl Ann Kennedy
Deceased ~~CONSERVATEE WARD~~

AFFIDAVIT OF MAILING ~~ORDER OR~~ NOTICE
OF ~~HEARING~~ informal probate of
will and informal appointment of personal representative and notice to
creditors

ATTACH COPY OF NOTICE OR ORDER HERE

STATE OF MINNESOTA
COUNTY OF HENNEPIN   } ss

Susan G. Browning
being first duly sworn on oath deposes and says that on
the ___21___ day of __September__ ,
19_77_ , at __Minneapolis__ in said
County and State ___he mailed a copy of the Order or
Notice hereto attached to each _devisee and heir
of said decedent, Cheryl Ann Kennedy

whose name and address are known to affiant, after exercising due diligence in ascertaining the correctness of
said name and address, by placing a true and correct copy
thereof in a sealed envelope, postage prepaid and depositing the same in the U. S. Mails at _____
Minneapolis, Minnesota
and addressed to the following named persons:
NOTE: (Instructions at bottom of page)

NAME	Street or Post Office	CITY	STATE
Cherry Kennedy	1010 Willow St.	Minneapolis	MN 55409
Cindy Kennedy	same		
Carl Kennedy	same		
Corey Kennedy	same		
Christopher Kennedy	same		
Karen Kelly	same		
Catherine Kelly	same		
Charles Kennedy	same		

Subscribed and sworn to before me this ___21___ day of
__September__ , 19_77_

/S/ Susan G. Browning

Astrid M. Martenssen/S/T/
Notary Public, Hennepin County, Minn.
My Commission expires March 3 , 19 80 .

SEAL

NOTED INSTRUCTION: In Estates To each heir, devisee, personal representative, the foreign consul pursuant to M.S. 524.3—306 and 524.3—403, and the Minnesota Attorney General, if
a devisee is the trustee of a charitable trust or if the decedent left no devisees or heirs.
In Conservatorships and Guardianships To each of persons as directed by the Court.

(Over)

Form 91 continued

AFFIDAVIT OF MAILING
ALLOWANCES TO SPOUSE AND/OR CHILDREN

When a decedent dies with or without a will the allowances to the spouse or children are as follows:

525.15 ALLOWANCES TO SPOUSE. When any person dies testate, or intestate,
(1) The surviving spouse shall be allowed from the personal property of which the decedent was possessed or to which he was entitled at the time of his death, the wearing apparel, and, as selected by him, furniture and household goods not exceeding $2,000 in value, and other personal property not exceeding $1,000 in value;

(2) When, except for one automobile, all of the personal estate of the decedent is allowed to the surviving spouse by clause (1), the surviving spouse shall also be allowed such automobile.

(3) If there be no surviving spouse, the minor children shall receive the property specified in clause (1) as selected in their behalf;

(4) During administration, but not exceeding 18 months, unless an extension shall have been granted by the court, or, if the estate be insolvent, not exceeding 12 months, the spouse or children, or both, constituting the family of the decedent shall be allowed reasonable maintenance.

(5) In the administration of an estate of a non-resident decedent, the allowances received in the domiciliary administration shall be deducted from the allowances under this section.

In all estates where there is a will the following rule applies to the spouse who has not consented to the will:

525.212 RENUNCIATION AND ELECTION. If a will make provision for a surviving spouse in lieu of the rights in the estate secured by statute, such spouse shall be deemed to have elected to take under the will, unless he shall have filed with the court and mailed or delivered to the personal representative, if any, within nine months after the date of death, or within six months after the probate of the decedent's will, whichever limitation last expires, an instrument in writing renouncing and refusing to accept the provisions in such will. For good cause shown, the court may permit an election within such further time as the court may determine. No devise to a surviving spouse shall be considered as adding to the rights in the estate secured by sections 525.145 and 525.16 to such spouse, unless it clearly appears from the contents of the will that such was the testator's intent.

STATE OF MINNESOTA
COUNTY OF__HENNEPIN____·____ ss.
__Charles Kennedy_____ being first duly sworn on oath deposes
and says that on the _21_ day of_September____, 19_77, at_Minneapolis_____ ___
in said County and State, he mailed a copy of Sections 525.15 and 525.212 of Minnesota Statutes as hereinbefore set out to decedent's spouse and children constituting the family of the decedent at their last known address after exercising due diligence and ascertaining the correctness of said addresses by placing a true and correct copy thereof in a sealed envelope, postage pre-paid and depositing the same in the U.S. mails at_ Minneapolis_____, Minnesota, and addressed to the following:

NAME	STREET or POST OFFICE	CITY	STATE
Charles Kennedy	1010 Willow Street	Minneapolis,	Minnesota

/S/ Susan G. Browning_____

Subscribed and sworn to be before me this
_21_ day of_September_____, 19_77_.

__Astrid M. Martensen /S/T/_____   (SEAL)
Notary Public_Hennepin____ County, Minn.
My Commission expires_March 3__, 19_80_.

Form 92 Acceptance of Appointment and Oath

OS201 (Rev. 7/76)   Form 524.3—601 # 1   UPC 43

STATE OF MINNESOTA   **PROBATE COURT**
                                                    COUNTY COURT—PROBATE DIVISION
COUNTY OF <u>HENNEPIN</u>

                                                    Court File No. <u>198540</u>
In Re: Estate of

<u>Cheryl Ann Kennedy</u>   **ACCEPTANCE OF APPOINTMENT**
                    Deceased   **AND OATH BY INDIVIDUAL**

TO THE ABOVE NAMED COURT:

STATE OF MINNESOTA
                                            } ss
COUNTY OF <u>HENNEPIN</u>

    I, <u>Charles Kennedy</u> ,
residing at <u>1010 Willow Street</u>
in the City of <u>Minneapolis</u>, County of <u>Hennepin</u>, State of <u>Minnesota</u>,
as a condition to receiving letters as <u>personal representative</u>
in the above entitled matter, hereby accept the duties of the office, agree to be bound by the provisions of the
statutes relating thereto and hereby submit to the jurisdiction of the Court in any proceeding relating to the said
matter that may be instuted by any person interested therein; and swear that I will faithfully and justly perform
all duties of the office and trust that I now assume as <u>personal representative</u>
in the above entitled matter to the best of my ability.

                          /S/ Charles Kennedy

Subscribed and sworn to before me this <u>7</u> day of
<u>September</u>, 19 <u>77</u>   **SEAL**

<u>Mariana S. Halsted /T/S/</u>
Notary Public, <u>Hennepin</u> County, Minn.
My Commission expires <u>April 2</u>, 19 <u>79</u>.

Form 93 Letters Testamentary

Form 4403 Rev. 6-76

524.3-601 #3   UPC 43

STATE OF MINNESOTA

COUNTY OF HENNEPIN

PROBATE COURT
COUNTY COURT-PROBATE DIVISION

In Re: Estate of

Court File No. 198540

LETTERS TESTAMENTARY

Cheryl Ann Kennedy
Deceased

The above named decedent having died on ___August 1___, 19 77 , and

Charles Kennedy, of Hennepin County, Minnesota

having been appointed and qualified, (is) (are) hereby authorized to act as personal representative(s) according to law.

Dated: September 7, 1977

/S/Lorina B. Arneson
Judge/Registrar

(COURT SEAL)

Form 94 Inventory and Appraisement

FORM 4428

| Form 524.3-706 | UPC 54 |

STATE OF MINNESOTA

COUNTY OF HENNEPIN

In Re: Estate of

Cheryl Ann Kennedy
                    Deceased

**PROBATE COURT
COUNTY COURT-PROBATE DIVISION**

Court File No. __198540__

INVENTORY AND APPRAISEMENT

Date of Death __August 1__ , 19 77
Social Security No. __217-48-4307__

TO THE HONORABLE JUDGE AND/OR REGISTRAR OF THE ABOVE NAMED COURT:

__Charles Kennedy__ , the undersigned personal representative, respectfully states:

1. That the following is a true and correct inventory and appraisement, at date of death values, of all the property of the above named estate, both real and personal, which has come into the possession of said representative and of which said representative has knowledge after diligent search and inquiry concerning the same, classified as follows, to-wit: (See instructions at end of last page.)

SCHEDULE A — Real Estate

Item number	Legal Description (Specify street address of city realty; acreage of rural land; and liens, if any)	Assessor's Estimated Market Value (Do not use "Green Acres" Value or Assessor's Limited Market Value)	GROSS APPRAISED VALUE
1	Homestead, being in the County of Hennepin , State of Minnesota: family residence located at 1010 Willow Street, Minneapolis, MN 55409 ~~Other Real Estate, being in the~~ ~~County of~~ _____ ~~State of Minnesota~~		$65,000.00

Form 94 continued

Real Estate SCHEDULE A — TOTAL $ 65,000.00

SCHEDULE B — Stocks and Bonds

Item number	Description (Specify face amount of bonds or number of shares and par value where needed for identification; and liens, if any)	GROSS APPRAISED VALUE
2	50 shares of Users, Inc. stock	$2,000.00

Personal Property SCHEDULE B — TOTAL $2,000.00

SCHEDULE C — Mortgages, Notes, and Cash

Item number	Description (Specify recording data; bank and account numbers; accrued interest; location of actual cash; and liens, if any)	GROSS APPRAISED

Personal Property SCHEDULE C — TOTAL $ --------

Form 94 continued

SCHEDULE D — Other Miscellaneous Property

Item number	Description (Specify location of property and liens, if any)	GROSS APPRAISED VALUE
	Furniture and Household goods:	
3		$ 5,000.00
	Wearing apparel and Ornaments:	
4	Diamond ring	4,000.00
5	Clothing	200.00
6	Wigs (2)	110.00
7	Mink Coat	4,000.00
	All other personal property (including partnership and business interests, insurance and annuities payable to estate, other receivables, farm crops, machinery, etc.):	
8	Automobile (1975 Ford Granada)	3,500.00
9	Miscellaneous	300.00

Personal Property SCHEDULE D — TOTAL $ 21,110.00

SUMMARY

Total Gross Value of Real Estate	$	65,000.00
Less Liens	$	0.00
Net Value of Real Estate	$	65,000.00
Total Gross Value of Personal Property	$	21,110.00
Less Liens	$	110.00
Net Value of Personal Property	$	21,000.00
TOTAL NET APPRAISEMENT	$	86,000.00

2. That a copy hereof has been mailed to the surviving spouse if there be one, and to all residuary distributees of the above named decedent and to interested persons or creditors who have requested the same.

Form 94 continued

FURTHER, under penalties for perjury for deliberate falsification therein, I declare or affirm that I have read the foregoing and to the best of my knowledge or information, its representations are true, correct and complete.

Dated: September 17, 1977

/S/ Charles Kennedy

Susan G. Browning

Attorney

1400 Main Street, Minneapolis, MN 55455

Address/Phone 773-3777

INSTRUCTIONS:

(1) The classification of assets herein is intended for them to be comparable to the Federal Estate Tax Return Form 706 with the exception of Schedule D herein which includes insurance and annuities payable to the estate and which are otherwise includable under separate Schedules of said Form 706.

(2) It is to be noted that the GROSS APPRAISED VALUE is requested of each asset without reduction by any lien requested to be specified as a part of its description. The reduction for liens is later taken under the Summary of Assets.

(3) It is also to be noted that each asset of a Schedule is to be given its "Item number" to facilitate a ready reference similar to the Estate Tax Form 706.

(4) Finally, it is to be noted that the Assessor's Estimated Market Value is requested. This information is always available to the Department of Revenue upon its request. The accurate furnishing of the information can result in better servicing of the inheritance tax returns.

(5) It is recommended that the appraisal report of any independent appraiser should be properly referenced and attached as an Exhibit including the name and address of any such appraisers.

Form 95 Written Statement of Claim

Form 4434

524.3-804 (1)   UPC 59

STATE OF MINNESOTA

COUNTY OF <u>HENNEPIN</u>

In Re: Estate of

<u>Cheryl Ann Kennedy</u>
       Deceased

PROBATE COURT
COUNTY COURT-PROBATE DIVISION

Court File No. <u>198540</u>

WRITTEN STATEMENT OF CLAIM

TO THE PERSONAL REPRESENTATIVE OF THE ABOVE NAMED ESTATE:

Claimant <u>Beauty Products, Inc.</u>, states:

1. Claimant's address <u>230 Dunkirk Lane, Minnetonka, MN 55606</u>;

2. Claimant claims that the estate is indebted ̶t̶o̶ ̶c̶l̶a̶i̶m̶a̶n̶t̶ ̶a̶s̶ ̶f̶o̶l̶l̶o̶w̶s̶ in the amount of $ <u>110.00</u>;

3. That the nature of the claim is merchandise (wigs) bought by decedent:

       Primavera (#7743) $ 64.00
       Carefree (#7739)   46.00
           TOTAL $110.00

4. That the claim arose prior to the death of the decedent on or about <u>July 27</u>,
19 <u>77</u>, ̶o̶r̶ ̶t̶h̶a̶t̶ ̶t̶h̶e̶ ̶c̶l̶a̶i̶m̶ ̶w̶i̶l̶l̶ ̶a̶r̶i̶s̶e̶ ̶a̶t̶ ̶a̶ ̶f̶u̶t̶u̶r̶e̶ ̶d̶a̶t̶e̶ ̶a̶s̶ ̶s̶e̶t̶ ̶o̶u̶t̶ ̶i̶n̶ ̶p̶a̶r̶a̶g̶r̶a̶p̶h̶,
̶X̶X̶;

5. That the claim is secured by <u>no security</u>;

6. That the claim was ̶o̶r̶ ̶w̶i̶l̶l̶ be due and payable on <u>August 27</u>, 19 <u>77</u>;

7. That if the claim is contingent or unliquidated, the nature of the uncertainty is as
follows: _____.

Dated: <u>September 18, 1977</u>

                   <u>/S/ Martin R. Kromstad</u>
                   Claimant /T/ Beauty Products, Inc.

<u>Rafael Y. Santelo</u>
Attorney for Claimant

<u>1341 Stevens Ave., Minneapolis, MN 55410</u>
Address/Phone   841-7662

Note: Claim may be presented to Personal
      Representative or filed with
      Clerk. _____
      Presentation of claim does **not**
      commence proceedings.
      See 3-806

Form 96 Informal Deed of Distribution

OS252 1/2 (Rev. 7/76)   Form 524.3-907 #1   UPC——

STATE OF MINNESOTA

COUNTY OF HENNEPIN

In Re: Estate of

Cheryl Ann Kennedy
                    Deceased

PROBATE COURT
COUNTY COURT—PROBATE DIVISION

Court File No. 198540

INFORMAL DEED OF DISTRIBUTION
(Individual Personal Representative)

This instrument dated this 8 day of January, 19 78, by and between Charles Kennedy, personal representative of the estate of Cheryl Ann Kennedy, decedent, first party, and Karen Kelly, of the County of Hennepin and State of Minnesota, second party;

WHEREAS, Cheryl Ann Kennedy, died on the 1 day of August, 19 77, and;

WHEREAS, thereafter, on the 7 day of September, 19 77, first party was duly appointed and qualified as personal representative of the above entitled estate, in an informal probate administration, and;

WHEREAS, the second party as a X/X/X/X (devisee) of the estate of Cheryl Ann Kennedy, deceased, is entitled to the property hereby distributed;

NOW, THEREFORE, in accordance with the laws of the State of Minnesota, first party hereby assigns, transfers, conveys, and releases to Karen Kelly all right, title and interest in the following described personal property located in the County of Hennepin and State of Minnesota, legally described as follows:

One blue-white marquise cut diamond ring, silver setting, valued at $4000.00

Dated: January 8, 1978

/S/ Charles Kennedy
Personal Representative

I, Charles Kennedy, spouse of the above named decedent, do hereby consent to the within conveyance.

/S/ Charles Kennedy

Form 96 continued

STATE OF MINNESOTA

COUNTY OF <u>HENNEPIN</u>   } ss.

The foregoing instrument was acknowledged before me this _____8_____ day of
<u>January</u> , 19 <u>78</u> , by <u>Charles Kennedy</u>
as _____ personal representative of the estate of <u>Cheryl Ann Kennedy</u>
_____ , deceased.

SEAL

<u>Georgeann Holtzer /T/S/</u>
Notary Public <u>Hennepin</u> County,____
My commission expires <u>November 3</u> , 19 <u>80</u>

THIS INSTRUMENT WAS DRAFTED BY

<u>Susan G. Browning /S/</u>
                              (Name)

<u>1400 Main Street</u>

<u>Minneapolis, MN 55455</u>
                              (Address)

Tax statements for the real property described in this instrument should be sent to:

_____   _____
            (Name)   (Address)

STATE DEED TAX
TRANSFER STAMPS DUE

_____

Doc. No. ____

INFORMAL DEED OF DISTRIBUTION
(Individual Personal Representative)

To

OFFICE OF COUNTY RECORDER
STATE OF MINNESOTA,

County of ____
I hereby certify that the within Deed
was filed in this office for record on
____ , 19 ____ ,
at ____ o'clock ____ M., and was
duly recorded in Book ____ of
Deeds, page ____ .
    OR
was duly recorded as instrument
No. ____

_____ County Recorder

By _____ Deputy.

No delinquent taxes and transfer entered.

Dated _____ , 19 ____ .

_____ County Auditor

By _____ Deputy.

Form 97 Receipt for Assets by Distributee

Form 524.3-1001 (4)
524.3-1003 (2)

OS272 1/2 (New 7/76)   UPC——

STATE OF MINNESOTA

COUNTY OF _HENNEPIN_

PROBATE COURT
COUNTY COURT—PROBATE DIVISION

Court File No. _198540_

In Re: Estate of

Cheryl Ann Kennedy
                    Deceased

RECEIPT FOR ASSETS BY DISTRIBUTEE

I, _Karen Kelly_ , the undersigned distributee, hereby acknowledge receipt from the personal representative(s) of the above entitled estate, of the following assets, to-wit:

1 marquise-cut blue diamond ring, silver setting, appraised value $4,000.00

in full satisfaction of the complete and final settlement of my distributive share of the above entitled estate.

Dated: _March 8, 1978_

/S/ Karen Kelly
Distributee

INSTRUCTIONS:

1. To be executed after Order or Decree of Distribution under 524.3-1001 (4) and furnished with petition for discharge Form 524.3-1001 #9.

2. To be executed under 524.3-1003 (2) prior to personal representative's closing statement Form 524.3-1003# 1.

Form 98 Informal Administration: Personal Representative's Statement to Close Estate

Form 4475

524.3-1003 #1   UPC --

STATE OF MINNESOTA

COUNTY OF <u>HENNEPIN</u>

PROBATE COURT
COUNTY COURT-PROBATE DIVISION

In Re: Estate of

Court File No. <u>198540</u>

INFORMAL ADMINISTRATION:
PERSONAL REPRESENTATIVE'S
STATEMENT TO CLOSE ESTATE

<u>Cheryl Ann Kennedy</u>
Deceased

TO THE HONORABLE REGISTRAR OF THE ABOVE NAMED COURT:

    <u>Charles Kennedy</u>   , the undersigned personal representative herein respectfully states that he or a prior personal representative whom he has succeeded has:

1. Published notice to creditors and that the date of the notice was more than six months prior to the date of this statement;

2. Fully administered the estate of the decedent by making payment, settlement or other disposition of all claims which were presented, expenses of administration and estate, inheritance and other taxes, except as specified in this statement, and that the assets of the estate have been inventoried and distributed to the persons entitled thereto. Listed below are unpaid claims, expenses or taxes which remain undischarged together with the detailed arrangements which have been made to accommodate all outstanding liabilities: (If none, so state)

3. Sent a copy of this statement to all distributees of the estate and to all creditors or other claimants of whom he is aware whose claims are neither paid or barred and has furnished a full account in writing of this administration to the distributees whose interests are affected thereby.

This statement is filed for the purpose of closing this estate and terminating the appointment of the undersigned.

DATED: <u>March 12, 1978</u>

<u>/S/ Charles Kennedy</u>
Personal Representative

STATE OF MINNESOTA   )
) ss.
COUNTY OF <u>HENNEPIN</u>   )

I, <u>Charles Kennedy</u>, being duly sworn state that I am the personal representative herein; that I have read the foregoing statement and know the contents thereof; that the same is true of my own knowledge, except as to those matters therein stated on information and belief, and as to those matters I believe it to be true.

<u>/S/ Charles Kennedy</u>
Personal Representative

Subscribed and sworn to before me this <u>12</u> day of <u>March</u>, 19<u>78</u>.

<u>Georgeann Holtzer /T/S/</u>
Notary Public, <u>Hennepin</u>County, Minnesota
My Commission expires <u>November 3</u>1980 .

(SEAL)

<u>Susan G. Browning</u>
Attorney for Personal Representative

<u>1400 Main St., Minneapolis, MN 55455</u>
Address/Phone   773-3777

Form 99 Application for Informal Appointment of Administrator

Form 4335 Rev. 6-76

524.3-301 #4	UPC 23

STATE OF MINNESOTA

COUNTY OF HENNEPIN

PROBATE COURT
COUNTY COURT-PROBATE DIVISION

In Re: Estate of

Court File No. __198541__

APPLICATION FOR
INFORMAL APPOINTMENT
OF ADMINISTRATOR

Cheryl Ann Kennedy
                  Deceased

TO THE HONORABLE REGISTRAR OF THE ABOVE NAMED COURT:

Applicant, __Charles Kennedy__ , respectfully states:

1. Applicant resides at __1010 Willow Street, Minneapolis, MN__ ;

2. Applicant has an interest herein as __spouse and heir__ ;
   and is, therefore, an interested person as defined by the laws of this State;

3. Decedent was born __January 13__ , 19 __44__ , at __Minneapolis, MN__ ;

4. Decedent died on __August 1__ , 19 __77__ , at __Minneapolis, MN__ ;

5. Decedent at the time of his death resided at __1010 Willow Street__ ;
   City of __Minneapolis__ , County of __Hennepin__ , State of __MN__ ;

6. That the names and addresses of decedent's spouse, children, heirs and devisees and other persons
   interested in this proceeding and the ages of any who are minors so far as known or ascertainable
   with reasonable diligence by the applicant are:
   NOTE: Classify the heirs and others entitled to take per stirpes and give the name, date of death,
        relationship/interest and address, if known, of their predeceased ancestor. Give the
        birthdate of any heir or devisee taking a life interest.

Name	Age	Relationship/Interest	Address
Charles Kennedy	34	born Feb. 3, 1943 spouse/heir	1010 Willow Street Minneapolis, MN
Cherry Kennedy	3	daughter/heir	same
Cindy Kennedy	3	daughter/heir	same
Carl Kennedy	5	son/heir	same
Corey Kennedy	9	son/heir	same
Christopher Kennedy	10	son/heir	same
Catherine Kelly	60	mother/heir	same
Karen Kelly	38	sister/heir	same

Decedent left no surviving children, other than herein named, and no

issue of deceased children.

---

7. That venue for this proceeding is in the above named County of the State of Minnesota, because the
   decedent was domiciled in such County at the time of his death, and was the owner of property
   located in the State of Minnesota. ~~because the property located in the State of Minnesota the~~
   ~~decedent was the owner of property located in the above named County at the time of his death. See~~
   ~~book.~~

Form 99 continued

8. That no personal representative of the decedent has been appointed in this State or elsewhere whose appointment has not been terminated.

9. That applicant has not received a demand for notice and is not aware of any demand for notice of any probate or appointment proceeding concerning the decedent that may have been filed in this State or elsewhere.

10. That the time limit for informal appointment proceeding as provided by the laws of this State has not expired because three years or less have passed since the decedent's death.

11. That after the exercise of reasonable diligence, applicant is unaware of any unrevoked testamentary instrument relating to property having a situs in this State under the laws of this State.

12. That applicant XXXXXXXXXXXXXXXXXXXXXXXXXXXXXX is entitled to priority and appointment as the administrator because applicant XXXXXXXXXXXXXXXXXXXXXXXXXXXXXXXXX (i) is the spouse _____ of the decedent, ((ii) is not disqualified to serve as a personal representative of the decedent, and (iii) there are no persons having a prior or equal right to the appointment under the laws of this State. XXXXXX XXXXXXXXXXXXXXXXXXXXXXXXXXXXXXXXXXXXXXXXXXXXXXXXXXXXXXXXXXXXXXXXXXXXXXX

13. That at least 120 hours have elapsed since decedent's death.

   WHEREFORE, your applicant request that applicant or XXXXXXXXXXXXXXXXXXXXXXXXXX be informally appointed as the administrator of said estate, with XXXX _$10,000.00_ bond, in an unsupervised administration; that, upon qualification and acceptance, letters of administration be issued to applicant XXXXXXXXXXXXXXXXXXX and granting such other and further relief as may be proper.

   FURTHER, under penalties for perjury for deliberate falsification therein, I declare or affirm that I have read the foregoing application and to the best of my knowledge or information, its representations are true, correct and complete.

Dated: ___August 30, 1977_____

                                             ___/S/ Charles Kennedy_____
                                             Applicant

   _Susan G. Browning_____
   Attorney for Applicant

   1400 Main Street, Minneapolis, MN
   Address/Phone   773-3777

                                   * ASSETS

                          Homestead $ _65,000.00_

                          Other Real Estate $ _____ (N.B. non-probate)

                          Personal Property $ _19,000.00_

Form 100 Order and Notice of Informal Appointment of Personal Representative and Notice to Creditors

OS143 (Rev. 7/76)

Form 524.3-310 #2
524.3-801 #2

UPC—

STATE OF MINNESOTA

COUNTY OF HENNEPIN

In Re: Estate of

Cheryl Ann Kennedy
                    Deceased

PROBATE COURT
COUNTY COURT—PROBATE DIVISION
Court File No. 198541

ORDER AND
NOTICE OF INFORMAL ~~PROBATE OF WILL~~
~~AND~~ APPOINTMENT OF PERSONAL
REPRESENTATIVE AND NOTICE TO CREDITORS

TO ALL INTERESTED PERSONS AND CREDITORS:

It is ordered and
Notice is hereby given, that an application for informal probate ~~of the estate named herein heretofore filed~~, ~~dated~~ ~~XXX~~, _____,

has been filed with the Registrar herein, and the application has been granted in formally probating such will. Any objections may be filed in the above named Court, and the same will be heard by the Court upon notice of hearing fixed for such purpose.

Notice is hereby further given that informal appointment of Charles Kennedy

whose address is 1010 Willow Street, Minneapolis, MN 55409

as personal representative of the estate of the above named decedent, has been made. Any heir, ~~devisee~~ or other interested person may be entitled to appointment as personal representative or may object to the appointment of the personal representative and the personal representative is empowered to fully administer the estate including, after 30 days from the date of issuance of his letters, the power to sell, encumber, lease or distribute real estate, unless objections thereto are filed with the Court (pursuant to Section 524.3-607) and the Court otherwise orders.

Notice is further given that ALL CREDITORS having claims against said estate are required to present the same to said personal representative or to the Clerk of the Court within four months after the date of this notice or said claims will be barred.

Dated: September 7, 1977

/S/ Lorina B. Arneson
Registrar

/S/ Bradford R. Mitlar
Clerk

Susan G. Browning
Attorney

1400 Main St., Minneapolis, MN 55455
Address

NOTE: If notice to creditors has been previously given, delete the Notice to Creditors herein.

Form 101 Bond

FORM 4411

Form 524.3-606 #2
Form 525.551 #5
Form 525.591 #9

UPC 49

STATE OF MINNESOTA

COUNTY OF HENNEPIN

IN THE MATTER OF THE (ESTATE (CONSERVATORSHIP (GUARDIANSHIP OF

Cheryl Ann Kennedy
         Deceased — Conservatee XXXXXXXXXXXXXXWard

PROBATE COURT
COUNTY COURT-PROBATE DIVISION

Court File No. 198541

BOND
(PERSONAL SURETIES)

KNOW ALL MEN BY THESE PRESENTS, That Charles Kennedy
of Minneapolis in the County of Hennepin ,
State of Minnesota as principal(s) and the Midwest Surety
Company
of said County and State as sureties, are held and firmly bound to the State of Minnesota for the benefit of the person interested in the above named estate in the sum of ($ 10,000.00)
Ten thousand 00/100------------ DOLLARS lawful money of the United States, to be paid to the said State of Minnesota; for which payment well and truly to be made, we bind ourselves, our and each of our heirs, executors and administrators, jointly and severally firmly by these presents.

The condition of this obligation is such that if the above bounden principal(s) who has (have) accepted his (her, their) appointment is personal representative of the estate of the above named decedent shall well and faithfully discharge all the duties of his (her, their) trust as such representative of said estate according to law then this obligation shall be void; otherwise it shall be and remain in full force and virtue.

WITNESS, Our hands and seals this 8 day of September , 19 77 .

/S/ Charles Kennedy
Principal(s)

/S/ Ira G. Benson
Attorney-in-Fact

Midwest Surety Company
Surety .

STATE OF MINNESOTA

COUNTY OF HENNEPIN

} ss.

ACKNOWLEDGEMENT

BE IT KNOWN, That on this 6 day of September , 19 77 , personally appeared before me Charles Kennedy

to me well known to be the same person who executed the foregoing bond, and they severally acknowledged the same to be their free act and deed, and that they executed the same for the purposes therein expressed.

Mariana S. Halsted /T/S/
Notary Public Hennepin County, Minnesota
My Commission expires April 2 , 19 78 .

SEAL

Form 102 Acceptance of Appointment and Oath

FORM 4401

Form 524.3-601 #1   UPC 43

STATE OF MINNESOTA

COUNTY OF HENNEPIN

In Re: Estate of

Cheryl Ann Kennedy
Deceased

PROBATE COURT
COUNTY COURT-PROBATE DIVISION

Court File No. 198541

ACCEPTANCE OF APPOINTMENT
AND OATH BY INDIVIDUAL

TO THE ABOVE NAMED COURT:

STATE OF MINNESOTA   )
) ss
COUNTY OF HENNEPIN   )

I, Charles Kennedy _____, residing at 1010 Willow Street
in the City of Minneapolis , County of Hennepin , State of Minnesota
as a condition to receiving letters as personal representative
in the above entitled matter, hereby accept the duties of the office, agree to be bound by the provisions
of the statutes relating thereto and hereby submit to the jurisdiction of the Court in any proceeding
relating to the said matter that may be instituted by any person interested therein; and swear that I
will faithfully and justly perform all duties of the office and trust that I now assume as _____
personal representative
in the above entitled matter to the best of my ability.

/S/Charles Kennedy _____

Subscribed and sworn to before me this
7 day of September , 19 77

Gordon Strommen
Notary Public, Hennepin County, Minn.   SEAL
My Commission Expires July 9 , 19 78

Form 103 Proof of Placing Order for Publication

STATE OF MINNESOTA

COUNTY OF HENNEPIN

PROBATE COURT - UNSUPERVISED

COURT FILE NO. 198541

In Re: Estate of

___Cheryl Ann Kennedy___
              Deceased

PROOF OF PLACING ORDER
FOR PUBLICATION

_____

_____

TO THE CLERK OF PROBATE COURT:

This is to verify that ___Susan G. Browning_____

_____

_____ Attorney for   , applicant(s)

has (have) made arrangements for the publication of:

[X] NOTICE OF INFORMAL APPOINTMENT OF PERSONAL
     REPRESENTATIVE(S) AND NOTICE TO CREDITORS

[ ] NOTICE OF INFORMAL PROBATE OF WILL AND APPOINTMENT OF
     PERSONAL REPRESENTATIVES(S) AND NOTICE TO CREDITORS

[ ]

once a week for two consecutive weeks in the __Legal Newsweekly_____

_____

and this is to confirm that the same will be published accordingly commencing

in the next available issue, and that arrangements for payment of the cost of

said publication have been made.

Dated: September 8, 1977

                                        __/S/ D.C. Morrison___
                                                 Publisher

Form 104 Affidavit of Mailing Notice of Appointment and Notice to Creditors

OS107 (Rev. 7/76)

Form 524.1—401 #2
525.83

UPC—

STATE OF MINNESOTA

COUNTY OF HENNEPIN

PROBATE COURT
COUNTY COURT—PROBATE DIVISION

Court File No. 198541

In Re: (ESTATE
          (CONSERVATORSHIP
          (GUARDIANSHIP

OF   Cheryl Ann Kennedy

Deceased—Conservatee Ward

AFFIDAVIT OF MAILING ORDER OR NOTICE
OF HEARING INFORMAL APPOINTMENT OF
PERSONAL REPRESENTATIVE
AND NOTICE TO CREDITORS

ATTACH COPY OF NOTICE OR ORDER HERE

STATE OF MINNESOTA
COUNTY OF HENNEPIN   } ss

Susan G. Browning

being first duly sworn on oath deposes and says that on the ___7___ day of __September__, 19_77_, at __Minneapolis__ in said County and State _She mailed a copy of the Order or Notice hereto attached to each _heir and personal representative_

whose name and address are known to affiant, after exercising due diligence in ascertaining the correctness of said name and address, by placing a true and correct copy thereof in a sealed envelope, postage prepaid and depositing the same in the U. S. Mails at _____ Minneapolis, Minnesota and addressed to the following named persons:

NOTE: (Instructions at bottom of page)

NAME	Street or Post Office	CITY	STATE
Charles Kennedy	1010 Willow Street	Minneapolis	MN 55409
Cindy Kennedy	same		
Cherry Kennedy	same		
Carl Kennedy	same		
Corey Kennedy	same		
Christopher Kennedy	same		
Catherine Kelly	same		
Karen Kelly	same		

Subscribed and sworn to before me this ___7___ day of __September__, 19_77_

Gordon Strommen
Notary Public, _Hennepin_ County, Minn.
My Commission expires _July 9_, 19_78_.

/S/ Susan G. Browning

SEAL

NOTED INSTRUCTION: In Estates To each heir, devisee, personal representative, the foreign consul pursuant to M.S. 524.3—306 and 524.3—403, and the Minnesota Attorney General, if a devisee is the trustee of a charitable trust or if the decedent left no devisees or heirs. In Conservatorships and Guardianships To each of persons as directed by the Court.

(Over)

Form 104 continued

AFFIDAVIT OF MAILING
ALLOWANCES TO SPOUSE AND/OR CHILDREN

When a decedent dies with or without a will the allowances to the spouse or children are as follows:

525.15 ALLOWANCES TO SPOUSE. When any person dies testate, or intestate,
(1) The surviving spouse shall be allowed from the personal property of which the decedent was possessed or to which he was entitled at the time of his death, the wearing apparel, and, as selected by him, furniture and household goods not exceeding $2,000 in value, and other personal property not exceeding $1,000 in value;

(2) When, except for one automobile, all of the personal estate of the decedent is allowed to the surviving spouse by clause (1), the surviving spouse shall also be allowed such automobile.

(3) If there be no surviving spouse, the minor children shall receive the property specified in clause (1) as selected in their behalf;

(4) During administration, but not exceeding 18 months, unless an extension shall have been granted by the court, or, if the estate be insolvent, not exceeding 12 months, the spouse or children, or both, constituting the family of the decedent shall be allowed reasonable maintenance.

(5) In the administration of an estate of a non-resident decedent, the allowances received in the domiciliary administration shall be deducted from the allowances under this section.

In all estates where there is a will the following rule applies to the spouse who has not consented to the will:

525.212 RENUNCIATION AND ELECTION. If a will make provision for a surviving spouse in lieu of the rights in the estate secured by statute, such spouse shall be deemed to have elected to take under the will, unless he shall have filed with the court and mailed or delivered to the personal representative, if any, within nine months after the date of death, or within six months after the probate of the decedent's will, whichever limitation last expires, an instrument in writing renouncing and refusing to accept the provisions in such will. For good cause shown, the court may permit an election within such further time as the court may determine. No devise to a surviving spouse shall be considered as adding to the rights in the estate secured by sections 525.145 and 525.16 to such spouse, unless it clearly appears from the contents of the will that such was the testator's intent.

STATE OF MINNESOTA
COUNTY OF _____ } ss

Susan G. Browning _____ being first duly sworn on oath deposes and says that on the ____7th____ day of ___September___ , 19 77 , at Minneapolis, Minn. in said County and State she mailed a copy of Sections 525.15 and 525.212 of Minnesota Statutes as hereinbefore set out to decedent's spouse and children constituting the family of decedent at their last known address after exercising due diligence and ascertaining the correctness of said addresses by placing a true and correct copy thereof in a sealed envelope, postage pre-paid and depositing the same in the U. S. Mails at _____ ___Minneapolis___ , Minnesota, and addressed to the following:

| NAME | STREET OR POST OFFICE | CITY | STATE |

Charles Kennedy and children (See reverse side)

/S/ Susan G. Browning

Subscribed and sworn to before me this __7th__ day of __September__ , 19 77

Gordon Strommen
Notary Public, ___Hennepin___ County, Minn.
My Commission expires ___July 9___ , 19 78 .   SEAL

Form 105 Letters of General Administration

OS204 (Rev. 7/76)   Form 524.3-601 #4   **UPC 43**

STATE OF MINNESOTA

COUNTY OF <u>HENNEPIN</u>

In Re: Estate of

<u>Cheryl Ann Kennedy</u>
                Deceased

**PROBATE COURT
COUNTY COURT—PROBATE DIVISION**

Court File No. <u>198541</u>

LETTERS OF GENERAL ADMINISTRATION

The above named decedent having died on <u>August 1</u> , 19<u>77</u> , and

<u>Charles Kennedy</u>

having been appointed and qualified, (is) (XX) hereby authorized to act as personal representative(X) according to law.

Dated: <u>September 7, 1977</u>

<u>/S/ Lorina B. Arneson</u>
Judge/Registrar

(COURT SEAL)

Form 106 Inventory and Appraisement

FORM 4428

Form 524.3-706

UPC 54

STATE OF MINNESOTA

COUNTY OF HENNEPIN

In Re: Estate of

Cheryl Ann Kennedy

Deceased

PROBATE COURT
COUNTY COURT-PROBATE DIVISION

Court File No. 198541

INVENTORY AND APPRAISEMENT

Date of Death August 1 _____, 19 77
Social Security No. 217-48-4307

TO THE HONORABLE JUDGE AND/OR REGISTRAR OF THE ABOVE NAMED COURT:

_____ Charles Kennedy _____, the undersigned personal representative, respectfully states:

1. That the following is a true and correct inventory and appraisement, at date of death values, of all the property of the above named estate, both real and personal, which has come into the possession of said representative and of which said representative has knowledge after diligent search and inquiry concerning the same, classified as follows, to-wit: (See instructions at end of last page.)

SCHEDULE A — Real Estate

Item number	Legal Description (Specify street address of city realty; acreage of rural land; and liens, if any)	Assessor's Estimated Market Value (Do not use "Green Acres" Value or Assessor's Limited Market Value)	GROSS APPRAISED VALUE
1	Homestead, being in the County of Hennepin _____, State of Minnesota: family residence, located at 1010 Willow St., Minneapolis, MN Lot 3, block 1, Loring Park Addition to Minneapolis		$65,000.00
	Other Real Estate being in the County of _____ State of Minnesota		

Form 106 continued

Real Estate SCHEDULE A — TOTAL $ 65,000.00

SCHEDULE B — Stocks and Bonds

Item number	Description (Specify face amount of bonds or number of shares and par value where needed for identification; and liens, if any)	GROSS APPRAISED VALUE
2	50 shares, Users, Inc. stock	$2,000.00

Personal Property SCHEDULE B — TOTAL $2,000.00

SCHEDULE C — Mortgages, Notes, and Cash

Item number	Description (Specify recording data; bank and account numbers; accrued interest; location of actual cash; and liens, if any)	GROSS APPRAISED

Personal Property SCHEDULE C — TOTAL $

Form 106 continued

SCHEDULE D — Other Miscellaneous Property

Item number	Description (Specify location of property and liens, if any)	GROSS APPRAISED VALUE
3	Furniture and Household goods:	$5,000.00
	Wearing apparel and Ornaments:	
4	Diamond ring	4,000.00
5	Clothing	200.00
6	Wigs (2)	110.00
7	Mink Coat	4,000.00
	All other personal property (including partnership and business interests, insurance and annuities payable to estate, other receivables, farm crops, machinery, etc.):	
8	Automobile (1975 Ford Granada)	3,500.00
9	Miscellaneous	300.00

Personal Property SCHEDULE D — TOTAL $21,110.00

SUMMARY

Total Gross Value of Real Estate	$ 65,000.00	
Less Liens	$ 0.00	
Net Value of Real Estate		$ 65,000.00
Total Gross Value of Personal Property	$ 21,110.00	
Less Liens	$ 110.00	
Net Value of Personal Property		$ 21,000.00
TOTAL NET APPRAISEMENT		$ 86,000.00

2. That a copy hereof has been mailed to the surviving spouse if there be one, and to all residuary distributees of the above named decedent and to interested persons or creditors who have requested the same.

Form 106 continued

FURTHER, under penalties for perjury for deliberate falsification therein, I declare or affirm that I have read the foregoing and to the best of my knowledge or information, its representations are true, correct and complete.

Dated: <u>September 17, 1977</u>

<u>/S/ Charles Kennedy</u>

<u>Susan G. Browning</u>
Attorney

<u>1400 Main St., Minneapolis, MN</u> <u>55455</u>
Address/Phone 773-3777

INSTRUCTIONS:

(1) The classification of assets herein is intended for them to be comparable to the Federal Estate Tax Return Form 706 with the exception of Schedule D herein which includes insurance and annuities payable to the estate and which are otherwise includable under separate Schedules of said Form 706.

(2) It is to be noted that the <u>GROSS</u> APPRAISED VALUE is requested of each asset without reduction by any lien requested to be specified as a part of its description. The reduction for liens is later taken under the Summary of Assets.

(3) It is also to be noted that each asset of a Schedule is to be given its "Item number" to facilitate a ready reference similar to the Estate Tax Form 706.

(4) Finally, it is to be noted that the Assessor's Estimated Market Value is requested. This information is always available to the Department of Revenue upon its request. The accurate furnishing of the information can result in better servicing of the inheritance tax returns.

(5) It is recommended that the appraisal report of any independent appraiser should be properly referenced and attached as an Exhibit including the name and address of any such appraisers.

Form 107 Written Statement of Claim

Form 4434 MILLER-DAVIS CO., MPLS.

524.3-804 (1)   UPC 59

STATE OF MINNESOTA

COUNTY OF __HENNEPIN__

PROBATE COURT
COUNTY COURT-PROBATE DIVISION

In Re: Estate of

Court File No. __198541__ _____

WRITTEN STATEMENT OF CLAIM

__Cheryl Ann Kennedy__
Deceased

TO THE PERSONAL REPRESENTATIVE OF THE ABOVE NAMED ESTATE:

Claimant __Beauty Products, Inc.__, states:

1. Claimant's address __230 Dunkirk Lane, Minnetonka, MN   55606_____;

2. Claimant claims that the estate is indebted or will become indebted in the amount of $ __110.00_____;

3. That the nature of the claim is __merchandise (wigs) bought by decedent:__

        Primavera (#7743) $ 64.00
        Carefree (#7739)   46.00
              TOTAL $110.00

4. That the claim arose prior to the death of the decedent on or about __July 27_____, 19 __77__, ~~or the claim arose at or after the death of the decedent, on or about~~ _____, 19 __;

5. That the claim is secured by __no security_____;

6. That the claim was ~~or will be~~ due and payable on __August 27_____, 19__77__;

7. That if the claim is contingent or unliquidated, the nature of the uncertainty is as follows: _____

Dated: __September 18, 1977_____

                                        /S/ Martin R. Kromstad_____
                                        Claimant /T/ Beauty Products, Inc.

Rafael Y. Santelo_____
Attorney for Claimant

1341 Stevens Ave., Minneapolis, MN 55410__
Address/Phone 841-7662

Note: Claim may be presented to Personal Representative or filed with Clerk._____
Presentation of claim does **not** commence proceedings.
See 3-806

Form 108 Informal Deed of Distribution

Form 4452

524.3-907 #1   UPC --

STATE OF MINNESOTA

COUNTY OF ___Hennepin___

PROBATE COURT
COUNTY COURT-PROBATE DIVISION

In Re: Estate of

Court File No. __198541__

INFORMAL DEED OF DISTRIBUTION
BY PERSONAL REPRESENTATIVE #15

___Cheryl Ann Kennedy___
Deceased

This instrument dated this __8th__ day of __January__ _____, 19 _78_, by and between __Charles Kennedy__ _____, personal representative of the estate of __Cheryl Ann Kennedy__ _____, decedent, first party, and __Charles Kennedy for__ __Christopher Kennedy, a minor__ _____, of the County of __Hennepin__ _____ and State of Minnesota, second party;

WHEREAS, __Cheryl Ann Kennedy__ _____ died on the __1st__ day of __August__ _____, 19 _77_, and;

WHEREAS, thereafter, on the __7th__ day of __September__ _____, 19 _77_, first party was duly appointed and qualified as personal representative of the above entitled estate in an informal probate administration, and;

WHEREAS, the second party as an (heir) (~~devisee~~) of the estate of __Cheryl Ann Kennedy__ _____, deceased, is entitled to the property hereby distributed;

NOW, THEREFORE, in accordance with the laws of the State of __Minnesota__ _____, first party hereby assigns, transfers, conveys, and releases to __Charles Kennedy for Christopher Kennedy,__ all the estate, right, title, interest, claims, and demand whatsoever, which the said decedent had at the __a minor__ time of death in the following described __real__ _____ property located in the County of __Hennepin__ _____ and State of Minnesota, legally described as follows:

Lot 1, Block 3, Loring Park Addition to Minneapolis:
To Charles Kennedy for Christopher Kennedy, a minor, son of the decedent: an undivided one fifth (1/5) of said homestead real estate, subject to the life estate of Charles Kennedy.

Dated: __January 8, 1978__

/S/ Charles Kennedy
Personal Representative

STATE OF MINNESOTA   )
) ss.
COUNTY OF __Hennepin__   )

The foregoing instrument was acknowledged before me this __8th__ _____ day of __January__ _____, 19 _78_, by __Charles Kennedy__ as personal representative of the estate of __Cheryl Ann Kennedy__ _____, deceased, for the purposes and consideration therein expressed.

Subscribed and sworn to before me this __8th__ day of __January__ _____, 19 _78_.

/S/ Burton J. McLane
Notary Public
My commission expires May 9, 1979

This instrument was drafted by:
/S/ Susan G. Browning
                        (Name)
1400 Main St.
Minneapolis, MN (Address)55455

Form 109 Receipt for Assets by Distributee

OS272 1/2 (New 7/76)

Form 524.3-1001 (4)
524.3-1003 (2)

UPC——

STATE OF MINNESOTA

COUNTY OF HENNEPIN

In Re: Estate of

Cheryl Ann Kennedy
_____
Deceased

**PROBATE COURT
COUNTY COURT—PROBATE DIVISION**

Court File No. 198541

RECEIPT FOR ASSETS BY DISTRIBUTEE

I, Charles Kennedy, for Christopher Kennedy, a minor , the undersigned distributee, hereby acknowledge receipt from the personal representative(s) of the above entitled estate, of the following assets, to-wit:

Lot 1, Block 3, Loring Park Addition to Minneapolis: an undivided one fifth (1/5) of said homestead real estate, subject to the life estate of Charles Kennedy.

in full satisfaction of the complete and final settlement of my distributive share of the above entitled estate.

Dated: January 8, 1978

/S/ Charles Kennedy for Christopher Kennedy
Distributee   (a minor)

INSTRUCTIONS:

1. To be executed after Order or Decree of Distribution under 524.3-1001 (4) and furnished with petition for discharge Form 524.3-1001 #9.

2. To be executed under 524.3-1003 (2) prior to personal representative's closing statement Form 524.3-1003# 1.

Form 110 Informal Administration: Personal Representative's Statement to Close Estate

S24 3-1003 #1   UPC--

STATE OF MINNESOTA

COUNTY OF HENNEPIN

**PROBATE COURT
COUNTY COURT-PROBATE DIVISION**

In Re: Estate of

Court File No. 198540

**INFORMAL ADMINISTRATION:
PERSONAL REPRESENTATIVE'S
STATEMENT TO CLOSE ESTATE**

Cheryl Ann Kennedy
                    Deceased

TO THE HONORABLE REGISTRAR OF THE ABOVE NAMED COURT:

Charles Kennedy , the undersigned personal representative herein respectfully states that he or a prior personal representative whom he has succeeded has:

1. Published notice to creditors and that the date of the notice was more than six months prior to the date of this statement;

2. Fully administered the estate of the decedent by making payment, settlement or other disposition of all claims which were presented, expenses of administration and estate, inheritance and other taxes, except as specified in this statement, and that the assets of the estate have been inventoried and distributed to the persons entitled thereto. Listed below are unpaid claims, expenses or taxes which remain undischarged together with the detailed arrangements which have been made to accommodate all outstanding liabilities: (If none, so state)

3. Sent a copy of this statement to all distributees of the estate and to all creditors or other claimants of whom he is aware whose claims are neither paid or barred and has furnished a full account in writing of this administration to the distributees whose interests are affected thereby.

This statement is filed for the purpose of closing this estate and terminating the appointment of the undersigned.

DATED: March 1, 1978

/S/ Charles Kennedy
Personal Representative

STATE OF MINNESOTA   )
) ss.
COUNTY OF HENNEPIN   )

I, Charles Kennedy , being duly sworn state that I am the personal representative herein; that I have read the foregoing statement and know the contents thereof; that the same is true of my own knowledge, except as to those matters therein stated on information and belief, and as to those matters I believe it to be true.

/S/ Charles Kennedy
Personal Representative

Subscribed and sworn to before me this 1st day of March , 19 78 .

Georgeann Holtzer /T/S/
Notary Public, Hennepin County, Minnesota
My Commission expires November 3 1980 .

(SEAL)

Susan G. Browning
Attorney for Personal Representative

1400 Main St., Minneapolis, MN 55455
Address/Phone   773-3777

Form 111 Application for Certificate from Registrar—Release of Bond

OS263 1/4 (New 7/76) Form 524.3-1007 #1 UPC—

STATE OF MINNESOTA PROBATE COURT

COUNTY OF HENNEPIN COUNTY COURT—PROBATE DIVISION
Court File No. 198541

In Re: Estate of

Cheryl Ann Kennedy
Deceased

APPLICATION FOR CERTIFICATE FROM
REGISTRAR THAT THE PERSONAL
REPRESENTATIVE APPEARS TO HAVE FULLY
ADMINISTERED THE ESTATE OF DECEDENT –
APPLICATION FOR RELEASE OF BOND

TO THE HONORABLE REGISTRAR OF THE ABOVE NAMED COURT:

Applicant, Charles Kennedy _____, respectfully states:

1. Applicant resides at 1010 Willow Street, Minneapolis, MN 55409 ;

2. Applicant has an interest herein as personal representative ,
and is, therefore, a proper applicant as defined by the laws of this State;

3. That Charles Kennedy (applicant) _____
(was) (were) the duly appointed personal representative(s) of the estate of decedent;

4. That the appointment of said personal representative(s) has terminated;

5. So far as known to applicant, no action concerning the estate of decedent is pending in any Court.

WHEREFORE, Your applicant requests the certificate from the Registrar that the personal representative(s) appear(s) to have fully administered the estate of decedent as evidence to discharge any lien on any property given to secure the obligation of the personal representative(s) in lieu of bond or any surety.

Dated: March 8, 1978

/S/ Charles Kennedy
Applicant

VERIFICATION

STATE OF MINNESOTA

COUNTY OF HENNEPIN } ss

I, Charles Kennedy _____,
being duly sworn state that I am the applicant herein; that I have read the foregoing application and know the contents thereof; that the same is true of my own knowledge, except as to those matters therein stated on information and belief, and as to those matters I believe them to be true, and I know and am informed that the penalties for perjury may follow from deliberate falsification therein.

Dated: March 8, 1978

/S/ Charles Kennedy
Applicant

Subscribed and sworn to before me this 8
day of March , 19 78 .

Gordon Strommen
Notary Public
Hennepin County, Minnesota
My Commission expires July 9 , 19 78 .

SEAL

Susan G. Browning
Attorney

1400 Main St., Minneapolis, MN 55455
Address/Phone 773-3777

Form 112 Certificate of Registrar—Release of Bond

OS263 1/2 (New 7/76)   Form 524.3-1007 #2   UPC——

STATE OF MINNESOTA

COUNTY OF HENNEPIN

In Re: Estate of

Cheryl Ann Kennedy
                    Deceased

PROBATE COURT
COUNTY COURT—PROBATE DIVISION

Court File No. 198541

CERTIFICATE OF REGISTRAR THAT PERSONAL
REPRESENTATIVE APPEARS TO HAVE FULLY
ADMINISTERED THE ESTATE OF DECEDENT-
RELEASE OF BOND

The application of Charles Kennedy   ,
dated March 8   , 19 78 , for the certificate from the Registrar that the personal representative appears to have fully administered the estate of the above named decedent having come before the
undersigned Registrar of the above named Court, the undersigned Registrar having considered such application
makes the following determinations:

1.   That the said application is complete.

2.   That the applicant has declared that the representations contained in the application are true, correct
     and complete to the best of his knowledge or information.

3.   That the applicant appears from the application to be an interested person as defined by the laws of
     this State.

4.   That, on the basis of the statements in the application and from the records on file herein, the appli-
     cation is proper.

Now, Therefore, it is CERTIFIED by the Registrar as follows:

1.   That the application is hereby granted.

2.   That Charles Kennedy   ,
     personal representative(s) of the estate of decedent appear(s) to have fully administered the estate
     of decedent.

3.   That this Certificate evidences discharge of any lien on any property given to secure the obligation of
     the personal representative(s) in lieu of bond or any surety, but does not preclude action against the
     personal representative(s) or the surety.

Dated: March 10, 1978

                              /s/ Lorina B. Arneson
                                  Registrar

Form 113 Statement of Claimant to Refund Due Deceased Taxpayer

Form **1310** (Rev. Oct. 1976) Department of the Treasury Internal Revenue Service	**Statement of Claimant to Refund Due—Deceased Taxpayer** For calendar year ...., or other taxable year beginning ...., 19......, and ending ...., 19......

Please type or print	Name of decedent		Name of claimant
	Date of death	Social security number	Number and street
	Number and street (Permanent residence or domicile on the date of death)		
	City or town, State, and ZIP code		City or town, State, and ZIP code

I am filing this statement as (check only one box):

A. ☐ Surviving spouse, claiming a refund based on a joint return.

B. ☐ Deceased's personal representative.[1] Attach a court certificate showing your appointment.

C. ☐ Claimant, for the estate of the decedent, other than above. Complete Schedule A and attach a copy of the death certificate or proof of death.[2]

Please attach requested information, complete Schedule A, if applicable, and sign below.

Schedule A. (To be completed only if C above is checked.)	Yes	No
1 Did the deceased leave a will?		
2(a) Has a deceased's personal representative been appointed for the estate of the decedent?		
(b) If "No," will one be appointed?		
If 2(a) or (b) is checked "Yes," do not file this form. The deceased's personal representative should file for the refund.		
3 Will you, as the claimant for the estate of the decedent, disburse the refund according to the law of the State in which the decedent was domiciled or maintained a permanent residence?		
If "No," payment of this claim will be withheld pending submission of proof of your appointment as the deceased's personal representative or other evidence showing that you are authorized under State law to receive payment.		

	Address
4 Name of widow or widower	
5 Names of surviving children	
6 Name of person supporting the children	
7 Names of decedent's living father and mother	Address
8 Names of decedent's living brothers and sisters	Address
9 Names of the living children of the decedent's deceased children	Address

Signature and Verification

I hereby make request for refund of taxes overpaid by or in behalf of the decedent and declare under penalties of perjury, that I have examined this claim and to the best of my knowledge and belief, it is true, correct and complete.

▶ Signature of claimant .... Date ....

[1] For purposes of this form, personal representative means the executor, executrix, administrator or administratrix of the decedent's estate; if no executor, executrix, administrator or administratrix is appointed, qualified and acting within the United States, personal representative means any person in actual or constructive possession of any property of the decedent.

[2] May be the original or an authentic copy of a telegram or letter from the Department of Defense notifying the next of kin of his or her death while in active service, or a death certificate issued by an appropriate officer of the Department of Defense.

Form 114 Statement of Claimant to Refund Due Deceased Taxpayer (Minnesota)

Minnesota Department of Revenue
Centennial Office Building — St. Paul, Minnesota 55145

FORM
M-506
(Rev. 3/76)

STATEMENT OF CLAIMANT TO REFUND DUE — DECEASED TAXPAYER

Name of Decedent			Name of Claimant		Social Security Number
Date of Death		Social Security Number	Address (Number and Street or Rural Route)		
Address (Permanent residence or domicile on date of death)			City, Town or Post Office		
City, Town or Post Office	State	Zip Code	State		Zip Code

(Print or Type shown in left margin)

I AM FILING THIS STATEMENT AS (check only one box):

A ☐ SURVIVING SPOUSE, claiming a refund based on a joint or combined Individual Income Tax Return.*

B ☐ SURVIVING SPOUSE, claiming a refund based on an Income-Adjusted Homestead Credit Return.*

C ☐ PERSONAL REPRESENTATIVE. Attach a court authorization showing your appointment.

D ☐ CLAIMANT OTHER THAN ABOVE. The Waiver on the reverse side of this form must be completed and signed by all persons who may be entitled to claim the refund due on behalf of the deceased taxpayer.*

* IMPORTANT NOTE: If A, B or D above is checked, you must attach a copy of the death certificate or proof of death. Proof of death may be the original or an authentic copy of a telegram or letter from the Department of Defense notifying the next of kin of a person's death while in active service, or a death certificate issued by an appropriate officer of the Department of Defense.

SCHEDULE A (To be completed only if A, B or D above is checked)

1. Did the Decedent leave a will? . . . .   Yes ☐   No ☐

2. Has an Executor or Administrator been appointed for the estate of the Decedent? . . . .   Yes ☐   No ☐

3. If the answer to question 2 is "No", will an Executor or Administrator be appointed? . . . .   Yes ☐   No ☐

4. Will the refund be disbursed according to the Laws of the State in which the Decedent was domiciled? . . .   Yes ☐   No ☐
   If no, payment of this claim may be withheld pending the appointment of claimant as administrator or executor and submission of court certificate showing the appointment unless claimant submits other satisfactory proof of right to receive payment.

	Address
5. Name of widow or widower	
6. Names of surviving children	
7. Name of person supporting the children	
8. Names of decedent's living father and mother	
9. Names of decedent's living brothers and sisters	
10. Names of the living children of the decedent's deceased children	

I hereby make request for refund of taxes due the above named decedent and declare under the penalties of perjury that I have examined this claim and it is true, correct and complete to the best of my knowledge and belief.

Sign Here → _____   Date _____
Signature of Claimant

Form 114 continued

WAIVER OF CLAIMANT TO REFUND DUE ON BEHALF OF DECEASED TAXPAYER

TO WHOM IT MAY CONCERN:

I/We hereby waive any and all right, title and interest that I/We have in the check representing over payment of

income tax for the year_____ , for_____, and it is with my/our permission that

said check be made payable to_____ , individually.

_____	_____		_____	_____
(Signature)	(Date)		(Signature)	(Date)
_____	_____		_____	_____
(Signature)	(Date)		(Signature)	(Date)
_____	_____		_____	_____
(Signature)	(Date)		(Signature)	(Date)

Form 115 Application for Extension of Time to File U.S. Individual Income Tax Return

Form **4868** Department of the Treasury Internal Revenue Service (0)	**Application for Automatic Extension of Time to File U.S. Individual Income Tax Return**	OMB No. 1545-0188 **1983** 71

	Your first name and initial (if joint return, also give spouse's name and initial)	Last name	Your social security number
Please Type or Print	Present home address (Number and street, including apartment number, or rural route)		Spouse's social security no.
	City, town or post office, State, and ZIP code		

Note: File this form with the Internal Revenue Service Center where you must file your income tax return and pay the amount shown on line 6 below. **This is not an extension of time for payment of tax.** You will be charged a penalty for late payment of tax and late filing unless you show reasonable cause for not paying or filing on time (see instructions).

If you expect to file a gift tax return (Form 709 or Form 709-A) for 1983, generally due by April 16, 1984, check this box . . . . ▶ ☐

I request an automatic 4-month extension of time to August 15, 1984, to file Form 1040A or Form 1040 for the calendar year 1983 (or if a fiscal year Form 1040 to _ _ _ _ _ _ _ _ _ _ _ _ _ _ _ _ _ _ , 19 _ _ _ _ _ , for the tax year ending _ _ _ _ _ _ _ _ _ _ _ _ _ _ _ _ , 19 _ _ _ _ _).

1	Total income tax liability for 1983. (You may estimate this amount.)		1	
	Note: You **must** enter an amount on line 1. If you do not expect to owe tax, enter zero (0).			
2	Federal income tax withheld	2		
3	1983 estimated tax payments (include 1982 overpayment allowed as a credit) .	3		
4	Other payments and credits you expect to show on Form 1040A or Form 1040 .	4		
5	Add lines 2, 3, and 4		5	
6	Income tax balance due (subtract line 5 from line 1). Pay in full with this form. (If line 5 is more than line 1, enter zero (0).). . . . . ▶		6	
7	Total gift tax you expect to owe for 1983 (see instructions) . . . . ▶		7	

If you send only one check for both income and gift tax due, attach a statement showing how much of the check applies to each type of tax.

Signature and Verification

If Prepared by Taxpayer.—Under penalties of perjury, I declare that I have examined this form, including accompanying schedules and statements, and to the best of my knowledge and belief, it is true, correct, and complete.

_ _
Your signature   Date

_ _
Spouse's signature (if filing jointly, BOTH must sign even if only one had income)   Date

If Prepared by Someone Other Than Taxpayer.—Under penalties of perjury, I declare that I have examined this form, including accompanying schedules and statements, and to the best of my knowledge and belief, it is true, correct, and complete; and that I am authorized to prepare this form.

_ _
Signature of preparer other than taxpayer   Date

Note: The person who signs this form may be an attorney or certified public accountant qualified to practice before the IRS, a person enrolled to practice before the IRS, or a person holding a power of attorney. If the taxpayer cannot sign because of illness, absence, or other good cause, a person in a close personal or business relationship to the taxpayer may sign this form.

For Paperwork Reduction Act Notice, see back of form.   Form **4868** (1983)

Form 115 continued

General Instructions

Paperwork Reduction Act Notice.—We ask for this information to carry out the Internal Revenue laws of the United States. We need it to ensure that taxpayers are complying with these laws and to allow us to figure and collect the right amount of tax. You are required to give us this information.

Purpose of Form.—Use Form 4868 to ask for an automatic 4-month extension of time to file **Form 1040A** or **Form 1040**. The 4-month extension period includes the automatic 2-month extension granted to U.S. citizens and resident aliens who are living or traveling outside the United States and Puerto Rico on the due date for filing their returns. Do not file this form if:

- You want the IRS to figure your tax, or
- You are under a court order to file your return by the regular due date.

The extension will be granted if you complete this form properly, file it on time, **and pay with it the amount of tax shown on line 6.** We will notify you **only** if your request for an extension is denied.

Note: *Any extension of time granted for filing your 1983 calendar year income tax return also extends the time for filing a gift tax return for 1983.*

Filing Form 2688.—Except in cases of undue hardship, we will not accept Form 2688, Application for Extension of Time to File U.S. Individual Income Tax Return, until you have first used Form 4868.

If you have filed Form 4868 and still need more time, use Form 2688 or write a letter of explanation. You must show reasonable cause. Send Form 2688 or the letter to the Internal Revenue Service Center where you file your Form 1040A or Form 1040. (See **Where to File**, below.)

If you need a further extension, ask for it early so that, if denied, you can still file your return on time.

When to File.— File Form 4868 by April 16, 1984. If you are filing a fiscal year Form 1040, file Form 4868 by the regular due date of your return. If you were granted the automatic 2-month extension explained above, file this form by the end of the 2-month period (June 15, 1984, for a 1983 calendar year return).

You may file Form 1040A or Form 1040 any time before the 4-month period ends.

Where to File.—Mail this form to the **Internal Revenue Service Center** for the place where you live.

If you are located in:	Use this address:
New Jersey, New York City and counties of Nassau, Rockland, Suffolk, and Westchester	Holtsville, NY 00501
New York (all other counties), Connecticut, Maine, Massachusetts, New Hampshire, Rhode Island, Vermont	Andover, MA 05501
Delaware, District of Columbia, Maryland, Pennsylvania	Philadelphia, PA 19255
Alabama, Florida, Georgia, Mississippi, South Carolina	Atlanta, GA 31101
Michigan, Ohio	Cincinnati, OH 45999
Arkansas, Kansas, Louisiana, New Mexico, Oklahoma, Texas	Austin, TX 73301

Alaska, Arizona, Colorado, Idaho, Minnesota, Montana, Nebraska, Nevada, North Dakota, Oregon, South Dakota, Utah, Washington, Wyoming	Ogden, UT 84201
Illinois, Iowa, Missouri, Wisconsin	Kansas City, MO 64999
California, Hawaii	Fresno, CA 93888
Indiana, Kentucky, North Carolina, Tennessee, Virginia, West Virginia	Memphis, TN 37501
American Samoa	Philadelphia, PA 19255
Guam	Commissioner of Revenue and Taxation Agana, GU 96910
Puerto Rico (or if excluding income under section 933) Virgin Islands: Nonpermanent residents	Philadelphia, PA 19255
Virgin Islands: Permanent residents	Bureau of Internal Revenue Charlotte Amalie St. Thomas, VI 00801
A.P.O. or F.P.O. address of:	Miami—Atlanta, GA 31101 New York—Holtsville, NY 00501 San Francisco—Fresno, CA 93888 Seattle—Ogden, UT 84201
Foreign country: U.S. citizens and those excluding income under section 911 or 931, or claiming the housing deduction under section 911	Philadelphia, PA 19255

Penalties.—You may be charged one or both of the following penalties.

Late payment penalty.—Form 4868 does not extend the time to pay income or gift tax. A penalty of 1/2 of 1% of any tax (other than estimated tax) not paid by the regular due date is charged for each month, or part of a month, that the tax remains unpaid. The penalty will not be charged if you can show reasonable cause for not paying on time. The penalty is limited to 25%.

You are considered to have reasonable cause for the period covered by this automatic extension if the amount you owe on Form 1040A, line 27, or Form 1040, line 68 (minus any estimated tax penalty):

- Is not more than 10% of the amount shown as total tax on Form 1040A, line 23, or Form 1040, line 56, and
- Is paid with Form 1040A or Form 1040.

If both of the above conditions are not met, the late payment penalty will apply, unless you show reasonable cause.

If you have reasonable cause, attach a statement to your return giving your reason.

If you cannot show reasonable cause, figure the penalty on the total tax due on Form 1040A, line 27, or Form 1040, line 68, from the regular due date of your return to the date of payment.

Late filing penalty.—A penalty is charged if your return is filed after the due date (including extensions), unless you can show reasonable cause for filing late. The penalty is 5% of the tax not paid by the regular due date for each month, or part of a month, that your return is late, but not more than 25%. If your return is more than 60 days late, the penalty will not be less than $100 or the balance of tax due on your return, whichever is smaller. If you file your return late, attach a full explanation with the return.

Interest.—Interest is charged from the regular due date of the return until the tax is paid. It will be charged even if:

- You have been granted an extension, or
- You show reasonable cause for not paying the tax on time.

Line-by-Line Instructions

At the top of this form, fill in the spaces for your name, address, social security number, and spouse's social security number if you are filing a joint return. If you expect to file a gift tax return (**Form 709 or Form 709-A**) for 1983, generally due by April 16, 1984, check the box on the front of this form. Below that, if you are on a fiscal year, fill in the date on which your 4-month extension will end and the date your tax year ends.

We have provided specific instructions for most of the lines on the form. Those lines that do not appear in these instructions are self-explanatory.

Note: *If you were granted the automatic 2-month extension and are filing Form 4868 to ask for an additional 2-month extension, write "Taxpayer Abroad" across the top of this form.*

Line 1.—Enter the total amount of income tax you expect to owe for 1983 (the amount you expect to enter on Form 1040A, line 23, or Form 1040, line 56, when you file your return). Be sure to estimate the amount correctly. If you underestimate this amount, you may be charged a penalty as explained earlier under **Penalties.**

Line 6.—Form 4868 does not extend the time to pay your income tax. Therefore, you must pay the amount of income tax shown on line 6 in full with this form.

Line 7.—If you plan to use the extension of time to file your gift tax return, enter the amount of gift tax you expect to owe for 1983. To avoid the late payment penalty, you must pay this amount in full with Form 4868 unless you specifically request an extension to pay the gift tax. To request an extension to pay the gift tax only, you must attach a statement to this form that paying the gift tax on the due date would cause you undue hardship (not merely inconvenience).

If your spouse is filing a separate Form 4868, enter on your form only the total gift tax **you** expect to owe.

If you are filing Form 4868 with your spouse, enter on line 7 the total gift tax the two of you expect to owe. However, if each of you expects to file a gift tax return, also show in the space to the right of line 7 how much gift tax each expects to owe for 1983.

Below line 7, sign and date the form. If someone else prepares the form for you, that person must sign and date the form.

How to Claim Credit for Payment Made With This Form.— If you file Form 1040A, include the amount paid (line 6) with this form in the total on Form 1040A, line 25. Also write "Form 4868" and the amount paid in the space to the left of line 25. If you file Form 1040, enter the amount paid (line 6) with this form on Form 1040, line 60.

If you and your spouse file separate Forms 4868 for 1983, but file a joint income tax return for the year, enter on the appropriate line of your Form 1040A or Form 1040, the total of the amounts paid on the separate Forms 4868. Also enter the social security numbers of both spouses in the spaces on your return.

If you and your spouse file a joint Form 4868 for 1983, but file separate income tax returns for the year, you may claim the total tax payment (line 6) on your separate return or on your spouse's separate return or you may divide it in any agreed amounts. Be sure to enter the social security numbers of both spouses on the separate returns.

Form 116 Application for Extension of Time to File Minnesota Income Tax Return

Form M-522E (Rev. 12/75)	**Minnesota Department of Revenue — Income Tax Division** **Centennial Office Building — St. Paul, Minnesota 55145** APPLICATION FOR EXTENSION OF TIME TO FILE MINNESOTA INCOME TAX RETURN – OTHER THAN CORPORATION (See Instructions on Reverse Side before Preparing this Form)	File in DUPLICATE on or before the due date for filing the tax return.

IMPORTANT: If you apply to the Internal Revenue Service for an extension of time to file your U.S. Individual, Fiduciary, Partnership or Electing Small Business Income Tax Return, do not make a separate extension application to Minnesota. See complete instructions on back of this form.

APPLICANT: Print or type name, address and zip code.
(If joint application, enter names of both spouses)

Indicate type of return to be filed:

☐ Form M-1, Individual - Soc. Sec. No. _____

☐ Form M-2, Fiduciary

☐ Form M-3, Partnership

☐ Form M-3S-4, Partnership (Electing Small Business Corporation)

☐ Form M-1HC, Income-Adjusted Homestead Credit

Name, address and zip code to whom extension should be forwarded, if not the applicant:

Extension Requested to _____
                                        (Date)

For ☐ Calendar Year Ended December 31, 19 ____
or
☐ Fiscal Year Ended _____

Application is hereby made for an extension for filing the return of the taxpayer named herein in accordance with the provisions of Section 290.42 of the Minnesota Income Tax Act.

An extension is necessary for the following reason:

Signature of Taxpayer or Representative	Date	Signature of Spouse if joint application	Social Security Number	Date

NOTICE TO APPLICANT:

☐ Your application is approved. This form must be attached to your income tax return when it is filed as evidence that the extension was granted.

☐ Your application cannot be considered since it was received in this office after the original or previously extended due date for filing the return. The return should be filed without further delay.

☐ Careful consideration has been given to the reasons and other data given in your application. It has been determined that the extension is not warranted. The return should be filed by the regular due date or within ten (10) days from the date stamped below, and MUST be accompanied by this extension form.

☐ Other:

Director		Date

Income Tax Division

Form 116 continued

IMPORTANT — Read these paragraphs first. It may not be necessary for you to make this application to Minnesota.

If you apply to the Internal Revenue Service for an extension of time to file your U.S. Individual Income Tax Return, do not make a separate extension application to Minnesota. Your Minnesota return in such case is considered due on the Federal extended due date and your Minnesota return must then be accompanied by a copy of the Federal "Automatic Extension" Form 4868, dated and signed. If you obtain an additional Federal extension or a Federal extension on some form other than Form 4868, your Minnesota return must be accompanied by a copy of that document showing that the Federal has acted upon the extension. Grace periods permitted on rejected Federal applications also apply to the Minnesota return.

If you apply to the Internal Revenue Service for an extension of time to file your U.S. Fiduciary, Partnership, or Electing Small Business (Partnership) Return, do not make a separate extension application to Minnesota. Attach a copy of the automatic or approved Federal extension to the Minnesota return.

If no Federal extension application is made, a Minnesota extension may be applied for by submitting this Form M-522E.

GENERAL INFORMATION

The Minnesota Income Tax Act does not require you to make a payment at the time you file an extension application. If you desire to make a payment, you should submit your payment with a letter stating your name, address, social security number and the purpose of the payment being "Extension payment on my 197__ Minnesota Individual Tax Return."

If you are outside the United States continuously for more than 90 days, an automatic extension of time for filing your return and paying the tax is granted to 6 months after your return. Attach a letter to your return giving dates of absence.

Armed forces personnel on active duty have an automatic extension of time to 6 months after termination of military service for filing their return and paying the tax, provided their ability to file their return and pay the tax is materially impaired by reason of such service. Attach a letter to your return giving dates of military service. This automatic extension does not apply to husbands or wives of armed forces personnel.

INTEREST — Interest accrues at the rate of 8% per year on any tax due for the year from the normal due date of the Return until the tax is paid.

INSTRUCTIONS IF FORM M-522E IS TO BE FILED

1. WHEN TO FILE — The application must be filed in DUPLICATE on or before the normal due date of the Return. The application should be submitted in sufficient time to enable this office to consider and to act on the application before the normal due date of the Return.

2. HOW AND WHERE TO FILE — A separate application must be made for each taxpayer and for each type of tax return to be filed. Blanket extension requests will NOT be granted. Complete this form in DUPLICATE and forward both copies to the Minnesota Department of Revenue, Income Tax Division, Centennial Office Bldg., St. Paul, Minnesota 55145. Mark the envelope "Extension Request" in the lower left corner. Do not include tax returns or other correspondence in the same envelope.

3. PERIOD OF EXTENSION — Generally, extensions of time on an initial application will be limited to a period of time not in excess of 60 days. Longer periods of time will not be granted unless sufficient need for such extended period is clearly shown. In no event will an extension be granted in excess of 6 months for taxpayers within the United States except for members of the Armed Forces.

4. SIGNATURE — The application must be signed by the taxpayer or a duly authorized agent. If it is signed by a person with a duly authorized power of attorney, a statement to that effect should be made. It will not be necessary to attach a copy of the power of attorney. If the taxpayer is unable to sign the application due to illness, absence or other good cause, any person standing in close personal or business relationship to the taxpayer may sign the application. However, the signer must state the reasons for his signature and his relationship to the taxpayer.

5. ADDITIONAL EXTENSIONS — Additional extensions require filing a new application in DUPLICATE. The new application should be marked "Additional Extension" and MUST BE ACCOMPANIED BY THE PREVIOUSLY GRANTED EXTENSION.

6. NOTICE TO APPLICANT — When a determination has been made, this form will be returned to you. The copy returned to you MUST BE ATTACHED TO YOUR INCOME TAX RETURN when it is filed.

If the application is rejected as not warranted by the reason given, you are allowed ten (10) days from the date of notice within which to file the Return. The rejected application MUST BE ATTACHED TO YOUR INCOME TAX RETURN when it is filed.

Form 117 Schedules A & B Itemized Deductions

SCHEDULES A&B **(Form 1040)** Department of the Treasury Internal Revenue Service (0)	**Schedule A—Itemized Deductions** (Schedule B is on back) ▶ Attach to Form 1040. ▶ See Instructions for Schedules A and B (Form 1040).	OMB No. 1545-0074 19**83** 07

Name(s) as shown on Form 1040 | Your social security number

Medical and Dental Expenses **(Do not include expenses reimbursed or paid by others.)** *(See page 18 of Instructions.)*	**1** Medicines and drugs	**1**		
	2 Write 1% of Form 1040, line 33	**2**		
	3 Subtract line 2 from line 1. If line 2 is more than line 1, write zero . .	**3**	
	4 Other medical and dental expenses:		
	a Doctors, dentists, nurses, hospitals, insurance premiums you paid for medical and dental care, etc.	**4a**	
	b Transportation	**4b**	
	c Other (list—include hearing aids, dentures, eyeglasses, etc.) ▶	**4c**	
	5 Add lines 3 through 4c	**5**	
	6 Multiply amount on Form 1040, line 33, by 5% (.05)	**6**	
	7 Subtract line 6 from line 5. If line 6 is more than line 5, write zero . . . . ▶	**7**	
Taxes *(See page 19 of Instructions.)*	**8** State and local income	**8**	
	9 Real estate	**9**	
	10 a General sales (see sales tax tables)	**10a**	
	b General sales on motor vehicles	**10b**	
	11 Other (list—include personal property) ▶	**11**	
	12 Add lines 8 through 11. Write your answer here . . . . ▶	**12**	
Interest Expense *(See page 20 of Instructions.)*	**13 a** Home mortgage interest paid to financial institutions	**13a**	
	b Home mortgage interest paid to individuals (show that person's name and address) ▶	**13b**	
	14 Credit cards and charge accounts	**14**	
	15 Other (list) ▶	**15**	
	16 Add lines 13a through 15. Write your answer here . . . . ▶	**16**	
Contributions *(See page 20 of Instructions.)*	**17 a** Cash contributions. (If you gave $3,000 or more to any one organization, report those contributions on line 17b.)	**17a**	
	b Cash contributions totaling $3,000 or more to any one organization. (Show to whom you gave and how much you gave.) ▶	**17b**	
	18 Other than cash (attach required statement)	**18**	
	19 Carryover from prior year	**19**	
	20 Add lines 17a through 19. Write your answer here . . . . ▶	**20**	
Casualty and Theft Losses	**21** Total casualty or theft loss(es) (attach Form 4684) (see page 20 of Instructions) . . . . ▶	**21**	
Miscellaneous Deductions *(See page 21 of Instructions.)*	**22** Union and professional dues	**22**	
	23 Tax return preparation fee	**23**	
	24 Other (list) ▶	**24**	
	25 Add lines 22 through 24. Write your answer here . . . . ▶	**25**	
Summary of Itemized Deductions *(See page 21 of Instructions.)*	**26** Add lines 7, 12, 16, 20, 21, and 25	**26**	
	27 If you checked Form 1040 { Filing Status box 2 or 5, write $3,400 Filing Status box 1 or 4, write $2,300 Filing Status box 3, write $1,700 }	**27**	
	28 Subtract line 27 from line 26. Write your answer here and on Form 1040, line 34a. (If line 27 is more than line 26, see the Instructions for line 28 on page 21.) . . . . ▶	**28**	

For Paperwork Reduction Act Notice, see Form 1040 Instructions.   Schedule A (Form 1040) 1983

Form 117 continued

Schedules A&B (Form 1040) 1983

Schedule B—Interest and Dividend Income   08

OMB No. 1545-0074   Page **2**

Name(s) as shown on Form 1040 (Do not enter name and social security number if shown on other side)   Your social security number

Part I **Interest Income** *(See pages 9 and 21 of Instructions.)* Also complete Part III.	If you received more than $400 in interest or you received any interest from an All-Savers Certificate, you must complete Part I and list ALL interest received. If you received interest as a nominee for another, or you received or paid accrued interest on securities transferred between interest payment dates, see page 22.	

Interest Income other than interest from All-Savers Certificates		Amount	
1 Interest income from seller-financed mortgages. (See Instructions and show name of payer.) ▶	**1**		
2 Other interest income (list name of payer) ▶			
....			
....			
....			
....	**2**		
....			
....			
....			
....			
3 Add lines 1 and 2	**3**		

Interest from All-Savers Certificates (ASCs). (See page 22.)		Amount	
4			
....	**4**		
....			
5 Add amounts on line 4	**5**		
6 Write the amount of your ASC exclusion from the worksheet on page 22 of Instructions .	**6**		
7 Subtract line 6 from line 5	**7**		
8 Add lines 3 and 7. Write your answer here and on Form 1040, line 8 . . . . . . ▶	**8**		

Part II **Dividend Income** *(See pages 9 and 22 of Instructions.)* Also complete Part III.	If you received more than $400 in gross dividends (including capital gain distributions) and other distributions on stock, or you are electing to exclude qualified reinvested dividends from a public utility, complete Part II. If you received dividends as a nominee for another, see page 22.	

Name of payer		Amount	
9			
....			
....			
....			
....	**9**		
....			
....			
....			
....			
10 Add amounts on line 9	**10**		
11 Capital gain distributions. Enter here and on line 15, Schedule D.*	**11**		
12 Nontaxable distributions. (See Instructions for adjustment to basis.)	**12**		
13 Exclusion of qualified reinvested dividends from a public utility. (See page 22 of Instructions.)	**13**		
14 Add lines 11, 12, and 13	**14**		
15 Subtract line 14 from line 10. Write your answer here and on Form 1040, line 9a . . ▶	**15**		

*If you received capital gain distributions for the year and you do not need Schedule D to report any other gains or losses, do not file that schedule. Instead, enter 40% of your capital gain distributions on Form 1040, line 14.

		Yes	No
Part III **Foreign Accounts and Foreign Trusts** *(See page 22 of Instructions.)*	If you received more than $400 of interest or dividends, OR if you had a foreign account or were a grantor of, or a transferor to, a foreign trust, you must answer both questions in Part III.		
	16 At any time during the tax year, did you have an interest in or a signature or other authority over a bank account, securities account, or other financial account in a foreign country? (See page 23 of the instructions for exceptions and filing requirements for Form 90-22.1.)		
	If "Yes," write the name of the foreign country ▶		
	17 Were you the grantor of, or transferor to, a foreign trust which existed during the current tax year, whether or not you have any beneficial interest in it? If "Yes," you may have to file Forms 3520, 3520-A, or 926		

For Paperwork Reduction Act Notice, see Form 1040 Instructions.   Schedule B (Form 1040) 1983

✿ U.S. GOVERNMENT PRINTING OFFICE: 1983-390-074 E.I. 43-0787287

Form 118 Application for Extension of Time to File U.S. Fiduciary Return

Form **2758**
(Rev. October 1976)
Department of the Treasury
Internal Revenue Service

Application for Extension of Time to File
U.S. Partnership, Fiduciary, and certain Exempt Organization Returns.
(Submit a separate application for each return)

Please type or print.

File in TRIPLICATE on or before the due date for filing the return. (See Instruction 3.)

Enter name and address exactly as it will appear on the return.

Name of taxpayer

Number and street

City or town, State, and ZIP code

Employer identification number

(See back for filing instructions and return address. Small Business Corporations filing Form 1120S, political or exempt organizations filing Form 1120–POL, or corporate exempt organizations filing Form 990–T, use Form 7004)

1. An extension of time until .... is hereby requested in which to file (check one):
   ☐ Partnership return of income, Form 1065.   ☐ Form 990   ☐ Form 990–PF
   ☐ Fiduciary income tax return, Form 1041 (estate).   ☐ Form 990–T (trust)
   ☐ Fiduciary income tax return, Form 1041 (trust).   ☐ Form 990–AR (or Own Report)
   ☐ Return of a section 4947(a) trust, Form 5227.   Check ☐ if organization does not have an office or place of business
   ☐ Return of Excise Tax under chapter 42, Form 4720. in the U.S.

2. For calendar year 19........, or other taxable year beginning .... and ending ....

3. Has an extension of time to file been previously granted for this taxable year? . . . . ☐ Yes ☐ No

4. State in detail why you need the extension, see instruction 4 on back: ....
....
....

5. IF THE EXTENSION IS FOR FORM 1041, 4720, 5227, 990–PF, or 990–T (Trust), FILL IN APPLICABLE AMOUNTS:
   (a) Tax estimated to be due on the return checked above . . . . $................................
   (b) Payment due with this application:
       (1) If an estate, at least one-quarter of the amount shown on line 5(a) above . . . . . . }
       (2) If a trust filing Form 1041 or 5227, an organization filing Form 990–PF or 990–T (Trust), . . $................................
           or an organization (or individual) filing Form 4720, enter amount shown on line 5(a), above }

Cautionary Note—*Interest accrues on any tax due on returns filed on forms listed on line 5 above, from the regular due date of the return until paid. For the rate of interest and amount of penalty due to late payment of tax, see instruction 1(a).*

Signature and Verification

Under penalties of perjury, I declare that to the best of my knowledge and belief the statements made herein are true, correct, and complete, that I am authorized to prepare this application, and that I am:

☐ A partner filing Form 1065.
☐ A fiduciary, trustee, or an officer representing the fiduciary or trustee filing Form 1041, 4720, or 5227.
☐ A fiduciary, trustee, or an officer representing the fiduciary or trustee of an exempt trust filing Form 990, 990–PF, 990–T (trust), or 990–AR.
☐ A principal officer of a corporate organization filing Form 4720, 990, 990–PF, or 990–AR.
☐ A member in good standing of the bar of the highest court of (specify jurisdiction) ....
☐ A foundation manager or disqualified person filing Form 4720 for my own liability.
☐ A certified public accountant duly qualified to practice in (specify jurisdiction) ....
☐ A person enrolled to practice before the Internal Revenue Service.
☐ A duly authorized agent holding a power of attorney. The power of attorney need not be submitted unless requested.

Signature ▶   Date ▶

THE INTERNAL REVENUE SERVICE WILL INDICATE BELOW WHETHER THE
EXTENSION IS GRANTED OR DENIED AND WILL RETURN THE ORIGINAL OF THIS APPLICATION

Notice to Applicant—To Be Completed By the Internal Revenue Service
☐ The application **IS** approved. (Please attach this form to the return.)
☐ The application **IS NOT** approved. (Please attach this form to the return.)
    However, in view of your reasons stated in the application, a 10-day grace period is granted from the date shown below or due date of the return, whichever is later. This 10-day grace period constitutes a valid extension of time for purposes of elections otherwise required to be made on timely filed returns.
☐ The application **IS NOT** approved.

    After consideration of the reasons stated in your application, we have determined the extension is not warranted. (The 10-day grace period is not granted.)
☐ The application cannot be considered, since you filed it after the due date of the return.
☐ Other ....

Director

Date   By: ....

Form 118 continued

If you want the original of this application returned to an address other than shown on page 1, please complete the section below:

Please Print or Type	Name
	Number and street
	City or town, State, and ZIP code

Instructions

1. Who may file.—You may use this application to request an extension of time to file any of the returns listed under line 1, page 1.

(a) An extension of time to file a return, unless it specifies otherwise, does not extend the time for payment of tax due. The law imposes a penalty for late payment of tax other than estimated tax figured at one-half percent a month or fractional part of a month, unless you can show reasonable cause for failure to pay when due.

Interest, which accrues from the regular due date of the return until the tax is paid, is charged whether or not an extension is granted. The interest will not be excused even if you show reasonable cause. The law provides for periodic adjustments of the interest rate, which is 7 percent for amounts outstanding on February 1, 1976 or arising thereafter.

(b) An extension of time for filing a partnership return will not apply to the individual income tax returns of the partners. If a partner desires an extension, the partner must file a separate application on Form 4868.

2. When to file.—You must file the application in sufficient time for the Internal Revenue Service to consider and act on it before the return's regular due date.

3. How and where to file.—Complete this form in triplicate and mail to the Internal Revenue Service office where you file your return. If you do not have a principal office or place of business in the United States, file this application with the Internal Revenue Service Center, 11601 Roosevelt Boulevard, Philadelphia, Pennsylvania 19155.

4. Reasons for extension.—The Internal Revenue Service will grant a reasonable extension of time for filing a return if you file a timely application that establishes you are unable to file the return by the due date because of circumstances beyond your control. Generally, an application will be considered on the basis of your efforts to fulfill your own filing responsibility, rather than on the convenience of anyone who assists you. However, consideration will be given to any circumstances that prevent your practitioner, for reasons beyond the practitioner's control, to file the return by the due date, and to circumstances in which you have been unable to get needed professional help in spite of timely efforts to do so.

You should clearly **describe** on line 4 the circumstances which will cause unavoidable delay in filing the return. Applications that give incomplete reasons, such as "illness" or "practitioner too busy," without adequate explanations, will not be approved. If

it is clear that a request for extension is frivolous, solely to gain time, the Internal Revenue Service will deny both the extension request and the 10-day grace period.

5. Extension period.—Except where an estate elects to pay tax in installments, an extension of time on an original application will generally be limited to not more than 60 days. For an estate paying tax in installments, an extension to the due date of the second installment may be allowed. A longer period of time will not be granted unless sufficient need for that extended period is clearly shown. In no event will an extension of more than 6 months be granted to an applicant within the United States.

6. Payment of tax.—The total amount of tax estimated to be due on Form 4720, 5227, 990–PF, 990–T (trust), or 1041 filed by a trust, must be paid in full on or before the normal due date of the return. The total tax estimated to be due on Form 1041 for an estate may be paid in full on or before the normal due date of the return or in four equal installments on or before the 15th day of the 4th, 7th, 10th, and 13th months following the close of the taxable year.

7. Blanket requests.—Blanket requests for extensions will not be granted. Submit a separate application for each return.

☆ U.S. GOVERNMENT PRINTING OFFICE: 1976—O-218-142— 52-0781521

Form 119 Federal (U.S.) Estate Tax Retrun

Form **706** (Rev. January 1984) Department of the Treasury Internal Revenue Service	**United States Estate Tax Return** Estate of a citizen or resident of the United States (see separate instructions) To be filed for Decedents dying after December 31, 1981, and before January 1, 1985. Section references are to the Internal Revenue Code.	OMB No. 1545-0015

Decedent's first name and middle initial (and maiden name, if any) JANE M.	Decedent's last name DOE		Date of death September 20, 1982
Domicile at time of death Minnesota	Year domicile established 1900	Date of Birth	Decedent's social security no. 000 : 00 : 0000
Name of executor John C. Doe	Executor's Address (Number and street including apartment number or rural route, city, town or post office, State and ZIP code) 1005 Easy Street, St. Paul, MN 07102 (Suggest mailing address c/o John Cranwall, 1st Trust Bldg., St. Paul, MN 55105)		
Executor's social security number (See instructions) : :			

Name and location of court where will was probated or estate administered Ramsey County Probate Court	Case number 999999

If decedent died testate check here ▶ ☒ and attach a certified copy of the will.   If Form 4768 is attached check here ▶ ☐

Authorization to receive confidential tax information under regulations section 601.502(c)(3)(ii), to act as the estate's representative before the Internal Revenue Service, and to make written or oral presentations on behalf of the estate if return prepared by an attorney, accountant, or enrolled agent for the executor:

Name of representative (print or type) John Cranwall	State MN	Address (Number and street, city, State and ZIP code) Cranwall & Schuster, 999 St. Paul Trust Company Building, St. Paul, MN 55105

I declare that I am the attorney/accountant/enrolled agent (strike out the words that do not apply) for the executor and prepared this return for the executor. I am not under suspension or disbarment from practice before the Internal Revenue Service and am qualified to practice in the State shown above—

Signature /s/ John Cranwall	Date June 20, 1983	Telephone Number 612-555-5555

Tax Computation

1	Total gross estate (from Recapitulation, page 3, line 10)	1	399,648
2	Total allowable deductions (from Recapitulation, page 3, line 20)	2	349,848
3	Taxable estate (subtract line 2 from line 1).	3	49,800
4	Adjusted taxable gifts (total taxable gifts (within the meaning of section 2503) made by the decedent after December 31, 1976, other than gifts that are includible in decedent's gross estate (section 2001(b))).	4	– –
5	Add line 3 and line 4	5	49,800
6	Tentative tax on the amount on line 5 from Table A in the instructions	6	10,552
7	Total gift taxes payable with respect to gifts by the decedent after December 31, 1976. Include gift taxes paid by the decedent's spouse for split gifts (section 2513) only if the decedent was the donor of these gifts and they are includible in the decedent's gross estate	7	
8	Gross estate tax (subtract line 7 from line 6)	8	10,552
9	Unified credit against estate tax from Table B in the instructions . . . . . [9] 62,800		
10	Adjustment to unified credit. See instructions . . . . [10] 0		
11	Allowable unified credit (subtract line 10 from line 9).	11	62,800
12	Subtract line 11 from line 8 (but do not enter less than zero).	12	0
13	Credit for State death taxes. Do not enter more than line 12. See Table C in the instructions and **attach credit evidence** (see instructions)	13	
14	Subtract line 13 from line 12.	14	
15	Credit for Federal gift taxes on pre-1977 gifts (section 2012) (attach computation) . [15]		
16	Credit for foreign death taxes (from Schedule(s) P). (Attach Form(s) 706CE) . . [16]		
17	Credit for tax on prior transfers (from Schedule Q) . . . . [17]		
18	Total (add lines 15, 16, and 17)	18	
19	Net estate tax (subtract line 18 from line 14)	19	
20	Prior payments. Explain in an attached statement . . . . [20]		
21	United States Treasury bonds redeemed in payment of estate tax. . . . . [21]		
22	Total (add lines 20 and 21)	22	
23	Balance due (subtract line 22 from line 19)	23	NONE

Note: *Please attach the necessary supplemental documents. You must attach the Death Certificate.*

Under penalties of perjury, I declare that I have examined this return, including accompanying schedules and statements, and to the best of my knowledge and belief, it is true, correct, and complete. Declaration of preparer other than the executor is based on all information of which preparer has any knowledge.

/s/ John C. Doe Signature(s) of executor(s) John C. Doe	June 20, 1983 Date

/s/ John Cranwall Signature of preparer other than executor John Cranwall	Cranwall & Schuster, 999 St. Paul Trust Co. Bldg., St. Paul, MN 55105 Address (and ZIP code)	June 20, 1983 Date

For Paperwork Reduction Act Notice, see page 1 of the instructions.   Form **706** (Rev. 1-84)

Form 119 continued

Form 706 (Rev. 1-84)

Estate of: JANE M. DOE

Elections by the Executor

Please check the "Yes" or "No" box for each question.	Yes	No
1 Do you elect the alternate valuation?		X
2 Do you elect the special use valuation?		X
If "Yes," complete and attach Schedule N and the agreements required by the instructions to Schedule N.		
3 Are you excluding from the decedent's gross estate the value of a lump-sum distribution described in section 2039(f)(2)?		X
If "Yes," you must attach the information required by the instructions.		
4 Do you elect to claim a marital deduction for an otherwise nondeductible interest under section 2056(b)(7)?		X
If "Yes," please attach the additional information required by the instructions.		
5 Do you elect to pay the tax in installments as described in section 6166?.		
6 Do you elect to postpone the part of the tax attributable to a reversionary or remainder interest as described in section 6163?		

General Information

1   Death certificate no. and issuing authority (attach a copy of the death certificate to this return).
    123456

2   Decedent's business or occupation. If retired check here ▶   [X]   and state decedent's former business or occupation.
    Real Estate Broker

3   Marital status of the decedent at time of death
    [X] Married
    ☐ Widow or widower—Name and date of death of deceased spouse ▶ _____

    ☐ Single
    ☐ Legally separated
    ☐ Divorced—Date divorce decree became final ▶

4a Surviving spouse's name	4b Social security number	4c Amount received (see instructions)
John C. Doe	111 11 1111	287,133.00

5   Individuals (other than the surviving spouse), trusts, or other estates who receive benefits from the estate (do not include charitable beneficiaries shown in Schedule O) (see instructions). For Privacy Act Notice, see the Instructions for Form 1040.

Name of individual, trust or estate receiving $1,000 or more	Identifying number	Relationship to decedent	Amount (see instructions)
Sandy R. Doe	222-22-2222	Daughter	35,000.00
Jay A. Doe	333-33-3333	Brother	10,000.00

All unascertainable beneficiaries and those who receive less than $1,000 . . . . ▶

Total 45,000.00

(Continued on next page)

Form 119 continued

Form 706 (Rev. 1-84)

Estate of: JANE M. DOE

Please check the "Yes" or "No" box for each question.

		Yes	No
6	Does the gross estate contain any section 2044 property?		X
7a	Have Federal gift tax returns ever been filed?.		X
	If "Yes," please attach copies of the returns, if available, and furnish the following information:		
7b	Period(s) covered 7c Internal Revenue office(s) where filed		

If you answer "Yes" to any of questions 8-15, you must attach additional information as described in the instructions.

		Yes	No
8a	Was there any insurance on the decedent's life that was not included on the return as part of the gross estate?		X
8b	Did the decedent own any insurance on the life of another that is not included in the gross estate?		X
9	Did the decedent at the time of death own any property as a joint tenant with right of survivorship in which (1) one or more of the other joint tenants was someone other than the decedent's spouse and (2) less than the full value of the property was included on the return as part of the gross estate?	X	
10	Did the decedent, at the time of death, own any interest in a partnership or unincorporated business or any stock in an inactive or closely held corporation?		X
11	Were any of the contents of any safe deposit box which the decedent either owned or had access to not included on the return as part of the gross estate?		X
12	Did the decedent make any transfer described in section 2035, 2036, 2037 or 2038 (see the instructions for Schedule G)?	X	
13	Were there in existence at the time of the decedent's death:		X
a	Any trusts created by the decedent during his or her lifetime?		X
b	Any trusts not created by the decedent under which the decedent possessed any power, beneficial interest or trusteeship?	X	
14	Did the decedent ever possess, exercise or release any general power of appointment?	X	
15	Was the marital deduction computed under the transitional rule of Public Law 97-34, section 403(e)(3) (Economic Recovery Tax Act of 1981)?		
	If "Yes," attach a separate computation of the marital deduction, enter the amount on line 18 of the Recapitulation, and note line 18 "computation attached."		

Recapitulation

Item number	Gross estate	Alternate value	Value at date of death
1	Schedule A—Real Estate		72,750
2	Schedule B—Stocks and Bonds		9,648
3	Schedule C—Mortgages, Notes, and Cash		76,350
4	Schedule D—Insurance on the Decedent's Life (attach Form(s) 712)		30,100
5	Schedule E—Jointly Owned Property (attach Form(s) 712 for life insurance)		80,000
6	Schedule F—Other Miscellaneous Property (attach Form(s) 712 for life insurance) . .		26,000
7	Schedule G—Transfers During Decedent's Life (attach Form(s) 712 for life insurance)		50,000
8	Schedule H—Powers of Appointment.		50,000
9	Schedule I—Annuities		4,800
10	Total gross estate (add items 1 through 9). Enter here and on page 1, line 1		399,648

Item number	Deductions		Amount
11	Schedule J—Funeral Expenses and Expenses Incurred in Administering Property Subject to Claims		4,125
12	Schedule K—Debts of the Decedent		2,610
13	Schedule K—Mortgages and Liens.		40,000
14	Total of Items 11 through 13		46,735
15	Allowable amount of deductions from item 14 (see the instructions for line 15 of the Recapitulation).		46,735
16	Schedule L—Net Losses During Administration		0
17	Schedule L—Expenses Incurred in Administering Property Not Subject to Claims		0
18	Schedule M—Bequests, etc., to Surviving Spouse		287,133
19	Schedule O—Charitable, Public, and Similar Gifts and Bequests		16,000
20	Total allowable deductions (add lines 15 through 19). Enter here and on page 1, line 2		349,848

Page **3**

Form 119 continued

Form 706 (Rev. 1-84)

Estate of: JANE M. DOE

SCHEDULE A—Real Estate

(For jointly owned property that must be disclosed on Schedule E, see the Instructions for Schedule E.)

Item number	Description	Alternate valuation date	Alternate value	Value at date of death
1	House and Lot, 1005 Easy Street, St. Paul, Minn., (Lot 615, Block 42 Reisers Addition to St. Paul, Ramsey County) in name of decedent. Copy of Appraisal attached as Exhibit _____.			50,000.000
2	An undivided one-fourth interest in Duplex and Lots, 776 Noname Road, St. Paul, Minn. (Lots 16 & 17, Block 20, Lovey's Addition to St. Paul, Ramsey County) in name of decedent. Copy of Appraisal attached as Exhibit _____. (1/4 x $91,000) (Assume all rent due and collected prior to death)			22,750.00
	Total from continuation schedule(s) (or additional sheet(s)) attached to this schedule			
	TOTAL. (Also enter on the Recapitulation, page 3, at item 1.)			72,750.00

(If more space is needed, attach the continuation schedule from the end of this package or additional sheets of the same size.)

Schedule A—Page 4

Form 119 continued

Form 706 (Rev. 1-84)

Estate of: JANE M. DOE

SCHEDULE B—Stocks and Bonds

(For jointly owned property that must be disclosed on Schedule E, see the Instructions for Schedule E.)

Item number	Description including face amount of bonds or number of shares and par value where needed for identification. Give CUSIP number if available.	Unit value	Alternate valuation date	Alternate value	Value at date of death
1	100 shares American Telephone and Telegraph, Common, NYSE	$50.00			5,000.00
2	1,000 shares Minnesota Co-op, Common, OTC	$ 4.50			4,500.00
3	$50.00 U.S. Government Savings Bond, Series E, No. R4502363E, Dated April 1963				74.00
4	$50.00 U.S. Government Savings Bond, Series E, No. R4502364E, Dated April 1963				74.00
	(Assume no accrued dividends on items 1 and 2)				
	Total from continuation schedules(s) (or additional sheet(s)) attached to this schedule . . .				
	TOTAL. (Also enter on the Recapitulation, page 3, at item 2.)				9,648.00

(If more space is needed, attach the continuation schedule from the end of this package or additional sheets of the same size.)

Schedule B—Page 5

Form 119 continued

Form 706 (Rev. 1-84)

Estate of: JANE M. DOE

SCHEDULE C—Mortgages, Notes, and Cash

(For jointly owned property that must be disclosed on Schedule E, see the Instructions for Schedule E.)

Item number	Description	Alternate valuation date	Alternate value	Value at date of death
1	American Express traveler's checks No. 10008 through 100017 in the amount of $100.00 each in name of decedent, uncashed at date of death			1,000.00
2	American National Bank of St. Paul, St. Paul, Minn., passbook savings certificate #44-444 dated 1/20/82 in name of decedent with interest at 5.5% per annum payable monthly to decedent. (Assume interest check in the amount of $68.75 payable 9/20/82 was received by decedent and deposited to checking account on 9/20/82			15,000.00
3	First National City Bank of St. Paul, St. Paul, Minn., checking account #55-5555 in name of decedent, reconciled balance as of date of death			50,000.00
4	$10,000 - Forrest Furriers Promissory Note dated 3/20/77 payable 3/20/84 with interest payable at 7% per annum on March 20			10,000.00
5	Interest accrued on Item 4 from 3/20/82 to 9/20/82			350.00
	Total from continuation schedule(s) (or additional sheet(s)) attached to this schedule . . .			76,350.00
	TOTAL. (Also enter on the Recapitulation, page 3, at item 3.)			

(If more space is needed, attach the continuation schedule from the end of this package or additional sheets of the same size.)

Form 119 continued

Form 706 (Rev. 1-84)

Estate of: JANE M. DOE

SCHEDULE D—Insurance on the Decedent's Life

Item number	Description	Alternate valuation date	Alternate value	Value at date of death
1	Prudential Life Insurance Company Policy #11-1111-123 Jay A. Dee, beneficiary Face Amount $10,000			10,000.00
2	Minnesota Life Insurance Company Policy #J 666221 Estate of Jane M. Doe, beneficiary Face Amount $20,000 Accumulated dividends 100 $20,100			20,100.00
	Total from continuation schedule(s) (or additional sheet(s)) attached to this schedule . . .			
	TOTAL. (Also enter on the Recapitulation, page 3, at item 4.)			30,100.00

(If more space is needed, attach the continuation schedule from the end of this package or additional sheets of the same size.)

Schedule D—Page 7

Form 119 continued

Form 706 (Rev. 1-84)

Estate of: JANE M. DOE

SCHEDULE E—Jointly Owned Property

PART I.— Qualified Joint Interests—Interests Held by the Decedent and His or Her Spouse as the Only Joint Tenants (Section 2040(b)(2))

Item number	Description For securities, give CUSIP number, if available.	Alternate valuation date	Alternate value	Value at date of death
Total from continuation schedule(s) (or additional sheet(s)) attached to this schedule.				
1(a)	Totals.			
1(b)	Amounts included in gross estate (½ of line 1(a))			NONE

PART II.— All Other Joint Interests

2(a) State the name and address of each surviving co-tenant. If there are more than 3 surviving co-tenants list the additional co-tenants on an attached sheet.

Name	Address (Number and street, city, State, and ZIP code)
A. John C. Doe	1005 Easy St., St. Paul, MN 07102
B. Sandy R. Doe	1005 Easy St., St. Paul, MN 07102

C.

Item number	Enter letter for co-tenant	Description (including alternate valuation date if any) For securities, give CUSIP number, if available.	Percentage includible	Includible alternate value	Includible value at date of death
1	A	1,000 shares American National Slide Rule Company, Common, NYSE at $75.00/share			75,000.00
2	B	100 shares Minnesota Company, Common, NYSE at $50.00/share			5,000.00
		(Assume surviving joint tenants provided no consideration)			
	Total from additional sheet(s) attached to this schedule				
2(b)	Total other joint interests				80,000.00
Total includible joint interests (add lines 1(b) and 2(b)). Also enter on the Recapitulation, page 3, at item 5					80,000.00

(If more space is needed, attach the continuation schedule from the end of this package or additional sheets of the same size.)

Schedule E—Page 8

Form 119 continued

Form 706 (Rev. 1-84)

Estate of: JANE M. DOE

SCHEDULE F—Other Miscellaneous Property Not Reportable Under Any Other Schedule

(For jointly owned property that must be disclosed on Schedule E, see the Instructions for Schedule E.)

		Yes	No
1	Did the decedent, at the time of death, own any articles of artistic or collectible value in excess of $3,000 or any collections whose artistic or collectible value combined at date of death exceeded $3,000? . . . . If "Yes," full details must be submitted on this schedule.		X
2	Has the decedent's estate, spouse, or any other person, received (or will receive) any bonus or award as a result of the decedent's employment or death?. . . . . If "Yes," full details must be submitted on this schedule.		X
3	Did the decedent at the time of death have, or have access to, a safe deposit box?. . . . . If "Yes," state location, and if held in joint names of decedent and another, state name and relationship of joint depositor. If any of the contents of the safe deposit box are omitted from the schedules in this return, explain fully why omitted.		X
4	Did the decedent, at the time of death, own any other miscellaneous property not reportable under any other schedule?. . . . . . If "Yes," full details must be submitted on this schedule.		X

Item number	Description For securities, give CUSIP number, if available.	Alternate valuation date	Alternate value	Value at date of death
1	Mink coat - Appraisal attached as Exhibit _____.			1,500.00
2	1978 Chevrolet - Nova, Vehicle Identification #6778899926 - Bluebook market value			2,000.00
3	Judgment dated February 19, 1978 against Forrest A. Redding, collected in full on Dec. 20, 1982			20,000.00
4	Clothing and personal effects			500.00
5	Furniture and household goods located at homestead			2,000.00
	Total from continuation schedule(s) (or additional sheet(s)) attached to this schedule			
	TOTAL. (Also enter on the Recapitulation, page 3, at item 6.)			26,000.00

(If more space is needed, attach the continuation schedule from the end of this package or additional sheets of the same size.)

Schedule F—Page 9

Form 119 continued

Form 706 (Rev. 1-84)

Estate of: JANE M. DOE

SCHEDULE G—Transfers During Decedent's Life

Item number	Description For securities, give CUSIP number, if available.	Alternate valuation date	Alternate value	Value at date of death
	A. Gift tax paid by the decedent or the estate for all gifts made by the decedent or his or her spouse within 3 years before the decedent's death (section 2035(c))	X X X X X		-0-
	B. Transfers includible under sections 2035(a), 2036, 2037 or 2038:			
1	Cash to John C. Doe, surviving spouse on April 20, 1982			20,000.00
2	Cash to Sandy R. Doe, daughter on April 20, 1982 Gift tax return filed on 2/15/83 for above gifts. Spouse jointed in on gift to daughter.			30,000.00
	Total from continuation schedule(s) (or additional sheet(s)) attached to this schedule			50,000.00
	TOTAL. (Also enter on the Recapitulation, page 3, at item 7.)			

SCHEDULE H—Powers of Appointment

Item number	Description	Alternate valuation date	Alternate value	Value at date of death
1	Trust created by decedent's uncle with income distributable to decedent for her lifetime and thereafter to her daughter; St. Paul Trust Co., trustee; decedent had no power of appointment nor other incidents of ownership, therefore trust assets are not taxable to decedent's estate			-0-
2	Trust created under agreement dated 12/2/50 by father of decedent for decedent's benefit under which she had a general power of appointment (to distribute income and/or principal) which power had not been exercised during her lifetime, but which decedent exercised under her will. Trust consists of 500 shares of Green Giant common stock and undistributed earnings (dividends) thereon	. . . .	. . . .	50,000.00
	Total from continuation schedule(s) (or additional sheet(s)) attached to this schedule			
	TOTAL. (Also enter on the Recapitulation, page 3, at item 8.)			50,000.00

(If more space is needed, attach the continuation schedule from the end of this package or additional sheets of the same size.)

Schedules G and H—Page 10

Form 119 continued

Form 706 (Rev. 1-84)

Estate of: JANE M. DOE

SCHEDULE I—Annuities

Note: *The total combined exclusion for lump sum distributions and "Annuities Under Approved Plans" is $100,000 for the estates of decedents dying after December 31, 1982 (see instructions).*

		Yes	No
1a	Was the decedent, immediately before death, receiving an annuity described in the "General" paragraph of the instructions for this schedule?.	X	
1b	If "Yes," was the annuity paid pursuant to an approved plan described in the instructions for this schedule?		X
1c	If the answer to "1b" is "Yes," state the ratio of the decedent's contribution to the total purchase price of the annuity.		
2a	If the decedent was employed at the time of death, did an annuity as described in paragraph (d) of the "Annuity defined" instructions for this schedule become payable to any beneficiary because the beneficiary survived the decedent?.		N/A
2b	If "Yes," state the ratio of the decedent's contribution to the total purchase price of the annuity.		
3a	Did an annuity under an individual retirement account, annuity, or bond described in section 2039(e) become payable to any beneficiary because the beneficiary survived the decedent?		X
3b	If "Yes," is the annuity payable to the beneficiary for life or for at least 36 months following decedent's death?.		N/A
3c	If the answer to "3a" is "Yes," state the ratio of the amount paid for the individual retirement account, annuity, or bond that was not allowable as an income tax deduction under section 219 (other than a rollover contribution) to the total amount paid for the account, annuity, or bond. N/A		

Item number	Description Show the entire value of the annuity before any exclusions.	Alternate valuation date	Includible alternate value	Includible value at date of death
1	Ecko Life Insurance Company Policy #99-9999. Annuity of $100 per month payable to decedent for life, thereafter to John C. Doe, husband of decedent (value of annuity based upon life expectancy of male age 77 is approximately 4.000 x 1,200)			4,800.00
	Total from continuation schedule(s) (or additional sheet(s)) attached to this schedule . . .			
	TOTAL. (Also enter on the Recapitulation, page 3, at item 9.)			4,800.00

(If more space is needed, attach the continuation schedule from the end of this package or additional sheets of the same size.)

Schedule I—Page 11

Form 119 continued

Form 706 (Rev. 1-84)

Estate of: JANE M. DOE

SCHEDULE J—Funeral Expenses and Expenses Incurred in Administering Property Subject to Claims

Note: *Do not list on this schedule expenses of administering property not subject to claims. For those expenses, see the Instructions for Schedule L.*

If executors' commissions, attorney fees, etc., are claimed and allowed as a deduction for estate tax purposes, they are not allowable as a deduction in computing the taxable income of the estate for Federal income tax purposes. They are allowable as an income tax deduction on Form 1041 if a waiver is filed to waive the deduction on Form 706 (see Form 1041 instructions).

Item number	Description		Amount
	A. Funeral expenses:		
1	Newark & Newark Funeral Home - funeral	2,500.00	
2	Morningside Florists - funeral flowers	100.00	
3	Happy Acres Cemetery - burial	1,000.00	
4	Stone Monument Company - gravestone	500.00	
5	Rev. B. Stone - funeral	25.00	
	Total	X X X X X	4,125.00
	B. Administration expenses:		
1	Executors' commissions—amount estimated/agreed upon/paid. (Strike out the words that do not apply.).	X X X X X	--
2	Attorney fees—amount estimated/agreed upon/paid. (Strike out the words that do not apply.)	X X X X X	--
3	Accountant fees—amount estimated/agreed upon/paid. (Strike out the words that do not apply.)	X X X X X	--
4	Miscellaneous expenses: Administration expenses claimed on estate's fiduciary income tax return		
	Total miscellaneous expenses.	X X X X X	

TOTAL. (Also enter on the Recapitulation, page 3, at item 11.) 4,125.00

(If more space is needed, attach additional sheets of the same size.)   **Schedule J—Page 12**

Form 119 continued

Form 706 (Rev. 1-84)

Estate of: JANE M. DOE

SCHEDULE K—Debts of the Decedent, and Mortgages and Liens

Item number	Debts of the Decedent—Creditor and nature of claim, and allowable death taxes	Amount
1	Porta Veta Hospital - last illness expense	850.00
2	Ace's Plumbing Co. - plumbing debt contract for by decedent, company claims $480.00 is owed, personal representative claims $230.00 is owed	230.00
3	St. Paul Telephone Company - telephone	50.00
4	St. Paul Electric Company - electric	100.00
5	Harvey's Garbage Pick-up - rubbish removal	50.00
6	Dr. Norma J. Dennison - medical	600.00
7	St. Paul Rents (wheelchair) - medical	50.00
8	Commissioner of Revenue - balance due on 1982 Minn. Gift Tax Return	680.00
	TOTAL. (Also enter on the Recapitulation, page 3, at item 12.)	2,610.00

Item number	Mortgages and Liens—Description	Amount
1	Mortgage on house and lot (Sched. A, Item 1) at St. Paul Bank and Trust Co. of St. Paul, including accrued interest to date of death	30,000.00
2	Mortgage on duplex and lots, (Sched. A, Item 2) at St. Paul Bank and Trust Co. of St. Paul, including accrued interest to date of death (1/4 x $40,000)	10,000.00
	TOTAL. (Also enter on the Recapitulation, page 3, at item 13.).	40,000.00

SCHEDULE L—Net Losses During Administration and Expenses Incurred in Administering Property Not Subject to Claims

Item number	Net losses during administration (**Note:** Do not deduct losses claimed on a Federal income tax return.)	Amount
1		
	TOTAL. (Also enter on the Recapitulation, page 3, at item 16.)	NONE

Item number	Expenses incurred in administering property not subject to claims (Indicate whether estimated, agreed upon, or paid.)	Amount
1		
	TOTAL. (Also enter on the Recapitulation, page 3, at item 17.).	NONE

(If more space is needed, attach additional sheets of the same size.)   **Schedules K and L—Page 13**

Form 119 continued

Form 706 (Rev. 1-84)

Estate of: JANE M. DOE

SCHEDULE M—Bequests, etc., to Surviving Spouse

		Yes	No
1 Did any property pass to the surviving spouse as a result of a qualified disclaimer?. . . . . If "Yes," attach a copy of the written disclaimer required by section 2518(b).			X

Item number	Description of property interests passing to surviving spouse		Value
1	Jointly owned property, Schedule E, Item 1		75,000.00
2	Transfers, Schedule G, Item 1		20,000.00
3	Property passing under will to spouse:		
	Real Estate, Sched. A	72,750.00	
	Stocks & Bonds, Sched. B	9,648.00	
	Mortgages, Notes & Cash, Sched. C	76,350.00	
	Insurance payable to estate, Sched. D. Item 2	20,100.00	
	Misc. Property, Sched. F	26,000.00	
	Powers of Appointment, Sched. H, Item 2	50,000.00	
		254,848.00	
	Less:		
	Deductions 46,735.00		
	Charitable devises 16,000.00	62,735.00	192,113.00

2 Total		287,113.00
3 (a) Federal estate tax payable out of property interests listed above		
(b) Other death taxes payable out of property interests listed above		
(c) Add items (a) and (b).		
4 Net value of property interests listed above (subtract 3(c) from 2). Also enter on the Recapitulation, page 3, at item 18. . . .		287,113.00

(If more space is needed, attach additional sheets of the same size.)   **Schedule M—Page 14**

Note: Annuity payable to spouse does not qualify for martial deduction
        (terminable interest)

Form 119 continued

Form 706 (Rev. 1-84)

Estate of: JANE M. DOE

SCHEDULE N—Section 2032A Valuation

Enter the requested information for each party who received any interest in the specially valued property. Also complete and attach the required agreements described in the instructions.

	Name	Address
A		
B		
C		
D		
E		
F		
G		
H		

	Identifying number	Relationship to decedent	Fair market value	Special use value
A				
B				
C				
D				
E				
F				
G				
H				

SCHEDULE O—Charitable, Public, and Similar Gifts and Bequests

		Yes	No
1(a)	If the transfer was made by will, has any action been instituted to have interpreted or to contest the will or any provision thereof affecting the charitable deductions claimed in this schedule?		X
	If "Yes," full details must be submitted with this schedule.		
1(b)	According to the information and belief of the person or persons filing the return, is any such action designed or contemplated? . . .		X
	If "Yes," full details must be submitted with this schedule.		
2	Did any property pass to charity as the result of a qualified disclaimer?		X
	If "Yes," attach a copy of the written disclaimer required by section 2518(b).		

Item number	Name and address of beneficiary	Character of institution	Amount
1	American Cancer Society	Medical Research	10,000.00
2	Girl's Clubs of America	Charitable	5,000.00
3	Newark Institute of Higher Learning	Educational Research	1,000.00

3 Total		16,000.00
4 (a) Federal estate tax payable out of property interests listed above	NONE	
(b) Other death taxes payable out of property interests listed above	NONE	
∗ Assume will provides for payment of all taxes out of residue		
(c) Add items (a) and (b).		
5 Net value of property interests listed above (subtract 4(c) from 3). Also enter on the Recapitulation, page 3, at item 19 . . .		16,000.00

(If more space is needed, attach additional sheets of the same size.)   **Schedules N and O—Page 15**

Form 119 continued

Form 706 (Rev. 1-84)

Estate of:

SCHEDULE P—Credit for Foreign Death Taxes

List all foreign countries to which death taxes have been paid and for which credit is claimed on this return.

If credit is claimed for death taxes paid to more than one foreign country, compute the credit for taxes paid to one country on this sheet and attach a separate copy of Schedule P for each of the other countries.

The credit computed on this sheet is for _____
(Name of death tax or taxes)

_____ imposed in _____
(Name of country)

Credit is computed under the _____
(Insert title of treaty or statute)

Citizenship (Nationality) of decedent at time of death _____

(All amounts and values must be entered in United States money)

1 Total of estate, inheritance, legacy and succession taxes imposed in the country named above attributable to property situated in that country, subjected to these taxes, and included in the gross estate (as defined by statute)	
2 Value of the gross estate (adjusted, if necessary, according to the instructions for item 2)	
3 Value of property situated in that country, subjected to death taxes imposed in that country, and included in the gross estate (adjusted, if necessary, according to the instructions for item 3)	
4 Tax imposed by section 2001 reduced by the total credits claimed under sections 2010, 2011, and 2012 (see instructions)	
5 Amount of Federal estate tax attributable to property specified at item 3. (Divide item 3 by item 2 and multiply the result by item 4.)	
6 Credit for death taxes imposed in the country named above (the smaller of item 1 or item 5). Also enter on page 1, line 16	

SCHEDULE Q—Credit for Tax on Prior Transfers

	Name of transferor	Social security number	IRS office where estate tax return was filed	Date of death
A				
B				
C				

Check here ▶ ☐ if section 2013(f) (special valuation of farm, etc., real property) adjustments to the computation of the credit were made (see instructions).

Check here ▶ ☐ if section 2013(g) (generation-skipping transfers) adjustments to the computation of the credit were made (see instructions).

Item	Transferor			Total A, B, & C
	A	B	C	
1 Transferee's tax as apportioned (from worksheet, (line 7 + line 8) x line 35 for each column) . . .				
2 Transferor's tax (from each column of worksheet, line 20)				
3 Maximum amount before percentage requirement (for each column, enter amount from line 1 or 2, whichever is smaller)				
4 Percentage allowed (each column) (see instructions).	%	%	%	
5 Credit allowable (line 3 x line 4 for each column)				
6 TOTAL Credit allowable (Add columns A, B, and C of line 5). Enter here and on line 17 of the Tax Computation.				

Schedules P and Q—Page 16

Appendix B

Sample Marital Deduction Testamentary Trust

LAST WILL AND TESTAMENT OF JOHN P. DOE

I, John P. Doe, a/k/a _____, of _____, City of _____, County of
_____, State of _____, being of sound and disposing mind and memory,
and not acting under undue influence of any person, do make, publish,
and declare this document to be my last will and testament, and do
hereby expressly revoke all wills and codicils previously made by me.

(alias)   (address)

Article I

I hereby direct my personal representative, hereinafter named, to
pay all my just debts, administrative expenses, and expenses for my last
illness, funeral, and burial out of my estate.

Article II

I give my homestead legally described as _____, which I own in
_____ County, State of _____, to my wife _____, in fee simple, if she
survives me.

Article III

I give my diamond ring to my son, _____, and my
collection of guns and rifles to my son, _____.

(name and address)

Article IV

I give all my other personal property including my automobiles, household furnishings, clothing, jewelry, ornaments, books, and personal effects of every kind used about my home or person to my wife, _____, to do with as she sees fit, if she survives me.

Article V

If my wife, _____, survives me, I give to the _____ of _____ as

(name of individual or corporate trustee, e.g., a bank)   (address), (city), and (state)

trustee of a trust to be known as "TRUST A", assets of my estate to be selected by my personal representative and having a value which, when added to the value of all interests in property passing to my wife, either by this will or by other means, in a manner which qualifies for the marital deduction under the provisions of the United States Internal Revenue Code in effect at the time of my death. Only assets qualifying for the marital deduction shall be allocated to Trust A. My personal representative shall satisfy the foregoing transfer (devise) with such assets as will qualify for said marital deduction and shall compute all values of assets for these purposes in accordance with the Federal Estate Tax values finally computed in my estate except the assets allocated to "TRUST A" shall have an aggregate market value which fairly represents the net appreciation or depreciation of the available property on the date or dates of distribution.

TRUST A shall be administered and distributed by my trustee as follows:

1. Beginning on the date of my death, the net income from TRUST A shall be paid to my wife, _____, in convenient installments to be determined by my trustee, but at least annually, during her life.

2. My trustee shall pay to my wife or apply for her benefit such amounts from the principal of TRUST A as she shall request in writing. In addition, my trustee may pay to my wife or apply for her benefit amounts of the principal of TRUST A as it determines is necessary or advisable for her care, comfort, support, maintenance and welfare, including reasonable luxuries.

3. Upon the death of my wife, my trustee shall distribute the entire assets in TRUST A, including income, to appointee or appointees in the manner and proportions as my wife may designate by her last will which shall expressly refer to this general power of appointment; included in the power shall be her right to appoint free of any other trust provisions hereunder. This general power of appointment conferred upon my wife shall exist immediately upon my death and shall be exercisable by my wife exclusively and in all events.

4. If, under the above provisions, any portion of TRUST A is not disposed of, it shall be added to TRUST B of ARTICLE VI and administered and distributed as a part of TRUST B.

5. It is my intention that TRUST A shall qualify for the marital deduction which is allowed under the Federal Estate Tax provisions of the Internal Revenue Code in effect at the time of my death. Any provisions of this will which relate to TRUST A shall be so construed and questions pertaining to TRUST A shall be resolved accordingly.

6. If my wife pre-deceases me or the creation of TRUST A does not effectively reduce the Federal Estate Tax payable by reason of my death, the devise and bequest of this ARTICLE IV shall lapse and no TRUST A shall be established.

Article VI

I hereby direct my personal representative to pay out of my residuary estate (and not from TRUST A) all estate, income, and inheritance taxes assessed against my taxable estate or the recipients thereof, whether passing by this will or by other means, without contribution or reimbursement from any person.

Article VII

I give the residue of my estate to _____
(name of individual or corporate trustee)

of _____, as trustee of a separate trust which shall be
(address, city, state)

known as "TRUST B", and which shall be administered and distributed by my trustee as follows:

1. During the life of my wife, _____:

   (a) Beginning on the date of my death, the net income from TRUST B shall be paid to my wife, _____, in convenient installments to be determined by my trustee, but at least annually, during her life.

   (b) If there are not sufficient principal funds readily available in TRUST A, then in addition to the net income from TRUST B, my trustee may pay to my wife or apply for her benefit sums from the principal of TRUST B as my trustee determines to be necessary or advisable to provide for her proper care, support, and maintenance.

   (c) My trustee may also pay to or apply for the benefit of any child or other issue of mine sums from the principal of TRUST B as my trustee determines to be necessary in order to provide for their proper care, support, maintenance and education. It is not required that such payments be for the equal benefit of my children and other issue.

2. After the death of my wife, _____, or in the event she does not survive me, then upon my death, my trustee shall administer and distribute TRUST B as follows:

   (a) Until my youngest living child reaches the age of twenty-five (25) years, my trustee may pay to or apply directly for the benefit of my children and other issue sums from the net income and principal of TRUST B as my trustee determines necessary to provide for their proper care, support, maintenance and education. It is not required that such payments be for the equal benefit of my children and other issue.

   (b) When my youngest living child has reached the age of twenty-five (25) years, my trustee shall divide TRUST B into equal shares and shall provide one share for each of my then living children, and one share to be divided equally among the living issue, collectively, of each deceased child of mine. In making such division, my trustee shall take into account all advances of principal to a child made after such child reached the age of twenty-five (25) years. It shall be within the discretion of my trustee to take into account some, none or all advances of principal to a child made before such child had reached the age of twenty-five (25) years. After such division has been made, said shares shall be distributed outright to such children and to the issue of deceased children by right of representation.

Article VIII

If at any time before final distribution of my estate or trust estate, it happens that there not be in existence anyone who is or might become entitled to receive benefits therefrom as hereinabove provided, then upon the occurrence of such event, all of my estate and trust estate then remaining shall be paid over and distributed outright to my heirs-at-law, in such proportions as though I had at that time died without a will, a resident of the State of _____, in accordance with the intestate succession laws of personal property of the State of _____ now/then in effect.

Article IX

It is an express condition of this will, which shall control over all other provisions, that in no event shall the duration of any trust created herein continue for a period longer than the lives of all of my wife, _____, and of any of my issue who may be living at the time of my death, and the survivor of all of them and twenty-one (21) years thereafter, and at the end of such time the trustee shall distribute the entire trust estate, principal and any undistributed income outright to the persons then entitled to receive the income therefrom or to have it accumulated for their benefit, in shares which shall be the same as those in which such income is then being distributed to, or accumulated for, them.

Article X

My trustee shall have all powers and authority necessary or advisable to ensure the proper administration and distribution of each trust created by my will. Except as I may otherwise expressly direct or require in my will and in extension but not in limitation of the powers provided by applicable _____ law, I hereby grant to my trustee as to
(state)
any properties, real, personal, or mixed, at any time constituting a part of any trust hereunder and without the necessity of notice to or license or approval of any court or person, full power and authority during the term of such and in the continuing sole discretion of my trustee:

1. To retain any assets, including cash, for so long as it deems advisable, whether or not such assets are hereinafter authorized for investment; to sell, exchange, mortgage, lease, or otherwise dispose of any assets of my trust estate for terms within and extending beyond the term of such trust; and to receive any additional properties acceptable to the trustee, from whatever source.

2. Within the trustee's discretion, to invest, reinvest, or exchange assets for, any securities and properties, including but not limited to common and preferred stocks, and no statutes, rules of law, custom or usage shall limit the selection of investments; and to commingle for the purpose of investment all or any part of the funds of said trust in any common trust fund or funds now or hereafter maintained by the trustee.

3. To collect, receive, and obtain receipts for any principal or income; to enforce, defend against, compromise or settle any claim by or against the trust; and to vote or issue proxies to vote, oppose or join in any plans for reorganization, and to exercise any other rights incident to the ownership of any stocks, bonds or other properties which constitute all or a part of the trust estate.

4. To hold assets in bearer form, in the name of the trustee, or in the name of the trustee's nominee or nominees without being required to disclose any fiduciary relationship; and to deposit cash assets as a general deposit in a special bank account without liability for interest thereon; provided that, at all times, such cash and assets shall be shown to be a part of the trust on the books of the trustee.

5. To charge premiums on bonds and other similar investments against principal. The trustee shall not be required to charge any depreciation or depletion against income from any real estate or personal property.

6. To make, without the necessity of intervention or consent of any legal guardian, any payments by the terms of this will payable to or for the benefit of any minor person in any or all of the following ways: (1) Directly for the maintenance, education and welfare of any such minor beneficiary; (2) To the parent or natural guardian of such minor beneficiary; or (3) To any person at that time having custody and care of the person of said minor beneficiary. The receipt of such person shall be full acquittance of the trustee and the trustee shall have no responsibility to oversee the application of the funds so paid.

7. To hold or make division or distribution whenever herein required in whole or in part in money, securities or other property, and in undivided interests therein, and to continue to hold any such undivided interest in any trust hereunder, and in such division or distribution the judgment of the trustee concerning the propriety thereof and the valuation of the properties and securities concerned shall be binding and conclusive on all persons in interest.

8. To charge against the trust principal and to receive on behalf of the trustee reasonable compensation for services hereunder and payment for all reasonable expenses and charges of the trust.

Article XI

In the event that my said wife, _____, predeceases me or should we both die in some common accident, even though she should survive me by an appreciable length of time, such as one-hundred twenty (120) days, then my wife shall be deemed to have survived me with regard to all dispositive provisions for her benefit in this, my last will and testament. In the event that one or more of my children does not survive me, then I hereby give, devise, and bequeath the share of my property which that child would normally have taken under this will, to the living issue, collectively, of each deceased child of mine.

Article XII

If assets of my estate are to become a part of any trust by the terms of this will, and if such assets will immediately distribute upon receipt thereof by the trustee, the trustee may distribute such assets in exactly the same manner as provided in such trust without requiring such trust to be established.

Article XIII

Except for the income and general testamentary power of appointment reserved to my wife in TRUST A of ARTICLE IX, no title in the trusts created by this will, or in the income from said trusts shall vest in any beneficiary and neither the principal nor the income of said trusts shall be liable for the debts of any beneficiary, and none of the beneficiaries herein shall have any power to sell, assign, transfer, encumber, or in any other manner to dispose of his or her interest in any such trust, or the income produced by such trust, prior to the actual distribution in fact, by the trustee to said beneficiary.

Article XIV

As used in this will, the singular includes the plural and the masculine includes the feminine, and the terms "issue" and "child" are defined as follows:

> **"issue"** means all persons who are descended from the persons referred to, either by legitimate birth to or legally adopted by him or any of his legitimately born or legally adopted descendants.

> **"child"** means an issue of the first generation.

Article XV

I hereby waive any and all requirements that any trust herein created be submitted to the jurisdiction of any court, that the trustee be appointed or confirmed by any court, that evidence of such appointment or confirmation be filed in any court, and that the trustee's accounts be examined, heard, filed with or allowed by any court. This provision shall be overridden by a request by any trust beneficiaries, trustees or executors to require the procedures waived in this article.

Article XVI

Any trusts herein created shall terminate if the trustee shall determine that the continued administration of such trusts could be unduly expensive or burdensome to the beneficiaries, and if such event should occur the assets of any such trusts shall be distributed to the beneficiaries then entitled to receive the net income of said trusts in such proportions as they are entitled to receive said net income.

Article XVII

If my estate includes any business, I hereby expressly authorize my personal representative and trustee to retain and carry on any such business regardless of the fact that such business may constitute a large or major portion of my estate or trust estate. My personal representative and trustee shall have all necessary powers to enable them to do any and all things deemed appropriate by them for the carrying on of such business, including the power to incorporate and reorganize the business, to put in additional capital, and to hire a business manager or other such employees as they shall deem necessary. My estate and trust estate shall bear the sole risk of any business interest so retained, and my personal representative and trustee shall not be liable for any loss incurred thereby except when such loss is caused by their own negligence. Because the desirability of retaining any such business interests may be affected by many factors, any powers given in this Article to my personal representative and trustee shall not be mandatory. My personal respresentative and trustee shall have the power to close out and liquidate or sell such business interests upon such terms as they in their sole discretion shall deem best.

Article XVIII

In the event that my trustee under this will is the beneficiary of proceeds of any pension, profit sharing or stock bonus plans which qualify under applicable provisions of the Internal Revenue Code, said trustee shall not use any of such proceeds to pay any taxes, debts or other obligations enforceable against my estate, including both probate and non-probate assets. Any such proceeds received from pension, profit sharing or stock bonus plans which qualify under applicable provisions of the Internal Revenue Code shall not be includable in my gross estate for Federal Estate Tax purposes nor shall they be subject to _____ Inheritance Tax to such extent that said proceeds are attributa-
<small>(state)</small>
ble to contributions by my employer to any such qualified pension, profit sharing or stock bonus plans. All such funds shall be allocated to "TRUST B" and none to "TRUST A" as created in this will.

Article XIX

The payment by an insurance company of the proceeds of any policy of insurance to my trustee under this will as beneficiary, shall fully discharge all obligation of such insurance company on account of such policy and such insurance company shall bear no responsibility for the proper discharge of my trust or any part thereof. I direct my trustee to administer and distribute such insurance proceeds as follows:

1. If my wife survives me, my trustee shall allocate said insurance proceeds between "TRUST A", and "TRUST B", according to provisions in this will and as directed by my personal representative.

2. When acting under this will with respect to insurance proceeds as insurance beneficiary, rather than as distributee of my probate estate, my trustee shall have all duties, powers, rights, privileges and discretions given to my personal representative, and I direct that my trustee shall cooperate with my personal representative to ensure the most efficient and economical administration of my total gross estate.

Article XX

In the event my wife, _____, does not survive me, I hereby nominate and appoint _____ as guardian of the person for
<small>(name and address)</small>
my minor child or children. The guardian may use the income from "TRUST B" for the support, education and well being of said child or children. In the event _____ is unable or unwilling to act as personal guardian, I hereby appoint _____ to serve in his place as
<small>(name and address)</small>
personal guardian.

Article XXI

I hereby nominate _____ of _____ as the personal representa-
(address)
tive of this my last will and testament, and I give and grant unto my personal representative with respect to my estate and to each and every portion thereof, real, personal, or mixed, all such duties, powers, and discretions herein given and granted to my trustee hereof with respect to my trust estate, all of which duties, powers, and discretions shall be in addition to and not in limitation of those which normally my personal representative would possess.

If at any time after my death, my wife shall file a request in writing with the herein named personal representative and trustee that she wishes to become a co-personal representative and/or co-trustee hereunder, I hereby nominate her as co-personal representative and/or co-trustee. Until such request if filed, the personal representative herein named shall be the sole personal representative and trustee.

Any trustee herein named may at any time after my death, resign by giving notice in writing to the then income beneficiary. The date of delivery shall be specified in such instrument of resignation, and such resignation shall take effect no earlier than thirty (30) days after delivery of such written resignation. Upon such effective resignation the resigning trustee shall be relieved of all further duties and responsibilities and shall bear no liability or responsibility for the acts of any successor trustee.

I hereby direct that my personal representative or trustee shall have custody and possession of all assets, shall bear the responsibility for all receipts and disbursements, and all accounting. I direct that bond shall not be required of my personal representative and trustee.

In witness whereof, I have hereunto set my hand to this my last will and testament, consisting of _____ typewritten pages, including this page and each bearing my signature, on this _____ day of _____, 198_ at _____, _____, in the presence of each and all the subscribing
(city)   (state)
witnesses, each of whom I have requested in the presence of the others to subscribe his/her name, with his/her address written opposite thereto, as an attesting witness, in my presence and in the presence of all the others.

_____

The above and foregoing instrument was on the date thereof, signed, published, sealed, and declared by the testator, _____, to be his last will and testament, in our presence, and we at his request and in his presence and in the presence of each other, have hereunto subscribed our names as witnesses thereto.

_____ Residing at _____

_____ Residing at _____

_____ Residing at _____

Appendix C

Uniform Probate Code

**Official Text Approved by the National
Conference of Commissioners on Uniform State Laws**

AN ACT

Relating to affairs of decedents, missing persons, protected persons, minors, incapacitated persons and certain others and constituting the Uniform Probate Code; consolidating and revising aspects of the law relating to wills and intestacy and the administration and distribution of estates of decedents, missing persons, protected persons, minors, incapacitated persons and certain others; ordering the powers and procedures of the Court concerned with the affairs of decedents and certain others; providing for the validity and effect of certain non-testamentary transfers, contracts and deposits which relate to death and appear to have testamentary effect; providing certain procedures to facilitate enforcement of testamentary and other trusts; making uniform the law with respect to decedents and certain others; and repealing inconsistent legislation.

Article I
General Provisions, Definitions
And Probate Jurisdiction of Court

Part 1
Short Title, Construction, General Provisions

Part 2
Definitions

Part 3
Scope, Jurisdiction and Courts

Part 4
Notice, Parties and Representation
in Estate Litigation and Other Matters

Part 1
Short Title, Construction, General Provisions

Section 1–101. [Short Title.]

This Act shall be known and may be cited as the Uniform Probate Code.

Section 1–102. [Purposes; Rule of Construction.]

(a) This Code shall be liberally construed and applied to promote its underlying purposes and policies.

(b) The underlying purposes and policies of this Code are:

(1) to simplify and clarify the law concerning the affairs of decedents, missing persons, protected persons, minors and incapacitated persons;

(2) to discover and make effective the intent of a decedent in the distribution of his property;

(3) to promote a speedy and efficient system for liquidating the estate of the decedent and making distribution to his successors;

(4) to facilitate use and enforcement of certain trusts;

(5) to make uniform the law among the various jurisdictions.

**Section 1–103. [Supplementary
General Principles of Law Applicable.]**

Unless displaced by the particular provisions of this Code, the principles of law and equity supplement its provisions.

Section 1–104. [Severability.]

If any provision of this Code or the application thereof to any person or circumstances is held invalid, the invalidity shall not affect other provisions or applications of the Code which can be given effect without the invalid provision or application, and to this end the provisions of this Code are declared to be severable.

**Section 1–105. [Construction
Against Implied Repeal.]**

This Code is a general act intended as a unified coverage of its subject matter and no part of it shall be deemed impliedly repealed by subsequent legislation if it can reasonably be avoided.

Section 1–106. [Effect of Fraud and Evasion.]

Whenever fraud has been perpetrated in connection with any proceeding or in any statement filed under this Code or if fraud is used to avoid or circumvent the provisions or purposes of this Code, any person injured thereby may obtain appropriate relief against the perpetrator of the fraud or restitution from any person (other than a bona fide purchaser) benefitting from the fraud, whether innocent or not. Any proceeding must be commenced within 2 years after the discovery of the fraud, but no proceeding may be brought against one not a perpetrator of the fraud later than 5 years after the time of commission of the fraud. This section has no bearing on remedies relating to fraud practiced on a decedent during his lifetime which affects the succession of his estate.

Section 1–107.   [Evidence as to Death or Status.]

In proceedings under this Code the rules of evidence in courts of general jurisdiction including any relating to simultaneous deaths, are applicable unless specifically displaced by the Code. In addition, the following rules relating to determination of death and status are applicable:

(1) a certified or authenticated copy of a death certificate purporting to be issued by an official or agency of the place where the death purportedly occurred is prima facie proof of the fact, place, date and time of death and the identity of the decedent;

(2) a certified or authenticated copy of any record or report of a governmental agency, domestic or foreign, that a person is missing, detained, dead, or alive is prima facie evidence of the status and of the dates, circumstances and places disclosed by the record or report;

(3) a person who is absent for a continuous period of 5 years, during which he has not been heard from, and whose absence is not satisfactorily explained after diligent search or inquiry is presumed to be dead. His death is presumed to have occurred at the end of the period unless there is sufficient evidence for determining that death occurred earlier.

Section 1–108.   [Acts by Holder of General Power.]

For the purpose of granting consent or approval with regard to the acts or accounts of a personal representative or trustee, including relief from liability or penalty for failure to post bond, to register a trust, or to perform other duties, and for purposes of consenting to modification or termination of a trust or to deviation from its terms, the sole holder or all co-holders of a presently exercisable general power of appointment, including one in the form of a power of amendment or revocation, are deemed to act for beneficiaries to the extent their interests (as objects, takers in default, or otherwise) are subject to the power.

Part 2
Definitions

Section 1–201. [General Definitions.]

Subject to additional definitions contained in the subsequent Articles which are applicable to specific Articles or parts, and unless the context otherwise requires, in this Code:

(1) "Application" means a written request to the Registrar for an order of informal probate or appointment under Part 3 of Article III.

(2) "Beneficiary", as it relates to trust beneficiaries, includes a person who has any present or future interest, vested or contingent, and also includes the owner of an interest by assignment or other transfer and as it relates to a charitable trust, includes any person entitled to enforce the trust.

(3) "Child" includes any individual entitled to take as a child under this Code by intestate succession from the parent whose relationship is involved and excludes any person who is only a stepchild, a foster child, a grandchild or any more remote descendant.

(4) "Claims", in respect to estates of decedents and protected persons, includes liabilities of the decedent or protected person whether arising in contract, in tort or otherwise, and liabilities of the estate which arise at or after the death of the decedent or after the appointment of a conservator, including funeral expenses and expenses of administration. The term does not include estate or inheritance taxes, or demands or disputes regarding title of a decedent or protected person to specific assets alleged to be included in the estate.

(5) "Court" means the Court or branch having jurisdiction in matters relating to the affairs of decedents. This Court in this state is known as [_____].

(6) "Conservator" means a person who is appointed by a Court to manage the estate of a protected person.

(7) "Devise", when used as a noun, means a testamentary disposition of real or personal property and when used as a verb, means to dispose of real or personal property by will.

(8) "Devisee" means any person designated in a will to receive a devise. In the case of a devise to an existing trust or trustee, or to a trustee on trust described by will, the trust or trustee is the devisee and the beneficiaries are not devisees.

(9) "Disability" means cause for a protective order as described by Section 5–401.

(10) "Distributee" means any person who has received property of a decedent from his personal representative other than as a creditor or purchaser. A testamentary trustee is a distributee only to the extent of distributed assets or increment thereto remaining in his hands. A beneficiary of a testamentary trust to whom the trustee has distributed property received from a personal representative is a distributee of the personal representative. For purposes of this provision, "testamentary trustee" includes a trustee to whom assets are transferred by will, to the extent of the devised assets.

(11) "Estate" includes the property of the decedent, trust, or other person whose affairs are subject to this Code as originally constituted and as it exists from time to time during administration.

(12) "Exempt property" means that property of a decedent's estate which is described in Section 2–402.

(13) "Fiduciary" includes personal representative, guardian, conservator and trustee.

(14) "Foreign personal representative" means a personal representative of another jurisdiction.

(15) "Formal proceedings" means those conducted before a judge with notice to interested persons.

(16) "Guardian" means a person who has qualified as a guardian of a minor or incapacitated person pursuant to testamentary or court appointment, but excludes one who is merely a guardian ad litem.

(17) "Heirs" means those persons, including the surviving spouse, who are entitled under the statutes of intestate succession to the property of a decedent.

(18) "Incapacitated person" is as defined in Section 5–101.

(19) "Informal proceedings" mean those conducted without notice to interested persons by an officer of the Court acting as a registrar for probate of a will or appointment of a personal representative.

(20) "Interested person" includes heirs, devisees, children, spouses, creditors, beneficiaries and any others having a property right in or claim against a trust estate or the estate of a decedent, ward or protected person which may be affected by the proceeding. It also includes persons having priority for appointment as personal representative, and other fiduciaries representing interested persons. The meaning as it relates to particular persons may vary from time to time and must be determined according to the particular purposes of, and matter involved in, any proceeding.

(21) "Issue" of a person means all his lineal descendants of all generations, with the relationship of parent and child at each

generation being determined by the definitions of child and parent contained in this Code.

(22) "Lease" includes an oil, gas, or other mineral lease.

(23) "Letters" includes letters testamentary, letters of guardianship, letters of administration, and letters of conservatorship.

(24) "Minor" means a person who is under [21] years of age.

(25) "Mortgage" means any conveyance, agreement or arrangement in which property is used as security.

(26) "Non resident decedent" means a decedent who was domiciled in another jurisdiction at the time of his death.

(27) "Organization" includes a corporation, government or governmental subdivision or agency, business trust, estate, trust, partnership or association, 2 or more persons having a joint or common interest, or any other legal entity.

(28) "Parent" includes any person entitled to take, or who would be entitled to take if the child died without a will, as a parent under this Code by intestate succession from the child whose relationship is in question and excludes any person who is only a stepparent, foster parent, or grandparent.

(29) "Person" means an individual, a corporation, an organization, or other legal entity.

(30) "Personal representative" includes executor, administrator, successor personal representative, special administrator, and persons who perform substantially the same function under the law governing their status. "General personal representative" excludes special administrator.

(31) "Petition" means a written request to the Court for an order after notice.

(32) "Proceeding" includes action at law and suit in equity.

(33) "Property" includes both real and personal property or any interest therein and means anything that may be the subject of ownership.

(34) "Protected person" is as defined in Section 5–101.

(35) "Protective proceeding" is as defined in Section 5–101.

(36) "Registrar" refers to the official of the Court designated to perform the functions of Registrar as provided in Section 1–307.

(37) "Security" includes any note, stock, treasury stock, bond, debenture, evidence of indebtness, certificate of interest or participation in an oil, gas or mining title or lease or in payments out of production under such a title or lease, collateral trust certificate, transferable share, voting trust certificate or, in general, any interest or instrument commonly known as a security, or any certificate of interest or participation, any temporary or interim certificate, receipt or certificate of deposit for, or any warrant or right to subscribe to or purchase, any of the foregoing.

(38) "Settlement," in reference to a decedent's estate, includes the full process of administration, distribution and closing.

(39) "Special administrator" means a personal representative as described by Sections 3–614 through 3–618.

(40) "State" includes any state of the United States, the District of Columbia, the Commonwealth of Puerto Rico, and any territory or possession subject to the legislative authority of the United States.

(41) "Successor personal representative" means a personal representative, other than a special administrator, who is appointed to succeed a previously appointed personal representative.

(42) "Successors" means those persons, other than creditors, who are entitled to property of a decedent under his will or this Code.

(43) "Supervised administration" refers to the proceedings described in Article III, Part 5.

(44) "Testacy proceeding" means a proceeding to establish a will or determine intestacy.

(45) "Trust" includes any express trust, private or charitable, with additions thereto, wherever and however created. It also includes a trust created or determined by judgment or decree under which the trust is to be administered in the manner of an express trust. "Trust" excludes other constructive trusts, and it excludes resulting trusts, conservatorships, personal representatives, trust accounts as defined in Article VI, custodial arrangements pursuant to [each state should list its legislation, including that relating to gifts to minors, dealing with special custodial situations], business trusts providing for certificates to be issued to beneficiaries, common trust funds, voting trusts, security arrangements, liquidation trusts, and trusts for the primary purpose of paying debts, dividends, interest, salaries, wages, profits, pensions, or employee benefits of any kind, and any arrangement under which a person is nominee or escrowee for another.

(46) "Trustee" includes an original, additional, or successor trustee, whether or not appointed or confirmed by court.

(47) "Ward" is as defined in Section 5–101.

(48) "Will" includes codicil and any testamentary instrument which merely appoints an executor or revokes or revises another will.

[FOR ADOPTION IN COMMUNITY PROPERTY STATES]

[(49) "Separate property" (if necessary, to be defined locally in accordance with existing concept in adopting state).

(50) "Community property" (if necessary, to be defined locally in accordance with existing concept in adopting state).]

Part 3
Scope, Jurisdiction and Courts

Section 1–301. [Territorial Application.]

Except as otherwise provided in this Code, this Code applies to (1) the affairs and estates of decedents, missing persons, and persons to be protected, domiciled in this state, (2) the property of nonresidents located in this state or property coming into the control of a fiduciary who is subject to the laws of this state, (3) incapacitated persons and minors in this state, (4) survivorship and related accounts in this state, and (5) trust subject to administration in this state.

Section 1–302. [Subject Matter Jurisdiction.]

(a) To the full extent permitted by the constitution, the Court has jurisdiction over all subject matter relating to (1) estates of decedents, including construction of wills and determination of heirs and successors of decedents, and estates of protected persons; (2) protection of minors and incapacitated persons; and (3) trusts.

(b) The Court has full power to make orders, judgments and decrees and take all other action necessary and proper to administer justice in the matters which come before it.

Section 1–303. [Venue;
Multiple Proceedings; Transfer.]

(a) Where a proceeding under this Code could be maintained in more than one place in this state, the Court in which the proceeding is first commenced has the exclusive right to proceed.

(b) If proceedings concerning the same estate, protected person, ward, or trust are commenced in more than one Court of this state, the Court in which the proceeding was first commenced shall continue to hear the matter, and the other courts shall hold the matter in abeyance until the question of venue is decided, and if the ruling Court determines that venue is properly in another Court, it shall transfer the proceeding to the other Court.

(c) If a Court finds that in the interest of justice a proceeding or a file should be located in another Court of this state, the Court making the finding may transfer the proceeding or file to the other Court.

Section 1–304. [Practice in Court.]

Unless specifically provided to the contrary in this Code or unless inconsistent with its provisions, the rules of civil procedure including the rules concerning vacation of orders and appellate review govern formal proceedings under this Code.

Section 1–305. [Records and Certified Copies.]

The [Clerk of Court] shall keep a record for each decedent, ward, protected person or trust involved in any document which may be filed with the Court under this Code, including petitions and applications, demands for notices or bonds, trust registrations, and of any orders or responses relating thereto by the Registrar or Court, and establish and maintain a system for indexing, filing or recording which is sufficient to enable users of the records to obtain adequate information. Upon payment of the fees required by law the clerk must issue certified copies of any probated wills, letters issued to personal representatives, or any other record or paper filed or recorded. Certificates relating to probated wills must indicate whether the decedent was domiciled in this state and whether the probate was formal or informal. Certificates relating to letters must show the date of appointment.

Section 1–306. [Jury Trial.]

(a) If duly demanded, a party is entitled to trial by jury in [a formal testacy proceeding and] any proceeding in which any controverted question of fact arises as to which any party has a constitutional right to trial by jury.

(b) If there is no right to trial by jury under subsection (a) or the right is waived, the Court in its discretion may call a jury to decide any issue of fact, in which case the verdict is advisory only.

Section 1–307. [Registrar; Powers.]

The acts and orders which this Code specifies as performable by the Registrar may be performed either by a judge of the Court or by a person, including the clerk, designated by the Court by a written order filed and recorded in the office of the Court.

Section 1–308. [Appeals.]

Appellate review, including the right to appellate review, interlocutory appeal, provisions as to time, manner, notice, appeal bond, stays, scope of review, record on appeal, briefs, arguments and power of the appellate court, is governed by the rules applicable to the appeals to the [Supreme Court] in equity cases from the [court of general jurisdiction], except that in proceedings where jury trial has been had as a matter of right, the rules applicable to the scope of review in jury cases apply.

Section 1–309. [Qualifications of Judge.]

A judge of the Court must have the same qualifications as a judge of the [court of general jurisdiction.]

Section 1–310. [Oath or Affirmation on Filed Documents.]

Except as otherwise specifically provided in this Code or by rule, every document filed with the Court under this Code including applications, petitions, and demands for notice, shall be deemed to include an oath, affirmation, or statement to the effect that its representations are true as far as the person executing or filing it knows or is informed, and penalties for perjury may follow deliberate falsification therein.

Part 4
Notice, Parties and Representation in Estate Litigation and Other Matters

Section 1–401. [Notice; Method and Time of Giving.]

(a) If notice of a hearing on any petition is required and except for specific notice requirements as otherwise provided, the petitioner shall cause notice of the time and place of hearing of any petition to be given to any interested person or his attorney if he has appeared by attorney or requested that notice be sent to his attorney. Notice shall be given:

(1) by mailing a copy thereof at least 14 days before the time set for the hearing by certified, registered or ordinary first class mail addressed to the person being notified at the post office address given in his demand for notice, if any, or at his office or place of residence, if known;

(2) by delivering a copy thereof to the person being notified personally at least 14 days before the time set for the hearing; or

(3) if the address, or identity of any person is not known and cannot be ascertained with reasonable diligence, by publishing at least once a week for 3 consecutive weeks, a copy thereof in a newspaper having general circulation in the county where the hearing is to be held, the last publication of which is to be at least 10 days before the time set for the hearing.

(b) The Court for good cause shown may provide for a different method or time of giving notice for any hearing.

(c) Proof of the giving of notice shall be made on or before the hearing and filed in the proceeding.

Section 1–402. [Notice; Waiver.]

A person, including a guardian ad litem, conservator, or other fiduciary, may waive notice by a writing signed by him or his attorney and filed in the proceeding.

Section 1–403. [Pleadings; When Parties Bound by Others; Notice.]

In formal proceedings involving trusts or estates of decedents, minors, protected persons, or incapacitated persons, and in judicially supervised settlements, the following apply:

(1) Interests to be affected shall be described in pleadings which give reasonable information to owners by name or class, by

reference to the instrument creating the interests, or in other appropriate manner.

(2) Persons are bound by orders binding others in the following cases:

(i) Orders binding the sole holder or all co-holders of a power of revocation or a presently exercisable general power of appointment, including one in the form of a power of amendment, bind other persons to the extent their interests (as objects, takers in default, or otherwise) are subject to the power.

(ii) To the extent there is no conflict of interest between them or among persons represented, orders binding a conservator bind the person whose estate he controls; orders binding a guardian bind the ward if no conservator of his estate has been appointed; orders binding a trustee bind beneficiaries of the trust in proceedings to probate a will establishing or adding to a trust, to review the acts or accounts of a prior fiduciary and in proceedings involving creditors or other third parties; and orders binding a personal representative bind persons interested in the undistributed assets of a decedent's estate in actions or proceedings by or against the estate. If there is no conflict of interest and no conservator or guardian has been appointed, a parent may represent his minor child.

(iii) An unborn or unascertained person who is not otherwise represented is bound by an order to the extent his interest is adequately represented by another party having a substantially identical interest in the proceeding.

(3) Notice is required as follows:

(i) Notice as prescribed by Section 1–401 shall be given to every interested person or to one who can bind an interested person as described in (2) (i) or (2) (ii) above. Notice may be given both to a person and to another who may bind him.

(ii) Notice is given to unborn or unascertained persons, who are not represented under (2) (i) or (2) (ii) above, by giving notice to all known persons whose interests in the proceedings are substantially identical to those of the unborn or unascertained persons.

(4) At any point in a proceeding, a court may appoint a guardian ad litem to represent the interest of a minor, an incapacitated, unborn, or unascertained person, or a person whose identity or address is unknown, if the Court determines that representation of the interest otherwise would be inadequate. If not precluded by conflict of interests, a guardian ad litem may be appointed to represent several persons or interests. The Court shall set out its

reasons for appointing a guardian ad litem as a part of the record of the proceeding.

Article II
Intestate Succession and Wills

Part 1
Intestate Succession

Part 2
Elective Share of Surviving Spouse

Part 3
Spouse and Children Unprovided For in Wills

Part 4
Exempt Property and Allowances

Part 5
Wills

Part 6
Rules of Construction

Part 1
Intestate Succession

Section 2–101. [Intestate Estate.]

Any part of the estate of a decedent not effectively disposed of by his will passes to his heirs as prescribed in the following sections of this Code.

Section 2–102. [Share of the Spouse.]

The intestate share of the surviving spouse is:

(1) if there is no surviving issue or parent of the decedent, the entire intestate estate;

(2) if there is no surviving issue but the decedent is survived by a parent or parents, the first [$50,000], plus one-half of the balance of the intestate estate;

(3) if there are surviving issue all of whom are issue of the surviving spouse also, the first [$50,000], plus one-half of the balance of the intestate estate;

(4) if there are surviving issue one or more of whom are not issue of the surviving spouse, one-half of the intestate estate.

ALTERNATIVE PROVISION FOR
COMMUNITY PROPERTY STATES

[Section 2–102A. [Share of the Spouse.]

The intestate share of the surviving spouse is as follows:

(1) as to separate property

(i) if there is no surviving issue or parent of the decedent, the entire intestate estate;

(ii) if there is no surviving issue but the decedent is survived by a parent or parents, the first [$50,000], plus one-half of the balance of the intestate estate;

(iii) if there are surviving issue all of whom are issue of the surviving spouse also, the first [$50,000], plus one-half of the balance of the intestate estate;

(iv) if there are surviving issue one or more of whom are not issue of the surviving spouse, one-half of the intestate estate.

(2) as to community property

(i) The one-half of community property which belongs to the decedent passes to the [surviving spouse].]

Section 2–103. [Share of Heirs Other Than Surviving Spouse.]

The part of the intestate estate not passing to the surviving spouse under Section 2–102, or the entire intestate estate if there is no surviving spouse, passes as follows:

(1) to the issue of the decedent; if they are all of the same degree of kinship to the decedent they take equally, but if of unequal degree, then those of more remote degree take by representation;

(2) if there is no surviving issue, to his parent or parents equally;

(3) if there is no surviving issue or parent, to the issue of the parents or either of them by representation;

(4) if there is no surviving issue, parent or issue of a parent, but the decedent is survived by one or more grandparents or issue of grandparents, half of the estate passes to the paternal grandparents if both survive, or to the surviving paternal grandparent, or to the issue of the paternal grandparents if both are deceased, the issue taking equally if they are all of the same degree of kinship to the decedent, but if of unequal degree those of more remote degree take by representation; and the other half passes to the maternal relatives in the same manner; but if there be no surviving grandparent or issue of grandparent on either the paternal or the maternal side, the entire estate passes to the relatives on the other side in the same manner as the half.

Section 2–104. [Requirement That Heir Survive Decedent For 120 Hours.]

Any person who fails to survive the decedent by 120 hours is deemed to have predeceased the decedent for purposes of homestead allowance, exempt property and intestate succession, and the decedent's heirs are determined accordingly. If the time of death of the decedent or of the person who would otherwise be an heir, or the times of death of both, cannot be determined, and it cannot be established that the person who would otherwise be an heir has survived the decedent by 120 hours, it is deemed that the person failed to survive for the required period. This section is not to be applied where its application would result in a taking of intestate estate by the state under Section 2–105.

Section 2–105. [No Taker.]

If there is no taker under the provisions of this Article, the intestate estate passes to the [state].

Section 2–106. [Representation.]

If representation is called for by this Code, the estate is divided into as many shares as there are surviving heirs in the nearest degree of kinship and deceased persons in the same degree who left issue who survive the decedent, each surviving heir in the nearest degree receiving one share and the share of each deceased person in the same degree being divided among his issue in the same manner.

Section 2–107.   [Kindred of Half Blood.]

Relatives of the half blood inherit the same share they would inherit if they were of the whole blood.

Section 2–108.   [Afterborn Heirs.]

Relatives of the decedent conceived before his death but born thereafter inherit as if they had been born in the lifetime of the decedent.

Section 2–109.   [Meaning of Child and Related Terms.]

If, for purposes of intestate succession, a relationship of parent and child must be established to determine succession by, through, or from a person,

(1) an adopted person is the child of an adopting parent and not of the natural parents except that adoption of a child by the spouse of a natural parent has no effect on the relationship between the child and either natural parent.

(2) In cases not covered by Paragraph (1), a person is the child of its parents regardless of the marital status of its parents and the parent and child relationship may be established under the [Uniform Parentage Act].

Alternative Subsection (2) for States That Have Not Adopted the Uniform Parentage Act.

[(2) In cases not covered by Paragraph (1), a person born out of wedlock is a child of the mother. That person is also a child of the father, if:

(i) the natural parents participated in a marriage ceremony before or after the birth of the child, even though the attempted marriage is void; or

(ii) the paternity is established by an adjudication before the death of the father or is established thereafter by clear and convincing proof, but the paternity established under this subparagraph is ineffective to qualify the father or his kindred to inherit from or through the child unless the father has openly treated the child as his, and has not refused to support the child.]

Section 2–110.   [Advancements.]

If a person dies intestate as to all his estate, property which he gave in his lifetime to an heir is treated as an advancement against the latter's share of the estate only if declared in a contemporaneous writing by the decedent or acknowledged in writing by the heir to be an advancement. For this purpose the property advanced is valued as of the time the heir came into possession or enjoyment of the property or as of the time of death of the decedent, whichever first occurs. If the recipient of the property fails to survive the decedent, the property is not taken into account in computing the intestate share to be received by the recipient's issue, unless the declaration or acknowledgment provides otherwise.

Section 2–111. [Debts to Decedent.]

A debt owed to the decedent is not charged against the intestate share of any person except the debtor. If the debtor fails to survive the decedent, the debt is not taken into account in computing the intestate share of the debtor's issue.

Section 2–112. [Alienage.]

No person is disqualified to take as an heir because he or a person through whom he claims is or has been an alien.

[Section 2–113. [Dower and Curtesy Abolished.]

The estates of dower and curtesy are abolished.]

Section 2–114. [Persons Related to Decedent Through Two Lines.]

A person who is related to the decedent through 2 lines of relationship is entitled to only a single share based on the relationship which would entitle him to the larger share.

Part 2
Elective Share of Surviving Spouse

Section 2–201. [Right to Elective Share.]

(a) If a married person domiciled in this state dies, the surviving spouse has a right of election to take an elective share of one-third of the augmented estate under the limitations and conditions hereinafter stated.

(b) If a married person not domiciled in this state dies, the right, if any, of the surviving spouse to take an elective share in property in this state is governed by the law of the decedent's domicile at death.

Section 2–202. [Augmented Estate.]

The augmented estate means the estate reduced by funeral and administration expenses, homestead allowance, family allowances and exemptions, and enforceable claims, to which is added the sum of the following amounts:

(1) The value of propery transferred to anyone other than a bona fide purchaser by the decedent at any time during marriage, to or for the benefit of any person other than the surviving spouse, to the extent that the decedent did not receive adequate and full consideration in money or money's worth for the transfer, if the transfer is of any of the following types:

(i) any transfer under which the decedent retained at the time of his death the possession or enjoyment of, or right to income from, the property;

(ii) any transfer to the extent that the decedent retained at the time of his death a power, either alone or in conjunction with any other person, to revoke or to consume, invade or dispose of the principal for his own benefit;

(iii) any transfer whereby property is held at the time of decedent's death by decedent and another with right of survivorship;

(iv) any transfer made to a donee within two years of death of the decedent to the extent that the aggregate transfers to any one donee in either of the years exceed $3,000.00.

Any transfer is excluded if made with the written consent or joinder of the surviving spouse. Property is valued as of the decedent's death except that property given irrevocably to a donee during lifetime of the decedent is valued as of the date the donee came into possession or enjoyment if that occurs first. Nothing herein shall cause to be included in the augmented estate any life insurance, accident insurance, joint annuity, or pension payable to a person other than the surviving spouse.

(2) The value of property owned by the surviving spouse at the decedent's death, plus the value of property transferred by the spouse at any time during marriage to any person other than the decedent which would have been includible in the spouse's augmented estate if the surviving spouse had predeceased the decedent to the extent the owned or transferred property is derived from the decedent by any means other than testate or intestate succession without a full consideration in money or money's worth. For purposes of this paragraph:

(i) Property derived from the decedent includes, but is not limited to, any beneficial interest of the surviving spouse in a trust created by the decedent during his lifetime, any property appointed to the spouse by the decedent's exercise of a general or special power of appointment also exercisable in favor of others than the spouse, any proceeds of insurance (including accidental death benefits) on the life of the decedent attributable to premiums paid by him, any lump sum immediately payable and the commuted value of the proceeds of annuity contracts under which the decedent was the primary annuitant attributable to premiums paid by him, the commuted value of amounts payable after the decedent's death under any public or private pension, disability compensation, death benefit or retirement plan, exclusive of the Federal Social Security system, by reason of service performed or disabilities incurred by the decedent, any property held at the time of decedent's death by decedent and the surviving spouse with right of survivorship, any property held by decedent and transferred by contract to the surviving spouse by reason of the decedent's death and the value of the share of the surviving spouse resulting from rights in community property in this or any other state formerly owned with the decedent. Premiums paid by the decedent's employer, his partner, a partnership of which he was a member, or his creditors, are deemed to have been paid by the decedent.

(ii) Property owned by the spouse at the decedent's death is valued as of the date of death. Property transferred by the spouse is valued at the time the transfer became irrevocable, or at the decedent's death, whichever occurred first. Income earned by included property prior to the decedent's death is not treated as property derived from the decedent.

(iii) Property owned by the surviving spouse as of the decedent's death, or previously transferred by the surviving spouse, is presumed to have been derived from the decedent except to the extent that the surviving spouse establishes that it was derived from another source.

(3) For purposes of this section a bona fide purchaser is a purchaser for value in good faith and without notice of any adverse claim. Any recorded instrument on which a state documentary fee is noted pursuant to [insert appropriate reference] is prima facie evidence that the transfer described therein was made to a bona fide purchaser.

Section 2-203. [Right of Election Personal to Surviving Spouse.]

The right of election of the surviving spouse may be exercised only during his lifetime by him. In the case of a protected person, the right of election may be exercised only by order of the court in which protective proceedings as to his property are pending, after finding that exercise is necessary to provide adequate support for the protected person during his probable life expectancy.

Section 2-204. [Waiver of Right to Elect and of Other Rights.]

The right of election of a surviving spouse and the rights of the surviving spouse to homestead allowance, exempt property and family allowance, or any of them, may be waived, wholly or partially, before or after marriage, by a written contract, agreement or waiver signed by the party waiving after fair disclosure. Unless it provides to the contrary, a waiver of "all rights" (or equivalent language) in the property or estate of a present or prospective spouse or a complete property settlement entered into after or in anticipation of separation or divorce is a waiver of all rights to elective share, homestead allowance, exempt property and family allowance by each spouse in the property of the other and a renunciation by each of all benefits which would otherwise pass to him from the other by intestate succession or by virtue of the provisions of any will executed before the waiver or property settlement.

Section 2–205. [Proceeding for Elective Share; Time Limit.]

(a) The surviving spouse may elect to take his elective share in the augmented estate by filing in the Court and mailing or delivering to the personal representative, if any, a petition for the elective share within 9 months after the date of death, or within 6 months after the probate of the decedent's will, whichever limitation last expires. However, that nonprobate transfers, described in Section 2–202(1), shall not be included within the augmented estate for the purpose of computing the elective share, if the petition is filed later than 9 months after death.

The Court may extend the time for election as it sees fit for cause shown by the surviving spouse before the time for election has expired.

(b) The surviving spouse shall give notice of the time and place set for hearing to persons interested in the estate and to the distributees and recipients of portions of the augmented net estate whose interests will be adversely affected by the taking of the elective share.

(c) The surviving spouse may withdraw his demand for an elective share at any time before entry of a final determination by the Court.

(d) After notice and hearing, the Court shall determine the amount of the elective share and shall order its payment from the assets of the augmented net estate or by contribution as appears appropriate under Section 2–207. If it appears that a fund or property included in the augmented net estate has not come into the possession of the personal representative, or has been distributed by the personal representative, the Court nevertheless shall fix the liability of any person who has any interest in the fund or property or who has possession thereof, whether as trustee or otherwise. The proceeding may be maintained against fewer than all persons against whom relief could be sought, but no person is subject to contribution in any greater amount than he would have been if relief had been secured against all persons subject to contribution.

(e) The order or judgment of the Court may be enforced as necessary in suit for contribution or payment in other courts of this state or other jurisdictions.

Section 2–206. [Effect of Election on Benefits by Will or Statute.]

A surviving spouse is entitled to homestead allowance, exempt property, and family allowance, whether or not he elects to take an elective share.

Section 2–207. [Charging Spouse With Gifts Received; Liability of Others For Balance of Elective Share.]

(a) In the proceeding for an elective share, values included in the augmented estate which pass or have passed to the surviving spouse, or which would have passed to the spouse but were renounced, are applied first to satisfy the elective share and to reduce any contributions due from other recipients of transfers included in the augmented estate. For purposes of this subsection, the electing spouse's beneficial interest in any life estate or in any trust shall be computed as if worth one half of the total value of the property subject to the life estate, or of the trust estate, unless higher or lower values for these interests are established by proof.

(b) Remaining property of the augmented estate is so applied that liability for the balance of the elective share of the surviving spouse is equitably apportioned among the recipients of the augmented estate in proportion to the value of their interests therein.

(c) Only original transferees from, or appointees of, the decedent and their donees, to the extent the donees have the property or its proceeds, are subject to the contribution to make up the elective share of the surviving spouse. A person liable to contribution may choose to give up the property transferred to him or to pay its value as of the time it is considered in computing the augmented estate.

Part 3
Spouse and Children Unprovided for in Wills

Section 2–301. [Omitted Spouse.]

(a) If a testator fails to provide by will for his surviving spouse who married the testator after the execution of the will, the omitted spouse shall receive the same share of the estate he would have received if the decedent left no will unless it appears from the will that the omission was intentional or the testator provided for the spouse by transfer outside the will and the intent that the transfer be in lieu of a testamentary provision is shown by statements of the testator or from the amount of the transfer or other evidence.

(b) In satisfying a share provided by this section, the devises made by the will abate as provided in Section 3–902.

Section 2–302. [Pretermitted Children.]

(a) If a testator fails to provide in his will for any of his children born or adopted after the execution of his will, the omitted child receives a share in the estate equal in value to that which he would have received if the testator had died intestate unless:

(1) it appears from the will that the omission was intentional;

(2) when the will was executed the testator had one or more children and devised substantially all his estate to the other parent of the omitted child; or

(3) the testator provided for the child by transfer outside the will and the intent that the transfer be in lieu of a testamentary provision is shown by statements of the testator or from the amount of the transfer or other evidence.

(b) If at the time of execution of the will the testator fails to provide in his will for a living child solely because he believes the child to be dead, the child receives a share in the estate equal in value to that which he would have received if the testator had died intestate.

(c) In satisfying a share provided by this section, the devises made by the will abate as provided in Section 3–902.

Part 4
Exempt Property and Allowances

Section 2–401. [Homestead Allowance.]

A surviving spouse of a decedent who was domiciled in this state is entitled to a homestead allowance of [$5,000]. If there is no surviving spouse, each minor child and each dependent child of the decedent is entitled to a homestead allowance amounting to [$5,000] divided by the number of minor and dependent children of the decedent. The homestead allowance is exempt from and has priority over all claims against the estate. Homestead allowance is in addition to any share passing to the surviving spouse or minor or dependent child by the will of the decedent unless otherwise provided, by intestate succession or by way of elective share.

[Section 2–401A. [Constitutional Homestead.]

The value of any constitutional right of homestead in the family home received by a surviving spouse or child shall be charged against that spouse or child's homestead allowance to the extent that the family home is part of the decedent's estate or would have been but for the homestead provision of the constitution.]

Section 2–402. [Exempt Property.]

In addition to the homestead allowance, the surviving spouse of a decedent who was domiciled in this state is entitled from the estate to value not exceeding $3,500 in excess of any security interests therein in household furniture, automobiles, furnishings, appliances and personal effects. If there is no surviving spouse, children of the decedent are entitled jointly to the same value. If encumbered chattels are selected and if the value in excess of security interests, plus that of other exempt property, is less than $3,500, or if there is not $3,500 worth of exempt property in the estate, the spouse or children are entitled to other assets of the estate, if any, to the extent necessary to make up the $3,500 value. Rights to exempt property and assets needed to make up a deficiency of exempt property have priority over all claims against the estate, except that the right to any assets to make up a deficiency of exempt property shall abate as necessary to permit prior payment of homestead allowance and family allowance. These rights are in addition to any benefit or share passing to the surviving spouse or children by the will of the decedent unless otherwise provided, by intestate succession, or by way of elective share.

Section 2–403. [Family Allowance.]

In addition to the right to homestead allowance and exempt property, if the decedent was domiciled in this state, the surviving spouse and minor children whom the decedent was obligated to support and children who were in fact being supported by him are entitled to a reasonable allowance in money out of the estate for their maintenance during the period of administration, which allowance may not continue for longer than one year if the estate is inadequate to discharge allowed claims. The allowance may be paid as a lump sum or in periodic installments. It is payable to the surviving spouse, if living, for the use of the surviving spouse and minor and dependent children; otherwise to the children, or persons having their care and custody; but in case any minor child or dependent child is not living with the surviving spouse, the allowance may be made partially to the child or his guardian or other person having his care and custody, and partially to the spouse, as their needs may appear. The family allowance is exempt from and has priority over all claims but not over the homestead allowance.

The family allowance is not chargeable against any benefit or share passing to the surviving spouse or children by the will of the decedent unless otherwise provided, by intestate succession, or by way of elective share. The death of any person entitled to family allowance terminates his right to allowances not yet paid.

Section 2–404. [Source, Determination and Documentation.]

If the estate is otherwise sufficient, property specifically devised is not used to satisfy rights to homestead and exempt property. Subject to this restriction, the surviving spouse, the guardians of the minor children, or children who are adults may select property of the estate as homestead allowance and exempt property. The personal representative may make these selections if the surviving spouse, the children or the guardians of the minor children are unable or fail to do so within a reasonable time or if there are no guardians of the minor children. The personal representative may execute an instrument or deed of distribution to establish the ownership of property taken as homestead allowance or exempt property. He may determine the family allowance in a lump sum not exceeding $6,000 or periodic installments not exceeding $500 per month for one year, and may disburse funds of the estate in payment of the family allowance and any part of the homestead allowance payable in cash. The personal representative or any interested person aggrieved by any selection, determination, payment, proposed payment, or failure to act under this section may petition the Court for appropriate relief, which relief may provide a family allowance larger or smaller than that which the personal representative determined or could have determined.

Part 5
Wills

Section 2–501. [Who May Make a Will.]

Any person 18 or more years of age who is of sound mind may make a will.

Section 2–502. [Execution.]

Except as provided for holographic wills, writings within Section 2–513, and wills within Section 2–506, every will shall be in writing signed by the testator or in the testator's name by some other person in the testator's presence and by his direction, and shall be signed by at least 2 persons each of whom witnessed either the signing or the testator's acknowledgment of the signature or of the will.

Section 2–503. [Holographic Will.]

A will which does not comply with Section 2–502 is valid as a holographic will, whether or not witnessed, if the signature and the material provisions are in the handwriting of the testator.

Section 2–504. [Self-proved Will.]

(a) Any will may be simultaneously executed, attested, and made self-proved, by acknowledgment thereof by the testator and affidavits of the witnesses, each made before an officer authorized to administer oaths under the laws of the state where execution occurs and evidenced by the officer's certificate, under official seal, in substantially the following form:

I, _____, the testator, sign my name to this instrument this _____ day of _____, 19__, and being first duly sworn, do hereby declare to the undersigned authority that I sign and execute this instrument as my last will and that I sign it willingly (or willingly direct another to sign for me), that I execute it as my free and voluntary act for the purposes therein expressed, and that I am eighteen years of age or older, of sound mind, and under no constraint or undue influence.

_____
Testator

We, _____, _____, the witnesses, sign our names to this instrument, being first duly sworn, and do hereby declare to the undersigned authority that the testator signs and executes this instrument as his last will and that he signs it willingly (or willingly directs another to sign for him), and that each of us, in the presence and hearing of the testator, hereby signs this will as witness to the testator's signing, and that to the best of our knowledge the testator is eighteen years of age or older, of sound mind, and under no constraint or undue influence.

_____
Witness

_____
Witness

The State of _____
County of _____

Subscribed, sworn to and acknowledged before me by _____, the testator and subscribed and sworn to before me by _____, and _____, witnesses, this ___ day of ___.

(Seal)   (Signed) _____

_____
(Official capacity of officer)

(b) An attested will may at any time subsequent to its execution be made self-proved by the acknowledgment thereof by the testator and the affidavits of the witnesses, each made before an officer authorized to administer oaths under the laws of the state where the acknowledgment occurs and evidenced by the officer's certificate, under the official seal, attached or annexed to the will in substantially the following form:

The State of _____
County of _____

We, _____, _____, and _____, the testator and the witnesses, respectively, whose names are signed to the attached or foregoing instrument, being first duly sworn, do hereby declare to the under-signed authority that the testator signed and executed the instrument as his last will and that he had signed willingly (or willingly directed another to sign for him), and that he executed it as his free and voluntary act for the purposes therein expressed, and that each of the witnesses, in the presence and hearing of the testator, signed the will as witness and that to the best of his knowledge the testator was at that time eighteen years of age or older, of sound mind and under no constraint or undue influence.

_____

Testator

_____

Witness

_____

Witness

Subscribed, sworn to and acknowledged before me by _____, the testator, and subscribed and sworn to before me by _____, and _____, witnesses, this ____ day of ____

(Seal)   (Signed) _____

_____

(Official capacity of officer)

Section 2–505. [Who May Witness.]

(a) Any person generally competent to be a witness may act as a witness to a will.

(b) A will or any provision thereof is not invalid because the will is signed by an interested witness.

Section 2–506.   [Choice of Law as to Execution.]

A written will is valid if executed in compliance with Section 2–502 or 2–503 or if its execution complies with the law at the time of execution of the place where the will is executed, or of the law of the place where at the time of execution or at the time of death the testator is domiciled, has a place of abode or is a national.

Section 2–507. [Revocation by Writing or by Act.]

A will or any part thereof is revoked

(1) by a subsequent will which revokes the prior will or part expressly or by inconsistency; or

(2) by being burned, torn, canceled, obliterated, or destroyed, with the intent and for the purpose of revoking it by the testator or by another person in his presence and by his direction.

Section 2–508. [Revocation by Divorce; No Revocation by Other Changes of Circumstances.]

If after executing a will the testator is divorced or his marriage annulled, the divorce or annulment revokes any disposition or appointment of property made by the will to the former spouse, any provision conferring a general or special power of appointment on the former spouse, and any nomination of the former spouse as executor, trustee, conservator, or guardian, unless the will expressly provides otherwise. Property prevented from passing to a former spouse because of revocation by divorce or annulment passes as if the former spouse failed to survive the decedent, and other provisions conferring some power or office on the former spouse are interpreted as if the spouse failed to survive the decedent. If provisions are revoked solely by this section, they are revived by testator's remarriage to the former spouse. For purposes of this section, divorce or annulment means any divorce or annulment which would exclude the spouse as a surviving spouse within the meaning of Section 2–802(b). A decree of separation which does not terminate the status of husband and wife is not a divorce for purposes of this section. No change of circumstances other than as described in this section revokes a will.

Section 2–509. [Revival of Revoked Will.]

(a) If a second will which, had it remained effective at death, would have revoked the first will in whole or in part, is thereafter revoked by acts under Section 2–507, the first will is revoked in whole or in part unless it is evident from the circumstances of the revocation of the second will or from testator's contemporary or subsequent declarations that he intended the first will to take effect as executed.

(b) If a second will which, had it remained effective at death, would have revoked the first will in whole or in part, is thereafter revoked by a third will, the first will is revoked in whole or in part, except to the extent it appears from the terms of the third will that the testator intended the first will to take effect.

Section 2–510. [Incorporation by Reference.]

Any writing in existence when a will is executed may be incorporated by reference if the language of the will manifests this intent and describes the writing sufficiently to permit its identification.

Section 2–511. [Testamentary Additions to Trusts.]

A devise or bequest, the validity of which is determinable by the law of this state, may be made by a will to the trustee of a trust established or to be established by the testator or by the testator and some other person or by some other person (including a funded or unfunded life insurance trust, although the trustor has reserved any or all rights of ownership of the insurance contracts) if the trust is identified in the testator's will and its terms are set forth in a written instrument (other than a will) executed before or concurrently with the execution of the testator's will or in the valid last will of a person who has predeceased the testator (regardless of the existence, size, or character of the corpus of the trust). The devise is not invalid because the trust is amendable or revocable, or because the trust was amended after the execution of the will or after the death of the testator. Unless the testator's will provides otherwise, the property so devised (1) is not deemed to be held under a testamentary trust of the testator but becomes a part of the trust to which it is given and (2) shall be administered and disposed of in accordance with the provisions of the instrument or will setting forth the terms of the trust, including any amendments thereto made before the death of the testator (regardless of whether made before or after the execution of the testator's will), and, if the testator's will so provides, including any amendments to the trust made after the death of the testator. A revocation or termination of the trust before the death of the testator causes the devise to lapse.

Section 2-512. [Events of Independent Significance.]

A will may dispose of property by reference to acts and events which have significance apart from their effect upon the dispositions made by the will, whether they occur before or after the execution of the will or before or after the testator's death. The execution or revocation of a will of another person is such an event.

Section 2-513. [Separate Writing Identifying Bequest of Tangible Property.]

Whether or not the provisions relating to holographic wills apply, a will may refer to a written statement or list to dispose of items of tangible personal property not otherwise specifically disposed of by the will, other than money, evidences of indebtedness, documents of title, and securities, and property used in trade or business. To be admissible under this section as evidence of the intended disposition, the writing must either be in the handwriting of the testator or be signed by him and must describe the items and the devisees with reasonable certainty. The writing may be referred to as one to be in existence at the time of the testator's death; it may be prepared before or after the execution of the will; it may be altered by the testator after its preparation; and it may be a writing which has no significance apart from its effect upon the dispositions made by the will.

Part 6
Rules of Construction

Section 2-601. [Requirement That Devisee Survive Testator by 120 Hours.]

A devisee who does not survive the testator by 120 hours is treated as if he predeceased the testator, unless the will of decedent contains some language dealing explicitly with simultaneous deaths or deaths in a common disaster, or requiring that the devisee survive the testator or survive the testator for a stated period in order to take under the will.

Section 2–602. [Choice of Law as to Meaning and Effect of Wills.]

The meaning and legal effect of a disposition in a will shall be determined by the local law of a particular state selected by the testator in his instrument unless the application of that law is contrary to the provisions relating to the elective share described in Part 2 of this Article, the provisions relating to exempt property and allowances described in Part 4 of this Article, or any other public policy of this State otherwise applicable to the disposition.

Section 2–603. [Rules of Construction and Intention.]

The intention of a testator as expressed in his will controls the legal effect of his dispositions. The rules of construction expressed in the succeeding sections of this Part apply unless a contrary intention is indicated by the will.

Section 2–604. [Construction That Will Passes All Property; After-Acquired Property.]

A will is construed to pass all property which the testator owns at his death including property acquired after the execution of the will.

Section 2–605. [Anti-lapse; Deceased Devisee; Class Gifts.]

If a devisee who is a grandparent or a lineal descendant of a grandparent of the testator is dead at the time of execution of the will, fails to survive the testator, or is treated as if he predeceased the testator, the issue of the deceased devisee who survive the testator by 120 hours take in place of the deceased devisee and if they are all of the same degree of kinship to the devisee they take equally, but if of unequal degree then those of more remote degree take by representation. One who would have been a devisee under a class gift if he had survived the testator is treated as a devisee for purposes of this section whether his death occurred before or after the execution of the will.

Section 2–606. [Failure of Testamentary Provision.]

(a) Except as provided in Section 2–605 if a devise other than a residuary devise fails for any reason, it becomes a part of the residue.

(b) Except as provided in Section 2–605 if the residue is devised to two or more persons and the share of one of the residuary devisees fails for any reason, his share passes to the other residuary devisee, or to other residuary devisees in proportion to their interests in the residue.

Section 2–607. [Change in
Securities; Accessions; Nonademption.]

(a) If the testator intended a specific devise of certain securities rather than the equivalent value thereof, the specific devisee is entitled only to:

(1) as much of the devised securities as is a part of the estate at time of the testator's death;

(2) any additional or other securities of the same entity owned by the testator by reason of action initiated by the entity excluding any acquired by exercise of purchase options;

(3) securities of another entity owned by the testator as a result of a merger, consolidation, reorganization or other similar action initiated by the entity; and

(4) any additional securities of the entity owned by the testator as a result of a plan of reinvestment if it is a regulated investment company.

(b) Distributions prior to death with respect to a specifically devised security not provided for in subsection (a) are not part of the specific devise.

Section 2–608. [Nonademption of Specific Devises
in Certain Cases; Unpaid Proceeds of Sale,
Condemnation or Insurance; Sale by Conservator.]

(a) A specific devisee has the right to the remaining specifically devised property and:

(1) any balance of the purchase price (together with any security interest) owing from a purchaser to the testator at death by reason of sale of the property;

(2) any amount of a condemnation award for the taking of the property unpaid at death;

(3) any proceeds unpaid at death on fire or casualty insurance on the property; and

(4) property owned by testator at his death as a result of foreclosure, or obtained in lieu of foreclosure, of the security for a specifically devised obligation.

(b) If specifically devised property is sold by a conservator, or if a condemnation award or insurance proceeds are paid to a conservator as a result of condemnation, fire, or casualty, the specific devisee has the right to a general pecuniary devise equal to the net sale price, the condemnation award, or the insurance proceeds. This subsection does not apply if after the sale, condemnation or casualty, it is adjudicated that the disability of the testator has ceased and the testator survives the adjudication by one year. The right of the specific devisee under this subsection is reduced by any right he has under subsection (a).

Section 2–609. [Non-Exoneration.]

A specific devise passes subject to any mortgage interest existing at the date of death, without right of exoneration, regardless of a general directive in the will to pay debts.

Section 2–610. [Exercise of Power of Appointment.]

A general residuary clause in a will, or a will making general disposition of all of the testator's property, does not exercise a power of appointment held by the testator unless specific reference is made to the power or there is some other indication of intention to include the property subject to the power.

Section 2–611. [Construction of Generic Terms to Accord with Relationships as Defined for Intestate Succession.]

Halfbloods, adopted persons, and persons born out of wedlock are included in class gift terminology and terms of relationship in accordance with rules for determining relationships for purposes of intestate succession. [However, a person born out of wedlock is not treated as the child of the father unless the person is openly and notoriously so treated by the father.]

Section 2–612. [Ademption by Satisfaction.]

Property which a testator gave in his lifetime to a person is treated as a satisfaction of a devise to that person in whole or in part, only if the will provides for deduction of the lifetime gift, or the testator declares in a contemporaneous writing that the gift is to be deducted from the devise or is in satisfaction of the devise, or the devisee acknowledges in writing that the gift is in satisfaction. For purpose of partial satisfaction, property given during lifetime is valued as of the time the devisee came into possession or enjoyment of the property or as of the time of death of the testator, whichever occurs first.

Part 7
Contractual Arrangements Relating to Death

(See also Article VI)

Section 2–701. [Contracts Concerning Succession.]

A contract to make a will or devise, or not to revoke a will or devise, or to die intestate, if executed after the effective date of this Act, can be established only by (1) provisions of a will stating material provisions of the contract; (2) an express reference in a will to a contract and extrinsic evidence proving the terms of the.contract; or (3) a writing signed by the decedent evidencing the contract. The execution of a joint will or mutual wills does not create a presumption of a contract not to revoke the will or wills.

Part 8
General Provisions

Section 2–801. [Renunciation of Succession.]

(a) A person or the representative of an incapacitated or protected person, who is an heir, devisee, person succeeding to a renounced interest, beneficiary under a testamentary instrument, or appointee under a power of appointment exercised by a testamentary instrument, may renounce in whole or in part the right of succession to any property or interest therein, including a future interest, by filing a written renunciation under this Act. The right to renounce does not survive the death of the person having it. The instrument shall (1) describe the property or interest renounced, (2) declare the renunciation and extent thereof, and (3) be signed by the person renouncing.

Comment to Subsection (a)

Who May Disclaim: At common law it was settled that the taker of property under a will had the right to accept or reject a legacy or devise (per Abbott, C.J. in Townson v. Tickell, 3 B & Ald 3, 136, 106 Eng.Rep. 575, 576). The same rule prevails in the United States (Peter v. Peter, 343 Ill. 493, 175 N.E. 846 (1931), 75 ALR 890). It is said that no one can make another an owner of an estate against his consent by devising it to him. See, for example, People v. Flanagin, 331 Ill. 203, 162 N.E. 848, (1928) 60 ALR 305:

> "The law is clear that a legatee or devisee is under no obligation to accept a testamentary gift . . . and he may renounce the gift, by which act the estate will descend to the heir or pass in some other direction under the will . . ."

Under the rule permitting the disclaimer of testate successions, the disclaimed interest related back to the date of the testator's death so that the interest did not vest in the grantee but remained in the original owner as if the will had never been executed (People v. Flanagin, *supra*).

Unlike the devisee or legatee, an heir had no common law power to prevent passage of title to himself by disclaimer. "An heir at law is the only person in whom the law of England vests property, whether he will or not," declares Williams on Real Property, and adds, "No disclaimer that he may make will have any effect, though, of course, he may as soon as he pleases dispose of the property by ordinary conveyance." (Williams on Law of Real Property 75 [2d Am.Ed.1857]. See also 6 Page on Wills [Bowe-Parker Revision] Section 49.1.)

The difference between testate and intestate successions in respect to the right to disclaim, has produced a number of illogical and undesirable consequences. An heir who sought to reject his inheritance was subjected to the Federal gift tax on the theory that since he could not prevent the passage of title to himself, any act done to rid himself of the interest necessarily involved a transfer subject to gift tax liability [Hardenberg v. Com'r, 198 F.2d 63 (8th Cir.) cert. denied, 344 U.S. 863, (1952) aff'g 17 T.C. 166 (1951); Maxwell v. Com'r, 17 T.C. 1589 (1952). See Lauritzen, Only God Can Make an Heir, 48 NWL Rev. 568; Annotation 170 ALR 435]. On the other hand, a legatee or devisee who rejected a legacy or devise under the will incurred no such tax consequences [Brown v. Routzahn, 63 F.2d 914 (6th Cir.) cert. denied, 290 U.S. 641 (1933)].

Subsection (a) places an heir on the same basis as a devisee or legatee and provides that he and others upon whom successions may devolve, have the full right to disclaim in whole or in part the passage of property to them, with the same legal consequences applying in all such cases.

Successive disclaimers are permitted by the express inclusion of "person succeeding to a disclaimed interest" among those who may disclaim.

Beneficiary: The term beneficiary is used in a broad sense to include any person entitled, but for his disclaimer, to possess or enjoy an equitable or legal interest, present or future, in the property or interest, including a power to consume, appoint, or apply it for any purpose or to enforce the transfer in any respect.

Subsection (a) extends the right to disclaim to the representative of an incapacitated or protected person. This accords with the general rule that the probate or surrogate court in the exercise of its traditional jurisdiction over the person and estate of a minor or incompetent may authorize or direct the guardian, conservator or committee to exercise the right on behalf of his ward when it is in the ward's interest to do so. Davis v. Mather, 309 Ill. 284, 141 N.E. 209 (1923).

On the other hand, absent a statute, the general rule is that the right to disclaim is personal to the person entitled to exercise it, and dies with him in the absence of fraud or concealment or conflict of interest of his representative, even though the time within which the right might have been utilized has not expired and even though he may be incompetent. Rock Island Bank & Trust Co. v. First Nat. Bank of Rock Island, 26 Ill.2d 47, 185 N.E.2d 890 (1962), 3 ALR 3d 114. Subsection (a) adopts this position by stating that the right to disclaim does not survive the death of the person having it.

The Act makes no provision here or elsewhere, for an extension of time to disclaim or other relief from a strict observance of the statutory requirements for disclaimer and the time limitations for expressing the right of disclaimer applies to persons under disability as well as to others.

What May be Disclaimed: Subsection (a) specifies that the "succession" to any property, real or personal or interest therein, may be disclaimed, and it is immaterial whether it derives by way of will, intestacy, exercise of a power of appointment or disclaimer. It would include the right to renounce any survivorship interest in the community in a community property state. *Cf.* U.S. v. Mitchell, 403 U.S. 190 (1971), rev'g 430 F.2d (5th Cir.1970), aff'g 51 T.C. 641 (1969).

Future Interests: Subsection (a) contemplates the disclaimer of future interests by reference to "beneficiary under a testamentary instrument" and "appointee under a power of appointment." The time for making such a disclaimer is dealt with in Subsection (b).

Partial Disclaimer: The status of partial disclaimers has been uncertain in many states. The result has often turned on whether the gift is "severable" or constitutes a "single, aggregate" gift [Olgesby v. Springfield Marine Bank, 395 Ill. 37, 69 N.E.2d 269 (1946); Brown v. Routzahn, *supra*]. Subsection (a) makes it clear that a partial, as well as a total, disclaimer is permitted.

Discretionary administrative and investment powers under a trust have been held to constitute a "severable" interest and subject to partial disclaimer. Estate of Harry C. Jaecker, 58 T.C. 166, CCH Dec. 31,356 (1972).

Method of Disclaiming: In many states no satisfactory case law has existed as to the form and manner of making disclaimers of devises or legacies under wills. See Annotation 93 ALR 2d 8—What Constitutes or Establishes Beneficiary's Acceptance of Renunciation of Bequest or Devise. Because certainty of titles and the expeditious administration of estates makes definiteness desirable in this area, Subsection (a) requires a disclaimer to (i) describe the property or interest disclaimed; (ii) declare the disclaimer and the extent thereof; and (iii) be signed by the disclaimant.

(b) (1) An instrument renouncing a present interest shall be filed not later than [9] months after the death of the decedent or the donee of the power.

(2) An instrument renouncing a future interest may be filed not later than [9] months after the event determining that the taker of the property or interest is finally ascertained and his interest is indefeasibly vested.

(3) The renunciation shall be filed in the [probate] court of the county in which proceedings have been commenced for the administration of the estate of the deceased owner or deceased donee of the power or, if they have not been commenced, in which they could be commenced. A copy of the renunciation shall be delivered in person or mailed by registered or certified mail to any personal representative, or other fiduciary of the decedent or donee of the power. If real property or an interest therein is renounced, a copy of the renunciation may be recorded in the office of the [Recorder of Deeds] of the county in which the real estate is situated.*

---

* If Torrens system is in effect, add provisions to comply with local law.

Comment to Subsection (b)

Time for Making Disclaimer. At common law, no specific time evolved within which disclaimer had to be made. The only requirement was that it be within a "reasonable" time (In re Wilson's Estate, 298 N.Y. 398, 83 N.E.2d 852 (1949); Ewing v. Rountree, 228 F.Supp. 137 (D.C. Tenn.1964). As a result, divergent holdings were reached by the courts (Brown v. Routzahn, 63 F.2d 914 (6th Cir.), cert. denied, 290 U.S. 641 (1933). Subsection (b) fixes a definite time for filing of disclaimers. This approach follows the pattern of the Federal estate tax law which prescribed the time for filing estate tax returns in terms of the decedent's death. The time allowed should overlast the time for filing claims and contesting the will and enable the executor or administrator to know with certainty who the takers of the estate will be. On the other hand, it should not be so long as to work against an early determination of the acceptance or rejection of succession to an estate, or increase the risk of inadvertent acceptance of the benefits of the property, creating an estoppel. In the case of future interests the disclaimer period should run from the time the takers of the interest are finally ascertained and their interests indefeasibly fixed. Seifner v. Weller, 171 S.W.2d 617 (Mo.1943). For the consequence of selecting too short a period, see Brodhag v. U.S., 319 F.Supp.747 (S.D.W.Va., 1970) involving a 2-month period fixed by West Virginia law.

In the case of future interests it should be noted that the person need not wait until the occurrence of the determinative event before filing a disclaimer, but may do so at any time after the death of the decedent or donee, so long as it is made "not later than" the prescribed period.

Federal Gift Tax Implications: Disclaimers have significance under the Federal gift tax law. Section 2511(a) of the Internal Revenue Code imposes a gift tax upon the transfer of property by gift whether the transfer is in trust or otherwise, and whether the gift is direct or indirect. The Treasury regulations under this section state that where local law gives the beneficiary, heir or next-of-kin an unqualified right to refuse to accept ownership of property transferred from a decedent, whether by will or by intestacy, a refusal to accept ownership does not constitute the making of a gift if the refusal is made within a "reasonable time" after knowledge of the existence of the transfer.

A "reasonable time" for gift tax purposes is not defined in the Code or regulations. It has been held that the courts will look to the law of the states in determining the question, (Brown v. Routzahn, 63 F.2d 914 (6th Cir.) cert. denied, 290 U.S. 641 (1933)), not conclusively, but as relevant and having probative value (Keinath v. C.I.R., 480 F.2d 57 (8th Cir.1973), rev'g 58 T.C. 352 (1972)), and that an unequivocal disclaimer filed within 6 months of the determinative event is made within a "reasonable time." It has been held, further, that as regards future interests, the "reasonable time" period runs from the termination of the preceding estate or interest, and not from the time the transfer was made, Keinath v. C.I.R., *supra.*

Place of Filing Disclaimer: Subsection (b) requires a disclaimer to be filed in the probate court. If real property or an interest therein is involved, a copy of the disclaimer may also be recorded in the office of the recorder of deeds or other appropriate office in the county in which the real estate is situated. If the Torrens system is in effect, appropriate provisions should be added to comply with local law.

Notice: A copy of the disclaimer is required to be delivered in person or mailed by registered or certified mail to the personal representative or other fiduciary of the decedent or of the donee of the power as the case may be.

(c) Unless the decedent or donee of the power has otherwise provided, the property or interest renounced devolves as though the person renouncing had predeceased the decedent or, if the appointment exercised by a testamentary instrument, as though the person renouncing had predeceased the donee of the power. A future interest that takes effect in possession or enjoyment after the termination of the estate or interest renounced takes effect as though the person renouncing had predeceased the decedent or the donee of the power. A renunciation relates back for all purposes to the date of the death of the decedent or the donee of the power.

Comment to Subsection (c)

Devolution of Disclaimed Property: When a beneficiary disclaims his interest under a will, the question arises as to what happens to the rejected interest. In People v. Flanagin, 331 Ill. 203, 162 N.E. 848 (1928), 60 ALR 305, the court, quoting the New York case of Burritt v. Sillman, 13 N.Y. 93 (1855) said that the disclaimed property will "descend to the heir or pass in some other direction under the will." From this, it may be assumed that the court meant that if the decedent left no will, the renounced interest passed according to the rules of descent, but if he left a will, it passed according to its terms.

It has been generally thought that devolution in the case of disclaimer should be the same as in the case of lapse, which is controlled by sections of the probate law. Subsection (c) takes this approach. It provides that unless the will of the decedent or the donee of the power has otherwise provided, the disclaimed interest devolves as if the disclaimant had predeceased the decedent or the donee of the power. In every case the disclaimer relates back to the date of the death of the decedent or of the donee. The provision that the disclaimer "relates back", codifies the rule that a renunciation of a devise or legacy relates to the date of death of the decedent or donee and prevents the succession from becoming operative in favor of the disclaimant. See In re Wilson's Estate, 298 N.Y. 398, 83 N.E.2d 852 (1949). Also, Bouse, for use of State v. Hull, 168 Md. 1, 176 A. 645 (1935).

Acceleration of Future Interests: If a life estate or other future interest is disclaimed, the problem is raised of whether succeeding interests or estates accelerate in possession or enjoyment or whether the disclaimed interest must be marshalled to await the actual happening of the contingency. Subsection (c) provides that remainder interests are accelerated, the second sentence specifically stating that any future interest which is to take effect in possession or enjoyment after the termination of the estate or interest disclaimed, takes effect as if the disclaimant had predeceased the deceased owner or deceased donee of the power. Thus, if T. leaves his estate in trust to pay the income to his son for life, remainder to his son's children who survive him, and S. disclaims with two children then living, the remainder in the children accelerates; the trust terminates and the children receive possession and enjoyment, even though the son may subsequently have other children or that one or more of the living children may die during their father's lifetime.

Effect of Death or Disability of Person Entitled to Disclaim: The effect of death of a person entitled to disclaim, including one under disability, is discussed under Subsection (a). A guardian or conservator of the estate of an incapacitated or protected person may disclaim for the ward. Subsection (b) makes no provision for an extension of time or for other relief in case of disability from the observance of the statutory requirements for effective disclaimer. The intent is that the period for disclaimer applies to a person under disability as well as to others, and includes a court which purports to act on behalf of one under disability in the absence of fraud, misconduct or other unusual circumstances. Pratt v. Baker, 48 Ill.App.2d 442, 199 N.E.2d 307 (1964).

Rights of Creditors and Others: As regards creditors, taxing authorities and others, the provision for "relation back" has the legal effect of preventing a succession from becoming operative in favor of the disclaimant. The relation back is "for all purposes" which would include, among others for the purpose of rights of creditors, taxing authorities and assertion of dower. It is immaterial that the effect is to avoid the imposition of a higher death tax than would be the case if the interest had been accepted: Estate of Aylsworth, 74 Ill.App.2d 375, 219 N.E.2d 779 (1966) [motive for the disclaimer is immaterial]; People v. Flanagin, 331 Ill. 203, 162 N.E. 848 (1928), 60 ALR 305; Cook v. Dove, 32 Ill.2d 109, 203 N.E.2d 892 (1965) [upholding for inheritance tax the right of appointees to take by default rather than under the power-holder's exercise of power]; Matter of Wolfe's Estate, 179 N.Y. 599, 72 N.E. 1152 (1904); eff'g 89 App.Div. 349, 83 N.Y.Supp. 949 (1903); Brown v. Routzahn, 63 F.2d 914 (6th Cir.), cert. denied 290 U.S. 641 (1933); In re Stone's Estate, 132 Ia. 136, 109 N.W. 455 (1906); Tax Commission v. Glass, 119 Ohio St. 389, 164 N.E. 425 (1929); U.S. v. McCrackin, 189 F.Supp. 632 (S.D.Ohio 1960).

Similarly, numerous cases have held that a devisee or legatee can disclaim a devise or legacy despite the claims of creditors: Hoecker v. United Bank of Boulder, 476 F.2d 838 (CA 10, 1973), aff'g 334 F.Supp. 1080 (D.Colo.1971) (bankruptcy); U.S. v. McCrackin, *supra* (Federal income tax liens); Shoonover v. Osborne, 193 Ia. 474, 187 N.W. 20

(1922); Bradford v. Calhoun, 120 Tenn. 53, 109 S.W. 502 (1908); Carter v. Carter, 63 N.J.Eq. 726, 53 A. 160 (1902); Estate of Hansen, 109 Ill. App.2d 283, 248 N.E.2d 709 (1969) (judgment creditor); 37 Mich.L.Rev. 1168; 43 Yale L J 1030; 27 ALR 477; 133 ALR 1428. A creditor is not entitled to notice of the disclaimer (In re Estate of Hansen, 109 Ill.App. 2d 283, 248 N.E.2d 709 (1969)).

(d) (1) The right to renounce property or an interest therein is barred by (i) an assignment, conveyance, encumbrance, pledge, or transfer of the property or interest, or a contract therefor, (ii) a written waiver of the right to renounce, (iii) an acceptance of the property or interest or benefit thereunder, or (iv) a sale of the property or interest under judicial sale made before the renunciation is effected.

(2) The right to renounce exists notwithstanding any limitation on the interest of the person renouncing in the nature of a spendthrift provision or similar restriction.

(3) A renunciation or a written waiver of the right to renounce is binding upon the person renouncing or person waiving and all persons claiming through or under him.

Comment to Subsection (d)

Bars to Disclaimer—Waiver—Estoppel: It may be necessary or advisable to sell real estate in a decedent's estate before the expiration of the period permitted for disclaimer. In such case, the possibility of a disclaimer being filed within the period, could be a deterrent to sale and delivery of good title. Subsection (d) expressly authorizes an heir, devisee, legatee or other person entitled to disclaim, to indicate in writing his intention to "waive" his right of disclaimer, and thus avoid any delay in the completion of a sale or other disposition of estate assets. The written waiver bars the right of the person subsequently to disclaim the property or interest therein and is binding on persons claiming through or under him.

Similarly, Subsection (d) provides that various acts of a person entitled to disclaim in regard to property or an interest therein, such as making an assignment, conveyance, encumbrance, pledge or transfer of the property or interest, or a contract therefor, bars the right of the person to disclaim and is binding on all persons claiming through or under him.

Spendthrift Provisions: The existence of a limitation on the interest of an heir, legatee, devisee or other disclaimant in the nature of a spendthrift provision or similar restriction is expressly declared not to affect the right to disclaim. Without this provision, there might be a question as to whether the beneficiary of a spendthrift trust can disclaim under the statute (Griswold, Spendthrift Trust [2d Ed.] Section 524, p. 603). If a person who is under no legal disability wishes to refuse a beneficial interest under a trust, he should not be powerless to make an effective disclaimer even though the intended interest once accepted by him would be inalienable. (Scott on Trusts, Section 337.7, p. 2683, 3d Ed.)

When a beneficial interest is accepted by a beneficiary, he cannot thereafter disclaim or release it (Griswold, supra, Section 534, p. 603, note 48). As to what conduct amounts to an acceptance, see In Re Wilson's Estate, 298 N.Y. 398, 83 N.E.2d 852 (1949).

Judicial Sale: The section provides that the right to disclaim is barred by a sale of the property or interest under a judicial sale. Judicial sales are ordered in many different types of proceeding such as foreclosure of mortgage or trust deed, enforcement of lien, partition proceedings and proceedings for the sale of real property of a decedent or ward for certain purposes. Probate laws frequently permit a representative to mortgage or pledge property of the decedent or ward in certain circumstances. Execution sales are made pursuant to a writ to satisfy a money judgment. Subsection (d) has the effect of providing that the making of a judicial sale for the account of the heir, devisee, or beneficiary, bars him from renouncing the property or interest. To be distinguished from a judicial sale, is a taking pursuant to eminent domain, which is considered to be a taking of property without the owner's consent and unrelated to his obligations or commitments. The right to disclaim the proceeds of a condemnation action if otherwise timely and in accordance with the Act, should not, therefore, be barred under this section.

(e) This Act does not abridge the right of a person to waive, release, disclaim, or renounce property or an interest therein under any other statute.

Comment to Subsection (e)

Subsection (e) provides that the right to disclaim under the law does not abridge the right of any person to waive, release, disclaim or renounce any property or interest therein under any other statute. The principal statutes to which this provision is pointed are those dealing with spousal renunciations and release of powers.

Being a codification of the common law in regard to the renunciation of the property, the Act is intended to constitute an *exclusive remedy* for the disclaimer of testamentary successions apart from those provided by other statutes, and supplants the common law right to disclaim.

(f) An interest in property existing on the effective date of this Act as to which, if a present interest, the time for filing a renunciation under this Act has not expired, or if a future interest, the interest has not become indefeasibly vested or the taker finally ascertained, may be renounced with [9] months after the effective date of this Act.

Comment to Subsection (f)

Subsection (f) deals with the application of the Act to property interests under instruments or in estates in existence on the effective date. If the interest is a present one and the filing time has not expired, the holder is given a full period after enactment within which to disclaim the interest. If the interest is a future one, the holder is given a full period after the interest becomes indefeasibly vested or the takers finally ascertained, after enactment in which to disclaim it. If T dies in 1960 trusteeing his estate to W for life, remainder to such of T's sons as are living at W's death and W dies in 1975, the Act permits a son to disclaim his remainder interest after it ripens even though it arises under an instrument predating the effective date of the Act. The application of statute to pre-existing instruments in like situations finds support in cases such as Will of Allis, 6 Wis.2d 1, 94 N.W.2d 226, (1959), 69 ALR2d 1128.

Comment to Section 2–801

The above text, consists of Sections 1 through 6 of Uniform Disclaimer of Transfers By Will, Intestacy or Appointment Act of 1973, redesignated as subsections (a) through (f).

The Comments following each subsection are the Official Comments to the 1973 statute. The word "renunciation" has been substituted for "disclaimer" because the original Section 2–801 used the term "renunciation" and several cross-references to this term appear in other sections of this Code. It is the view of the Joint Editorial Board that the terms "renunciation" and "disclaimer" have the same meaning.

The principal substantive difference between original Section 2–801 and the 1973 replacement therefor is that the former permitted renunciation by the personal representative of a person who might have renounced during his lifetime. Under the new uniform act which is now the official text of Section 2–801, the right to renounce terminates upon the death of the person who might have renounced during his lifetime. Also, the original version was less precise than the present version in the important provisions of subsection (b) which govern the time for renunciation.

(The balance of the comment is the same as the original comment to Section 2–801.)

This section is designed to facilitate renunciation in order to aid postmortem planning. Although present law in all states permits renunciation of a devise under a will, the common law did not permit renunciation of an intestate share. There is no reason for such a distinction, and some states have already adopted legislation permitting renunciation of an intestate share. Renunciation may be made for a variety of reasons, including carrying out the decedent's wishes not expressed in a properly executed will.

Under the rule of this section, renounced property passes as if the renouncing person had failed to survive the decedent. In the case of intestate property, the heir who would be next in line in succession would take; often this will be the issue of the renouncing person, taking by representation. For consistency the same rule is adopted for renunciation by a devisee; if the devisee is a relative who leaves issue surviving the testator, the issue will take under Section 2–605; otherwise disposition will be governed by Section 2–606 and general rules of law.

The section limits renunciation to nine months after the death of the decedent or if the taker of the property is not ascertained at that time, then nine months after he is ascertained. If the personal representative is concerned about closing the estate within that nine months period in order to make distribution, he can obtain a waiver of the right to renounce. Normally this should be no problem, since the heir or devisee cannot renounce once he has taken possession of the property.

The presence of a spendthrift clause does not prevent renunciation under this section.

Section 2–802. [Effect of Divorce, Annulment, and Decree of Separation.]

(a) A person who is divorced from the decedent or whose marriage to the decedent has been annulled is not a surviving spouse unless, by virtue of a subsequent marriage, he is married to the decedent at the time of death. A decree of separation which does not terminate the status of husband and wife is not a divorce for purposes of this section.

(b) For purposes of Parts 1, 2, 3 & 4 of this Article, and of Section 3–203, a surviving spouse does not include:

(1) a person who obtains or consents to a final decree or judgment of divorce from the decedent or an annulment of their marriage, which decree or judgment is not recognized as valid in this state, unless they subsequently participate in a marriage ceremony purporting to marry each to the other, or subsequently live together as man and wife;

(2) a person who, following a decree or judgment of divorce or annulment obtained by the decedent, participates in a marriage ceremony with a third person; or

(3) a person who was a party to a valid proceeding concluded by an order purporting to terminate all marital property rights.

[Section 2–803. [Effect of Homicide on Intestate Succession, Wills, Joint Assets, Life Insurance and Beneficiary Designations.]

(a) A surviving spouse, heir or devisee who feloniously and intentionally kills the decedent is not entitled to any benefits under the will or under this Article, and the estate of decedent passes as if the killer had predeceased the decedent. Property appointed by the will of the decedent to or for the benefit of the killer passes as if the killer had predeceased the decedent.

(b) Any joint tenant who feloniously and intentionally kills another joint tenant thereby effects a severance of the interest of the decedent so that the share of the decedent passes as his property and the killer has no rights by survivorship. This provision applies to joint tenancies [and tenancies by the entirety] in real and personal property, joint and multiple-party accounts in banks, savings and loan associations, credit unions and other institutions, and any other form of co-ownership with survivorship incidents.

(c) A named beneficiary of a bond, life insurance policy, or other contractual arrangement who feloniously and intentionally kills the principal obligee or the person upon whose life the policy is issued is not entitled to any benefit under the bond, policy or other contractual arrangement, and it becomes payable as though the killer had predeceased the decedent.

(d) Any other acquisition of property or interest by the killer shall be treated in accordance with the principles of this section.

(e) A final judgment of conviction of felonious and intentional killing is conclusive for purposes of this section. In the absence of a conviction of felonious and intentional killing the Court may determine by a preponderance of evidence whether the killing was felonious and intentional for purposes of this section.

(f) This section does not affect the rights of any person who, before rights under this section have been adjudicated, purchases from the killer for value and without notice property which the killer would have acquired except for this section, but the killer is liable for the amount of the proceeds or the value of the property. Any insurance company, bank, or other obligor making payment according to the terms of its policy or obligation is not liable by reason of this section unless prior to payment it has received at its home office or principal address written notice of a claim under this section.]

Part 9
Custody and Deposit of Wills

Section 2–901. [Deposit of Will With Court in Testator's Lifetime.]

A will may be deposited by the testator or his agent with any Court for safekeeping, under rules of the Court. The will shall be kept confidential. During the testator's lifetime a deposited will shall be delivered only to him or to a person authorized in writing signed by him to receive the will. A conservator may be allowed to examine a deposited will of a protected testator under procedures designed to maintain the confidential character of the document to the extent possible, and to assure that it will be resealed and left on deposit after the examination. Upon being informed of the testator's death, the Court shall notify any person designated to receive the will and deliver it to him on request; or the Court may deliver the will to the appropriate Court.

Section 2–902. [Duty of Custodian of Will; Liability.]

After the death of a testator and on request of an interested person, any person having custody of a will of the testator shall deliver it with reasonable promptness to a person able to secure its probate and if none is known, to an appropriate Court. Any person who wilfully fails to deliver a will is liable to any person aggrieved for the damages which may be sustained by the failure. Any person who wilfully refuses or fails to deliver a will after being ordered by the Court in a proceeding brought for the purpose of compelling delivery is subject to penalty for contempt of Court.

[Part 10]
[Uniform International Wills Act];
International Will Information Registration]

Prefatory Note

Introduction

The purpose of the Washington Convention of 1973 concerning international wills is to provide testators with a way of making wills that will be valid as to form in all countries joining the Convention. As proposed by the Convention, the objective would be achieved through uniform local rules of form, rather than through local or international law that makes recognition of foreign wills turn on choice of law rules involving possible application of foreign law. The international will provisions, prepared for the National Conference of Commissioners on Uniform State Laws by the Joint Editorial Board for the Uniform Probate Code which has functioned as a special committee of the Conference for the project, should be enacted by all states, including those that have not accepted the Uniform Probate Code. To that end, the proposal being submitted to the National Conference is framed both as a free-standing act and as an added part of the Uniform Probate Code. The bracketed headings and numbers fit the proposal into UPC; the others present the proposal as a free-standing act.

Uniform state enactment of these provisions will permit the Washington Convention of 1973 to be implemented through state legislaton familiar to will draftsmen. Thus, local proof of foreign law and reliance on federal legislation regarding wills can be avoided when foreign wills come into our states to be implemented. Also, the citizens of all states will have a will form available that should greatly reduce perils of proof and risks of invalidity that attend proof of American wills abroad.

History of the International Will

Discussions about possible international accord on an acceptable form of will led the Governing Council of UNIDROIT (International Institute for the Unification of Private Law) in 1960 to appoint a small committee of experts from several countries to develop proposals. Following week-long meetings at the Institute's quarters in Rome in 1963, and on two occasions in 1965, the Institute published and circulated a Draft Convention of December 1966 with an annexed uniform law that would be required to be enacted locally by those countries agreeing to the convention. The package and accompanying explanations were reviewed in this country by the Secretary of State's Advisory Committee on Private International Law. In turn, it referred the proposal to a special committee of American probate specialists drawn from members of NCCUSL's Special Committee on the Uniform Probate Code and its advisors and reporters. The resulting reports and recommendations were affirmative and urged the State Department to cooperate in continuing efforts to develop the 1966 Draft Convention, and to endeavor to interest other countries in the subject.

Encouraged by support for the project from this country and several others, UNIDROIT served as host for a 1971 meeting in Rome of an expanded group that included some of the original panel of experts and others from several countries that were not represented in the early drafting sessions. The result of this meeting was a revised draft of the proposed convention and annexed uniform law and this, in turn, was the subject of study and discussion by many more persons in this country. In mid-1973, the proposal from UNIDROIT was discussed in a joint program of the Real Property Probate and Trust Law Section, and the Section of International Law at the American Bar Association's annual meeting held that year in Washington, D.C. By late 1973, the list of published, scholarly discussions of the International Will proposals included Fratcher, "The Uniform Probate Code and the International Will", 66 Mich.L.Rev. 469 (1968); Wellman, "Recent Unidroit Drafts on the International Will", 6 The International Lawyer 205 (1973); and Wellman, "Proposed International Convention Concerning Wills", 8/4 Real Property, Probate and Trust Journal 622 (1973).

In October 1973, pursuant to a commitment made earlier to UNIDROIT representatives that it would provide leadership for the international will proposal if sufficient interest from other countries became evident, the United States served as host for the diplomatic Conference on Wills which met in Washington from October 10 to 26, 1973. 42 governments were represented by delegations, 6 by observers. The United States delegation of 8 persons plus 2 Congressional advisers and 2 staff advisers, was headed by Ambassador Richard D. Kearney, Chairman of the Secretary of State's Advisory Committee on Private

International Law who also was selected president of the Conference. The result of the Conference was the Convention of October 26, 1973 Providing a Uniform Law on the Form of an International Will, an appended Annex, Uniform Law on the Form of an International Will, and a Resolution recommending establishment of state assisted systems for the safekeeping and discovery of wills. These three documents are reproduced at the end of these preliminary comments.

A more detailed account of the UNIDROIT project and the 1973 Convention, together with recommendations regarding United States implementation of the Convention, appears in Nadelmann, "The Formal Validity of Wills and the Washington Convention 1973 Providing the Form of an International Will", XXII The American Journal of Comparative Law, 365 (1974).

Description of the Proposal

The 1973 Convention obligates countries becoming parties to make the annexed uniform law a part of their local law. The proposed uniform law contemplates the involvement in will executions under this law of a state-recognized expert who is referred to throughout the proposals as the "authorized person". Hence, the local law called for by the Convention must designate authorized persons, and prescribe the formalities for an international will and the role of authorized persons relating thereto. The Convention binds parties to respect the authority of another party's authorized persons and this obligation, coupled with local enactment of the common statute prescribing the role of those persons and according finality to their certificates regarding due execution of wills, assures recognition of international wills under local law in all countries joining the Convention.

The Convention and the annexed uniform law deal only with the formal validity of wills. Thus, the proposal is entirely neutral in relation to local laws dealing with revocation of wills, or those defining the scope of testamentary power, or regulating the probate, interpretation, and construction of wills, and the administration of decedents' estates. The proposal describes a highly formal mode of will execution; one that is sufficiently protective against imposition and mistake to command international approval as being safe enough. However, failure to meet the requirements of an international will does not necessarily result in invalidity, as the mode of execution described for an international will does not pre-empt or exclude other standards of testamentary validity.

The details of the prescribed mode of execution reflect a blend of common- and civil-law elements. Two attesting witnesses are required in the tradition of the English Statute of Wills of 1837 and its American counterparts. The authorized person whose participation in the ceremony of execution is required, and whose certificate makes the will self-proved, plays a role not unlike that of the civil law notary, though he is not required to retain custody of the will as is customary with European notaries.

The question of who should be given state recognition as authorized persons was resolved by designation of all licensed attorneys. The reasons for this can be seen in the observations about the role of Kurt H. Nadelmann, writing in The American Journal of Comparative Law:

> The duties imposed by the Uniform Law upon the person doing the certifying go beyond legalization of signatures, the domain of the notary public. At least paralegal training is a necessity. Abroad, in countries with the law trained notary, the designation is likely to go to this class or at least to include it. Similarly, in countries with a closely supervised class of solicitors, their designation may be expected.

Attorneys are subject to training and licensing requirements everywhere in this country. The degree to which they are supervised after qualification varies considerably from state to state, but the trend is definitely in the direction of more rather than less supervision. Designation of attorneys in the uniform law permits a state to bring the statute into its local law books without undue delay.

Roles for Federal and State Law in Relation to International Will

Several alternatives are available for arranging federal and state laws on the subject of international wills. The 1973 Convention obligates nations becoming parties to introduce the annexed uniform law into their local law, and to recognize the authority, *vis a vis* will executions and certificates relating to wills, of persons designated as authorized by other parties to the Convention. But, the Convention includes a clause for federal states that may be used by the United States as it moves, through the process of Senate Advice and Consent, to accept the international compact. Through it, the federal government may limit the areas in this country to which the Convention will be applicable. Thus, Article XIV of the 1973 Convention provides:

> 1. If a state has two or more territorial units in which different systems of law apply in relation to matters respecting the form of wills, it may at the time of signature, ratification, or accession, declare that this Convention shall extend to all its territorial units or only to one or more of them, and may modify its declaration by submitting another declaration at any time.
>
> 2. These declarations shall be notified to the Depositary Government and shall state expressly the territorial units to which the Convention applies.

One alternative would be for the federal government to refrain from use of Article XIV and to accept the Convention as applicable to all areas of the country. The obligation to introduce the uniform law into local law then could be met by passage of a federal statute incorporating the uniform law and designating authorized persons who can assist testators desiring to use the international format, possibly leaving it open for state legislatures, if they wish, to designate other or additional groups of authorized persons. As to constitutionality, the federal statute on wills could be rested on the power of the federal government to bind the states by treaty and to implement a treaty obligation to bring agreed upon rules into local law by any appropriate method. Missouri v. Holland, 252 U.S. 416, 40 S.Ct. 382, 64 L.Ed. 641 (1920); Nadelmann, "The Formal Validity of Wills and the Washington Convention 1973 Providing the Form of An International Will", XXII The Am.Jn'l of Comp.L. 365, 375 (1974). Prof. Nadelmann favors this approach, arguing that new risks of invalidity of wills would arise if the treaty were limited so as to be applicable only in designated areas of the country, presumably those where state enactment of the uniform law already had occurred.

One disadvantage of this approach is that it would place a potentially important method for validating wills in federal statutes where probate practitioners, long accustomed to finding the statutes pertinent to their specialty in state compilations, simply would not discover it. Another, of course, relates to more generalized concerns that would attend any move by the federal government into an area of law traditionally reserved to the states.

Alternatively, the federal government might accept the Convention and uniform law as applicable throughout the land, so that international wills executed with the aid of authorized persons of other countries would be good anywhere in this country, but refrain from any designation of authorized persons, other than possibly of some minimum federal cadre, or of those who could function within the District of Columbia, leaving the selection of more useful groups of authorized persons entirely to the states. One result would be to narrow greatly the advantage of international wills to American testators who wanted to execute their instruments at home. In probable consequence, there would be pressure on state legislatures to enact the uniform law so as to make the advantages of the system available to local testators. Assuming some state legislatures respond to the pressure affirmatively and others negatively, a crazy-quilt pattern of international-will states would develop, leading possibly to some of the confusion and risk of illegality feared by Prof. Nadelmann. On the other hand, since execution of an international will involves use of an authorized person who derives authority from (on this assumption) state legislation, it seems somewhat unlikely that testators in states that have not designated authorized persons will be led to believe they can make an international will unless they go to a state where authorized persons have been designated. Hence, the confusion may not be as great as if the Convention were inapplicable to portions of the country.

Finally, the federal government might use Article XIV, as suggested earlier, and designate some but not all states as areas of the country in which the Convention applies. This seems the least desirable of all alternatives because it subjects international wills from abroad to the risk of non-recognition in some states, and offers the risk of confusion of American testators regarding the areas of the country where they can execute a will that will be received outside this country as an international will.

Under any of the approaches, the desirability of widespread enactment of state statutes, embodying the uniform law and designating authorized persons, seems clear, as does the necessity for this project of the National Conference of Commissioners on Uniform State Laws.

Style

In preparing the International Will proposal, the special committee, after considerable discussion and consideration of alternatives, decided to adhere as closely as possible to the wording of the Annex to the Convention of October 26, 1973.   The Convention and its Annex were written in the English, French, Russian and Spanish languages, each version, as declared by Article XVI of the Convention, being equally authentic.   Not surprisingly, the English version of the Annex has a style that is somewhat different than that to which the National Conference is accustomed.   Nonetheless, from the view of those using languages other than English who may be reviewing our state statutes on the International Will to see if they adhere to the Annex, it is more important to accept the agreed formulations than it is to re-style these expressions to suit our traditions.   However, some changes from the Annex were made in the interests of clarity, and because some of the language of the Annex is plainly inappropriate in a local enactment. These changes are explained in the Comments.

Will Registration

A bracketed Section 9[2–1009], is included in the International Will proposal to aid survivors in locating international and other wills that have been kept secret by testators during their lives.   Differing from the Section 2–901 of the Uniform Probate Code and the many existing statutes from which that section was derived which designate the probate court as an agency for the safe-keeping of wills deposited by living testators, the bracketed proposal is for a system of registering certain minimum information about wills, including where the instrument will be kept pending the death of the testator.   It can be separated or omitted from the rest of the Act.

This provision for a state will-registration system is derived from recommendations by the Council of Europe for common market countries.   Those recommendations were urged on the group that assembled in Rome in 1971, and were received with interest by representatives of United Kingdom, Canada and United States, where will-making laws and customs have not included any officially-sanctioned system for safekeeping of wills or for locating information about wills, other than occasional statutes providing for ante-mortem deposit of wills with probate courts.   Interest was expressed also by the notaries from civil law countries who have traditionally aided will-making both by formalizing execution and by being the source thereafter of official certificates about wills, the originals of which are retained with the official records of the notary and carefully protected and regulated by settled customs of the profession. All recognized that acceptance of the international will would tend to increase the frequency with which owners of property in several different countries relied on a single will to control all of their properties. This prospect, plus increasing mobility of persons between countries, indicates that new methods for safekeeping and locating wills after death should be developed. The Resolution adopted as the final act of the 1973 Conference on Wills shows that the problem also attracted the interest and attention of that assembly.

Apart from problems of wills that may have effect in more than one country, Americans are moving from state to state with increasing frequency. As the international will statute becomes enacted in most if not all states, our laws will tend to induce persons to rely on a single will as sufficient even though they may own land in two or more states, and to refrain from making new wills when they change domicile from one state to another. The spread of the Uniform Probate Code, tending as it does to give wills the same meaning and procedural status in all states, will have a similar effect.

General enactment of the will-registration section should lead to development of new state and interstate systems to meet the predictable needs of testators and survivors that will follow as the law of wills is detached from provincial restraints. It is offered with the international-will provisions because both meet obvious needs of the times.

Documents from 1973 Convention

Three documents representing the work of the 1973 Convention are reproduced here for ready reference.

CONVENTION PROVIDING A UNIFORM LAW ON THE FORM OF AN INTERNATIONAL WILL

The States signatory to the present Convention,

DESIRING to provide to a greater extent for the respecting of last wills by establishing an additional form of will hereinafter to be called an "international will' which, if employed, would dispense to some extent with the search for the applicable law;

HAVE RESOLVED to conclude a Convention for this purpose and have agreed upon the following provisions:

Article I 1. Each Contracting Party undertakes that not later than six months after the date of entry into force of this Convention in respect of that Party it shall introduce into its law the rules regarding an international will set out in the Annex to this Convention.

2. Each Contracting Party may introduce the provisions of the Annex into its law either by reproducing the actual text, or by translating it into its official language or languages.

3. Each Contracting Party may introduce into its law such further provisions as are necessary to give the provisions of the Annex full effect in its territory.

4. Each Contracting Party shall submit to the Depositary Government the text of the rules introduced into its national law in order to implement the provisions of this Convention.

Article II 1. Each Contracting Party shall implement the provisions of the Annex in its law, within the period provided for in the preceding article, by designating the persons who, in its territory, shall be authorized to act in connection with international wills. It may also designate as a person authorized to act with regard to its nationals its diplomatic or consular agents abroad insofar as the local law does not prohibit it.

2. The Party shall notify such designation, as well as any modifications thereof, to the Depositary Government.

Article III The capacity of the authorized person to act in connection with an international will, if conferred in accordance with the law of a Contracting Party, shall be recognized in the territory of the other Contracting Parties.

Article IV The effectiveness of the certificate provided for in Article 10 of the Annex shall be recognized in the territories of all Contracting Parties.

Article V 1. The conditions requisite to acting as a witness of an international will shall be governed by the law under which the authorized person was designated. The same rule shall apply as regards an interpreter who is called upon to act.

2. Nonetheless no one shall be disqualified to act as a witness of an international will solely because he is an alien.

Article VI 1. The signature of the testator, of the authorized person, and of the witnesses to an international will, whether on the will or on the certificate, shall be exempt from any legalization or like formality.

2. Nonetheless, the competent authorities of any Contracting Party may, if necessary, satisfy themselves as to the authenticity of the signature of the authorized person.

Article VII The safekeeping of an international will shall be governed by the law under which the authorized person was designated.

Article VIII No reservation shall be admitted to this Convention or to its Annex.

Article IX 1. The present Convention shall be open for signature at Washington from October 26, 1973, until December 31, 1974.

2. The Convention shall be subject to ratification.

3. Instruments of ratification shall be deposited with the Government of the United States of America, which shall be the Depositary Government.

Article X   1.   The Convention shall be open indefinitely for accession.

2.   Instruments of accession shall be deposited with the Depositary Government.

Article XI   1.   The present Convention shall enter into force six months after the date of deposit of the fifth instrument of ratification or accession with the Depositary Government.

2.   In the case of each State which ratifies this Convention or accedes to it after the fifth instrument of ratification or accession has been deposited, this Convention shall enter into force six months after the deposit of its own instrument of ratification or accession.

Article XII   1.   Any Contracting Party may denounce this Convention by written notification to the Depositary Government.

2.   Such denunciation shall take effect twelve months from the date on which the Depositary Government has received the notification, but such denunciation shall not affect the validity of any will made during the period that the Convention was in effect for the denouncing State.

Article XIII   1.   Any State may, when it deposits its instrument of ratification or accession or at any time thereafter, declare, by a notice addressed to the Depositary Government, that this Convention shall apply to all or part of the territories for the international relations of which it is responsible.

2.   Such declaration shall have effect six months after the date on which the Depositary Government shall have received notice thereof or, if at the end of such period the Convention has not yet come into force, from the date of its entry into force.

3.   Each Contracting Party which has made a declaration in accordance with paragraph 1 of this Article may, in accordance with Article XII, denounce this Convention in relation to all or part of the territories concerned.

Article XIV   1.   If a State has two or more territorial units in which different systems of law apply in relation to matters respecting the form of wills, it may at the time of signature, ratification, or accession, declare that this Convention shall extend to all its territorial units or only to one or more of them, and may modify its declaration by submitting another declaration at any time.

2.   These declarations shall be notified to the Depositary Government and shall state expressly the territorial units to which the Convention applies.

Article XV   If a Contracting Party has two or more territorial units in which different systems of law apply in relation to matters respecting the form of wills, any reference to the internal law of the place where the will is made or to the law under which the authorized person has been appointed to act in connection with international wills shall be construed in accordance with the constitutional system of the Party concerned.

Article XVI 1. The original of the present Convention, in the English, French, Russian and Spanish languages, each version being equally authentic, shall be deposited with the Government of the United States of America, which shall transmit certified copies thereof to each of the signatory and acceding States and to the International Institute for the Unification of Private Law.

2. The Depositary Government shall give notice to the signatory and acceding States, and to the International Institute for the Unification of Private Law, of:

(a) any signature;

(b) the deposit of any instrument of ratification or accession;

(c) any date on which this Convention enters into force in accordance with Article XI;

(d) any communication received in accordance with Article I, paragraph 4;

(e) any notice received in accordance with Article II, paragraph 2;

(f) any declaration received in accordance with Article XIII, paragraph 2, and the date on which such declaration takes effect;

(g) any denunciation received in accordance with Article XII, paragraph 1, or Article XIII, paragraph 3, and the date on which the denunciation takes effect;

(h) any declaration received in accordance with Article XIV, paragraph 2, and the date on which the declaration takes effect.

IN WITNESS WHEREOF, the undersigned Plenipotentiaries, being duly authorized to that effect, have signed the present Convention.

DONE at Washington this twenty-sixth day of October, one thousand nine hundred and seventy-three.

Annex

UNIFORM LAW ON THE FORM OF AN INTERNATIONAL WILL

Article 1 1. A will shall be valid as regards form, irrespective particularly of the place where it is made, of the location of the assets and of the nationality, domicile or residence of the testator, if it is made in the form of an international will complying with the provisions set out in Articles 2 to 5 hereinafter.

2. The invalidity of the will as an international will shall not affect its formal validity as a will of another kind.

Article 2 This law shall not apply to the form of testamentary dispositions made by two or more persons in one instrument.

Article 3 1. The will shall be made in writing.

2. It need not be written by the testator himself.

3. It may be written in any language, by hand or by any other means.

Article 4 1. The testator shall declare in the presence of two witnesses and of a person authorized to act in connection with international wills that the document is his will and that he knows the contents thereof.

2. The testator need not inform the witnesses, or the authorized person, of the contents of the will.

Article 5 1. In the presence of the witnesses and of the authorized person, the testator shall sign the will or, if he has previously signed it, shall acknowledge his signature.

2. When the testator is unable to sign, he shall indicate the reason therefor to the authorized person who shall make note of this on the will. Moreover, the testator may be authorized by the law under which the authorized person was designated to direct another person to sign on his behalf.

3. The witnesses and the authorized person shall there and then attest the will by signing in the presence of the testator.

Article 6 1. The signatures shall be placed at the end of the will.

2. If the will consists of several sheets, each sheet shall be signed by the testator or, if he is unable to sign, by the person signing on his behalf or, if there is no such person, by the authorized person. In addition, each sheet shall be numbered.

Article 7 1. The date of the will shall be the date of its signature by the authorized person.

2. This date shall be noted at the end of the will by the authorized person.

Article 8 In the absence of any mandatory rule pertaining to the safekeeping of the will, the authorized person shall ask the testator whether he wishes to make a declaration concerning the safekeeping of his will. If so and at the express request of the testator the place where he intends to have his will kept shall be mentioned in the certificate provided for in Article 9.

Article 9 The authorized person shall attach to the will a certificate in the form prescribed in Article 10 establishing that the obligations of this law have been complied with.

Article 10 The certificate drawn up by the authorized person shall be in the following form or in a substantially similar form:

CERTIFICATE

(Convention of October 26, 1973)

1. I, _____ (name, address and capacity), a person authorized to act in connection with international wills

2. Certify that on _____ (date) at _____ (place)

3. (testator) _____ (name, address, date and place of birth) in my presence and that of the witnesses

4. (a) _____ (name, address, date and place of birth)
    (b) _____ (name, address, date and place of birth) has declared that the attached document is his will and that he knows the contents thereof.

5. I furthermore certify that:

6. (a) in my presence and in that of the witnesses
        (1) the testator has signed the will or has acknowledged his signature previously affixed.
      * (2) following a declaration of the testator stating that he was unable to sign his will for the following reason _____
        –I have mentioned this declaration on the will
       *–the signature has been affixed by _____
        (name, address)

7. (b) the witnesses and I have signed the will;

8. *(c) each page of the will has been signed by _____
        _____ and numbered;

9. (d) I have satisfied myself as to the identity of the testator and of the witnesses as designated above;

10. (e) the witnesses met the conditions requisite to act as such according to the law under which I am acting;

11. * (f) the testator has requested me to include the following statement concerning the safekeeping of his will:

_____

_____

12.   PLACE

13.   DATE

14.   SIGNATURE and, if necessary, SEAL

* To be completed if appropriate

Article 11 The authorized person shall keep a copy of the certificate and deliver another to the testator.

Article 12 In the absence of evidence to the contrary, the certificate of the authorized person shall be conclusive of the formal validity of the instrument as a will under this Law.

Article 13 The absence or irregularity of a certificate shall not affect the formal validity of a will under this Law.

Article 14 The international will shall be subject to the ordinary rules of revocation of wills.

Article 15 In interpreting and applying the provisions of this law, regard shall be had to its international origin and to the need for uniformity in its interpretation.

RESOLUTION

The Conference

Considering the importance of measures to permit the safeguarding of wills and to find them after the death of the testator;

Emphasizing the special interest in such measures with respect to the international will, which is often made by the testator far from his home;

RECOMMENDS to the States that participated in the present Conference

  • that they establish an internal system, centralized or not, to facilitate the safekeeping, search and discovery of an international will as well as the accompanying certificate, for example, along the lines of the Convention on the Establishment of a Scheme of Registration of Wills, concluded at Basel on May 16, 1972;

  • that they facilitate the international exchange of information in these matters and, to this effect, that they designate in each state an authority or a service to handle such exchanges.

Section [1] [2–1001].   [Definitions.]

In this [Act] [Part]:

(1) "international will" means a will executed in conformity with Sections [2] [2–1002] through [5] [2–1005].

(2) "Authorized person" and "person authorized to act in connection with international wills" means a person who by Section [9] [2–1009], or by the laws of the United States including members of the diplomatic and consular service of the United States designated by Foreign Service Regulations, is empowered to supervise the execution of international wills.   Added 1977.

Section [2] [2–1002].   [International Will; Validity.]

(a) A will is valid as regards form, irrespective particularly of the place where it is made, of the location of the assets and of the nationality, domicile, or residence of the testator, if it is made in the form of an international will complying with the requirements of this [Act] [Part].

(b) The invalidity of the will as an international will does not affect its formal validity as a will of another kind.

(c) This [Act] [Part] does not apply to the form of testamentary dispositions made by 2 or more persons in one instrument.   Added 1977.

Section [3] [2–1003]. [International Will; Requirements.]

(a) The will must be made in writing. It need not be written by the testator himself. It may be written in any language, by hand or by any other means.

(b) The testator shall declare in the presence of two witnesses and of a person authorized to act in connection with international wills that the document is his will and that he knows the contents thereof. The testator need not inform the witnesses, or the authorized person, of the contents of the will.

(c) In the presence of the witnesses, and of the authorized person, the testator shall sign the will or, if he has previously signed it, shall acknowledge his signature.

(d) If the testator is unable to sign, the absence of his signature does not affect the validity of the international will if the testator indicates the reason for his inability to sign and the authorized person makes note thereof on the will. In that case, it is permissible for any other person present, including the authorized person or one of the witnesses, at the direction of the testator, to sign the testator's name for him if the authorized person makes note of this on the will, but it is not required that any person sign the testator's name for him.

(e) The witnesses and the authorized person shall there and then attest the will by signing in the presence of the testator. Added 1977.

Section [4] [2–1004]. [International Wills; Other Points of Form.]

(a) The signatures must be placed at the end of the will. If the will consists of several sheets, each sheet must be signed by the testator or, if he is unable to sign, by the person signing on his behalf or, if there is no such person, by the authorized person. In addition, each sheet must be numbered.

(b) The date of the will must be the date of its signature by the authorized person. That date must be noted at the end of the will by the authorized person.

(c) The authorized person shall ask the testator whether he wishes to make a declaration concerning the safekeeping of his will. If so and at the express request of the testator, the place where he intends to have his will kept must be mentioned in the certificate provided for in Section 5.

(d) A will executed in compliance with Section 3 is not invalid merely because it does not comply with this section. Added 1977.

Section [5] [2–1005]. [International Will; Certificate.]

The authorized person shall attach to the will a certificate to be signed by him establishing that the requirements of this [Act] [Part] for valid execution of an international will have been fulfilled. The authorized person shall keep a copy of the certificate and deliver another to the testator. The certificate must be substantially in the following form:

CERTIFICATE

(Convention of October 26, 1973)

1. I, _____ (name, address, and capacity), a person authorized to act in connection with international wills,

2. certify that on _____ (date) at _____ (place)

3. (testator) _____
   (name, address, date and place of birth) in my presence and that of the witnesses

4. (a) _____ (name, address, date and place of birth)
   (b) _____ (name, address, date and place of birth) has declared that the attached document is his will and that he knows the contents thereof.

5. I furthermore certify that:

6. (a) in my presence and in that of the witnesses

   (1) the testator has signed the will or has acknowledged his signature previously affixed.

   * (2) following a declaration of the testator stating that he was unable to sign his will for the following reason _____, I have mentioned this declaration on the will,

      * and the signature has been affixed by _____
      (name and address)

7. (b) the witnesses and I have signed the will;

8. *(c) each page of the will has been signed by _____
   and numbered;

9. (d) I have satisfied myself as to the identity of the testator and of the witnesses as designated above;

10. (e) the witnesses met the conditions requisite to act as such according to the law under which I am acting;

11. * (f) the testator has requested me to include the following statement concerning the safekeeping of his will:

---

12.   PLACE OF EXECUTION
13.   DATE
14.   SIGNATURE and, if necessary, SEAL
* To be completed if appropriate

Added 1977.

Section [6] [2–1006]. [International Will; Effect of Certificate.]

In the absence of evidence to the contrary, the certificate of the authorized person is conclusive of the formal validity of the instrument as a will under this [Act] [Part]. The absence or irregularity of a certificate does not affect the formal validity of a will under this [Act] [Part]. Added 1977.

Section [7] [2–1007]. [International Will; Revocation.]

An international will is subject to the ordinary rules of revocation of wills. Added 1977.

Section [8] [2–1008]. [Source and Construction.]

Sections [1] [2–1001] through [7] [2–1007] derive from Annex to Convention of October 26, 1973, Providing a Uniform Law on the Form of an International Will. In interpreting and applying this [Act] [Part], regard shall be had to its international origin and to the need for uniformity in its interpretation. Added 1977.

Section [9] [2–1009]. [Persons Authorized to Act in Relation to International Will; Eligibility; Recognition by Authorizing Agency.]

Individuals who have been admitted to practice law before the courts of this State and are currently licensed so to do are authorized persons in relation to international wills. Added 1977.

Section [10] [2–1010]. [International Will Information Registration.]

The [Secretary of State] shall establish a registry system by which authorized persons may register in a central information center, information regarding the execution of international wills, keeping that information in strictest confidence until the death of the maker and then making it available to any person desiring information about any will who presents a death certificate or other satisfactory evidence of the testator's death to the center. Information that may be received, preserved in confidence until death, and reported as indicated is limited to the name, social-security or any other individual-identifying number established by law, address, and date and place of birth of the testator, and the intended place of deposit or safekeeping of the instrument pending the death of the maker. The [Secretary of State], at the request of the authorized person, may cause the information it receives about execution of any international will to be transmitted to the registry system of another jurisdiction as identified by the testator, if that other system adheres to rules protecting the confidentiality of the information similar to those established in this State.] Added 1977.

Article III
Probate of Wills and Administration

Part 1
General Provisions

Part 2
Venue for Probate and Administration; Priority to Administer; Demand for Notice

Part 3
Informal Probate and Appointment Proceedings

Part 4
Formal Testacy and Appointment Proceedings

Part 5
Supervised Administration

Part 6
Personal Representative; Appointment, Control and Termination of Authority

Part 7
Duties and Powers of Personal Representatives

Part 8
Creditors' Claims

Part 9
Special Provisions Relating to Distribution

Part 10
Closing Estates

Part 11
Compromise of Controversies

Part 12
Collection of Personal Property by
Affidavit and Summary Administration
Procedure for Small Estates

Part 1
General Provisions

Section 3–101. [Devolution of Estate at Death; Restrictions.]

The power of a person to leave property by will, and the rights of creditors, devisees, and heirs to his property are subject to the restrictions and limitations contained in this Code to facilitate the prompt settlement of estates. Upon the death of a person, his real and personal property devolves to the person to whom it is devised by his last will or to those indicated as substitutes for them in cases involving lapse, renunciation, or other circumstances affecting the devolution of testate estate, or in the absence of testamentary disposition, to his heirs, or to those indicated as substitutes for them in cases involving renunciation or other circumstances affecting devolution of intestate estates, subject to homestead allowance, exempt property and family allowance, to rights of creditors, elective share of the surviving spouse, and to administration.

ALTERNATIVE SECTION FOR COMMUNITY PROPERTY STATES

[Section 3–101A. [Devolution of Estate at Death; Restrictions.]

The power of a person to leave property by will, and the rights of creditors, devisees, and heirs to his property are subject to the restrictions and limitations contained in this Code to facilitate the prompt settlement of estates. Upon the death of a person, his separate property devolves to the persons to whom it is devised by his last will, or to those indicated as substitutes for them in cases involving lapse, renunciation or other circumstances affecting the devolution of testate estates, or in the absence of testamentary disposition to his heirs, or to those indicated as substitutes for them in cases involving renunciation or other circumstances affecting the devolution of intestate estates, and upon the death of a husband or wife, the decedent's share of their community property devolves to the persons to whom it is devised by his last will, or in the absence of testamentary disposition, to his heirs, but all of their community property which is under the management and control of the decedent is subject to his debts and administration, and that portion of their community property which is not under the management and control of the decedent but which is necessary to carry out the provisions of his will is subject to adminstration; but the devolution of all the above described property is subject to rights to homestead allowance, exempt property and family allowances, to renunciation to rights of creditors, [elective share of the surviving spouse] and to administration.]

Section 3–102. [Necessity of Order of Probate For Will.]

Except as provided in Section 3–1201, to be effective to prove the transfer of any property or to nominate an executor, a will must be declared to be valid by an order of informal probate by the Registrar, or an adjudication of probate by the Court, except that a duly executed and unrevoked will which has not been probated may be admitted as evidence of a devise if (1) no Court proceeding concerning the succession or administration of the estate has occurred, and (2) either the devisee or his successors and assigns possessed the property devised in accordance with the provisions of the will, or the property devised was not possessed or claimed by anyone by virtue of the decedent's title during the time period for testacy proceedings.

Section 3–103. [Necessity of Appointment For Administration.]

Except as otherwise provided in Article IV, to acquire the powers and undertake the duties and liabilities of a personal representative of a decedent, a person must be appointed by order of the Court or Registrar, qualify and be issued letters. Administration of an estate is commenced by the issuance of letters.

Section 3-104. [Claims Against Decedent; Necessity of Administration.]

No proceeding to enforce a claim against the estate of a decedent or his successors may be revived or commenced before the appointment of a personal representative. After the appointment and until distribution, all proceedings and actions to enforce a claim against the estate are governed by the procedure prescribed by this Article. After distribution a creditor whose claim has not been barred may recover from the distributees as provided in Section 3–1004 or from a former personal representative individually liable as provided in Section 3–1005. This section has no application to a proceeding by a secured creditor of the decedent to enforce his right to his security except as to any deficiency judgment which might be sought therein.

Section 3–105. [Proceedings Affecting Devolution and Administration; Jurisdiction of Subject Matter.]

Persons interested in decedents' estates may apply to the Registrar for determination in the informal proceedings provided in this Article, and may petition the Court for orders in formal proceedings within the Court's jurisdiction including but not limited to those described in this Article. The Court has exclusive jurisdiction of formal proceedings to determine how decedents' estates subject to the laws of this state are to be administered, expended and distributed. The Court has concurrent jurisdiction of any other action or proceeding concerning a succession or to which an estate, through a personal representative, may be a party, including actions to determine title to property alleged to belong to the estate, and of any action or proceeding in which property distributed by a personal representative or its value is sought to be subjected to rights of creditors or successors of the decedent.

Section 3–106. [Proceedings Within the Jurisdiction of Court; Service; Jurisdiction Over Persons.]

In proceedings within the exclusive jurisdiction of the Court where notice is required by this Code or by rule, and in proceedings to construe probated wills or determine heirs which concern estates that have not been and cannot now be opened for administration, interested persons may be bound by the orders of the Court in respect to property in or subject to the laws of this state by notice in conformity with Section 1–401. An order is binding as to all who are given notice of the proceeding though less than all interested persons are notified.

Section 3–107. [Scope of Proceedings; Proceedings Independent; Exception.]

Unless supervised administration as described in Part 5 is involved, (1) each proceeding before the Court or Registrar is independent of any other proceeding involving the same estate; (2) petitions for formal orders of the Court may combine various requests for relief in a single proceeding if the orders sought may be finally granted without delay. Except as required for proceedings which are particularly described by other sections of this Article, no petition is defective because it fails to embrace all matters which might then be the subject of a final order; (3) proceedings for probate of wills or adjudications of no will may be combined with proceedings for appointment of personal representatives; and (4) a proceeding for appointment of a personal representative is concluded by an order making or declining the appointment.

Section 3–108. [Probate, Testacy and Appointment Proceedings; Ultimate Time Limit.]

No formal probate or appointment proceeding or formal testacy or appointment proceeding, other than a proceeding to probate a will previously probated at the testator's domicile and appointment proceedings relating to an estate in which there has been a prior appointment, may be commenced more than 3 years after the decedent's death, except (1) if a previous proceeding was dismissed because of doubt about the fact of the decedent's death, appropriate probate, appointment or testacy proceedings may be maintained at any time thereafter upon a finding that the decedent's death occurred prior to the initiation of the previous proceeding and the applicant or petitioner has not delayed unduly in initiating the subsequent proceeding; (2) appropriate probate, appointment or testacy proceedings may be maintained in relation to the estate of an absent, disappeared or missing person for whose estate a conservator has been appointed, at any time within three years after the conservator becomes able to establish the death of the protected person; and (3) a proceeding to contest an informally probated will and to secure appointment of the person with legal priority for appointment in the event the contest is successful, may be commenced within the later of twelve months from the informal probate or three years from the decedent's death. These limitations do not apply to proceedings to construe probated wills or determine heirs of an intestate. In cases under (1) or (2) above, the date on which a testacy or appointment proceeding is properly commenced shall be deemed to be the date of the decedent's death for purposes of other limitations provisions of this Code which relate to the date of death.

Section 3–109. [Statutes of Limitation on Decedent's Cause of Action.]

No statute of limitation running on a cause of action belonging to a decedent which had not been barred as of the date of his death, shall appy to bar a cause of action surviving the decedent's death sooner than four months after death. A cause of action which, but for this section, would have been barred less than four months after death, is barred after four months unless tolled.

Part 2
Venue for Probate and Administration;
Priority to Administer; Demand for Notice

Section 3–201. [Venue for First and Subsequent Estate Proceedings; Location of Property.]

(a) Venue for the first informal or formal testacy or appointment proceedings after a decedent's death is:

    (1) in the [county] where the decedent had his domicile at the time of his death; or

    (2) if the decedent was not domiciled in this state, in any [county] where property of the decedent was located at the time of his death.

(b) Venue for all subsequent proceedings within the exclusive jurisdiction of the Court is in the place where the initial proceeding occurred, unless the initial proceeding has been transferred as provided in Section 1–303 or (c) of this section.

(c) If the first proceeding was informal, on application of an interested person and after notice to the proponent in the first proceeding, the Court, upon finding that venue is elsewhere, may transfer the proceeding and the file to the other court.

(d) For the purpose of aiding determinations concerning location of assets which may be relevant in cases involving non-domiciliaries, a debt, other than one evidenced by investment or commercial paper or other instrument in favor of a non-domiciliary, is located where the debtor resides or, if the debtor is a person other than an individual, at the place where it has its principal office. Commercial paper, investment paper and other instruments are located where the instrument is. An interest in property held in trust is located where the trustee may be sued.

Section 3–202. [Appointment or Testacy Proceedings; Conflicting Claim of Domicile in Another State.]

If conflicting claims as to the domicile of a decedent are made in a formal testacy or appointment proceeding commenced in this state, and in a testacy or appointment proceeding after notice pending at the same time in another state, the Court of this state must stay, dismiss, or permit suitable amendment in, the proceeding here unless it is determined that the local proceeding was commenced before the proceeding elsewhere. The determination of domicile in the proceeding first commenced must be accepted as determinative in the proceeding in this state.

Section 3–203. [Priority Among Persons Seeking Appointment as Personal Representative.]

(a) Whether the proceedings are formal or informal, persons who are not disqualified have priority for appointment in the following order:

(1) the person with priority as determined by a probated will including a person nominated by a power conferred in a will;

(2) the surviving spouse of the decedent who is a devisee of the decedent;

(3) other devisees of the decedent;

(4) the surviving spouse of the decedent;

(5) other heirs of the decedent;

(6) 45 days after the death of the decedent, any creditor.

(b) An objection to an appointment can be made only in formal proceedings. In case of objection the priorities stated in (a) apply except that

(1) if the estate appears to be more than adequate to meet exemptions and costs of administration but inadequate to discharge anticipated unsecured claims, the Court, on petition of creditors, may appoint any qualified person;

(2) in case of objection to appointment of a person other than one whose priority is determined by will by an heir or devisee appearing to have a substantial interest in the estate, the Court may appoint a person who is acceptable to heirs and devisees whose interests in the estate appear to be worth in total more than half of the probable distributable value, or, in default of this accord any suitable person.

(c) A person entitled to letters under (2) through (5) of (a) above, and a person aged [18] and over who would be entitled to letters but for his age, may nominate a qualified person to act as personal representative. Any person aged [18] and over may renounce his right to nominate or to an appointment by appropriate writing filed with the Court. When two or more persons share a priority, those of them who do not renounce must concur in nominating another to act for them, or in applying for appointment.

(d) Conservators of the estates of protected persons, or if there is no conservator, any guardian except a guardian ad litem of a minor or incapacitated person, may exercise the same right to nominate, to object to another's appointment, or to participate in determining the preference of a majority in interest of the heirs and devisees that the protected person or ward would have if qualified for appointment.

(e) Appointment of one who does not have priority, including priority resulting from renunciation or nomination determined pursuant to this section, may be made only in formal proceedings. Before appointing one without priority, the Court must determine that those having priority, although given notice of the proceedings, have failed to request appointment or to nominate another for appointment, and that administration is necessary.

(f) No person is qualified to serve as a personal representative who is:

(1) under the age of [21];

(2) a person whom the Court finds unsuitable in formal proceedings.

(g) A personal representative appointed by a court of the decedent's domicile has priority over all other persons except where the decedent's will nominates different persons to be personal representative in this state and in the state of domicile. The domiciliary personal representative may nominate another, who shall have the same priority as the domiciliary personal representative.

(h) This section governs priority for appointment of a successor personal representative but does not apply to the selection of a special administrator.

Section 3-204. [Demand for Notice of Order or Filing Concerning Decedent's Estate.]

Any person desiring notice of any order or filing pertaining to a decedent's estate in which he has a financial or property interest, may file a demand for notice with the Court at any time after the death of the decedent stating the name of the decedent, the nature of his interest in the estate, and the demandant's address or that of his attorney. The clerk shall mail a copy of the demand to the personal representative if one has been appointed. After filing of a demand, no order or filing to which the demand relates shall be made or accepted without notice as prescribed in Section 1-401 to the demandant or his attorney. The validity of an order which is issued or filing which is accepted without compliance with this requirement shall not be affected by the error, but the petitioner receiving the order or the person making the filing may be liable for any damage caused by the absence of notice. The requirement of notice arising from a demand under this provision may be waived in writing by the demandant and shall cease upon the termination of his interest in the estate.

Part 3
Informal Probate and Appointment Proceedings

Section 3-301. [Informal Probate or Appointment Proceedings; Application; Contents.]

(a) Applications for informal probate or informal appointment shall be directed to the Registrar, and verified by the applicant to be accurate and complete to the best of his knowledge and belief as to the following information:

(1) Every application for informal probate of a will or for informal appointment of a personal representative, other than a special or successor representative, shall contain the following:

(i) a statement of the interest of the applicant;

(ii) the name, and date of death of the decedent, his age, and the county and state of his domicile at the time of death, and the names and addresses of the spouse, children, heirs and devisees and the ages of any who are minors so far as known or ascertainable with reasonable diligence by the applicant;

(iii) if the decedent was not domiciled in the state at the time of his death, a statement showing venue;

(iv) a statement identifying and indicating the address of any personal representative of the decedent appointed in this state or elsewhere whose appointment has not been terminated;

(v) a statement indicating whether the applicant has received a demand for notice, or is aware of any demand for notice of any probate or appointment proceeding concerning the decedent that may have been filed in this state or elsewhere; and

(vi) that the time limit for informal probate or appointment as provided in this Article has not expired either because 3 years or less have passed since the decedent's death, or, if more than 3 years from death have passed, circumstances as described by Section 3–108 authorizing tardy probate or appointment have occurred.

(2) An application for informal probate of a will shall state the following in addition to the statements required by (1):

(i) that the original of the decedent's last will is in the possession of the court, or accompanies the application, or that an authenticated copy of a will probated in another jurisdiction accompanies the application;

(ii) that the applicant, to the best of his knowledge, believes the will to have been validly executed;

(iii) that after the exercise of reasonable diligence, the applicant is unaware of any instrument revoking the will, and that the applicant believes that the instrument which is the subject of the application is the decedent's last will.

(3) An application for informal appointment of a personal representative to adminster an estate under a will shall describe the will by date of execution and state the time and place of probate or the pending application or petition for probate. The application for appointment shall adopt the statements in the application or petition for probate and state the name, address and priority for appointment of the person whose appointment is sought.

(4) An application for informal appointment of an administrator in intestacy shall state in addition to the statements required by (1):

(i) that after the exercise of reasonable diligence, the applicant is unaware of any unrevoked testamentary instrument relating to property having a situs in this state under Section 1–301, or, a statement why any such instrument of which he may be aware is not being probated;

(ii) the priority of the person whose appointment is sought and the names of any other persons having a prior or equal right to the appointment under Section 3–203.

(5) An application for appointment of a personal representative to succeed a personal representative appointed under a different testacy status shall refer to the order in the most recent testacy proceeding, state the name and address of the person whose appointment is sought and of the person whose appointment will be terminated if the application is granted, and describe the priority of the applicant.

(6) An application for appointment of a personal representative to succeed a personal representative who has tendered a resignation as provided in Section 3–610(c), or whose appointment has been terminated by death or removal, shall adopt the statements in the application or petition which led to the appointment of the person being succeeded except as specifically changed or corrected, state the name and address of the person who seeks appointment as successor, and describe the priority of the applicant.

(b) By verifying an application for informal probate, or informal appointment, the applicant submits personally to the jurisdiction of the court in any proceeding for relief from fraud relating to the application, or for perjury, that may be instituted against him.

Section 3–302. [Informal Probate; Duty of Registrar; Effect of Informal Probate.]

Upon receipt of an application requesting informal probate of a will, the Registrar, upon making the findings required by Section 3–303 shall issue a written statement of informal probate if at least 120 hours have elapsed since the decedent's death. Informal probate is conclusive as to all persons until superseded by an order in a formal testacy proceeding. No defect in the application or procedure relating thereto which leads to informal probate of a will renders the probate void.

Section 3–303. [Informal Probate; Proof and Findings Required.]

(a) In an informal proceeding for original probate of a will, the Registrar shall determine whether:

(1) the application is complete;

(2) the applicant has made oath or affirmation that the statements contained in the application are true to the best of his knowledge and belief;

(3) the applicant appears from the application to be an interested person as defined in Section 1–201(20);

(4) on the basis of the statements in the application, venue is proper;

(5) an original, duly executed and apparently unrevoked will is in the Registrar's possession;

(6) any notice required by Section 3–204 has been given and that the application is not within Section 3–304; and

(7) it appears from the application that the time limit for original probate has not expired.

(b) The application shall be denied if it indicates that a personal representative has been appointed in another [county] of this state or except as provided in subsection (d) below, if it appears that this or another will of the decedent has been the subject of a previous probate order.

(c) A will which appears to have the required signatures and which contains an attestation clause showing that requirements of execution under Section 2–502, 2–503 or 2–506 have been met shall be probated without further proof. In other cases, the Registrar may assume execution if the will appears to have been properly executed, or he may accept a sworn statement or affidavit of any person having knowledge of the circumstances of execution, whether or not the person was a witness to the will.

(d) Informal probate of a will which has been previously probated elsewhere may be granted at any time upon written application by any interested person, together with deposit of an authenticated copy of the will and of the statement probating it from the office or court where it was first probated.

(e) A will from a place which does not provide for probate of a will after death and which is not eligible for probate under subsection (a) above, may be probated in this state upon receipt by the Registrar of a duly authenticated copy of the will and a duly authenticated certificate of its legal custodian that the copy filed is a true copy and that the will has become operative under the law of the other place.

Section 3–304. [Informal Probate; Unavailable in Certain Cases.]

Applications for informal probate which relate to one or more of a known series of testamentary instruments (other than a will and its codicil), the latest of which does not expressly revoke the earlier, shall be declined.

Section 3–305. [Informal Probate; Registrar Not Satisfied.]

If the Registrar is not satisfied that a will is entitled to be probated in informal proceedings because of failure to meet the requirements of Sections 3–303 and 3–304 or any other reason, he may decline the application. A declination of informal probate is not an adjudication and does not preclude formal probate proceedings.

Section 3–306. [Informal Probate; Notice Requirements.]

[*] The moving party must give notice as described by Section 1–401 of his application for informal probate to any person demanding it pursuant to Section 3–204, and to any personal representative of the decedent whose appointment has not been terminated. No other notice of informal probate is required.

[(b) If an informal probate is granted, within 30 days thereafter the applicant shall give written information of the probate to the heirs and devisees. The information shall include the name and address of the applicant, the name and location of the court granting the informal probate, and the date of the probate. The information shall be delivered or sent by ordinary mail to each of the heirs and devisees whose address is reasonably available to the applicant. No duty to give information is incurred if a personal representative is appointed who is required to give the written information required by Section 3–705. An applicant's failure to give information as required by this section is a breach of his duty to the heirs and devisees but does not affect the validity of the probate.]

Section 3–307. [Informal Appointment Proceedings; Delay in Order; Duty of Registrar; Effect of Appointment.]

(a) Upon receipt of an application for informal appointment of a personal representative other than a special administrator as provided in Section 3–614, if at least 120 hours have elapsed since the decedent's death, the Registrar, after making the findings required by Section 3–308, shall appoint the applicant subject to qualification and acceptance; provided, that if the decedent was a non-resident, the Registrar shall delay the order of appointment until 30 days have elapsed since death unless the personal representative appointed at the decedent's domicile is the applicant, or unless the decedent's will directs that his estate be subject to the laws of this state.

(b) The status of personal representative and the powers and duties pertaining to the office are fully established by informal appointment. An appointment, and the office of personal representative created thereby, is subject to termination as provided in Sections 3–608 through 3–612, but is not subject to retroactive vacation.

---

* This paragraph becomes (a) if optional subsection (b) is accepted.

Section 3–308. [Informal Appointment Proceedings; Proof and Findings Required.]

(a) In informal appointment proceedings, the Registrar must determine whether:

(1) the application for informal appointment of a personal representative is complete;

(2) the applicant has made oath or affirmation that the statements contained in the application are true to the best of his knowledge and belief;

(3) the applicant appears from the application to be an interested person as defined in Section 1–201(20);

(4) on the basis of the statements in the application, venue is proper;

(5) any will to which the requested appointment relates has been formally or informally probated; but this requirement does not apply to the appointment of a special administrator;

(6) any notice required by Section 3–204 has been given;

(7) from the statements in the application, the person whose appointment is sought has priority entitling him to the appointment.

(b) Unless Section 3–612 controls, the application must be denied if it indicates that a personal representative who has not filed a written statement of resignation as provided in Section 3–610(c) has been appointed in this or another [county] of this state, that (unless the applicant is the domiciliary personal representative or his nominee) the decedent was not domiciled in this state and that a personal representative whose appointment has not been terminated has been appointed by a Court in the state of domicile, or that other requirements of this section have not been met.

Section 3–309. [Informal Appointment Proceedings; Registrar Not Satisfied.]

If the Registrar is not satisfied that a requested informal appointment of a personal representative should be made because of failure to meet the requirements of Sections 3–307 and 3–308, or for any other reason, he may decline the application. A declination of informal appointment is not an adjudication and does not preclude appointment in formal proceedings.

Section 3–310. [Informal Appointment Proceedings; Notice Requirements.]

The moving party must give notice as described by Section 1–401 of his intention to seek an appointment informally: (1) to any person demanding it pursuant to Section 3–204; and (2) to any person having a prior or equal right to appointment not waived in writing and filed with the Court. No other notice of an informal appointment proceeding is required.

Section 3–311. [Informal Appointment Unavailable in Certain Cases.]

If an application for informal appointment indicates the existence of a possible unrevoked testamentary instrument which may relate to property subject to the laws of this state, and which is not filed for probate in this court, the Registrar shall decline the application.

Part 4
Formal Testacy and Appointment Proceedings

Section 3–401. [Formal Testacy Proceedings; Nature; When Commenced.]

A formal testacy proceeding is litigation to determine whether a decedent left a valid will. A formal testacy proceeding may be commenced by an interested person filing a petition as described in Section 3–402(a) in which he requests that the Court, after notice and hearing, enter an order probating a will, or a petition to set aside an informal probate of a will or to prevent informal probate of a will which is the subject of a pending application, or a petition in accordance with Section 3–402(b) for an order that the decedent died intestate.

A petition may seek formal probate of a will without regard to whether the same or a conflicting will has been informally probated. A formal testacy proceeding may, but need not, involve a request for appointment of a personal representative.

During the pendency of a formal testacy proceeding, the Registrar shall not act upon any application for informal probate of any will of the decedent or any application for informal appointment of a personal representation of the decedent.

Unless a petition in a formal testacy proceeding also requests confirmation of the previous informal appointment, a previously appointed personal representative, after receipt of notice of the commencement of a formal probate proceeding, must refrain from exercising his power to make any further distribution of the estate during the pendency of the formal proceeding. A petitioner who seeks the appointment of a different personal representative in a formal proceeding also may request an order restraining the acting personal representative from exercising any of the powers of his office and requesting the appointment of a special administrator. In the absence of a request, or if the request is denied, the commencement of a formal proceeding has no effect on the powers and duties of a previously appointed personal representative other than those relating to distribution.

Section 3–402. [Formal Testacy or Appointment Proceedings; Petition; Contents.]

(a) Petitions for formal probate of a will, or for adjudication of intestacy with or without request for appointment of a personal representative, must be directed to the Court, request a judicial order after notice and hearing and contain further statements as indicated in this section. A petition for formal probate of a will

(1) requests an order as to the testacy of the decedent in relation to a particular instrument which may or may not have been informally probated and determining the heirs,

(2) contains the statements required for informal applications as stated in the six subparagraphs under Section 3–301(1), the statements required by subparagraphs (ii) and (iii) of Section 3–301(2), and

(3) states whether the original of the last will of the decedent is in the possession of the Court or accompanies the petition.

If the original will is neither in the possession of the Court nor accompanies the petition and no authenticated copy of a will probated in another jurisdiction accompanies the petition, the petition also must state the contents of the will, and indicate that it is lost, destroyed, or otherwise unavailable.

(b) A petition for adjudication of intestacy and appointment of an administrator in intestacy must request a judicial finding and order that the decedent left no will and determining the heirs, contain the statements required by (1) and (4) of Section 3–301 and indicate whether supervised administration is sought. A petition may request an order determining intestacy and heirs without requesting the appointment of an administrator, in which case, the statements required by subparagraph (ii) of Section 3–301(4) above may be omitted.

Section 3–403. [Formal Testacy Proceedings; Notice of Hearing on Petition.]

(a) Upon commencement of a formal testacy proceeding, the Court shall fix a time and place of hearing. Notice shall be given in the manner prescribed by Section 1–401 by the petitioner to the persons herein enumerated and to any additional person who has filed a demand for notice under Section 3–204 of this Code.

Notice shall be given to the following persons: the surviving spouse, children, and other heirs of the decedent, the devisees and executors named in any will that is being, or has been, probated, or offered for informal or formal probate in the [county,] or that is known by the petitioner to have been probated, or offered for informal or formal probate elsewhere, and any personal representative of the decedent whose appointment has not been terminated. Notice may be given to other persons. In addition, the petitioner shall give notice by publication to all unknown persons and to all known persons whose addresses are unknown who have any interest in the matters being litigated.

(b) If it appears by the petition or otherwise that the fact of the death of the alleged decedent may be in doubt, or on the written demand of any interested person, a copy of the notice of the hearing on said petition shall be sent by registered mail to the alleged decedent at his last known address. The Court shall direct the petitioner to report the results of, or make and report back concerning, a reasonably diligent search for the alleged decedent in any manner that may seem advisable, including any or all of the following methods:

(1) by inserting in one or more suitable periodicals a notice requesting information from any person having knowledge of the whereabouts of the alleged decedent;

(2) by notifying law enforcement officials and public welfare agencies in appropriate locations of the disappearance of the alleged decedent;

(3) by engaging the services of an investigator. The costs of any search so directed shall be paid by the petitioner if there is no administration or by the estate of the decedent in case there is administration.

Section 3–404. [Formal Testacy Proceedings; Written Objections to Probate.]

Any party to a formal proceeding who opposes the probate of a will for any reason shall state in his pleadings his objections to probate of the will.

Section 3–405. [Formal Testacy Proceedings; Uncontested Cases; Hearings and Proof.]

If a petition in a testacy proceeding is unopposed, the Court may order probate or intestacy on the strength of the pleadings if satisfied that the conditions of Section 3–409 have been met, or conduct a hearing in open court and require proof of the matters necessary to support the order sought. If evidence concerning execution of the will is necessary, the affidavit or testimony of one of any attesting witnesses to the instrument is sufficient. If the affidavit or testimony of an attesting witness is not available, execution of the will may be proved by other evidence or affidavit.

Section 3–406. [Formal Testacy Proceedings; Contested Cases; Testimony of Attesting Witnesses.]

(a) If evidence concerning execution of an attested will which is not self-proved is necessary in contested cases, the testimony of at least one of the attesting witnesses, if within the state competent and able to testify, is required. Due execution of an attested or unattested will may be proved by other evidence.

(b) If the will is self-proved, compliance with signature requirements for execution is conclusively presumed and other requirements of
execution are presumed subject to rebuttal without the testimony of
any witness upon filing the will and the acknowledgment and affidavits
annexed or attached thereto, unless there is proof of fraud or forgery
affecting the acknowledgment or affidavit.

Section 3–407. [Formal Testacy Proceedings; Burdens in Contested Cases.]

In contested cases, petitioners who seek to establish intestacy have the
burden of establishing prima facie proof of death, venue, and heirship.
Proponents of a will have the burden of establishing prima facie proof
of due execution in all cases, and, if they are also petitioners, prima
facie proof of death and venue. Contestants of a will have the burden
of establishing lack of testamentary intent or capacity, undue influence,
fraud, duress, mistake or revocation. Parties have the ultimate burden
of persuasion as to matters with respect to which they have the initial
burden of proof. If a will is opposed by the petition for probate of a
later will revoking the former, it shall be determined first whether the
later will is entitled to probate, and if a will is opposed by a petition for
a declaration of intestacy, it shall be determined first whether the will
is entitled to probate.

Section 3–408. [Formal Testacy Proceedings; Will Construction; Effect of Final Order in Another Jurisdiction.]

A final order of a court of another state determining testacy, the
validity or construction of a will, made in a proceeding involving notice
to and an opportunity for contest by all interested persons must be
accepted as determinative by the courts of this state if it includes, or is
based upon, a finding that the decedent was domiciled at his death in
the state where the order was made.

Section 3–409. [Formal Testacy Proceedings; Order; Foreign Will.]

After the time required for any notice has expired, upon proof of notice,
and after any hearing that may be necessary, if the Court finds that the
testator is dead, venue is proper and that the proceeding was commenced within the limitation prescribed by Section 3–108, it shall
determine the decedent's domicile at death, his heirs and his state of
testacy. Any will found to be valid and unrevoked shall be formally
probated. Termination of any previous informal appointment of a
personal representative, which may be appropriate in view of the relief
requested and findings, is governed by Section 3–612. The petition
shall be dismissed or appropriate amendment allowed if the court is not
satisfied that the alleged decedent is dead. A will from a place which
does not provide for probate of a will after death, may be proved for
probate in this state by a duly authenticated certificate of its legal

custodian that the copy introduced is a true copy and that the will has become effective under the law of the other place.

Section 3–410. [Formal Testacy Proceedings; Probate of More Than One Instrument.]

If two or more instruments are offered for probate before a final order is entered in a formal testacy proceeding, more than one instrument may be probated if neither expressly revokes the other or contains provisions which work a total revocation by implication. If more than one instrument is probated, the order shall indicate what provisions control in respect to the nomination of an executor, if any. The order may, but need not, indicate how any provisions of a particular instrument are affected by the other instrument. After a final order in a testacy proceeding has been entered, no petition for probate of any other instrument of the decedent may be entertained, except incident to a petition to vacate or modify a previous probate order and subject to the time limits of Section 3–412.

Section 3–411. [Formal Testacy Proceedings; Partial Intestacy.]

If it becomes evident in the course of a formal testacy proceeding that, though one or more instruments are entitled to be probated, the decedent's estate is or may be partially intestate, the Court shall enter an order to that effect.

Section 3–412. [Formal Testacy Proceedings; Effect of Order; Vacation.]

Subject to appeal and subject to vacation as provided herein and in Section 3–413, a formal testacy order under Sections 3–409–3–411, including an order that the decedent left no valid will and determining heirs, is final as to all persons with respect to all issues concerning the decedent's estate that the court considered or might have considered incident to its rendition relevant to the question of whether the decedent left a valid will, and to the determination of heirs, except that:

(1) the court shall entertain a petition for modification or vacation of its order and probate of another will of the decedent if it is shown that the proponents of the later-offered will were unaware of its existence at the time of the earlier proceeding or were unaware of the earlier proceeding and were given no notice thereof, except by publication.

(2) If intestacy of all or part of the estate has been ordered, the determination of heirs of the decedent may be reconsidered if it is shown that one or more persons were omitted from the determination and it is also shown that the persons were unaware of their relationship to the decedent, were unaware of his death or were

given no notice of any proceeding concerning his estate, except by publication.

(3) A petition for vacation under either (1) or (2) above must be filed prior to the earlier of the following time limits:

(i) If a personal representative has been appointed for the estate, the time of entry of any order approving final distribution of the estate, or, if the estate is closed by statement, 6 months after the filing of the closing statement.

(ii) Whether or not a personal representative has been appointed for the estate of the decedent, the time prescribed by Section 3–108 when it is no longer possible to initiate an original proceeding to probate a will of the decedent.

(iii) 12 months after the entry of the order sought to be vacated.

(4) The order originally rendered in the testacy proceeding may be modified or vacated, if appropriate under the circumstances, by the order of probate of the later-offered will or the order redetermining heirs.

(5) The finding of the fact of death is conclusive as to the alleged decedent only if notice of the hearing on the petition in the formal testacy proceeding was sent by registered or certified mail addressed to the alleged decedent at his last known address and the court finds that a search under Section 3–403(b) was made.

If the alleged decedent is not dead, even if notice was sent and search was made, he may recover estate assets in the hands of the personal representative. In addition to any remedies available to the alleged decedent by reason of any fraud or intentional wrongdoing, the alleged decedent may recover any estate or its proceeds from distributees that is in their hands, or the value of distributions received by them, to the extent that any recovery from distributees is equitable in view of all of the circumstances.

Section 3–413. [Formal Testacy Proceedings; Vacation of Order For Other Cause.]

For good cause shown, an order in a formal testacy proceeding may be modified or vacated within the time allowed for appeal.

Section 3–414. [Formal Proceedings Concerning Appointment of Personal Representative.]

(a) A formal proceeding for adjudication regarding the priority or qualification of one who is an applicant for appointment as personal representative, or of one who previously has been appointed personal representative in informal proceedings, if an issue concerning the testacy of the decedent is or may be involved, is governed by Section 3–402, as well as by this section. In other cases, the petition shall contain or adopt the statements required by Section 3–301(1) and describe the question relating to priority or qualification of the personal representative which is to be resolved. If the proceeding precedes any appointment of a personal representative, it shall stay any pending informal appointment proceedings as well as any commenced thereafter. If the proceeding is commenced after appointment, the previously appointed personal representative, after receipt of notice thereof, shall refrain from exercising any power of administration except as necessary to preserve the estate or unless the Court orders otherwise.

(b) After notice to interested persons, including all persons interested in the administration of the estate as successors under the applicable assumption concerning testacy, any previously appointed personal representative and any person having or claiming priority for appointment as personal representative, the Court shall determine who is entitled to appointment under Section 3–203, make a proper appointment and, if appropriate terminate any prior appointment found to have been improper as provided in cases of removal under Section 3–611.

Part 5
Supervised Administration

Section 3–501. [Supervised Administration; Nature of Proceeding.]

Supervised administration is a single in rem proceeding to secure complete administration and settlement of a decedent's estate under the continuing authority of the Court which extends until entry of an order approving distribution of the estate and discharging the personal representative or other order terminating the proceeding. A supervised personal representative is responsible to the Court, as well as to the interested parties, and is subject to directions concerning the estate made by the Court on its own motion or on the motion of any interested party. Except as otherwise provided in this Part, or as otherwise ordered by the Court, a supervised personal representative has the same duties and powers as a personal representative who is not supervised.

Section 3–502. [Supervised Administration; Petition; Order.]

A petition for supervised administration may be filed by any interested person or by a personal representative at any time or the prayer for supervised administration may be joined with a petition in a testacy or appointment proceeding. If the testacy of the decedent and the priority and qualification of any personal representative have not been adjudicated previously, the petition for supervised administration shall include the matters required of a petition in a formal testacy proceeding and the notice requirements and procedures applicable to a formal testacy proceeding apply. If not previously adjudicated, the Court shall adjudicate the testacy of the decedent and questions relating to the priority and qualifications of the personal representative in any case involving a request for supervised administration, even though the request for supervised administration may be denied. After notice to interested persons, the Court shall order supervised administration of a decedent's estate: (1) if the decedent's will directs supervised administration, it shall be ordered unless the Court finds that circumstances bearing on the need for supervised administration have changed since the execution of the will and that there is no necessity for supervised administration; (2) if the decedent's will directs unsupervised administration, supervised administration shall be ordered only upon a finding that it is necessary for protection of persons interested in the estate; or (3) in other cases if the Court finds that supervised administration is necessary under the circumstances.

Section 3–503. [Supervised Administration; Effect on Other Proceedings.]

(a) The pendency of a proceeding for supervised administration of a decedent's estate stays action on any informal application then pending or thereafter filed.

(b) If a will has been previously probated in informal proceedings, the effect of the filing of a petition for supervised administration is as provided for formal testacy proceedings by Section 3–401.

(c) After he has received notice of the filing of a petition for supervised administration, a personal representative who has been appointed previously shall not exercise his power to distribute any estate. The filing of the petition does not affect his other powers and duties unless the Court restricts the exercise of any of them pending full hearing on the petition.

Section 3–504. [Supervised Administration; Powers of Personal Representative.]

Unless restricted by the Court, a supervised personal representative has, without interim orders approving exercise of a power, all powers of personal representatives under this Code, but he shall not exercise his power to make any distribution of the estate without prior order of the Court. Any other restriction on the power of a personal representative which may be ordered by the Court must be endorsed on his letters of appointment and, unless so endorsed, is ineffective as to persons dealing in good faith with the personal representative.

Section 3–505. [Supervised Administration; Interim Orders; Distribution and Closing Orders.]

Unless otherwise ordered by the Court, supervised administration is terminated by order in accordance with time restrictions, notices and contents of orders prescribed for proceedings under Section 3–1001. Interim orders approving or directing partial distributions or granting other relief may be issued by the Court at any time during the pendency of a supervised administration on the application of the personal representative or any interested person.

Part 6
Personal Representative; Appointment, Control and Termination of Authority

Section 3–601. [Qualification.]

Prior to receiving letters, a personal representative shall qualify by filing with the appointing Court any required bond and a statement of acceptance of the duties of the office.

Section 3–602. [Acceptance of Appointment; Consent to Jurisdiction.]

By accepting appointment, a personal representative submits personally to the jurisdiction of the Court in any proceeding relating to the estate that may be instituted by any interested person. Notice of any proceeding shall be delivered to the personal representative, or mailed to him by ordinary first class mail at his address as listed in the application or petition for appointment or as thereafter reported to the Court and to his address as then known to the petitioner.

Section 3–603. [Bond Not Required Without Court Order, Exceptions.]

No bond is required of a personal representative appointed in informal proceedings, except (1) upon the appointment of a special administrator; (2) when an executor or other personal representative is appointed to administer an estate under a will containing an express requirement of bond or (3) when bond is required under Section 3–605. Bond may be required by court order at the time of appointment of a personal representative appointed in any formal proceeding except that bond is not required of a personal representative appointed in formal proceedings if the will relieves the personal representative of bond, unless bond has been requested by an interested party and the Court is satisfied that it is desirable. Bond required by any will may be dispensed with in formal proceedings upon determination by the Court that it is not necessary. No bond is required of any personal representative who, pursuant to statute, has deposited cash or collateral with an agency of this state to secure performance of his duties.

Section 3–604. [Bond Amount; Security; Procedure; Reduction.]

If bond is required and the provisions of the will or order do not specify the amount, unless stated in his application or petition, the person qualifying shall file a statement under oath with the Registrar indicating his best estimate of the value of the personal estate of the decedent and of the income expected from the personal and real estate during the next year, and he shall execute and file a bond with the Registrar, or give other suitable security, in an amount not less than the estimate. The Registrar shall determine that the bond is duly executed by a corporate surety, or one or more individual sureties whose performance is secured by pledge of personal property, mortgage on real property or other adequate security. The Registrar may permit the amount of the bond to be reduced by the value of assets of the estate deposited with a domestic financial institution (as defined in Section 6–101) in a manner that prevents their unauthorized disposition. On petition of the personal representative or another interested person the Court may excuse a requirement of bond, increase or reduce the amount of the bond, release sureties, or permit the substitution of another bond with the same or different sureties.

Section 3–605. [Demand For Bond by Interested Person.]

Any person apparently having an interest in the estate worth in excess of [$1000], or any creditor having a claim in excess of [$1000], may make a written demand that a personal representative give bond. The demand must be filed with the Registrar and a copy mailed to the personal representative, if appointment and qualification have occurred. Thereupon, bond is required, but the requirement ceases if the person demanding bond ceases to be interested in the estate, or if bond is excused as provided in Section 3–603 or 3–604. After he has received notice and until the filing of the bond or cessation of the requirement of bond, the personal representative shall refrain from exercising any powers of his office except as necessary to preserve the estate. Failure of the personal representative to meet a requirement of bond by giving suitable bond within 30 days, after receipt of notice is caused for his removal and appointment of a successor personal representative.

Section 3–606. [Terms and Conditions of Bonds.]

(a) The following requirements and provisions apply to any bond required by this Part:

(1) Bonds shall name the [state] as obligee for the benefit of the persons interested in the estate and shall be conditioned upon the faithful discharge by the fiduciary of all duties according to law.

(2) Unless otherwise provided by the terms of the approved bond, sureties are jointly and severally liable with the personal representative and with each other. The address of sureties shall be stated in the bond.

(3) By executing an approved bond of a personal representative, the surety consents to the jurisdiction of the court which issued letters to the primary obligor in any proceedings pertaining to the fiduciary duties of the personal representative and naming the surety as a party. Notice of any proceeding shall be delivered to the surety or mailed to him by registered or certified mail at his

address as listed with the court where the bond is filed and to his address as then known to the petitioner.

(4) On petition of a successor personal representative, any other personal representative of the same decedent, or any interested person, a proceeding in the Court may be initiated against a surety for breach of the obligation of the bond of the personal representative.

(5) The bond of the personal representative is not void after the first recovery but may be proceeded against from time to time until the whole penalty is exhausted.

(b) No action or proceeding may be commenced against the surety on any matter as to which an action or proceeding against the primary obligor is barred by adjudication or limitation.

Section 3–607. [Order Restraining Personal Representative.]

(a) On petition of any person who appears to have an interest in the estate, the Court by temporary order may restrain a personal representative from performing specified acts of administration, disbursement, or distribution, or exercise of any powers or discharge of any duties of his office, or make any other order to secure proper performance of his duty, if it appears to the Court that the personal representative otherwise may take some action which would jeopardize unreasonably the interest of the applicant or of some other interested person. Persons with whom the personal representative may transact business may be made parties.

(b) The matter shall be set for hearing within 10 days unless the parties otherwise agree. Notice as the Court directs shall be given to the personal representative and his attorney of record, if any, and to any other parties named defendant in the petition.

Section 3–608. [Termination of Appointment; General.]

Termination of appointment of a personal representative occurs as indicated in Sections 3–609 to 3–612, inclusive. Termination ends the right and power pertaining to the office of personal representative as conferred by this Code or any will, except that a personal representative, at any time prior to distribution or until restrained or enjoined by court order, may perform acts necessary to protect the estate and may deliver the assets to a successor representative. Termination does not discharge a personal representative from liability for transactions or omissions occurring before termination, or relieve him of the duty to preserve assets subject to his control, to account therefor and to deliver the assets. Termination does not affect the jurisdiction of the Court over the personal representative, but terminates his authority to represent the estate in any pending or future proceeding.

Section 3–609. [Termination of Appointment; Death or Disability.]

The death of a personal representative or the appointment of a conservator for the estate of a personal representative, terminates his appointment. Until appointment and qualification of a successor or special representative to replace the deceased or protected representative, the representative of the estate of the deceased or protected personal representative, if any, has the duty to protect the estate possessed and being administered by his decedent or ward at the time his appointment terminates, has the power to perform acts necessary for protection and shall account for and deliver the estate assets to a successor or special personal representative upon his appointment and qualification.

Section 3–610. [Termination of Appointment; Voluntary.]

(a) An appointment of a personal representative terminates as provided in Section 3–1003, one year after the filing of a closing statement.

(b) An order closing an estate as provided in Section 3–1001 or 3–1002 terminates an appointment of a personal representative.

(c) A personal representative may resign his position by filing a written statement of resignation with the Registrar after he has given at least 15 days written notice to the persons known to be interested in the estate. If no one applies or petitions for appointment of a successor representative within the time indicated in the notice, the filed statement of resignation is ineffective as a termination of appointment and in any event is effective only upon the appointment and qualification of a successor representative and delivery of the assets to him.

Section 3–611. [Termination of Appointment by Removal; Cause; Procedure.]

(a) A person interested in the estate may petition for removal of a personal representative for cause at any time. Upon filing of the petition, the Court shall fix a time and place for hearing. Notice shall be given by the petitioner to the personal representative, and to other persons as the Court may order. Except as otherwise ordered as provided in Section 3–607, after receipt of notice of removal proceedings, the personal representative shall not act except to account to correct maladministration or preserve the estate. If removal is ordered, the Court also shall direct by order the disposition of the assets remaining in the name of, or under the control of, the personal representative being removed.

(b) Cause for removal exists when removal would be in the best interests of the estate, or if it is shown that a personal representative or the person seeking his appointment intentionally misrepresented material facts in the proceedings leading to his appointment, or that the personal representative has disregarded an order of the Court, has become incapable of discharging the duties of his office, or has mismanaged the estate or failed to perform any duty pertaining to the office.

Unless the decedent's will directs otherwise, a personal representative appointed at the decedent's domicile, incident to securing appointment of himself or his nominee as ancillary personal representative, may obtain removal of another who was appointed personal representative in this state to administer local assets.

Section 3–612. [Termination of Appointment; Change of Testacy Status.]

Except as otherwise ordered in formal proceedings, the probate of a will subsequent to the appointment of a personal representative in intestacy or under a will which is superseded by formal probate of another will, or the vacation of an informal probate of a will subsequent to the appointment of the personal representative thereunder, does not terminate the appointment of the personal representative although his powers may be reduced as provided in Section 3–401. Termination occurs upon appointment in informal or formal appointment proceedings of a person entitled to appointment under the later assumption concerning testacy. If no request for new appointment is made within 30 days after expiration of time for appeal from the order in formal testacy proceedings, or from the informal probate, changing the assumption concerning testacy, the previously appointed personal representative upon request may be appointed personal representative under the subsequently probated will, or as in intestacy as the case may be.

Section 3–613. [Successor Personal Representative.]

Parts 3 and 4 of this Article govern proceedings for appointment of a personal representative to succeed one whose appointment has been terminated. After appointment and qualification, a successor personal representative may be substituted in all actions and proceedings to which the former personal representative was a party, and no notice, process or claim which was given or served upon the former personal representative need be given to or served upon the successor in order to preserve any position or right the person giving the notice or filing the claim may thereby having obtained or preserved with reference to the former personal representative. Except, as otherwise ordered by the Court, the successor personal representative has the powers and duties in respect to the continued administration which the former personal representative would have had if his appointment had not been terminated.

Section 3–614. [Special Administrator; Appointment.]

A special administrator may be appointed:

(1) informally by the Registrar on the application of any interested person when necessary to protect the estate of a decedent prior to the appointment of a general personal representative or if a prior appointment has been terminated as provided in Section 3–609;

(2) in a formal proceeding by order of the Court on the petition of any interested person and finding, after notice and hearing, that

appointment is necessary to preserve the estate or to secure its proper administration including its administration in circumstances where a general personal representative cannot or should not act. If it appears to the Court that an emergency exists, appointment may be ordered without notice.

Section 3–615. [Special Administrator; Who May Be Appointed.]

(a) If a special administrator is to be appointed pending the probate of a will which is the subject of a pending application or petition for probate, the person named executor in the will shall be appointed if available, and qualified.

(b) In other cases, any proper person may be appointed special administrator.

Section 3–616. [Special Administrator; Appointed Informally; Powers and Duties.]

A special administrator appointed by the Registrar in informal proceedings pursuant to Section 3–614(1) has the duty to collect and manage the assets of the estate, to preserve them, to account therefor and to deliver them to the general personal representative upon his qualification. The special administrator has the power of a personal representative under the Code necessary to perform his duties.

Section 3–617. [Special Administrator; Formal Proceedings; Power and Duties.]

A special administrator appointed by order of the Court in any formal proceeding has the power of a general personal representative except as limited in the appointment and duties as prescribed in the order. The appointment may be for a specified time, to perform particular acts or on other terms as the Court may direct.

Section 3–618. [Termination of Appointment; Special Administrator.]

The appointment of a special administrator terminates in accordance with the provisions of the order of appointment or on the appointment of a general personal representative. In other cases, the appointment of a special administrator is subject to termination as provided in Sections 3–608 through 3–611.

Part 7
Duties and Powers of Personal Representatives

Section 3–701. [Time of Accrual of Duties and Powers.]

The duties and powers of a personal representative commence upon his appointment. The powers of a personal representative relate back in time to give acts by the person appointed which are beneficial to the estate occurring prior to appointment the same effect as those occurring thereafter. Prior to appointment, a person named executor in a will may carry out written instructions of the decedent relating to his body, funeral and burial arrangements. A personal representative may ratify and accept acts on behalf of the estate done by others where the acts would have been proper for a personal representative.

Section 3–702. [Priority Among Different Letters.]

A person to whom general letters are issued first has exclusive authority under the letters until his appointment is terminated or modified. If, through error, general letters are afterwards issued to another, the first appointed representative may recover any property of the estate in the hands of the representative subsequently appointed, but the acts of the latter done in good faith before notice of the first letters are not void for want of validity of appointment.

Section 3–703. [General Duties; Relation and Liability to Persons Interested in Estate; Standing to Sue.]

(a) A personal representative is a fiduciary who shall observe the standards of care applicable to trustees as described by Section 7–302. A personal representative is under a duty to settle and distribute the estate of the decedent in accordance with the terms of any probated and effective will and this Code, and as expeditiously and efficiently as is consistent with the best interests of the estate. He shall use the authority conferred upon him by this Code, the terms of the will, if any, and any order in proceedings to which he is party for the best interests of successors to the estate.

(b) A personal representative shall not be surcharged for acts of administration or distribution if the conduct in question was authorized at the time. Subject to other obligations of administration, an informally probated will is authority to administer and distribute the estate according to its terms. An order of appointment of a personal representative, whether issued in informal or formal proceedings, is authority to distribute apparently intestate assets to the heirs of the decedent if, at the time of distribution, the personal representative is not aware of a pending testacy proceeding, a proceeding to vacate an order entered in an earlier testacy proceeding, a formal proceeding questioning his appointment or fitness to continue, or a supervised administration proceeding. Nothing in this section affects the duty of the personal representative to administer and distribute the estate in accordance with the rights of claimants, the surviving spouse, any minor and dependent children and any pretermitted child of the decedent as described elsewhere in this Code.

(c) Except as to proceedings which do not survive the death of the decedent, a personal representative of a decedent domiciled in this state at his death has the same standing to sue and be sued in the courts of this state and the courts of any other jurisdiction as his decedent had immediately prior to death.

Section 3–704. [Personal Representative to Proceed Without Court Order; Exception.]

A personal representative shall proceed expeditiously with the settlement and distribution of a decedent's estate and, except as otherwise specified or ordered in regard to a supervised personal representative, do so without adjudication, order, or direction of the Court, but he may invoke the jurisdiction of the Court, in proceedings authorized by this Code, to resolve questions concerning the estate or its administration.

Section 3–705. [Duty of Personal Representative; Information to Heirs and Devisees.]

Not later than 30 days after his appointment every personal representative, except any special administrator, shall give information of his appointment to the heirs and devisees, including, if there has been no formal testacy proceeding and if the personal representative was appointed on the assumption that the decedent died intestate, the devisees in any will mentioned in the application for appointment of a personal representative. The information shall be delivered or sent by ordinary mail to each of the heirs and devisees whose address is reasonably available to the personal representative. The duty does not extend to require information to persons who have been adjudicated in a prior formal testacy proceeding to have no interest in the estate. The information shall include the name and address of the personal representative, indicate that it is being sent to persons who have or may have some interest in the estate being administered, indicate whether bond has been filed, and describe the court where papers relating to the estate are on file. The personal representative's failure to give this information is a breach of his duty to the persons concerned but does not affect the validity of his appointment, his powers or other duties. A personal representative may inform other persons of his appointment by delivery or ordinary first class mail.

Section 3–706. [Duty of Personal Representative; Inventory and Appraisement.]

Within 3 months after his appointment, a personal representative, who is not a special administrator or a successor to another representative who has previously discharged this duty, shall prepare and file or mail an inventory of property owned by the decedent at the time of his death, listing it with reasonable detail, and indicating as to each listed item, its fair market value as of the date of the decedent's death, and the type and amount of any encumbrance that may exist with reference to any item.

The personal representative shall send a copy of the inventory to interested persons who request it. He may also file the original of the inventory with the court.

Section 3–707. [Employment of Appraisers.]

The personal representative may employ a qualified and disinterested appraiser to assist him in ascertaining the fair market value as of the date of the decedent's death of any asset the value of which may be subject to reasonable doubt. Different persons may be employed to appraise different kinds of assets included in the estate. The names and addresses of any appraiser shall be indicated on the inventory with the item or items he appraised.

Section 3–708. [Duty of Personal Representative; Supplementary Inventory.]

If any property not included in the original inventory comes to the knowledge of a personal representative or if the personal representative learns that the value or description indicated in the original inventory for any item is erroneous or misleading, he shall make a supplementary inventory or appraisement showing the market value as of the date of the decedent's death of the new item or the revised market value or descriptions, and the appraisers or other data relied upon, if any, and file it with the Court if the original inventory was filed, or furnish copies thereof or information thereof to persons interested in the new information.

Section 3–709. [Duty of Personal Representative; Possession of Estate.]

Except as otherwise provided by a decedent's will, every personal representative has a right to, and shall take possession or control of, the decedent's property, except that any real property or tangible personal property may be left with or surrendered to the person presumptively entitled thereto unless or until, in the judgment of the personal representative, possession of the property by him will be necessary for purposes of administration. The request by a personal representative for delivery of any property possessed by an heir or devisee is conclusive evidence, in any action against the heir or devisee for possession thereof, that the possession of the property by the personal representative is necessary for purposes of administration. The personal representative shall pay taxes on, and take all steps reasonably necessary for the management, protection and preservation of, the estate in his possession. He may maintain an action to recover possession of property or to determine the title thereto.

Section 3–710. [Power to Avoid Transfers.]

The property liable for the payment of unsecured debts of a decedent includes all property transferred by him by any means which is in law void or voidable as against his creditors, and subject to prior liens, the right to recover this property, so far as necessary for the payment of unsecured debts of the decedent, is exclusively in the personal representative.

Section 3–711. [Powers of Personal Representatives; In General.]

Until termination of his appointment a personal representative has the same power over the title to property of the estate that an absolute owner would have, in trust however, for the benefit of the creditors and others interested in the estate. This power may be exercised without notice, hearing, or order of court.

Section 3–712. [Improper Exercise of Power; Breach of Fiduciary Duty.]

If the exercise of power concerning the estate is improper, the personal representative is liable to interested persons for damage or loss resulting from breach of his fiduciary duty to the same extent as a trustee of an express trust. The rights of purchasers and others dealing with a personal representative shall be determined as provided in Sections 3–713 and 3–714.

Section 3–713. [Sale, Encumbrance or Transaction Involving Conflict of Interest; Voidable; Exceptions.]

Any sale or encumbrance to the personal representative, his spouse, agent or attorney, or any corporation or trust in which he has a substantial beneficial interest, or any transaction which is affected by a substantial conflict of interest on the part of the personal representative, is voidable by any person interested in the estate except one who has consented after fair disclosure, unless

(1) the will or a contract entered into by the decedent expressly authorized the transaction; or

(2) the transaction is approved by the Court after notice to interested persons.

Section 3–714. [Persons Dealing with Personal Representative; Protection.]

A person who in good faith either assists a personal representative or deals with him for value is protected as if the personal representative properly exercised his power. The fact that a person knowingly deals with a personal representative does not alone require the person to inquire into the existence of a power or the propriety of its exercise. Except for restrictions on powers of supervised personal representatives which are endorsed on letters as provided in Section 3–504, no provision in any will or order of court purporting to limit the power of a personal representative is effective except as to persons with actual knowledge thereof. A person is not bound to see to the proper application of estate assets paid or delivered to a personal representative. The protection here expressed extends to instances in which some procedural irregularity or jurisdictional defect occurred in proceedings leading to the issuance of letters, including a case in which the alleged decedent is found to be alive. The protection here expressed is not by substitution for that provided by comparable provisions of the laws relating to commercial transactions and laws simplifying transfers of securities by fiduciaries.

Section 3–715. [Transactions Authorized for Personal Representatives; Exceptions.]

Except as restricted or otherwise provided by the will or by an order in a formal proceeding and subject to the priorities stated in Section 3–902, a personal representative, acting reasonably for the benefit of the interested persons, may properly:

(1) retain assets owned by the decedent pending distribution or liquidation including those in which the representative is personally interested or which are otherwise improper for trust investment;

(2) receive assets from fiduciaries, or other sources;

(3) perform, compromise or refuse performance of the decedent's contracts that continue as obligations of the estate, as he may determine under the circumstances. In performing enforceable contracts by the decedent to convey or lease land, the personal representative, among other possible courses of action, may:

(i) execute and deliver a deed of conveyance for cash payment of all sums remaining due or the purchaser's note for the sum remaining due secured by a mortgage or deed of trust on the land; or

(ii) deliver a deed in escrow with directions that the proceeds, when paid in accordance with the escrow agreement, be paid to the successors of the decedent, as designated in the escrow agreement;

(4) satisfy written charitable pledges of the decedent irrespective of whether the pledges constituted binding obligations of the decedent or were properly presented as claims, if in the judgment of the personal representative the decedent would have wanted the pledges completed under the circumstances;

(5) if funds are not needed to meet debts and expenses currently payable and are not immediately distributable, deposit or invest liquid assets of the estate, including moneys received from the sale of other assets, in federally insured interest-bearing accounts, readily marketable secured loan arrangements or other prudent investments which would be reasonable for use by trustees generally;

(6) acquire or dispose of an asset, including land in this or another state, for cash or on credit, at public or private sale; and manage, develop, improve, exchange, partition, change the character of, or abandon an estate asset;

(7) make ordinary or extraordinary repairs or alterations in buildings or other structures, demolish any improvements, raze existing or erect new party walls or buildings;

(8) subdivide, develop or dedicate land to public use; make or obtain the vacation of plats and adjust boundaries; or adjust differences in valuation on exchange or partition by giving or receiving considerations; or dedicate easements to public use without consideration;

(9) enter for any purpose into a lease as lessor or lessee, with or without option to purchase or renew, for a term within or extending beyond the period of administration;

(10) enter into a lease or arrangement for exploration and removal of minerals or other natural resources or enter into a pooling or unitization agreement;

(11) abandon property when, in the opinion of the personal representative, it is valueless, or is so encumbered, or is in condition that it is of no benefit to the estate;

(12) vote stocks or other securities in person or by general or limited proxy;

(13) pay calls, assessments, and other sums chargeable or accruing against or on account of securities, unless barred by the provisions relating to claims;

(14) hold a security in the name of a nominee or in other form without disclosure of the interest of the estate but the personal representative is liable for any act of the nominee in connection with the security so held;

(15) insure the assets of the estate against damage, loss and liability and himself against liability as to third persons;

(16) borrow money with or without security to be repaid from the estate assets or otherwise; and advance money for the protection of the estate;

(17) effect a fair and reasonable compromise with any debtor or obligor, or extend, renew or in any manner modify the terms of any obligation owing to the estate. If the personal representative holds a mortgage, pledge or other lien upon property of another person, he may, in lieu of foreclosure, accept a conveyance or transfer of encumbered assets from the owner thereof in satisfaction of the indebtedness secured by lien;

(18) pay taxes, assessments, compensation of the personal representative, and other expenses incident to the administration of the estate;

(19) sell or exercise stock subscription or conversion rights; consent, directly or through a committee or other agent, to the reorganization, consolidation, merger, dissolution, or liquidation of a corporation or other business enterprise;

(20) allocate items of income or expense to either estate income or principal, as permitted or provided by law;

(21) employ persons, including attorneys, auditors, investment advisors, or agents, even if they are associated with the personal representative, to advise or assist the personal representative in the performance of his administrative duties; act without independent investigation upon their recommendations; and instead of acting per-

sonally, employ one or more agents to perform any act of administration, whether or not discretionary;

(22) prosecute or defend claims, or proceedings in any jurisdiction for the protection of the estate and of the personal representative in the performance of his duties;

(23) sell, mortgage, or lease any real or personal property of the estate or any interest therein for cash, credit, or for part cash and part credit, and with or without security for unpaid balances;

(24) continue any unincorporated business or venture in which the decedent was engaged at the time of his death (i) in the same business form for a period of not more than 4 months from the date of appointment of a general personal representative if continuation is a reasonable means of preserving the value of the business including good will, (ii) in the same business form for any additional period of time that may be approved by order of the Court in a formal proceeding to which the persons interested in the estate are parties; or (iii) throughout the period of administration if the business is incorporated by the personal representative and if none of the probable distributees of the business who are competent adults object to its incorporation and retention in the estate;

(25) incorporate any business or venture in which the decedent was engaged at the time of his death;

(26) provide for exoneration of the personal representative from personal liability in any contract entered into on behalf of the estate;

(27) satisfy and settle claims and distribute the estate as provided in this Code.

Section 3–716. [Powers and Duties of Successor Personal Representative.]

A successor personal representative has the same power and duty as the original personal representative to complete the administration and distribution of the estate, as expeditiously as possible, but he shall not exercise any power expressly made personal to the executor named in the will.

Section 3–717. [Co-representatives; When Joint Action Required.]

If two or more persons are appointed co-representatives and unless the will provides otherwise, the concurrence of all is required on all acts connected with the administration and distribution of the estate. This restriction does not apply when any co-representative receives and receipts for property due the estate, when the concurrence of all cannot readily be obtained in the time reasonably available for emergency action necessary to preserve the estate, or when a co-representative has been delegated to act for the others. Persons dealing with a co-representative if actually unaware that another has been appointed to serve with him or if advised by the personal representative with whom they deal that he has authority to act alone for any of the reasons mentioned herein, are as fully protected as if the person with whom they dealt had been the sole personal representative.

Section 3–718. [Powers of Surviving Personal Representative.]

Unless the terms of the will otherwise provide, every power exercisable by personal co-representatives may be exercised by the one or more remaining after the appointment of one or more is terminated, and if one of 2 or more nominated as co-executors is not appointed, those appointed may exercise all the powers incident to the office.

Section 3–719. [Compensation of Personal Representative.]

A personal representative is entitled to reasonable compensation for his services. If a will provides for compensation of the personal representative and there is no contract with the decedent regarding compensation, he may renounce the provision before qualifying and be entitled to reasonable compensation. A personal representative also may renounce his right to all or any part of the compensation. A written renunciation of fee may be filed with the Court.

Section 3–720. [Expenses in Estate Litigation.]

If any personal representative or person nominated as personal representative defends or prosecutes any proceeding in good faith, whether successful or not he is entitled to receive from the estate his necessary expenses and disbursements including reasonable attorneys' fees incurred.

Section 3–721. [Proceedings for Review of Employment of Agents and Compensation of Personal Representatives and Employees of Estate.]

After notice to all interested persons, on petition of an interested person or on appropriate motion if administration is supervised, the propriety of employment of any person by a personal representative including any attorney, auditor, investment advisor or other specialized agent or assistant, the reasonableness of the compensation of any person so employed, or the reasonableness of the compensation determined by the personal representative for his own services, may be reviewed by the Court. Any person who has received excessive compensation from an estate for services rendered may be ordered to make appropriate refunds.

Part 8
Creditors' Claims

Section 3–801. [Notice to Creditors.]

Unless notice has already been given under this section, a personal representative upon his appointment shall publish a notice once a week for 3 successive weeks in a newspaper of general circulation in the [county] announcing his appointment and address and notifying creditors of the estate to present their claims within 4 months after the date of the first publication of the notice or be forever barred.

Section 3–802. [Statutes of Limitations.]

Unless an estate is insolvent the personal representative, with the consent of all successors whose interests would be affected, may waive any defense of limitations available to the estate. If the defense is not waived, no claim which was barred by any statute of limitations at the time of the decedent's death shall be allowed or paid. The running of any statute of limitations measured from some event other than death and advertisement for claims against a decedent is suspended during the 4 months following the decedent's death but resumes thereafter as to claims not barred pursuant to the sections which follow. For purposes of any statute of limitations, the proper presentation of a claim under Section 3–804 is equivalent to commencement of a proceeding on the claim.

Section 3–803. [Limitations on Presentation of Claims.]

(a) All claims against a decedent's estate which arose before the death of the decedent, including claims of the state and any subdivision thereof, whether due or to become due, absolute or contingent, liquidated or unliquidated, founded on contract, tort, or other legal basis, if not barred earlier by other statute of limitations, are barred against the estate, the personal representative, and the heirs and devisees of the decedent, unless presented as follows:

(1) within 4 months after the date of the first publication of notice to creditors if notice is given in compliance with Section 3–801; provided, claims barred by the non-claim statute at the decedent's domicile before the first publication for claims in this state are also barred in this state.

(2) within [3] years after the decedent's death, if notice to creditors has not been published.

(b) All claims against a decedent's estate which arise at or after the death of the decedent, including claims of the state and any subdivision thereof, whether due or to become due, absolute or contingent, liquidated or unliquidated, founded on contract, tort, or other legal basis, are barred against the estate, the personal representative, and the heirs and devisees of the decedent, unless presented as follows:

(1) a claim based on a contract with the personal representative, within four months after performance by the personal representative is due;

(2) any other claim, within 4 months after it arises.

(c) Nothing in this section affects or prevents:

(1) any proceeding to enforce any mortgage, pledge, or other lien upon property of the estate; or

(2) to the limits of the insurance protection only, any proceeding to establish liability of the decedent or the personal representative for which he is protected by liability insurance.

Section 3–804. [Manner of Presentation of Claims.]

Claims against a decedent's estate may be presented as follows:

(1) The claimant may deliver or mail to the personal representative a written statement of the claim indicating its basis, the name and address of the claimant, and the amount claimed, or may file a written statement of the claim, in the form prescribed by rule, with the clerk of the Court. The claim is deemed presented on the first to occur of receipt of the written statement of claim by the personal representative, or the filing of the claim with the Court. If a claim is not yet due, the date when it will become due shall be stated. If the claim is contingent or unliquidated, the nature of the uncertainty shall be stated. If the claim is secured, the security shall be described. Failure to describe correctly the security, the nature of any uncertainty, and the due date of a claim not yet due does not invalidate the presentation made.

(2) The claimant may commence a proceeding against the personal representative in any Court where the personal representative may be subjected to jurisdiction, to obtain payment of his claim against the estate, but the commencement of the proceeding must occur within the time limited for presenting the claim. No presentation of claim is required in regard to matters claimed in proceedings against the decedent which were pending at the time of his death.

(3) If a claim is presented under subsection (1), no proceeding thereon may be commenced more than 60 days after the personal representative has mailed a notice of disallowance; but, in the case of a claim which is not presently due or which is contingent or unliquidated, the personal representative may consent to an extension of the 60-day period, or to avoid injustice the Court, on petition, may order an extension of the 60-day period, but in no event shall the extension run beyond the applicable statute of limitations.

Section 3–805. [Classification of Claims.]

(a) If the applicable assets of the estate are insufficient to pay all claims in full, the personal representative shall make payment in the following order:

(1) costs and expenses of administration;

(2) reasonable funeral expenses;

(3) debts and taxes with preference under federal law;

(4) reasonable and necessary medical and hospital expenses of the last illness of the decedent, including compensation of persons attending him;

(5) debts and taxes with preference under other laws of this state;

(6) all other claims.

(b) No preference shall be given in the payment of any claim over any other claim of the same class, and a claim due and payable shall not be entitled to a preference over claims not due.

Section 3–806. [Allowance of Claims.]

(a) As to claims presented in the manner described in Section 3–804 within the time limit prescribed in 3–803, the personal representative may mail a notice to any claimant stating that the claim has been disallowed. If, after allowing or disallowing a claim, the personal representative changes his decision concerning the claim, he shall notify the claimant. The personal representative may not change a disallowance of a claim after the time for the claimant to file a petition for allowance or to commence a proceeding on the claim has run and the claim has been barred. Every claim which is disallowed in whole or in part by the personal representative is barred so far as not allowed unless the claimant files a petition for allowance in the Court or commences a proceeding against the personal representative not later than 60 days after the mailing of the notice of disallowance or partial allowance if the notice warns the claimant of the impending bar. Failure of the personal representative to mail notice to a claimant of action on his claim for 60 days after the time for original presentation of the claim has expired has the effect of a notice of allowance.

(b) Upon the petition of the personal representative or of a claimant in a proceeding for the purpose, the Court may allow in whole or in part any claim or claims presented to the personal representative or filed with the clerk of the Court in due time and not barred by subsection (a) of this section. Notice in this proceeding shall be given to the claimant, the personal representative and those other persons interested in the estate as the Court may direct by order entered at the time the proceeding is commenced.

(c) A judgment in a proceeding in another court against a personal representative to enforce a claim against a decedent's estate is an allowance of the claim.

(d) Unless otherwise provided in any judgment in another court entered against the personal representative, allowed claims bear interest at the legal rate for the period commencing 60 days after the time for original presentation of the claim has expired unless based on a contract making a provision for interest, in which case they bear interest in accordance with that provision.

Section 3–807.   [Payment of Claims.]

(a) Upon the expiration of 4 months from the date of the first publication of the notice to creditors, the personal representative shall proceed to pay the claims allowed against the estate in the order of priority prescribed, after making provision for homestead, family and support allowances, for claims already presented which have not yet been allowed or whose allowance has been appealed, and for unbarred claims which may yet be presented, including costs and expenses of administration. By petition to the Court in a proceeding for the purpose, or by appropriate motion if the administration is supervised, a claimant whose claim has been allowed but not paid as provided herein may secure an order directing the personal representative to pay the claim to the extent that funds of the estate are available for the payment.

(b) The personal representative at any time may pay any just claim which has not been barred, with or without formal presentation, but he is personally liable to any other claimant whose claim is allowed and who is injured by such payment if

(1) the payment was made before the expiration of the time limit stated in subsection (a) and the personal representative failed to require the payee to give adequate security for the refund of any of the payment necessary to pay other claimants; or

(2) the payment was made, due to the negligence or wilful fault of the personal representative, in such manner as to deprive the injured claimant of his priority.

Section 3–808.   [Individual Liability of Personal Representative.]

(a) Unless otherwise provided in the contract, a personal representative is not individually liable on a contract properly entered into in his fiduciary capacity in the course of administration of the estate unless he fails to reveal his representative capacity and identify the estate in the contract.

(b) A personal representative is individually liable for obligations arising from ownership or control of the estate or for torts committed in the course of administration of the estate only if he is personally at fault.

(c) Claims based on contracts entered into by a personal representative in his fiduciary capacity, on obligations arising from ownership or control of the estate or on torts committed in the course of estate administration may be asserted against the estate by proceeding against the personal representative in his fiduciary capacity, whether or not the personal representative is individually liable therefor.

(d) Issues of liability as between the estate and the personal representative individually may be determined in a proceeding for accounting, surcharge or indemnification or other appropriate proceeding.

Section 3–809. [Secured Claims.]

Payment of a secured claim is upon the basis of the amount allowed if the creditor surrenders his security; otherwise payment is upon the basis of one of the following:

(1) if the creditor exhausts his security before receiving payment, [unless precluded by other law] upon the amount of the claim allowed less the fair value of the security; or

(2) if the creditor does not have the right to exhaust his security or has not done so, upon the amount of the claim allowed less the value of the security determined by converting it into money according to the terms of the agreement pursuant to which the security was delivered to the creditor, or by the creditor and personal representative by agreement, arbitration, compromise or litigation.

Section 3–810. [Claims Not Due and Contingent or Unliquidated Claims.]

(a) If a claim which will become due at a future time or a contingent or unliquidated claim becomes due or certain before the distribution of the estate, and if the claim has been allowed or established by a proceeding, it is paid in the same manner as presently due and absolute claims of the same class.

(b) In other cases the personal representative or, on petition of the personal representative or the claimant in a special proceeding for the purpose, the Court may provide for payment as follows:

(1) if the claimant consents, he may be paid the present or agreed value of the claim, taking any uncertainty into account;

(2) arrangement for future payment, or possible payment, on the happening of the contingency or on liquidation may be made by creating a trust, giving a mortgage, obtaining a bond or security from a distributee, or otherwise.

Section 3–811. [Counterclaims.]

In allowing a claim the personal representative may deduct any counterclaim which the estate has against the claimant. In determining a claim against an estate a Court shall reduce the amount allowed by the amount of any counterclaims and, if the counterclaims exceed the claim, render a judgment against the claimant in the amount of the excess. A counterclaim, liquidated or unliquidated, may arise from a transaction other than that upon which the claim is based. A counterclaim may give rise to relief exceeding in amount or different in kind from that sought in the claim.

Section 3–812. [Execution and Levies Prohibited.]

No execution may issue upon nor may any levy be made against any property of the estate under any judgment against a decedent or a personal representative, but this section shall not be construed to prevent the enforcement of mortgages, pledges or liens upon real or personal property in an appropriate proceeding.

Section 3–813.   [Compromise of Claims.]

When a claim against the estate has been presented in any manner, the personal representative may, if it appears for the best interest of the estate, compromise the claim, whether due or not due, absolute or contingent, liquidated or unliquidated.

Section 3–814.   [Encumbered Assets.]

If any assets of the estate are encumbered by mortgage, pledge, lien, or other security interest, the personal representative may pay the encumbrance or any part thereof, renew or extend any obligation secured by the encumbrance or convey or transfer the assets to the creditor in satisfaction of his lien, in whole or in part, whether or not the holder of the encumbrance has presented a claim, if it appears to be for the best interest of the estate.   Payment of an encumbrance does not increase the share of the distributee entitled to the encumbered assets unless the distributee is entitled to exoneration.

Section 3–815.   [Administration in More Than One State; Duty of Personal Representative.]

(a) All assets of estates being administered in this state are subject to all claims, allowances and charges existing or established against the personal representative wherever appointed.

(b) If the estate either in this state or as a whole is insufficient to cover all family exemptions and allowances determined by the law of the decedent's domicile, prior charges and claims, after satisfaction of the exemptions, allowances and charges, each claimant whose claim has been allowed either in this state or elsewhere in administrations of which the personal representative is aware, is entitled to receive payment of an equal proportion of his claim.   If a preference or security in regard to a claim is allowed in another jurisdiction but not in this state, the creditor so benefited is to receive dividends from local assets only upon the balance of his claim after deducting the amount of the benefit.

(c) In case the family exemptions and allowances, prior charges and claims of the entire estate exceed the total value of the portions of the estate being administered separately and this state is not the state of the decedent's last domicile, the claims allowed in this state shall be paid their proportion if local assets are adequate for the purpose, and the balance of local assets shall be transferred to the domiciliary personal representative.   If local assets are not sufficient to pay all claims allowed in this state the amount to which they are entitled, local assets shall be marshalled so that each claim allowed in this state is paid its proportion as far as possible, after taking into account all dividends on claims allowed in this state from assets in other jurisdictions.

Section 3–816. [Final Distribution to Domiciliary Representative.]

The estate of a non-resident decedent being administered by a personal representative appointed in this state shall, if there is a personal representative of the decedent's domicile willing to receive it, be distributed to the domiciliary personal representative for the benefit of the successors of the decedent unless (1) by virtue of the decedent's will, if any, and applicable choice of law rules, the successors are identified pursuant to the local law of this state without reference to the local law of the decedent's domicile; (2) the personal representative of this state, after reasonable inquiry, is unaware of the existence or identity of a domiciliary personal representative; or (3) the Court orders otherwise in a proceeding for a closing order under Section 3–1001 or incident to the closing of a supervised administration. In other cases, distribution of the estate of a decedent shall be made in accordance with the other Parts of this Article.

Part 9
Special Provisions Relating to Distribution

Section 3–901. [Successors' Rights if No Administration.]

In the absence of administration, the heirs and devisees are entitled to the estate in accordance with the terms of a probated will or the laws of intestate succession. Devisees may establish title by the probated will to devised property. Persons entitled to property by homestead allowance, exemption or intestacy may establish title thereto by proof of the decedent's ownership, his death, and their relationship to the decedent. Successors take subject to all charges incident to administration, including the claims of creditors and allowances of surviving spouse and dependent children, and subject to the rights of others resulting from abatement, retainer, advancement, and ademption.

Section 3–902. [Distribution; Order in Which Assets Appropriated; Abatement.]

(a) Except as provided in subsection (b) and except as provided in connection with the share of the surviving spouse who elects to take an elective share, shares of distributees abate, without any preference or priority as between real and personal property, in the following order: (1) property not disposed of by the will; (2) residuary devises; (3) general devises; (4) specific devises. For purposes of abatement, a general devise charged on any specific property or fund is a specific devise to the extent of the value of the property on which it is charged, and upon the failure or insufficiency of the property on which it is charged, a general devise to the extent of the failure or insufficiency. Abatement within each classification is in proportion to the amounts of property each of the beneficiaries would have received if full distribution of the property had been made in accordance with the terms of the will.

(b) If the will expresses an order of abatement, or if the testamentary plan or the express or implied purpose of the devise would be defeated by the order of abatement stated in subsection (a), the shares of the distributees abate as may be found necessary to give effect to the intention of the testator.

(c) If the subject of a preferred devise is sold or used incident to administration, abatement shall be achieved by appropriate adjustments in, or contribution from, other interests in the remaining assets.

[Section 3-902A. [Distribution; Order in Which Assets Appropriated; Abatement.]

(addendum for adoption in community property states)

[(a) and (b) as above.]

(c) If an estate of a decedent consists partly of separate property and partly of community property, the debts and expenses of administration shall be apportioned and charged against the different kinds of property in proportion to the relative value thereof.

[(d) same as (c) in common law state.]]

Section 3-903. [Right of Retainer.]

The amount of a non-contingent indebtedness of a successor to the estate if due, or its present value if not due, shall be offset against the successor's interest; but the successor has the benefit of any defense which would be available to him in a direct proceeding for recovery of the debt.

Section 3-904. [Interest on General Pecuniary Devise.]

General pecuniary devises bear interest at the legal rate beginning one year after the first appointment of a personal representative until payment, unless a contrary intent is indicated by the will.

Section 3-905. [Penalty Clause for Contest.]

A provision in a will purporting to penalize any interested person for contesting the will or instituting other proceedings relating to the estate is unenforceable if probable cause exists for instituting proceedings.

Section 3–906. [Distribution in Kind; Valuation; Method.]

(a) Unless a contrary intention is indicated by the will, the distributable assets of a decedent's estate shall be distributed in kind to the extent possible through application of the following provisions:

(1) A specific devisee is entitled to distribution of the thing devised to him, and a spouse or child who has selected particular assets of an estate as provided in Section 2–402 shall receive the items selected.

(2) Any homestead or family allowance or devise payable in money may be satisfied by value in kind provided

(i) the person entitled to the payment has not demanded payment in cash;

(ii) the property distributed in kind is valued at fair market value as of the date of its distribution, and

(iii) no residuary devisee has requested that the asset in question remain a part of the residue of the estate.

(3) For the purpose of valuation under paragraph (2) securities regularly traded on recognized exchanges, if distributed in kind, are valued at the price for the last sale of like securities traded on the business day prior to distribution, or if there was no sale on that day, at the median between amounts bid and offered at the close of that day. Assets consisting of sums owed the decedent or the estate by solvent debtors as to which there is no known dispute or defense are valued at the sum due with accrued interest or discounted to the date of distribution. For assets which do not have readily ascertainable values, a valuation as of a date not more than 30 days prior to the date of distribution, if otherwise reasonable, controls. For purposes of facilitating distribution, the personal representative may ascertain the value of the assets as of the time of the proposed distribution in any reasonable way, including the employment of qualified appraisers, even if the assets may have been previously appraised.

(4) The residuary estate shall be distributed in kind if there is no objection to the proposed distribution and it is practicable to distribute undivided interests. In other cases, residuary property may be converted into cash for distribution.

(b) After the probable charges against the estate are known, the personal representative may mail or deliver a proposal for distribution to all persons who have a right to object to the proposed distribution. The right of any distributee to object to the proposed distribution on the basis of the kind or value of asset he is to receive, if not waived earlier in writing, terminates if he fails to object in writing received by the personal representative within 30 days after mailing or delivery of the proposal.

Section 3–907. [Distribution in Kind; Evidence.]

If distribution in kind is made, the personal representative shall execute an instrument or deed of distribution assigning, transferring or releasing the assets to the distributee as evidence of the distributee's title to the property.

Section 3–908. [Distribution; Right or Title of Distributee.]

Proof that a distributee has received an instrument or deed of distribution of assets in kind, or payment in distribution, from a personal representative, is conclusive evidence that the distributee has succeeded to the interest of the estate in the distributed assets, as against all persons interested in the estate, except that the personal representative may recover the assets or their value if the distribution was improper.

Section 3–909. [Improper Distribution; Liability of Distributee.]

Unless the distribution or payment no longer can be questioned because of adjudication, estoppel, or limitation, a distributee of property improperly distributed or paid, or a claimant who was improperly paid, is liable to return the property improperly received and its income since distribution if he has the property. If he does not have the property, then he is liable to return the value as of the date of disposition of the property improperly received and its income and gain received by him.

Section 3–910. [Purchasers from Distributees Protected.]

If property distributed in kind or a security interest therein is acquired for value by a purchaser from or lender to a distributee who has received an instrument or deed of distribution from the personal representative, or is so acquired by a purchaser from or lender to a transferee from such distributee, the purchaser or lender takes title free of rights of any interested person in the estate and incurs no personal liability to the estate, or to any interested person, whether or not the distribution was proper or supported by court order or the authority of the personal representative was terminated before execution of the instrument or deed. This section protects a purchaser from or lender to a distributee who, as personal representative, has executed a deed of distribution to himself, as well as a purchaser from or lender to any other distributee or his transferee. To be protected under this provision, a purchaser or lender need not inquire whether a personal representative acted properly in making the distribution in kind, even if the personal representative and the distributee are the same person, or whether the authority of the personal representative had terminated before the distribution. Any recorded instrument described in this section on which a state documentary fee is noted pursuant to [insert appropriate reference] shall be prima facie evidence that such transfer was made for value.

Section 3–911. [Partition for Purpose of Distribution.]

When two or more heirs or devisees are entitled to distribution of undivided interests in any real or personal property of the estate, the personal representative or one or more of the heirs or devisees may petition the Court prior to the formal or informal closing of the estate, to make partition. After notice to the interested heirs or devisees, the Court shall partition the property in the same manner as provided by the law for civil actions of partition. The Court may direct the personal representative to sell any property which cannot be partitioned without prejudice to the owners and which cannot conveniently be allotted to any one party.

Section 3–912. [Private Agreements Among Successors to Decedent Binding on Personal Representative.]

Subject to the rights of creditors and taxing authorities, competent successors may agree among themselves to alter the interests, shares, or amounts to which they are entitled under the will of the decedent, or under the laws of intestacy, in any way that they provide in a written contract executed by all who are affected by its provisions. The personal representative shall abide by the terms of the agreement subject to his obligation to administer the estate for the benefit of creditors, to pay all taxes and costs of administration, and to carry out the responsibilities of his office for the benefit of any successors of the decedent who are not parties. Personal representatives of decedents' estates are not required to see to the performance of trusts if the trustee thereof is another person who is willing to accept the trust. Accordingly, trustees of a testamentary trust are successors for the purposes of this section. Nothing herein relieves trustees of any duties owed to beneficiaries of trusts.

Section 3–913. [Distributions to Trustee.]

(a) Before distributing to a trustee, the personal representative may require that the trust be registered if the state in which it is to be administered provides for registration and that the trustee inform the beneficiaries as provided in Section 7–303.

(b) If the trust instrument does not excuse the trustee from giving bond, the personal representative may petition the appropriate Court to require that the trustee post bond if he apprehends that distribution might jeopardize the interests of persons who are not able to protect themselves, and he may withhold distribution until the Court has acted.

(c) No inference of negligence on the part of the personal representative shall be drawn from his failure to exercise the authority conferred by subsections (a) and (b).

[Section 3–914. [Disposition of Unclaimed Assets.]

(a) If an heir, devisee or claimant cannot be found, the personal representative shall distribute the share of the missing person to his conservator, if any, otherwise to the [state treasurer] to become a part of the [state escheat fund].

(b) The money received by [state treasurer] shall be paid to the person entitled on proof of his right thereto or, if the [state treasurer] refuses or fails to pay, the person may petition the Court which appointed the personal representative, whereupon the Court upon notice to the [state treasurer] may determine the person entitled to the money and order the [treasurer] to pay it to him. No interest is allowed thereon and the heir, devisee or claimant shall pay all costs and expenses incident to the proceeding. If no petition is made to the [court] within 8 years after payment to the [state treasurer], the right of recovery is barred.]

Section 3–915. [Distribution to Person Under Disability.]

A personal representative may discharge his obligation to distribute to any person under legal disability by distributing to his conservator, or any other person authorized by this Code or otherwise to give a valid receipt and discharge for the distribution.

Section 3–916. [Apportionment of Estate Taxes.]

(a) For purposes of this section:

(1) "estate" means the gross estate of a decedent as determined for the purpose of federal estate tax and the estate tax payable to this state;

(2) "person" means any individual, partnership, association, joint stock company, corporation, government, political subdivision, governmental agency, or local governmental agency;

(3) "person interested in the estate" means any person entitled to receive, or who has received, from a decedent or by reason of the death of a decedent any property or interest therein included in the decedent's estate. It includes a personal representative, conservator, and trustee;

(4) "state" means any state, territory, or possession of the United States, the District of Columbia, and the Commonwealth of Puerto Rico;

(5) "tax" means the federal estate tax and the additional inheritance tax imposed by _____ and interest and penalties imposed in addition to the tax;

(6) "fiduciary" means personal representative or trustee.

(b) Unless the will otherwise provides, the tax shall be apportioned among all persons interested in the estate. The apportionment is to be made in the proportion that the value of the interest of each person interested in the estate bears to the total value of the interests of all persons interested in the estate. The values used in determining the tax are to be used for that purpose. If the decedent's will directs a method of apportionment of tax different from the method described in this Code, the method described in the will controls.

(c)(1) The Court in which venue lies for the administration of the estate of a decedent, on petition for the purpose may determine the apportionment of the tax.

(2) If the Court finds that it is inequitable to apportion interest and penalties in the manner provided in subsection (b), because of special circumstances, it may direct apportionment thereof in the manner it finds equitable.

(3) If the Court finds that the assessment of penalties and interest assessed in relation to the tax is due to delay caused by the negligence of the fiduciary, the Court may charge him with the amount of the assessed penalties and interest.

(4) In any action to recover from any person interested in the estate the amount of the tax apportioned to the person in accordance with this Code the determination of the Court in respect thereto shall be prima facie correct.

(d)(1) The personal representative or other person in possession of the property of the decedent required to pay the tax may withhold from any property distributable to any person interested in the estate, upon its distribution to him, the amount of tax attributable to his interest. If the property in possession of the personal representative or other person required to pay the tax and distributable to any person interested in the estate is insufficient to satisfy the proportionate amount of the tax determined to be due from the person, the personal representative or other person required to pay the tax may recover the deficiency from the person interested in the estate. If the property is not in the possession of the personal representative or the other person required to pay the tax, the personal representative or the other person required to pay the tax may recover from any person interested in the estate the amount of the tax apportioned to the person in accordance with this Act.

(2) If property held by the personal representative is distributed prior to final apportionment of the tax, the distributee shall provide a bond or other security for the apportionment liability in the form and amount prescribed by the personal representative.

(e)(1) In making an apportionment, allowances shall be made for any exemptions granted, any classification made of persons interested in the estate and for any deductions and credits allowed by the law imposing the tax.

(2) Any exemption or deduction allowed by reason of the relationship of any person to the decedent or by reason of the purposes of the gift inures to the benefit of the person bearing such relationship or receiving the gift; but if an interest is subject to a prior present interest which is not allowable as a deduction, the tax apportionable against the present interest shall be paid from principal.

(3) Any deduction for property previously taxed and any credit for gift taxes or death taxes of a foreign country paid by the

decedent or his estate inures to the proportionate benefit of all persons liable to apportionment.

(4) Any credit for inheritance, succession or estate taxes or taxes in the nature thereof applicable to property or interests includable in the estate, inures to the benefit of the persons or interests chargeable with the payment thereof to the extent proportionately that the credit reduces the tax.

(5) To the extent that property passing to or in trust for a surviving spouse or any charitable, public or similar purpose is not an allowable deduction for purposes of the tax solely by reason of an inheritance tax or other death tax imposed upon and deductible from the property, the property is not included in the computation provided for in subsection (b) hereof, and to that extent no apportionment is made against the property. The sentence immediately preceding does not apply to any case if the result would be to deprive the estate of a deduction otherwise allowable under Section 2053(d) of the Internal Revenue Code of 1954, as amended, of the United States, relating to deduction for state death taxes on transfers for public, charitable, or religious uses.

(f) No interest in income and no estate for years or for life or other temporary interest in any property or fund is subject to apportionment as between the temporary interest and the remainder. The tax on the temporary interest and the tax, if any, on the remainder is chargeable against the corpus of the property or funds subject to the temporary interest and remainder.

(g) Neither the personal representative nor other person required to pay the tax is under any duty to institute any action to recover from any person interested in the estate the amount of the tax apportioned to the person until the expiration of the 3 months next following final determination of the tax. A personal representative or other person required to pay the tax who institutes the action within a reasonable time after the 3 months' period is not subject to any liability or surcharge because any portion of the tax apportioned to any person interested in the estate was collectible at a time following the death of the decedent but thereafter became uncollectible. If the personal representative or other person required to pay the tax cannot collect from any person interested in the estate the amount of the tax apportioned to the person, the amount not recoverable shall be equitably apportioned among the other persons interested in the estate who are subject to apportionment.

(h) A personal representative acting in another state or a person required to pay the tax domiciled in another state may institute an action in the courts of this state and may recover a proportionate amount of the federal estate tax, of an estate tax payable to another state or of a death duty due by a decedent's estate to another state, from a person interested in the estate who is either domiciled in this state or who owns property in this state subject to attachment or execution. For the purposes of the action the determination of apportionment by the Court having jurisdiction of the administration of the decedent's estate in the other state is prima facie correct.

Part 10
Closing Estates

Section 3–1001. [Formal Proceedings Terminating Administration; Testate or Intestate; Order of General Protection.]

(a) A personal representative or any interested person may petition for an order of complete settlement of the estate. The personal representative may petition at any time, and any other interested person may petition after one year from the appointment of the original personal representative except that no petition under this section may be entertained until the time for presenting claims which arose prior to the death of the decedent has expired. The petition may request the Court to determine testacy, if not previously determined, to consider the final account or compel or approve an accounting and distribution, to construe any will or determine heirs and adjudicate the final settlement and distribution of the estate. After notice to all interested persons and hearing the Court may enter an order or orders, on appropriate conditions, determining the persons entitled to distribution of the estate, and, as circumstances require, approving settlement and directing or approving distribution of the estate and discharging the personal representative from further claim or demand of any interested person.

(b) If one or more heirs or devisees were omitted as parties in, or were not given notice of, a previous formal testacy proceeding, the Court, on proper petition for an order of complete settlement of the estate under this section, and after notice to the omitted or unnotified persons and other interested parties determined to be interested on the assumption that the previous order concerning testacy is conclusive as to those given notice of the earlier proceeding, may determine testacy as it affects the omitted persons and confirm or alter the previous order of testacy as it affects all interested persons as appropriate in the light of the new proofs. In the absence of objection by an omitted or unnotified person, evidence received in the original testacy proceeding shall constitute prima facie proof of due execution of any will previously admitted to probate, or of the fact that the decedent left no valid will if the prior proceedings determined this fact.

Section 3–1002. [Formal Proceedings Terminating Testate Administration; Order Construing Will Without Adjudicating Testacy.]

A personal representative administering an estate under an informally probated will or any devisee under an informally probated will may petition for an order of settlement of the estate which will not adjudicate the testacy status of the decedent. The personal representative may petition at any time, and a devisee may petition after one year, from the appointment of the original personal representative, except that no petition under this section may be entertained until the time for presenting claims which arose prior to the death of the decedent has expired. The petition may request the Court to consider the final account or compel or approve an accounting and distribution, to construe the will and adjudicate final settlement and distribution of the estate. After notice to all devisees and the personal representative and hearing, the Court may enter an order or orders, on appropriate conditions, determining the persons entitled to distribution of the estate under the will, and, as circumstances require, approving settlement and directing or approving distribution of the estate and discharging the personal representative from further claim or demand of any devisee who is a party to the proceeding and those he represents. If it appears that a part of the estate is intestate, the proceedings shall be dismissed or amendments made to meet the provisions of Section 3–1001.

Section 3–1003. [Closing Estates; By Sworn Statement of Personal Representative.]

(a) Unless prohibited by order of the Court and except for estates being administered in supervised administration proceedings, a personal representative may close an estate by filing with the court no earlier than 6 months after the date of original appointment of a general personal representative for the estate, a verified statement stating that he, or a prior personal representative whom he has succeeded, has or have:

> (1) published notice to creditors as provided by Section 3–801 and that the first publication occurred more than 6 months prior to the date of the statement.

> (2) fully administered the estate of the decedent by making payment, settlement or other disposition of all claims which were presented, expenses of administration and estate, inheritance and other death taxes, except as specified in the statement, and that the assets of the estate have been distributed to the persons entitled. If any claims remain undischarged, the statement shall state whether the personal representative has distributed the estate subject to possible liability with the agreement of the distributees or it shall state in detail other arrangements which have been made to accommodate outstanding liabilities; and

> (3) sent a copy thereof to all distributees of the estate and to all creditors or other claimants of whom he is aware whose claims are neither paid nor barred and has furnished a full account in writing of his administration to the distributees whose interests are affected thereby.

(b) If no proceedings involving the personal representative are pending in the Court one year after the closing statement is filed, the appointment of the personal representative terminates.

Section 3–1004. [Liability of Distributees to Claimants.]

After assets of an estate have been distributed and subject to Section 3–1006, an undischarged claim not barred may be prosecuted in a proceeding against one or more distributees. No distributee shall be liable to claimants for amounts received as exempt property, homestead or family allowances, or for amounts in excess of the value of his distribution as of the time of distribution. As between distributees, each shall bear the cost of satisfaction of unbarred claims as if the claim had been satisfied in the course of administration. Any distributee who shall have failed to notify other distributees of the demand made upon him by the claimant in sufficient time to permit them to join in any proceeding in which the claim was asserted against him loses his right of contribution against other distributees.

Section 3–1005. [Limitations on Proceedings Against Personal Representative.]

Unless previously barred by adjudication and except as provided in the closing statement, the rights of successors and of creditors whose claims have not otherwise been barred against the personal representative for breach of fiduciary duty are barred unless a proceeding to assert the same is commenced within 6 months after the filing of the closing statement. The rights thus barred do not include rights to recover from a personal representative for fraud, misrepresentation, or inadequate disclosure related to the settlement of the decedent's estate.

Section 3–1006. [Limitations on Actions and Proceedings Against Distributees.]

Unless previously adjudicated in a formal testacy proceeding or in a proceeding settling the accounts of a personal representative or otherwise barred, the claim of any claimant to recover from a distributee who is liable to pay the claim, and the right of any heir or devisee, or of a successor personal representative acting in their behalf, to recover property improperly distributed or the value thereof from any distributee is forever barred at the later of (1) three years after the decedent's death; or (2) one year after the time of distribution thereof. This section does not bar an action to recover property or value received as the result of fraud.

Section 3–1007. [Certificate Discharging Liens Securing Fiduciary Performance.]

After his appointment has terminated, the personal representative, his sureties, or any successor of either, upon the filing of a verified application showing, so far as is known by the applicant, that no action concerning the estate is pending in any court, is entitled to receive a certificate from the Registrar that the personal representative appears to have fully administered the estate in question. The certificate evidences discharge of any lien on any property given to secure the obligation of the personal representative in lieu of bond or any surety, but does not preclude action against the personal representative or the surety.

Section 3–1008. [Subsequent Administration.]

If other property of the estate is discovered after an estate has been settled and the personal representative discharged or after one year after a closing statement has been filed, the Court upon petition of any interested person and upon notice as it directs may appoint the same or a successor personal representative to administer the subsequently discovered estate. If a new appointment is made, unless the Court orders otherwise, the provisions of this Code apply as appropriate; but no claim previously barred may be asserted in the subsequent administration.

Part 11
Compromise of Controversies

Section 3–1101. [Effect of Approval of Agreements Involving Trusts, Inalienable Interests, or Interests of Third Persons.]

A compromise of any controversy as to admission to probate of any instrument offered for formal probate as the will of a decedent, the construction, validity, or effect of any probated will, the rights or interests in the estate of the decedent, of any successor, or the administration of the estate, if approved in a formal proceeding in the Court for that purpose, is binding on all the parties thereto including those unborn, unascertained or who could not be located. An approved compromise is binding even though it may affect a trust or an inalienable interest. A compromise does not impair the rights of creditors or of taxing authorities who are not parties to it.

Section 3–1102. [Procedure for Securing Court Approval of Compromise.]

The procedure for securing court approval of a compromise is as follows:

(1) The terms of the compromise shall be set forth in an agreement in writing which shall be executed by all competent persons and parents acting for any minor child having beneficial interests or having claims which will or may be affected by the compromise. Execution is not required by any person whose identity cannot be ascertained or whose whereabouts is unknown and cannot reasonably be ascertained.

(2) Any interested person, including the personal representative or a trustee, then may submit the agreement to the Court for its approval and for execution by the personal representative, the

trustee of every affected testamentary trust, and other fiduciaries and representatives.

(3) After notice to all interested persons or their representatives, including the personal representative of the estate and all affected trustees of trusts, the Court, if it finds that the contest or controversy is in good faith and that the effect of the agreement upon the interests of persons represented by fiduciaries or other representatives is just and reasonable, shall make an order approving the agreement and directing all fiduciaries subject to its jurisdiction to execute the agreement. Minor children represented only by their parents may be bound only if their parents join with other competent persons in execution of the compromise. Upon the making of the order and the execution of the agreement, all further disposition of the estate is in accordance with the terms of the agreement.

Part 12
Collection of Personal Property by Affidavit and Summary Administration Procedure for Small Estates

Section 3–1201.   [Collection of Personal Property by Affidavit.]

(a) Thirty days after the death of a decedent, any person indebted to the decedent or having possession of tangible personal property or an instrument evidencing a debt, obligation, stock or chose in action belonging to the decedent shall make payment of the indebtedness or deliver the tangible personal property or an instrument evidencing a debt, obligation, stock or chose in action to a person claiming to be the successor of the decedent upon being presented an affidavit made by or on behalf of the successor stating that:

(1) the value of the entire estate, wherever located, less liens and encumbrances, does not exceed $5,000;

(2) 30 days have elapsed since the death of the decedent;

(3) no application or petition for the appointment of a personal representative is pending or has been granted in any jurisdiction; and

(4) the claiming successor is entitled to payment or delivery of the property.

(b) A transfer agent of any security shall change the registered ownership on the books of a corporation from the decedent to the successor or successors upon the presentation of an affidavit as provided in subsection (a).

Section 3–1202. [Effect of Affidavit.]

The person paying, delivering, transferring, or issuing personal property or the evidence thereof pursuant to affidavit is discharged and released to the same extent as if he dealt with a personal representative of the decedent. He is not required to see to the application of the personal property or evidence thereof or to inquire into the truth of any statement in the affidavit. If any person to whom an affidavit is delivered refuses to pay, deliver, transfer, or issue any personal property or evidence thereof, it may be recovered or its payment, delivery, transfer, or issuance compelled upon proof of their right in a proceeding brought for the purpose by or on behalf of the persons entitled thereto. Any person to whom payment, delivery, transfer or issuance is made is answerable and accountable therefor to any personal representative of the estate or to any other person having a superior right.

Section 3–1203. [Small Estates; Summary Administrative Procedure.]

If it appears from the inventory and appraisal that the value of the entire estate, less liens and encumbrances, does not exceed homestead allowance, exempt property, family allowance, costs and expenses of administration, reasonable funeral expenses, and reasonable and necessary medical and hospital expenses of the last illness of the decedent, the personal representative, without giving notice to creditors, may immediately disburse and distribute the estate to the persons entitled thereto and file a closing statement as provided in Section 3–1204.

Section 3–1204. [Small Estates; Closing by Sworn Statement of Personal Representative.]

(a) Unless prohibited by order of the Court and except for estates being administered by supervised personal representatives, a personal representative may close an estate administered under the summary procedures of Section 3–1203 by filing with the Court, at any time after disbursement and distribution of the estate, a verified statement stating that:

(1) to the best knowledge of the personal representative, the value of the entire estate, less liens and encumbrances, did not exceed homestead allowance, exempt property, family allowance, costs and expenses of administration, reasonable funeral expenses, and reasonable, necessary medical and hospital expenses of the last illness of the decedent;

(2) the personal representative has fully administered the estate by disbursing and distributing it to the persons entitled thereto; and

(3) the personal representative has sent a copy of the closing statement to all distributees of the estate and to all creditors or other claimants of whom he is aware whose claims are neither paid

nor barred and has furnished a full account in writing of his administration to the distributees whose interests are affected.

(b) If no actions or proceedings involving the personal representative are pending in the Court one year after the closing statement is filed, the appointment of the personal representative terminates.

(c) A closing statement filed under this section has the same effect as one filed under Section 3–1003.

Article IV
Foreign Personal Representatives;
Ancillary Administration

Part 1
Definitions

Part 2
Powers of Foreign Personal Representatives

Part 3
Jurisdiction Over Foreign Representatives

Part 4
Judgments and Personal Representative

4–401. [Effect of Adjudication for or Against Personal Representative.]

Part 1
Definitions

Section 4–101. [Definitions.]

In this Article

(1) "local administration" means administration by a personal representative appointed in this state pursuant to appointment proceedings described in Article III.

(2) "local personal representative" includes any personal representative appointed in this state pursuant to appointment proceedings described in Article III and excludes foreign personal representatives who acquire the power of a local personal representative pursuant to Section 4–205.

(3) "resident creditor" means a person domiciled in, or doing business in this state, who is, or could be, a claimant against an estate of a non-resident decedent.

Part 2
Powers of Foreign Personal Representatives

Section 4–201. [Payment of Debt and Delivery of Property to Domiciliary Foreign Personal Representative Without Local Administration.]

At any time after the expiration of sixty days from the death of a nonresident decedent, any person indebted to the estate of the nonresident decedent or having possession or control of personal property, or of an instrument evidencing a debt, obligation, stock or chose in action belonging to the estate of the nonresident decedent may pay the debt, deliver the personal property, or the instrument evidencing the debt, obligation, stock or chose in action, to the domiciliary foreign personal representative of the nonresident decedent upon being presented with proof of his appointment and an affidavit made by or on behalf of the representative stating:

(1) the date of the death of the nonresident decedent,

(2) that no local administration, or application or petition therefor, is pending in this state,

(3) that the domiciliary foreign personal representative is entitled to payment or delivery.

Section 4–202. [Payment or Delivery Discharges.]

Payment or delivery made in good faith on the basis of the proof of authority and affidavit releases the debtor or person having possession of the personal property to the same extent as if payment or delivery had been made to a local personal representative.

Section 4–203. [Resident Creditor Notice.]

Payment or delivery under Section 4–201 may not be made if a resident creditor of the nonresident decedent has notified the debtor of the nonresident decedent or the person having possession of the personal property belonging to the nonresident decedent that the debt should not be paid nor the property delivered to the domiciliary foreign personal representative.

Section 4–204. [Proof of Authority-Bond.]

If no local administration or application or petition therefor is pending in this state, a domiciliary foreign personal representative may file with a Court in this State in a [county] in which property belonging to the decedent is located, authenticated copies of his appointment and of any official bond he has given.

Section 4–205. [Powers.]

A domiciliary foreign personal representative who has complied with Section 4–204 may exercise as to assets in this state all powers of a local personal representative and may maintain actions and proceedings in this state subject to any conditions imposed upon nonresident parties generally.

Section 4–206. [Power of Representatives in Transition.]

The power of a domiciliary foreign personal representative under Section 4–201 or 4–205 shall be exercised only if there is no administration or application therefor pending in this state. An application or petition for local administration of the estate terminates the power of the foreign personal representative to act under Section 4–205, but the local Court may allow the foreign personal representative to exercise limited powers to preserve the estate. No person who, before receiving actual notice of a pending local administration, has changed his position in reliance upon the powers of a foreign personal representative shall be prejudiced by reason of the application or petition for, or grant of, local administration. The local personal representative is subject to all duties and obligations which have accrued by virture of the exercise of the powers by the foreign personal representative and may be substituted for him in any action or proceedings in this state.

Section 4–207. [Ancillary and Other Local Administrations; Provisions Governing.]

In respect to a non-resident decedent, the provisions of Article III of this Code govern (1) proceedings, if any, in a Court of this state for probate of the will, appointment, removal, supervision, and discharge of the local personal representative, and any other order concerning the estate; and (2) the status, powers, duties and liabilities of any local personal representative and the rights of claimants, purchasers, distributees and others in regard to a local administration.

Part 3
Jurisdiction Over Foreign Representatives

Section 4–301. [Jurisdiction by Act of Foreign Personal Representative.]

A foreign personal representative submits personally to the jurisdiction of the Courts of this state in any proceeding relating to the estate by (1) filing authenticated copies of his appointment as provided in Section 4–204, (2) receiving payment of money or taking delivery of personal property under Section 4–201, or (3) doing any act as a personal representative in this state which would have given the state jurisdiction over him as an individual. Jurisdiction under (2) is limited to the money or value of personal property collected.

Section 4–302. [Jurisdiction by Act of Decedent.]

In addition to jurisdiction conferred by Section 4–301, a foreign personal representative is subject to the jurisdiction of the courts of this state to the same extent that his decedent was subject to jurisdiction immediately prior to death.

Section 4–303. [Service on Foreign Personal Representative.]

(a) Service of process may be made upon the foreign personal representative by registered or certified mail, addressed to his last reasonably ascertainable address, requesting a return receipt signed by addressee only. Notice by ordinary first class mail is sufficient if registered or certified mail service to the addressee is unavailable. Service may be made upon a foreign personal representative in the manner in which service could have been made under other laws of this state on either the foreign personal representative or his decedent immediately prior to death.

(b) If service is made upon a foreign personal representative as provided in subsection (a), he shall be allowed at least [30] days within which to appear or respond.

Part 4
Judgments and Personal Representative

Section 4–401. [Effect of Adjudication for or Against Personal Representative.]

An adjudication rendered in any jurisdiction in favor of or against any personal representative of the estate is as binding on the local personal representative as if he were a party to the adjudication.

Article V
Protection of Persons Under Disability and Their Property

Part 1
General Provisions

Section

Part 2
Guardians of Minors

Part 3
Guardians of Incapacitated Persons

Part 4
Protection of Property of
Persons Under Disability and Minors

Part 5
Powers of Attorney

Part 1
General Provisions

Section 5–101. [Definitions and Use of Terms.]

Unless otherwise apparent from the context, in this Code:

(1) "incapacitated person" means any person who is impaired by reason of mental illness, mental deficiency, physical illness or disability, advanced age, chronic use of drugs, chronic intoxication, or other cause (except minority) to the extent that he lacks sufficient understanding or capacity to make or communicate responsible decisions concerning his person;

(2) a "protective proceeding" is a proceeding under the provisions of Section 5–401 to determine that a person cannot effectively manage or apply his estate to necessary ends, either because he lacks the ability or is otherwise inconvenienced, or because he is a minor, and to secure administration of his estate by a conservator or other appropriate relief;

(3) a "protected person" is a minor or other person for whom a conservator has been appointed or other protective order has been made;

(4) a "ward" is a person for whom a guardian has been appointed. A "minor ward" is a minor for whom a guardian has been appointed solely because of minority.

Section 5–102. [Jurisdiction of Subject Matter; Consolidation of Proceedings.]

(a) The Court has jurisdiction over protective proceedings and guardianship proceedings.

(b) When both guardianship and protective proceedings as to the same person are commenced or pending in the same court, the proceedings may be consolidated.

Section 5–103. [Facility of Payment or Delivery.]

Any person under a duty to pay or deliver money or personal property to a minor may perform this duty, in amounts not exceeding $5,000 per annum, by paying or delivering the money or property to, (1) the minor, if he has attained the age of 18 years or is married; (2) any person having the care and custody of the minor with whom the minor resides; (3) a guardian of the minor; or (4) a financial institution incident to a deposit in a federally insured savings account in the sole name of the minor and giving notice of the deposit to the minor. This section does not apply if the person making payment or delivery has actual knowledge that a conservator has been appointed or proceedings for appointment of a conservator of the estate of the minor are pending. The persons, other than the minor or any financial institution under (4) above, receiving money or property for a minor, are obligated to apply the money to the support and education of the minor, but may not pay themselves except by way of reimbursement for out-of-pocket expenses for goods and services necessary for the minor's support. Any excess sums shall be preserved for future support of the minor and any balance not so used and any property received for the minor must be turned over to the minor when he attains majority. Persons who pay or deliver in accordance with provisions of this section are not responsible for the proper application thereof.

Section 5–104. [Delegation of Powers by Parent or Guardian.]

A parent or a guardian of a minor or incapacitated person, by a properly executed power of attorney, may delegate to another person, for a period not exceeding 6 months, any of his powers regarding care, custody, or property of the minor child or ward, except his power to consent to marriage or adoption of a minor ward.

Part 2
Guardians of Minors

Section 5–201. [Status of Guardian of Minor; General.]

A person becomes a guardian of a minor by acceptance of a testamentary appointment or upon appointment by the Court. The guardianship status continues until terminated, without regard to the location from time to time of the guardian and minor ward.

Section 5–202. [Testamentary Appointment of Guardian of Minor.]

The parent of a minor may appoint by will a guardian of an unmarried minor. Subject to the right of the minor under Section 5–203, a testamentary appointment becomes effective upon filing the guardian's acceptance in the Court in which the will is probated, if before acceptance, both parents are dead or the surviving parent is adjudged incapacitated. If both parents are dead, an effective appointment by the parent who died later has priority. This state recognizes a testamentary appointment effected by filing the guardian's acceptance under a will probated in another state which is the testator's domicile. Upon acceptance of appointment, written notice of acceptance must be given by the guardian to the minor and to the person having his care, or to his nearest adult relation.

Section 5–203. [Objection by Minor of Fourteen or Older to Testamentary Appointment.]

A minor of 14 or more years may prevent an appointment of his testamentary guardian from becoming effective, or may cause a previously accepted appointment to terminate, by filing with the Court in which the will is probated a written objection to the appointment before it is accepted or within 30 days after notice of its acceptance. An objection may be withdrawn. An objection does not preclude appointment by the Court in a proper proceeding of the testamentary nominee, or any other suitable person.

Section 5–204. [Court Appointment of Guardian of Minor; Conditions for Appointment.]

The Court may appoint a guardian for an unmarried minor if all parental rights of custody have been terminated or suspended by circumstances or prior Court order. A guardian appointed by will as provided in Section 5–202 whose appointment has not been prevented or nullified under 5–203 has priority over any guardian who may be appointed by the Court but the Court may proceed with an appointment upon a finding that the testamentary guardian has failed to accept the testamentary appointment within 30 days after notice of the guardianship proceeding.

Section 5–205. [Court Appointment of Guardian of Minor; Venue.]

The venue for guardianship proceedings for a minor is in the place where the minor resides or is present.

Section 5–206. [Court Appointment of Guardian of Minor; Qualifications; Priority of Minor's Nominee.]

The Court may appoint as guardian any person whose appointment would be in the best interests of the minor. The Court shall appoint a person nominated by the minor, if the minor is 14 years of age or older, unless the Court finds the appointment contrary to the best interests of the minor.

Section 5–207. [Court Appointment of Guardian of Minor; Procedure.]

(a) Notice of the time and place of hearing of a petition for the appointment of a guardian of a minor is to be given by the petitioner in the manner prescribed by Section 1–401 to:

(1) the minor, if he is 14 or more years of age;

(2) the person who has had the principal care and custody of the minor during the 60 days preceding the date of the petition; and

(3) any living parent of the minor.

(b) Upon hearing, if the Court finds that a qualified person seeks appointment, venue is proper, the required notices have been given, the requirements of Section 5–204 have been met, and the welfare and best interests of the minor will be served by the requested appointment, it shall make the appointment. In other cases the Court may dismiss the proceedings, or make any other disposition of the matter that will best serve the interest of the minor.

(c) If necessary, the Court may appoint a temporary guardian, with the status of an ordinary guardian of a minor, but the authority of a temporary guardian shall not last longer than six months.

(d) If, at any time in the proceeding, the Court determines that the interests of the minor are or may be inadequately represented, it may appoint an attorney to represent the minor, giving consideration to the preference of the minor if the minor is fourteen years of age or older.

Section 5–208. [Consent to Service by Acceptance of Appointment; Notice.]

By accepting a testamentary or court appointment as guardian, a guardian submits personally to the jurisdiction of the Court in any proceeding relating to the guardianship that may be instituted by any interested person. Notice of any proceeding shall be delivered to the guardian, or mailed to him by ordinary mail at his address as listed in the Court records and to his address as then known to the petitioner. Letters of guardianship must indicate whether the guardian was appointed by will or by court order.

Section 5-209. [Powers and Duties of Guardian of Minor.]

A guardian of a minor has the powers and responsibilities of a parent who has not been deprived of custody of his minor and unemancipated child, except that a guardian is not legally obligated to provide from his own funds for the ward and is not liable to third persons by reason of the parental relationship for acts of the ward. In particular, and without qualifying the foregoing, a guardian has the following powers and duties:

(a) he must take reasonable care of his ward's personal effects and commence protective proceedings if necessary to protect other property of the ward.

(b) He may receive money payable for the support of the ward to the ward's parent, guardian or custodian under the terms of any statutory benefit or insurance system, or any private contract, devise, trust, conservatorship or custodianship. He also may receive money or property of the ward paid or delivered by virtue of Section 5-103. Any sums so received shall be applied to the ward's current needs for support, care and education. He must exercise due care to conserve any excess for the ward's future needs unless a conservator has been appointed for the estate of the ward, in which case excess shall be paid over at least annually to the conservator. Sums so received by the guardian are not to be used for compensation for his services except as approved by order of court or as determined by a duly appointed conservator other than the guardian. A guardian may institute proceedings to compel the performance by any person of a duty to support the ward or to pay sums for the welfare of the ward.

(c) The guardian is empowered to facilitate the ward's education, social, or other activities and to authorize medical or other professional care, treatment, or advice. A guardian is not liable by reason of this consent for injury to the ward resulting from the negligence or acts of third persons unless it would have been illegal for a parent to have consented. A guardian may consent to the marriage or adoption of his ward.

(d) A guardian must report the condition of his ward and of the ward's estate which has been subject to his possession or control, as ordered by Court on petition of any person interested in the minor's welfare or as required by Court rule.

Section 5-210. [Termination of Appointment of Guardian; General.]

A guardian's authority and responsibility terminates upon the death, resignation or removal of the guardian or upon the minor's death, adoption, marriage or attainment of majority, but termination does not affect his liability for prior acts, nor his obligation to account for funds and assets of his ward. Resignation of a guardian does not terminate the guardianship until it has been approved by the Court. A testamentary appointment under an informally probated will terminates if the will is later denied probate in a formal proceeding.

Section 5–211. [Proceedings Subsequent to Appointment; Venue.]

(a) The Court where the ward resides has concurrent jurisdiction with the Court which appointed the guardian, or in which acceptance of a testamentary appointment was filed, over resignation, removal, accounting and other proceedings relating to the guardianship.

(b) If the Court located where the ward resides is not the Court in which acceptance of appointment is filed, the Court in which proceedings subsequent to appointment are commenced shall in all appropriate cases notify the other Court, in this or another state, and after consultation with that Court determine whether to retain jurisdiction or transfer the proceedings to the other Court, whichever is in the best interest of the ward. A copy of any order accepting a resignation or removing a guardian shall be sent to the Court in which acceptance of appointment is filed.

Section 5–212. [Resignation or Removal Proceedings.]

(a) Any person interested in the welfare of a ward, or the ward, if 14 or more years of age, may petition for removal of a guardian on the ground that removal would be in the best interest of the ward. A guardian may petition for permission to resign. A petition for removal or for permission to resign may, but need not, include a request for appointment of a successor guardian.

(b) After notice and hearing on a petition for removal or for permission to resign, the Court may terminate the guardianship and make any further order that may be appropriate.

(c) If, at any time in the proceeding, the Court determines that the interests of the ward are, or may be, inadequately represented, it may appoint an attorney to represent the minor, giving consideration to the preference of the minor if the minor is 14 or more years of age.

Part 3
Guardians of Incapacitated Persons

Section 5–301. [Testamentary Appointment of Guardian For Incapacitated Person.]

(a) The parent of an incapacitated person may by will appoint a guardian of the incapacitated person. A testamentary appointment by a parent becomes effective when, after having given 7 days prior written notice of his intention to do so to the incapacitated person and to the person having his care or to his nearest adult relative, the guardian files acceptance of appointment in the court in which the will is informally or formally probated, if prior thereto, both parents are dead or the surviving parent is adjudged incapacitated. If both parents are dead, an effective appointment by the parent who died later has priority unless it is terminated by the denial of probate in formal proceedings.

The spouse of a married incapacitated person may by will appoint a guardian of the incapacitated person. The appointment becomes effective when, after having given 7 days prior written notice of his intention to do so to the incapacitated person and to the person having his care or to his nearest adult relative, the guardian files acceptance of appointment in the Court in which the will is informally or formally probated. An effective appointment by a spouse has priority over an appointment by a parent unless it is terminated by the denial of probate in formal proceedings.

(c) This state shall recognize a testamentary appointment effected by filing acceptance under a will probated at the testator's domicile in another state.

(d) On the filing with the Court in which the will was probated of written objection to the appointment by the person for whom a testamentary appointment of guardian has been made, the appointment is terminated. An objection does not prevent appointment by the Court in a proper proceeding of the testamentary nominee or any other suitable person upon an adjudication of incapacity in proceedings under the succeeding sections of this Part.

Section 5–302. [Venue.]

The venue for guardianship proceedings for an incapacitated person is in the place where the incapacitated person resides or is present. If the incapacitated person is admitted to an institution pursuant to order of a Court of competent jurisdiction, venue is also in the county in which that Court sits.

Section 5–303. [Procedure For Court Appointment of a Guardian of an Incapacitated Person.]

(a) The incapacitated person or any person interested in his welfare may petition for a finding of incapacity and appointment of a guardian.

(b) Upon the filing of a petition, the Court shall set a date for hearing on the issues of incapacity and unless the allegedly incapacitated person has counsel of his own choice, it shall appoint an appropriate official or attorney to represent him in the proceeding, who shall have the powers and duties of a guardian ad litem. The person alleged to be incapacitated shall be examined by a physician appointed by the Court who shall submit his report in writing to the Court and be interviewed by a visitor sent by the Court. The visitor also shall interview the person seeking appointment as guardian, and visit the present place of abode of the person alleged to be incapacitated and the place it is proposed that he will be detained or reside if the requested appointment is made and submit his report in writing to the Court. The person alleged to be incapacitated is entitled to be present at the hearing in person, and to see or hear all evidence bearing upon his condition. He is entitled to be represented by counsel, to present evidence, to cross-examine witnesses, including the Court-appointed physician and the visitor [, and to trial by jury]. The issue may be determined at a closed hearing [without a jury] if the person alleged to be incapacitated or his counsel so requests.

Section 5–304. [Findings; Order of Appointment.]

The Court may appoint a guardian as requested if it is satisfied that the person for whom a guardian is sought is incapacitated and that the appointment is necessary or desirable as a means of providing continuing care and supervision of the person of the incapacitated person. Alternatively, the Court may dismiss the proceeding or enter any other appropriate order.

Section 5–305. [Acceptance of Appointment; Consent to Jurisdiction.]

By accepting appointment, a guardian submits personally to the jurisdiction of the Court in any proceeding relating to the guardianship that may be instituted by any interested person. Notice of any proceeding shall be delivered to the guardian or mailed to him by ordinary mail at his address as listed in the Court records and to his address as then known to the petitioner.

Section 5–306. [Termination of Guardianship for Incapacitated Person.]

The authority and responsibility of a guardian for an incapacitated person terminates upon the death of the guardian or ward, the determination of incapacity of the guardian, or upon removal or resignation as provided in Section 5–307. Testamentary appointment under an informally probated will terminates if the will is later denied probate in a formal proceeding. Termination does not affect his liability for prior acts nor his obligation to account for funds and assets of his ward.

Section 5–307. [Removal or Resignation of Guardian; Termination of Incapacity.]

(a) On petition of the ward or any person interested in his welfare, the Court may remove a guardian and appoint a successor if in the best interests of the ward. On petition of the guardian, the Court may accept his resignation and make any other order which may be appropriate.

(b) An order adjudicating incapacity may specify a minimum period, not exceeding one year, during which no petition for an adjudication that the ward is no longer incapacitated may be filed without special leave. Subject to this restriction, the ward or any person interested in his welfare may petition for an order that he is no longer incapacitated, and for removal or resignation of the guardian. A request for this order may be made by informal letter to the Court or judge and any person who knowingly interferes with transmission of this kind of request to the Court or judge may be adjudged guilty of contempt of Court.

(c) Before removing a guardian, accepting the resignation of a guardian, or ordering that a ward's incapacity has terminated, the Court, following the same procedures to safeguard the rights of the ward as apply to a petition for appointment of a guardian, may send a visitor to the residence of the present guardian and to the place where the ward resides or is detained, to observe conditions and report in writing to the Court.

Section 5-308. [Visitor in Guardianship Proceeding.]

A visitor is, with respect to guardianship proceedings, a person who is trained in law, nursing or social work and is an officer, employee or special appointee of the Court with no personal interest in the proceedings.

Section 5-309. [Notices in Guardianship Proceedings.]

(a) In a proceeding for the appointment or removal of a guardian of an incapacitated person other than the appointment of a temporary guardian or temporary suspension of a guardian, notice of hearing shall be given to each of the following:

(1) the ward or the person alleged to be incapacitated and his spouse, parents and adult children;

(2) any person who is serving as his guardian, conservator or who has his care and custody; and

(3) in case no other person is notified under (1), at least one of his closest adult relatives, if any can be found.

(b) Notice shall be served personally on the alleged incapacitated person, and his spouse and parents if they can be found within the state. Notice to the spouse and parents, if they cannot be found within the state, and to all other persons except the alleged incapacitated person shall be given as provided in Section 1-401. Waiver of notice by the person alleged to be incapacitated is not effective unless he attends the hearing or his waiver of notice is confirmed in an interview with the visitor. Representation of the alleged incapacitated person by a guardian ad litem is not necessary.

Section 5–310.   [Temporary Guardians.]

If an incapacitated person has no guardian and an emergency exists, the Court may exercise the power of a guardian pending notice and hearing.   If an appointed guardian is not effectively performing his duties and the Court further finds that the welfare of the incapacitated person requires immediate action, it may, with or without notice, appoint a temporary guardian for the incapacitated person for a specified period not to exceed 6 months.   A temporary guardian is entitled to the care and custody of the ward and the authority of any permanent guardian previously appointed by the Court is suspended so long as a temporary guardian has authority.   A temporary guardian may be removed at any time.   A temporary guardian shall make any report the Court requires.   In other respects the provisions of this Code concerning guardians apply to temporary guardians.

Section 5–311.   [Who May Be Guardian;   Priorities.]

(a) Any competent person or a suitable institution may be appointed guardian of an incapacitated person.

(b) persons who are not disqualified have priority for appointment as guardian in the following order:

(1) the spouse of the incapacitated person;

(2) an adult child of the incapacitated person;

(3) a parent of the incapacitated person, including a person nominated by will or other writing signed by a deceased parent;

(4) any relative of the incapacitated person with whom he has resided for more than 6 months prior to the filing of the petition;

(5) a person nominated by the person who is caring for him or paying benefits to him.

Section 5–312.   [General Powers and Duties of Guardian.]

(a) A guardian of an incapacitated person has the same powers, rights and duties respecting his ward that a parent has respecting his unemancipated minor child except that a guardian is not liable to third persons for acts of the ward solely by reason of the parental relationship.   In particular, and without qualifying the foregoing, a guardian has the following powers and duties, except as modified by order of the Court:

(1) to the extent that it is consistent with the terms of any order by a court of competent jurisdiction relating to detention or commitment of the ward, he is entitled to custody of the person of his ward and may establish the ward's place of abode within or without this state.

(2) If entitled to custody of his ward he shall make provision for the care, comfort and maintenance of his ward, and whenever appropriate, arrange for his training and education.   Without

regard to custodial rights of the ward's person, he shall take reasonable care of his ward's clothing, furniture, vehicles and other personal effects and commence protective proceedings if other property of his ward is in need of protection.

(3) A guardian may give any consents or approvals that may be necessary to enable the ward to receive medical or other professional care, counsel, treatment or service.

(4) If no conservator for the estate of the ward has been appointed, he may:

(i) institute proceedings to compel any person under a duty to support the ward or to pay sums for the welfare of the ward to perform his duty;

(ii) receive money and tangible property deliverable to the ward and apply the money and property for support, care and education of the ward; but, he may not use funds from his ward's estate for room and board which he, his spouse, parent, or child have furnished the ward unless a charge for the service is approved by order of the Court made upon notice to at least one of the next of kin of the ward, if notice is possible. He must exercise care to conserve any excess for the ward's needs.

(5) A guardian is required to report the condition of his ward and of the estate which has been subject to his possession or control, as required by the Court or court rule.

(6) If a conservator has been appointed, all of the ward's estate received by the guardian in excess of those funds expended to meet current expenses for support, care, and education of the ward must be paid to the conservator for management as provided in this Code, and the guardian must account to the conservator for funds expended.

(b) Any guardian of one for whom a conservator also has been appointed shall control the custody and care of the ward, and is entitled to receive reasonable sums for his services and for room and board furnished to the ward as agreed upon between him and the conservator, provided the amounts agreed upon are reasonable under the circumstances. The guardian may request the conservator to expend the ward's estate by payment to third persons or institutions for the ward's care and maintenance.

Section 5–313. [Proceedings Subsequent to Appointment; Venue.]

(a) The Court where the ward resides has concurrent jurisdiction with the Court which appointed the guardian, or in which acceptance of a testamentary appointment was filed, over resignation, removal, accounting and other proceedings relating to the guardianship.

(b) If the Court located where the ward resides is not the Court in which acceptance of appointment is filed, the Court in which proceedings subsequent to appointment are commenced shall in all appropriate cases notify the other Court, in this or another state, and after consultation with that Court determine whether to retain jurisdiction or transfer the proceedings to the other Court, whichever may be in the best interest of the ward. A copy of any order accepting a resignation or removing a guardian shall be sent to the Court in which acceptance of appointment is filed.

Part 4
Protection of Property of
Persons Under Disability and Minors

Section 5–401. [Protective Proceedings.]

Upon petition and after notice and hearing in accordance with the provisions of this Part, the Court may appoint a conservator or make other protective order for cause as follows:

(1) Appointment of a conservator or other protective order may be made in relation to the estate and affairs of a minor if the Court determines that a minor owns money or property that requires management or protection which cannot otherwise be provided, has or may have business affairs which may be jeopardized or prevented by his minority, or that funds are needed for his support and education and that protection is necessary or desirable to obtain or provide funds.

(2) Appointment of a conservator or other protective order may be made in relation to the estate and affairs of a person if the court determines that (i) the person is unable to manage his property and affairs effectively for reasons such as mental illness, mental deficiency, physical illness or disability, advanced age, chronic use of drugs, chronic intoxication, confinement, detention by a foreign power, or disappearance; and (ii) the person has property which will be wasted or dissipated unless proper management is provided, or that funds are needed for the support, care and welfare of the person or those entitled to be supported by him and that protection is necessary or desirable to obtain or provide funds.

Section 5–402. [Protective Proceedings; Jurisdiction of Affairs of Protected Persons.]

After the service of notice in a proceeding seeking the appointment of a conservator or other protective order and until termination of the proceeding, the Court in which the petition is filed has:

(1) exclusive jurisdiction to determine the need for a conservator or other protective order until the proceedings are terminated;

(2) exclusive jurisdiction to determine how the estate of the protected person which is subject to the laws of this state shall be managed, expended or distributed to or for the use of the protected person or any of his dependents;

(3) concurrent jurisdiction to determine the validity of claims against the person or estate of the protected person and his title to any property or claim.

Section 5–403. [Venue.]

Venue for proceedings under this Part is:

(1) In the place in this state where the person to be protected resides whether or not a guardian has been appointed in another place; or

(2) If the person to be protected does not reside in this state, in any place where he has property.

Section 5–404. [Original Petition for Appointment or Protective Order.]

(a) The person to be protected, any person who is interested in his estate, affairs or welfare including his parent, guardian, or custodian, or any person who would be adversely affected by lack of effective management of his property and affairs may petition for the appointment of a conservator or for other appropriate protective order.

(b) The petition shall set forth to the extent known, the interest of the petitioner; the name, age, residence and address of the person to be protected; the name and address of his guardian, if any; the name and address of his nearest relative known to the petitioner; a general statement of his property with an estimate of the value thereof, including any compensation, insurance, pension or allowance to which he is entitled; and the reason why appointment of a conservator or other protective order is necessary. If the appointment of a conservator is requested, the petition also shall set forth the name and address of the person whose appointment is sought and the basis of his priority for appointment.

Section 5–405. [Notice.]

(a) On a petition for appointment of a conservator or other protective order, the person to be protected and his spouse or, if none, his parents, must be served personally with notice of the proceeding at least 14 days before the date of hearing if they can be found within the state, or, if they cannot be found within the state, they must be given notice in accordance with Section 1–401. Waiver by the person to be protected is not effective unless he attends the hearing or, unless minority is the reason for the proceeding, waiver is confirmed in an interview with the visitor.

(b) Notice of a petition for appointment of a conservator or other initial protective order, and of any subsequent hearing, must be given to any person who has filed a request for notice under Section 5–406 and to interested persons and other persons as the Court may direct. Except as otherwise provided in (a), notice shall be given in accordance with Section 1–401.

Section 5–406. [Protective Proceedings; Request for Notice; Interested Person.]

Any interested person who desires to be notified before any order is made in a protective proceeding may file with the Registrar a request for notice subsequent to payment of any fee required by statute or Court rule. The clerk shall mail a copy of the demand to the conservator if one has been appointed. A request is not effective unless it contains a statement showing the interest of the person making it and his address, or that of his attorney, and is effective only as to matters occurring after the filing. Any governmental agency paying or planning to pay benefits to the person to be protected is an interested person in protective proceedings.

Section 5–407. [Procedure Concerning Hearing and Order on Original Petition.]

(a) Upon receipt of a petition for appointment of a conservator or other protective order because of minority, the Court shall set a date for hearing on the matters alleged in the petition. If, at any time in the proceeding, the Court determines that the interests of the minor are or may be inadequately represented, it may appoint an attorney to represent the minor, giving consideration to the choice of the minor if fourteen years of age or older. A lawyer appointed by the Court to represent a minor has the powers and duties of a guardian ad litem.

(b) Upon receipt of a petition for appointment of a conservator or other protective order for reasons other than minority, the Court shall set a date for hearing. Unless the person to be protected has counsel of his own choice, the Court must appoint a lawyer to represent him who then has the powers and duties of a guardian ad litem. If the alleged disability is mental illness, mental deficiency, physical illness or disability, advanced age, chronic use of drugs, or chronic intoxication, the Court may direct that the person to be protected be examined by a physician designated by the Court, preferably a physician who is not connected with any institution in which the person is a patient or is detained. The Court may send a visitor to interview the person to be protected. The visitor may be a guardian ad litem or an officer or employee of the Court.

(c) After hearing, upon finding that a basis for the appointment of a conservator or other protective order has been established, the Court shall make an appointment or other appropriate protective order.

Section 5–408.   [Permissible Court Orders.]

The Court has the following powers which may be exercised directly or through a conservator in respect to the estate and affairs of protected persons;

(1) While a petition for appointment of a conservator or other protective order is pending and after preliminary hearing and without notice to others, the Court has power to preserve and apply the property of the person to be protected as may be required for his benefit or the benefit of his dependents.

(2) After hearing and upon determining that a basis for an appointment or other protective order exists with respect to a minor without other disability, the Court has all those powers over the estate and affairs of the minor which are or might be necessary for the best interests of the minor, his family and members of his household.

(3) After hearing and upon determining that a basis for an appointment or other protective order exists with respect to a person for reasons other than minority, the Court has, for the benefit of the person and members of his household, all the powers over his estate and affairs which he could exercise if present and not under disability, except the power to make a will.   These powers include, but are not limited to power to make gifts, to convey or release his contingent and expectant interests in property including marital property rights and any right of survivorship incident to joint tenancy or tenancy by the entirety, to exercise or release his powers as trustee, personal representative, custodian for minors, conservator, or donee of a power of appointment, to enter into contracts, to create revocable or irrevocable trusts of property of the estate which may extend beyond his disability or life, to exercise options of the disabled person to purchase securities or other property, to exercise his rights to elect options and change beneficiaries under insurance and annuity policies and to surrender the policies for their cash value, to exercise his right to an elective share in the estate of his deceased spouse and to renounce any interest by testate or intestate succession or by inter vivos transfer.

(4) The Court may exercise or direct the exercise of, its authority to exercise or release powers of appointment of which the protected person is donee, to renounce interests, to make gifts in trust or otherwise exceeding 20 percent of any year's income of the estate or to change beneficiaries under insurance and annuity policies, only if satisfied, after notice and hearing, that it is in the best interests of the protected person, and that he either is incapable of consenting or has consented to the proposed exercise of power.

(5) An order made pursuant to this section determining that a basis for appointment of a conservator or other protective order exists, has no effect on the capacity of the protected person.

Section 5–409. [Protective Arrangements and Single Transactions Authorized.]

(a) If it is established in a proper proceeding that a basis exists as described in Section 5–401 for affecting the property and affairs of a person the Court, without appointing a conservator, may authorize, direct or ratify any transaction necessary or desirable to achieve any security, service, or care arrangement meeting the foreseeable needs of the protected person. Protective arrangements include, but are not limited to, payment, delivery, deposit or retention of funds or property, sale mortgage, lease or other transfer of property, entry into an annuity contract, a contract for life care, a deposit contract, a contract for training and education, or addition to or establishment of a suitable trust.

(b) When it has been established in a proper proceeding that a basis exists as described in Section 5–401 for affecting the property and affairs of a person the Court, without appointing a conservator, may authorize, direct or ratify any contract, trust or other transaction relating to the protected person's financial affairs or involving his estate if the Court determines that the transaction is in the best interests of the protected person.

(c) Before approving a protective arrangement or other transaction under this section, the Court shall consider the interests of creditors and dependents of the protected person and, in view of his disability, whether the protected person needs the continuing protection of a conservator. The Court may appoint a special conservator to assist in the accomplishment of any protective arrangement or other transaction authorized under this section who shall have the authority conferred by the order and serve until discharged by order after report to the Court of all matters done pursuant to the order of appointment.

Section 5–410. [Who May Be Appointed Conservator; Priorities.]

(a) The Court may appoint an individual, or a corporation with general power to serve as trustee, as conservator of the estate of a protected person. The following are entitled to consideration for appointment in the order listed:

> (1) a conservator, guardian of property or other like fiduciary appointed or recognized by the appropriate court of any other jurisdiction in which the protected person resides;

> (2) an individual or corporation nominated by the protected person if he is 14 or more years of age and has, in the opinion of the Court, sufficient mental capacity to make an intelligent choice;

> (3) the spouse of the protected person;

> (4) an adult child of the protected person;

> (5) a parent of the protected person, or a person nominated by the will of a deceased parent;

(6) any relative of the protected person with whom he has resided for more than 6 months prior to the filing of the petition;

(7) a person nominated by the person who is caring for him or paying benefits to him.

(b) A person in priorities (1), (3), (4), (5), or (6) may nominate in writing a person to serve in his stead. With respect to persons having equal priority, the Court is to select the one who is best qualified of those willing to serve. The Court, for good cause, may pass over a person having priority and appoint a person having less priority or no priority.

Section 5–411. [Bond.]

The Court may require a conservator to furnish a bond conditioned upon faithful discharge of all duties of the trust according to law, with sureties as it shall specify. Unless otherwise directed, the bond shall be in the amount of the aggregate capital value of the property of the estate in his control plus one year's estimated income minus the value of securities deposited under arrangements requiring an order of the Court for their removal and the value of any land which the fiduciary, by express limitation of power, lacks power to sell or convey without Court authorization. The Court in lieu of sureties on a bond, may accept other security for the performance of the bond, including a pledge of securities or a mortgage of land.

Section 5–412. [Terms and Requirements of Bonds.]

(a) The following requirements and provisions apply to any bond required under Section 5–411:

(1) Unless otherwise provided by the terms of the approved bond, sureties are jointly and severally liable with the conservator and with each other;

(2) By executing an approved bond of a conservator, the surety consents to the jurisdiction of the Court which issued letters to the primary obligor in any proceeding pertaining to the fiduciary duties of the conservator and naming the surety as a party defendant. Notice of any proceeding shall be delivered to the surety or mailed to him by registered or certified mail at his address as listed with the court where the bond is filed and to his address as then known to the petitioner;

(3) On petition of a successor conservator or any interested person, a proceeding may be initiated against a surety for breach of the obligation of the bond of the conservator;

(4) The bond of the conservator is not void after the first recovery but may be proceeded against from time to time until the whole penalty is exhausted.

(b) No proceeding may be commenced against the surety on any matter as to which an action or proceeding against the primary obligor is barred by adjudication or limitation.

Section 5–413. [Acceptance of Appointment; Consent to Jurisdiction.]

By accepting appointment, a conservator submits personally to the jurisdiction of the Court in any proceeding relating to the estate that may be instituted by any interested person. Notice of any proceeding shall be delivered to the conservator, or mailed to him by registered or certified mail at his address as listed in the petition for appointment or as thereafter reported to the Court and to his address as then known to the petitioner.

Section 5–414. [Compensation and Expenses.]

If not otherwise compensated for services rendered, any visitor, lawyer, physician, conservator or special conservator appointed in a protective proceeding is entitled to reasonable compensation from the estate.

Section 5–415. [Death, Resignation or Removal of Conservator.]

The Court may remove a conservator for good cause, upon notice and hearing, or accept the resignation of a conservator. After his death, resignation or removal, the Court may appoint another conservator. A conservator so appointed succeeds to the title and powers of his predecessor.

Section 5–416. [Petitions for Orders Subsequent to Appointment.]

(a) Any person interested in the welfare of a person for whom a conservator has been appointed may file a petition in the appointing court for an order (1) requiring bond or security or additional bond or security, or reducing bond, (2) requiring an accounting for the administration of the trust, (3) directing distribution, (4) removing the conservator and appointing a temporary or successor conservator, or (5) granting other appropriate relief.

(b) A conservator may petition the appointing court for instructions concerning his fiduciary responsibility.

(c) Upon notice and hearing, the Court may give appropriate instructions or make any appropriate order.

Section 5–417. [General Duty of Conservator.]

In the exercise of his powers, a conservator is to act as a fiduciary and shall observe the standards of care applicable to trustees as described by Section 7–302.

Section 5–418. [Inventory and Records.]

Within 90 days after his appointment, every conservator shall prepare and file with the appointing Court a complete inventory of the estate of the protected person together with his oath or affirmation that it is complete and accurate so far as he is informed. The conservator shall provide a copy thereof to the protected person if he can be located, has attained the age of 14 years, and has sufficient mental capacity to understand these matters, and to any parent or guardian with whom the protected person resides. The conservator shall keep suitable records of his administration and exhibit the same on request of any interested person.

Section 5–419. [Accounts.]

Every conservator must account to the Court for his administration of the trust upon his resignation or removal, and at other times as the Court may direct. On termination of the protected person's minority or disability, a conservator may account to the Court, or he may account to the former protected person or his personal representative. Subject to appeal or vacation within the time permitted, an order, made upon notice and hearing, allowing an intermediate account of a conservator, adjudicates as to his liabilities concerning the matters considered in connection therewith; and an order, made upon notice and hearing, allowing a final account adjudicates as to all previously unsettled liabilities of the conservator to the protected person or his successors relating to the conservatorship. In connection with any account, the Court may require a conservator to submit to a physical check of the estate in his control, to be made in any manner the Court may specify.

Section 5–420. [Conservators; Title by Appointment.]

The appointment of a conservator vests in him title as trustee to all property of the protected person, presently held or thereafter acquired, including title to any property theretofore held for the protected person by custodians or attorneys in fact. The appointment of a conservator is not a transfer or alienation within the meaning of general provisions of any federal or state statute or regulation, insurance policy, pension plan, contract, will or trust instrument, imposing restrictions upon or penalties for transfer or alienation by the protected person of his rights or interest, but this section does not restrict the ability of persons to make specific provision by contract or dispositive instrument relating to a conservator.

Section 5–421. [Recording of Conservator's Letters.]

Letters of conservatorship are evidence of transfer of all assets of a protected person to the conservator. An order terminating a conservatorship is evidence of transfer of all assets of the estate from the conservator to the protected person, or his successors. Subject to the requirements of general statutes governing the filing or recordation of documents of title to land or other property, letters of conservatorship, and orders terminating conservatorships, may be filed or recorded to give record notice of title as between the conservator and the protected person.

Section 5–422. [Sale, Encumbrance or Transaction Involving Conflict of Interest; Voidable; Exceptions.]

Any sale or encumbrance to a conservator, his spouse, agent or attorney, or any corporation or trust in which he has a substantial beneficial interest, or any transaction which is affected by a substantial conflict of interest is voidable unless the transaction is approved by the Court after notice to interested persons and others as directed by the Court.

Section 5–423. [Persons Dealing with Conservators; Protection.]

A person who in good faith either assists a conservator or deals with him for value in any transaction other than those requiring a Court order as provided in Section 5–408, is protected as if the conservator properly exercised the power. The fact that a person knowingly deals with a conservator does not alone require the person to inquire into the existence of a power or the propriety of its exercise, except that restrictions on powers of conservators which are endorsed on letters as provided in Section 5–426 are effective as to third persons. A person is not bound to see to the proper application of estate assets paid or delivered to a conservator. The protection here expressed extends to instances in which some procedural irregularity or jurisdictional defect occurred in proceedings leading to the issuance of letters. The protection here expressed is not by substitution for that provided by comparable provisions of the laws relating to commercial transactions and laws simplifying transfers of securities by fiduciaries.

Section 5–424. [Powers of Conservator in Administration.]

(a) A conservator has all of the powers conferred herein and any additional powers conferred by law on trustees in this state. In addition, a conservator of the estate of an unmarried minor under the age of 18 years, as to whom no one has parental rights, has the duties and powers of a guardian of a minor described in Section 5–209 until the minor attains the age of 18 or marries, but the parental rights so conferred on a conservator do not preclude appointment of a guardian as provided by Part 2.

(b) A conservator has power without Court authorization or confirmation, to invest and reinvest funds of the estate as would a trustee.

(c) A conservator, acting reasonably in efforts to accomplish the purpose for which he was appointed, may act without Court authorization or confirmation, to

(1) collect, hold and retain assets of the estate including land in another state, until, in his judgment, disposition of the assets

should be made, and the assets may be retained even though they include an asset in which he is personally interested;

(2) receive additions to the estate;

(3) continue or participate in the operation of any business or other enterprise;

(4) acquire an undivided interest in an estate asset in which the conservator, in any fiduciary capacity, holds an undivided interest;

(5) invest and reinvest estate assets in accordance with subsection (b);

(6) deposit estate funds in a bank including a bank operated by the conservator;

(7) acquire or dispose of an estate asset including land in another state for cash or on credit, at public or private sale; and to manage, develop, improve, exchange, partition, change the character of, or abandon an estate asset;

(8) make ordinary or extraordinary repairs or alterations in buildings or other structures, to demolish any improvements, to raze existing or erect new party walls or buildings;

(9) subdivide, develop, or dedicate land to public use; to make or obtain the vacation of plats and adjust boundaries; to adjust differences in valuation on exchange or to partition by giving or receiving considerations; and to dedicate easements to public use without consideration;

(10) enter for any purpose into a lease as lessor or lessee with or without option to purchase or renew for a term within or extending beyond the term of the conservatorship;

(11) enter into a lease or arrangement for exploration and removal of minerals or other natural resources or enter into a pooling or unitization agreement;

(12) grant an option involving disposition of an estate asset, to take an option for the acquisition of any asset;

(13) vote a security, in person or by general or limited proxy;

(14) pay calls, assessments, and any other sums chargeable or accruing against or on account of securities;

(15) sell or exercise stock subscription or conversion rights; to consent, directly or through a committee or other agent, to the reorganization, consolidation, merger, dissolution, or liquidation of a corporation or other business enterprise;

(16) hold a security in the name of a nominee or in other form without disclosure of the conservatorship so that title to the security may pass by delivery, but the conservator is liable for any act of the nominee in connection with the stock so held;

(17) insure the assets of the estate against damage or loss, and the conservator against liability with respect to third persons;

(18) borrow money to be repaid from estate assets or otherwise; to advance money for the protection of the estate or the protected person, and for all expenses, losses, and liability sustained in the administration of the estate or because of the holding or ownership of any estate assets and the conservator has a lien on the estate as against the protected person for advances so made;

(19) pay or contest any claim; to settle a claim by or against the estate or the protected person by compromise, arbitration, or otherwise; and to release, in whole or in part, any claim belonging to the estate to the extent that the claim is uncollectible;

(20) pay taxes, assessments, compensation of the conservator, and other expenses incurred in the collection, care, administration and protection of the estate;

(21) allocate items of income or expense to either estate income or principal, as provided by law, including creation of reserves out of income for depreciation, obsolescence, or amortization, or for depletion in mineral or timber properties;

(22) pay any sum distributable to a protected person or his dependent without liability to the conservator, by paying the sum to the distributee or by paying the sum for the use of the distributee either to his guardian or if none, to a relative or other person with custody of his person;

(23) employ persons, including attorneys, auditors, investment advisors, or agents, even though they are associated with the conservator to advise or assist him in the performance of his administrative duties; to act upon their recommendation without independent investigation; and instead of acting personally, to employ one or more agents to perform any act of administration, whether or not discretionary;

(24) prosecute or defend actions, claims or proceedings in any jurisdiction for the protection of estate assets and of the conservator in the performance of his duties; and

(25) execute and deliver all instruments which will accomplish or facilitate the exercise of the powers vested in the conservator.

Section 5–425. [Distributive Duties and Powers of Conservator.]

(a) A conservator may expend or distribute income or principal of the estate without Court authorization or confirmation for the support, education, care or benefit of the protected person and his dependents in accordance with the following principles:

(1) The conservator is to consider recommendations relating to the appropriate standard of support, education and benefit for the protected person made by a parent or guardian, if any. He may not be surcharged for sums paid to persons or organizations actually furnishing support, education or care to the protected person

pursuant to the recommendations of a parent or guardian of the protected person unless he knows that the parent or guardian is deriving personal financial benefit therefrom, including relief from any personal duty of support, or unless the recommendations are clearly not in the best interests of the protected person.

(2) The conservator is to expend or distribute sums reasonably necessary for the support, education, care or benefit of the protected person with due regard to (i) the size of the estate, the probable duration of the conservatorship and the likelihood that the protected person, at some future time, may be fully able to manage his affairs and the estate which has been conserved for him; (ii) the accustomed standard of living of the protected person and members of his household; (iii) other funds or sources used for the support of the protected person.

(3) The conservator may expend funds of the estate for the support of persons legally dependent on the protected person and others who are members of the protected person's household who are unable to support themselves, and who are in need of support.

(4) Funds expended under this subsection may be paid by the conservator to any person, including the protected person to reimburse for expenditures which the conservator might have made, or in advance for services to be rendered to the protected person when it is reasonable to expect that they will be performed and where advance payments are customary or reasonably necessary under the circumstances.

(b) If the estate is ample to provide for the purposes implicit in the distributions authorized by the preceding subsections, a conservator for a protected person other than a minor has power to make gifts to charity and other objects as the protected person might have been expected to make, in amounts which do not exceed in total for any year 20 percent of the income from the estate.

(c) When a minor who has not been adjudged disabled under Section 5–401(2) attains his majority, his conservator, after meeting all prior claims and expenses of administration, shall pay over and distribute all funds and properties to the former protected person as soon as possible.

(d) When the conservator is satisfied that a protected person's disability (other than minority) has ceased, the conservator, after meeting all prior claims and expenses of administration, shall pay over and distribute all funds and properties to the former protected person as soon as possible.

(e) If a protected person dies, the conservator shall deliver to the Court for safekeeping any will of the deceased protected person which may have come into his possession, inform the executor or a beneficiary named therein that he has done so, and retain the estate for delivery to a duly appointed personal representative of the decedent or other persons entitled thereto. If after [40] days from the death of the protected person no other person has been appointed personal representative and no application or petition for appointment is before the Court, the conservator may apply to exercise the powers and duties of a personal representative so that he may proceed to administer and distribute the decedent's estate without additional or further appointment. Upon application for an order granting the powers of a personal representative to a conservator, after notice to any person demanding notice under Section 3–204 and to any person nominated executor in any will of which the applicant is aware, the Court may order the conferral of the power upon determining that there is no objection, and endorse the letters of the conservator to note that the formerly protected person is deceased and that the conservator has acquired all of the powers and duties of a personal representative. The making and entry of an order under this section shall have the effect of an order of appointment of a personal representative as provided in Section 3–308 and Parts 6 through 10 of Article III except that estate in the name of the conservator, after administration, may be distributed to the decedent's successors without prior re-transfer to the conservator as personal representative.

Section 5–426. [Enlargement or Limitation of Powers of Conservator.]

Subject to the restrictions in Section 5–408(4), the Court may confer on a conservator at the time of appointment or later, in addition to the powers conferred on him by Sections 5–424 and 5–425, any power which the Court itself could exercise under Sections 5–408(2) and 5–408(3). The Court may, at the time of appointment or later, limit the powers of a conservator otherwise conferred by Sections 5–424 and 5–425, or previously conferred by the Court, and may at any time relieve him of any limitation. If the Court limits any power conferred on the conservator by Section 5–424 or Section 5–425, the limitation shall be endorsed upon his letters of appointment.

Section 5–427. [Preservation of Estate Plan.]

In investing the estate, and in selecting assets of the estate for distribution under subsections (a) and (b) of Section 5–425, in utilizing powers of revocation or withdrawal available for the support of the protected person, and exercisable by the conservator or the Court, the conservator and the Court should take into account any known estate plan of the protected person, including his will, any revocable trust of which he is settlor, and any contract, transfer or joint ownership arrangement with provisions for payment or transfer of benefits or interests at his death to another or others which he may have originated. The conservator may examine the will of the protected person.

Section 5-428. [Claims Against Protected Person; Enforcement.]

(a) A conservator must pay from the estate all just claims against the estate and against the protected person arising before or after the conservatorship upon their presentation and allowance. A claim may be presented by either of the following methods: (1) the claimant may deliver or mail to the conservator a written statement of the claim indicating its basis, the name and address of the claimant and the amount claimed; (2) the claimant may file a written statement of the claim, in the form prescribed by rule, with the clerk of Court and deliver or mail a copy of the statement to the conservator. A claim is deemed presented on the first to occur of receipt of the written statement of claim by the conservator, or the filing of the claim with the Court. A presented claim is allowed if it is not disallowed by written statement mailed by the conservator to the claimant within 60 days after its presentation. The presentation of a claim tolls any statute of limitation relating to the claim until thirty days after its disallowance.

(b) A claimant whose claim has not been paid may petition the Court for determination of his claim at any time before it is barred by the applicable statute of limitation, and, upon due proof, procure an order for its allowance and payment from the estate. If a proceeding is pending against a protected person at the time of appointment of a conservator or is initiated against the protected person thereafter, the moving party must give notice of the proceeding to the conservator if the outcome is to constitute a claim against the estate.

(c) If it appears that the estate in conservatorship is likely to be exhausted before all existing claims are paid, preference is to be given to prior claims for the care, maintenance and education of the protected person or his dependents and existing claims for expenses of administration.

Section 5-429. [Individual Liability of Conservator.]

(a) Unless otherwise provided in the contract, a conservator is not individually liable on a contract properly entered into in his fiduciary capacity in the course of administration of the estate unless he fails to reveal his representative capacity and identify the estate in the contract.

(b) The conservator is individually liable for obligations arising from ownership or control of property of the estate or for torts committed in the course of administration of the estate only if he is personally at fault.

(c) Claims based on contracts entered into by a conservator in his fiduciary capacity, on obligations arising from ownership or control of the estate, or on torts committed in the course of administration of the estate may be asserted against the estate by proceeding against the conservator in his fiduciary capacity, whether or not the conservator is individually liable therefor.

(d) Any question of liability between the estate and the conservator individually may be determined in a proceeding for accounting, surcharge, or indemnification, or other appropriate proceeding or action.

Section 5–430. [Termination of Proceeding.]

The protected person, his personal representative, the conservator or any other interested person may petition the Court to terminate the conservatorship. A protected person seeking termination is entitled to the same rights and procedures as in an original proceeding for a protective order. The Court, upon determining after notice and hearing that the minority or disability of the protected person has ceased, may terminate the conservatorship. Upon termination, title to assets of the estate passes to the former protected person or to his successors subject to provision in the order for expenses of administration or to conveyances from the conservator to the former protected persons or his successors, to evidence the transfer.

Section 5–431. [Payment of Debt and Delivery of Property to Foreign Conservator Without Local Proceedings.]

Any person indebted to a protected person, or having possession of property or of an instrument evidencing a debt, stock, or chose in action belonging to a protected person may pay or deliver to a conservator, guardian of the estate or other like fiduciary appointed by a court of the state of residence of the protected person, upon being presented with proof of his appointment and an affidavit made by him or on his behalf stating:

(1) that no protective proceeding relating to the protected person is pending in this state; and

(2) that the foreign conservator is entitled to payment or to receive delivery.

If the person to whom the affidavit is presented is not aware of any protective proceeding pending in this state, payment or delivery in response to the demand and affidavit discharges the debtor or possessor.

Section 5–432. [Foreign Conservator; Proof of Authority; Bond; Powers.]

If no local conservator has been appointed and no petition in a protective proceeding is pending in this state, a domiciliary foreign conservator may file with a Court in this State in a [county] in which property belonging to the protected person is located, authenticated copies of his appointment and of any official bond he has given. Thereafter, he may exercise as to assets in this State all powers of a local conservator and may maintain actions and proceedings in this State subject to any conditions imposed upon non-resident parties generally.

Part 5
Powers of Attorney

Section 5–501. [When Power of Attorney Not Affected by Disability.]

Whenever a principal designates another his attorney in fact or agent by a power of attorney in writing and the writing contains the words "This power of attorney shall not be affected by disability of the principal," or "This power of attorney shall become effective upon the disability of the principal," or similar words showing the intent of the principal that the authority conferred shall be exercisable notwithstanding his disability, the authority of the attorney in fact or agent is exercisable by him as provided in the power on behalf of the principal notwithstanding later disability or incapacity of the principal at law or later uncertainty as to whether the principal is dead or alive. All acts done by the attorney in fact or agent pursuant to the power during any period of disability or incompetence or uncertainty as to whether the principal is dead or alive have the same effect and inure to the benefit of and bind the principal or his heirs, devisees and personal representative as if the principal were alive, competent and not disabled. If a conservator thereafter is appointed for the principal, the attorney in fact or agent, during the continuance of the appointment, shall account to the conservator rather than the principal. The conservator has the same power the principal would have had if he were not disabled or incompetent to revoke, suspend, or terminate all or any part of the power of attorney or agency.

Section 5–502. [Other Powers of Attorney Not Revoked Until Notice of Death or Disability.]

(a) The death, disability, or incompetence of any principal who has executed a power of attorney in writing other than a power as described by Section 5–501, does not revoke or terminate the agency as to the attorney in fact, agent or other person who, without actual knowledge of the death, disability, or incompetence of the principal, acts in good faith under the power of attorney or agency. Any action so taken, unless otherwise invalid or unenforceable, binds the principal and his heirs, devisees, and personal representatives.

(b) An affidavit, executed by the attorney in fact or agent stating that he did not have, at the time of doing an act pursuant to the power of attorney, actual knowledge of the revocation or termination of the power of attorney by death, disability or incompetence, is, in the absence of fraud, conclusive proof of the nonrevocation or nontermination of the power at that time.   If the exercise of the power requires execution and delivery of any instrument which is recordable, the affidavit when authenticated for record is likewise recordable.

(c) This section shall not be construed to alter or affect any provision for revocation or termination contained in the power of attorney.

Article VI
Non-Probate Transfers

Part 1
Multiple-Party Accounts

Part 2
Provisions Relating to Effect of Death

Part 1
Multiple-Party Accounts

Section 6–101.   [Definitions.]

In this part, unless the context otherwise requires:

(1) "account" means a contract of deposit of funds between a depositor and a financial institution, and includes a checking account, savings account, certificate of deposit, share account and other like arrangement;

(2) "beneficiary" means a person named in a trust account as one for whom a party to the account is named as trustee;

(3) "financial institution" means any organization authorized to do business under state or federal laws relating to financial institutions, including, without limitation, banks and trust companies, savings banks, building and loan associations, savings and loan companies or associations, and credit unions;

(4) "joint account" means an account payable on request to one or more of two or more parties whether or not mention is made of any right of survivorship;

(5) A "multiple-party account" is any of the following types of account: (i) a joint account, (ii) a P.O.D. account, or (iii) a trust account. It does not include accounts established for deposit of funds of a partnership, joint venture, or other association for business purposes, or accounts controlled by one or more persons as the duly authorized agent or trustee for a corporation, unincorporated association, charitable or civic organization or a regular fiduciary or trust account where the relationship is established other than by deposit agreement;

(6) "net contribution" of a party to a joint account as of any given time is the sum of all deposits thereto made by or for him, less all withdrawals made by or for him which have not been paid to or applied to the use of any other party, plus a pro rata share of any interest or dividends included in the current balance. The term includes, in addition, any proceeds of deposit life insurance added to the account by reason of the death of the party whose net contribution is in question;

(7) "party" means a person who, by the terms of the account, has a present right, subject to request, to payment from a multiple-party account. A P.O.D. payee or beneficiary of a trust account is a party only after the account becomes payable to him by reason of his surviving the original payee or trustee. Unless the context otherwise requires, it includes a guardian, conservator, personal representative, or assignee, including an attaching creditor, of a party. It also includes a person identified as a trustee of an account for another whether or not a beneficiary is named, but it does not include any named beneficiary unless he has a present right of withdrawal;

(8) "payment" of sums on deposit includes withdrawal, payment on check or other directive of a party, and any pledge of sums on deposit by a party and any set-off, or reduction or other disposition of all or part of an account pursuant to a pledge;

(9) "proof of death" includes a death certificate or record or report which is prima facie proof of death under Section 1–107;

(10) "P.O.D. account" means an account payable on request to one person during his lifetime and on his death to one or more P.O.D. payees, or to one or more persons during their lifetimes and on the death of all of them to one or more P.O.D. payees;

(11) "P.O.D. payee" means a person designated on a P.O.D. account as one to whom the account is payable on request after the death of one or more persons;

(12) "request" means a proper request for withdrawal, or a check or order for payment, which complies with all conditions of the account, including special requirements concerning necessary signatures and regulations of the financial institution; but if the financial institution conditions withdrawal or payment on advance notice, for purposes of this part the request for withdrawal or payment is treated as immediately effective and a notice of intent to withdraw is treated as a request for withdrawal;

(13) "sums on deposit" means the balance payable on a multiple-party account including interest, dividends, and in addition any deposit life insurance proceeds added to the account by reason of the death of a party;

(14) "trust account" means an account in the name of one or more parties as trustee for one or more beneficiaries where the relationship is established by the form of the account and the deposit agreement with the financial institution and there is no subject of the trust other than the sums on deposit in the account; it is not essential that payment to the beneficiary be mentioned in the deposit agreement. A trust account does not include a regular trust account under a testamentary trust or a trust agreement which has significance apart from the account, or a fiduciary account arising from a fiduciary relation such as attorney-client;

(15) "withdrawal" includes payment to a third person pursuant to check or other directive of a party.

Section 6–102. [Ownership As Between Parties, and Others; Protection of Financial Institutions.]

The provisions of Sections 6–103 to 6–105 concerning beneficial ownership as between parties, or as between parties and P.O.D. payees or beneficiaries of multiple-party accounts, are relevant only to controversies between these persons and their creditors and other successors, and have no bearing on the power of withdrawal of these persons as determined by the terms of account contracts. The provisions of Sections 6–108 to 6–113 govern the liability of financial institutions who make payments pursuant thereto, and their set-off rights.

Section 6–103. [Ownership During Lifetime.]

(a) A joint account belongs, during the lifetime of all parties, to the parties in proportion to the net contributions by each to the sums on deposit, unless there is clear and convincing evidence of a different intent.

(b) A P.O.D. account belongs to the original payee during his lifetime and not to the P.O.D. payee or payees; if two or more parties are named as original payees, during their lifetimes rights as between them are governed by subsection (a) of this section.

(c) Unless a contrary intent is manifested by the terms of the account or the deposit agreement or there is other clear and convincing evidence of an irrevocable trust, a trust account belongs beneficially to the trustee during his lifetime, and if two or more parties are named as trustee on the account, during their lifetimes beneficial rights as between them are governed by subsection (a) of this section. If there is an irrevocable trust, the account belongs beneficially to the beneficiary.

Section 6–104. [Right of Survivorship.]

(a) Sums remaining on deposit at the death of a party to a joint account belong to the surviving party or parties as against the estate of the decedent unless there is clear and convincing evidence of a different intention at the time the account is created. If there are 2 or more surviving parties, their respective ownerships during lifetime shall be in proportion to their previous ownership interests under Section 6–103 augmented by an equal share for each survivor of any interest the decedent may have owned in the account immediately before his death; and the right of survivorship continues between the surviving parties.

(b) If the account is a P.O.D. account;

(1) on death of one of 2 or more original payees the rights to any sums remaining on deposit are governed by subsection (a);

(2) on death of the sole original payee or of the survivor of two or more original payees, any sums remaining on deposit belong to the P.O.D. payee or payees if surviving, or to the survivor of them if one or more die before the original payee; if 2 or more P.O.D. payees survive, there is no right of survivorship in the event of death of a P.O.D. payee thereafter unless the terms of the account or deposit agreement expressly provide for survivorship between them.

(c) If the account is a trust account;

(1) on death of one of 2 or more trustees, the rights to any sums remaining on deposit are governed by subsection (a);

(2) on death of the sole trustee or the survivor of 2 or more trustees, any sums remaining on deposit belong to the person or persons named as beneficiaries, if surviving, or to the survivor of them if one or more die before the trustee, unless there is clear evidence of a contrary intent; if 2 or more beneficiaries survive, there is no right of survivorship in event of death of any beneficiary thereafter unless the terms of the account on deposit agreement expressly provide for survivorship between them.

(d) In other cases, the death of any party to a multiple-party account has no effect on beneficial ownership of the account other than to transfer the rights of the decedent as part of his estate.

(e) A right of survivorship arising from the express terms of the account or under this section, a beneficiary designation in a trust account, or a P.O.D. payee designation, cannot be changed by will.

Section 6–105. [Effect of
Written Notice to Financial Institution.]

The provisions of Section 6–104 as to rights of survivorship are determined by the form of the account at the death of a party. This form may be altered by written order given by a party to the financial institution to change the form of the account or to stop or vary payment under the terms of the account. The order or request must be signed by a party, received by the financial institution during the party's lifetime, and not countermanded by other written order of the same party during his lifetime.

Section 6–106. [Accounts and Transfers Nontestamentary.]

Any transfers resulting from the application of Section 6–104 are effective by reason of the account contracts involved and this statute and are not to be considered as testamentary or subject to Articles I through IV, except as provided in Sections 2–201 through 2–207, and except as a consequence of, and to the extent directed by, Section 6–107.

Section 6–107. [Rights of Creditors.]

No multiple-party account will be effective against an estate of a deceased party to transfer to a survivor sums needed to pay debts, taxes, and expenses of administration, including statutory allowances to the surviving spouse, minor children and dependent children, if other assets of the estate are insufficient. A surviving party, P.O.D. payee, or beneficiary who receives payment from a multiple-party account after the death of a deceased party shall be liable to account to his personal representative for amounts the decedent owed beneficially immediately before his death to the extent necessary to discharge the claims and charges mentioned above remaining unpaid after application of the decedent's estate. No proceeding to assert this liability shall be commenced unless the personal representative has received a written demand by a surviving spouse, a creditor or one acting for a minor or dependent child of the decedent, and no proceeding shall be commenced later than two years following the death of the decedent. Sums recovered by the personal representative shall be administered as part of the decedent's estate. This section shall not affect the right of a financial institution to make payment on multiple-party accounts according to the terms thereof, or make it liable to the estate of a deceased party unless before payment the institution has been served with process in a proceeding by the personal representative.

Section 6–108. [Financial Institution Protection; Payment on Signature of One Party.]

Financial institutions may enter into multiple-party accounts to the same extent that they may enter into single-party accounts. Any multiple-party account may be paid, on request, to any one or more of the parties. A financial institution shall not be required to inquire as to the source of funds received for deposit to a multiple-party account, or to inquire as to the proposed application of any sum withdrawn from an account, for purposes of establishing net contributions.

Section 6–109. [Financial Institution Protection; Payment After Death or Disability; Joint Account.]

Any sums in a joint account may be paid, on request, to any party without regard to whether any other party is incapacitated or deceased at the time the payment is demanded; but payment may not be made to the personal representative or heirs of a deceased party unless proofs of death are presented to the financial institution showing that the decedent was the last surviving party or unless there is no right of survivorship under Section 6–104.

Section 6–110. [Financial Institution Protection; Payment of P.O.D. Account.]

Any P.O.D. account may be paid, on request, to any original party to the account. Payment may be made, on request, to the P.O.D. payee or to the personal representative or heirs of a deceased P.O.D. payee upon presentation to the financial institution of proof of death showing that the P.O.D. payee survived all persons named as original payees. Payment may be made to the personal representative or heirs of a deceased original payee if proof of death is presented to the financial institution showing that his decedent was the survivor of all other persons named on the account either as an original payee or as P.O.D. payee.

Section 6–111. [Financial Institution Protection; Payment of Trust Account.]

Any trust account may be paid, on request, to any trustee. Unless the financial institution has received written notice that the beneficiary has a vested interest not dependent upon his surviving the trustee, payment may be made to the personal representative or heirs of a deceased trustee if proof of death is presented to the financial institution showing that his decedent was the survivor of all other persons named on the account either as trustee or beneficiary. Payment may be made, on request, to the beneficiary upon presentation to the financial institution of proof of death showing that the beneficiary or beneficiaries survived all persons named as trustees.

Section 6–112. [Financial Institution Protection; Discharge.]

Payment made pursuant to Sections 6–108, 6–109, 6–110 or 6–111 discharges the financial institution from all claims for amounts so paid whether or not the payment is consistent with the beneficial ownership of the account as between parties, P.O.D. payees, or beneficiaries, or their successors. The protection here given does not extend to payments made after a financial institution has received written notice from any party able to request present payment to the effect that withdrawals in accordance with the terms of the account should not be permitted. Unless the notice is withdrawn by the person giving it, the successor of any deceased party must concur in any demand for withdrawal if the financial institution is to be protected under this section. No other notice or any other information shown to have been available to a financial institution shall affect its right to the protection provided here. The protection here provided shall have no bearing on the rights of parties in disputes between themselves or their successors concerning the beneficial ownership of funds in, or withdrawn from, multiple-party accounts.

Section 6–113. [Financial Institution Protection; Set-off.]

Without qualifying any other statutory right to set-off or lien and subject to any contractual provision, if a party to a multiple-party account is indebted to a financial institution, the financial institution has a right to set-off against the account in which the party has or had immediately before his death a present right of withdrawal. The amount of the account subject to set-off is that proportion to which the debtor is, or was immediately before his death, beneficially entitled, and in the absence of proof of net contributions, to an equal share with all parties having present rights of withdrawal.

Part 2
Provisions Relating to Effect of Death

Section 6–201. [Provisions for Payment or Transfer at Death.]

(a) Any of the following provisions in an insurance policy, contract of employment, bond, mortgage, promissory note, deposit agreement, pension plan, trust agreement, conveyance or any other written instrument effective as a contract, gift, conveyance, or trust is deemed to be nontestamentary, and this Code does not invalidate the instrument or any provision:

    (1) that money or other benefits theretofore due to, controlled or owned by a decedent shall be paid after his death to a person designated by the decedent in either the instrument or a separate writing, including a will, executed at the same time as the instrument or subsequently;

(2) that any money due or to become due under the instrument shall cease to be payable in event of the death of the promisee or the promissor before payment or demand; or

(3) that any property which is the subject of the instrument shall pass to a person designated by the decedent in either the instrument or a separate writing, including a will, executed at the same time as the instrument or subsequently.

(b) Nothing in this section limits the rights of creditors under other laws of this state.

Article VII
Trust Administration

Part 1
Trust Registration

Part 2
Jurisdiction of Court Concerning Trusts

Part 3
Duties and Liabilities of Trustees

7–305. [Trustee's Duties; Appropriate Place of Administration; Deviation.]

7–306. [Personal Liability of Trustee to Third Parties.]

7–307. [Limitations on Proceedings Against Trustees After Final Account.]

Part 1
Trust Registration

Section 7–101. [Duty to Register Trusts.]

The trustee of a trust having its principal place of administration in this state shall register the trust in the Court of this state at the principal place of administration. Unless otherwise designated in the trust instrument, the principal place of administration of a trust is the trustee's usual place of business where the records pertaining to the trust are kept, or at the trustee's residence if he has no such place of business. In the case of co-trustees, the principal place of administration, if not otherwise designated in the trust instrument, is (1) the usual place of business of the corporate trustee if there is but one corporate co-trustee, or (2) the usual place of business or residence of the individual trustee who is a professional fiduciary if there is but one such person and no corporate co-trustee, and otherwise (3) the usual place of business or residence of any of the co-trustees as agreed upon by them. The duty to register under this Part does not apply to the trustee of a trust if registration would be inconsistent with the retained jurisdiction of a foreign court from which the trustee cannot obtain release.

Section 7–102. [Registration Procedures.]

Registration shall be accomplished by filing a statement indicating the name and address of the trustee in which it acknowledges the trusteeship. The statement shall indicate whether the trust has been registered elsewhere. The statement shall identify the trust: (1) in the case of a testamentary trust, by the name of the testator and the date and place of domiciliary probate; (2) in the case of a written inter vivos trust, by the name of each settlor and the original trustee and the date of the trust instrument; or (3) in the case of an oral trust, by information identifying the settlor or other source of funds and describing the time and manner of the trust's creation and the terms of the trust, including the subject matter, beneficiaries and time of performance. If a trust has been registered elsewhere, registration in this state is ineffective until the earlier registration is released by order of the Court where prior registration occurred, or an instrument executed by the trustee and all beneficiaries, filed with the registration in this state.

Section 7–103. [Effect of Registration.]

(a) By registering a trust, or accepting the trusteeship of a registered trust, the trustee submits personally to the jurisdiction of the Court in any proceeding under 7–201 of this Code relating to the trust that may be initiated by any interested person while the trust remains registered. Notice of any proceeding shall be delivered to the trustee, or mailed to him by ordinary first class mail at his address as listed in the registration or as thereafter reported to the Court and to his address as then known to the petitioner.

(b) To the extent of their interests in the trust, all beneficiaries of a trust properly registered in this state are subject to the jurisdiction of the court of registration for the purposes of proceedings under Section 7–201, provided notice is given pursuant to Section 1–401.

Section 7–104. [Effect of Failure to Register.]

A trustee who fails to register a trust in a proper place as required by this Part, for purposes of any proceedings initiated by a beneficiary of the trust prior to registration, is subject to the personal jurisdiction of any Court in which the trust could have been registered. In addition, any trustee who, within 30 days after receipt of a written demand by a settlor or beneficiary of the trust, fails to register a trust as required by this Part is subject to removal and denial of compensation or to surcharge as the Court may direct. A provision in the terms of the trust purporting to excuse the trustee from the duty to register, or directing that the trust or trustee shall not be subject to the jurisdiction of the Court, is ineffective.

Section 7–105. [Registration, Qualification of Foreign Trustee.]

A foreign corporate trustee is required to qualify as a foreign corporation doing business in this state if it maintains the principal place of administration of any trust within the state. A foreign co-trustee is not required to qualify in this state solely because its co-trustee maintains the principal place of administration in this state. Unless otherwise doing business in this state, local qualification by a foreign trustee, corporate or individual, is not required in order for the trustee to receive distribution from a local estate or to hold, invest in, manage or acquire property located in this state, or maintain litigation. Nothing in this section affects a determination of what other acts require qualification as doing business in this state.

Part 2
Jurisdiction of Court Concerning Trusts

Section 7–201. [Court; Exclusive Jurisdiction of Trusts.]

(a) The Court has exclusive jurisdiction of proceedings initiated by interested parties concerning the internal affairs of trusts. Proceedings which may be maintained under this section are those concerning the administration and distribution of trusts, the declaration of rights and the determination of other matters involving trustees and beneficiaries of trusts. These include, but are not limited to, proceedings to:

(1) appoint or remove a trustee;

(2) review trustees' fees and to review and settle interim or final accounts;

(3) ascertain beneficiaries, determine any question arising in the administration or distribution of any trust including questions of construction of trust instruments, to instruct trustees, and determine the existence or nonexistence of any immunity, power, privilege, duty or right; and

(4) release registration of a trust.

(b) Neither registration of a trust nor a proceeding under this section result in continuing supervisory proceedings. The management and distribution of a trust estate, submission of accounts and reports to beneficiaries, payment of trustee's fees and other obligations of a trust, acceptance and change of trusteeship, and other aspects of the administration of a trust shall proceed expeditiously consistent with the terms of the trust, free of judicial intervention and without order, approval or other action of any court, subject to the jurisdiction of the Court as invoked by interested parties or as otherwise exercised as provided by law.

Section 7–202. [Trust Proceedings; Venue.]

Venue for proceedings under Section 7–201 involving registered trusts is in the place of registration. Venue for proceedings under Section 7–201 involving trusts not registered in this state is in any place where the trust properly could have been registered, and otherwise by the rules of civil procedure.

Section 7–203. [Trust Proceedings; Dismissal of Matters Relating to Foreign Trusts.]

The Court will not, over the objection of a party, entertain proceedings under Section 7–201 involving a trust registered or having its principal place of administration in another state, unless (1) when all appropriate parties could not be bound by litigation in the courts of the state where the trust is registered or has its principal place of administration or (2) when the interests of justice otherwise would seriously be impaired. The Court may condition a stay or dismissal of a proceeding under this section on the consent of any party to jurisdiction of the state in which the trust is registered or has its principal place of business, or the Court may grant a continuance or enter any other appropriate order.

Section 7–204. [Court; Concurrent Jurisdiction of Litigation Involving Trusts and Third Parties.]

The Court of the place in which the trust is registered has concurrent jurisdiction with other courts of this state of actions and proceedings to determine the existence or nonexistence of trusts created other than by will, of actions by or against creditors or debtors of trusts, and of other actions and proceedings involving trustees and third parties. Venue is determined by the rules generally applicable to civil actions.

Section 7–205. [Proceedings for Review of Employment of Agents and Review of Compensation of Trustee and Employees of Trust.]

On petition of an interested person, after notice to all interested persons, the Court may review the propriety of employment of any person by a trustee including any attorney, auditor, investment advisor or other specialized agent or assistant, and the reasonableness of the compensation of any person so employed, and the reasonableness of the compensation determined by the trustee for his own services. Any person who has received excessive compensation from a trust may be ordered to make appropriate refunds.

Section 7–206. [Trust Proceedings; Initiation by Notice; Necessary Parties.]

Proceedings under Section 7–201 are initiated by filing a petition in the Court and giving notice pursuant to Section 1–401 to interested parties. The Court may order notification of additional persons. A decree is valid as to all who are given notice of the proceeding though fewer than all interested parties are notified.

Part 3
Duties and Liabilities of Trustees

Section 7–301. [General Duties Not Limited.]

Except as specifically provided, the general duty of the trustee to administer a trust expeditiously for the benefit of the beneficiaries is not altered by this Code.

Section 7–302. [Trustee's Standard of Care and Performance.]

Except as otherwise provided by the terms of the trust, the trustee shall observe the standards in dealing with the trust assets that would be observed by a prudent man dealing with the property of another, and if the trustee has special skills or is named trustee on the basis of representations of special skills or expertise, he is under a duty to use those skills.

Section 7–303. [Duty to Inform and Account to Beneficiaries.]

The trustee shall keep the beneficiaries of the trust reasonably informed of the trust and its administration. In addition:

(a) Within 30 days after his acceptance of the trust, the trustee shall inform in writing the current beneficiaries and if possible, one or more persons who under Section 1–403 may represent beneficiaries with future interests, of the Court in which the trust is registered and of his name and address.

(b) Upon reasonable request, the trustee shall provide the beneficiary with a copy of the terms of the trust which describe or affect his interest and with relevant information about the assets of the trust and the particulars relating to the administration.

(c) Upon reasonable request, a beneficiary is entitled to a statement of the accounts of the trust annually and on termination of the trust or change of the trustee.

Section 7–304. [Duty to Provide Bond.]

A trustee need not provide bond to secure performance of his duties unless required by the terms of the trust, reasonably requested by a beneficiary or found by the Court to be necessary to protect the interests of the beneficiaries who are not able to protect themselves and whose interests otherwise are not adequately represented. On petition of the trustee or other interested person the Court may excuse a requirement of bond, reduce the amount of the bond, release the surety, or permit the substitution of another bond with the same or different sureties. If bond is required, it shall be filed in the Court of registration or other appropriate Court in amounts and with sureties and liabilities as provided in Sections 3–604 and 3–606 relating to bonds of personal representatives.

Section 7–305. [Trustee's Duties; Appropriate Place of Administration; Deviation.]

A trustee is under a continuing duty to administer the trust at a place appropriate to the purposes of the trust and to its sound, efficient management. If the principal place of administration becomes inappropriate for any reason, the Court may enter any order furthering efficient administration and the interests of beneficiaries, including, if appropriate, release of registration, removal of the trustee and appointment of a trustee in another state. Trust provisions relating to the place of administration and to changes in the place of administration or of trustee control unless compliance would be contrary to efficient administration or the purposes of the trust. Views of adult beneficiaries shall be given weight in determining the suitability of the trustee and the place of administration.

Section 7–306. [Personal Liability of Trustee to Third Parties.]

(a) Unless otherwise provided in the contract, a trustee is not personally liable on contracts properly entered into in his fiduciary capacity in the course of administration of the trust estate unless he fails to reveal his representative capacity and identify the trust estate in the contract.

(b) A trustee is personally liable for obligations arising from ownership or control of property of the trust estate or for torts committed in the course of administration of the trust estate only if he is personally at fault.

(c) Claims based on contracts entered into by a trustee in his fiduciary capacity, on obligations arising from ownership or control of the trust estate, or on torts committed in the course of trust administration may be asserted against the trust estate by proceeding against the trustee in his fiduciary capacity, whether or not the trustee is personally liable therefor.

(d) The question of liability as between the trust estate and the trustee individually may be determined in a proceeding for accounting, surcharge or indemnification or other appropriate proceeding.

Section 7–307. [Limitations on Proceedings Against Trustees After Final Account.]

Unless previously barred by adjudication, consent or limitation, any claim against a trustee for breach of trust is barred as to any beneficiary who has received a final account or other statement fully disclosing the matter and showing termination of the trust relationship between the trustee and the beneficiary unless a proceeding to assert the claim is commenced within [6 months] after receipt of the final account or statement. In any event and notwithstanding lack of full disclosure a trustee who has issued a final account or statement received by the beneficiary and has informed the beneficiary of the location and availability of records for his examination is protected after 3 years. A beneficiary is deemed to have received a final account or statement if, being an adult, it is received by him personally or if, being a minor or disabled person, it is received by his representative as described in Section 1–403(1) and (2).

Article VIII
Effective Date and Repealer

Section
8–101. [Time of Taking Effect; Provisions for Transition.]
8–102. [Specific Repealer and Amendments.]

Section 8–101. [Time of Taking Effect; Provisions for Transition.]

(a) This Code takes effect on January 1, 19__.

(b) Except as provided elsewhere in this Code, on the effective date of this Code:

(1) the Code applies to any wills of decedents dying thereafter;

(2) the Code applies to any proceedings in Court then pending or thereafter commenced regardless of the time of the death of

decedent except to the extent that in the opinion of the Court the former procedure should be made applicable in a particular case in the interest of justice or because of infeasibility of application of the procedure of this Code;

(3) every personal representative including a person administering an estate of a minor or incompetent holding an appointment on that date, continues to hold the appointment but has only the powers conferred by this Code and is subject to the duties imposed with respect to any act occurring or done thereafter;

(4) an act done before the effective date in any proceeding and any accrued right is not impaired by this Code. If a right is acquired, extinguished or barred upon the expiration of a prescribed period of time which has commenced to run by the provisions of any statute before the effective date, the provisions shall remain in force with respect to that right;

(5) any rule of construction or presumption provided in this Code applies to instruments executed and multiple party accounts opened before the effective date unless there is a clear indication of a contrary intent;

(6) a person holding office as judge of the Court on the effective day of this Act may continue the office of judge of this Court and may be selected for additional terms after the effective date of this Act even though he does not meet the qualifications of a judge as provided in Article I.

Section 8–102. [Specific Repealer and Amendments.]

(a) The following Acts and parts of Acts are repealed:

 (1)

 (2)

 (3)

(b) The following Acts and parts of Acts are amended:

 (1)

 (2)

 (3)

Glossary

A

abatement The process for determining the order in which property in a decedent's estate will be applied to the payment of decedent's debts, taxes, and expenses, which may cause the reduction or elimination of gifts made by will.

accelerated remainder In the event the income or the preceding beneficiary fails, the property passes to the remainderman.

acceleration Hastening the enjoyment of an estate which was otherwise postponed to a later period.

accounting A report given to heirs, beneficiaries, and the probate court of all items of property, income, and expenses prepared by a personal representative, trustee, or guardian.

accumulated income The part of the income from a trust which is kept in the account.

active trust A trust that imposes on the trustee the duty of being active in the execution of the trust, with management and administrative duties.

ademption Revocation, recalling, or cancellation of a gift through the will by an *act* of the testate with the intention to do so.

adjusted gross estate The value of the decedent's estate after administration expenses, funeral expenses, creditors' claims, and casualty losses have been subtracted from the value of the gross estate. The value of the adjusted gross estate is used for computing the federal estate tax.

ad litem Meaning "for the suit"; "for the purposes of a law suit" (see Guardian ad Litem).

administration of estate The management of an estate by a representative, guardian, or trustee.

817

administrative-control rule   A rule that makes the grantor of a trust liable for the tax if the grantor retains control that may be exercised primarily for the grantor's own benefit (I.R.C. § 675).

administrator   A male personal representative appointed by the probate court to handle the estate of an intestate decedent.

administrator(-trix) *cum testamento annexo*   Also called administrator C.T.A. (administrator with the will annexed). The personal representative appointed by the court in two situations: where the maker of the will does not name an executor or executrix, or where the maker of the will does name an executor or executrix but the latter cannot serve due to deficiency in qualification or competency.

administrat-or(-trix) *de bonis non*   Also called administrator D.B.N. (administrator of goods not administered). A court-appointed personal representative who replaces a previous administrator who has begun but failed to complete the administration of an intestate estate for any reason, including death.

administratrix   A female personal representative appointed by the probate court to handle the estate of an intestate decedent.

ad valorem **taxes**   Taxes assessed in proportion to the value of the property.

advancement   Money or property given by a parent to a child in anticipation of the share that child will inherit from the parent's estate and in advance of the proper time for receipt of such property. It is intended to be deducted from the share of the parent's estate which the child receives.

affinity   Relationship by marriage.

after-acquired property   All property obtained by the maker of a will after the date of the formal execution of a will.

after-born child   A child born after the parent's will has been executed.

agency   An account in which the title to the property constituting the agency remains in the owner of the property and does not pass to the trust institution, and in which the agent is charged with certain duties regarding the property.

agent   A person authorized by another person—called the principal—to act in place of the principal. The distinguishing characteristics of an agent are (1) that he or she acts on behalf of and subject to the control of his or her principal, (2) that he or she does not have title to the property of his or her principal, and (3) that he or she owes the duty of obedience to his or her principal's orders.

alienability   Transferability.

alienation   In the law of real property, alienation is the conveyance or transfer of the property from one person to another.

allocation   The crediting of a receipt or the charging of a disbursement in its entirety to one account, as to the principal account or the income account.

allowance   The sum awarded by the court to a fiduciary as compensation for its services.

alternate valuation date   The representative's choice of a date six months after a decedent's death when all the assets of the decedent may be valued.

ambulatory will   A will subject to change, the phrase merely denoting the power a testator possesses of altering the will during his or her lifetime.

amendment   Change in a legal document, either by an addition, deletion, or correction.

amortization The operation of paying off an indebtedness by installments or by a sinking fund.

ancestor Also ascendant. Claimant to an intestate's share related to the decedent in an ascending lineal bloodline.

ancillary administrator(-trix) The personal representative appointed by the court overseeing the distribution of that part of a decedent's estate located in a jurisdiction (state) different from the one of the main administration, which is the decedent's domicile at the time of death.

annual exclusion The purpose of the annual exclusion is to eliminate the administrative inconvenience of taxing numerous small gifts by excluding the gifts to each donee during the calendar year below a certain amount, e.g., $10,000.

annuitant One who is entitled to an annuity, a beneficiary.

annuity A fixed sum to be paid at regular intervals, such as annually, for a certain or indefinite period, as for a stated number of years or for life.

antenuptial contract A contract made by a man and woman before their marriage in contemplation of that marriage whereby the property rights of either or both the prospective husband or wife are determined.

apportionment A division, partition, or distribution of property into proportionate parts.

approved list A list of authorized investments that a fiduciary may acquire. It may or may not be a statutory list.

ascendant Also ancestor. Claimant to an intestate's share related to the decedent in an ascending lineal bloodline.

assets All property of the deceased, real or personal, tangible or intangible, legal or equitable, which can be made available for or appropriated to payment of debts.

assignee The person to whom an assignment (transfer) is made.

assignment A transfer from one person to another of the whole of any property, real or personal, or of any estate or right therein.

assignor The person making a transfer.

attachment In property law, the act by a sheriff of seizing property from a judgment debtor by virtue of a judicial order or summons, thereby bringing the property under the jurisdiction of the court as security for payment of the debt.

attest To witness the making of the final draft of a will (see sample clause).

attestation clause Witnesses to a will must state that they have attested the maker's signature. Ordinarily they sign a clause to this effect.

B

bailment The delivery of goods or personal property by one person to another for some specific purpose but without passing title to the property or goods. The person delivering the goods is known as the *bailor*; the person receiving it is the *bailee*.

basis Original basis is usually an asset's cost, which may be adjusted later when improvements are made to the asset, e.g., the addition of a new roof to a home. Basis is important in tax calculations since capital gain is the excess of selling price over basis.

beneficial title See **Equitable Title.**

beneficiary In the terminology of wills, the person or institution to whom the maker of a will gives personal property through the will.

beneficiary of a trust During the existence of the trust, the person or institution to whom the trustee distributes the income earned from the trust property. When the trust terminates, the trustee conveys legal title to the property held in trust to the beneficiary or to some other person designated by the settlor (grantor) by a deed (inter vivos trust) or by a will (testamentary trust).

bequest A gift of personal property, other than money, through a will.

bona fide In good faith.

bond A certificate whereby a surety company agrees to pay money if the personal representative of a deceased fails to faithfully perform the duties of administering the decedent's estate.

budget (1) A statement of estimated receipts and expenditures. (2) A statement of funds available and needed for the payment of claims, taxes, and cash bequests in an estate.

business trust The managers are principals, and the shareholders are beneficiaries.

buy-sell agreement An agreement among co-owners of a business promising to buy out one of their number upon death, disability or retirement.

C

capacity The legal power and ability to make a valid will, e.g., being sane and of adult age.

capital gain The profit realized by the sale of capital assets, e.g., assets owned for more than one year.

case law See Common law. The law created by judges' decisions is Case Law.

cash surrender value In ordinary (straight) life insurance, the cash reserve that increases (builds) each year the policy remains in force as a minimum savings feature. After the policy has been in force for a period specified by the insurer (company), the policyholder may borrow an amount not to exceed the cash value.

causa mortis In contemplation of approaching death.

cause of action The right of a person to commence a lawsuit.

caveat "Let him beware."

caveator An interested party who gives a formal notice or warning to a court or judge against the performance of certain acts within his or her power and jurisdiction. This process may be used in the proper courts to prevent (temporarily or provisionally) the proving of a will.

certified copy An authoritative endorsement or guarantee that the copy is accurate, i.e., the same as the original.

cestui que trust Beneficiary of a trust, person having the enjoyment of property (real or personal) of which a trustee, executor, etc., has the legal title. The beneficiary is said to hold equitable title to the trust property.

charitable deduction A deduction allowed in computing "net gifts" for the full value of all gifts made to public, religious, charitable, scientific, literary, and educational institutions which meet the specified tests in the statute.

charitable trust A charitable (public) trust is an express trust established for the purpose of accomplishing social benefit for the public or the community.

chattel Generally, any item of personal property.

citation The reference to legal authorities such as constitutions, statutes, case decisions, etc., in arguments made to a court or in legal textbooks to identify the source of the authority.

civil action A lawsuit brought to remedy a private, individual wrong, such as a breach of contract or tort.

civil court Civil matters, i.e., breach of contract and personal injury (tort) cases, must be brought before a civil court. A civil court has no power to hear criminal cases.

class gift A gift of an aggregate sum to a body of persons, uncertain in number, as, for example, the class consisting of the children of the same parents.

"clean hands" doctrine Equitable relief may be denied to a person who has been guilty of unjust or unfair conduct.

Clifford trust See **Short-Term Trust.**

closely held corporation A corporation whose shares of stock are not traded on any recognized stock exchange, and are thus said to be "closely held."

codicil A supplement or addition to a will which may modify or revoke provisions in the will but does not cancel (invalidate) the will. A codicil must be executed with the same formalities as a will.

codification A systemization. One of the common features of probate codes.

collateral heir A person not in a direct line of lineal ascent or descent tracing a kinship relationship to an intestate decedent through a common ancestor (e.g., brothers, sisters, aunts, uncles, nieces, nephews, cousins), forming a collateral line of relationship.

collaterals of the half-blood Persons related to an intestate through only one common ancestor. Example: Having the same father or mother, but not both parents, in common.

commission Compensation a fiduciary receives for its services, based on a percentage of the principal or of the income or both.

common disaster clause A clause used in a will to avoid an undesirable result where the order of death of two or more persons cannot be established by proof. Simultaneous deaths (e.g., in an automobile accident) are deaths in a common disaster (see sample clause).

common law Common law is based on the unwritten principles of law that had their origin in England. These principles were developed according to the customs and traditions of the community or on what was "equitable," "fair," or "just."

common law state The 42 states of the United States which are not community property states and which take their marital property law from the English common law.

common probate procedure An informal probate. Referring to one of the two probate procedures included in the Uniform Probate Code; the other procedure is the formal, or solemn, procedure.

complaint In a civil action, the written pleadings or claims the person suing (plaintiff) lists against the defendant and has served on him or her.

concurrent ownership One of the various forms of property ownership. Concurrent ownership is a situation where two or more persons share rights as co-owners.

conditional gift A gift of property that is subject to the performance of a condition specified in a will or trust.

condition precedent A condition that must occur before an agreement or obligation becomes binding.

condition subsequent A condition that will continue or terminate an existing agreement once the condition does or does not occur. See also Defeasance.

consanguinity Relationship by blood through at least one common ancestor.

conservator (1) A court-appointed individual or a trust institution to care for and manage property, specifically the property of an incompetent person.

consideration (1) In contract terminology, the benefit requested and received by a person making a promise in return for that promise. The benefit may be an act, forbearance, or return promise given to the original promisor (person making the promise). In sales contracts, the consideration for each party is either the price or the delivery of the goods; however, initially the consideration is the exchange of promises. (2) The cause, motive, impelling influence (i.e., something of value) which induces two or more contracting parties to enter into a contract.

constructive trust A remedial device invoked by courts of equity to obtain title from a person who ought not to have it and force him or her to convey that title to the one who should have it.

"contemplation of death" gift In tax law, a gift made within three years of the donor's death.

contingent remainder A remainder is contingent if the right to possession is dependent or conditional on the happening of some event in addition to the termination of the preceding estate.

contract for deed An agreement or contract to sell real property on an installment basis. On payment of the last installment, the title to the property is transferred by delivery of the deed to the purchaser (see Form 18).

conveyance Any transfer by deed or will of legal or equitable title to real property from one party to another, e.g., from one person to another person, a corporation, or the government.

copyright A government grant to an author of an exclusive right to publish, reprint, and sell a manuscript for a period of the life of the author plus 50 years after the author's death for works written after January 1, 1978.

court of equity The court that administers justice according to the rules of equity and fairness. Examples of remedies from this court include a court order forbidding the person sued (defendant) from doing some act, i.e., an injunction, or a reforming of a contract by the court to conform the contract to the parties' intentions.

court of law The court that administers justice according to the rules and practices of both statutory law and common law. An example of a remedy that a court of law grants is damages (money) as compensation for personal injury or breach of contract.

covenant A promise of two or more parties, incorporated in a trust indenture or other formal instrument, to perform certain acts or to refrain from the performance of certain acts.

creditor's claim A document that must be filed by the creditors of a decedent in order to be paid from the assets of the decedent's estate.

creditor's notice In probate proceedings, the notice that is published stating the decedent's death and the name of the executor or the administrator to whom claims should be presented for payment.

credits Subtractions made directly from a tax that is owed which are more beneficial than deductions.

Crummy trust An irrevocable life insurance trust that permits premiums to be paid with dollars given to the trust free of gift tax.

curator A court-appointed individual or a trust institution to care for the property of a minor or an incompetent person. In some states it is the same as a temporary administrator or a temporary guardian.

curtesy In common law, the right of the husband to a life estate in all of his wife's real property owned during marriage. A husband was entitled to curtesy only if the married couple had a child born alive.

cy-pres doctrine *Cy-pres* means "as near as possible." Where a testator or settlor makes a gift to a charity or for a charitable purpose and subsequently it becomes impossible or impractical to apply the gift to that particular charity, the equity court may order it applied to another charity "as near as may be possible" to the one designated by the settlor.

D

damages The monetary remedy from a court of law that can be recovered by the person who has suffered loss or injury to his or her person, property, or rights by the unlawful act, omission, or negligence of another.

death transfer taxes A government levy (rate or amount of taxation) on property transferred to others by an individual on his or her death. Such taxes include estate, inheritance and/or gift taxes.

decedent The deceased person, referred to as having died testate or intestate.

declaration of trust The act by which the person who holds legal title to property or an estate acknowledges and declares that he or she holds the same in trust for the use of another person or for certain specified purposes.

decree The written judgment (decision) of the court.

decree of distribution A decree whereby the court determines the persons entitled to the estate, names the heirs or devisees, states their relationship to the decedent, describes the property, determines the property to which each person is entitled, and gives other findings of fact.

deductions Items that may be subtracted from taxable income, the taxable estate, or taxable gifts, thereby lowering the amount on which the tax is due.

deed A written, signed document that transfers title or ownership of real property, such as land.

deed of trust An instrument in writing duly executed and delivered by which the legal title to real property is placed in one or more trustees.

deemed transferor An ancestor of the beneficiary of a generation-skipping transfer who is of a generation younger than the grantor and whose taxable estate at death forms the basis for the generation-skipping transfer tax.

defeasance   See **Condition Subsequent.**

defeasible   Capable of being defeated, annulled, revoked, or undone upon the happening of a future event or the performance of a condition subsequent, or by a conditional limitation, as a defeasible title to property.

degree of kinship   The relationship of surviving relatives to a decedent who dies intestate.

demonstrative gift (legacy)   A bequest of a sum of money, with a direction that it be paid out of a particular fund, or from the general assets of the estate in the event the fund designated is not sufficient.

dependent   One who derives support from another; to be distinguished from one who merely derives a benefit from the earnings of the deceased.

deposition   A written declaration of a witness, under oath and before a qualified officer, to be used in place of the oral testimony of the witness at a trial or other hearing.

depreciation   A deduction allowed against the income produced by property in the amount of the property's original cost divided by its estimated useful life.

descendant   Claimant to an intestate's share related to the decedent in a descending lineal bloodline.

descent   Succession to the ownership of an estate by inheritance.

devise   A gift of real property through a will.   In U.P.C. terminology, "devise" refers to gifts of both real and personal property.

devisee   The recipient of a devise.

devolution   The passing of property by inheritance, including both descent of real property and distribution of personal property.

direct heir   In the direct line of ascent or descent of the decedent, such as father, mother, son, daughter.

disclaimer   A document that will allow an heir or beneficiary to give up the right to inherit or receive property without any adverse tax consequences.

discretionary trust   A trust that provides the trustee with direction as to the management of the fund.   This entitles the beneficiary to only so much of the income or principal as the trustee in its uncontrolled discretion shall see fit to give the beneficiary or to apply for his or her use.

disposition   The parting with, transfer of, or conveyance of property.

dissent   Refusal to agree with something already stated or to an act previously performed.   For example, a widow refusing to take the share provided for her in her husband's will and assertion of her rights under the law are known as her "dissent from the will."

distributee or next-of-kin   The person to whom personal property of the intestate decedent is distributed (orthodox terminology).

distribution   The apportionment and division, under authority of a court, of the remainder of the estate of an intestate, after payment of the debts and charges, among those who are legally entitled to share in the same.

distributive share   A recipient's portion of property left by a decedent who died intestate, as determined by state intestate succession laws.

divest   "To take away."   Usually referring to an authority, power, property, or title, as to take away a vested right.

dividend The share of profits or property to which the owners of a business are entitled, e.g., stockholders are entitled to dividends authorized by a corporation in proportion to the number of shares they own.

domicile The place where a person has a true, fixed, and permanent home and to which the person intends to return when absent. A temporary residence, such as a summer home, is not a domicile. A person may have only one domicile but could have more than one residence. Domicile and residence are frequently used interchangeably, but they are distinguished in that domicile is the legal home, the fixed permanent place of habitation, while residence is a transient place of dwelling. Domicile, not residence, determines venue.

domiciliary administration Administration in the state where a person was domiciled at time of death.

donee One to whom a gift is made or a bequest given.

donor One who makes a gift or who creates a trust.

double indemnity Payment of double the face amount of a life insurance policy if the death of the insured (policyholder) is caused by an accident.

dower At common law, the wife's right to a life estate in one-third of the real property her husband owned during the marriage. Most states (except community property states) have replaced common law dower with statutes that give one spouse (wife or husband) the right to an "elective" share of the other spouse's property. The spouse may renounce the will and "elect" to take the statutory share.

E

ejectment In the law of real property, a civil action for the recovery of the possession of land and for damages for the unlawful detention of its possession.

eleemosynary Relating to the distribution of charity, as an eleemosynary institution.

emergency provision The provision of a will or trust agreement that gives the trustee power to pay over or apply principal or accumulated income to meet emergencies in the life of the beneficiary due to unforeseeable events.

encumbrance (incumbrance) A claim or lien against real property, e.g., mortgages, easements, or a judgment, tax, or mechanic's lien.

endowment insurance An insurance contract in which the insurance company agrees to pay a stipulated amount when the policyholder reaches a specified age or upon the policyholder's death if that occurs earlier.

enjoyment-control rule One of the five rules that a grantor in a trust is required to meet in order to avoid taxation as the owner of all or a portion of the trust property. This rule makes the grantor liable for the tax if the grantor retains the power to control the beneficial enjoyment of the trust income or property.

equitable title The party to whom equitable title belongs can have the legal title transferred to him or her; e.g., a person in possession of real property such as a home who has equitable title while that person pays off the installment (on a mortgage) on the home to the legal title owner, e.g., the bank. Once the last payment is made, legal title will be transferred to the possessor by the delivery of a deed.

equity A system of laws or judicial remedies granted by certain courts, called courts of equity (chancery), distinct from the common-law courts. Examples of such judicial remedies, granted when no adequate remedy from a court of law is available, are injunctions, reformation of contracts, and specific performance.

escheat   The process by which property passes to the state when an intestate decedent leaves no surviving relatives entitled to inherit the intestate's estate.

estate   The whole of the property, real and personal, owned by any person. Also called the *gross estate*.

estate plan   An arrangement for the disposition of a person's assets during life and at death using wills and trusts.

estate tax (or transfer tax)   A tax imposed on the privilege of passing on an estate at death. The rate of tax is ordinarily based on the size of the estate and does not depend on the shares of the individual beneficiaries or their relationship to the decedent. To be distinguished from an inheritance tax.

estoppel   Words or acts which prohibit a person from alleging or denying certain facts.

exculpatory provision   A clause in favor of a trustee in a will or trust instrument which implies that the trustee has the power he or she purports to execute and clears him or her of all responsibility where this power is exercised in good faith. Sometimes called an immunity provision.

execution   The completed or finished product, e.g., an executed contract.

execution of a will   Writing, signing, attesting, and publishing the will in order to give it legal validity.

executor   A man named by the maker in the will to be the personal representative of the decedent's estate and to carry out the provisions of the will.

executrix   The woman named by the maker in the will to be the personal representative of the decedent's estate and to carry out the provisions of the will.

exordium clause   The beginning or introductory clause of a will.

express trust   A trust established by voluntary action and represented by a written document or an oral declaration.

F

fair market value   The monetary amount that an item of property, e.g., a house, would bring if sold on the open market. Generally, the price agreed to by a willing seller and willing buyer, neither party being compelled to offer a price above or below the average price for such an item.

family allowance   The portion of personal property of the deceased which is distributed to the spouse and children before any debts are paid or distribution made under a will or without a will.

federal estate tax   A tax imposed on the transfer of the total taxable estate and not on any particular legacy, devise, or distributive share. It is neither a property tax nor an inheritance tax and is imposed solely on the "testamentary transfer."

fee simple   A freehold estate that is absolute and unqualified; the largest estate and the most extensive interest that can be enjoyed in real property. It is not limited in duration or in the owner's method of disposition.

fee tail   An estate limited or restrained to particular heirs, exclusive of others; fee tail male if male heirs, fee tail female if female heirs.

feoffee   The person to whom a fee simple is conveyed.

feoffee to uses   The person to whom land was conveyed for the use of a third party. (The latter was called "*cestui que use.*") One holding the same position with reference to a use that a trustee holds with reference to a trust.

fiduciary   A person who has a duty of trust and loyalty and the obligation to act in good faith for the benefit of another. An example would be a trustee acting for the benefit of a trust beneficiary. Other examples would be a guardian acting for a minor, and a partner acting for fellow partners.

fiduciary capacity   The legal capability of a person or institution such as a bank to act as a fiduciary.

fiduciary duty   A duty or obligation that arises out of a position of loyalty, trust, and confidence. In the law of trusts, it is a duty that a trustee owes to the beneficiary of a trust.

forced heirship   Forced share. The absolute right of an heir (e.g., spouse) to receive a statutory share of a decedent's estate.

foreclosure   The termination of all rights in property of the person (the mortgagor) who, in writing, pledges the property for the purpose of securing a debt.

formal probate   A supervised probate proceeding by the probate court in the administration of a decedent's estate, with or without a will.

fraud in the execution   There is fraud when the testator is deceived about the character or contents of the document he or she is signing.

fraud in the inducement   In this case, the testator makes the will or provision relying on a false representation of a material fact made to him or her by one who knows it to be false.

freehold estate   A right of title to land; an estate in land or other real property, of uncertain duration. There are three freehold estates: fee simple, fee tail, and life estate.

future estate or interest   Any fixed estate or interest, except a reversion, in which the privilege of possession or enjoyment is future and not present.

G

garnishment   A three-party statutory proceeding in which a judgment creditor may demand that an employer who owes wages to an employee (the judgment debtor) pay these wages to the creditor to satisfy the creditor's claim against the employee (debtor).

general power of appointment   A donee (the one who is given the power) who has a general power of appointment has the right to pass on an interest in property to whomever he chooses, including himself or his estate, his creditors, or creditors of his estate.

generation-skipping trust   A trust whereby property or benefits transferred by a grantor are split between persons (beneficiaries) from two or more generations that are younger than the generation of the grantor of the trust.

gift *causa mortis*   A gift of personalty made in expectation of death, completed by actual delivery of the property, and effective only if the donor dies.

gift *inter vivos*   Gifts between the living. To be effective, there must be actual delivery of the property during the lifetime of the donor and without reference to the donor's death.

gift tax A graduated tax imposed by the federal government on transfers of property by gift during the donor's lifetime.

grantee The person to whom the conveyance of real property is made.

grantor The person who makes a conveyance (transfer) of real property to another. Also, the testator or donor who creates a trust.

grantor-taxable Any portion (all or part) of the trust property of which the grantor is treated as the owner for income tax purposes.

gross estate All a person's property before deductions (debts, taxes, and other expenses or liabilities).

guardian The person or institution named by the maker of a will to care for the person and/or property of a minor, handicapped, or incompetent person.

guardian *ad litem* A person appointed by the court to represent and defend a minor or an incompetent person.

H

half-blood A term denoting the degree of relationship that exists between those who have the same mother *or* the same father, but not both parents in common.

heir or heir-at-law In orthodox terminology, a person entitled by statute to the real property of an intestate decedent.

hereditament Things capable of being inherited, be they corporeal or incorporeal, real, personal, or mixed, and including not only lands and everything thereon, but also heirlooms and certain furniture which by custom may descend to the heir together with the land.

holographic will A will drawn entirely in the maker's own handwriting. State laws establish the conditions for a valid holographic will.

homestead The house and the adjoining land (within statutory limits) where the head of the family lives; the family's fixed place of residence.

"hose and spray" power The power of a trustee to sprinkle the trust income among various persons and decide how much to distribute to each (only someone other than the grantor can have this power as trustee).

I

implied trust Implied trust are trusts imposed on property by the courts when trust intent is lacking. These trusts are subdivided into resulting and constructive trusts. Both types are also passive trusts, and are said to be created by "operation of law."

inchoate Incomplete, partial, unfinished; begun but not completed.

inchoate dower At common law, the wife's interest in the property owned by her husband during his life while the husband is still alive. It is a claim contingent on the wife's surviving her husband.

incidents of ownership This pertains to the right of the insured or his or her estate to the economic benefits of the insurance policy. This right includes the options to change the beneficiary, to surrender or cancel the policy, to assign the policy, to pledge the policy for a loan, or to obtain a loan from the insurer (insurance company) against the cash surrender value of the policy.

income beneficiary The beneficiary who is entitled to receive the income produced from trust property.

incorporation by reference   A situation where the testator by provision in his or her will has legally made reference in one document to the contents of another document in such a manner as to give legal effect to the material to which reference is made as if it were the incorporating document.

incorporeal hereditament   Anything inheritable and not tangible or visible, such as a right to rent or a promise to pay money.

increment   An increase; that which is gained or added.

indefeasible   That which cannot be defeated, revoked, or made void.

indenture   A deed to which two or more persons are parties and in which these persons enter into reciprocal and corresponding grants or obligations toward each other.

individual retirement accounts (IRAs)   Retirement funds allowed to any wage earner who can contribute up to $2,000 per year tax deductible or $2,250 per year if a nonworking spouse joins in the account.

informal probate   An unsupervised probate proceeding. This requires the proponent of the will to produce the will and living testator's witnesses before the court. The will is proved after the witnesses have given testimony under oath.

inheritance tax (or "succession tax")   A tax on the right to receive property from a decedent at death. Usually graduated by the size of the share of the particular beneficiary and his or her relationship to the decedent. To be distinguished from an estate tax.

injunction   A remedy from a court of equity which consists of a court order forbidding the performance of some act.

in loco parentis   In the place of a parent; with a parent's rights, duties, and responsibilities.

in personam **proceeding**   Courts have authority over the individual against whom a lawsuit is brought, i.e., the defendant, in order to have *in personam* jurisdiction.

in rem **proceeding**   Courts must have the authority over the thing ("res") concerning which the lawsuit is brought in order to have *in rem* jurisdiction. A probate court is empowered to hear cases concerning decedents' wills, instruments by which decedents direct the transfer of property or "things." Therefore, the jurisdiction of a probate court is basically *in rem.*

insurable interest   An interest in the life of an individual or in property by which there will be financial loss if the insured dies or in the case of property if it is damaged, lost, or destroyed. Such an interest will entitle the person possessing the interest to obtain insurance on it.

intangible personal property   A personal property interest that can not be touched or moved, such as a right to sue another person.

interest-free loan   A popular method of shifting income taxes to lower-bracket taxpayers.

interested party   A person including heirs, devisees, children, spouses, creditors, beneficiaries, and any others having a property right in or claim to the estate of the decedent.

inter vivos   "Between the living."

inter vivos **gift** A voluntary transfer of property by a living person, called the donor, to a recipient, called the donee. Consideration is not required of an *inter vivos* gift, as it would be in the case of a contract.

inter vivos **trust** A trust created by a maker (settlor) during the maker's lifetime. It becomes operative during the lifetime of the settlor. A "living trust."

intestate Meaning "without a will"; as a noun, meaning a person who died without a valid will.

intestate succession The manner in which a decedent's property will be distributed when death occurs without a valid will, determined by state law.

intestate succession laws Laws passed in each state determining the manner in which a decedent's property will be distributed when death occurs without a valid will.

inventory A complete physical check of all the assets of the decedent and a listing of said assets and their value at the time of decedent's death on the forms provided for the inventory.

irrevocable trust According to the terms of an irrevocable trust, the trust cannot be revoked by the settlor, or it can be terminated by the settlor only with the consent of someone who has an adverse interest in the trust.

issue All persons who have descended from a common ancestor; a broader term than "children." Includes lineal descendants of any degree (children, grandchildren, etc.), natural, legitimate issue only, excluding adopted or illegitimate children.

J

joint tenancy The ownership of real or personal property by two or more persons (joint tenants) by gift, sale, or inheritance. Joint tenants have the same interest, acquired by the same conveyance, commencing at the same time, held by the same undivided possession, and each has the *right of survivorship* by which a deceased joint tenant's interest in the property automatically goes to the surviving joint tenant or tenants.

joint will A will written on a single piece of paper and executed by two or more persons as the wills of both or all of them.

judgment The official decision of a court of justice establishing the rights and claims of parties in a lawsuit submitted to the court for determination.

jurisdiction The authority by which a particular court is empowered by statute to decide a certain kind of case and to have its decision enforced.

K

kin Relationship by blood.

L

lapsed devise A devise that fails, or takes no effect, by reason of the death, unwillingness, or incapacity of the donee during the testator's lifetime.

lapsed legacy When the legatee dies before the testator, or before the legacy is payable, the bequest is said to lapse, as it then falls into the residuary fund of the estate.

last will and testament A legally enforceable declaration of one's intention to dispose of one's property, both real and personal, after death. It is revocable or amendable by means of a codicil up to the time of a person's death or loss of mental capacity to make a valid will.

laws of descent   Rules by which inheritances are regulated. These laws govern the descent of real property from ancestor to heir.

laws of distribution   See **Statutes of Distribution**.

leasehold estate   One of the categories into which the law of real property divides the rights of ownership, the other being a freehold estate. The categories are distinguished by the extent and duration of the individual's interest or according to how long and how much an interest a person has in realty.

legacy   A gift of money through a will.

legal description of real estate   A description recognized by law which definitely locates real property by reference to government surveys or recorded maps.

legal entity   Something having legal existence, e.g., a natural or artificial person (corporation) that can sue or be sued.

legal investments   Investments by trustees and other fiduciaries governed by statutes.

legal title   In trust law, the form of ownership of trust property held by the trustee giving the trustee the right to control the property. Legal title is the antithesis of equitable title.

legatee   The person to whom a legacy is given.

Letters of Administration   The formal instrument of authority and appointment given to an administrator by the proper court to carry out the administration of the estate as prescribed by law (in the case of intestacy).

Letters Testamentary   The formal instrument of authority and appointment given to an executor by the proper court to carry out the administration of the estate as prescribed by law (in the case of a will).

lien   A claim or charge on property for payment of some debt. An estate in real property includes the right to possession and enjoyment of it, while a lien on real property is the right to have it sold or otherwise applied in satisfaction of a debt.

life estate   A freehold estate in which a person, called the life tenant, holds an interest in land during his or her own or someone else's lifetime.

life in being   A phrase used in the common-law and statutory rules against perpetuities, meaning the remaining duration of the life of a person who is in existence at the time the deed or will takes effect.

life insurance   A contract, a legally binding agreement, by which promise is made by one party (the insurance company) to pay another (the policyholder or the designated beneficiary) a certain sum of money if the policyholder sustains a specific loss (i.e., death or total disability). For this protection on a regular basis, such as annually, the policyholder makes a payment, called a premium, to the insurance company.

life interest   A claim or interest not amounting to ownership and limited by a term of life, either that of the person in whom the right is vested or that of another.

limited power of appointment   Power of appointment is limited when it can be exercised only in favor of persons or a class of persons designated in the instrument creating the power.

lineal   A lineal is a person related to an intestate decedent in a direct line of kinship either upward in an ascending bloodline (e.g. , parents, grandparents, or great-grandparents) or downward in a descending bloodline (e.g., children, grandchildren, or great-grandchildren).

lineal ascendants   Persons with whom one is related in the ascending line— one's parents, grandparents, great-grandparents, etc.

lineal descendant   Persons with whom one is related in the descending line, as from father or grandfather to son or grandson.

living trust   A trust that is created and becomes operative during the lifetime of the settlor. The same as an *inter vivos* trust.

M

maintenance allowance   An allowance provided by state statutes to the surviving spouse and minor children, which gives them reasonable maintenance during the administration of the decedent's estate for a statutory time period, e.g., 12 to 18 months.

marital deduction   Half the decedent's adjusted gross estate, which may be given to the surviving spouse without becoming subject to the federal estate tax levied against the decedent's estate.

marshaling of assets   The arrangement or ranking of assets in a certain order toward the payment of debts, taking into consideration which claims have priority over others.

mortgage   A contract by which a person pledges property to another as security in order to obtain a loan.

mortgagee   The person who takes or receives a mortgage from the borrower.

mortgagor   The person who gives a mortgage to the lender.

N

natural guardian   The father of the child, or the mother if the father is dead.

necessaries   Necessary items that supply the personal needs of an individual or family, such as food, clothing, or shelter.

net estate   Under estate tax statutes "net estate" means that which is left of the gross estate after various deductions allowed by statute in the course of settlement.

next-of-kin   In the law of descent and distribution, this term properly denotes the persons nearest of kindred to the decedent, those who are most nearly related to him or her by blood.

nomination   The act of suggesting or proposing a person for an office, position, or duty; to be distinguished from appointment. Thus, the testator nominates, but the court appoints, the executor under a will.

non-adverse party   Any person having a substantial beneficial interest in the trust which would be adversely affected by the exercise or nonexercise of the power which he or she possesses respecting the trust.

non-probate asset   This type of property will pass by operation of law.

notary public   A public officer who administers oaths and attests and certifies by signature and seal documents, deeds, and the like.

notice to creditors A written notice posted in public places or by notice in newspapers to creditors of an estate to present their claims for what the executor or administator owes them. It is also a notice to debtors to come in and pay what they owe the estate.

notice to surviving spouse Notification to surviving spouse or minor children regarding what allowances of personal property from the decedent's estate they are entitled to. In addition, a renunciation and election rule applying to the spouse who has not consented to the will, giving him or her the right to file a statement in writing renouncing and refusing to accept the provisions of such a will.

nuncupative will An oral will spoken in the presence of a witness or witnesses which is valid only under exceptional circumstances, such as the impending death of the person "speaking" the will. Nuncupative wills are prohibited in some jurisdictions.

O

olographic testament A will that is written by the testator himself (or herself). In order to be valid it must be entirely written, dated, and signed by the hand of the testator.

operation of law The manner in which rights pass to a person by the application of the established rules of law, without the act, knowledge, or cooperation of the person.

operative Taking effect, e.g., when a will becomes operative, the maker of the will has died, and the will is now in operation.

ordinary (straight) life insurance Life insurance that combines protection with a minimum savings feature called cash surrender value. Premium payments are required throughout the policyholder's lifetime. The cash value slowly increases until it equals the face amount of the policy. The policyholder may surrender the policy at any time and take out the money (cash value) for his or her own use or retain the policy until death for the benefit of the named beneficiary.

orphan's court Another name for the probate court in some states.

orthodox terminology Traditional definitions of words relating to wills and probate matters, used universally before the adoption into law of the Uniform Probate Code.

P

parol evidence rule A general rule of contract law that oral or written evidence (testimony) is not allowed to vary, change, alter, or modify any terms or provisions of a written contract (agreement).

partition The dividing of lands by joint tenants, co-partners, or tenants in common into distinct portions so that they may hold them in severalty. It does not create or convey a new or additional title or interest, but merely severs the unity of possession.

passive trust An implied, resulting, constructive trust, or a trust that does not give oral or written affirmative powers and duties to a trustee to perform discretionary acts of management or administration for the benefit of named beneficiaries. A passive trust commissions the trustee to perform only minor acts of a mechanical or formal nature and often creates no administrative duties at all.

patent   A government grant to an inventor of an exclusive right to make, use, and sell an invention for a nonrenewable period of 17 years.

pecuniary legacy   A bequest of a sum of money or of an annuity.

per capita   "Individually." When all heirs entitled to a portion of an intestate decedent's estate are related to the deceased in the same degree of relationship (same-generation ascendants or descendants), each receives an identical portion, all sharing equally.

perpetuity   Any limitation or condition that may take away or suspend the power of alienation for a period beyond life or lives in being and 21 years thereafter.

personal guardian   A court-appointed individual or trust institution to care for the person of a minor or an incompetent.

personal property   Also referred to as "chattels personal" or movable property. Everything subject to ownership which is not real estate; includes such items as clothing, household furnishings, stocks, money, contract rights, life insurance, and similar holdings.

personal representative   A person who acts as liaison between the decedent's estate and the court to which the decedent's will is submitted. If the personal representative has been named in the will to carry out such liaison duties, he is called an executor (a woman is an executrix); if the court appoints the personal representative because no valid will exists, he is an administrator (administratrix, in the case of a woman). Generally, the executor and administrator perform similar duties, face similar liabilities, and hold similar powers. In sum, the court that has jurisdiction over the estate of the decedent manages this estate through the personal representative.

per stirpes   When heirs entitled to a portion of an intestate decedent's estate are related to the deceased in different degrees of relationship (intergenerational ascendants or descendants) with some heirs having predeceased the intestate, the descendants of such persons receive their shares through the predeceased heirs.

petition for probate   An application to the proper court (probate court) from the person seeking to validate a will or to administer the decedent's estate asking the court to grant the request sought in the application.

posthumous child   A child born after the death of its father or, when the caesarean operation is performed, after that of the mother.

pour-over   A "pour-over" provision refers to the transfer of property from an estate or trust to another estate or trust upon the happening of an event as provided in the instrument.

power of appointment   A power or authority conferred by one person by deed or will on another (called the "donee") to select and nominate the person or persons who are to receive and enjoy an estate or an income therefrom or from a fund, after the testator's death or the donee's death, or after the termination of an existing right or interest.

power of attorney   A document, witnessed and acknowledged, authorizing another to act as one's agent or attorney.

power in trust   A power that the donee (the trustee) must exercise in favor of the beneficiary of the trust.

present value   In the law of trusts, the present value is the value to the beneficiaries of the trust property for gift tax purposes. The present value varies with the length of time the trust runs and is a percentage of the full value of the trust property.

precatory trust A trust created by certain words, which are more like words of entreaty and permission than words of command or certainty. Examples of such words are "wish and request," "have fullest confidence," "heartily beseech," and the like.

the premium-payment rule One of the five rules that a grantor in a trust is required to meet in order to avoid taxation as the owner of all or a portion of the trust property. This rule makes the grantor liable for the tax if the trust income may be used for the benefit of the grantor. The grantor may not use the income from a trust to pay premiums of insurance policies on the grantor's or the grantor's spouse's life, nor may any other person have a power to make the trust pay such premiums without the consent of an adverse party.

pretermitted heir A child or other descendant omitted by a testator.

prima facie At first sight; on the face of it. A fact presumed to be true unless disproved by evidence to the contrary.

primary beneficiary The person selected by the policyholder of a life insurance contract who is given a superior claim to the benefits of the insurance over all others.

primogeniture The state of being the firstborn among several children of the same parents; seniority by birth in the same family.

principal The capital or property of an estate or trust, as opposed to the income, which is the fruit of capital.

private trust A trust established or created for the benefit of a certain designated individual or individuals, or a known person or class of persons, clearly identified or capable of being identified by the terms of the instrument creating the trust.

probate Procedure by which a document alleged to be a will is established judicially as a valid testamentary disposition. The process by which a proper court declares the will to be a valid testamentary disposition.

probate assets Property passed by will or descended as intestate property.

probate court A court having jurisdiction over the probate of wills, the grant of administration, and supervision of the management and settlement of the estates of decedents, including the collection of assets, the allowance of claims, and the distribution of the estate. In some states probate courts also have jurisdiction over the estates of minors, including the appointment of guardians and the settlement of their accounts, and the estates of lunatics, habitual drunkards, and spendthrifts.

probate estate This includes assets that are solely owned and property held as tenants-in-common.

probate in common form An informal proceeding in court without notice to the interested parties. Probate in common form is revocable.

property guardian A court-appointed individual or trust institution to care for the property of a minor or an incompetent. The same individual can be both personal and property guardian and is then called simply the guardian.

pro rata According to a certain rate or percentage.

prorate To divide, share, or distribute proportionally.

prudent-man rule for trust investment   This rule is used in states that have statutes governing investments by trustees. It was originally stated in 1830 by the Supreme Judicial Court of Massachusetts that, in investing, all that is required of trustees is that they conduct themselves faithfully and exercise a sound discretion and observe how people of prudence, discretion, and intelligence manage their own affairs not in regard to speculation but in regard to the permanent disposition of their funds, considering the probable income as well as the probable safety of the capital to be invested. This is also used in states where there is no statute governing investments.

publication   In the law of wills, publication is the formal declaration made by a testator at the time of signing a will that it is his or her last will and testament.

public trust   A trust constituted for the social benefit either of the public at large or of some considerable portion of it answering a particular description. May be considered a charitable trust.

purchase-money resulting trust   In this trust, property is purchased and paid for by one person and title is taken in the name of someone else.

Q

QTIP trust (Qualified Terminal Interest Property Trust)   A type of trust that will qualify for the marital deduction even though under the trust a spouse is given the income of the trust for life.

R

ratification   The confirmation, approval, or sanction of a previous act done either by persons themselves or by another.

real property   Realty or real estate. Land, and generally whatever is built or growing on or affixed to land. It includes land, buildings and fixtures. A fixture is real property that may once have been personal property but now is permanently attached to land or buildings. An example of a fixture on land is a tree. In a building, a fixture could be the carpeting nailed to a floor, a built-in dishwasher, and the like.

recapture rule   One of the five fundamental requirements of a short-term trust which the grantor must meet to avoid taxation. The rule makes the grantor liable for the tax if the income from the trust may be used for the benefit of the grantor or the grantor's spouse. If the income of an interest in a trust may be paid to the grantor during any time period of the trust, i.e., recaptured by the grantor, that income is grantor-taxable.

receivables   Debts (promissory notes and the like) established in the course of business, due from others at present or within a certain time period.

receiver   An indifferent person between the parties to a cause, appointed by the court to receive and preserve the property or fund in litigation, receive its rents, issues, and profits, and apply or dispose of them at the direction of the court when it does not seem reasonable that either party should hold them or where a party is incompetent to do so, as in the case of an infant.

receivership   An extraordinary remedy of an ancillary character, the chief reason for its allowance being to husband property in litigation for benefit of a person who may ultimately be found entitled to it.

reformation of contracts   Equitable remedy to conform a written agreement to the actual intention of the contracting parties.

registrar The judge of the court or the person designated by the court to perform the functions of the court in informal proceedings.

relationship by affinity A connection by ties of marriage.

relationship by consanguinity Blood relationship; the relationship of persons descended from the same common ancestor.

remainder In the law of wills, the remainder is the balance of an estate after all the other provisions of the will have been satisfied. Also referred to as "rest" and "residue."

remaindermen Persons entitled to the remainder of an estate after a particular estate carved out of it has expired.

renounce To reject, disclaim, abandon. To divest oneself of a right, power, or privilege.

renunciation The act by which a person abandons a right acquired without transferring it to another.

republication The reexecution or reestablishment by a testator of a will he or she had once revoked. A second publication of a will, either expressly or by construction.

res A thing; an object. The phrase "trust res" means trust property. Everything that may form an "object" of rights.

residence That place (locality) in which one lives or resides. "Residence" is not always synonymous with "domicile," although the terms are frequently interchanged. "Residence" may imply a temporary dwelling, whereas "domicile" always denotes a permanent dwelling.

residual devise A gift of all the testator's estate not otherwise effectively disposed of by a will.

residuary clause A clause in a will that disposes of the remaining assets (residue) of the decedent after all debts and gifts in the will are discharged.

residue of estate The surplus of a testator's or testatrix's estate remaining after all the debts have been discharged and specific property transferred.

Restatement of Trusts In 1935, recognizing the need to simplify and clarify the law of trusts, a group of trust experts working for the American Law Institute set forth the existing rules of law affecting trust creation and administration and included illustrations and comments. The completed work was called the Restatement of the American Law of Trusts. In 1957, the original Restatement was revised and the revisions were incorporated into the Restatement of Trusts, Second. Throughout the trust chapters of this book, relevant sections of the Restatement (Second) of Trusts will be cited.

resulting trust Resulting trusts are based on presumed or implied intent. These trusts arise by operation of law rather than as the result of any intentional act by the trustor where it appears that the trustor, in conveying away the property, did not make an effective disposition of the beneficial interest or did not intend that the person taking or holding title should have the beneficial interest.

reversion or reversionary interest The interest in real property that a grantor retains when a conveyance of the property by deed or by will transfers an estate smaller than what the grantor owns. At some future time the real property reverts back to the grantor.

revocable Susceptible of being revoked, annulled, or made void by canceling, rescinding, repealing, or reversing.

revocable trust   A trust that the creator (settlor) has a right or power to revoke (cancel). Generally, such a power must be expressly reserved by the settlor in the trust instrument.

revocation of will   Recalling, annulling, or rendering inoperative an existing will by some subsequent act of the testator or testatrix.

right of election   The right of a surviving husband or wife to choose to take, under the decedent's estate law, his or her intestate share in preference to the provision made in the deceased person's will.

right of succession   The right of a successor to share in a decedent's estate, determined by degree of kinship.

right of survivorship   An important characteristic of a joint tenancy which, upon the death of one joint tenant, passes the decedent's interest in the property to the surviving joint tenants, with the last joint tenant entitled to the whole property.

royalty   A payment made to an author, composer, or inventor by a company that has been licensed to either publish or manufacture the manuscript or invention of that author, composer, or inventor.

rule against perpetuities   A rule of common law prohibiting the title to real property from settling (vesting) absolutely in a beneficiary when a certain length of time has elapsed after the making of the original grant or trust. Today, most of the states have enacted this rule into statutory law.

S

savings bank trust   See **Totten Trust.**

secondary beneficiary   The person selected by the policyholder as a successor to the benefits of a life insurance policy whenever the proceeds of the policy are not paid to the primary beneficiary.

seisin (or seizin)   Actual possession, where the possessor intends to claim the land as a fee simple or life estate. Seisin is not the same as legal title. The difference between legal title and seisin is that the person who holds seisin over the land does not necessarily hold legal title to it.

separate property   The property one person owns free from any rights or control of others; as the property of either husband or wife, that which he or she owned at the time of the marriage and what he or she acquired during marriage by inheritance, will, or gift.

settlement   The final distribution of an estate by an executor or an administrator.

settlement option   One of a number of alternatives that parties to an insurance contract agree to follow to discharge their agreement.

settlor   A person who creates a trust; also called donor, grantor, creator, and trustor.

severalty   Property in severalty is that held by one person only, without any other person having an interest or right in the property.

severance   Act of severing, separating, or partitioning; with respect to joint tenancy, severance is the destruction of any one of the four essential unities accomplished by one of the joint tenants transferring inter vivos the interest in real property to another by deed.

short-term trust   An irrevocable trust running for at least ten years or more, or for the life of the beneficiary, in which the income is payable to a person other than the settlor. The income from a trust of this kind is taxable to the income beneficiary and not to the settlor. Also known as a Clifford, come-back, give and keep, and reversionary trust.

soldiers' and sailors' wills Several states have statutes relaxing statutory requirements for wills of soldiers and sailors. They usually require that the will be made by soldiers in actual military service or sailors while at sea. These wills are usually limited to disposing of personalty.

solemn probate procedure Formal probate.

sovereign (governmental) immunity A common law rule that exempts or frees the government from tort liability. Many states have limited or abolished this immunity.

special administrator An administrator appointed by the court to take over and safeguard an estate pending the appointment of an executor or administrator.

special power of appointment The power of the donee to pass on an interest in property that is limited as to whom or for whom and to the time within which he or she must exercise this power.

specific devise A gift, by will, of lands particularly specified.

specific legacy A gift, by will, of a particular article of personal property.

specific performance A remedy from a court of equity requiring the parties to a contract to do what they promised, e.g., perform their contract according to its terms.

spendthrift One who spends money unwisely and wastefully.

spendthrift clause A clause in a will which prevents the beneficiary from having the power to transfer his or her interest in the principal or income of a trust in any manner stating that such interest be subject to the claims of his or her creditors, attachment, execution, or other process of law.

spendthrift trust A trust created to provide a fund for the maintenance of a beneficiary and at the same time to secure it against his or her improvidence or incapacity.

spouse's allowance Allowance made by the court to the surviving husband or wife for the purpose of providing him or her with funds for living expenses during the period of settlement of the estate.

sprinkling trusts A trust in which the income or principal is distributed among the members of a designated class in amounts and proportions determined by the discretion of the trustee. Also called spraying trusts.

stare decisis The practice of following previous court decisions. A Latin term meaning "to stand by decisions."

statute Law. Statutory law is one source of law, i.e., state statutes, federal statutes. State and federal governments publish books on law which are called statutes.

Statute of Frauds State laws which provide that no suit or civil action shall be maintained on certain classes of *oral* contracts unless the agreement is put in writing and signed by the party to be charged, i.e., the person being sued, or by an authorized agent of that person. Each state has its own Statute of Frauds patterned on the medieval English statute of the same name.

statute of limitations   Each state has its own statute of limitations which bars suits on valid claims after the expiration of a specified period of time.   The period varies for different kinds of claims.

Statute of Uses   An English statute enacted in 1536 directed against the practice of creating "uses" in land.   It converted the purely equitable title of persons (beneficiaries) entitled to a use into a legal title or absolute ownership with right of possession.   The statute is said to "execute the use," that is, it turned equitable estates into legal estates.

statutes of descent   Statutes that govern the descent of real property under intestacy.

statutes of distribution   Laws prescribing the manner of the distribution of personal property under intestacy.

statutes of mortmain   As far back as the thirteenth century, various English statutes were enacted which restricted or forbade charitable and religious societies or corporations from holding property.   *Mortmain* means "dead hand." These statutes were intended to prevent land from becoming perpetually controlled by one dead hand, that of the charitable entity.   Many states have "mortmain"-type statutes, which limit the power of a testator to make charitable gifts.   Modern mortmain statutes are usually for the purpose of protecting the family of a decedent from disinheritance by deathbed gifts to charity.

statutory investment   An investment that a trustee is specifically authorized to make under the terms of the statutes governing investments by trustees.

statutory lists   Lists of conservative investments set forth by statute in which a trustee is to invest.   These statutes are of two types: (1) "permissive," where the trustee may invest outside the list but has the burden of justifying any investments not on the list; (2) "mandatory," where the trustee is liable for any investment not on the list.   These lists are also known as "legal lists."

stepped-up basis   A provision whereby the heir's basis in inherited property is equal to its value at the date of the decedent's death.

straw man   A person used to accomplish creation of a joint tenancy of real property between the existing owner of the property and one or more other persons.   The owner transfers a deed to the straw man, and the straw man immediately reconveys, by a second deed, the property back to the original owner and the new co-owner as joint tenants.

subrogation   The substitution of one person in the place of another with reference to a lawful claim, demand, or right.   An equitable remedy borrowed from civil law to compel the ultimate discharge of a debt or obligation by a person who in good conscience should pay it.

subject matter jurisdiction   The power a court must have to render the kind of judgment requested by a party to an action-at-law.

subscribing witness   One who sees a writing executed, or hears it acknowledged, and at the request of the party thereupon signs his or her name as a witness.

subscription   The act of signing one's name to a written document.

succession   The act of acquiring property of a deceased person, whether by operation of law upon the person's dying intestate or by taking under a will.

succession tax A tax imposed on the privilege of receiving property from a decedent by devise or inheritance. It is imposed on each legacy or distributive share of the estate as it is received.

successive beneficiary One who takes the place of another beneficiary by succession. For example, under a will in which property is left to A for life, then to B for life, and then to C outright, B and C are successive beneficiaries.

successors An all-inclusive term meaning those persons, other than creditors, who are entitled to real or personal property of a decedent either under the will or through intestate succession.

summary proceeding Any proceeding by which a controversy is settled, a case is disposed of, or trial is conducted in a prompt and simple manner without the aid of a jury, without presentment or indictment, or in other respects out of the regular course of common law. An example would be a process used to settle an estate without the probate procedure.

summons In a civil action (lawsuit), the notification to a defendant that he or she is being sued and that he or she must answer it at a time or place named in the notice document.

supernumerary witnesses Where more than the required number of witnesses attest a will (e.g., three sign instead of the required two) and it turns out that one of them is "beneficially interested," that witness is regarded as a supernumerary.

support trust A trust containing a direction that the trustee shall pay or apply only so much of the income and principal as is necessary for the education and support of the beneficiary and to spend the income only for that purpose. This type of trust can be used where spendthrift trusts are not recognized.

surcharge An overcharge beyond what is just and right, e.g., an amount the fiduciary is required by court decree to make good because of negligence or other failure of duty.

surety An individual or company that, at the request of another, usually called the principal, agrees to undertake to pay money or to do any other act in event that the principal fails to perform as agreed. An example would be the surety on an administrator's or guardian's bond.

surrogate The name given in some of the states to the judge or judicial officer who has the administration of probate matters, guardianships, etc.

T

taxable distribution A payment other than from income from a generation-skipping trust to a younger-generation beneficiary prior to termination of the interest of an older-generation beneficiary.

taxable estate The balance of an estate after the various deductions allowed by the statute are subtracted from the gross estate.

taxable gift A transfer of property that is both voluntary and complete by an individual for less than an adequate and full consideration in money or money's worth which is not a bona fide business transfer at arm's length.

taxable termination Termination of a property interest of a beneficiary of a younger generation than the grantor and its passing to a beneficiary of a still younger generation.

tax waiver A written consent from the state tax department allowing the withdrawal of property belonging to the estate of a decedent by the administrator or the executor for the purpose of assembling the assets and to permit distribution.

tenancy An interest in or ownership of property by any kind of legal right or title. Not necessarily limited to the more restricted meaning of one (called a tenant) who has temporary use and possession of real property, e.g., an apartment, owned by another (called the landlord).

tenancy at sufferance When one has tenancy at sufferance, one has come into possession of land by lawful title and continues to hold the property even after his or her title or interest has terminated.

tenancy at will When one has tenancy at will, one holds possession of premises by permission of the owner or landlord but without fixed term. The person has no sure estate because he or she is at the will or pleasure of the owner.

tenancy by the entireties An estate available only to a husband and wife. It is essentially a *joint tenancy* modified by the common-law theory that husband and wife are one person, but it is distinguished from the usual joint tenancy in that it cannot be terminated by one joint tenant's inter vivos conveyance of his or her interest. Neither one of the tenants by the entireties can convey (transfer) the property or sever the tenancy by the entireties without the consent of the other spouse. The predominant and distinguishing feature of both joint tenancy and tenancy by the entireties is the "right of survivorship."

tenancy for years The temporary use and possession of lands or tenements not one's own, for a determinate period of time, as for a year or a fixed number of years.

tenancy-in-common The ownership of real or personal property by two or more persons under different titles but by unity of possession. Each person has the right to hold or occupy the whole property in common with the other co-tenants, and each is entitled to share in the profits derived from the property. There is no right of survivorship in tenancy-in-common. Therefore, unlike a joint tenancy, when a tenant-in-common dies, the decedent's interest goes to an heir or as directed in a will.

term insurance Life insurance that is pure protection without savings (cash value). It is also the cheapest insurance. It requires the insurance company to pay the face amount of insurance, i.e., the proceeds, to the beneficiary if the policyholder dies within a given time period (term).

territorial jurisdiction A court has authority only over matters affecting persons and property within the geographic limits assigned to the court by statute.

testament A will.

testamentary capacity That measure of mental ability which is recognized in law as sufficient for the making of a will.

testamentary devise In orthodox terminology, a transfer of real property through a will.

testamentary disposition A disposition of property by way of gift which is not to take effect unless or until the grantor dies.

testamentary guardian A guardian of a minor or an incompetent person appointed in the decedent's last will.

testamentary trust A trust created in a will. It becomes operative only after death.

testate As an adjective, having made a valid will; as a noun, one, either a man or a woman, who has made a valid will.

testator The maker of a will when a man.

testatrix The maker of a will when a woman.

testimonium clause This clause in a will contains a statement by the maker that the will has been freely signed and a request of the proper number of witnesses to do the same.

throw-back rule Any property transferred to the trust which reverts to the grantor less than ten years after the transfer is taxable to the grantor.

"tickler" system Chronologically lists all the important steps and dates in the stages of the administration of the estate.

title The right to or ownership of property.

too-temporary rule The fifth of the five rules that a grantor must meet in order to avoid taxation as the owner of all or part of a trust property. This rule makes the grantor liable for the tax if the grantor retains a reversionary interest to take effect in less than ten years and a day. Also known as the *duration rule.*

Torrens title proceeding A judicial proceeding for the registration of title to real property in which all interests, encumbrances, and estates in the property are determined and entered on the record and on the legal document called the certificate of title which is used to transfer ownership.

tort A private or civil wrong or injury independent of contract law.

Totten trust A trust created by the deposit by one person of his or her own money in his or her own name as a trustee for another. It is a tentative trust revocable at will until the depositor dies or completes the gift in his or her lifetime by some unequivocal act or declaration, such as a delivery of the passbook or notice to the beneficiary. The depositor may withdraw all or any part of the funds during his or her lifetime and on death the beneficiary may enforce the trust as to any part remaining on deposit at the death. The word "Totten" refers to a famous case establishing this principle.

transfer An act of the parties (e.g., individuals, corporations, or the government) by which the title to property is conveyed from one party to another.

transfer tax A tax on the passing of the title to property or a valuable interest out of or from the estate of a decedent by inheritance, devise, or bequest.

trust A right of property, real or personal, held by one person (trustee) for the benefit of another (beneficiary). The trustee holds legal title to the property; the beneficiary holds equitable title.

trust account This general term includes all types of accounts in a trust department, such as agencies, guardianships, estates, etc.

trust capital All extraordinary receipts, such as proceeds from the sale or the exchange of assets, settlement of claims for injury to trust property, etc.

trustee The person or institution named by the maker of a will to administer property for the benefit of another according to provisions in a testamentary trust or an inter vivos trust.

trust estate Either the estate of the trustee, i.e., the legal title, the estate of the beneficiary, or the corpus of the property which is the subject of the trust.

trust fund   All the property held in trust in a given account.

trust income   All ordinary receipts from use or investment of the trust property, such as interest, rents, and dividends.

trust instrument   Any writing under which a trust is created, such as a will, trust agreement, deed of trust, declaration of trust, or court order.

trust investments   A broad term that includes not just securities but all kinds of property in which trust funds are invested.

trustor   A person who intentionally creates a trust. Also known as settlor, feoffor, grantor, testator.

trust powers   The authority to engage in the trust business.

trust property   Also called the trust corpus, res, fund, estate, or subject matter of the trust. The property interest which the trustee holds subject to the right of someone else.

U

ultra vires   Acts beyond the express and implied powers of a corporation.

undivided interest   A right to an undivided portion of property that is owned by one of two or more tenants-in-common or joint tenants before the property is divided (partitioned).

undue influence   The influence one person exerts over another person to the point where the latter is overpowered and induced to do or forbear an act that he or she would not do or would do if left to act freely.

unified credit   The credit given against the federal estate tax for certain transfers prior to death or pursuant to the will.

Uniform Anatomical Gift Act   Any individual who is competent and of legal age may give all or a part of his or her body to any hospital, surgeon, physician, accredited medical or dental school, college or university, or any bank or storage facility for education, research, advancement of medical or dental science, therapy or transplantation, or to any specified individual for therapy or transplantation. The gift of all or part of the body may be made by a document other than a will, e.g., a card designed to be carried on the person which must be signed by the donor in the presence of witnesses, who in turn must sign the card in the presence of the donor.

Uniform Gift to Minors Act   A law that enables a gift of specified types of property to be given to a custodian or guardian and held for a minor until the minor reaches adulthood.

Uniform Probate Code   To help alleviate the confusion of having 50 states with different procedures for handling decedents' estates, the National Conference of Commissioners on Uniform State Laws and the American Law Institute prepared model uniform statutes and recommended their adoption by the states. The Uniform Probate Code is one such model. These codes are not the law of a particular state until that state adopts them. The current trend of state legislatures is to adopt the Uniform Probate Code.

Uniform Simultaneous Death Act   An act which provides that where the inheritance of property depends on the priority of death of the decedents and where there is no sufficient evidence that the decedents have died other than simultaneously, the property of each decedent involved shall be distributed as if each had survived the other.

unity of possession   One of the essential elements of concurrent forms of ownership, i.e., ownership involving two or more persons.   It requires that concurrent owners must hold the same undivided possession of the whole property and that each owner has the right to share proportionately in profits derived from it, e.g., cultivated crops, livestock, and the like.

uses   The early medieval English forerunner of a trust (specifically a passive trust) based on the principle of separation of the legal title to an estate from the equitable (beneficial) title.   The person who legally owned the estate (i.e., had legal title) did not have the right to gain benefits from it (a considerable right in the Middle Ages), and the person who had the right to the benefits did not legally own it.   In feudal society, uses were valuable to landowners as means of assigning or avoiding the responsibilities of landowners, e.g., their obligations to their lords for military support, for payment of a portion of their crops, and the like.   Consequently, many landowners abused this practice by creating uses. The Statute of Uses abolished "uses," which were equivalent to modern-day passive trusts, and put an end to the practice described above.

V

venue   The particular place, county or city, in which a court with jurisdiction may hear and decide a case.

vested interest   An interest in which there is a present fixed right in real or personal property although the right of possession and enjoyment may be postponed until some future date or until the happening of some event.

vested remainder   An estate by which a present interest passes to the party, with the right of possession and enjoyment postponed until the termination of the prior estate.

voluntary trust   A trust created by the voluntary act of the settlor and not conditioned upon his or her death.   The actual title passes to a cestui que trust while the legal title is retained by the settlor, to be held by him or her for the purposes of the trust.

W

widow's allowance   An allowance consisting of personal property made by the court to a widow to cover immediate needs after her husband's death.

widow's exemption   For the purpose of computing the state inheritance tax, a certain amount is allowed as a deduction on the widow's share of her husband's estate.   This is known as the widow's exemption.

will   A legally enforceable written declaration stating how the maker wishes property distributed after death.

will contest   Litigation to overturn a decedent's will.

Y

younger-generation beneficiary   Any beneficiary who is assigned to a generation younger than the grantor's generation.

Index